More praise for

THE HOUSE

"*The House* is an exceptional achievement—a 500-page history of the House of Representatives that effectively describes and explains its role in America's democratic experiment. Remini's book will be the standard study of this vital national institution for years to come. It is a must-read for anyone interested in American government."
— Robert Dallek, author of *Nixon and Kissinger*

"Robert Remini has done a wonderful job, covering with rich detail and compelling prose the sweep of history of the House of Representatives— warts, majesty, and all—from its colonial roots all the way up to the election of George W. Bush. This is a book to read and savor, and then keep handy on the desk as a ready reference."
— Norman Ornstein, *Roll Call*

"In a clear and concise page-turning narrative of the people's house, Robert V. Remini . . . has written a volume that will appeal alike to specialists and a wider American public. It is the very best volume of its kind thus far presented to the vast constituency of the House."
— Richard Lowitt, author of *George W. Norris*

"Highly readable . . . the definitive history of 'the People's House.'"
— *Publishers Weekly*, Starred Review

"Only a historian of Robert Remini's stature could encompass more than two centuries of the dramatic experience of the House of Representatives so vividly in so few pages. From the convention of 1787 to the impeachment of Bill Clinton, he takes the reader on an exhilarating ride."
— William E. Leuchtenburg,
author of *The White House Looks South*

"[Remini] conveys the color along with the consequence of the House. He is an entertaining writer, and his extensive research is complemented by an eye for the telling anecdote."
— Lee Hamilton, *An American Interest/Center on Congress*

THE
HOUSE

The History of the
House of Representatives

Robert V. Remini

 The LIBRARY of CONGRESS

 Smithsonian Books

Collins
An Imprint of HarperCollinsPublishers

For my children:

Elizabeth, Joan and Bob

HarperCollins books may be purchased for educational, business, or sales promotional use. For information please write: Special Markets Department, HarperCollins Publishers, 10 East 53rd Street, New York, NY 10022.

First Smithsonian Books paperback edition published 2007

Library of Congress Cataloging-in-Publication data is available upon request.

ISBN 978-0-06-134111-3 (pbk.)

07 08 09 10 11   ID/RRD   10 9 8 7 6 5 4 3 2 1

Contents

Foreword

THE IDEA FOR this book originated with Congressman John Larson of Connecticut, a former high school teacher of American history, who, with the encouragement and support of other members of the Congress from both parties, including the Speaker, J. Dennis Hastert, won passage in 1999 of Public Law 106–99, the History of the House Awareness and Preservation Act. This act directed the Library of Congress to have prepared a complete narrative history of the House of Representatives. I therefore want to take this opportunity to publicly thank Congressman Larson, Speaker Hastert and the other members of Congress for their efforts in making this project possible. It has long been overdue.

Immediately thereafter, Dr. James Billington, the librarian of Congress, established an advisory committee to help in planning the work. It consisted of scholars in American history and political science, along with several members of Congress, including John Larson, David Dreier and John Dingell, and members of the Congressional Research Service. It was this committee that decided the book should be a single-, not a multi-, volume work, and be written by one author, not a team of scholars with a general editor. In addition, the committee felt that the history should be aimed at the general reading public, as well as members of Congress, and have value for scholars.

Sometime later Dr. Billington invited me to undertake this task, and I immediately accepted, even though I fully realized what an enormous assignment it would be. I was expected to cover the entire history of the House of Representatives from 1789 to the present in a single volume, complete with notes and illustrations, giving due attention to the important contributions to the development of the House resulting from the experiences of the colonial assemblies, the two Continental Congresses, and the Constitutional Convention. In addition, an account of national and international events during the entire period, as appropriate, needed to be sketched into the text, along with brief descriptions of the cities where the capital was located at various times and the physical structures in which the House functioned. Moreover, several members of the advisory committee urged that notice of the rules and procedures that have controlled the operation of the House over the past two centuries be included.

It would be a monumental undertaking! It was particularly challenging in that I needed to balance all these disparate parts and yet maintain a steady focus on the House and its members. It seemed like an impossible task, especially for me, who has only written biographies, never an institutional history. But now that it is over, I confess that I have thoroughly enjoyed writing this book. I shall always feel immensely grateful to Dr. Billington for his invitation. I learned an enormous amount of congressional history over the past five years. It has been a wonderful, if at times daunting, experience.

To make my task easier, Dr. Billington appointed me a Kluge Scholar in the John W. Kluge Center of the library, with an office in the center, and he assigned W. Ralph Eubanks, the director of publications, as my liaison with the library. I was also provided with the help of several research assistants, and given Library of Congress borrowing privileges. That meant that every published and unpublished work concerning the House and its history was within easy reach.

The first thing I had to decide was my ultimate goal in writing such a work. There is so much to say about the House and its history and traditions, so many themes and variations of those themes, so many fascinating individuals who served as representatives. It didn't take long for me to realize that for a single volume it would be best to concentrate on explaining to the average reader how the House evolved from a fragile union of a handful of states in 1789 into the towering edifice for democracy and liberty that it is today. I was especially anxious to capture as much as possible the human drama involved in that evolution. Despite the many mistakes and failings committed over the past two centuries, despite the numerous incidents of mayhem on the floor of the House, despite the poisonous atmosphere generated from time to time among the members, this splendid institution has had notable triumphs in realizing the national objectives as spelled out in the preamble of the Constitution. All of this I have endeavored to capture.

In undertaking this assignment, I started off by obtaining an interview with Speaker Hastert to invite his help—which he gladly provided. So that I would have some idea of the duties of the Speaker, he permitted me to follow him around as he went about his various tasks—one of the first of which was visiting the White House while he met with the President. And I was present when the Speaker greeted the Dalai Lama in his office. That was a very special moment. He also arranged, through Theodore J. Van Der Meid, his legal counsel and director of floor operations in the House, for me to have floor privileges, which meant I could come and go into the chamber and cloak rooms to listen to debates, mingle with the members, and learn firsthand how the House operates. The Speaker and his counsel could not have been more cooperative.

I am especially indebted to the former Clerk of the House, Jeff Trandahl, for his extraordinary support on many fronts. He provided me with several pieces of necessary equipment, along with passes to hear the President's State of the Union address, Prime Minister Tony Blair's speech to the Joint Meeting of Congress, the opening organizational meetings of the House for the 108th and 109th Congresses, and the counting of electoral ballots by Congress following the presidential election of 2004. The Clerk also allowed me access to the orientation sessions for new members of Congress, and, when possible, to the meetings of the Democratic Caucus and Republican Conference.

Shortly after being selected as the writer for this history, I asked that Sara Day be assigned to the project as lead researcher. She has vast experience as an editor, researcher and staff member of the office of publications at the Library. I knew her ability as a result of our work together for a book entitled *Gathering History*, which she edited for the Library and to which I contributed an introductory essay. It was in writing that essay that I came to appreciate Ms. Day's many talents, and I was delighted when she agreed to temporarily put aside her own research and contribute her knowledge and experience to the preparation of this volume. Without her many skills, it would have been impossible to cover so much history in such a short period of time.

Supporting me and Sara Day were a group of dedicated young research assistants, including Colin Gilbert, Sara Gregg, Stephanie Richmond and especially Rachel Shapiro, who stayed with the project to the very end. I also had help from members of the Office of the House Historian, including Fred Beuttler, Michael Cronin and Anthony Wallis. They were all indispensable in gathering the information I needed to write this book. I deeply appreciate their extraordinary efforts in digging through original sources, memoirs, government documents, newspapers, articles in learned journals and published histories and biographies. It would take many more pages were I to attempt a complete bibliography of all the works consulted for this book. Suffice it to say that little of importance dealing with the House of Representatives among the holdings of the Library of Congress escaped the attention of Sara Day and her research staff.

The architectural historian of the Capitol, William C. Allen, provided a memorable guided tour of the building. And Jay Pierson, House floor assistant, arranged a tour by which I was able to climb to the top of the Capitol

dome and see the Brumidi fresco up close and then view the city of Washington from the base of the Statue of Freedom. Jonathan Hanley, a Capitol
guide, conducted the tour and provided interesting and valuable information about the dome.

Naturally I owe a special debt to the many individuals who agreed to an
interview about their knowledge and experience as members, or former
members, of the House. I thank them all: Vice President Richard Cheney;
Secretary of Defense Donald Rumsfeld; Speaker J. Dennis Hastert; former
Speakers Jim Wright, Thomas Foley and Newt Gingrich; the majority whip
and currently temporary majority leader, Roy Blunt; Congressmen John Dingell, John Murtha, Henry Hyde and John Larson; former congressmen and
congresswomen Lindy Boggs, Victor Fazio, Robert Livingston, Robert Michel, Dan Rostenkowski and Pat Schroeder; and Charles Johnson, the former
parliamentarian, who served in that post from 1994 to 2004. In addition, I
want to acknowledge the valuable information provided by former clerks of
the House Donnald K. Anderson and Jeff Trandahl, and such present and
former staff members as Barry Jackson, Jim Oliver, William Pitts and Theodore J. Van Der Meid. Jim Oliver, assistant manager, Republican cloakroom,
responded to repeated requests for information about the House pages, as did
Wren Ivester, who is Oliver's opposite number on the Democratic side. And
Darren Nowels, a page, conducted me through the school for pages located in
the Library of Congress. I am happy to report that the teachers, classrooms
and equipment at the school are of the highest quality possible.

Jay Eagen, chief administrative officer of the House, and Kenneth Kato,
former chief of the Office of History and Preservation of the House, were
particularly helpful with information and documentary material.

There are many other individuals I had hoped to interview for this book,
but for one reason or another the meetings could not be arranged in time.

Quite obviously, the amount of history generated by the House of Representatives over the last two hundred and more years is vast. Any number of
events had to be excluded because of space limitation, but I was determined
to make this a narrative history of the House that provided due attention to
the men and women who have made important contributions to its development and evolution or who have given it character and life and flavor.

I cannot close without stating as emphatically as possible that although
I have had considerable help from many people in Washington in preparing this book, I was never pressured to give it a particular slant or interpretation. The narrative as presented here is totally my own, good or bad. In
any event, I hope this book will prove valuable to present and future members of the House, and most especially to the American people.

Robert V. Remini
Wilmette, Illinois

Prologue

THE UNITED STATES House of Representatives is regarded by many as the finest deliberative body in human history. A grand conceit, to be sure. But one that is not far from the mark. It is an extraordinary instrument for legislating the will of the American people. Through an electoral process it regularly absorbs fresh blood and fresh ideas so that it can reflect popular needs and demands. Every one of its members from 1789 to the present—over ten thousand individuals!—has been elected. Not one has been appointed. It has been said many times that the United States House of Representatives is the "People's House," and as such it has endured for more than two centuries.

Any history of this institution should begin with a reminder that many of the traditions and practices of the American system of government originated in Great Britain, a country ruled by a monarch and a two-house Parliament: the House of Lords and the House of Commons. As England expanded its empire into the New World in the seventeenth and eighteenth centuries and colonies of transplanted settlers were established, the king, or corporate or individual entrepreneurs who subsidized the colonization, appointed governors to represent their will and execute their instructions. To assist them in their responsibilities, these governors chose advisory councils of distinguished residents and over time allowed them to offer suggestions by which the colonies could be administered.

More particularly, in 1619, the stockholders of the company that maintained settlers in what was the colony of Virginia in North America ordered the governor to summon two landowning representatives from each of the small settlements in the colony to meet in Jamestown. These representatives were told to provide advice only. Twenty-two men gathered in a tiny church and forthwith ignored the company's instructions and enacted a series of laws for the colony against gambling, drunkenness, idleness and the breaking of the Sabbath. The House of Burgesses, as it came to be called, then adjourned. But, by its action, this house gave notice that it was prepared to go its own way and assume authority to legislate on matters that it regarded as beneficial for the community. It demonstrated a degree of independence that would be repeated many times in the future by other colonial legislative bodies. When, in 1639, the king instructed the Virginia governor to summon the Burgesses together each year, he was simply acknowledging what had been going on for quite some time. Nonetheless, final authority in the colony still rested with the governor and his council of prominent planters.

With the arrival of the Pilgrims at Plymouth on November 21, 1620, some forty-one settlers aboard the vessel, the *Mayflower*, signed a compact by which they pledged allegiance to their "dread sovereign, the King," and did "covenant and combine ourselves together into a civil Body Politik." They further promised to obey whatever laws were thought to be "meet and convenient for the general Good of the Colony."[1] This Mayflower Compact thus became the authority by which the settlers made their own laws and chose their own officials. At first every settler had the right to vote, but later religious and property qualifications were added to the requirements for suffrage.

Other Puritans, led by John Winthrop, undertook the first "Great Migration" to America in 1630 and landed in Boston. Winthrop assured the settlers that if they bound themselves together "as one man," God would protect them and provide for their prosperity. "We shall be as a city upon a hill," he preached, "the eyes of all people are upon us."[2]

In this Massachusetts Bay Colony the governor and eighteen assistants elected by the freemen, called the General Court, administered the community. But dissatisfaction with this arrangement caused the General Court in 1634 to permit the towns to elect deputies to sit with the assistants. Then, ten years later, the court divided into two houses and thereby created a bicameral commonwealth based on representative government.

Virginia and Massachusetts were only two of the colonies established under British rule; nearly a dozen more followed over the next century. Some were founded and governed by a proprietor or by stockholders in a company, but ultimately most of them evolved into colonies under royal control with a governor and one or two houses of appointed and elected officials. Legislative assemblies, representing the people, became an integral part of the governmental operation.

As the number of immigrants to the New World increased and the frontier moved steadily westward, the colonists became increasingly detached from the Mother Country. Far from England, they lacked regular direction from a ruling body in London, and they needed laws by which they could thrive in a hostile environment—where Native Americans regularly thwarted their efforts to obtain additional land. Thus, the settlers relied on their local assemblies to address their concerns. The colonies had no real representation in Parliament and therefore they became more and more independent, especially in their thinking about raising taxes to operate their local governments, paying the salaries of their officials, increasing the size of the militia to fight Indians and generally settling local disputes. Most important, the colonists thrived under this policy of "salutary neglect" by the Mother Country.

The rivalry between England and France that developed into a hundred years of warfare, starting in the late seventeenth century and extending well into the eighteenth century, forced the colonies to confront the danger of the French presence in Canada and their intrusion into territory across the Allegheny Mountains. To counter this threat, representatives from seven colonies—Massachusetts, Rhode Island, Connecticut, New Hampshire, New York, Pennsylvania and Maryland—met in Albany in June 1754, along with over a hundred Iroquois chiefs, and discussed a Plan of Union for the common defense. Formulated by Benjamin Franklin of Pennsylvania, it recommended the establishment of a continental government with representatives from each colony. It included a president-general to be appointed by the king, who had authority to veto bills passed by the representatives. It would meet annually to regulate such matters as Indian affairs, public lands and a colonial militia. This was the first effort in America to bring about a continental assembly to act for the entire population, but both the Crown and the several colonial legislatures rejected the plan.

The defeat of France and the acquisition of Canada by Great Britain led to problems in administering an expanded empire, and the Parliament in London ended the policy of "salutary neglect" and enacted a series of laws by which duties were levied on English imports into America, with part of the revenue to go toward paying the salaries of royal officials in the colonies. Not only did these laws tax Americans without their consent (according to their view), but they also eliminated the one lever of power the colonists had over their royal governors—namely, the appropriation of their salaries and the salaries of their advisers and other officials.

In protesting these actions taken by Parliament, the colonists insisted they were simply claiming their rights as Englishmen to manage their internal affairs through their duly elected assemblies. Predictably, the British Parliament rejected this argument.

A contest of will ensued, and violence soon erupted. The Boston Massacre, the Boston Tea Party and the resulting Coercive Acts of 1774 (which closed the port of Boston, forbade town meetings and quartered soldiers among civilians, along with other things) further exacerbated the problem. These Intolerable Acts, as the colonists dubbed them, triggered the convocation of delegates assembled from all the colonies, save Georgia, to agree on demands and devise strategy to pressure Britain into recognizing the rights of colonists. When the First Continental Congress convened in Carpenter's Hall in Philadelphia in September 1774, most delegates had no intention of initiating rebellion. They were still, by and large, loyal to the Crown.

It is important to note that they used the word "Congress" to describe this assembly. That word did not mean a legislative body as it is used today. A congress in the eighteenth and nineteenth centuries usually denoted a diplomatic assembly of sovereign national states, such as the Congress of Vienna in 1815 that arranged the peace following the Napoleonic Wars. The countries taking part in the Congress of Vienna were independent nations. So the delegates at the First Continental Congress represented a collection of individual entities, each of which had special needs and interests. And although they had separate concerns and separate governing bodies, they had a common purpose and goal which bound them together.

In addressing their deeply felt grievance, the First Continental Congress executed a number of important actions. It demanded the repeal of the Intolerable Acts, the repeal of all taxes and a return to a policy of "salutary neglect." Furthermore, it agreed to collective economic sanctions against Great Britain, namely, the imposition of a policy of nonimportation of British goods, starting on December 1, 1774, and nonexportation of American goods on September 1, 1775. This Continental Association was to be enforced by committees within each colony chosen by those qualified to participate in assembly elections, thereby involving the entire electorate in the effort. However, merchants and planters failed to carry out the nonimportation and nonexportation agreements, and Parliament refused to accept the claims of the colonists, or relax its rule.

So the crisis escalated, and a Second Continental Congress convened in the State House in Philadelphia in 1775. Some of the members of this Congress favored the radical cause of independence; they included John Adams and Samuel Adams of Massachusetts, Richard Henry Lee and George Wythe of Virginia, and Christopher Gadsden of South Carolina, but they were balanced by moderates such as John Dickinson and James Wilson of Pennsylvania, and John Jay of New York. Even so, most of these delegates realized that if conflict or revolution ensued it must not come from any action by Congress but from the continued provocations of Great Britain. The delegates must stand together and project the appearance of unanimity, not disagreement or discord.

As subsequently happened, Britain played into the hands of the radicals. It pushed the delegates into adopting revolutionary action. Bloodshed occurred at Lexington and Concord and at Bunker Hill in Massachusetts, whereupon these delegates dared to proceed further to seek redress of their grievances. They raised an army, issued Continental currency and opened negotiations with foreign powers to win support and intervention.

As the fighting continued, the move toward independence accelerated. In 1776, North Carolina instructed its delegates in Congress to seek separation, and on June 7, Richard Henry Lee of Virginia submitted a resolution which declared that the colonies are "and of right ought to be, free and independent states."[3] A committee was formed to write a justification of the action to be taken should Congress vote to adopt the resolution. Thomas Jefferson, the principal author of the document, wrote an eloquent statement about human liberty and equality. On July 2, 1776, the Lee resolution was passed, and on July 4, the Declaration of Independence was adopted without dissent.

These delegates were united in the single goal of winning independence from Britain, but they had little enthusiasm for creating a controlling central government. After all they were committed to their individual "sovereign" states. Still they needed a central authority of some sort to attend to such problems as providing military and financial resources for their common goal. So another committee prepared a proposal outlining the structure of a national government. This was the Articles of Confederation, a document written mainly by Dickinson. It constituted a major breakthrough in the development of representative government for a collection of sovereign entities. It declared that the several states were to be joined in a "perpetual union" and a "firm league of friendship." But it also admitted that each state would retain its "sovereignty, freedom, and independence." And it created a unicameral Congress representing all the states.[4]

But the Articles failed. The document lacked the instruments of government essential to make it work effectively. It lacked the ability to coerce or enforce its laws and the power to tax; it forbade any commercial treaty that might limit the right of individual states to levy their own import duties; and it required a unanimous vote by the states to amend the Articles, something that proved to be impossible. In other words, this central government was subservient to thirteen other governmental bodies.

It took until March 1, 1781, for the Articles of Confederation to be ratified, since ratification also required unanimous approval. Maryland refused its consent until all the states ceded their western lands to the central government.

Meanwhile, in mid-October 1781, the British army surrendered at Yorktown and the struggle for independence came to an end. The following year a provisional peace treaty was signed in Paris and later ratified by Congress.

During the era of the Confederation from 1781 to 1789, Congress approved one important piece of legislation: the Northwest Ordinance of 1787. This ordinance provided the formula by which future states could be added to the Union. It also supported public education and outlawed slavery in the Northwest Territory.

But the states quarreled with one another over boundaries, commerce, currency, debts and a host of other concerns that had national implications. To add to these failings, an economic depression resulted during the 1780s that provided additional evidence that the Articles of Confederation needed to be revised.

Virginia and Maryland made the first move in that direction and met in 1787 at Mount Vernon to tackle the problem of interstate matters. It soon became obvious that Pennsylvania and Delaware had an interest in the issue and wished to join in the effort. So Virginia invited all the states to assemble in Annapolis, Maryland, in 1786 and see what could be done. Unfortunately, delegates from only five states appeared at this convention, whereupon Alexander Hamilton of New York proposed something far more comprehensive. He suggested that the Annapolis delegates invite the states to send representatives to attend a special convention in Philadelphia in 1787 for the purpose of devising such "provisions as shall appear to them necessary to render the constitution of the Federal Government adequate to the exigencies of the Union." The Congress under the Articles added its support and called on the states to appoint delegates to the Philadelphia convention "for the sole and express purpose of revising the Articles of Confederation."[5]

All the states, save Rhode Island, responded, and fifty-five representatives appeared in Philadelphia in May of 1787, including many notables, such as George Washington, James Madison, Benjamin Franklin and Alexander Hamilton. They met in secret,[6] if for no other reason, because they decided at the start of their deliberations to scrap the Articles and prepare an entirely new document. Had their action been known, several states might well have recalled their delegation.

Shortly after the convention began, Governor Edmund Randolph of Virginia introduced a plan prepared by Madison that would create a national government based on the people and not the states. This "Virginia Plan," as it was called, established three separate branches of the government (legislative, executive and judicial), each of which would serve as a check against the others. The legislative branch—the centerpiece of this government—consisted of two houses in which the lower house would be proportionate to population and would elect the members of the upper house. The plan conferred broad legislative powers on the Congress and the right to nullify state law.[7]

The delegates from small states were distressed over this arrangement and supported a proposal offered by William Patterson of New Jersey. This New Jersey Plan imitated the Articles by calling for a unicameral legislature in which each state would have one vote. The state governments, not the people, would elect the representatives. And it provided additional authority to tax and regulate trade. Clearly the New Jersey Plan proposed a mere modification of the Articles, while the Virginia Plan offered an entirely new form of government.

The delegates debated the two proposals and finally worked out a series of compromises to satisfy both the small and large states. Congress would consist of two houses, in which the lower chamber would be elected by the people on the basis of population, and the upper house would be elected by the states with two delegates representing each state. Other compromises included the counting of three-fifths of slaves in determining population for a state's representation in the lower house, and allowing the national legislature to regulate trade (which the North wanted) but forbidding the imposition of duties on exports (which the South demanded to protect its export of cotton), and prohibiting interference in the slave trade for twenty years. The final Constitution also forbade the states from issuing paper money or infringing on the obligation of contracts.

The document went on at length to describe the powers delegated to Congress, but said little about the other two branches, except how the President would be elected (by a College of Electors chosen in each state) and the justices appointed. It gave the chief executive veto and appointive powers, and named him commander in chief of the armed forces of the United States. It also said that the judicial power shall be invested in one Supreme Court and such inferior courts as Congress shall from time to time establish. Furthermore, it defined the original jurisdiction of the Supreme Court and declared that the judicial power shall extend to all cases in law and equity. Most important, it stipulated that the members of Congress, the President and federal judges were to receive compensation from the national treasury, not from the states.

The preamble of the document declared, "We the people of the United States" established this Constitution, not "we the states," as given in the Articles. In addition, it stated that the Constitution, the treaties and the laws of the United States "shall be the supreme Law of the Land."[8]

The Constitution emphasized the principle of compromise in providing for a viable government. By balancing powers among the three branches and between the central government and the states, it established a federal system in which compromise would be essential for its success.

These Founders believed with Aristotle that there were basically three forms of government: monarchy, oligarchy and democracy. In establishing a republic they put together elements from these three types to create a "mixed government": the executive imitated the monarchy form, the Senate reflected the oligarchy and the House democracy. But within a generation the republic slowly began to evolve into a democracy.

The document, signed on September 17, 1787, by thirty-nine delegates[9] from twelve states, went forth with a recommendation that the states call special conventions elected by the people to approve or reject the instrument. When nine states ratified, the Constitution would replace the Articles and go into operation in those states.

By July 1788, eleven of the thirteen states had ratified the Constitution,[10] whereupon the Congress under the Articles decreed that on the first Wednesday of January 1789 electors would be chosen in the several states who would vote for President and Vice President; that on the first Wednesday of February 1789 these electors would cast their ballots; and that on the first Wednesday of March 1789—March 4[11]—the newly elected Congress would assemble in New York City, the seat of the American government since 1785, tabulate the ballots and announce the victors, thereby inaugurating the new administration.

The Constitution may have been imperfect (slavery was like a poison pill embedded in the system) but it did propose a workable plan for a national government. And it had been written by men schooled in a long tradition of legislative assemblies that went far back to their colonial origins. The procedures and practices mandated by the Constitution reflected that tradition.

Many invaluable lessons were learned from the colonial and early national experiences. Since a republican form of government had been established, in contrast to the many European monarchies that feared and resented this "experiment in freedom," unity was essential for success. And that unity could best be accomplished through compromise, the only proven method for working out problems in which there were conflicting views. The Framers of the Constitution also understood that legitimate government must be grounded in the consent of the people who are empowered to express their will through the selection of their representatives. What resulted over the next two hundred years was a steady enlargement of the electorate by which universal white manhood suffrage was quickly achieved, followed later when voting rights were conferred on African-Americans, women, Asian-Americans and Native Americans. If nothing else, the colonial experience demonstrated the need to keep a distance between the legislative and executive functions of government, and the importance of maintaining a protective eye on the rights of the legislature to prevent their infringement.

But could this republican government bind the sovereign states into a lasting Union that would protect the liberties of the American people and provide for their safety and welfare? That was the hope of these "Founding Fathers."

The months and years ahead provided the answer.

1

Inaugurating a New Government,
March–April 1789

THE GUNS AT the Battery in New York City shattered the stillness of the morning with an eleven-gun salute to announce to a barely awakened population that this was March 4, 1789, the day the new government, formed by the recently ratified Constitution, would be inaugurated.

Then church bells around the city added to the din, setting up a joyful cry to remind everyone that at eleven o'clock both houses of Congress would meet and count the electoral ballots submitted by each state and announce to the world that the great hero of their Revolution had been elected President of the United States. Even without an electoral count everyone knew that George Washington would head—indeed, must head—the new government. He was so much beloved and honored that it was inconceivable that anyone else should or could be selected President. It was also expected that John Adams of Massachusetts would be chosen Vice President. His remarkable career and his northern connection, despite his monarchical leanings, made him the appropriate choice.

Virtually every building in the city hung flags to celebrate the momentous event, and as each hour passed people poured into the streets and headed for Federal Hall, where Congress would assemble. "Marks of evident satisfaction were visibly imprinted on every countenance," wrote a reporter for the *Massachusetts (Boston) Centinel*.[1] In a city of a little less than thirty thousand individuals, with approximately two thousand black slaves, a city recovering from the effects of British occupation during much of the Revolution, it seemed that most of the population joined in the celebration. In part the excitement centered on the fact that a republican form of government had been established that was indeed representative of the people and their states. True, this tripartite form of government contained traces of a monarchical system with its office of chief executive, along with elements of oligarchy or aristocracy in the structure of the Senate. But the House of Representatives was truly democratic since it was composed of members chosen directly by the electorate, either at large or from districts in each state. Every two years the representatives of the House had to go before their constituents and win approval for another two years in office or be replaced by someone else. It had taken more than a century and a half of colonial government for Americans to appreciate the need, and invent the way, to provide for democratic rule. As George Mason, who framed the Virginia Declaration of Rights, declared, the House is "the grand repository of the democratic principle of the Government."[2] As such it was totally unique, and everyone at the time knew it and hoped and prayed it would work.

In the national elections that followed the ratification of the Constitution, the friends of this new document, called Federalists, fortunately won an overwhelming majority in the local and state contests, rather than its critics, the Anti-Federalists, who fought to defeat ratification of the Constitution because it failed to provide a Bill of Rights and conferred what seemed like enormous powers on the central government and thereby weakened the states. Disputed contests for House seats occurred in only fifteen out of forty-three districts, but forty-nine out of fifty-nine Federalists were elected.[3] Now these congressmen had the enormous responsibility of implementing the Constitution. They had to flesh out the bare bones of a governmental structure that contained any number of ambiguities and inherent problems. And the Framers of the Constitution had to guess at state populations in apportioning the number of seats for each state in the first House of Representatives.[4]

So, THERE WAS fear and expectation, excitement and hope as the elected members of Congress filed into Federal Hall, a building at the corner of Wall and Nassau Streets, which served as New York's City Hall. Major Pierre-Charles L'Enfant, a young French architect and engineer who had fought in the Revolution as a volunteer, had been hired to convert the building into a handsome and appropriate site for the nation's new government. At a cost of $65,000, financed by a local tax and lotteries,[5] the structure measured 95 feet in width and 145 feet in depth.[6] With large portals off the covered walkway on the street level, it sported four columns on the second floor and a huge American eagle on the pediment of the portico. Rather strikingly, the building marked the beginning of the country's commitment to the uniquely Federal style of architecture.

As congressmen entered the building they found a three-story central vestibule with a marble floor and a splendidly decorated skylight under a small cupola. The House chamber was located off this vestibule; it was a handsomely adorned two-story octagonal hall, with committee rooms and an office for a clerk connected to it. Senators found their chamber on the second floor via two stairways, one of which was reserved for congressmen, and was almost immediately referred to as the upper house.[7] "It is very true," wrote Peter Muhlenberg to Benjamin Rush, "that the appellation of Lower House will perfectly apply at present to the House of Representatives, but in this case, the upper and lower House derive their different rank from the whim or pleasure of the Architect."[8]

The building won instant praise as a "superb edifice," one worthy of the greatest and best cities of Europe.[9] "Let us all hope," editorialized the *New York Morning Post and Daily Advertiser* on March 14, "that as the Building of this House has been attended with singular success so may our wishes be fulfilled in every respect . . . by a swift and successful administration of Government."[10]

WORKMEN WERE STILL putting the final touches to L'Enfant's elegant structure when the representatives arrived on March 4, so the congressmen had to temporarily find makeshift space in another part of the building.

An early print of the interior of Federal Hall, where the 1st Congress met.

Some sixty-five representatives were expected on that first day but only thirteen showed up, and most of them came from Massachusetts, Connecticut and Pennsylvania, with single members from Virginia and South Carolina. Fisher Ames and Elbridge Gerry of Massachusetts, Jonathan Trumbull of Connecticut and Frederick A. Muhlenberg of Pennsylvania were among the more notable men to put in an appearance. But without a quorum to do business they simply adjourned after agreeing to meet the following day at eleven o'clock in the morning. They grumbled their annoyance but there was nothing they could do.

The missing members were delayed on account of roads frequently mired in mud, riddled with potholes or washed away by floodwaters. Ice-packed rivers also hampered travel and some members had to slog their way through a wilderness because there were no roads at all. "So very bad is the traveling even from Philadelphia to this city," wrote one, "that a gentleman who came to town yesterday was three days on his journey from that place. This is the SOLE CAUSE of the members not attending."[11]

Many of these congressmen traveled extraordinary distances—a thousand miles for some—to reach the capital over impossible or nonexistent roads. The very idea of creating and sustaining a union of sovereign states that stretched from the Atlantic Ocean to the Mississippi River and from the thirty-second parallel (the border of the Spanish colony of Florida) northward to New England and the Great Lakes seemed impossible, even ludicrous.[12]

The following day five more representatives showed up, most of them again from Massachusetts and Pennsylvania, but still Congress lacked a quorum. For the next week not a single additional representative appeared. Frustration and mounting anger registered on the members' faces as day after weary day they met and promptly adjourned. "This morning," wrote Fisher Ames on March 25, "we have twenty-six representatives; and as thirty are necessary to make a quorum, we are still in a state of inaction. This is a very mortifying situation. . . . I am inclined to believe that the languor of the old Confederation [under the Articles] is transfused into the members of the new Congress." Just think of the cost of doing nothing and the loss of revenue, he growled. "We lose credit, spirit, every thing. The public will forget the government before it is born. The resurrection of the infant will come before it is born."[13]

And many of the arriving members found New York "a dirty city," with pigs roaming loose to eat garbage thrown in the streets. The stench, especially for those from country areas, was "so apparent," wrote Representative Elias Boudinot of New Jersey to his wife, "as to effect our smelling Faculties greatly."[14] The members were obliged to take up residence in whatever nearby boardinghouse they could find. What a place to live and work in, they moaned.

Not until April 1, 1789, with the arrival of Thomas Scott from western

ELIAS BOUDINOT
OF NEW JERSEY
Elected November 4, 1782

Elias Boudinot of New Jersey, member of the 1st Congress, who was amused that the House finally had a quorum to begin its first session on April Fool's Day.

Pennsylvania, did the House finally have a quorum of thirty. It was April Fool's Day, noted Boudinot.[15] Imagine! April Fool's Day. What an inauspicious day to inaugurate the People's House!

Even so, said Ames, there was a sense among the members that the "great business before us will soon make us sufficiently serious," although if truth be told, he added, there were "few shining geniuses among us." Still there was enough virtue and "habits of business" to make the House of Representatives in this 1st Congress a truly "republican assembly."[16] For the most part, Ames continued, they are "sober, solid, old-charter folks" with considerable experience as legislators. After all, nine members attended the Convention in Philadelphia that wrote the Constitution, and thirty-three took part in one of the Continental Congresses, their state's ratifying convention or both. All but five had served in a colonial assembly or their state legislatures and were highly trained.[17] Of the entire group in this 1st Congress only two members lacked previous public service.[18] As a body they had been thoroughly indoctrinated in British parliamentary procedures and traditions and they therefore provided important continuity with their colonial past. Most of them were lawyers, southern planters and merchants of high social standing and varied educational background. Many of them were men of means, a few having risen from poverty. Conservative in their politics and fiercely republican, averaging forty-three years of age, they were determined to make the Constitution succeed. "They will be inclined," remarked Ames, "to a temperate, guarded policy."[19]

And there actually were a few "shining" lights. Ames himself was one of them. Son of an innkeeper, he entered Harvard at the age of twelve and was admitted to the bar in 1781. He served in the Massachusetts convention to ratify the Constitution and won election to the 1st Federal Congress over

Samuel Adams. A brilliant intellectual, graceful speaker and effective debater, he participated in most of the debates. Admired for his candor, integrity and extensive knowledge, he along with James Madison would dominate the 1st Congress.

And dominate is precisely what James Madison of Virginia did. He stood head and shoulders above most of the other members. He was a little man, wrote Ames, and seemingly quite ordinary, but a man of remarkable common sense, wide reading and outstanding integrity. Painfully shy, he spoke low, but his words were always "pure, perspicuous," and to the point. "Very much Frenchified in his politics," he was a "book politician" who had devoured all the great works of political science, but he did not live and breathe the art of politics.[20] Educated at the College of New Jersey (later Princeton), he served in the Continental Congress and helped draft the Virginia constitution and the federal Constitution. Indeed, he is properly regarded as the "Father of the Constitution."

Other men of note in this first House were Roger Sherman and Jonathan Trumbull of Connecticut, Abraham Baldwin of Georgia, Elbridge Gerry and Theodore Sedgwick of Massachusetts, Elias Boudinot of New Jersey, Frederick A. Muhlenberg of Pennsylvania and William Branch Giles of Virginia. Catherine Greene, widow of General Nathanael Greene, told Jeremiah Wadsworth of Virginia, "I think . . . that the representatives are a little better than the Senators."[21]

ROUGHLY HALF THE members of the House said nothing at all during the debates in this 1st Congress, but most of them were reported as hardworking.[22] Elias Boudinot told his wife that once the House began its operation, "I am up at 7 oClock or a little after; spend half an hour in my Room—dress

Fisher Ames of Massachusetts, one of the wisest and most valuable members of the 1st Congress.

Frederick Muhlenberg of Pennsylvania had a "clear, penetrating" voice, which probably helped win him election as the first Speaker of the House of Representatives.

& breakfast by half past eight—in Committee at 9—from thence immediately to the House—adjourn at 3 oClock—In Committee ag. at 6—return at 8—and write til 12 at Night—This has been my Course for some Time, except when I dine out, which to me is harder service."[23]

The first thing the members did now that they had a quorum was elect the "rotund and dignified" Frederick Augustus Conrad Muhlenberg to preside as Speaker. He had a "clear penetrating voice" which added to his attractiveness.[24] Since it was generally understood that a Virginian and a Massachusetts man would be elected President and Vice President, political sense dictated that the Speaker come from one of the middle states, like Pennsylvania. In addition, Muhlenberg had served as speaker of the Pennsylvania Assembly and had acquitted himself with some distinction. A Lutheran minister and a Federalist who spoke with a slight German accent, having been educated in Germany, he seemed ideally suited to preside over the House.

Once elected, Muhlenberg was escorted to the chair, where he acknowledged the "distinguished" honor that had been bestowed upon him. The members then elected John Beckley, a young Virginian, as clerk.[25] He had served in his state's legislature and was a friend of Thomas Jefferson and James Madison. Unfortunately he was neither an archivist nor a historian, and as clerk he was a disaster since he discarded many original documents once they had been copied or were no longer needed. As a consequence, the processes by which bills were introduced, written and enacted during this most important first session of the House of Representatives have been lost. To a large extent, information on the workings of the House must be gleaned from contemporary newspapers and letters written by the members to family and friends back home.

Although the Constitution required each branch of Congress to keep and publish a journal of its proceedings, the document did not stipulate that the content of the debates be made public. Therefore, newspaper reporters attended the House proceedings and took notes that were subsequently published. John Fenno's *Gazette of the United States* provided the most extensive coverage of the debates. Thomas Lloyd, a shorthand expert, sold subscriptions to his *Congressional Register* to anyone who was interested and his shorthand notes, now housed in the Library of Congress, have recently been transcribed and provide additional information on the early proceedings of the House.[26]

DURING THE NEXT several days the representatives spent their time on housekeeping chores, and for the first week the sessions were held in secret. Unlike the Senate, whose proceedings remained secret until 1795, following the example of most colonial assemblies, Continental Congresses, and the Constitutional Convention, the House opened its doors on April 9 to an eager and interested public. As a result, public interest centered on the House, not the Senate, and its members enjoyed added notoriety and authority. The visitors watched from two overhanging galleries at the back of the second level.[27] Since this House was closest to the people and judged the centerpiece of government, many citizens wished to attend its sessions and hear and observe what their representatives planned to do. Alexander Hamilton, a leading figure in the Constitutional Convention, and James Kent, a future jurist and early commentator on the Constitution, watched the proceedings from the gallery. "I considered it to be a proud & glorious day," Kent wrote, "the consummation of our wishes, & that I was looking upon an organ of popular will, just beginning to breathe the Breath of Life, & which might in some future age, much more truly than the Roman Senate, be regarded as the refuge of nations."[28]

Members regularly complained that the crowd in the gallery cracked nuts during the debates, much to their annoyance, and well-to-do visitors frequently found that pickpockets had relieved them of their valuables, discarding empty wallets at the Battery.

What visitors in the gallery saw during the sessions were the members sitting in semicircles facing the Speaker, and wearing their hats! But when they rose and spoke they removed their hats, a practice that continued for many years. "The pleasure which our open Doors, and the knowledge of our Debates obtained by that means, has given the People, can hardly be conceived," wrote Representative Alexander White of Virginia. "The different conduct of the Senate must of course have a contrary effect."[29]

On beginning regular business the members appointed a committee, which Madison chaired, to "prepare and report such standing rules and orders of proceedings as may be proper to be observed in the House."[30] And until this committee made its report, said John Page of Virginia, "& the House agree to it; we can do nothing; for the Members have had in the difft. Assemblies such various Rules & are all so fond of their own, that it is a most unruly Assembly we are all in."[31]

The Madison committee acted quickly and submitted its report, which the House accepted without amendment. According to these early rules no one was permitted to talk, read or move about while a member addressed the House; bills were to be read three times, and the Committee of the Whole House would function "for considering and perfecting legislation."[32] Then it spelled out the duties of a sergeant at arms,[33] describing what he must do when the anticipated physical and verbal brawls broke out. Speaker Muhlenberg authorized a mace for this officer, who would brandish it to quell disruptive behavior by the members. The House also decided to have a doorkeeper with an assistant, along with a chaplain and a clerk with two assistants. They named Joseph Wheaton as sergeant at arms, Gifford Dalley as doorkeeper[34] with Thomas Claxton as his assistant, and William Lynn of Philadelphia, a Dutch Reformed Presbyterian, as chaplain.[35]

After that, the House agreed on the oath (or affirmation) of office in which each representative would declare the following: "I [name], a Representative of the United States in the Congress thereof, do solemnly swear [or affirm] in the presence of Almighty God, that I will support the Constitution of the United States—so help me God."[36] This oath was important because it ensured the members' loyalty to the national government. Later, in an even more crucial action, the Congress passed the Oath Act, which required all members of the state executive, legislative and judicial branches to also swear to uphold the Constitution. By legislating this uniform pledge, the Federalists clearly intended to affirm the primacy of the central government.[37]

The profundity of the wisdom displayed by members of the 1st Congress in organizing themselves, establishing rules of procedure and conducting their operations is truly remarkable.[38]

FIVE DAYS AFTER the House started to function as a legislative body, the Senate achieved a quorum and the Congress of the United States was finally launched. Speaker Muhlenberg informed the House that the Senate was organized and ready to count the electoral ballots in the choice of President and Vice President. Each elector had two votes: one for President, the second for Vice President. The candidate with the highest majority of electoral votes would be declared President and the candidate with the next-highest count Vice President. Under this clearly "defective" system there was the danger of a tie vote. As a result some of the electors realized they must throw away their second vote rather than risk a tie.

The House and Senate met together and a list of the votes of the electors from the several states was then delivered to the clerk. Not surprisingly, all sixty-nine electors voted for "His Excellency George Washington," while thirty-four electors cast their ballots for the "Honorable John Adams," who was declared Vice President. Nine other candidates, including John Jay, John Rutledge, John Hancock and George Clinton, among others, received scattered votes, not one more than nine.

Not everyone was happy about voting for Adams since, as his most recent biographer has written, he "could be blunt, stubborn, opinionated, vain, and given to jealousy."[39] Often cranky and suspicious, he himself admitted that he was considered by many "the most vain, conceited, impudent, arrogant Creature in the World."[40] But he was also a man of great learning who had a distinguished career of service in negotiating the treaty that ended the Revolution and in representing the Republic in France, Holland and England.

Only ten of the eleven states voted for Washington and Adams. New York, which had duly ratified the Constitution, found its legislature locked in an internal squabble about the kind of ballot to be employed and so no electors were chosen. The periodic quirkiness of New York politics surfaced right at the start of this new government as it failed to join the rest of the nation in approving George Washington for President.

Messengers were immediately dispatched to inform the two men of their election. The impatient John Adams was already packed when he received the news, but Washington, who knew he had no rival for the presidency, waited at his home until he had been officially informed of his election before preparing to start for New York.

IN THE MEANTIME, the lower chamber returned to its housekeeping chores and settled on the duties of the Speaker. These included presiding, maintaining order, deciding points of order, appointing committees of not more than three members, putting questions and announcing results. The House also determined the rules of decorum and debate (they really worried about rowdyism, which says something about what usually went on in state legislatures), the rights of the members and the method of selecting committees of more than three individuals. Although they were particularly fond of their own colonial and state practices, they nonetheless set aside their differences and settled the procedure for introducing bills and in forming themselves into a Committee of the Whole House.

There was only one standing, that is, permanent, committee: the Committee on Elections. Established on April 13, it was charged with examining certificates of election presented by each member. Thus all of the 143 bills introduced during this 1st Congress emanated from select, that is, temporary, committees in the House, either appointed or elected, on an ad hoc basis. The duration of these committees was sometimes only a few days. The Senate introduced only 24 bills, demonstrating very clearly the dominance of the House in the legislative process at this time.

For the most part the House adopted relatively simple rules of procedure—compared to today's complex and involved regulations. To start, general principles or guidelines involved for each bill were determined by the Committee of the Whole. Then the measure was referred to a select committee to gather facts and work out the details, after which it was returned to the full House for action. All bills required three readings before passage. The first reading involved obtaining information, and if there was no opposition it went to a second reading. After that the Speaker announced whether the bill was to be sent to a committee or engrossed. If engrossed it was read a third time and the bill was "executed in a fair round hand," and certified by the clerk. If sent to a committee it could be a select committee or the Committee of the Whole. Either way it was finally taken up by the Committee of the Whole for discussion and consideration of amendments. The entire House then heard another reading, decided on amendments and finally voted on its passage or rejection.[41]

Within a few years the tremendous increase of legislation made it virtually impossible for the Committee of the Whole to decide on principles and guidelines before the facts had been gathered. As a result, use of the Committee of the Whole declined and standing committees were created to provide the House with information it needed for each major bill, along with a detailed proposal. Ultimately the Committee of the Whole became a reviewer of the recommendations of its standing and select committees.

Because the Constitution established a bicameral legislature, some form of communication between the two chambers had to be decided. Within a few weeks the House and Senate met in joint session, set up joint committees to consider legislation in which they differed and agreed on joint rules. The House also determined the ways in which it would go about communicating with both the Senate and the executive.[42]

Once these preliminary organizational matters were resolved the members invited the chief justice of the state of New York to administer the oath of office to each individual.

DURING THE EARLY Congresses, and especially the 1st Congress, one of the most important means of initiating legislation came from petitions sent in from individuals and groups seeking relief, assistance or redress of grievances. These petitions represented a long tradition in Britain and America for bringing particular issues to the attention of legislators. Received with respect and attention, they were referred to an appropriate committee and frequently resulted in successful legislation. They not only aided the House in understanding the wishes of their constituents, but confirmed the popular notion that the House was the branch expected to consider those issues of immediate concern to the electorate.

The first such petition to be considered by the House came from "tradesmen, manufacturers, and others, of the town of Baltimore, in the state of Maryland . . . praying an imposition of such duties on all foreign articles which can be made in America." On April 28, a select committee, acting on the petition, recommended impost duties on a long list of goods such as soap, cheese, candles, boots, hemp, pickled fish, leather gloves, saddles, canes and ready-made clothing. The impost bill that was subsequently passed levied a 5 percent tax on these goods.[43]

With the President-elect and the Vice President–elect expected at any moment, the House also busied itself with the necessary "ceremonials" for receiving them. John Adams arrived first on April 20, and a congressional delegation escorted him to the home of John Jay at the present intersection of Varick and Charlton Streets. The next day he appeared at Federal Hall and was escorted to the chair of the presiding officer in the Senate chamber, where he "cheerfully and readily" accepted the duties of his office.[44]

Two days later, on April 23, General George Washington arrived, following a long eight-day triumphal march from his home at Mount Vernon through Philadelphia to New Jersey. Everywhere he stopped crowds greeted and cheered him with receptions, dinners and displays of fireworks. When he reached the New Jersey shore he boarded a specially constructed barge for his entrance into the capital. It was a splendid vessel, its decks were lined with velvet, and an awning stretched over the main deck with red curtains hanging from it. Thirteen pilots dressed in white uniforms rowed this extraordinary craft. A committee of House and Senate members, along with representatives from the city and state governments, provided an official escort. "When I saw Washington," Fisher Ames wrote enthusiastically, "I felt very strong emotions. I believe that no man ever had so fair a claim to veneration as he."[45]

The barge landed at Murray's Wharf at the foot of Wall Street, where Washington mounted carpeted steps to be greeted by Governor George Clinton. The deafening screams from an adoring crowd of spectators welcomed the hero to New York as he paraded on foot to a mansion on Cherry Street that had been elegantly appointed for his use. The house was decorated with the finest wallpaper, rugs and china available.

However, Washington was not inaugurated until April 30, 1789. During the intervening week the Congress fussed and debated over how they would address him. The Constitution called him the President of the United States but that was not good enough for men like John Adams, who preferred "His Most Benign Highness." Other members of the Senate opted for "His Highness the President of the United States of America and Protector of the Rights of the Same."[46] Washington himself rather liked "His High

Mightiness" and in his public documents frequently referred to himself in the third person, imitating royalty. But House members were outraged by the "aristocratic" pretensions of the Senate. Any other title than President of the United States, they said, was unwarranted by the Constitution, "repugnant to republican principles; dangerous, vain, ridiculous, arrogant, and damnable."[47] And that settled that.

THE DAY OF the inaugural ceremony began with thirteen cannon blasts, followed by the ringing of church bells. It was a bright, sunshiny day, and at 12:30 p.m. Washington rode to Federal Hall in a yellow carriage drawn by six white horses and attended by four footmen in livery. Members of Congress and the New York militia marched behind. Dressed in a suit (not a military uniform) with silver buttons embossed with eagles, and wearing white silk stockings and pumps with silver buckles, the President-elect looked every inch an elegant (if not an English) gentleman of high society, especially with his powdered hair and dress sword buckled around his waist. Tall and thin-lipped with a prominent Roman nose, the most distinguishing feature of his slightly pockmarked face, he behaved as though he had been elected a monarch and was headed for his coronation. This first inaugural parade established the traditional route from the President's mansion to the Capitol.

Once Washington reached Federal Hall he strode directly to the Senate chamber upstairs, where Adams greeted him and informed him that the

An artist's conception of the ever-aristocratic George Washington as he prepares to take the oath as the first President.

members of Congress were ready for him to take the oath of office as prescribed by the Constitution. There was a good bit of bowing and scraping
all around, after which Washington declared, "I am ready to proceed."[48]
Obviously they had no precedent for inaugurating a President, and the
bowing and such was only one small indication of that problem. As Madison later told Thomas Jefferson, we are "in a wilderness without a single
footstep to guide us. Our successors will have an easier task. And by de-
grees the way will become smooth short and certain."[49]

The committee assigned to conduct the inaugural arrangements had
decided that the ceremony of the oath should take place in full view of the
public, not in either the House or Senate chamber. So Adams led Washington to the outer gallery, which looked over the street at the second-story
level. Below a cheering crowd saluted him in a thunderous outburst that
overwhelmingly demonstrated their faith in him as well as their love and
respect.

The highest legal officer in New York, the chancellor, Robert R. Livingston, stepped forward, held up a Bible and intoned the words of the oath
as prescribed in the Constitution. "Do you solemnly swear," rumbled the
chancellor, "that you will faithfully execute the office of President of the
United States, and will, to the best of your ability, preserve, protect, and
defend the Constitution of the United States?"

"I solemnly swear," responded Washington. Whereupon he repeated
the oath. Then he bowed down and kissed the book.

"It is done," cried Livingston, "Long live George Washington, President
of the United States."[50] The crowd screamed their approval, and cannons in
the harbor added to the uproar with big booming explosions. The scene was
one great and glorious beginning to a history whose direction few could
begin to guess or imagine. But Senator Robert Morris of Pennsylvania
hoped that "the 4th of March 1789 . . . will hereafter be celebrated as a New
Era in the Annals of the World."[51]

Then the assembly returned to the Senate chamber, where the President addressed the two houses, his mood solemn, his voice deep, "his aspect grave," almost to the point of "sadness."[52] Although he was very
conscious of his position and its importance, still "this great Man was agitated and embarrassed," recorded Senator William Maclay of Pennsylvania. ". . . he trembled and several times could scarce make out to read."[53]

"I was summoned" to this office, Washington began, "by my country,
whose voice I can never hear but with veneration and love."[54] Then he spoke
in the most general terms about virtue, prosperity, duty and the need for
providential guidance. He called for a Bill of Rights to be added to the Constitution, although he opposed any other change to that document until
time and experience dictated otherwise.[55]

The members of Congress listened with rapt attention. Here was virtue personified, declared Ames. Here stood the man who had literally created this nation and whose influence won ratification of the Constitution. In his person he represented a Union of states. Without him any Union seemed unthinkable.

The entire audience was moved to tears. The speech lasted about twenty minutes, and when the great man finished he shook hands with those around him. Then the President left Federal Hall and walked up the hill to St. Paul's Chapel, where the Episcopal bishop conducted services and asked divine blessing on this new administration. The day concluded with receptions and fireworks.

The new government under a new Constitution was at last under way. "The Rooff is now raised & the federal Edifice compleated," wrote Representative Henry Wynkoop of Pennsylvania.[56] The most productive legislative session in the entire history of the House of Representatives was about to begin.

2

The First Session of the 1st Congress, March–September 1789

THE FRAMERS OF the Constitution were absolutely committed to the belief that a representative body, accountable to its constituents, was the surest means of protecting liberty and individual rights. So anxious were they to affirm legislative supremacy in the new government that they failed to flesh out the executive and judicial departments, leaving that task to Congress, and thereby assuring that the legislature would retain control of the structure and authority of both those branches. In addition, they provided the House of Representatives with three important and exclusive rights: impeachment; election of the President if any candidate failed to obtain a majority of electoral votes; and origination of all revenue bills.

The colonial assemblies had asserted their exclusive right to originate and control revenue bills, and the Framers of the Constitution demanded that this right be written into the final document. They also insisted that candidates for office in the House come from the widest pool available, with the fewest possible limitations. Thus, qualifications to serve in the House were reduced to an absolute minimum. To wit: candidates must be residents of the states from which they are chosen, at least twenty-five years of age and seven years a citizen of the United States. Unlike most states in 1789, there were no property or religious qualifications, a rather extraordinary and advanced notion at that time.

Once the government had begun functioning and the housekeeping duties completed, the most pressing need was money. The government had absolutely nothing except a debt that ran to over $50 million, accumulated since the Revolution. To pay it meant levying taxes, and James Madison set about trying to move the House to pass the necessary legislation as fast as possible. In fact, he opened the legislative agenda of the 1st Congress on April 8, 1789, and rose 124 times during the next five months to plead for action on a variety of measures, but most particularly the elimination of the national debt and the establishment of the nation's credit, both at home and abroad. No other member spoke more than 60 times during that same period. Obviously Madison had become the floor leader. The *Massachusetts Centinel* reported on April 22, 1789, that "The Hon. MR. MADISON, is very active—and takes the lead in publick business." "He is our first man," admitted Fisher Ames.[1]

Meanwhile, a series of bills were introduced in the House to address the matter of revenue. The Congress under the Articles of Confederation had no power to raise money. It was obliged to rely on the states to pay its bills, and frequently the states refused to shoulder their share, or did not have the money to do so, or even chose to contribute less than what was requested. It was different now. The Union under the Constitution had recovered "from the state of imbecility that heretofore prevented a performance of its duty," said Madison to his colleagues. We must "revive those principles of honor and honesty that have long been lain dormant."[2]

Naturally, certain states sought to shield their citizens from taxes that would weaken their financial interests. And the people of those states expected their representatives in this 1st Congress to see to it that these interests were protected. For example, New England opposed any tax on the importation of molasses since it needed the molasses to manufacture rum. "We are not . . . at church or school to listen to harangues of speculative piety", lectured Fisher Ames, "we are to talk of the political interests of our charge."[3] So ardent was his appeal that Alexander White of Virginia dubbed him "a Sweet Stickler for Molosses."[4] Another representative moved a tax of $10 for every imported slave, a proposal that brought angry protests from southerners. Still other representatives called for tariff duties to protect infant industries within their communities, particularly to prevent dumping of manufactured goods by Great Britain.

An impost bill was introduced in the House on May 5 and was debated for several weeks, the members dawdling over minor details or sometimes bickering over procedures. "I felt chagrined at the yawning listlessness of many here, in regard to the great objects of the government," fussed the irritated Ames; "their . . . State prejudices; their overrefining spirit in relation to trifles; their attachment to some very distressing formalities in doing business." He added, "It is the most dilatory assembly in the universe."[5]

Finally, under prodding from Madison, and after agreeing on several compromises, the first revenue bill passed and went to the Senate. This was followed by a series of related bills, but not until August were they all enacted by Congress and signed by the President.

These measures included the impost bill, which levied a 5 percent tax on all imported goods, except for a long list of items on which specific duties were assigned. Then the tonnage bill placed a duty on ships entering the United States, with a lower rate for American-owned and American-built ships. Madison tried to provide a lower rate for those nations that had commercial treaties with this country, such as France. "It is a favorite point with the Frenchmen in town," sneered the pro-British Ames.[6] Obviously Madison was trying to force Great Britain into abandoning its restrictive policies toward noncolonial countries. "I wish to teach those nations who have declined to enter into commercial treaties with us," he declared, "that we have the power to extend or withhold advantages as their conduct may deserve."[7] But the Senate refused to accept Madison's ploy and the bill died. "The Senate, God bless them," Ames exclaimed, "as if designated by Providence to keep rash and frolicsome brats out of the fire, have demolished the absurd, impolitic, and mad discrimination of foreigners in alliance from other foreigners."[8]

In settling the conflict over these duties, "the ideas of different quarters N[orther]n Southn. Eastern & Western," reported Madison, "do not entirely accord; but the difficulties are adjusted as easily as could be well expected." In general, he said, "the temper of the Congress seems to be propitious."[9] Clearly the majority was determined to make the Constitution succeed by attempting to accommodate individual prejudices and local loyalties of as many members as possible. The debates, though extremely animated at times, were conducted, wrote William Smith of South Carolina, with "much harmony, politeness and good humor . . . with a moderation and ability extremely unusual in so large a body. . . . How long this delightful accommodation will continue is uncertain: I sincerely wish I shall never see it interrupted." Outside observers in the gallery agreed. "I have constantly attended the debates of the House of Representatives," wrote one visitor from North Carolina, "& have received great pleasure from observing the great liberality of sentiment & spirit of mutual concession which appear from their debates to actuate every member of the House & I have not observed the least attempt to create a party or to divide the house by setting up the southern in opposition to the eastern interest."[10]

To enforce the revenue laws the House passed a collection bill in July that designated ports of entry into the United States. It called for the appointment of one hundred federal officials with powers of "search and seizure" to collect the duties. This important act initiated both the bureaucracy and patronage system of the federal government.[11]

The lighthouse bill of August 1789 absorbed jurisdiction over all exist-ing lighthouses in the United States and directed the construction of a new lighthouse at the entrance of Chesapeake Bay. Then, in the second session of this 1st Congress, the United States Coast Guard was established with authorization for the building of ten revenue cutters.

AT THE SAME time that revenue finally started arriving—and that took months—the government also began dispersing it. During the first session of Congress in 1789, $639,000 was appropriated to run the government; in the second session, $541,395.70 was approved to pay a wide variety of other commitments, including pensions, salaries and the maintenance of light-houses.[12] Congress agreed to pay members of the House and Senate a salary of $6 a day during the session plus travel expenses. Senators demanded a dollar more as a sign of their supposedly more exalted status. After all, the qualifications spelled out by the Constitution to win election to the Senate were more demanding and selective. Finally, following several disputes, the House agreed to an increase for the Senate beginning in 1795 with the un-derstanding that it would remain in effect until March 4, 1796. When that date arrived, Congress decided on equal pay for both houses.

But the pay did not begin to meet the needs of the members. Unless a decent salary was provided for them to give up their "Estates or Profes-sions" and attend "wholly to the public Service in Congress," argued John Page, the result would be the election of "Fools or knaves or Nabobs." Fools would "bungle & perplex [matters] & cost more Money," while knaves would "spin out their Time . . . to the Number of Dollars they wished for & Nabobs would establish the Aristocracy" they all dreaded.[13]

The failure to set a respectable salary for representatives and senators explains in part why there was a tremendous turnover of membership dur-ing the early Congresses.

In addition to fixing their own salaries, members of Congress appro-priated $1,500 a year for the clerk of the House and secretary of the Senate, plus $2 a day for each day they attended the sessions of Congress. The ser-geant at arms received $4 a day, the doorkeeper $3, and the chaplain $500 per annum. For the President, a salary of $20,000 was fixed, while the Vice President received $5,000. The President was also granted a contingency fund of $10,000 as well as money for furniture, horses and carriages. In ad-dition, special appropriations were enacted to cover a variety of activities as recommended by Alexander Hamilton after he had been appointed secre-tary of the treasury by President Washington. All told, the 1st Congress spent $2,154,344.20 to operate the government from 1789 to 1791.[14]

THE RELATION BETWEEN the executive and the legislative branches had not been made clear in the Constitution. But Madison had no fear. "In our government," he said, it was "less necessary to guard against the abuse in the Executive Department . . . because it is not the stronger branch of the system, but the weaker."[15] Little did he know what the future would bring. Under the Articles of Confederation there were executive committees; the Constitution referred to them without including any further provision. On May 19, Madison proposed the formation of executive departments: foreign affairs, treasury and war, each to be headed by a secretary appointed by the President with the advice and consent of the Senate, and removable by the President. Jealous of the House's impeachment power, several representatives objected to the latter provision. According to their view, removal always necessitated impeachment. But Madison took the position that it was "absolutely necessary that the president should have the power [of removal] . . . ; it will make him, in a peculiar manner, responsible for their conduct, and subject him to impeachment himself, if he suffers them to perpetuate with impunity high crimes or misdemeanors against the United States, or neglects to superintend their conduct, so as to check their excesses."[16]

Here was a clear constitutional problem. Who has the power to remove executive officers? Impeachment aside—since it is the exclusive right of the House—can the President remove those he has appointed for any reason short of malfeasance? Must the Senate also advise and consent to removal? "The meddling of the Senate in appointments," grumbled Ames, was bad enough. "I would not extend their power any further."[17]

The Constitution deliberately left the matter to Congress to decide. And Congress ultimately decided to duck the question—a practice habitually adopted in the future—and allowed the bill to establish the Department of Foreign Affairs to pass on July 27 without any mention of removal.[18] Today Presidents usually get rid of unwanted executive officers by asking for their resignation.

Later that summer the name of the Department of Foreign Affairs was changed to the Department of State. During the discussion there was even a proposal to limit the life of the department to one or two years. Some representatives felt that American "intercourse" with foreign nations would gradually decline. They argued that in a short time there would be no need for such a department. Wishful thinking, responded others, and the proposal failed to pass.

The bills to create the Treasury and War Departments were less controversial and won easy approval. With the Treasury there was some discussion about having a board of three instead of a single secretary, such as it had under the Articles of Confederation—that is, a secretary, a comptroller and an auditor. Presumably such a board would prevent any one individual from acquiring paramount financial authority. Again Madison argued convincingly that a single head was preferable in that the comptroller and the auditor could keep a check on the secretary, which would be unlikely with a three-headed board. The House agreed.

Since all revenue bills originate in the House, another concern centered on whether the secretary of the treasury should have direct access to Congress and make his reports in person and even draft legislation. In the final bill signed by the President on September 2, the secretary was directed to prepare reports and give information to both houses in person or in writing "as he may be required." However, drafting legislation would remain a prerogative of the lower chamber. The House made it very explicit that the secretary was not to submit unsolicited bills for legislation regarding revenue.

The War Department was established on August 7, and Henry Knox, who had served under the Articles as secretary of war since 1785, was asked by Washington to continue in that post, a position that placed all military matters under his supervision. One of Washington's more trusted advisers during the Revolution, General Knox distinguished himself as an artillery commander, figuring prominently in the battles of Princeton, Germantown and Yorktown. But Congress seemed to think that this position was less important than the secretaries of state or the treasury because it set the War Department secretary's salary at $3,000, $500 less than those authorized for State and Treasury.[19]

President Washington immediately invited Thomas Jefferson, then serving as minister to France, to become secretary of state. Trained in the law and a former governor of Virginia, Jefferson was happy to return home, arriving in New York in March 1790 to take up his duties.[20]

The brilliant, young and soon-to-be controversial Alexander Hamilton was asked to take over the Treasury Department. Born in the island of Nevis in the West Indies, he was educated at King's College (later Columbia), and married Elizabeth, the daughter of Philip Schuyler, a wealthy New York landowner and that state's newly elected senator to the 1st Congress. Hamilton was one of the principal authors of *The Federalist Papers* (along with James Madison), which had been so instrumental in winning ratification of the Constitution.

While the House concentrated on the questions of the revenue and executive departments, the Senate focused on the judiciary branch. The Constitution established the Supreme Court and assigned its original jurisdiction but then left to Congress the task of creating such inferior courts as changing times necessitated. It was all very vague. But the Judiciary Act of 1789 rectified the ambiguity once and for all. It passed Congress and was signed by the President on September 24. This act provided for a Supreme Court consisting of a chief justice and five associate justices. It also created district courts with a single judge for each state in the Union and three circuit courts of appeal composed of two Supreme Court judges and the judge of the district court in which the case was being heard. In other words, Supreme Court justices had to "ride the circuit." In addition, the jurisdictions of the district and circuit courts were defined and the office of attorney general was established.

This basic structure has remained in place to the present day, although the number of circuit and district courts has increased tremendously. From time to time the number of members of the Supreme Court has varied and was finally set at nine. The passage of this Judiciary Act was one of the major accomplishments of the first session of the 1st Congress.

On July 21, the House accepted the Northwest Ordinance[21] as federal law. Among other things, this ordinance established a government for this territory and the procedure by which additional states could be carved from it and added to the Union. It forbade slavery in the territory, supported education and guaranteed trial by jury and freedom of religion. It provided the model for dealing with future territorial expansion and the admission of new states. Congress passed this Northwest Territory Act and Washington signed it into law on August 7, 1789.

FLOOR MANAGER JAMES Madison caused a stir when he announced to the House on May 4, 1789, that he intended to introduce constitutional amendments that would include a Bill of Rights. The Framers of the Constitution had considered including such a bill in the document but decided against it for the simple reason that the proposed government had only delegated powers and therefore would not concern itself with personal rights. But there was another consideration. In preparing such a list, how could they make it comprehensive? How many rights are there? Ten? Fifteen? Twenty? And if one was inadvertently overlooked, did that mean Congress had the power to legislate on it?

But the failure to include a Bill of Rights almost resulted in the rejection of the Constitution by several states. Anti-Federalists hammered away at this omission and called for another convention to write a proper document. Madison, who originally opposed the idea of such a bill, found his constituents decidedly in its favor. Thomas Jefferson added his voice of approval by reminding Madison that the American people, having endured the Revolution, expected a written statement confirming their rights and placing restraints on the ability of the central government to legislate on them.

The arguments, and especially the overwhelming will of his constituents, convinced Madison to change his position, and he pledged to introduce the necessary amendments. But it would be no easy task. Both Federalists and Anti-Federalists were chagrined by his announcement. The Federalists argued that such a bill had no place in a document that simply described the mechanics of government and gave it limited powers. Bring-

James Madison is not only the Father of the Constitution and the author of the Bill of Rights but the steady hand that guided the House during all three sessions of the 1st Congress.

ing it up at this time, argued Theodore Sedgwick of Massachusetts, "was in my opinion unwise and will not produce those beneficial effects which its advocates predicted. Before we could be said to have a government to attempt to amend the constitution argues a frivolity of character very inconsistent with national dignity."[22] Madison responded by declaring that since power is subject to abuse, did it not make sense to amend the document "in a more secure manner than is now done?"[23]

Anti-Federalists, on the other hand, feared that such amendments would prevent the calling of another convention by which they could strengthen the rights of the states and lessen the powers of the central government. "Antifederals in our House," declared William Smith of South Carolina, "have thrown difficulties in the way of these Amendmts, merely because they can't carry alterations which wod... overturn the Governmt."[24]

The possibility of a second convention frightened those who were concerned about having a strong government. "The Voice of Congress," Richard Bland Lee of Virginia wrote, "is almost unanimous against a Second Convention, as leading directly to anarchy & the most fatal discord."[25]

Madison realized that if the new government was to be protected from emasculation or replacement he would have to prepare a list of changes that would appease both the friends and the enemies of the Constitution. He also realized that by allowing amendments that protected individual liberties he would safeguard the basic structure of the government from further tampering by its enemies. Once converted, he convinced Washington to include a call for such amendments in his inaugural address. Indeed, he helped write the address. Having the President as an ally provided enormous help in convincing his colleagues to accept his changes.

Madison had his work cut out for him. He had on hand more than two hundred amendments that had been submitted by the states over the past two years, many of which altered the fundamental structure of the government and restored important authorities to the states. Still he was determined to achieve his goal. Fortunately he had a solid basis to start: George Mason's Virginia Declaration of Rights of 1776.

On June 8 Madison "introduced his long expected amendments. They are the fruit of much labor and research," declared Fisher Ames. "He has hunted up all the grievances and complaints of newspapers, all the articles of conventions, and the small talk of their debates. It contains a bill of rights, the right of enjoying property, of changing the government at pleasure, freedom of the press, of conscience, of juries, exemption from general warrants, gradual increase of representatives.... This is the substance. There is too much of it. Oh! I had forgot, the right of the people to bear arms."[26]

Madison put forward nineteen amendments. He wanted them woven into the text of the Constitution, with a preface to be added that would emphasize the sovereignty of the people and state the principles of republican government. But he wisely held off pushing for consideration of these amendments early on so that important pending legislation, such as the revenue bills, could be completed and sent along to the Senate. Finally, on July 21, he "begged the house to indulge him."[27]

On a motion from Fisher Ames the House agreed to refer the matter to a select committee. Ames dreaded the idea that the amendments would be considered by the Committee of the Whole and consume valuable time. "I dislike the committee of the whole more than ever," he wrote. "We could not be so long doing so little, by any other expedient." Members of the committee "indulge a very minute criticism upon its style. We correct spelling, or erase *may* and insert *shall,* and quibble little improprieties. Our great committee is too unwieldly for this operation. A great, clumsy machine is applied to the slightest and most delicate operations—the hoof of an elephant to the strokes of messotinto."[28]

Bypassing the Committee of the Whole was a wise decision. The select committee took only a week to come back to the full House on July 28 with a recommendation favoring what Madison had introduced.

The Anti-Federalists sneered. One of them, Aedanus Burke of South Carolina, said the amendments were "little better than whipsyllabub, frothy and full of wind, formed only to please the palate." They resembled "a tub thrown out to a whale, to secure the freight of the ship and its peaceable voyage."[29]

For the most part the amendments dealt with personal liberties and forbade the government from legislating on any of them. They dealt with basic freedoms, such as speech, press, religion, the rights of assembly and petition, and the right to bear arms. They also guaranteed fair trial. And Madison went out of his way to include what Anti-Federalists insisted upon—namely, that those powers not delegated by the Constitution to the national government were reserved to the "States respectively, or to the people."

At times the debate became rather heated "so that a frequent call to Order became absolutely necessary."[30] Not until August 24 did the members exhaust the arguments for and against the proposals. To Madison's intense satisfaction, they agreed to seventeen of them without a declaration of principles. On a motion from Roger Sherman it was decided to group the amendments together at the end of the Constitution rather than incorporate them into the text itself. In this form the Congress created an actual "Bill of Rights."

The package was sent to the Senate, where through combinations and deletion—a guarantee of protection of the right of conscience and a statement on the separation of powers were deleted—their number was reduced to twelve and passed. On September 28, the day before this first session of the 1st Congress ended, they were submitted to the states for ratification. Not until December 15, 1791, did the states ratify ten of the twelve. Amendments regarding congressional salaries and the apportionment of House seats failed to pass. However the salaries amendment proposed in 1789 was finally ratified in 1992 as the 27th Amendment to the Constitution.

On the whole, thought Fisher Ames, these changes might "do some good towards quieting men, who attend to sounds only."[31] Otherwise they seemed unnecessary. Of course, he was quite wrong. If nothing else, the Bill of Rights effectively blocked any concerted effort to call a second constitutional convention to create still another national government.

ONE OTHER TROUBLESOME matter kept disturbing the general unanimity of the members. During this first session there were constant rumblings about deciding on a permanent residence for this new government. Throughout the Revolution the seat of government had moved from place to place and finally came to rest in New York in 1785. But there had been no commitment, and the Constitution said nothing about it. Naturally New York hoped to retain the residence because of the many financial benefits that would ensue, which is why it went to the expense of remodeling Federal Hall. But the Pennsylvania delegation felt that the honor belonged to Philadelphia since it was more centrally located in the country and because the Declaration of Independence and the Constitution itself had been written and adopted in that city. Southerners hoped to bring the government farther south and contended for a location on the Potomac River. Others even opted for Trenton since that city had served briefly as the seat of government in 1784.[32]

"Special interest, always more active than public interest," wrote one foreign observer, "was at the point yesterday of inciting a great tumult in Congress at its very debut. The Pennsylvanians . . . want this sovereign Assembly to reside in their State at all costs. . . . It was only with difficulty that they decided to defer this distinct measure."[33]

At the start of the session, Madison, who supported the Potomac River site, dreaded any discussion of a permanent residence because he knew it would trigger controversy and delay action on what he considered more important matters. But he promised the Philadelphians that the question would be addressed before the end of the session. By the time the other issues were resolved it was clear to many that such a residence would have to encompass a considerable expanse of territory—that is, if the government expected to function independently. Certainly a town or city like New York or Philadelphia or Trenton would never do, particularly since Congress would have only limited authority in those places. It had become obvious that a hundred-square-mile federal district was required to mount the central government, over which land Congress would exercise exclusive jurisdiction.

As the first session neared an end, the Pennsylvania delegation, accepting the fact that Philadelphia was out of the question, negotiated an arrangement with several northern representatives whereby the permanent capital would be located on the Susquehanna River in Pennsylvania after remaining in New York for a few more years while the new site was being built. But southerners insisted on an area near Georgetown, Maryland, on the Potomac. Madison, as leader of the Potomac faction, strongly objected to the Susquehanna location and, as a result, a sectional squabble broke out on the floor. Despite his best efforts, Madison could not convince his colleagues to support his position, and the House therefore passed a bill designating the Susquehanna River as the site for the new capital.

To foil the Pennsylvanians, Madison concocted a plan by which the New York senators were talked into helping put off final action on the bill until the next session. This would, for the time being, keep the capital in New York. And Madison's scheme worked. The Senate postponed final action.

With that problem temporarily resolved the first session of the 1st Congress came to an end on September 29, 1789. The second session would begin four months later on January 4, 1790.

DURING THE LONG, hot and humid days of this summer—"the Hottest weather I ever experienced," complained George Leonard of Massachusetts—the members tried to find some diversion besides the many parties and balls they attended. In late July a group of them took a boat trip up the Hudson River to West Point on board the *Captain North*. They left on a Friday and after a delightful outing returned to the city on Saturday evening. They were a mixed bunch, representing northern, middle and southern states. They got to know one another personally and found they enjoyed each other's company, despite the fact that they were "men under the influence of such jarring interests coming from such different countries and climates and accustomed to such different manners."[34] They initiated a sense of collegiality that marked many periods of congressional history.

THE TREMENDOUS SUCCESS of this first session—securing revenue, establishing executive departments, creating the judicial system and enacting the Bill of Rights—was due principally to the determination by most members of the House to make the Constitution work.[35] A Union of states had been achieved with the federal government exercising supreme jurisdiction. The members truly worried that the Constitution might fail, as had the Articles of Confederation, and if it did, not only would foreign powers mock American attempts at establishing a republican form of government, but they would also be encouraged to take advantage of the failure and reassert their influence on and control of American affairs. Worse, it might prove impossible to discover the necessary ingredients to establish a lasting government based on liberty, justice and the protection of private property.

A Union of states and people under the Constitution had been created, and that is what had to be perpetuated. "I wish to have every American think the Union so indissoluble and integral," wrote Ames, "that the corn would not grow, nor the pot boil, if it should be broken."[36]

The members disagreed at times, and even quarreled, but never to the point of creating irreconcilable factions within the House. This cooperation and harmony, which existed despite sectional and economic differences, would not last long. But it was essential in the beginning. The members knew it and therefore worked together to provide a proper start to this "new experiment in freedom."

So they put partisanship aside. As Fisher Ames said, "There is less party spirit, less of the acrimony of pride when disappointed of success, less personality, less intrigue, cabal, management, or cunning than I ever saw in a public assembly." Even more astounding, the members took their responsibilities very seriously by showing up each day and on time. There was "the most punctual attendance of the members at the hour of meeting. Three or four have had leave of absence, but every other member actually attends daily, till the hour of adjourning."[37] Small wonder they completed so much in such a short time—and all this without a staff of assistants to aid them or offices where they could prepare their speeches or attend to their correspondence.

There were other reasons for this prodigious accomplishment. The House was fortunate to have James Madison as floor manager. He understood the importance of compromise in resolving problems. His experience at the Constitutional Convention in Philadelphia taught him the value of reconciling the needs and demands of opponents. Directing the majority in the House to run roughshod over opposing views was not the way to go. By acceding, where possible, to other proposals or suggestions put forward by Anti-Federalists or hostile voices, by building coalitions with members from different sections of the country and by being conciliatory, he could complete a legislative program that would flesh out the Constitution and ensure its workability.

The people, too, fervently desired the success of the Constitution. They were encouraged by what was reported in the newspapers. Most particularly they rejoiced that the Bill of Rights had been passed and sent to the states for ratification.

When Congress adjourned in late September the members knew they had made tremendous strides in completing much of the structure for a strong central government that could—and later would—command respect in the country and around the world.

3

New York, Philadelphia and Ideological Conflict, 1790–1797

T HE HARMONY THAT characterized the opening session of the 1st Congress soon faded. Regional jealousies, sectional disagreements and ideological differences mounted and created divisions that locked the members of Congress into opposing groups that at times threatened to tear the Union apart. The first stirrings of party activity became manifest.

AFTER COMPLETING THEIR initial work of erecting a federal government, the members scrambled to get out of town and enjoy a brief respite at home. New York, said Representative John Page of Virginia, "is not half so large as Philadelphia; nor in any manner to be compared to it for Beauty & Elegance. . . . The streets here are badly paved, very dirty & narrow as well as crooked, & filled up with strange Variety of wooden & Stone & brick Houses & full of Hogs and mud." However, he allowed that "the College, St. Paul's Church, & the Hospital are elegant Buildings."[1]

Actually, New York boasted many attractive sites. Although the catastrophic fire of 1776 and a second conflagration two years later had destroyed over a thousand buildings in a wide swath in lower Manhattan, by 1790 "elegant brick houses" had replaced them. The imposing homes of wealthy merchants and lawyers could be found on Broadway, Whitehall, Broad, Water, Vesey and Barclay Streets. Most of them showed a distinct

Georgian or Colonial style in architecture, but the Dutch influence could still be detected and admired.

Broadway attracted visitors because of its wide, paved expanse and its walkway laid with bricks. Business and family dwellings lined both sides and some of them enjoyed kitchen gardens with a section reserved for the cultivation of flowers. Although most congressmen lived in boarding-houses, they frequently attended lavish parties thrown by the leaders of New York society, such as the Schuylers, the Verplancks, the Livingstons, the Duanes, the Jays, the Bleeckers, the Beekmans, the Stuyvesants, the Bayards and the Duers.

At his residence, Macomb House, President Washington enjoyed and encouraged elaborate ceremonies, and held a "levee" on Tuesday after-noons, with as much royal trappings as seemed suitable. His wife, Martha, conducted Friday evening receptions at 8:00 p.m. "The form of the Recep-tion is this," reported Abigail Adams, the wife of the Vice President: "the servants announce & Col. Humphries or Mr. Lear, receive every Lady at the door, & Hands her up to Mrs. Washington to whom she makes a most Re-spectfull courtsey and then is seated. . . . The President then comes up, and speaks to the Lady, which he does with a grace dignity & ease, that leaves Royal George far behind him. The company are entertained with Ice creems & Lemonade, and return at their pleasure performing the same ceremony when they quit the Room."[2]

Speaker Muhlenberg, too, was frequently busy in giving "oyster sup-pers." "Some amusement from the Business of the day is necessary," com-mented Abigail Adams, "and can there be a more Innocent one than that of meeting at Gentlemens Houses and conversing together?" She herself en-tertained company on Monday evenings. "All other ladies who have pub-lick Evenings," she said, "give Tea, Coffee & Lemonade, but one only who introduces cards, and she is frequently put to difficulty to make up one table at whist. Pray is not this better than resorting to Taverns, or even having supper partys?"[3]

Numerous taverns did act as gathering places for various societies and clubs, the most famous of which was Fraunces Tavern, the terminus for the Boston, Albany and Philadelphia stagecoaches. At these taverns, as well as the parties and balls, personal alliances were forged, networks created and political influence exercised. Frequently, at these gatherings, men and even women "lobbied" for different causes or needs. It was very informal, unor-ganized and spontaneous for the most part—nowhere near the lobbying operation that functions today—but it did operate and was sometimes quite effective.[4] The term "lobbying" itself originated in Great Britain, where journalists would stand around the lobby of the House of Commons, wait-ing to interview the members as they emerged from the hall. In the United States the term was expanded to include a wide variety of individuals intent

on influencing legislation. The procedure would later become public, organized and produce both benefits and problems for the members of Congress.

For theater, New Yorkers and congressmen attended the Old American
Company, which offered not only the classics, especially Shakespeare, but
also American works by such aspiring dramatists as William Dunlap. President Washington frequented the theater quite often, lending it a high degree of respectability among the more fastidious. Musical entertainments
were provided by concerts and recitals that attracted gifted artists to the
city along with circus performers such as acrobats, contortionists, jugglers,
dancers and comedians.

THE SECOND SESSION of the 1st Congress was scheduled to reconvene on
Monday, January 4, 1790. True to form the House lacked a quorum on that
day and had to wait until Thursday, January 7, before a sufficient number of
representatives arrived to commence operations. A few, like Madison, were
delayed on account of illness; others found it difficult to leave the restful
surroundings of home or the demands of their profession. "Ah, politics!"
sighed Fisher Ames, "how have they spoiled me for my profession. . . . Either I must become a mere politician, and think of my profession as a secondary matter, or renounce politics, and devote myself to the humble
drudgery of earning bread."[5]

The session began with Washington's address to Congress on January
8, or, as Ames called it, "the King's speech."[6] The President acknowledged
North Carolina's ratification of the Constitution[7] and the improved "credit
and respectability of our country." He noted with pleasure the many successes of the first session and mentioned that "adequate provision for the
support of the public credit, is a matter of high importance to the national
honor and prosperity."[8]

On the recommendation of several House members of a need to form a
committee to advise it on fiscal matters, a select Committee of Ways and
Means had been appointed on July 24, 1789, during the debate on the establishment of the Treasury Department. This committee consisted of one
member from each state. But the committee was discharged from its responsibility on September 17 and the secretary of the treasury was invited
to report on the state of the public credit.[9]

Throughout the fall and early winter of 1789 Alexander Hamilton had
studied a number of fiscal tracts and had consulted with several individuals, including Madison. There was considerable speculation about the secretary's likely report, which set off a buying spree of depreciated government
and state securities.

When Hamilton notified Congress that his "Report on Public Credit"
was ready for presentation, the members took immediate alarm over the

fear of executive encroachment on the rights of Congress; they quickly decided against allowing him to appear in person to present the fifty-one-page
document. Instead it was read on January 14, 1790, by a clerk, page after
tedious page, while the representatives sat and listened in "stupefied silence."[10]

The report revealed a national debt of $54,124,464.56, of which
$11,710,378 was owed to foreigners, mostly French and Dutch. The secre-
tary recommended that it be funded along with state debts that amounted
to $25 million, which would be paid by instituting an excise tax. The na-
tional debt represented obligations for supplies and services contracted
during the war, along with 6 percent certificates issued to pay the army. In
asking that state debts be assumed Hamilton hoped to bind the loyalty of
state creditors to the national government.[11]

By funding the debt, Hamilton knew he could establish the nation's financial credit. And the funding would involve no distinction between the
original and the present holders of these debts, despite the fact that speculators had been buying them up at bargain rates ever since they first got wind
of Hamilton's intended proposal.

The report, on its face, was bound to cause problems. Funding the national debt was one thing, but assuming state debts was quite another, particularly when some of the states had already paid off a considerable amount
of their debt by selling their western lands. It struck Madison, who arrived
to take his seat on January 21, as penalizing states, such as Virginia, that
had met their obligations, and rewarding those who had shirked their responsibility. In addition, it seemed unfair to many congressmen to line the
pockets of speculators by providing full face value to the debts they held
while the original holders received nothing. Ever since this report became
public, thundered Representative James Jackson of Georgia on the floor in
late January, "a spirit of havoc, speculation, and ruin, has arisen, and been
cherished by people who had an access to the information. . . . My soul rises
indignant at the avaricious and immoral turpitude which so vile a conduct
displays."[12]

When the debate on the report began in the House on February 8, the
public jammed the gallery. They were "all in a flame about funding."[13] Madison immediately voiced his objections. He insisted that original holders,
such as soldiers and patriotic merchants who had provided food and supplies during the Revolution, be given full value while the present holders,
those greedy, opportunistic speculators, receive less. "The only point on
which we can deliberate," he argued, "is, to whom the payment is really
due."[14] In addition, he opposed assuming state debts as another example of
injustice.

Just how the government would go about distinguishing between original and secondary holders and trying to adjust a fair balance between

them struck most representatives as unworkable, and so Madison's motion for discrimination was resoundingly defeated on February 22, 1790, by the vote of 36 to 13, in part because many northerners regarded this kind of speculation as both legitimate and admirable. Nine Virginians and four other southerners voted for the defeated measure.

Madison sat at his desk mortified. It was a stinging defeat. Thirty-six to 13. That hurt. But he had some satisfaction in knowing that many people around the country applauded his efforts. "Happy there is a Madison," editorialized the Boston's *Columbian Centinel* on February 24, "who fearless of the blood suckers will step forward and boldly vindicate the rights of the widows and orphans, the original creditors and the war worn soldier."[15]

Hamilton was puzzled by Madison's position. He had always regarded him as an ally in the important task of creating a strong national government. Had he deserted this noble cause simply to appease the interest of his state? Theodore Sedgwick declared the Virginian "an apostate from all his former principles. . . . Whether he means to put himself at the head of the discontented in America time will discover."[16] Fisher Ames was also shocked. Madison "hangs heavy on us. If he is a friend, he is more troublesome than a declared foe."[17] According to Irving Brant, his biographer, Madison sacrificed his leadership in the House by initiating this contest. Worse, he caused a split within the Federalist ranks by which one small part of that group now sided with "the radical wing of the vanishing Antifederalists."[18] The youthful John Quincy Adams, son of the Vice President, recognized that the "seeds of two contending factions appear to be plentifully sown. The names Federalist and Antifederalist are no longer expressive of the sentiments which they were so lately supposed to contain, and I expect soon to hear a couple of new names, which will designate the respective friends of the national and particular systems. The people are evidently dividing into these two parties."[19]

To exacerbate the dissension, Quakers from New York and Philadelphia petitioned Congress to abolish the slave trade. But the Pennsylvania Abolition Society went one step further and demanded the outright abolition of slavery. It was signed by the society's president, Benjamin Franklin. These petitions could not have come at a worse time. They caused a major uproar. Southerners protested that any discussion of the question could jeopardize the Union. They quoted the Bible to support their moral right to hold slaves. William Smith of South Carolina reminded his colleagues that "We took each other, with our mutual bad habits and respective evils, for better, for worse, the Northern States adopted us with our slaves, and we adopted them with their Quakers."[20] Northerners, of course, cited the Declaration of Independence in their arguments against the institution. Some opted for gradual emancipation with compensation to the slaveholders. But finding the funds to implement this suggestion also provoked division.

Senator William Maclay heard there was "warmth in the House of Representatives, on the Quaker memorial," so he visited the lower chamber to
see for himself. He was shocked. "The house have certainly greatly debased
their dignity," he recorded. "Using base invective indecorous language 3 or
4 up at a time. manifest signs of passion. the most disorderly Wandering, in
their Speeches, telling Stories, private anecdotes &ca &ca. I know not What
may come of it. but there seems a General discontent among the Members,
and many of them do not Hesitate to declare, that the Union Must fall to
pieces, at the rate we go on."[21] The collegiality of the first session had evaporated, replaced by angry voices who threatened the life of the Union if the
question of slavery, ever again, became a matter of debate. The issue was
finally referred to a committee, where it was buried and subsequently
died.

BY THE TIME the House returned to Hamilton's report the atmosphere in
the chamber had grown increasingly quarrelsome. And although Madison
had sustained a stinging defeat on funding, he fared better on the question
of the assumption of state debts. Not only would those states, north and
south, that had paid some or most of their debts feel cheated, but if the
national government paid these debts, it would gobble up most of the revenue.

These concerns, plus the realization that the North Carolina delegation
would soon arrive and join Virginia, Maryland and Georgia in opposition
to his proposals, worried Hamilton enough, according to Senator Maclay,
to require the application of extreme measures. "I do not know what pecu-

*Unfortunately, Senator William Maclay
of Pennsylvania served only one term in
Congress. His diary provides a critical
glimpse of what transpired in Congress
during the formation of the federal government under the Constitution.*

niary influence has actually been Used, but I am certain, That every kind of management has been practised, and Every tool at Work that could be thought of. Officers of Government, Clergy Citizens Cincinnati, and every Person under the influence of the Treasury." Worse, Representatives Theodorick Bland of Virginia and Daniel Huger of South Carolina were literally carried into the chamber to help with their votes, the "one lame, the other sick."[22]

But together these worthies could not stem the tide of opposition to assumption and, on April 12, the Committee of the Whole House rejected it by a vote of 31 to 29, a two-vote difference.[23] Hamilton's friends broke down in tears, their faces "reddened like Scarlet . . . or [turned] deadly White." George Clymer of Pennsylvania could scarcely believe what had happened. His "lips quavered" and his lower jaw shook convulsively. "His head neck & Breast consented to Gesticulations resembling those of a Turkey or Goose, nearly strangled in the Act of deglutition."[24] Sedgwick stood up and ranted that the people of Massachusetts had "implored" the members "to relieve us from the pressure of intolerable burdens—burdens incurred in support of your freedom and independence."[25] According to Representative Abraham Baldwin of Georgia, "the N Carolina members turned the scale against it, but they are still trying to cook the dish so as to make it more palatable, and intend to bring it forward again."[26]

THE HOUSE HAD reached a critical moment in its history. Because several other issues awaited resolution—such as the temporary and permanent residences of the capital—and because northern congressmen continued to entertain petitions against slavery and the slave trade, there was increasing talk about dissolving the Union and starting over. "People almost seem ripe for a national division of North & South," Representative Benjamin Goodhue of Massachusetts was told by one constituent.[27] Northerners resented the unwillingness of southerners to agree to assumption, while southerners berated northerners for presuming they had the right to even discuss petitions involving slavery. As for the residence question, it had been left unfinished when the first session of this Congress adjourned. Then, in the opening of the second session, the House adopted a new joint rule by which any business left unfinished at the end of one session must begin all over again at the next session, thereby killing the bill that had selected Pennsylvania for the site of the new capital. It was a neat bit of "skullduggery" that naturally infuriated the Pennsylvania delegation.[28]

The government hovered on the threshold of convulsion, or so President Washington reported to the Marquis de la Luzerne.[29] Madison claimed that a number of "eastern members" had sworn to oppose all provision for the public debt unless it included assumption, even intimating "danger to the Union from a refusal to assume."[30]

At this point Thomas Jefferson arrived in New York to take up his duties as secretary of state, knowing little about the several issues that were embroiling Congress. He later wrote in his "Anas" that he was going to meet the President, and while on his way he ran into Hamilton on the street. They continued walking toward Washington's home, and when they arrived at the door, Hamilton paced back and forth for a full half hour, haranguing Jefferson about "the temper into which the legislature had been wrought" and the "danger of the *secession* of their members and the separation of the states."

That brought Jefferson up short. Could you, would you, pleaded Hamilton, speak to some of your friends and help resolve the crisis? Responding as best he could, Jefferson invited him to dinner the next day, at which time he felt certain, "by some mutual sacrifices of opinion," a compromise could be found so as "to save the Union."[31]

Jefferson also invited Madison to attend the dinner in the hope that he could be of some help in finding a solution to the problem. When the three men met, Jefferson pointed out that passage of assumption would be bitter medicine for many southerners. He then suggested that the bitterness could be sweetened by locating the seat of government in Philadelphia for ten years, after which it would be moved permanently to a site along the Potomac. It could be accomplished, Jefferson continued, because two Virginia members, Richard Bland Lee and Alexander White, would change their vote on assumption in return for which Hamilton would be expected to obtain support from northern delegates for the Potomac location. For his part, Madison consented to the arrangement though he said he would refuse to vote for assumption. Still he would "not be strenuous" in his opposition.[32]

Jefferson's undoubtedly exaggerated and oversimplified account of what happened at the dinner party and the role he played in arranging a compromise has been challenged by more than one historian.[33] There was indeed a dinner, but whether it occurred before or after these critical issues were resolved, or whether assumption and the permanent residence were linked, are still disputed. Whatever the facts, Madison did convince Senator Charles Carroll of Carrollton, a wealthy Maryland landowner, and four representatives to change their vote on assumption. These four included Representatives Daniel Carroll and George Gale, whose districts bordered the Potomac, in addition to Lee and White. For his part, Hamilton convinced several northerners to accept a permanent residence on the Potomac after an extended temporary residence in Philadelphia. "Intrigues, cabals & combinations," Elbridge Gerry told James Monroe, "are the consequence."[34] But they produced the desired result. As such, the so-called Compromise of

1790 gave southerners the capital they wanted with its supposed economic benefits, and provided northerners with the assumption of state debts.

On a motion by Charles Carroll in the Senate, the bill enacted in the first session to locate the capital in Pennsylvania was amended on June 28. It substituted a site on the Potomac between the Anacostia River and Conococheague Creek at Williamsport, Maryland. The question of a temporary residence of ten years during the period when the new capital was being constructed set off a heated argument; but on July 1, the upper house agreed to locate it in Philadelphia. It passed the Senate by a single vote.

The House took up the issue on July 6 and enacted it on July 9 without amendment by a vote of 32 to 29. Perhaps Pennsylvanians accepted the arrangement in the vain hope that once the capital was located in Philadelphia it would be next to impossible to dislodge it after ten years. In any event, the bill went to the President, who immediately signed it, no doubt delighted that the permanent capital would spread across some of his property and provide easy access from his home in Mount Vernon.

But New Yorkers were naturally infuriated. Here, stormed Philip Schuyler, they had raised a large amount of money to provide adequate and comfortable quarters for Congress only to have this generosity repaid by a want of "decency which was due to a City whose citizens made very capital exertions for the accommodation of Congress." Some worried about what action the New York members would take on this account, "but Hamilton has kept them with us," wrote the much-relieved William Smith of South Carolina.[35]

Once the residence question had been settled, the Senate amended the House funding bill to include the assumption of state debts by a vote of 14 to 12. Charles Carroll switched his earlier position and provided the winning margin. The House modified this amendment and approved assumption on July 24 when Lee, White, Carroll and Gale all gave their approval. The vote was 34 to 28. Madison voted against it, but said nothing in opposition.

Later Jefferson came to appreciate exactly what he had done. He said he was "most ignorantly and innocently made to hold the candle" for Hamilton's elaborate scheme of "plunder."[36] The important speculators of the public debt had gambled heavily in state debts. Had assumption failed they would have been wiped out. Instead they reaped a tremendous financial reward and the Union survived its first major crisis.

President Washington let out a sigh of relief. "I hope they [the debt and residence questions] are now settled in as satisfactory a manner as could have been expected," he wrote, "and that we have a prospect of enjoying peace abroad, with tranquility at home."[37]

•   •   •

DURING THESE DEBATES on the residency bill the filibuster* tactic was frequently applied in the House to delay or halt action. But as time passed and the size of the House increased in number, the rules were changed to restrict this practice. For example, a rule was adopted in which calling the previous question could permit a majority of the House to shut off debate. Furthermore, by limiting the time each member could speak and insisting that representatives stay focused on the issue at hand, the filibuster had a fitful history in the lower chamber. But from time to time it reemerged to produce havoc in the House.

Congress also passed the enumeration bill in this second session to provide for a census as required by the Constitution so that an accurate apportionment of seats in the House could be determined. The result of the first census revealed many inequities that Madison hoped to rectify with a constitutional amendment that would call for one representative for every 30,000 inhabitants until the membership of the House reached 100, after which the population figure would be raised to 40,000 until the members numbered 200, and thereafter 50,000. But the states failed to ratify this amendment and Congress was obliged to pass another apportionment bill for the second census, which Washington vetoed—his first such—because it allowed additional seats for fractions of inhabitants over a half. Consequently Congress directed a fixed ratio of one seat for every 33,000 without fractions. Thus, a state like Delaware got only one representative for its 58,000 inhabitants.[38] This reapportionment went into effect in 1793 and increased House membership to 106. It remained in force until the 1840s. Virginia had the largest delegation with 19 representatives, followed by Massachusetts with 14, Pennsylvania with 13 and New York with 10. Rhode Island had 2, as did Vermont, which entered the Union on March 4, 1791, and Kentucky, which entered on June 1, 1792. When Tennessee joined the Union in 1796 it had one representative: Andrew Jackson.

THE SECOND SESSION of the 1st Congress ended on August 12, 1790, by which time it had become clear that the unanimity of the first session had faded with the struggle over funding, assumption, abolition of slavery and the permanent residence of the government. The initial split between Federalists and Anti-Federalists had now expanded to include rivalry between the north and south, between those who favored national over states' rights and between those who entertained an expanded versus a restricted interpretation of the Constitution. "Already we begin to perceive the collision of

---

*A filibuster is a delaying tactic involving prolonged oratory by the opposition, to prevent a vote on a legislative matter that would pass if a vote were permitted. *The Encyclopedia of the United States Congress* (New York, 1995), 2:833.

the Government of the United States with that of the individual States," worried Senator William Few of Georgia.[39] Even within the country as a whole there was deep concern over the proceedings of Congress. Northern Federalists no longer looked to Madison as their leader. They were alienated by his strong pro-southern and pro-Virginia arguments during the several debates. Robert R. Livingston reported to Jefferson that northerners were dissatisfied with the outcome of several issues, to which the secretary of state replied that there was also "a vast mass of discontent" in the South.[40]

The situation grew worse when the third session began in Philadelphia on December 6, 1790. And wonder of wonders, the House had a quorum on December 7, a day after its scheduled starting date. The members complained about the difficulty of finding adequate quarters at reasonable prices in Philadelphia. As for the city itself, the ever-critical Senator Maclay thought that the influence of Quakers made it a gloomy place that lacked fashionable dress and entertainments.[41] Others, like Theodore Sedgwick, disagreed, claiming that "every day almost I have an invitation to dine and spend the evening." Such prominent Philadelphia families as the McKeans, the Dallases, the Binghams, the Chews and the Clymers regularly gave dancing parties. Abigail Adams found Philadelphia society "brilliant" even though she missed New York. "When all is done," she sighed, "it will not be Broadway."[42]

George and Martha Washington rented Robert Morris's mansion at 190 Market Street, near Sixth. The President held his levees on Tuesdays from 3:00 to 4:00 p.m., which were attended only by men. Martha Washington gave her customary Friday evening levee, which attracted "all the Beauties of Philadelphia." Sedgwick attended one such levee and could hardly get over "the stupid formality of a great number of well dressed people assembled together for the unmeaning purpose of seeing and being seen."[43]

John and Abigail Adams rented Bush Hill for $400 a month. Unfortunately it was two miles from the city and created problems, especially in winter or inclement weather. Abigail said Philadelphia was much more expensive than New York, "horse keeping in particular, which we sensibly feel, as we are obliged to keep four, for during the sitting of Congress they frequently go six times to the city in the course of the day. We cannot purchase any marketting but by going into the city."[44] Those who could afford them rented houses, but most representatives messed together in hotels, taverns or boardinghouses. Theodore Sedgwick moved into a boardinghouse with five other House members. A "motley mixture" to be sure, he remarked.[45]

Philadelphia was undoubtedly the most cosmopolitan city in the United States, boasting cultural and educational institutions that rivaled many European cities. Its population numbered approximately forty-three thousand

and its many economic advantages in commerce and industry attracted a constant flow of immigrants not only from Europe but from surrounding states. Its streets were straight and provided sidewalks of raised bricks.

Having hosted the Continental Congresses, the second of which produced the Declaration of Independence, as well as the Constitutional Convention, the city, in a real sense, represented the country's national past. Known for its "Beauty & Elegance," Philadelphia boasted museums, a circus where equestrian spectacles dazzled audiences and the country's first free lending library. According to Abigail Adams there was "one continued scene of Parties upon Parties, Balls and entertainments equal to any European city." However, "The Public amusements tis True are few. No Theatre here this winter . . . but the more general Method for those who have Houses calculated for it, is to give Balls at their own Houses."[46]

CONGRESS MET IN the County Courthouse at the corner of Sixth and Chestnut Streets, a relatively newly built structure that required only minor changes to meet the needs of the two chambers and was renamed Congress Hall. It was only a short distance from Independence Hall, where the Declaration of Independence had been signed. The House occupied an unadorned first floor while the Senate took the more elaborately furnished second floor. The House chamber had two rows of semicircular desks, which was a tight fit, especially after the census raised the number of representatives to 106. There was a balcony within the chamber that accommodated five hundred spectators. Each member had an inkstand, a sandbox, pens and paper. In front of the members was a raised platform for the Speaker, along with two tables on which law books were laid. Four stoves at strategic locations kept the chamber warm during the winter.[47] The building was "neat, elegant & convenient," according to Sedgwick, but it lacked the "splendid grandeur" of Federal Hall in New York.[48]

The serious work of this third and final session of the 1st Congress began on December 6, 1790, after hearing a "speech from the throne."[49] In issuing a reply to the "King's speech," the House inaugurated the practice of responding to it with elaborate ceremonials that resembled those conducted by the British Parliament. Each chamber composed a reply to the message and then members of Congress paraded through the streets of Philadelphia to the President's residence and assured him that the issues raised in his speech would be given due consideration. Washington rather liked the deference paid him and the practice continued for the first six Congresses. It ended when Jefferson became President.

Congress finally got down to business when Secretary Hamilton recommended the establishment of a national bank—"the linchpin of his entire program," according to one historian[50]—to provide sound credit and currency in the country, and passage of an excise tax on imported spirits

Interior of Philadelphia's Congress Hall, where the government resided for ten years.

and domestic liquor stills to ease the burden created by the assumption of state debts. In an instant, there was opposition. Fisher Ames recognized that "the southern people dread" the excise and contend that it "is an odious, unpopular tax, and will fall unequally on them. They are afraid for their Whiskey."[51] But southerners were not alone in their dislike of an excise tax. There were thousands of stills all over the country, and James Jackson of Georgia vehemently insisted that his constituents claimed "a right to get drunk, that they have been long in the habit of getting drunk, and that they will get drunk in defiance of all the excise duties which Congress might be weak or wicked enough to impose."[52]

Despite this opposition and after a protracted debate, the bill passed the House on January 27, 1791, by a large majority, 35 to 21. As expected, this tax proved to be very unpopular, especially among the farmers in western Pennsylvania who were accustomed to shipping their surplus grain to eastern markets in liquid form as whiskey. So they refused to pay the tax and attacked the federal revenue officers who tried to collect it. Frightened that this might become another Shays Rebellion, which occurred in Massachusetts in 1786 and led to the overthrow of the government, President Washington overreacted and in 1794 sent some thirteen thousand militiamen to crush the uprising. This so-called Whiskey Rebellion dissolved upon the arrival of the troops, but it had the excellent effect of reaffirming the authority of the central government (acting with the support of the state militia), something that had to be visibly demonstrated sooner or later. It proved that the administration had the will and the power to enforce the government's laws.[53]

OF GREATER MOMENT was the uproar over Hamilton's request on December 13, 1790, that Congress charter a central banking system for twenty years with a parent bank in Philadelphia and branch banks in the major cities throughout the nation. This Bank of the United States (BUS) would be a quasi-private operation with a capital stock of $10 million, four-fifths of which would be subscribed by private investors and one-fifth by the government. Its management would consist of a president and a board of twenty-five directors, twenty of whom would be elected by the stockholders and five appointed by the government. The bank with its branches would act as an agent for the collection of taxes and serve as a depository of federal funds. It would be authorized to issue banknotes, redeemable in specie and acceptable in the payment of taxes, thus increasing the money supply with which to finance the nation's economic growth. Hamilton believed the BUS would not only provide the country with sound and flexible currency and credit, but also further unify and strengthen it.[54]

However, one problem for many, especially those in major cities, was the fact that a twenty-year charter meant that Philadelphia would remain the financial center of the country, even after the capital had moved to its permanent site on the Potomac. Senator Maclay thought it would operate "like a Tax in favor of the Rich against the poor, tending to the Accumulating in a few hands."[55] William Few of Georgia considered it "a Dangerous combination of the monied interests of the United States and a monopoly of extensive advantages."[56] The "talkative and pugnacious" William Branch Giles of Virginia was outspoken in condemning the bank bill as yet another federal grab for power.[57] Still, the fight over the issue did not really get started until James Madison rose and questioned its constitutionality. Congress did not have the authority, he insisted, to charter a bank because such power had been rejected in the Constitutional Convention.

Ames, Sedgwick, Boudinot and others answered the objection by pointing to the clause in the Constitution that allows Congress to pass "all laws necessary and proper" for the execution of its delegated powers. The bank was certainly necessary and proper, they chorused, and on February 8, 1791, the House passed the bill by a vote of 39 to 20, thanks in large part to Hamilton's influence at the private caucuses he held with his supporters in Congress, something his opponents regarded as a clear violation of the separation of powers as established by the Constitution.

The Senate had already passed the measure, but the question of consti-

Hon. Theodore Sedgwick.

Federalist Theodore Sedgwick of Massachusetts thoroughly enjoyed the social life of Philadelphia.

tutionality troubled President Washington enough for him to consult with his cabinet. Jefferson submitted his reasons for rejecting the bill by arguing the doctrine of "strict construction" of the Constitution. He insisted that powers not specifically delegated to the government, such as the authority of granting charters of incorporation, were reserved to the states and the people.[58] Hamilton composed a masterful "Defense of the Constitutionality of the Bank" by providing a "loose construction" of the Constitution. He said that the "implied powers" clause gave Congress the power to pass the bank bill for the simple reason that it was necessary to implement the funding and assumption laws.[59] Still uncertain, Washington nevertheless signed the measure on February 25 because he felt obliged to support the secretary whose department was directly involved.

WHEN THE THIRD session of the 1st Congress concluded on March 3, 1791, the House unanimously voted its thanks to Frederick Augustus Muhlenberg for the "execution of the difficult and important trust reposed in him, as Speaker." Muhlenberg replied that "this unexpected mark of your approbation" made such an "impression on my mind, that I cannot find words to express the high sense of gratitude I entertain on this occasion. . . . Gentlemen, I most sincerely thank you. May every possible happiness attend you and every individual of this body—and may your zealous endeavors to promote the welfare of our beloved country . . . be crowned with unbounded success."[60]

Without question the 1st Congress, despite growing partisan discord, ended its work with "unbounded success." Just think. It had inaugurated a strong central government under the Constitution, administered the election and inauguration of President George Washington, established the first executive departments, created the Supreme Court and a federal judiciary system, passed the Bill of Rights and submitted it to the states for ratification, erected a revenue system, provided for the "uniform regulation of commerce," fixed the permanent residence of the capital, guaranteed the payment of the national debt, established a national bank, commissioned a regular census and admitted Kentucky and Vermont to statehood.[61] Quite an achievement in just two short years.

Still, there were divisions. There would always be divisions, but House members over time learned to work around them to "promote the welfare" of their "beloved country." The times they failed would invite catastrophe.

THESE INCREASING IDEOLOGICAL divisions within Congress over economic issues, the powers of government, the rights of the people and the relationship between the central and state governments, among others, resulted in attempts at organizing support groups or voting blocs. Not that the members of Congress were thinking of organizing political parties. Most of the founders had a perfect horror of political parties, calling them cabals of greedy men intent on achieving their own selfish ends without any consideration for the good of society as a whole. Washington said that political parties were instruments of discord and dissension, and John Adams declared that the "division of the republic into two great parties . . . is to be dreaded as the greatest political evil under our Constitution."[62] But the two groups taking shape felt that only their program and their view of government would benefit the American people, protect their liberties and advance the well-being of all. Moreover, they each saw the opposition as dangerous to the preservation of the Union.

Because of his stand on assumption and the permanent residence of the government, Madison may have alienated many northerners, who more and more looked to Alexander Hamilton for leadership, but the Virginian found much encouragement from agricultural districts in the South and the West. He and Jefferson regarded the Hamiltonian fiscal policy as a reach for power, motivated by aristocratic and British notions about who should rule in a republic. For their part Hamilton and his many northern allies in commerce and industry feared that any opposition to their goals and purposes would surely result in the collapse of the new government. Hamilton believed that only a government that guaranteed the financial interests of its citizens was likely to succeed.

Newspapers became the principal means by which these differing views of government were conveyed to the electorate. Hamilton enjoyed the very active support of John Fenno, publisher of the *Gazette of the United States,* and the secretary rendered invaluable assistance by awarding him many printing contracts from the Treasury Department as well as contributing ideas and articles. Eager to get their own message across to the public, Madison and Jefferson enticed Philip Freneau, a poet and printer, to establish the *National Gazette* in Philadelphia and present an opposing view from the one advanced by Fenno. To assist Freneau financially, Jefferson appointed him a clerk in the State Department. He and Madison also contributed short essays to the journal, offering a different set of political and economic ideas to Hamilton's proposals. During May and June of 1791, Jefferson and Madison took a trip to New York to talk with George Clinton, Robert R. Livingston and Aaron Burr, the political leaders in that state, and solicit their help in forming a coalition along national lines against the Hamiltonian agenda.

Of enormous assistance to Jefferson and Madison in the development of partisan politics was the work of their close friend John Beckley, the clerk of the House. He not only supplied them with useful information and gossip about the activities of the opposition, but he also took an active role in writing political pamphlets and circulating them among friends in New York, Pennsylvania and Virginia. He toured New York during the election of 1792 and conferred with Aaron Burr, informing Jefferson and Madison of his conversations. He was particularly effective in coordinating political campaigns among several states.[63] Societies were formed with a political bias, and such newspapers as the Fenno and Freneau journals, Benjamin F. Bache's *Aurora* and others were extremely important in urging voters to join these societies.

What came to be known as Jeffersonian democracy emphasized the value and need of local autonomy in order to preserve individual freedom. There was a real concern about the overconcentration of power in the central government and a belief that people should be left to govern themselves as much as possible. There was also a commitment to agrarian needs and a distrust of organized finance, such as banks.

Hamilton, on the other hand, believed in a strong central government, one that would support commerce, industry and shipping. He distrusted the people's ability to govern, and favored rule by an elite. In his final *Report on Manufactures,* submitted to the House during the first session of the 2nd Congress on December 5, 1791, he urged the passage of tariffs to protect American industries, a recommendation that won immediate ap-

proval in the North, but alarmed southerners who would have to buy manufactured goods from a protected market and yet sell their cotton and
tobacco in an open market worldwide.[64]

It was these ideological differences that would slowly but inevitably
lead to the formation of a two-party system: the Hamiltonian or Federalist
Party and the Jeffersonian-Madisonian or Democratic-Republican Party.

CONCERNED OVER THE increased authority of the executive branch, yet
respectful of Washington's position, the Republicans aimed their attacks at
the treasury secretary. During the 2nd Congress that began its session on
October 24, 1791, an open contest between the legislative and executive
branches evolved when the governor of the Northwest Territory, General
Arthur St. Clair, led a poorly equipped and inadequately trained force
against the Ohio Indians and suffered a humiliating defeat on November 4,
1791. Some 657 U.S. soldiers were killed and 271 wounded.

When word of this disaster reached Philadelphia, Representative William Branch Giles introduced a resolution in the House calling on the President to initiate an investigation. Giles had a reputation for opposing
Hamilton's policies, and he may have been motivated in part by the hope of
smearing the treasury secretary with the disgrace. But the House members
felt that instructing the President to undertake an investigation was disrespectful, if not improper, and defeated Giles's motion by a vote of 35 to 21.
Instead, on March 27, 1792, the House approved the appointment of a select
committee of seven to look into the expenditure of appropriated funds for
this expedition, and it authorized the committee to call for such persons,
records and papers as might be necessary to complete the inquiry.[65]

Concerned about the precedent this request might set, President Washington consulted his cabinet, and they unanimously agreed that the House
had the authority to conduct such an investigation and request relevant
documents. The subsequent hearings resulted in a report delivered by Representative Thomas Fitzsimons of Pennsylvania on May 8, 1792, in which
St. Clair and his officers and troops were exonerated but the quartermaster
general, and indirectly the secretary of war, were faulted for the defeat. The
committee reported repeated complaints about the fatal mismanagement
of military stores and supplies. Muskets were said to be defective and the
gunpowder was judged of poor quality.

This was the first investigation by the House into the operations of the
executive branch and it set a precedent for all future inquiries—namely,
that executive officers would appear before select House committees and
not the entire body.

This 2nd Congress also passed the first Coinage Act, providing full-
weight gold and silver coins that were declared legal tender and were to be
minted at the ratio of 15 to 1. Because this act undervalued gold—a ratio of

15.5 to 1 would have been closer to the market value—it drove gold out of circulation as a medium of exchange.[66] At the time the Coinage Act won passage there was heated debate over whether the likeness of George Washington's head should decorate these coins. But ever fearful that monarchical trappings could damage the image and reputation of a Republic, Congress substituted Liberty's head.

The 2nd Congress also established a uniform militia and empowered the President to summon it to suppress insurrections, resist invasions and enforce federal law. In addition, it created the post office department under the direction of a postmaster general (not yet of cabinet rank)[67] and answerable to Congress. The act also rewarded congressmen with the all-important franking privilege by which the members could more readily communicate with their constituents and encourage them to identify with a particular political party.

THE RIVALRY BETWEEN Federalists and Republicans intensified, although parties, as such, were still in a very formative stage. In the hope of lessening tensions, George Washington agreed to run for a second term and was re-elected in 1792 when he received 132 electoral votes with 3 abstentions. In an effort to unseat John Adams as Vice President, Jefferson and Madison urged John Beckley to consult with their allies in New York and Pennsylvania and come up with a more appropriate candidate. These conspirators decided on George Clinton of New York, a leading Anti-Federalist and opponent of Alexander Hamilton. The strategy failed when Adams was re-elected Vice President with 77 votes against 50 cast for Clinton.

Nevertheless, the campaign against Hamilton and the Treasury Department continued without letup, and on January 24, 1793, Representative William Branch Giles of Virginia, with help from Secretary Jefferson, introduced five resolutions in the House demanding that Hamilton produce documentation of his operations, especially information regarding foreign loans and the sinking fund to pay the debt. "I cannot help remarking," Giles declared on the House floor on January 30, 1793, ". . . that we have been legislating for some years without competent official knowledge of the state of the treasury or revenues. . . . It is now time that this information be officially laid before this house."[68]

Although Hamilton made a detailed and compelling case in defense of his activities, it was unacceptable to Giles, who introduced additional resolutions on February 27 seeking the secretary's censure and removal. The resolutions failed, but they inaugurated the unfortunate, if inevitable, development of intense political partisanship within Congress. Now political leaders used their position in the House to verbally attack opponents and their programs. "Madison," commented Fisher Ames, "is become a desperate party leader." He and his friends have, "like toads, sucked poison from the earth. They thirst for vengeance. The Secretary of the Treasury is one whom they would immolate; Knox another. The President is not to be spared. His popularity is a fund of strength to that cause which they would destroy."[69]

The growing split between the emerging Federalist and Republican parties widened over foreign affairs, specifically the armed hostility that broke out on February 1, 1793, when France declared war against Great Britain, Spain and Holland. The French had inaugurated a revolution that ended the monarchy and established a republic. Since France had helped the American colonies win their independence there was considerable French sympathy in the United States, especially among Republicans. But New England merchants and shippers found England a much better "market for our exports, better than the French . . . and for many of our products, the only one," and therefore a better ally.[70] Hamilton and his Federalist friends sought to encourage friendship with Great Britain in the hope of securing trade concessions, and this became another issue separating the two political groups.

Although the United States was still formally allied to France under the Treaty of 1778, signed during the American Revolution, the outbreak of war in Europe prompted Washington to issue a Proclamation of Neutrality on April 22, 1793, in which he declared that this country wished to remain at peace with both Britain and France and therefore Americans should avoid any action, pro or con, toward either belligerent. When the new minister of the French Republic to the United States, the brilliant, impulsive and indiscreet Edmond-Charles Édouard Genêt, attempted to encourage Americans to attack British vessels along the coast, Washington demanded his recall. By this time the President leaned more toward the Federalists' position and frequently consulted Hamilton on foreign affairs, a situation that ultimately resulted in Jefferson's resignation as secretary of state on December 31. He was succeeded by Edmund Randolph.

In June and November of 1793, England issued orders in council authorizing the seizures of U.S. vessels and the impressment of American seamen. Moreover, it continued to incite Indian nations in the Ohio Valley to attack American frontiersmen, and refused to evacuate military posts along the northern frontier within the territorial limits of the United States as required by the peace treaty that ended the Revolution. "I do not believe that Great Britain intends to force us into war," commented Fisher Ames; "but she intends to make our neutrality unpleasant to our feelings and unprofitable to our navigation, &c.; and in doing this, she probably cares little whether it is war or peace."[71]

In the hope of avoiding war, Washington dispatched Chief Justice John Jay as a special envoy to England to negotiate these complaints. The resulting treaty, signed on November 19, 1794, was released without authority to the press. Its humiliating terms shocked and angered many Americans, especially Republicans. The treaty favored British interests in almost every particular. It said nothing about impressment, and although the British West Indies was opened to American ships, these ships could not exceed seventy tons. Worse, the United States was required to abandon its carrying trade of such staples as cotton, sugar and molasses. Even Federalists felt humiliated by the treaty, and Washington himself judged it unsatisfactory. The outrage generated public protests, and Jay himself was pilloried for accepting such a damnable agreement. Memorials and petitions from all over the country inundated the President, begging him to reject the insulting document. John Jay was burned in effigy in New York, Philadelphia and Boston. Hamilton tried to defend the treaty and was hit by a rock.[72] Still, Washington submitted it to the Senate for ratification because he believed it would prevent a disastrous war with Great Britain. The Senate ratified it after a protracted debate by only a bare two-thirds vote, but rejected the West Indian trade provision.

The House tried to go further and nullify the treaty altogether by refusing to appropriate the funds necessary to implement it. To argue that the House must of necessity vote funds to enforce a treaty with which it had no involvement would destroy the appropriation power, claimed John Swanwick of Pennsylvania. "In such a case the House become mere automatons, mere Mandarine members, like those who nod on a chimney-piece, as directed by a power foreign to themselves."[73] The members requested copies of the instructions that Jay had been given when he accepted the mission, and the documents and correspondence relating to the treaty.[74] Washington, asserting his executive privilege, refused to provide them, thus setting an important precedent. Said the President: "It does not occur that the inspection of the papers asked for can be relative to any purpose under the cognizance of the House of Representatives, except that of an impeachment, which the resolution has not expressed."[75]

The stinging tone and manner of the President's response, according to Madison, was "improper and indelicate."[76] And the reference to impeachment must have panicked any number of representatives. The incident resulted in the first party caucus in the House, a meeting of Republicans to discuss their next move. According to Albert Gallatin of Pennsylvania, the caucus failed to reach a consensus; however, it did inaugurate organized party action within Congress in an attempt to agree on a partisan policy.

Determined to challenge the President on the issue of the role to be played by the House in foreign affairs, Madison drew up a set of resolutions that were introduced by Thomas Blount of North Carolina affirming the right of the lower chamber to consider a treaty that required enabling legislation. It passed on April 9, 1796, by a majority of twenty-two votes.

Meanwhile, Hamilton mobilized his supporters, and the ailing Fisher

Ames delivered an impassioned speech in favor of the treaty. He wanted his words to reach across the mountains to the frontier and speak to the people living in the West, he said. Without a treaty, he argued, the safety of the frontier is in jeopardy. "In the day time, your path through the woods is ambushed; the darkness of midnight will glitter with the blaze of your dwellings. You are a father: the blood of your sons shall fatten your corn-field! You are a mother: the war-whoop shall wake the sleep of the cradle. . . . I can fancy that I listen to the yells of savage vengeance and the shrieks of torture." Should the members deny the appropriation, "even I, slender and almost broken as my hold on life is, may outlive the Government and Con-stitution of my country."[77]

There was not a dry eye in the chamber, noted John Adams. Where-upon the House Committee of the Whole approved the appropriation for the Jay Treaty on April 30, 1796, by the tie-breaking vote of Frederick Muhlenberg, a vote that cost him his reelection to Congress. Worse, his brother-in-law, a rabid Republican, attacked and stabbed him for his treach-ery, but he survived.[78]

At least the People's House had asserted its prerogatives against both the President and Senate, but they were not able to settle the constitutional question of its proper role in treaty making, a problem that would recur many times in the future.

THE CONTROVERSY OVER the Jay Treaty helped stimulate the final emer-gence of two distinct political parties in the United States. Each side at-tacked the other, and in the chorus of criticism, protest meetings and near riots over the treaty that reverberated across the nation, even the sainted Washington felt the lash of abuse. At a dinner party in Virginia a toast was offered to a "speedy death to General Washington."[79] Deeply offended, he resolved not to stand for a third term.

Alexander Hamilton also fell. The constant barrage of charges of cor-ruption and the disclosure of an affair with a married woman, Mrs. Maria Reynolds, convinced him to resign his office on January 31, 1795, although he continued to exercise a great deal of influence in the formulation of ad-ministration policy. He was succeeded in the Treasury Department by Oli-ver Wolcott, Jr.

In the presidential election of 1796, the Republicans agreed to support Jefferson against the Federalist John Adams. Adams won by three votes, 71 to 68. Jefferson, as runner-up, was elected Vice President.

Fisher Ames despaired over Jefferson's election. "His Vice-Presidency is a most formidable danger," he wrote. If the Republicans have their way "they would Frenchify and democratize us."[80]

Within the House this partisanship now developed into a struggle to control the office of the Speaker and with it his authority to appoint committee members. This in turn meant directing legislative policy. When the Federalist Theodore Sedgwick won election as Speaker over Republican Nathaniel Macon of North Carolina in 1799, he appointed Federalist chairmen and members to the standing and select committees in an effort to guarantee his party's dominance over all important legislation.[81] His office had now become a political prize.

The rise of political parties and the introduction of partisan politics into the operation of the House of Representatives began a new era in American history. By this time the House had acquired direction and purpose. It had rules and precedents;[82] it had a history, however short, that gave it life. It had developed into an active, breathing institution that men, and later women, would learn to love. The members discovered that in a very real sense the House of Representatives had a soul.

4

A New Beginning in Washington, 1798–1807

THE JAY TREATY proved disastrous for Franco-American relations. The French attacked U.S. shipping headed for Great Britain and seized those ships that entered French ports. The problem mounted when the French government attempted to extort a bribe from American diplomats as the price for recognizing them and their mission. The resulting furor in the United States almost led to war. The so-called XYZ Affair (letters were substituted for the names of the French agents involved in the attempted bribery) generated the cry "Millions for defense but not one penny for tribute." What resulted was a "Quasi-War" between the two nations in which their ships regularly attacked one another on the high seas. There was genuine fear of invasion, and the Federalists seemed anxious to pressure President Adams into asking Congress for a declaration of war. Indeed, Alexander Hamilton looked forward to donning a military uniform and leading American forces into battle.[1]

As the war fever mounted the hatred toward the French redounded against Republicans and the party suffered heavy electoral losses in 1798. Taking full advantage of their political strength, the Federalists in Congress won approval for the creation of a Department of the Navy and the building of a fleet of warships. The size of the army was also expanded.

During the first four Congresses (1789–1797) an opposition to the administration's program had formed in the House around James Madison.

His vast knowledge, particularly the work of the Constitutional Convention, and his experience provided his supporters with leadership, invaluable information and powerful arguments during protracted debates on the floor. At first the Federalists called this opposition the "Madison party," but in 1797 the little man retired to his home in Virginia, leaving the House Republican organization considerably weakened.

The only other Republican of real stature in the House at this time was Albert Gallatin. Born in Switzerland and French accented, he first came to Massachusetts and then settled in western Pennsylvania, where he won election as a Republican to the state legislature. An opponent of the excise tax, he helped prevent bloodshed in the Whiskey Rebellion. Elected to the House in 1794, he quickly demonstrated his command of finance and was one of the few Republicans who could intelligently challenge the policies of the Treasury Department now that Hamilton had retired. He led the opposition to the Jay Treaty and defended the right of the House to request documents from the President.[2]

A year later, in 1795, Gallatin also called for the creation of a standing committee of Ways and Means to reassert House control over the purse, and although that committee had a majority of Federalists, it nevertheless included Gallatin and Madison before he retired, and became a powerful instrument for formulating spending and revenue policies. Sixteen members, one from each state, served on the committee, but the number was reduced to nine in 1798. The first two chairmen were Federalists: William Loughton Smith and Robert Goodloe Harper, both of South Carolina. At first the committee dealt only with taxation and revenue, but its duties were

Albert Gallatin was one of the few Republicans in the House who could match Alexander Hamilton's understanding of finance and business.

later expanded to include appropriations and oversight of government departments. In 1802 it was formally incorporated into the Standing Rules of the House, and was soon followed by other standing committees, such as the Committee of Commerce and Manufactures established in December 1795. As the number of standing committees increased over the years, the number of select committees steadily declined.

THE DANGER TO the country of being drawn into the European war, and the fear, distrust and anger it produced among congressmen, brought about one of the first and most disgraceful altercations in the history of the House. On January 30, 1798, Representative Matthew Lyon, a Republican of Vermont, got into a shouting match with Federalist Roger Griswold of Connecticut. It climaxed when Lyon spat tobacco juice in the face of Griswold, who calmly took his handkerchief out of his pocket and wiped the filth away. The Committee on Breach of Privileges recommended that Lyon be expelled and the House interrupted its ordinary business to spend the next fourteen days arguing the case. Federalists were unable to come up with the two-thirds majority necessary for expulsion, whereupon Griswold decided to take the matter into his own hands.

On the morning of February 15, following prayers, and before the House was called to order, Griswold found Lyon sitting alone at his desk writing letters. He walked boldly toward the unsuspecting man and struck him repeatedly over the head and shoulders "with all his force," using "a large yellow hickory cane."[3] Lyon staggered to his feet, seized a pair of tongs at a nearby fireplace and swung it at his attacker. The two men grappled and fell to the floor in a wrestling match as their partisans cheered them on. Desperately the Speaker ordered bystanders to separate the two men. After several more minutes of this nonsense, the two were pulled apart, but the fracas continued as members struck "at each other with sticks in the lobbies and about the House at intervals through the day." Several representatives shook their heads with dismay over such appalling behavior by supposedly civilized men. Later, after the commotion had been quelled, a motion to expel both members failed. To some it was a ridiculous interlude, but to others, like Albert Gallatin, "it is indeed the most unpleasant and unprofitable business that ever a respectable representative body did pursue."[4]

It was the first of many more to come.

Another unsavory event took place when the House charged Senator William Blount of Tennessee, a former governor of the Tennessee territory and an insatiable land speculator, with conspiring with British agents to finance military expeditions against Spanish-held Louisiana and Florida. This was the first instance in which the House exercised its impeachment authority. The British rejected Blount's scheme, but his letter of April 21, 1797, to one James Carey in which he admitted his role in the conspiracy

The first but certainly not the last physical violence that occurred in the House, when Matthew Lyon and Roger Griswold assaulted each other to the delight of some of their colleagues.

came into the possession of the Adams administration and was turned over to Congress. A select committee of the House initiated an inquiry and reported that Blount "did conspire, and contrive to create, promote, and set on foot within the jurisdiction of the United States and to conduct and carry on from thence a military hostile expedition against the territories and dominions of His said Catholic Majesty in the Floridas and Louisiana, or a part thereof, for the purpose of conquering the same for the King of Great Britain."[5] The House, with the support and advice of the attorney general, adopted impeachment charges against Blount and asked that his seat be "sequestered." But the Senate, in an effort to avoid a trial, simply expelled him on July 8, 1797. As a result, rather than engage in the messy and protracted business of impeachment and trial, it became a practice in the future for each branch of the legislature to discipline its own members.

AMERICAN INVOLVEMENT IN foreign intrigues, and most particularly fears about French (Jacobin) influence on Republican policy, encouraged the Federalist majority in Congress to introduce a series of laws in the summer of 1798 known as the Alien and Sedition Acts. These acts belied everything this country professed about liberty and democracy. Since many members of the Republican press were immigrants, like Matthew Lyon, Congress felt obliged to impose restrictions on both citizens and aliens. In the Naturalization Act the period of residence in the United States required to become a citizen was raised from five to fourteen years;[6] the Alien[7] and Alien Enemies Acts authorized the President to imprison or deport anyone he deemed a threat to the peace and safety of the nation; and the Sedition Act provided fines and imprisonment of both citizens and aliens convicted of publishing any "false, scandalous and malicious writing" against the government, Congress or the President.[8]

In the House, Representative Robert Goodloe Harper of South Carolina, James A. Bayard of Delaware and John Allen of Connecticut led the Federalist drive for passage of these laws, while Albert Gallatin, whose election in 1793 to the U.S. Senate had been voided on the grounds that he had not been a citizen long enough to qualify, spoke vehemently in opposition. Harper insisted that those who opposed these bills, especially aliens, were in league with the enemies of the country and should be treated as criminals, a statement that caused Gallatin to lose his temper. If the members can criminalize the actions of aliens, Gallatin warned, "he had no doubt they would be equally ready to do it against citizens whenever they shall wish to do so." He was certain that this particular act was directed against him personally.[9]

Another Republican leader in the House, Edward Livingston of New York, blasted the alien bill for allowing John Adams "to expel without notice and without a hearing, any non-citizen who excited the President's suspicions." Who knows, he exclaimed, what conduct will arouse suspicion—perhaps "a careless word, perhaps misrepresented or never spoken may be sufficient evidence, a look . . . an idle gesture. . . . Judiciary power is taken from the courts and given to the Executive. . . . The trial by jury is abolished. . . . All is dark, silence, mystery, and suspicion."[10]

As for the Sedition Act, Gallatin argued that its supporters suppose "that whoever dislikes the measures of the Administration . . . and shall, either by speaking or writing, express his disapprobation, and his want of confidence in the men now in power, is seditious, is an enemy, not of Administration, but of the Constitution, and is liable to punishment."[11] He spoke so forcefully and so long and so often that Federalists amended the rules of the House to deny a member the right to talk more than once on any given subject. Gallatin's stature continued to rise in the House until by 1800 he was recognized as the leading Republican in Congress.[12]

Federalists insisted a sedition act was necessary for the security of the nation. "Let gentlemen look at certain papers printed in this city and elsewhere," said the towering John Allen of Connecticut, "and ask ourselves whether an unwarrantable and dangerous combination does not exist to overturn and ruin the Government by publishing the most shameful falsehoods against the Representatives of the people of all denominations."[13]

The Federalist Congress agreed and passed the Alien and Sedition Acts in June and July of 1798, and President Adams signed them. Subsequently, the government indicted fifteen men under the Sedition Act and convicted ten of them, including Matthew Lyon, who was imprisoned for four months and fined $1,000 for his published attack against President Adams. The injustice of this law prompted Lyon's constituents to reelect him to the House even though he was incarcerated.

Jefferson and Madison responded by writing resolutions passed by the Kentucky and Virginia legislatures. These Kentucky and Virginia Resolutions of 1798 condemned the Alien and Sedition Acts as unconstitutional. And they affirmed the right of the states to judge for themselves "the mode and measure of redress" as well as the duty to "interpose for arresting the progress of the evil."[14]

ALTHOUGH A NUMBER of leading Federalists, especially Hamilton, were anxious for the President to ask Congress for a declaration of war against France, President Adams was determined to avoid conflict. Without consulting his cabinet he sent a new diplomatic mission to France, which helped to ease tensions and bring the Quasi-War to an end. It was a gesture that marked "the expulsion from power of the Hamiltonian wing of the party and the end of their whole system of politics." Federalist anger against the President and the mounting public abhorrence of the Alien and Sedition Acts produced a "violent schism in the Federal ranks" and presaged "the overthrow of that party in the next election."[15]

Encouraged by popular support, especially their victory in New York in the spring election, the Republicans in Congress organized themselves further by holding their first nominating caucus during the evening of May 11, 1800. They chose Thomas Jefferson and Aaron Burr as their national candidates. This practice of holding a congressional caucus to nominate the party's presidential and vice presidential nominees remained in force through the election of 1824 when, after many cries that it was undemocratic, it came to an unlamented end.

In late 1799, just after the 6th Congress had reassembled, the American people were momentarily distracted from the turmoil of domestic and foreign politics by the death of George Washington on December 14. The one man most responsible for the success of America's "experiment in freedom" had departed and the nation felt his tremendous loss. Who could possibly replace this extraordinary man and hold the Union together? Surely no one currently visible could match his unique gifts and heroic stature.

AS THOUGH TO inaugurate the new century with a new beginning, several events of particular importance occurred in 1800. First, both Republicans and Federalists in Congress voted to disband the army by summer, an army that had been raised to ward off a possible French invasion. Richard Brent, a Republican of Virginia, advised the House that if we "go on and make the people salutary laws [and] let the people experience the blessings of a good government" then "you will not require a standing army either to defend the country against internal or external enemies."[16]

A standing army never did sit well with the American people in the early national period, and, during the summer of 1800, it was disbanded.

The next and more important change came when the ten years in Philadelphia mandated by the Residence Act had expired, and President Adams, on April 24, 1800, signed the legislation that directed the removal of the government to the new Federal City on the banks of the Potomac River. On May 13, Congress stipulated that the second session of the 6th Congress would commence on November 17, 1800, in its new location.[17] A sum of $9,000 was appropriated to furnish the Capitol building and transport papers, records and books to the Federal City. An additional $5,000 was approved to buy books for the Library of Congress, which was established by this legislation.[18]

When the Residence Act of 1790 settled the question of a permanent location for the capital, Congress also authorized President Washington to select the precise spot for the federal district on the Potomac, which he did; he also appointed a three-man commission to arrange its planning and building.[19] Then, on September 8, 1791, the commissioners met with Jefferson and Madison in Georgetown to decide the names for the city and the district. It seemed automatic that the city could not be called anything but "Washington" after the revered first President. As for the district itself, the commissioners decided on a symbol that had been used regularly to represent this country—namely, "Columbia." So the District of Columbia was carved out of Maryland property and Alexandria from the Virginia location. Later the land from Virginia was returned to that state.[20]

The city had been laid out on a grand scale by Pierre-Charles L'Enfant, stretching in every direction on a grid street pattern and laced with broad diagonal avenues and spacious roundabouts, many of which, when constructed, were muddy and lined with tree stumps. According to the plan, the avenues would radiate from two central buildings: the Executive Mansion and the Capitol. The mansion was a little more than a mile west of the Capitol and these two buildings were connected by Pennsylvania Avenue, then scarcely more than a footpath slicing through bushes and briars.

There were nearly 400 dwellings scattered about the area, only 109 of which were built of brick or stone and therefore might be considered "permanent." The rest were hardly more than shacks.[21] A few stores, hotels and boardinghouses dotted the landscape, but not a single church or school had been erected. It was a cultural wasteland compared to New York and Philadelphia, carved out of a hilly countryside. Some congressmen referred to it as a "howling, malarious wilderness."[22] As early as March 19, 1789, Dr. Benjamin Rush had warned John Adams that after a removal to Philadelphia

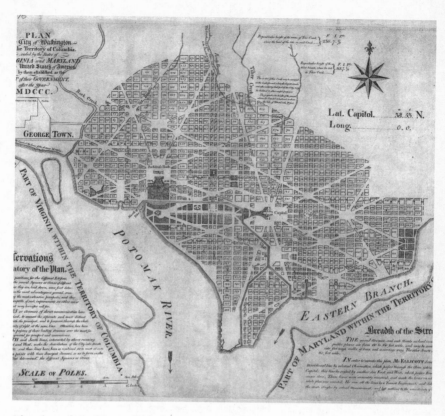

The plan of the "City of Washington in the Territory of Columbia" ceded by Virginia and Maryland as laid out by Pierre L'Enfant.

"you will probably be dragged in a few years to the banks of the Potowmac where Negro Slaves will be your Servants by day . . . mosquitoes your centinels by night, and bilious fevers your companions every Summer & fall— and pleurisies, every Spring."[23] Hardly a recommendation for northern congressmen.

The district was ringed by the Potomac and Anacostia Rivers and by the shallow waters of Rock Creek. Terribly hot and humid for many months of the year, the weather was frequently unbearable. Still, many Congressmen were happy to vacate Philadelphia, a city that had been plagued for the past few years by outbreaks of yellow fever.

Congressmen residing in the new capital messed together in boardinghouses, most of them leaving their families home. In time they hoped the city would be more livable and attractive. "We only need here houses, cellars, kitchens, scholarly men, amiable women and a few other such trifles to possess a perfect city," enthused Senator Gouverneur Morris of New York.

". . . I hasten to assure you that . . . we are not wanting in sites for magnificent mansions, that projected canals will give birth to a large commerce, that as a consequence riches will bring forth a taste for the fine arts; in a word, that this is the best city in the world to live in—in the future."[24]

In early June of 1800, President Adams traveled to Washington to inspect the unfinished buildings scattered around the district's ten-mile square. He was given an appropriate welcome by the native population. Only the Treasury, a two-story brick structure next to the Executive Mansion, had been completed. The President's house was not ready for occupancy, although Adams liked what he saw and thought it suitably grand to house the august presence of the President of the United States. Actually, Washington was not yet ready to absorb a functioning government. In ten years the commissioners had only built what looked to one congressman like a city in "ruins."[25]

The Capitol building, made of brick and sandstone, was still under construction. It was designed by William Thornton, who combined the increasingly popular neoclassicism with the familiar Georgian style of architecture. The land was part of a manor owned by Daniel Carroll of Duddington and purchased from him for $66.66 an acre. The building itself sat on Jenkins Hill, which rose eighty-eight feet from the river and was meant to provide space for the House and Senate, the Supreme Court and the Library of Congress. L'Enfant told President Washington that the area resembled "a pedestal waiting for a monument."[26] Built for the most part by slave labor—"slave labor to build the home of a free government"[27]—the Capitol was laid out on a north-south axis in which the Senate would occupy the north wing and the House the south. The north end (the Senate wing) rose three stories, and because the south wing had not yet been built, save for the foundation, the House, after the removal from Philadelphia, occupied the west side (front) of the second floor of the north wing (the area intended for the Library of Congress). The Senate met on the east side of the first floor. Later the Senate moved to the second floor, leaving the first floor to the Supreme Court.

The centerpiece of the building was a domed Rotunda with a portico supported by twelve Corinthian columns. The portico stood on a one-story arcade and provided a sheltered carriageway and balcony, somewhat similar to Federal Hall in New York City but on a grander scale.[28]

The House assembled in the library because it was the largest room in the building. It measured 86 feet long, 35 feet wide and 36 feet high. In the winter it was heated by four fireplaces and a stove. Five windows on the west side of the library overlooked an undulating countryside that stretched down to the Potomac. But light and heat were frequently substandard and smoking was permitted on the floor until 1871, further polluting the air in the chamber. A regular din of conversation in violation of the rules added to the general discomfort. Vendors peddled their wares of food and drink outside the chamber and liquor was consumed in prodigious amounts, both on and off the floor.

"Around the Capitol," according to Gallatin, "are seven or eight boarding-houses, one taylor, one shoemaker, one printer, a washing-woman, a grocery shop, a pamphlets and stationery shop, a small dry-goods shop, and an oyster house." He himself rented a room in a boardinghouse at the southeast corner of New Jersey Avenue and C Street SW. It was expensive, he told his wife, and only moderately comfortable. The members, all men save for two wives, dined together. The company was good enough, Gallatin reported, but always the same. "I would rather now and then see other persons," he sighed. A great many imbibed and some gambled, "but the majority drink naught but politics."[29]

Josiah Quincy of Massachusetts, a Federalist, later reported that his relations with other members in Washington was "regulated by party rather than by personal friendship. . . . Our association on the floor, and at times in our respective lodgings, led to the reciprocation of friendship which remained intimate and cordial." As for Republicans, he said, "my intercourse for the most part was polite, but cold and general." Southern and western leaders of that party, he continued, "were violent, overbearing, and insolent, both in manner and language." Slaveholders were accustomed to "speak in the tone of masters." They were always "ready to construe contradiction into insult" and "would on the slightest provocation tender a duel, which they knew they could do with impunity." Westerners were also overbearing, he declared, "not from the habits of masterdom, but from their education and habits of professional life. For the most part they were lawyers accustomed to speak at barbeques and electioneering canvassings."[30]

In no time a "Washington Etiquette" developed. It was deemed proper for the general public and wives of Congressmen to make first visits or courtesy calls on those individuals who ranked above them, starting with the President's family, and including the wives of cabinet members and the diplomatic corps. Courtesy calls were considered a mark of good breeding.[31]

IT WAS A motley group of congressmen representing all sections of the country that converged on Jenkins Hill to inaugurate the beginning of government in this unlikely capital. They formally reconvened on November 17, 1800, although the House did not have a quorum until November 21. They gathered in an unfinished city and in an unfinished Capitol only to discover that their first important decision involved settling an unfinished presidential election.

For the first and last time in American history the election of 1800 pitted the President against the Vice President, Adams versus Jefferson. The Federalists naturally offered Adams for a second term, along with General

Charles Cotesworth Pinckney of South Carolina for the vice presidency. But the friends of Alexander Hamilton despised the President, and toward the end of the campaign Hamilton himself published a fifty-four-page pamphlet excoriating Adams for his public conduct and defects of character, citing his reputed weakness, vacillation and ungovernable temper. Worse, Hamilton conspired to have a few Federalist electors withhold their votes for Adams so that the more acceptable Pinckney would be elected President.

Republicans reveled over this catastrophic split in their opponent's ranks. Madison, in a jubilant letter to Jefferson, said, "I rejoice with you that Republicanism is likely to be so *completely* triumphant."[32]

In what turned out to be a vicious campaign, Republicans accused Federalists of aristocratic leanings and pro-British sympathies, that they were the enemies of freedom as demonstrated by the Alien and Sedition Acts. Federalists responded by warning that a Republican victory meant rule by a gang of radicals who, like the Jacobins of France, would introduce a reign of terror in the United States.

Not until December 1800, after the removal to Washington, did the outcome of the election become known. And it proved to be closer than anyone expected. Jefferson captured 73 electoral votes, while Adams won 65. Trailing them stood Pinckney with 63, and John Jay with 1. But in their determination to seize the presidency from the Federalists, the Republicans failed to hold back a few votes for Burr, and so he ended up with the exact same electoral count as Jefferson. To the shock of some and the delight of others it was a tie, and, according to Article II of the Constitution, the House of Representatives had to decide which of the two would be President and which Vice President. To complicate matters the lame-duck* House would make that decision—not the new Congress in which Republicans had won sizable majorities in both houses.

Since they could not have Adams, Federalists now had the unbelievable opportunity to wreak revenge on Jefferson, the leader of their hated opposition, by preventing his election and possibly, with the help of a few Republicans, elect Burr. And that is exactly what a number of them planned to do since Burr, to the disbelief of Jefferson and his staunch supporters, steadfastly refused to promise that he would not accept a presidential election by the House.

There were sixteen states in the Union in 1800, the original thirteen

---

*Lame ducks were members of Congress who were defeated for reelection or about to retire but continued to serve until March 4, when their replacements took office. A lame-duck session included the months from the reconvening of Congress, usually December, to March 4.

plus Vermont, Kentucky and Tennessee. Federalists in the House controlled six of them and Republicans eight. Together the parties split two other states. Nine states were necessary for election with each state having one vote determined by its delegation. According to the rules adopted by the House Committee of the Whole, the balloting would continue without adjournment until the President was elected, the doors of the House would be shut during balloting and the delegations of the states would sit together and ballot.[33]

Alexander Hamilton hated the idea of Burr's election and spent weeks writing to Federalist friends urging them to support Jefferson. It was not that he liked Jefferson (the Virginian was a "contemptible hypocrite," Hamilton ranted) but he feared Burr. Jefferson, he claimed, "is by far not so dangerous a man and he has pretensions to character," but Burr had "no other spring or aim than his own aggrandisement."[34] Hamilton worked particularly hard on James Bayard, the sole representative from Delaware, assuring him that Jefferson did not favor an all-powerful House of Representatives at the expense of executive authority. He believed that the Virginian would "temporize" and not attempt a "violent" overthrow of the existing system.[35]

On February 11, in a howling snowstorm, members trudged from their boardinghouses to the Capitol. Congress met in the Senate chamber and counted the electoral ballots. The House then withdrew to the library, where it was agreed the members would ballot for President *"and shall not adjourn until a choice is made."*[36] On the first ballot, Jefferson took eight states—New York, New Jersey, Pennsylvania, Virginia, North Carolina, Kentucky, Georgia and Tennessee—while Burr had six—New Hampshire, Massachusetts, Rhode Island, Connecticut, Delaware and South Carolina. Two states, Vermont and Maryland, were split. Since neither man had the required nine states, the House continued balloting for the remainder of the day and night and into the next morning, all with the same result. Obviously Federalist New England was determined to deny Jefferson the presidency either by necessitating another election or by adjourning without making a decision, thus instituting an interregnum. There was real danger that the government might collapse.

The members were exhausted as the polling continued, and they entertained no other business. Periodically they took breaks to consume the food they had ordered from their boardinghouses or attempt to catnap on blankets brought in for that purpose. At midnight on February 12, after twenty-eight failures, it was decided to adjourn and resume the balloting at eleven o'clock the following morning.

But the members were deadlocked. Day after weary day they repeated the procedure. Still no decision. Attempts at arranging deals were constant. Even Jefferson was approached. "I have declared to them unequivocally," he indignantly responded, "that I would not receive the government on capitulation, that I would not go into it with my hands tied."[37]

Finally, perhaps influenced by Hamilton's urging but more likely concerned that the crisis was headed toward a national catastrophe that would totally discredit the government, James Bayard announced on Saturday, February 14, to some of his Federalist colleagues, that he would end the contest by voting for Jefferson, thus giving the Virginian the nine needed states. But on Monday, the sixteenth, he did not make good his threat. The reason, said Gallatin, was Bayard's attempt to bring "the whole Federalist party" with him.[38]

That evening the Federalists met "to agree upon a mode of surrendering," necessitated by Bayard's announcement. "It occurred to us that . . . we might obtain terms of capitulation."[39] According to Bayard, he spoke to several Republican representatives who were close to Jefferson and requested assurances that the Hamiltonian system would not be dismantled and that officeholders would not be removed because they were Federalists. He mentioned in particular the collectors of the ports of Philadelphia and Wilmington.[40]

The assurances were given, but without Jefferson's involvement, and the following day, February 17, after thirty-six ballots, the members finally chose Thomas Jefferson as President.

What happened turned out to be quite clever. Representative Lewis R. Morris of Vermont withdrew, allowing his colleague, Matthew Lyon, to cast Vermont's vote for Jefferson. Representatives George Baer, William Craik, John Dennis and John C. Thomas, all from Maryland, cast blank votes, allowing the Republicans to carry that state for the Virginian. Bayard of Delaware also cast a blank vote, as did the South Carolina members. The four New England states, however, stuck with Burr to the end. The final vote gave Jefferson ten states and Burr four. Delaware and South Carolina chose not to vote. Jefferson was now the President-elect and Burr the Vice President–elect.

In December 1803, Congress proposed the 12th Amendment to the Constitution, providing separate balloting by electors for President and Vice President. It was ratified on September 25, 1804.

As one of his last official acts, President Adams filled a great number of judicial positions created by the Judiciary Act that had been passed only five days before his administration expired. This act created sixteen circuit courts of appeal (one for each state) and reduced the number of justices on the Supreme Court to five, thus effectively delaying Jefferson's opportunity to appoint a new member. The act also eliminated the onerous circuit duty for Supreme Court judges. Adams also nominated, and the Senate quickly confirmed, John Marshall as chief justice of the United States. Still at his desk at 9:00 p.m. on March 3, the last day of his administration, Adams kept bombarding the Senate with these "midnight" nominations.

Around noon on Wednesday, March 4, the fifty-eight-year-old Jefferson walked from his boardinghouse to the Capitol and entered the Senate chamber on the ground floor and was duly sworn in as President. His predecessor chose not to attend, a discourtesy that was repeated by his son, John Quincy Adams, when Andrew Jackson was inaugurated in 1829.

In his inaugural address, Jefferson made a valiant effort to heal the many wounds inflicted by the election. "We are all Republicans, we are all Federalists," he said. "If there be any among us who would wish to dissolve the Union or change its republican form, let them stand undisturbed as monuments of the safety with which error of opinion may be tolerated where reason is left free to combat it."[41]

It was a revolution. The government had been turned over by one political party to another without dissent or conflict. Margaret Bayard Smith, wife of the owner of a newly established Washington newspaper the *National Intelligencer,* wrote that once the result of the election had been made known, the "dark and threatening cloud that had hung over the political horrison rolled harmlessly away, and the sunshine of prosperity and gladness broke forth."[42]

ON THIS HIGH note the 6th Congress ended. And since the census of 1800 was certain to increase the membership of the House, the board of commissioners asked James Hoban, winner of the competition to design the President's mansion, to plan a temporary wooden chamber on the existing foundations of the south wing to serve as the House of Representatives.

Hoban prepared three possible plans with cost estimates. Jefferson opted for the least expensive, which was the construction of an elliptical room measuring 94 feet long and 70 feet wide with sixteen arches and fourteen windows. It had a 120-foot-long gallery fitted with three rows of seats. Contracts were signed on June 20, 1801, with the agreement that the room had to be completed by November 1801, prior to the return of Congress. The room was to be connected to the north (Senate) wing by a one-story wooden passageway 145 feet long that stretched across a vacant yard intended for a domed centerpiece that would link the House and Senate wings. The passageway also housed three water closets.[43]

The room was hastily built and of poor construction. In fact, much of the city showed signs of shoddy workmanship and inferior building materials. The representatives dubbed their new chamber the "Oven" because its shape resembled a Dutch oven and because it was exceptionally stuffy, indeed suffocating at times, despite the fourteen windows. Later, ventilators were installed on the roof, but they never worked properly and members had to endure the discomfort. Truly, they worked in an oven.

It was a weird-looking Capitol with its long corridor connecting the south wing to the north wing. It looked even weirder when outside braces to support the walls were added to the House's elliptical Oven in 1803. The room had been so poorly constructed that these buttresses were essential to keep the walls from collapsing.

Because of the lack of churches in Washington, public religious services began in the Capitol as soon as the government moved to Washington. Held in the House chamber, these services proved so popular that the House became a rendezvous for the "youth, beauty and fashion" of the capital. This practice continued well into the 1850s, even though by that time the district "teemed with churches." Music was provided by the Marine Band. "Their scarlet uniform, their various instruments, make quite a dazzling appearance in the gallery," reported Margaret Bayard Smith. "The marches they played were good and inspiring, but in their attempts to accompany the psalm-singing of the congregation, they completely failed and after a while, the practice was discontinued,—it was *too* ridiculous."[44]

Not infrequently, money was raised during the services for missionary purposes, and ministers of various denominations preached in the House: Presbyterians, Methodists, Baptists, Episcopalians, an Anglican, a Unitarian (that caused an uproar) and in 1825 the Catholic bishop of Charleston, South Carolina. And, to the amazement of many, Dorothy Ripley preached a sermon in the House on January 12, 1806, the first female to speak officially in the chamber.[45]

WHEN THE 7TH Congress convened in December 1801, about 70 of the 106 members were Republican. That total swelled with the reapportionment resulting from the census of 1800, which increased the size of the House to 142. Unlike Washington and Adams, who personally read their addresses to the members, Jefferson chose to have his annual message read by the clerk. And this action ended once and for all the practice of the members parading to the Executive Mansion to acknowledge the President's wishes and show due deference. Not until Woodrow Wilson became

The House chamber in Washington, otherwise known as the "Oven," with its walls buttressed to keep them from collapsing.

President in 1913 did the chief executive again begin to read his message personally to Congress. And there is no longer a parade to the Executive Mansion.

The Republicans in the House immediately elected Nathaniel Macon of North Carolina as Speaker, and he in turn chose John Randolph of Roanoke as chairman of the increasingly powerful Ways and Means Committee. Randolph was kin to Jefferson, extremely partisan and recognized as majority leader because of his chairmanship. He replaced Albert Gallatin, whom Jefferson appointed secretary of the treasury. Committed to the Republican doctrines of states' rights and a rigid economy, Randolph had a sharp tongue that frequently sliced apart the arguments and character of his opponents. He had a high, weird-sounding feminine voice—it resembled the screech of a peacock, claimed one observer[46]—but no one laughed or mocked him for fear of a devastating personal attack in response. Tall and extremely thin, he usually wore a floor-length overcoat with an upright-standing collar pulled tight around his neck so that his head looked like it was mounted on the collar of the coat. As he grew more arrogant and contentious he often brought his favorite foxhound with him, and anyone who protested the presence of the animal was threatened with his riding whip.

Such a leader proved extremely problematic. Still, Jefferson sought to direct the operations of Congress as much as possible to win approval of his recommendations—especially the lower chamber, because it held the purse strings. But he found that Republican members were unable or unwilling to exercise leadership. They looked to him for guidance since it was he, they believed, who had created their overwhelming victory in 1800. In effect they abdicated responsibility for directing national policy.

Jefferson wheedled Randolph into becoming the administration's spokesman in the House. The relationship worked for a time until Randolph became resentful and broke loose. Spitefully, in a speech before the House in March 1806, he lambasted the "back-stairs influence of men who bring messages to this House, which, although they do not appear on the Journals, govern its decisions."[47] Jefferson was shocked. "We never heard this while the declaimer was himself a backstairs man as he called it."[48]

Randolph had a better relationship with Secretary Gallatin and they proved to be an effective pair in achieving the economic goals of the President's first administration. But as Josiah Quincy, a Federalist from Massachusetts, commented, "all the great political questions are settled somewhere else."[49]

Jefferson also worked through other committee chairmen in both houses. Representatives Caesar A. Rodney of Delaware and Barnabas Bidwell of Massachusetts, along with Senators William Branch Giles and Wilson Cary Nicholas, both of Virginia, became floor leaders for the President's program. These men frequently met at the home of Albert Gallatin.

Most important of all, perhaps, were the regular dinner parties Jefferson hosted in the Executive Mansion. Three times a week during the congressional session the President entertained members of Congress. Dinners were held around three or four in the afternoon, and the guests sat at an oval table so as to encourage a feeling of equality and comradeship. Prepared by a French chef, the meals alone provided an attraction that few legislators could resist. "The Jacobins," groused the Federalist Roger Griswold of Connecticut, ". . . have adopted the plan of meeting in divan and agreeing on measures to be pursued and passed in the House and they vote in mass without admitting any alteration in the plan proposed." Their behavior is scandalous, he went on. "The wickedness of such a course has never been equaled but by the Jacobin club in Paris. The spirit is intolerant and must lead to ruin."[50]

Like other Presidents, Jefferson also regularly proposed a legislative agenda in his annual messages to Congress, various parts of which were referred to select committees, and he himself actually prepared a number of bills that he sent to supporters for introduction to either the House or the Senate. During a period when the separation of branches was held sacrosanct and the idea of a President actually writing the legislation he wanted passed was anathema, this practice not only undermined the centrality of the legislature in the American system but greatly increased the power and authority of the chief executive. It was the beginning of executive encroachment on the powers of Congress.

Here, then, is one of the most important themes woven into the history of Congress. The founders had created a government with three separate branches in which the legislature was the centerpiece and given delegated powers to run the country. But in time, presidents attempted to gain control of national policy by exercising congressional powers, such as the power of the purse through "backdoor spending" and impoundment, and the right to declare war. Periodically, a contest would develop between the two branches over which one should run the country. In the course of two hundred years, the pendulum of control would swing back and forth.

BECAUSE OF THE high turnover of representatives in these early Congresses, a chairman of a standing committee held that office no longer than two or four years on average. And this fact also added to the President's ability to influence and control legislation. Even so, these chairmen wielded immense authority. In 1802 there were five such standing committees: Ways and Means, Elections, Claims, Commerce and Manufacturing, and Revisal and Unfinished Business. Over the next six years, four more standing committees were formed: Accounts, Public Lands, District of Columbia, and Post Office and Post Roads. But of these nine, only Ways and Means, Commerce and Manufactures, and Public Lands dealt with issues of major importance. And in the rules revision of 1802, the authority of Ways and Means was expanded to include appropriations.

At the very start of his administration, Jefferson decided to terminate the practice of bribing the Barbary nations of Algiers, Morocco, Tunis and Tripoli to keep them from seizing U.S. merchant ships in the Mediterranean and holding American seamen for ransom. When the pasha of Tripoli declared war against the United States on May 14, 1801, by ordering his soldiers to chop down the flagpole at the American consulate in Tripoli, Congress was not in session. Nevertheless, Jefferson decided to dispatch a squadron of warships to the area without summoning Congress into special session. When Congress returned to the Capitol there was no effort by the administration to seek its consent to the hostilities that had occurred with a formal declaration of war. Instead, the House Ways and Means Committee, working closely with Gallatin, raised import duties to provide the necessary funds to finance the war. After several years of intermittent fighting, the pasha finally sued for peace and was paid a ransom of $60,000 for the release of American prisoners. But payments to the other Barbary States continued until 1816.

This war was a stunning example of executive encroachment on congressional authority, and it only encouraged Jefferson to further efforts. The next one involved the purchase of Louisiana, which set off a major row in the House of Representatives over its role in foreign affairs.

NAPOLÉON PLANNED TO revive the French colonial empire in North America, and when Jefferson learned early in 1802 that Spain had agreed to cede Louisiana to France in the Treaty of San Ildefonso in October 1800, and that the port of New Orleans had been closed to American trade by Spanish officials, he recognized it as a threat to the safety of the United States. "There is on the globe one single spot, the possessor of which is our natural and habitual enemy," he said. "It is New Orleans." From the moment France took possession of New Orleans, he continued, "we must marry ourselves to the British fleet and nation."[51]

The House immediately passed a resolution requesting that the President provide all the documents relating to the closing of the New Orleans port. Some Federalists in the House were spoiling for a fight and demanded that military action be taken to reopen the port. Griswold introduced a series of resolutions requiring presidential action, but the Republicans defeated the motions and reaffirmed their commitment to free access of the Mississippi River. In a closed session, the House agreed, by a vote of 50 to 25 on January 7, 1803, to give the President authority to take such measures as necessary "for asserting the rights and vindicating the injuries of the United States."[52] Several days later, again during a closed session, Samuel Smith of Maryland, prompted by the chief executive, proposed an appropriation of

$2 million to defray all expenses involving this country's relations with foreign powers. It was shepherded safely through a committee chaired by a Republican loyalist, Joseph H. Nicholson of Maryland. Jefferson immediately notified the U.S. minister to France, Robert R. Livingston, to begin negotiations for the purchase of a portion of Louisiana, including the city of New Orleans, and he dispatched James Monroe as an envoy extraordinary with instructions to offer $2 million for New Orleans and West Florida. The President was willing to go as high as $10 million.

By this time Napoléon had abandoned his plan for a colonial empire in the New World following the disastrous defeat of his army in Haiti while attempting to put down a slave revolt. The likelihood of a new war with Great Britain also shaped his decision. On April 11, 1803, the French foreign minister, Talleyrand, asked Livingston how much the United States was willing to pay for the entire territory of Louisiana. The ministers agreed on 60 million francs, or approximately $15 million, as the price for all of Louisiana, and the treaty of cession was signed on April 30. Of the $15 million, $11,250,000 went directly to France in 6 percent stock, not redeemable for fifteen years, and $3,750,000 was assumed by the United States to pay claims of its citizens against France. It was also agreed that the inhabitants of Louisiana would become American citizens in due course.[53]

It was an incredible bargain. It doubled the size of the country. As soon as Jefferson heard on July 3 that the treaty was signed he summoned Congress into session, three weeks before it was due to return. The President wanted quick action in ratifying the treaty since it called for the exchange of ratifications within six months of the date of signing. Also, he desperately needed to forestall a possible change of heart by Napoleon.

But he faced an opposition that seemed determined to block the acquisition. Federalists argued that the Constitution provided no specific grant of authority to increase the size of the country, and Congress had no constitutional authority to incorporate the territory and its people into the Union without the express consent of existing states. Jefferson himself had doubts about the constitutionality of the purchase. "The Constitution," he told Senator John Breckinridge, "has made no provision for our holding foreign territory, still less for incorporating foreign nations into our Union."[54] But in his haste to get the treaty ratified he put those doubts aside and warned the floor managers in both houses against raising the issue.

Recognizing that the role of the House in treaty making was still debatable, Jefferson decided to involve the House in a forthright manner since the enabling appropriation would have to originate in the lower chamber. Still, he withheld from the House the correspondence and various documents that he forwarded to the Senate. This provided Federalists with ammunition to demand copies of the official documents, including the Treaty of San Ildefonso, by which Louisiana had been retroceded by Spain to France, but the resolution was defeated 59 to 57.

In the Senate, the overwhelming majority of Republicans quickly ratified the treaty on October 20 by a vote of 24 to 7, four days after it had been submitted to them. All the Federalists, but one, voted against the treaty. Senator William Plumer of New Hampshire complained that they took less time to approve this important treaty than they did "on the most trivial Indian contract."[55]

It was a different story in the House. There the Federalists argued the question of constitutionality. Nowhere did the Constitution speak of expanding the size of the country, but if any such power had been delegated it would have been given to Congress since new states are admitted into the Union by the legislature, not the President. The chief executive acted unlawfully, Gaylord Griswold of New York angrily complained, and it was the duty of the House "to resist the usurped power exercised by the Executive." The treaty promised to incorporate Louisiana into the Union and grant its inhabitants the rights and privileges of American citizens, and that cannot be done, Griswold insisted, without the consent of the states.[56]

Randolph responded by needling the opposition about how they championed the Jay Treaty, which was an insult to the American people, but now denounced a treaty that would add territory of "enormous magnitude" at a trifling cost. Further, he insisted that since the executive is the branch by which this country communicates with foreign nations, it stood to reason that if any territory is to be acquired from such states, the President must be the prime agent in negotiating such an acquisition.[57]

The House agreed, and on November 10, after a long and stormy debate, it approved the certificates of stock to be paid the French, and it authorized the President to take command of Louisiana. The American flag was raised above New Orleans on December 30, 1803.

Earlier, shortly after requesting $2 million to undertake the Louisiana negotiations, Jefferson asked Congress in a confidential message to appropriate $2,500 for an expedition to explore the Missouri River to its source. Rather than arouse French and Spanish suspicions, he suggested that the appropriation be designated "for the purpose of extending the external commerce of the United States." Congress obliged him, but by the time Meriwether Lewis and William Clark began their journey, Louisiana had been acquired, although its exact boundaries to the north and west were unknown. When Robert Livingston asked about the boundaries, Talleyrand responded that the United States had concluded a notable bargain and would surely make the most of it.

The great Lewis and Clark Expedition of 1803–1806 not only provided an overland route to the Pacific Ocean (they pushed west of the Louisiana

Purchase) and gained much scientific knowledge, but it also stimulated western settlement and gave the United States a claim to the Oregon country that lay beyond the Louisiana Territory.

THE LOUISIANA PURCHASE placed a severe crimp in Secretary Gallatin's plan to reduce the national debt, one of the President's prime objectives. Gallatin also wished to reduce taxes. This program was cordially endorsed by Chairman Randolph and it largely succeeded, despite the Louisiana Purchase. Gallatin was able to reduce defense expenditures, eliminate the direct tax for the military and revise the schedule of debt payments. The debt, thanks to him, shrank from $82 million in 1801 to $57 million in 1808. With increased revenue from imposts and the sale of public land, Gallatin arranged that $8 million would be applied annually to the payment of interest and principal of the debt.[58]

In another action to extend executive authority, Jefferson demanded the repeal of the Judiciary Act of 1801 by which President Adams had loaded the judiciary department with Federalists. These offensive "midnight appointments" had to be vacated. At Jefferson's insistence, the act was repealed on March 8, 1801, despite the negative vote by Vice President Aaron Burr, who tried to block action on the bill. It was replaced by the Judiciary Act of 1802, which restored a six-member Supreme Court and created six circuit courts.

WILLIAM MARBURY WAS one of the midnight appointees whose commission as justice of the peace had been signed and sealed but not delivered before the Jefferson administration took office. Acting at the direction of the President, Secretary of State James Madison withheld the commission, whereupon Marbury sued in the Supreme Court for a writ of mandamus, requiring delivery. Chief Justice John Marshall recognized that Jefferson would probably defy any order to deliver the commission. He also understood that the court lacked the prestige, importance and authority of the other two branches, a situation that he hoped to remedy. So inconsequential was the court's reputation that it held its session in a clerk's office in the basement of the Capitol and met only six weeks a year.

This was Marshall's dilemma, which he skillfully resolved in the case *Marbury v. Madison*. On February 24, 1803, he dismissed Marbury's suit on the grounds that the court did not have the authority to act. It lacked jurisdiction because Section 13 of the Judiciary Act of 1789, which granted the court such authority, was unconstitutional. This was the first instance of a congressional statute voided by the high court—it would not happen again for another fifty years—and it subsequently raised the judiciary to a level of equality with the other two branches. He had pronounced the doctrine of judicial review.

A confrontation between the court and the executive seemed imminent; it came very quickly. It was not enough to repeal the Judiciary Act of
1801; Jefferson wanted to clear out as many Federalist judges as possible.
And to do so he chose the route of impeachment. No doubt he had John
Marshall in his sights, especially after the Marbury decision.

On February 3, 1803, Jefferson sent a letter and affidavits to the House
charging district court judge John Pickering of New Hampshire, a Federalist and a midnight appointee, with improper conduct on the bench, mental
instability and intoxication. The President asked that proceedings of redress be instituted if warranted. The matter was referred to a select committee, which reported its recommendation to the Committee of the Whole
on February 18, and Pickering was impeached. There was hardly any discussion. Pickering proved to be an easy mark since he was not only an alcoholic but probably insane. His son admitted that his father was too
"deranged" to appear in his own defense. The Senate tried him, found him
guilty by a vote of 19 to 7 on March 12, 1804, and ordered him removed
from office.[59] All the negative votes were cast by Federalists, who argued
that insanity was not a "high crime or misdemeanor."

Jefferson then sought bigger targets and found one in the person of an
associate justice of the Supreme Court, Samuel Chase. It was not a difficult
search. Chase had a reputation of delivering political harangues to grand
juries. His behavior during the prosecution of Republican journalists for
violations of the Sedition Act of 1798 marked him as a rabid partisan without a shred of discretion or judicious regard for the rights of the accused.
But it was his wild accusations against the Jefferson administration to a
Baltimore grand jury in which he denounced the Republican leadership for
annulling basic security of property and personal liberty that got him into
trouble. Worse, he raged, the independence of the national judiciary had
been "shaken to its foundation." Those remarks prompted Jefferson to write
to Congressman Joseph Nicholson and ask if such "seditious" talk should
"go unpunished."[60]

John Randolph demanded the appointment of a committee to investigate Chase's conduct. Acting on the recommendation of a seven-man committee, the House, on March 12, 1804, voted 73 to 32 to impeach Chase on
eight counts based on his Baltimore grand jury remarks and those uttered
in a number of circuit-court cases.

Federalists called it a dastardly act of deliberate sabotage, destroying
in effect the judiciary by using the threat of impeachment to silence judges.
Chase spoke in his own defense and a battery of the best Federalist lawyers
in the country offered him their free services, most notably Luther Martin
of Maryland. In the Senate trial, Vice President Aaron Burr presided, as
one of his last official acts. Randolph headed the House prosecutorial team
but was no match for Martin and company. Let Chase "speak, and write,

John Randolph of Roanoke was one of the most contentious and remarkable members in the entire history of the House.

and publish, as he pleases," intoned Randolph. "This is his right in common with his fellow-citizens. . . . But shall a judge declaim on these topics from his seat of office? Shall he not put off the political partisan when he ascends the tribune? Or shall we have the pure stream of public justice polluted with the venom of party violence?"[61] The defense responded by pointing out that Chase had not committed a crime and the Constitution clearly states that "high crimes and misdemeanors" are the only reasons for removal.

As the trial proceeded the prosecution literally fell to pieces. Randolph frequently lost control of himself. He screamed and groaned; he was forgetful and unprepared. He began one speech of about two and a half hours long, reported Senator John Quincy Adams of Massachusetts, "with as little relation to the subject matter as possible, without order, connection or argument."[62]

The defense had no problem in convincing the Senate that the charges against Chase were little more than political vindictiveness that could severely damage the constitutional system if they voted to remove. Although a majority of Republican senators found Chase guilty on three of the eight charges against him, not one charge received the necessary two-thirds majority for conviction. Several Republicans voted to acquit.

Chase's acquittal on March 1, 1805, was a blow to Jefferson and his party, and they excoriated Randolph for his incompetence. But many Americans saw the defeat as a victory for judicial independence. Never again would a justice of the Supreme Court suffer the indignity of impeachment because of his outspoken political views. But Chase's behavior in court would not be tolerated today, and such recent jurists as Chief Justice William Rehnquist have expressed belief that Chase was indeed guilty on some of the counts brought against him.[63]

The very partisan Senator John Quincy Adams summed up the feeling of most Federalists when he said that the upper chamber had fulfilled its "most important purpose" by "putting a check upon the impetuous violence of the House of Representatives."[64]

THE TREMENDOUS SUCCESS of Jefferson's first administration resulted in his reelection in 1804 over the Federalist Charles Cotesworth Pinckney of South Carolina, by an electoral vote of 162 to 14. Jefferson captured all but two states, Connecticut and Delaware. But the second administration brought one disaster after another. The first sign of trouble came with the election of the Speaker. Nathaniel Macon of North Carolina was challenged by a northerner, Joseph B. Varnum of Massachusetts, and it took four ballots for Macon to win reelection. The challenge may also have been an attempt to bring stronger leadership in the House to curtail continued executive encroachment of congressional authority.

Further trouble resulted from an intraparty collision when John Randolph broke with the President and formed a faction within the Republican Party. In December 1805 Jefferson informed his congressional leaders that he wanted $2 million to purchase West Florida. In the House the request was referred to the Ways and Means Committee, whose chairman, Randolph, refused to consent to it, insisting that the territory was part of the Louisiana Purchase. Why pay for what we already owned? he protested. Besides, he regarded the money as a bribe, which, if granted, "would disgrace us forever."[65]

The Ways and Means Committee agreed with its chairman and refused the request, but the full House approved the appropriation and that action brought about Randolph's final break with the President. Now it became imperative to remove the obstreperous chairman from Ways and Means. But as long as Macon was Speaker there was no way that could be done.

After several false starts, Jefferson finally got his wish. At the opening of the 10th Congress in 1807, the Republicans elected Joseph Varnum as Speaker and Randolph lost his chairmanship. Only a few members, called Quids, rallied to Randolph's support. They set up a constant barrage of criticism of the President for his abandonment of what they regarded as the "true" and orthodox creed of the Republican faith.

The split among Republicans, like the earlier split among Federalists, produced interparty and intraparty discord and became the harbinger of further changes in the political system. A new phase of party government was about to begin, and a new figure would appear in the House of Representatives who would restore control of national policy to the Congress.

5

Henry Clay and the Ascendancy of the House of Representatives, 1806–1821

MORE THREATENING THAN the interparty and intraparty squabbles that marred the second Jefferson administration was the continued harassment by Great Britain of American ships in the Atlantic Ocean and the impressment of American seamen. The renewal of the war between France and England served as justification for both countries to prey upon neutral shipping. British ships patrolled much of the eastern coastline and virtually shut down the port of New York with a blockade. On May 16, 1806, the British foreign minister also declared a blockade of the European coast from Brest to the Elbe River, to which Napoléon responded on November 21 by issuing the Berlin Decree, which prescribed a blockade of Great Britain. Less than two months later, Britain announced an order in council that barred all ships from French coastal trade. Not to be outmatched, Napoléon replied with the Milan Decree, which promised the seizure of any foreign vessel that obeyed the British order.

IN THE MIDST of these developments, the House of Representatives changed its location in the Capitol. From 1801 to 1804 it had met in the Oven. Then, on November 5, 1804, the members returned to the north wing in the room they originally occupied, and the Oven was dismantled so that the south wing of the Capitol could be constructed. They remained in the north-wing chamber until March 3, 1807, at which time they occupied the newly built room, on the second floor of the south wing. This room, completed under the direction of Benjamin Latrobe, was elliptically shaped and "consisted of two semi-circles 60 feet in diameter ... united by straight lines 25 feet in length," thus creating an internal space of nearly 85 by 60 feet. A seven-foot wall supported twenty-four Corinthian columns that were 26 feet 8 inches high. They in turn supported a 6-foot-high entablature. There were extensive carvings by the Italian artist Giuseppe Franzoni over the main entrance to the room, representing Art, Science, Agriculture and Commerce.[1]

Sitting in a semicircle, the representatives faced the Speaker's podium positioned on a dais under a splendid canopy of crimson silk held aloft by four posts. "A colossal eagle in the act of rising" decorated the frieze above the Speaker's rostrum. Behind the podium rested an eight-and-a-half-foot statue of Liberty, represented by a seated female figure holding a liberty cap in one hand and a scroll in the other. To one side was an eagle with its claw wrapped around a crown as though in the act of crushing it.

Everyone agreed that the room was probably the most beautiful in the country and truly representative of the American Republic. But it was an acoustical horror. Echoes bouncing around the chamber drowned out a speaker's voice. Members had difficulty hearing the debates, and, despite an investigation by a "sound committee," no remedy could be found to correct the problem. To make matters worse, only $25,000 had been appropriated in 1807 for this marvel, but the final cost came to $60,000.[2]

Now, after more than a decade of construction, the U.S. Capitol consisted of north and south wings joined by a two-story wooden walkway across an area intended for a Rotunda. Much work remained to complete the structure, especially the north wing, only half of which had been rebuilt.

BY THE TIME the members assembled into what they thought would be their permanent chamber for the first session of the 10th Congress on October 26, 1807, they were fighting mad over what had happened the previous June. The USS *Chesapeake,* on its maiden voyage, was attacked by the British frigate *Leopard* when it refused to allow a search for supposed deserters from the English navy. Three Americans were killed and eighteen wounded. The *Chesapeake* was searched and four sailors were removed. In retaliation, Jefferson ordered all British warships out of American ports and summoned Congress to an early session to address the crisis. He asked the legislature to enact an embargo on all foreign trade, an action that would surely cripple American commerce since it forbade all American

The northern half of the Capitol housed the Senate, House and Library of Congress from 1805 to 1807, when the Oven was dismantled in order to begin construction of the southern half of the building.

ships to leave for foreign ports and outlawed foreign ships from departing U.S. ports with American goods. The Senate passed the measure on the very day the President asked for it, but in the House, John Randolph, the Quids and the remaining Federalists voiced their protest, claiming the action was unconstitutional.

George Campbell of Tennessee, chairman of Ways and Means and Jefferson's latest floor manager, argued the Hamiltonian loose interpretation of the Constitution, and, after several delays initiated by its opponents, the Embargo Act finally passed the House by a vote of 82 to 44 on December 22, 1807.

But the embargo proved to be a disaster for the nation. And it did not adversely affect England or France one iota. American shippers howled their pain as their commerce all but disappeared. Large coastal cities like Portsmouth, Boston, New York and Philadelphia suffered tremendous losses, and the New England states seemed close to rebellion. The Federalist Party was resuscitated by the furor. Some of its members ranted about nullifying the embargo within their states and even seceding from the Union. Southern states also suffered as their crops rotted on the wharves.

During the heated debates, Barent Gardinier of New York got into a nasty altercation with Campbell and they decided to settle the matter on the field of honor. The people in Georgetown got wind of the intended duel and "were so anxious *to see the sport*" that 150 men, women and children showed up "on the spot marked out for the bloody arena." When the intended combatants saw the crowd they were so outraged that a private matter had now become a public spectacle that they refused to fight. They would not satisfy the bloodlust of the crowd and "were obliged to retire," reported Josiah Quincy. But thanks to "a private gentleman . . . who happens to be a violent Federalist," and who offered them ground on his private estate in Bladensburg, Maryland, just fifteen miles north of Washington, the two men conducted their "affair of honor" on March 2, 1808, in the proper manner, and the skillful Tennessean critically wounded the inexperienced New Yorker, who fortunately survived. "Congress," pleaded Gardinier, "will certainly grant me a pension for known wounds received in the service of the United States."[3]

In 1808 Jefferson decided to follow George Washington's example and step down as President. Some 89 out of 149 Republicans in Congress held an ad hoc caucus and nominated James Madison to replace him. But the small number of those in attendance at the caucus indicated the growing disruption within the party. Randolph and his Quids denounced the nominating procedure, a criticism that would be repeated many times in future elections. They turned to James Monroe of Virginia as their presidential candidate, but that candidacy eventually faded. The Federalists put forward Charles Cotesworth Pinckney of South Carolina, who was hardly an attractive alternate. In the fall election, Madison received 122 electoral votes to 47 for Pinckney, while George Clinton was reelected Vice President.

As one of his final acts in office, Jefferson signed a Non-Intercourse Act, which repealed the embargo and reopened trade with all nations except France and England. It also authorized the President to reinstate trade with either of those two belligerents if they first agreed to respect neutral rights. It was a face-saving retreat from the much-maligned embargo.

But Jefferson had one last victory before he left office. In his message to Congress on December 2, 1806, he pointed out that the Constitution forbade the termination of the African slave trade prior to 1808. He therefore strongly recommended that the trade be ended on January 1, 1808. Naturally there were objections and serious questions about where such a law would lead—to say nothing about the coastal slave trade between states. In a strident and almost hysterical address, John Randolph warned that the bill could become "the pretext of universal emancipation" and if that happened it would "blow up the Constitution."[4] But the House approved the bill, as did the Senate, and the prohibition against the further importation of slaves into the United States passed on March 2, 1807, to go into effect on January 1, 1808.

To JAMES MADISON, "a withered little apple-john," as Washington Irving derisively called him, Jefferson left a country beset with problems abroad and at home. The Federalists had made serious inroads in the Republican majority in Congress and the President's party had been fractured. Madison offered no leadership and instilled no party discipline. Gone were the days when he provided direction for the Congress. Maverick Republicans, called Malcontents, who included Wilson Cary Nichols of Virginia and Senators William Branch Giles and Michael Leib of Pennsylvania, talked Madison out of nominating Albert Gallatin as secretary of state and into accepting in his place Nichols's brother-in-law, the duplicitous Robert Smith, who was also the brother of the crooked senator from Maryland, Samuel Smith. This cozy family arrangement saddled Madison with an incompetent secretary.

To add to Madison's woes, there were increasing cries to end the humiliation suffered at the hands of Great Britain by declaring war. "I am for resistance by the *sword*," Senator Henry Clay of Kentucky bellowed. "No man in the nation wants peace more than I; but I prefer the troubled ocean of war . . . to the tranquil putrescent pool of ignominious peace." If we must choose an enemy between France and England, he continued, "then am I for war with Britain; because I believe her prior in aggression, and her injuries and insults to us were atrocious in character."[5]

With the President willing to take direction from Congress, but the legislature accustomed to leadership from the chief executive, the country floundered. Then, in April 1810, the House passed a bill, introduced by Nathaniel Macon, chairman of the Foreign Affairs Committee, which, when altered by the Senate, did no more than restrict British and French warships from American waters. A younger generation of legislators, like Henry Clay, demanded stronger action. He wanted armed conflict, and he asked it from the veterans of the Revolution seated around him. No, cried the congressional majority, war was not the answer. The upshot was passage on May 1, 1810, by both houses of Macon's Bill No. 2, which removed all trade restrictions against the two belligerents but further declared that if either one revoked its edicts, the United States would reimpose nonintercourse against the other belligerent. Forthwith, Napoléon duped the "withered little apple-john" into believing he would revoke the Berlin and Milan Decrees, whereupon Madison announced the reopening of trade with France and its closing with Great Britain. In fact, Napoléon had no intention of taking such action and Madison soon realized he had been hoodwinked.

The British responded by renewing their blockade of New York City and redoubling their impressment of American seamen.

The 11th Congress further demonstrated its incompetence by allowing the charter of the Bank of the United States to expire, despite the need for a central bank to address such problems as reduced revenues and the likelihood of increased expenditures to cope with foreign hostility. The electorate showed its displeasure by replacing more than seventy members with a younger generation of nationalists, including John C. Calhoun, William C. Lowndes and Langdon Cheves from South Carolina; Richard M. Johnson of Kentucky; Felix Grundy from Tennessee; Peter B. Porter from New York; Ezekiel Bacon from Massachusetts; William W. Bibb from Georgia; John Adams Harper of New Hampshire; and Henry Clay, who chose to run for a House seat rather than the Senate because he preferred the "turbulence . . . of a numerous body to the solemn stillness of the Senate Chamber."[6] This group represented one of the most important, if not the most famous legislative team, in the history of the House. They were young and determined and fiercely intelligent. Randolph dubbed them the "War Hawks" because of their vociferous demands for redress against Great Britain unless the orders in council were revoked. They met in caucus prior to the convening of Congress to evaluate the situation and to choose their nominee for Speaker. They agreed that they needed someone to preside who could enforce the rules and bridle Randolph, "for he disregards all rules." Then their Speaker must "be a man who can meet John Randolph on the floor or on the field, for he may have to do both." But who could fill such qualifications?

"I'll tell you," called out Jonathan Roberts of Pennsylvania. "Young Henry Clay . . . is the very man to do it." All in the room who knew Clay as as a senator shouted their agreement, and thus Clay was chosen.[7]

The next day, Monday, November 4, 1811, the House met, and on the first ballot Clay was elected Speaker. He garnered 75 votes to 38 for William W. Bibb of Georgia, 3 for Macon, 2 for Hugh Nelson of Virginia and 1 for Burwell Bassett of Virginia. And this was Clay's first term as a member of the House! It was an astounding feat.

Born in Virginia, Clay studied law with Chancellor George Wythe and the state's attorney general, Robert Brooke. He migrated west to Kentucky to advance his career, married into one of the leading families of the state and won election to the Kentucky assembly in 1803, where he demonstrated his unique public speaking ability and legislative skills. He won a seat in the U.S Senate in 1806 at the age of twenty-nine, despite the fact that he was constitutionally underage for the position. Senators must be at least thirty. In a Congress that was short on talent, Clay made an immediate and very forceful impression. He was a consummate actor as well as an outstanding debater, and he launched his congressional career with flashes of brilliance that amazed all who heard and saw him.

Arguably the greatest Speaker to preside over the House of Representatives, the formidable, quick-witted and brilliant Henry Clay of Kentucky dominated Congress.

And now, at the age of thirty-four, he was Speaker of the House of Representatives. No impartial presiding officer, he. Clay moved quickly to establish his role as the unchallenged leader of the legislative agenda. He started off by assigning War Hawks to the chairmanships of all the important committees. Porter headed Foreign Relations; Bacon, skilled in finance, took over Ways and Means; Cheves chaired Naval Affairs; and David R. Williams of South Carolina controlled the committee on Miliary Affairs. For the most part the Speaker used Bacon, Cheves and Williams as his floor leaders. He put Randolph on Foreign Relations along with Calhoun, Grundy and Harper, who were expected to keep the wild man in line or at least outvote him.

Clay had every intention of determining policy and the legislation to come before the House. More than any of his predecessors he regularly took part in debates and voted on all legislative bills. He enforced the rules of the House (in the long history of the lower chamber few Speakers have really been able to do this) and he did not hesitate to cut off debate by the opposition when necessary. The brilliance of his leadership was best demonstrated by his treatment of his colleagues. He went out of his way to assure experienced legislators that they would be consulted and that their influence would not be diminished simply because younger men chaired the important committees. In his long career as Speaker, he was eminently fair and evenhanded in his relations with the other members. Yet he could be "haughty and imperious." He delighted in anecdote and regularly mesmerized an audience with his storytelling. Added to this was his quick wit, sharp tongue and histrionic talents as an orator. He was the first truly great Speaker of the House of Representatives.[8]

Of course some congressmen, like Josiah Quincy of Massachusetts, thought his style and manner coarse: "Bold, aspiring, presumptuous, with a rough, overbearing eloquence, neither exact nor comprehensive, which he had cultivated and formed in the contests with the half-civilized wranglers in the county courts of Kentucky, and quickened into confidence and readiness by successful declamations at barbecues and electioneering struggles, he had not yet the polish of language and refinement of manners which he afterwards acquired by familiarity and attrition with highly cultivated men."[9] True, Clay represented a new type of politician just beginning to appear on the American scene, one that appreciated the importance of reflecting the needs and thinking of ordinary citizens, not just those of wealth and position.

The new Speaker's first assignment was putting John Randolph in his place. That meant ordering the doorkeeper to remove the hunting dogs that regularly accompanied the representative from Virginia. Animals were not permitted in the House, Clay declared.

On hearing the Speaker's decree, Randolph bounded to his feet and objected. He was ruled out of order. He appealed to his colleagues to overrule the chair, but they sustained Clay's ruling in the hope that the outrageous eccentricities of Randolph would at last be contained.

The two men clashed repeatedly—even outside the chamber. One day Randolph saw Clay walking down the street toward him. Neither man was willing to step aside and let the other pass. Finally, when they came within a few feet of each other, Randolph stopped in his tracks, looked straight into Clay's eyes and snarled, "I never side-step skunks."

Clay quickly responded, "I always do," and jumped to one side.[10]

In time, even Randolph acknowledged Clay's mastery. The "Speaker of the Ho of Representatives was the second man in the Nation," he reluctantly admitted.[11]

Clay's strong leadership would soon be challenged in the Senate, where many of the Malcontents attempted to weaken or turn back measures approved by the lower chamber. With foreign relations steadily eroding and the likelihood of war with Great Britain rapidly increasing, Madison finally called the 12th Congress into session a full month ahead of schedule. In his message the President asked the Congress to prepare the nation for possible war.

Clay promptly ordered the message to be taken up by two standing committees, Ways and Means and Commerce and Manufacturing, and by six select committees, among them Foreign Affairs and Military Affairs. And he asked for immediate action. Within a month and in concert with the new secretary of state, James Monroe, the chairman of the Foreign Affairs Committee, Peter B. Porter, prepared legislation to arm the merchant fleet and increase the size of the regular army. Unfortunately, Congress had allowed the charter of the Bank of the United States to expire and the nation therefore lacked an adequate supply of ready cash. The secretary of the treasury, Albert Gallatin, had to rely on congressionally approved loans to meet the country's looming crisis.

Working closely with the administration, the House turned out a series of war measures to hurry the nation into a state of readiness. In raising troops, the President had asked for a modest ten thousand. But others in both the House and Senate thought twenty-five thousand a more sensible number. So did Clay. Vacating the chair, he strode to the well of the chamber and within minutes revealed his burgeoning lust for war. "The difference," he declared, "between those who were for 15,000, and those who were for 25,000, appeared to him to resolve itself into the question merely of a short or protracted war, a war of vigor, or a war of languor and imbecility." To him, fifteen thousand was "too great for peace, and . . . too small for war." And make no mistake. War was inevitable. The impressment of seamen and seizure of American property were bad enough, but when "we are called upon to submit to debasement, dishonor, and disgrace—to bow the neck to royal insolence," we cannot submit. We must stand and fight. "It was not by submission," he reminded his colleagues, "that our fathers achieved our independence."[12]

Intense love of country exuded from "every line and word" of the Speaker's speech, declared *Niles' Weekly Register,* the Baltimore newspaper, on January 4, 1812. It "breathes the language of an independent patriot." Clay convinced his colleagues. The bill for the larger army passed overwhelmingly; and Madison accepted what the House had forced upon him. Shortly thereafter, Congress approved the raising of a one-hundred-thousand-man militia for a six-month tour of duty.

In advancing the war hysteria, Clay met with Secretary Monroe on March 15 to work out a strategy to produce a declaration of war. He suggested that Madison first recommend to Congress another embargo, one of

thirty days, which would provide enough time for American ships to return home safely. It would be followed by a message asking for a declaration
of war. The President, now convinced that war was inevitable, went along,
but instead of a thirty-day embargo he extended it to sixty days in the hope
that the delay would pressure Great Britain into suspending its orders in
council. Despite the change, Clay vigorously supported the measure, but
Randolph condemned it as a violation of the traditional Republican opposition to standing armies and armed conflict. War will bring military defeat,
he warned, and the destruction of the Union.[13]

The House approved a sixty-day embargo, which the War Hawks understood to be a prelude to armed conflict, by the vote of 70 to 41. The Senate further increased the time to ninety days and, after considerable
haggling, the House consented to the change. Madison signed the bill on
April 1, 1812.

As the administration lurched hesitantly toward war, eighty-three Republicans from both houses met in a party caucus on May 18 and unanimously nominated James Madison for a second term as President, along
with Elbridge Gerry as Vice President. DeWitt Clinton of New York was
nominated by the antiwar Republicans of his state, and in a secret meeting
the Federalists threw their support to him. Charles J. Ingersoll, a moderate
Federalist, completed the Clinton ticket.

Then, on June 1, Madison sent a secret message to Congress, which was
read behind closed doors, asking for a consideration of a declaration of war
against Great Britain. He expressed his belief that "the decision will be worthy of the enlightened and patriotic councils, of a virtuous, a free, and powerful Nation."[14]

The message was referred to a select committee chaired by John C. Calhoun. Two days later, the House debated the committee's "war manifesto,"
which declared that this was the nation's "second war of independence."
Under Clay's tight control, the debate on the manifesto moved along swiftly,
but courtesy among members gave way to "partisan rudeness," a situation
that would arise again and again over the next two centuries. On the question of war, Clay kept the House in session "several weeks, day and night,
without recess or respite." Federalists tried to block its progress with a filibuster. They organized a phalanx of orators who spelled one another and
prevented a vote. Into the night they droned. Most of the members fell
asleep, including the Speaker. The clerk's head slowly came to rest on the
journal he was writing.

And then it happened. Suddenly down the aisles came shattering, rat-
tling, smashing sounds. Spittoons sailed through the air and crashed to the
floor, "reverberating their sounds like thunders among the crags of the Alps."
Clay and the clerk bolted to attention. "Order! Order! Order!" came the cry
from every corner of the room. It was chaotic. The Federalist orator who held

A rather wizened-looking John C. Calhoun when he served in the Senate, still battling for southern rights and the protection of slavery.

the floor and had been droning on for hours raced to his seat from fright. At that point, in their prearranged scenario, one Republican addressed the chair and moved "the previous question," which would shut off further debate. It was immediately seconded. Clay overruled objections and put the measure to a vote.[15] On June 4, the House, for the first time, voted a declaration of war by a count of 79 to 49. The Federalists and the Malcontents naturally opposed it, especially those from New England and some parts of New York and New Jersey. The South and the West solidly supported it.[16]

The bill languished in the Senate for nearly two weeks. Not until June 17 did the upper house give its consent to war by a vote of 19 to 13. The following day, June 18, Madison signed it and proclaimed a state of war with Great Britain.

Two days later, Lord Castlereagh, the foreign secretary, agreed to suspend the orders in council.

IN THE FALL election, Clinton came within a whisker of victory. He won all of New England, except Vermont, and the middle states with the exception

of Pennsylvania for a total of 89 electoral votes. Madison took the South
and the West for 128 votes. Had Clinton carried Pennsylvania he would
have unseated the "apple-john." Still, the tremendous Federalist victory in
the East virtually doubled the numerical strength of their party in the next
Congress.

The war proved to be a disaster for the United States—at least in the
beginning. The long planned three-pronged invasion of Canada by American troops ended in defeat on all fronts. General William Hull not only
retreated but surrendered Detroit to the British and their Indian allies in
the hope of preventing the massacre of women and children in the town by
Native Americans. He was later court-martialed and sentenced to death for
cowardice and neglect of duty, but the sentence was suspended because of
his illustrious record during the Revolution. Meanwhile, the British block-
aded the East Coast from New York to the mouth of the Mississippi River.
At first New England was exempt from the blockade in the hope that it
would secede from the Union. At the same time a series of naval raids along
the upper Chesapeake, commanded by Rear Admiral Sir George Cockburn,
kept Washington in a state of panic, fearing not only the British military
but the possibility of a slave revolt.[17]

Shortly after the United States declared war, Napoléon invaded Russia.
Now an ally of Britain, the czar initiated steps to end the Anglo-American
conflict in order to help crush the French. He spoke to the U.S. minister,
John Quincy Adams, and offered to act as mediator, a proposal Madison
quickly accepted. But the British balked at Russian involvement and suggested instead that commissioners meet in Ghent, in what is now Belgium,
to work out a peace treaty. The President chose Adams to head a U.S. delegation that included Henry Clay, Albert Gallatin, James A. Bayard and
Jonathan Russell.

To add to the nation's misery, the Creek Indians in the Alabama
Country began a general uprising along the frontier and on August 30,
1813, massacred approximately three hundred Americans at Fort Mims,
about thirty-five miles north of Mobile. The governor of Tennessee dispatched the state's militia under the command of General Andrew Jackson to quell the uprising. After a series of engagements, the Creeks were
defeated at the Battle of Horseshoe Bend along the Tallapoosa River on
March 27, 1814.

With the defeat of Napoléon's army in Russia and his subsequent abdication, the British now felt secure in launching a major offensive against the
United States from three separate areas: Lake Champlain, Chesapeake Bay
and New Orleans. Thousands of veterans of the Duke of Wellington's army
were transported to America, and on June 24, 1814, a force of four thousand
troops under the command of General Robert Ross left France for the
Chesapeake invasion. Together with Cockburn's fleet, Ross and his crack

The torching of Washington by the British during the War of 1812.

army entered the bay and moved quickly up to the mouth of the Patuxent River and landed at Benedict in Maryland. They marched on Washington and easily defeated a superior number of American militiamen gathered at Bladensburg. "Their army composed of conquering veterans," wrote Margaret Bayard Smith, "ours of young mechanics and farmers, many of whom had never before carried a musket." They will make us "a martial people," she continued, "for never, never will Americans give up their liberty."[18] The U.S. Army and the government, with President Madison at its head, fled to Virginia and the British entered the unprotected city on the evening of August 24, 1814.

Congress was not in session and the militia had abandoned what hastily constructed fortifications existed. The inhabitants, those who had not deserted their homes, could do nothing to defend themselves. Then snipers opened fire and killed four British soldiers and General Ross's horse just a few blocks from the Capitol. "I imagine Genl. R. thought that his life was particularly aim'd at," commented Mrs. Smith, "for while his troops remained in the city he never made his appearance, altho' Cochburn [sic] and the other officers often rode through the avenue."[19] In retaliation, the commanding officers ordered the destruction of both the White House and the Capitol, along with all public buildings. The Patent Office was spared because William Thornton, the superintendent of patents, convinced the British officers that the destruction of the records contained within the building would rank with the barbaric act of the Saracens who burned the library at Alexandria. Nevertheless, the British did not hesitate to torch any private dwelling harboring snipers.

The burning of the House chamber was especially severe. All the mahogany furniture was piled high in the room and ignited with rocket fuel. The blaze consumed everything but the outer walls. Worse, the Library of Congress in the north wing was destroyed. Patrick Magruder, the clerk of the House and the librarian of Congress, had left town for reasons of health, but before leaving he issued instructions to subordinates that with the approach of the British army they were to evacuate the records of the House and the books in the library as soon as the War Department began moving its documents to safety.

On the morning of Monday, August 22, the staff at the War Department began their evacuation, and as soon as the House staff heard this they started moving their records. But they had trouble finding transport. The streets were "fill'd with carriages bringing out citizens and Baggage waggons and troops."[20] Residents and other government employees had commandeered all the wagons and horses available. Only one cart and a team of oxen was located on the outskirts of the city. By the time these clerks got back to the Capitol with the cart, the British had started their invasion. In a panic they quickly transferred what documents were easily seized and secured them in houses across the street from the Capitol. Unfortunately, when the Capitol was torched, sparks from the flames destroyed these houses and the enormous mass of historical documents with them, including the secret journals of the House, the earliest petitions submitted to the House from 1789 to 1799 and the contingent expenses for the present Congress. Later a select committee investigated the loss and found Magruder guilty of neglect of duty. He protested his innocence and resigned his office on January 28, 1815, while a resolution was pending to remove him from office.

Fortunately, a violent storm struck during the middle of the night— Mrs. Smith called it a hurricane—and prevented the entire city from being incinerated. A day or two later she inspected the damage to the public buildings, but none, she reported, "were so thoroughly destroy'd as the House of Representatives and the Presidents House. Those beautiful pillars in that Representatives Hall were crack'd and broken, the roof, that noble dome, painted and carved with such beauty and skill, lay in ashes in the cellars beneath the smouldering ruins, were yet smoking."[21]

The British continued their march toward Baltimore but were repulsed on September 13 by thirteen thousand Americans who had fortified the

The Capitol, seen from the southern end, as it appeared after the fires set by the British had been extinguished.

heights around the city. In the engagement General Ross was killed. Fort McHenry was bombarded by a British fleet, but when the defenders refused to surrender, the fleet and army withdrew. These invading forces were then ordered to head for New Orleans to participate in the capture of that vital city.

THE THIRD SESSION of the 13th Congress met, according to schedule, on September 19, 1814. Without a Capitol building the members were forced to meet in the Patent Office and Blodgett's Hotel at Eighth and E Streets NW. The President took up residence in the Octagon House on New York Avenue. One of the first things the congressional leaders considered was moving the capital to a less vulnerable site farther north and west. But the humiliation involved and its effect on the public prompted the House to vote to remain in Washington.

Congress then set about rebuilding the city. A $500,000 loan from Washington banks started the process, which the citizens of the town aided by raising $25,000 for the construction of a temporary structure near the ruins of the Capitol to serve as the seat of government. This was a brick hall located at First and A Street NE, on the site of the present Supreme Court building. The Senate assembled on the first floor of this "Old Brick Capitol" while the House met on the second floor.[22]

A new Capitol building on the old site was soon under construction. It was not completed until 1825, although it was ready for partial use in December 1819. The Brick Capitol then became a boardinghouse. As for the President's Mansion, it was repainted and refurbished, and received its new occupants in September 1817.

To replenish its library, Congress agreed to pay former President Jefferson $23,900 for his extensive collection of books, despite the fears of some who thought they might be too philosophical to have much value. This collection became the core of what is today the world's largest library. In the rebuilding of the city, it was decided to replace all public buildings on the sites on which they previously stood.

It was very painful for congressmen to go about their business, particularly when they heard rumors that delegates from a convention held in Hartford, Connecticut, representing the New England states, were headed for Washington with demands for constitutional changes as the price for their continued allegiance to the Union. Worse, they knew that a tremendous invasion at New Orleans had taken place involving thousands of British veterans who faced a "rag-tag" army of American militia, regulars, pirates, Indians and townspeople commanded by General Andrew Jackson. If the British defeated the Americans, they could easily march up the Mississippi River valley and establish a buffer state to block the westward expansion of the country.

To add to the gloom in the capital a severe snowstorm inundated Washington on January 23 and continued for three days. Not until February 4 did word arrive that Jackson and his troops had decimated the invading army on January 8, 1815. Over two thousand British were killed, wounded or missing, while the Americans suffered only a dozen or so casualties. The city exploded out of its gloom and fear. "ALMOST INCREDIBLE VICTORY!!!" trumpeted the *Washington National Intelligencer* on February 7. "Enemy . . . beaten and repulsed . . . with great slaughter." Celebrants thronged the house where the President now lived and the homes of the cabinet officers. The mayor issued a proclamation for the illumination of the city.

Nine days later came word that the commissioners in Ghent had signed a peace treaty on Christmas Eve, ending the war between Great Britain and the United States once the document was ratified by both countries. Citizens ran through the street screaming, "Peace! Peace!" It seemed like a miracle that the war had ended without any loss of territory and with a glorious military victory. "The last six months is the proudest period in the history of the republic," exclaimed *Niles' Weekly Register. "Who would not be an American? Long live the Republic."*[23]

From the House Committee on Military Affairs, George M. Troup of Georgia reported resolutions about "the glorious termination of the most glorious war ever waged by any people."[24] A gold medal was ordered to be struck and presented to General Jackson. The nation had at last found another illustrious hero.

The text of the Treaty of Ghent ending the war arrived in Washington and was submitted to the Senate on February 15, 1815. The following day it was ratified and the war officially came to an end.

WITH THE VICTORY at New Orleans and the conclusion of the War of 1812 the delegation from the Hartford Convention realized their mission was now hopeless, so they turned around and went home. The Hartford Convention was never in the hands of secessionists, but suspicions of treason on the part of its participants lingered for many years, and the Federalist Party, accused of participating in this disloyalty, lost popular support and slowly declined. It dragged on for several more years in a few northern states but finally disappeared.

There followed a suspension of party strife—what one contemporary described as "a calm after the storm."[25] It marked the beginning of what would be known as "the Era of Good Feelings." The country was in the throes of massive changes, marked by a heightened sense of nationalism. The original thirteen states had grown to nineteen and a new era of expansion and prosperity was about to begin.

The war convinced President Madison and any number of other Republicans that the nation suffered many weaknesses that had to be remedied immediately. Thus, in the President's annual message to Congress in December 1815, he emphasized the importance of increased government responsibility for establishing an independent domestic economy. He urged Congress to recharter the national bank and thereby restore a uniform national currency, impose a protective tariff to assist the establishment and growth of native manufactures and encourage westward expansion by supporting internal improvements, such as roads, bridges and canals. The whole idea was to strengthen the nation in order to safeguard its liberties. It was Federalist dogma now mouthed by ardent nationalists who reiterated the cry for a new concept of accelerating government's role in advancing the emerging market revolution. "England is the most formidable power in the world," declared Representative John C. Calhoun of South Carolina. "We, on the contrary, are the most growing nation on earth."[26]

Fortunately, at the start of the 14th Congress, Henry Clay returned to the House, following his sojourn in Europe, and he easily won election as Speaker. Once more he manned the committees with reliable allies. And to regain and maintain control of the House, he increasingly depended on standing committees whose members and work could be monitored and directed. Indeed, during his tenure as Speaker, the number of standing committees increased dramatically from eleven to twenty-four. Such matters as Indian affairs, military affairs, the judiciary, public lands, revolutionary war claims, agriculture, foreign affairs and naval affairs required the special attention that only standing committees could provide. And, in 1819, one of the earliest standing committees, Commerce and Manufacturing, was split into two committees in order to cope with these two important areas of national development. Although the Commerce and Manufacturing Committee was chaired by a protectionist, Thomas Newton of Georgia, its members lacked the enthusiasm for a higher tariff that Clay desired. So the Speaker divided the committee, over Newton's protests, and he staffed the new Committee on Manufactures with strong protectionists, headed by Henry Baldwin of Pennsylvania, a manufacturer of glass products. This committee presumed to write a new tariff bill in 1820, much to the displeasure of the Ways and Means Committee.

The House now came to rely on standing committees to draft legislation. When Clay resigned from the House in 1825, almost 90 percent of all bills were reported from these committees. The number of these bills grew from 153 in the 10th Congress to 454 in the 18th Congress (1823–1825).[27] By this time, standing committees had been institutionalized and select committees were used only for special purposes such as investigating actions taken by the executive branch. As a consequence, the House now asserted its authority into all functions of the federal government.[28]

The 14th Congress (1815–1817) inaugurated many of these remarkable changes and produced some of the most important legislation to be initiated by the House. Various standing committees put forward legislation to increase the size of the navy, create an army of ten thousand men, construct military roads and canals, charter a national bank and subsidize industry. Most of these proposals violated traditional Republican dogma, but times had changed, and the party, these nationalists argued, had to change with them.

THE WAYS AND Means Committee drafted the first protective tariff in U.S. history, and it was enacted into law on April 27, 1816. Thanks to the lobbying efforts by Francis Cabot Lowell and Nathaniel Appleton of the Boston Manufacturing Company, who came down to Washington and exerted their influence on the members, the bill established a 25 percent duty on woolen and cotton goods and 30 percent on iron products. The success of Lowell and Appleton encouraged other manufacturers to send lobbying agents to the capital, thus establishing a practice that continued to grow over the next several decades. Southerners like Calhoun supported the measure for nationalistic reasons but would later reverse themselves in the belief that the tariff harmed cotton interests. On the other hand, Daniel Webster, a Federalist, opposed the tariff as detrimental to the shipping and commercial interests he represented, but, following his removal to Massachusetts from New Hampshire, he would later switch his position and become a strong advocate for tariff protection of manufactures.

Next, Calhoun and his Committee on the National Currency brought in a bill on January 8, 1816, for the incorporation of the Second National Bank of the United States. It approved a twenty-year charter for a bank to be located in Philadelphia with branches in other cities. It would have a capital stock of $35 million, of which one-fifth would be purchased by the government, the rest sold to the public. It would be operated by a board of twenty-five directors, five of whom would be appointed by the President, the other twenty elected by the stockholders. This bank would become the custodian of public funds, and its notes would be acceptable for debts owed the government. In return, the bank would transact all government business free of charge and pay the Treasury a bonus of $1.5 million in three installments over five years.[29]

In a close vote, 80 to 71, the bill passed the House on March 14, 1816. It had an easier time in the Senate, and Madison signed it on May 10. The Bank went into operation on January 1, 1817. As for the bonus, Calhoun concocted a plan by which it would serve as a permanent fund, along with dividends from the government-owned stock, to construct roads and canals that were so necessary for the expansion of the country and commercial development. "Let us then bind the Republic together with a perfect system of roads and canals," he pleaded in presenting the bill. "Let us conquer space." The measure passed on March 1, 1817, but Madison vetoed it on constitutional grounds the day before he left office. Clay pleaded with him to leave the question to his successor, but he was wasting his breath. An attempt to override the veto failed in the House by a vote of 60 to 56.[30]

The National Road, which extended westward from Cumberland, Maryland, had been authorized in 1806 and appropriations for further construction had been approved several times thereafter. Now, in 1816, federally funded internal improvements, like tariff protection and support for a strong banking institution, had become part of what Clay later called his "American System."

BY THIS TIME it was clear to most Americans that the nation had entered a new era of development. The Industrial Revolution burst upon the country and a market revolution produced a conversion that would move the United States from a purely agricultural to an industrial society. The building of bridges, roads, canals, highways and finally railroads, financed mainly by the states and private investors, resulted in a transportation revolution. And Americans had already begun their long trek westward to the Pacific Ocean. Following the war, thousands of emigrants from Europe arrived and fanned out into the seemingly endless landscape.

In addition, political attitudes had changed dramatically. Where the

Founders decried parties, by 1816, with the retirement and/or death of most of the Founders, a new group of political leaders appeared who maintained that parties were essential for achieving those ends of government that would benefit the nation as a whole and safeguard liberty.

The leadership in the House of Representatives—Clay, Calhoun, William Lowndes, Richard M. Johnson, Peter B. Porter and others—represented this second generation of American statesmen. They provided the impetus and legislation that assisted the nation in this transformation. Calhoun was particularly active as chairman of the Committee on National Currency. "Not a cent of money ought to be applied but by our direction and under our control," he exclaimed.[31]

The leadership stumbled only once. Colonel Richard M. Johnson of Kentucky, the supposed slayer of the Indian chief Tecumseh in hand-to-hand combat, moved to change congressional compensation from a per diem rate, established by the 1st Congress in 1789, to a fixed salary. There was no question that the pay was inadequate and that the members deserved a raise. After all, they were paid less than the President, the cabinet officers and the members of the Supreme Court. From a select committee he chaired, Johnson reported a bill that changed the $6 per day compensation to an annual salary of $1,500. Since Clay would receive double compensation as Speaker, he demonstrated either remarkable courage or insensitivity by vigorously arguing for the bill's passage. In the debate that followed, Calhoun and Randolph insisted on a higher sum. They suggested $2,500, and Randolph thought that implementation should wait until after the next election. But the House rejected both suggestions and on March 19, by a bipartisan vote of 81 to 67, decided on an immediate increase to $1,500.[32]

The electorate was outraged by this "Salary Grab," as they called it. And they promised an appropriate revenge. This was a presidential election year and the Republicans put forward James Monroe of Virginia—thereby continuing the so-called Virginia Dynasty—while the Federalists backed Rufus King of New York. In the fall election the voters demonstrated their anger with Congress by ousting fully two-thirds of the House and half the members of the Senate. Even Clay felt the sting of their anger, but he did manage to survive the congressional slaughter. And Monroe easily defeated King, who received the support of only Massachusetts, Connecticut and Delaware. The electoral count was 183 to 34. Clearly the Federalist Party was moribund.

The first thing Congress did when it reconvened was repeal the Compensation Act in January 1817. The per diem method was reimposed, but the rate was raised from $6 to $8.

The leaders in the House then renewed their focus on domestic issues. As Joseph Story, an associate justice, rightly remarked, "the Executive has no longer a commanding influence; the House of Representatives has absorbed . . . all the effective power of the country. Even the Senate cowers under its lofty pretensions to be the guardians of the people and their rights."[33]

CLAY'S DESIRE TO initiate and control legislation without deference to the Monroe administration may have been prompted in part by his anger and disappointment at not being appointed secretary of state. That office had become the stepping-stone to the presidency, which he desperately desired. Instead, Monroe appointed John Quincy Adams to head the State Department. Adams's sage advice and direction enabled the President to concentrate on foreign affairs. Throughout the eight years of Monroe's presidential term, Clay became a nagging critic, particularly in his outspoken support of the newly independent Latin American republics and his mistaken and unfortunate condemnation of the invasion of Spanish-held Florida by General Andrew Jackson in 1818.

The Seminole Indians in Florida regularly crossed the border and attacked American settlements in Georgia and Alabama, then retreated to what they felt was the safety of their towns in Spanish territory. Unwilling to allow this violation to continue, the President instructed his secretary of war, the newly appointed John C. Calhoun, to direct Jackson to pursue the Indians and put a halt to their invasions once and for all. Not content with just subduing Native Americans, the general asked permission to seize Florida and, as far as can be determined, he received it, although the language of Monroe's letter was guarded. In any event, Jackson not only pursued the Seminoles, killed a number of them and burned their towns, but he also executed two British subjects accused of aiding the Indians and captured St. Marks and Pensacola, the two important seats of Spanish authority in Florida.

This invasion and seizure of Florida without a declaration of war by Congress, and the execution of the British nationals by an army court-martial, triggered an international crisis. Without wasting a moment, Clay demanded the punishment of Jackson and an apology to Britain and Spain. He deliberately used the general as the instrument to wreak revenge against the administration.

The Committee on Military Affairs condemned the executions and Jackson's handling of the Florida expedition. In one of his most powerful speeches, Clay verbally crucified the general. The chamber was jammed; the city's social elite crowded into the gallery; the Senate adjourned to hear him; and foreign ministers vied with one another for seats.

He did not disappoint. In a two-hour speech, Clay compared Jackson to many of the tyrants of history. "Beware how you give a fatal sanction, in this infant period of our republic, scarcely yet two score years old, to military insubordination. Remember that Greece had her Alexander, Rome her Caesar, England her Cromwell, France her Bonaparte, and, that if we would escape the rock on which they split, we must avoid their errors." This military chieftain had ridden roughshod over law and the Constitution. The assault on Spanish authority, he ranted, "was open, undisguised and unauthorized hostility."[34]

Nevertheless, the members of the House understood only too well the retribution the public would exact on them if the Hero of New Orleans was punished or even censured. So, on February 8, 1819, they voted down the recommendation of their committee by the count of 107 to 63.

Clay's unfortunate speech began a long controversy with a powerful enemy in the person of General Jackson, who could and would do him great injury in the future. And just a few weeks later, on February 22, 1819, Spain signed a treaty with the United States in which it ceded Florida in return for which the United States assumed the claims by American citizens against Spain to the extent of $5 million. It was an achievement that greatly enhanced the reputation of Jackson and the secretary of state, John Quincy Adams, who had defended the general's actions before the President and cabinet and convinced the Spanish that it served their interests to relinquish Florida to the United States.

THANKS TO MEN like Jackson, Adams, Clay and Calhoun, the United States was growing in size and power. New states had been admitted to the Union: Louisiana in 1810, Indiana in 1816, Mississippi in 1817 and Illinois in 1818. Then in February 1819, the House took up the question of admitting Alabama and Missouri. Alabama's admission came without difficulty, but Missouri's application unleashed a storm that almost brought about the breakup of the Union.

The Missouri Territory had been carved out of the Louisiana Purchase and, if admitted as a slave state, would be the first such state located completely west of the Mississippi River. Moreover, it would upset the numerical balance between free and slave states. So on February 13, 1819, Representative James Tallmadge of New York offered an amendment to the enabling act, prohibiting the further introduction of slaves into Missouri and mandating the emancipation of all slaves subsequently born in the state on reaching the age of twenty-five.

That did it. The question of the constitutional right of Congress to outlaw slavery in the territories was hotly disputed. It had begun in Congress under the Articles of Confederation with the passage of the Northwest Ordinance of 1787, which forbade slavery north of the Ohio River. Now it had risen again, and southerners were determined to establish their right under the Constitution to take their slaves anywhere in the territories. Representative Thomas W. Cobb of Georgia shook his fist at Tallmadge. "If you persist," he cried, "the Union will be dissolved. You have kindled a fire which all the waters of the ocean cannot put out, which seas of blood can only extinguish."

So be it, screamed Tallmadge in response. "Let it come."[35]

Despite these dire predictions and over the protests of southerners, the Tallmadge amendment to the enabling act passed by a vote of 79 to 67. But the Senate shot it down by the overwhelming vote of 31 to 7. And on that quarrelsome note, the 15th Congress adjourned on March 3, 1819.

Over the summer the question generated petitions from northern groups demanding that Congress outlaw slavery in Missouri, while southerners warned that any such action could trigger secession. The public discussion had become so heated that by the time the 16th Congress convened on December 6, 1819, the two sides were primed for battle.

ON ARRIVING IN Washington, the members finally moved into their new quarters in the restored wings of the Capitol. Latrobe had resigned as architect in November 1817, a disheartened and discouraged man whose genius was only later recognized. He had been replaced by Charles Bulfinch of Boston. But the plan of the south wing remained virtually unchanged from its earlier design, except that Latrobe proposed a semicircular chamber with an imposing colonnade to be covered by a dome of brick and masonry. Unfortunately, to save money and speed completion of the building, President Monroe ordered a wooden dome instead. As a result the room, once again, was an acoustical disaster; the high smooth arched ceiling acted as a sounding board and redirected voices.

Still, the sweeping colonnade added a touch of the magnificent. Also commanding notice was the renowned *Car of History* carved in marble by Carlo Franzoni and positioned above the entrance of the House. It was a statue of Clio, the muse of history, in billowing drapery standing on a winged chariot. The chariot included a bas-relief portrait of George Washington and a figure of Fame blowing a horn. The wheel of the chariot was the face of an enormous clock. Simon Willard of Roxbury, Massachusetts, crafted the workings of the clock itself.

Every member had an easy chair and a desk. The gallery had a ladies' section. This gorgeous room housed 192 members when first occupied, but a year later, following the census of 1820, the capacity of the chamber was increased to 216.

Less than a month after Bulfinch assumed the position of architect of the Capitol, the building commissioners asked him to design a structure between the north and south wings. In the design he was required to provide as many committee rooms as possible. It was to be a grand vestibule in which artist John Trumbull would display a group of four paintings of historical scenes, including the signing of the Declaration of Independence.

The Car of History *depicts Clio, the muse of history, seemingly taking notes as she observes the debates in the old House chamber.*

Bulfinch designed a Rotunda that rose 96 feet to match its diameter exactly, and the double dome above it rose 140 feet above the ground. The cornerstone was laid at noon on August 24, 1818, the fourth anniversary of the burning of the Capitol. It was completed in 1827.[36]

THE HOUSE MEMBERS assembled in their splendid new quarters to begin debate on potentially the most lethal issue to arise since the inauguration of the government. "The words, civil war, and disunion," Henry Clay told a friend, "are uttered almost without emotion." Not surprisingly, emotion spilled out on the floor day and night as the members struggled with the problem. Clay himself feared that at the very least, *"sectional"* political parties would arise.[37]

A glimmer of hope suddenly appeared when Maine, the northern district of Massachusetts, petitioned for admission as a separate (free) state in the Union. Clay immediately saw the possibility of compromise by tying Missouri to Maine in an enabling act. But he did not have the votes to pass it, so he wisely waited for the Senate to do it for him. On February 16, 1820, the upper house united the two bills of admission into one and, as an amendment offered by Senator Jesse Thomas of Illinois, prohibited the extension of slavery in the Louisiana Territory north of 36° 30′, with the exception of Missouri itself. [38]

In an impassioned four-hour speech that completely consumed the entire sitting of the House, Speaker Clay wheedled and cajoled and threatened and even resorted to a "repulsive gesture" to prevent what looked like a headlong rush toward disunion. Still, radicals on both sides refused to budge from their positions and denounced the compromise. "God has given us Missouri," shrieked Randolph in his earsplitting voice, "and the devil shall not take it from us."[39]

The House subsequently rejected the Senate compromise, whereupon Clay appointed a committee of conciliators who favored compromise to meet jointly with a Senate committee and work out a solution. On March 2, 1820, this joint committee reported out three separate bills (instead of the single enabling act passed by the Senate) in which Maine's admission constituted one part, Missouri's a second, and the prohibition of slavery north of 36° 30′ a third. And, miraculously, what had been unacceptable as one bill now passed as three. "The Southern & Western people talked so much, threatened so loudly, & predicted such dreadful consequences," declared Representative William Plumer of New Hampshire, ". . . that they fairly frightened our weak-minded members into an abandonment" of their stand against slavery in the territories. These "weak-minded members" were "dough faces," according to John Randolph. "They were scared at their own dough faces."[40]

But Randolph was not ready to admit defeat. The following day he rose in the House and asked for a reconsideration of the Missouri vote. Clay ruled him out of order until the ordinary business of the House was concluded. Meanwhile, as Speaker, he signed the Missouri bill and had it rushed to the Senate. Randolph rose again when the ordinary business of the House had ended, whereupon Clay calmly informed him that the bill had already gone to the Senate and could not be retrieved. Randolph appealed to his colleagues, but the thought of enduring another round of angry debate convinced the members to be done with this ghastly problem. By a vote of 71 to 61 they refused to reconsider. It was the one of the niftiest sleight-of-hand tricks ever pulled in the House of Representatives.

However, passage of the Missouri Compromise of 1820 failed to bring a final solution to the problem because in writing its constitution, Missouri, to show its resentment against congressional dictation, inserted a clause that required the legislature to forbid "free negroes and mulattoes" from entering the state. This was a clear violation of the U.S. Constitution because free Negroes were citizens in some states.

Northern representatives erupted. The compromise must be scrapped, they argued. "Missouri is still a territory."

And so another pitched battle ensued. Unfortunately, Clay had resigned as Speaker to attend to personal business in Kentucky, and the House needed twenty-two ballots—the most prolonged struggle to name a Speaker thus far—before electing John Taylor of New York over William Lowndes of South Carolina. But Taylor did not have the skill to handle a situation that daily ran out of control. "A fixed and settled majority is hard to move, especially if power is the object," commented Nathaniel Macon. "They want the guidance of such a man as Mr. Clay," said William Plumer of New Hampshire, "who, with all his violence & impetuosity, knew better how to control & direct his party, than any man they now have here."[41]

Fortunately, Clay had not resigned his seat in the House, and when he returned many members sighed with relief. "His coming was universally and anxiously awaited."[42] He quickly arranged a second compromise by which Missouri would be admitted provided its legislature solemnly agreed that laws would never be enacted to deprive any citizen of any state the rights and privileges that were protected by the U.S. Constitution. The measure passed both houses and on August 10, 1821, President Monroe declared that Missouri was the twenty-fourth state in the Union.

Thereafter Henry Clay was known as the Great Compromiser or the Great Pacificator. "The Constitution of the Union was in danger," cried one congressman, "& has been Saved," thanks to Henry Clay. Missouri was brought into the Union without bloodshed or the dismemberment of the American nation.[43]

Secession had been averted, but the central question regarding the right of Congress to forbid slavery in the territories remained. It would haunt the country for the next forty years. Yet as long as Henry Clay remained alive he could always find a compromise to keep it from exploding into civil war.

6

A Democratized House,
1822–1846

THE ERA FOLLOWING the War of 1812 was one of intense nationalism, a sense that the nation was capable of extraordinary feats in advancing freedom and democracy. The size of the electorate among white males increased markedly and changed the conduct of elections at both the state and national level. Americans reveled in the diplomatic triumphs achieved by President Monroe and his secretary of state, John Quincy Adams. Not only did Monroe and Adams acquire Florida, settle the western boundary for the Louisiana Purchase and recognize the independence of Latin American republics, but they also put forward the Monroe Doctrine, which would constitute a fundamental American precept with respect to European involvement in the Western Hemisphere.

But Secretary Adams delivered a warning to his countrymen. On July 4, 1821, from the rostrum of the House of Representatives, he declared that the United States would always be "the well-wisher to the freedom and independence of all" nations, but that it must not go "abroad in search of monsters to destroy" by enlisting under banners other "than our own." Such a policy, he insisted, would inaugurate America's search for "dominion and power" in the world, and would ultimately result in the loss of our own "freedom and independence."[1]

• • •

THE YEARS BETWEEN the War of 1812 and the Civil War also became
known as the Age of Jackson, in which the hero of the Battle of New Orleans
first won election to the presidency, despite his limited qualifications, and
then went on to symbolize an age in which the common man intruded more
aggressively into the political scene. Party loyalty became more pronounced,
and the question of slavery began to tear apart the bonds of Union.

In the chamber of the House the personnel and especially the manners
of the members underwent profound alteration. On a social note, Mrs. Smith
reported that gentlemen in the House had "grown very gallant and attentive." For example, they invented a new mode of supplying ladies seated in
the gallery with oranges, cakes and other sweets. They tied them up in handkerchiefs and included a note designating the person to whom the goodies
were intended and then fastened the bundle to a long pole. "This was taken
on the floor of the house and handed up to the ladies who sat in front of the
gallery. . . . These presentations were frequent and quite amusing, even in
the midst" of one of Henry Clay's most electrifying speeches.[2]

Obviously, conduct on the floor of the House had become quite informal. On one occasion two reporters from New York newspapers got into a
heated argument and attempted to cane each other. The sergeant at arms
took them into custody and they were denied further access to the floor, a
mild punishment, according to John Fairfield of Maine, "considering how
indignant the members were at the outrage."

On another occasion a Quaker lady sitting in the gallery rose from her
seat before the House had been called into session and "in the most sepulchral tones" preached "a sermon or exhortation." The doorkeeper hauled
her out of the chamber.[3]

Members could be quite fastidious about certain things, however. For
example, they continued to sit in the House with their hats on, except when
they rose to speak, a custom that went back to the Continental Congresses.
It was considered a distinct honor for the members to "uncover for anything
or anybody." Throughout the session the Speaker would preside, wearing his
hat. He would remove it only when he rose to recognize a member or call the
attention of the House to a particular matter. Not until "cloak rooms" were
introduced around 1830 did the members gradually give up the practice of
wearing hats during the session. But they continued using snuff, containers
of which were strategically located around the House. It was not uncommon
for a member to interrupt his oration, walk over to a silver urn, sample the
fragrant Maccaboy or Old Scotch in the urn, let fire with a sneeze or two,
wipe his nose and calmly resume his tirade. And the members rather liked a
drink called Switchell, a concoction of molasses, ginger and water, laced
with pure Jamaica rum, which was readily at hand and supplied at taxpayers' expense. Oh, how a few glasses of Switchell could enliven a debate![4]

And congressmen never read their speeches. Although they often spent hours preparing them, "they would have been laughed out of the House had they come into the hall with, and attempted to *read* a written speech." In fact they could not conceive "that such a thing could be done. . . . These men met one another face to face" and argued their case with great passion and conviction and with a verbal power that would rarely again be equaled in American history.[5]

Outside the chamber, Anne Royall, the novelist, was frequently seen tramping through the halls, umbrella in hand, and confronting every passerby to urge them to buy her latest romance. "She was the terror of politicians, and especially of Congressmen." Any public man, including justices of the Supreme Court, who refused to buy her wares was "certain of a severe philippic in her newspaper." Justice Joseph Story told his wife that "we have the famous Mrs. Royall here with her new novel, 'The Tennessean,' which she has compelled the Chief Justice and myself to buy to avoid a castigation. I shall bring it home for your edification."[6]

Few wives of congressmen came to Washington with their husbands in these early days, and even fewer children. Most of the women in the district were local residents, spouses and daughters of civil officers of the government, or the families of officers in the army and the navy stationed or temporarily resident in the capital, or those of foreign ministers.[7]

ALTHOUGH CLAY RETIRED from Congress with the conclusion of the second session of the 16th Congress, he returned at the start of the 18th Congress on December 1, 1823, and was again elected Speaker. Indeed, he served longer as Speaker than anyone else in the nineteenth century. Only Sam Rayburn in the twentieth century held the office longer. Clay's service in the 18th Congress was one of his most outstanding. He helped win passage of the Tariff of 1824, which increased the protective rates on imported goods; and he announced what he called the American System of economic nationalism: specifically, the importance of a strong national bank, protective tariffs and support of internal improvements. And, most important, he played a vital role in the outcome of the presidential election of 1824–1825.

James Monroe had been reelected as chief executive in 1820 without any organized opposition. The Federalist Party had ceased to exist on the national level. Only New Hampshire kept him from receiving a unanimous electoral vote when one elector cast his ballot for John Quincy Adams. In 1824 Monroe did not designate a successor, and since only one party existed, the contest was restricted to candidates of the Republican Party. In the past, the party held a congressional caucus to choose its candidate, but that procedure was now condemned as undemocratic in that it would eliminate the electorate in choosing the President.

Nonetheless, Senator Martin Van Buren, a master politician and one typical of the new generation of statesmen who emphasized the importance of party organization in local and national politics, followed the traditional procedure and called a meeting of the congressional caucus to be held on February 14, 1824, in the House chamber. His candidate for the nomination was the secretary of the treasury, William H. Crawford, a very popular leader who seemed certain to triumph in the caucus. Other possible candidates were dead set against having the meeting. Henry Clay was one; John C. Calhoun, the secretary of war, another. Because the office of secretary of state had become a stepping-stone to the presidency, it was expected that John Quincy Adams would also run. Finally, there was strong support building throughout the country for General Andrew Jackson, the Hero of New Orleans.

Not surprisingly, therefore, only 66 out of 261 members attended the meeting. "King Caucus is dead," cried the supporters of the other candidates, and "persuasions, threats, coaxing, entreaties were unsparingly used" to keep congressmen from attending. Even so, the meeting took place and the balloting began. To the "heavy groans in the Gallery," Crawford was announced as the Republican candidate, having received sixty-two votes, while Adams had two and Andrew Jackson and Nathaniel Macon obtained one apiece.[8] Whereupon all the other candidates—Adams, Jackson, Calhoun and Clay—received their nominations from state legislatures.

During the course of the campaign, if it could be called one, Calhoun accepted a nomination for the vice presidency when his northern support evaporated in favor of Andrew Jackson. Four candidates remained, and in the fall elections Jackson won both the popular and electoral pluralities. This was the first election in which the popular vote was recorded. Jackson garnered 152,901 popular and 99 electoral votes; Adams came next with 114,023 popular and 84 electoral votes; Crawford won 46,979 and 41 electoral votes; and Clay trailed behind with 47,217 and 37 electoral votes. No one had the constitutionally required majority of electoral votes, so the final decision went to the House of Representatives.

According to the 12th Amendment, the House must choose the President from among the three persons with the highest electoral votes. Clay, being the fourth, was automatically excluded, even though he received more popular votes than Crawford. Yet he, of all men, could have won a House election. Now he was in the position to decide which one of the three remaining candidates would be elected. He let out a sigh. "I only wish that I could have been spared such a painful duty."[9]

Actually, it proved to be a lot easier than one might expect. Clay dismissed Jackson as a candidate because he was a "military chieftain" who defied the law and might develop into another Napoléon. Besides, his speech on the floor attacking Jackson had produced an unbridgeable chasm between them. He also dismissed Crawford, who had suffered a debilitating stroke and had temporarily lost the power of speech and was partially paralyzed. That left Adams, and although he and the secretary had clashed previously, the two men were both nationalists and Adams could be expected to endorse Clay's American System.

On Sunday, January 9, 1825, Clay sent a note to Adams asking to see him that very evening. The Speaker arrived at six o'clock and spent the next three hours exploring "the past and prospective of the future." When their discussion ended, Clay made it clear he would support the New Englander for the presidency. Unfortunately, rumors of the meeting caused the friends of Jackson to suspect a "corrupt bargain," namely, that Clay would champion Adams for the presidency, in return for which Adams would appoint Clay his secretary of state.[10]

The day of the election fell on February 9, 1825. A heavy snowfall blanketed Washington. At noon the Senate joined the House to count the electoral votes. Then the Senate left the chamber and the House proceeded to make the final selection.

The gallery was jammed with spectators when the balloting began. Each state had one vote to be decided by its delegation, and a majority of thirteen states was necessary for election. One of the representatives, Stephen Van Rensselaer of New York, had promised Van Buren to vote for Crawford, but when the ballot box reached his desk he spotted a ticket on the floor bearing the name of John Quincy Adams. Being an intensely religious man, he reckoned it a divinely sent directive. He picked up the ballot and thrust it into the box. According to Van Buren, that single vote gave Adams the thirteenth state he needed to be elected the sixth President of the United States.

It is a delightful story. But more likely is the fact that Van Rensselaer believed that the Clay forces were unstoppable and therefore felt obliged "to allay the excitement."[11] Jackson received the votes of seven states and Crawford four.

Jackson roared his rage. The people had obviously selected him as their President, but a "corrupt bargain" hatched by two "poltroons" had denied them their choice. When Adams subsequently appointed Clay his secretary of state, the Jacksonians angrily shrieked their belief that the election had been rigged. "So you see," Jackson cried, "the Judas of the West has closed the contract and will receive the thirty pieces of silver. . . . Was there ever witnessed such a bare faced corruption in any country before?"[12]

Clay left the House of Representatives in 1825 to assume his new duties and never returned to the institution he had done so much to shape. And his contribution was tremendous. Most important, he had introduced a new system of legislative government. Few Speakers before or since equaled his influence in directing the affairs of the House. Few were as important in transforming a body of delegates into a modern forum for the pursuit of the people's business. His reliance on standing committees made them increasingly active in drafting legislation and establishing policy.

And there were other important innovations. Where in the past the Ways and Means Committee, for example, would report appropriation items without indicating specific amounts, now the committee brought forward bills that carried precise amounts for each item. Also, in the past, a single omnibus bill would lump together the needs of all departments; but starting in 1823 separate bills were reported for each department and each division within departments. This allowed the House to exercise greater control of government expenses. Throughout the rest of the century these procedures remained pretty much as Henry Clay had established them.

The Kentuckian brought with him to his new post his abiding commitment to ideas contained in his American System, ideas that were made specific in President Adams's first message to Congress in December 1825. The message requested the building of an extensive system of roads and canals, the founding of a national university and a naval academy similar to West Point, and the "erection of an astronomical observatory" to observe the "phenomena of the heavens." In a burst of nationalistic enthusiasm, the President insisted that "the great object of the institution of civil government is the improvement of the condition of those who are parties to the social compact."[13]

The Jacksonians angrily disagreed. Some thought Adams had lost his senses. The proposals were preposterous because of their cost, they argued, if not clearly unconstitutional. Only a corrupt administration spawned by a "monstrous union" between "the puritan and black-leg," as John Randolph called Adams and Clay, could advance such nonsense.[14] Clay challenged Randolph to a duel over these remarks, but fortunately neither man was injured in the ensuing engagement.

Over the next several years those hostile to the administration organized themselves under the direction of Senator Van Buren with the active help of Vice President Calhoun in support of the candidacy of Andrew Jackson for President in the 1828 election. They came to be called Democratic-Republicans, or simply Democrats, and emphasized the importance of states' rights and fiscal responsibility. Those who agreed with the administration and its nationalistic program called themselves National Republicans and looked to Secretary Clay and President Adams for leadership. So ended the Era of Good Feelings in which one party controlled the government. The two-party system reemerged.

One of the most important changes to occur in the 1820s was the increased number of voters in state and national elections. The newer western states—Illinois, Missouri, Indiana, Ohio—entered the Union with constitutions that granted voting rights to all adult white male citizens, and this trend was imitated by the older states, which summoned conventions to revise their constitutions and broadened the suffrage. As a result, universal white manhood suffrage was achieved in this Age of Jackson. The nation had begun the process of evolving into a more democratic system, and with each expansion of the suffrage in the future the evolution accelerated.

These changes were reflected in what was probably the most disgraceful campaign in American history. The two parties, bolstered by an enlarged electorate, set about organizing the country politically by establishing electioneering committees of one kind or another and founding newspapers to attack each other. Adams and Clay were pummeled for "stealing" the 1824 election, and the President was even accused of pimping for the czar of Russia when he served as the U.S. minister to that country. Jackson, on the other hand, was denounced as a murderer and wife-stealer, having married Rachel Donelson Robards while she was still married to her first husband, Lewis Robards. And his mother was called a prostitute, brought to this country to service British soldiers.

In Congress, the two parties vied for control of legislation, and over the next four years the Jacksonians managed to block the administration's efforts to implement the American System. Only a tariff bill was allowed to pass, and that resulted because the Democrats turned it into an "electioneering engine" to unseat the President.

THE DEMAND FOR greater tariff protection had increased since the passage of the Tariff of 1824, and when the 20th Congress convened in December 1827 there was little doubt that new protective rates would be introduced. The Committee on Manufactures, chaired by Rollin C. Mallary of Vermont, a friend of the administration and a strong protectionist, was actually controlled by a majority of Jacksonians whose leading member was Silas Wright, Jr., of New York, a close associate of Senator Van Buren.

The recommendations of the committee were laid before the House on March 3, 1828, and many members howled their dismay over what they read. The committee had jacked up the rates on those products from states that Jackson needed to win election in 1828, and refused adequate protection to those industries from states and sections favorable to President Adams, such as New England. That meant that manufactured woolens did not have nearly the protection they required. The committee started, explained Wright to his friends in New York, by raising the rates upon "all kinds of woolen cloths" as "high as *our own friends* in Pennsylvania, Kentucky & Ohio would vote them." Then it jumped the molasses, flax, hemp and lead rates to attract votes from western states; and the high duty on iron was "the Sine qua non with Pennsylvania."[15] In other words, raw materials received higher protection while manufactured goods did not. The committee members had concocted a "lopsided" bill.

But the recommendations hurt southern planters who had come to believe (wrongly) that the tariff had caused a decline in the price of cotton when sold abroad. Besides, protective tariffs favored northern industry, they insisted, and not southern planters. Since virtually all the southern states supported Jackson, there was no need to satisfy their demands to win their allegiance. Consequently, southerners agreed among themselves that if they voted in favor of the provisions of this ghastly measure, New Englanders, among others, would turn against it and defeat it on the final vote.

Chairman Mallary disowned the bill since his recommendations had been completely disregarded by the other members of his committee. He therefore offered a series of amendments to improve the bill, raising rates on manufactured items and even lowering some on raw materials. During the voting on the amendments, a solid phalanx of southerners voted against them and these changes went down to defeat. At that moment, southerners burst out with shouts of joy, certain that the entire bill was now lost. They foolishly announced to New Englanders that "they voted for molasses, & some other articles with a view of making the Bill odious to them." By revealing their scheme they had stupidly ruined their single hope of killing the tariff in the House. "We have not only disclosed our plan," groaned Augustine H. Shepperd of North Carolina, "but defeated its success."[16]

Indeed. "Can we go the *hemp*, iron, spirit and molasses," asked Daniel Webster of Massachusetts, "for the sake of any woolen bill?"[17] Northern House members decided that yes they could, and the tariff passed on April 22 by the vote of 105 to 94.

To make the bill more palatable to New Englanders, the Senate increased the woolen rates to 40 percent ad valorum with a 5 percent increase each year until it reached 50 percent. On May 13, the upper house passed the bill 26 to 21. The amended bill then went back to the House, where George McDuffie of South Carolina and Richard Wilde of Georgia attempted to defeat the Senate changes. But, by a vote of 85 to 44, the amendments were sustained and President Adams signed the measure.[18] Now, thanks to the Jacksonians, Pennsylvania enjoyed higher rates for its iron and Ohio and Kentucky the duties for their flax, hemp and molasses, just as the House committee had planned.[19]

The reaction in the South bordered on violence. The bill was called a Tariff of Abominations. Vice President Calhoun returned home after the adjournment to write his "Exposition and Protest," in which he argued that the states could nullify any federal law that they perceived violated their rights. This doctrine of nullification was intended by Calhoun to prevent secession, although he did not deny that each state still retained the right to withdraw from the Union if compelled to do so in defense of its rights.

•   •   •

IT IS NOT certain how much the Tariff of 1828 affected the presidential election. Suffice it to say that Jackson won the South, the West and the Northwest for a total of 178 electoral votes. Adams garnered 83 votes, almost all of which came from New England. In the election some 1,155,340 white males went to the polls out of a total population of approximately 13 million, a jump of 800,000 voters over the previous presidential election of 1824. Of the total popular vote, Jackson received 647,276 and Adams 508,064.[20]

The overwhelming enthusiasm of the public for their Hero of New Orleans was reflected in his inauguration on March 4, 1829, when twenty thousand of them surrounded the Capitol to cheer his victory. Later they poured through the White House, "scrambling, fighting, romping." Jackson was "almost suffocated & torn to pieces by the people in their eagerness to shake hands with Old Hickory."[21]

The strength of this new administration became immediately obvious with the appearance of a new group of leaders in both houses of Congress. The reelection of Andrew Stevenson of Virginia as Speaker and the presence of such men as James Knox Polk of Tennessee, Churchill C. Cambreleng of New York and Richard M. Johnson of Kentucky in the House, and Thomas Hart Benton of Missouri and Edward Livingston of Louisiana in the Senate, provided organized and articulate leadership. They were different from their forebears in that most of them believed in the importance of party for the proper governing of the nation. And they worked closely with a President who had a definite reform program he wanted enacted.

In his first message to Congress, Jackson made it clear that he hoped to settle any existing differences with foreign countries, especially over American claims for property depredations during the Napoleonic Wars. He also proposed a constitutional amendment to prevent a repeat of the disaster of 1824–1825 so that the "fair expression of the will of the majority" will decide who serves as President.[22] As for the tariff, he favored a "middle and just" course and felt that "adjustments" in some of the provisions of the existing law were necessary so that all sections of the country might prosper. He also favored Indian removal beyond the Mississippi River and the reform of the Bank of the United States, inasmuch as it had failed, he said, to establish "a uniform and sound currency."[23]

The first important piece of legislation to be enacted by this administration was the Indian Removal Act, something Jackson felt essential for national security and the preservation of Indian life and culture. Many members of Congress disagreed, and in the House the bill came close to defeat. The debate began on May 15, 1830, with a powerful speech by Henry R. Storrs of New York, who accused the President of attempting to overthrow the constitutional authority of the states as well as assume the right to arbitrarily cancel treaties with the Indians. William Ellsworth of

Connecticut fretted about the cost of removal, arguing that it could run into the millions. And any number of House members worried about the justice of forcing thousands of men, women and children to leave their tribal homes and seek new quarters in an unfriendly environment. Religious groups in the country were shocked by the inhumanity of removal. Finally, Joseph Hemphill of Pennsylvania, sensitive to the bill's opposition by many of his constituents, proposed a substitute measure that would postpone removal for a year so that a commission could gather information about the country to which the Indians would be sent.

This substitute almost passed. A large number of Democrats supported it, and the vote was 98 in favor, 98 opposed. It took the vote of the Speaker, Andrew Stevenson, to defeat the substitute measure. Jackson applied considerable pressure on House Democrats during the debate, and, in the final vote, the bill narrowly passed, 102 to 97.[24] The Senate agreed, and the Indian Removal Act of 1830 was signed by the President on May 28, 1830. According to this legislation the chief executive was authorized to exchange unorganized public land beyond the Mississippi River for Indian land in the East. The cost of removal would be assumed by the federal government and the tribes would be given "support and subsistence" for the first year after their removal.[25]

The removal itself, extending over several years, proved to be a horror. Many Indians died in their trek to the west. The Cherokees called it the "Trail of Tears." By the close of Jackson's administration some 45,690 Indians had been relocated beyond the Mississippi and something like 100 million acres of eastern land was acquired for approximately $68 million plus 32 million acres of western land.

BESIDES HAVING TO contend with the Committee on Manufactures in devising a tariff, the Ways and Means Committee encountered challenges to its authority over banking from the Currency Committee and over the regulation of tonnage duties from the Committee on Foreign Affairs. This overlap of jurisdictions proved to be quite troublesome during the Jacksonian era since Ways and Means could and did argue its right to initiate legislation dealing with a wide variety of matters, including postal rates, pensions, appropriations to Native Americans in the execution of Indian treaties, salaries for consular and diplomatic service, and military appropriations. Obviously, because of its extensive authority and control of the purse strings, Ways and Means had become the most important House committee in shaping and directing legislation.

The turbulence that frequently broke out in the lower chamber among competing committees helped convince the members to reform their rules. In 1837 the House adopted Thomas Jefferson's *Manual of Parliamentary Practice,* written during his term as Vice President from 1797 to 1801. First published in 1801, it went through numerous revisions in the following years. It proved to be highly valuable to the House in settling quarrels, and today the current rules stipulate that the manual "shall govern the House in all cases in which they are applicable, and in which they are not inconsistent with the standing rules and orders of the House."[26] In the words of one former member, "the Manual is still the foundation on which House practice is built."[27]

With the ongoing evolution of democracy in the United States, along with the continued growth of the two-party system in the 1830s, House committees began to reflect some of these changes by including minority representation among its members and even permitting minority reports of the committees to reach the floor. It was an important change. In addition, selection of members to a particular committee now involved "party loyalty, ideological alliances, political expediency" and even, on occasion, "competence."[28] This explains why the crafty Jacksonian leadership in the House chose John Quincy Adams to chair the Committee on Manufactures, knowing he would be obliged to handle a very hot potato that could provoke a confrontation between the national government and South Carolina over the tariff.

Adams had hardly returned home after his devastating defeat for a second term as President when the people of his congressional district overwhelmingly elected him to the House of Representatives. He took his seat at the start of the 22nd Congress in December 1831, and once appointed chairman of the Committee on Manufactures turned to his responsibility with his customary zeal and dedication. He thoroughly researched the subject of protection and met repeatedly with Jackson's secretary of the treasury, Louis McLane, to discuss particulars of pending legislation. His committee finally wrote a tariff bill that was expected to be more amenable to the South. But George McDuffie beat him to the floor. His Ways and Means Committee reported a measure on February 8, 1832, which stated that protective tariffs "ought to be abandoned."[29]

The House chose to ignore the McDuffie bill because of its extreme position and accepted instead the bill reported by Adams's Committee on Manufactures. This measure eliminated some of the "abominations" of the 1828 tariff by deleting a few articles from the schedule and lowering the duties on noncompetitive goods; but it remained a relatively high level of protection on everything else. Adams claimed it had the support of the treasury secretary, and so the bill subsequently passed both houses, and Jackson signed it on July 14, 1832. It was the last tariff bill the Committee on Manufactures would write.

The South Carolina delegation in the House denounced the measure as inadequate and reported to their constituents that they could expect no relief from Congress. Forthwith, the state legislature called a convention that declared both the Tariff of 1832 and the "abominable" Tariff of 1828 violations of its sovereignty. It therefore nullified them, which meant that collection of custom duties within South Carolina was forbidden. Furthermore, the convention proposed the secession of the state if the federal government attempted to impose compliance by force.

At the same time this tariff worked its way through Congress, the House responded to a request by Nicholas Biddle, the president of the Second National Bank of the United States, to recharter the institution even though its present charter had four more years to run. President Jackson had called for modifications in the bank's operation, which were ignored. Among other things, he felt the bank used its money to influence legislation and the election of favored members of Congress. It was, he later contended, a "hydra of corruption."[30]

Both Ways and Means in the House and the Senate Committee on Finance dismissed these accusations and reported favorably on recharter. Henry Clay, now returned to Congress as a senator from Kentucky, was anxious to use the issue to his advantage in the fast-approaching presidential election of 1832, in which he was the candidate of the National Republican Party. Under his leadership, therefore, the Senate passed recharter on June 11, 1832, by a vote of 28 to 20, followed by the House on July 3 by a count of 107 to 85.[31] The bill had solid support from New England and the middle states and determined opposition from the South. The Northwest and the Southwest were divided.

Jackson vetoed the measure on July 10 in a message that warned against those institutions and individuals who through money and influence would use the government to advance their own selfish purposes.[32] Congress could not override the veto, so Biddle called in loans and instituted a tight money policy that touched off an economic panic. In the election of 1832, Jackson won an overwhelming victory over Clay on a ticket that called for the total destruction of the U.S. bank.

To begin the process of annihilating this "hydra," Jackson ordered his secretary of the treasury to remove the government's deposits from the bank—that is, cease making additional deposits and exhaust government's funds in the institution through normal expenditures. The government's funds would hereafter be deposited in state (pet) banks.

Meanwhile, with the beginning of the 23rd Congress (1833–1835), Speaker Andrew Stevenson appointed a Ways and Means Committee that included James Knox Polk, one of Jackson's staunchest allies in Congress, as chair, along with a majority of loyal Democrats as members. This committee ultimately reported a series of resolutions to the full House against recharter and against restoring government deposits in the bank. It also called for the formation of a committee to investigate the bank's practices. These resolutions passed the House on April 4, 1834, and spelled the bank's doom. The subsequent investigation found Biddle unwilling to cooperate, and he barely escaped being held in contempt of Congress. But his actions and the economic panic he had triggered, commented William Rives, proved "to the people never again to give themselves such a master."[33]

During the debates over the bank, the near violence of opinion in both chambers demonstrated that the character of these bodies had changed considerably, most particularly in the House. When the Democrats captured the government in 1829 they described their victory as the defeat of elitist, aristocratic rule and the triumph of democracy.

DEMOCRACY! IT WAS the start of a new age in which the republican form of government was giving way to a more democratic one. This, in turn, altered the composition and operation of the House of Representatives. By the end of the Jacksonian era, the House had evolved from a small body of sixty-five relatively well-off and well-educated individuals in 1789 to a heterogeneous mass of several hundred men representing a diverse group of social, economic and cultural classes. Lacking the political credentials of the generation of the Founders, this new generation advanced their careers through the party structure which they diligently built by creating mass electorates. But they went further. In a speech on the House floor in 1826, Churchill C. Cambreleng of New York declared that parties were "essential to the existence of our institutions."[34] Parties and the operation of government were intertwined. As a result, partisan wrangling became so pronounced during the years prior to the Civil War that one foreign observer of House debates, Frederick Marryat, said the squabbles were "full of eagles, star-spangled banners, sovereign people, claptrap, flattery, and humbug."[35] Another distinguished observer, Alexis de Tocqueville, author of *Democracy in America,* visited Congress during the Jacksonian era and commented on the extraordinary dissimilarity between the House and Senate. "On entering the House of Representatives at Washington," he reported, "one is struck by the vulgar demeanor of that great assembly. Often there is not a distinguished man in the whole number. Its members are almost all obscure individuals, whose names bring no associations to mind. They are mostly village lawyers, men in trade, or even persons belonging to the lower classes of society," unlike the Senate, where such men as Clay, Webster, Calhoun and Thomas Hart Benton of Missouri held forth. Indeed, their "arguments would do honor to the most remarkable parliamentary debates of Europe." Why the difference? Because, explained Tocqueville, representatives were elected directly by the people and senators were elected by other elected bodies, namely, state legislatures.[36]

The city of Washington was also evolving. By the mid-1830s it had become a more livable community. Around all the public buildings and the whole length of Pennsylvania Avenue, wrote John Fairfield, a new House member from Maine, "much attention has been paid to the planting of trees." In April they began leafing out and the apricots and peach trees blossomed. "This will be a beautiful City in a few weeks," he added. Pennsylvania Avenue had been macadamized, but it was "done with so soft a stone that it grinds into dust which is between one & two inches deep at all times when dry, and after a rain we have that depth of mud." And because of this condition, "we begin to find our situation rather uncomfortable in one respect; to wit, the great quantities of dust continually floating in the air."[37]

There was now a theater in the district in which plays were sometimes performed. And the circus came to town every so often, attracting both natives and congressmen. On one occasion Davy Crockett of Tennessee and Warren R. Davis of South Carolina went to the circus together. Crockett was fascinated with the appearance of a "large baboon dressed in uniform riding a little pony in the ring." The animal reminded him of a member of Congress, and Crockett spoke the individual's name. Davis whispered to his friend that the congressman he had just mentioned was standing behind him and had heard every word. Best to apologize to him, advised Davis. To whom shall I apologize, Crockett asked, "the monkey or the member of Congress?"[38]

By the mid-1830s, besides trees, Pennsylvania Avenue was lined with boardinghouses, many of which had shops on the ground floor. Fairfield reported finding suitable lodging at Mrs. S. F. Hill's house after checking out a number of possible establishments. He took a room on the fourth floor and paid $8 a week. Prices ranged from $8 to $12, and because his room was rather small and four flights up he paid the lower rate. The rent included furniture, "a fire, and lights, to wit two spermaceti candles and a wood fire" instead of coal. The following session he took a room at Mrs. Pitman's house on Third Street, which was "regarded as about No. 1 in the City." He paid only $9 because he had a small room, twelve feet square, on the third floor in the back. His furniture consisted of "a table, 3 chairs, a bed and a wash stand." He confessed it was not what he would like, but it was relatively inexpensive.

Both times Fairfield joined groups of men of the same political persuasion. About fifteen congressmen messed together in these houses, which made for pleasant companionship and conversation. And the food was generally good, without being outstanding. For breakfast at Mrs. Hill's, Fairfield listed "coffee, tea, green and black, beefsteak, mutton cutlet, sausage meat, hominy, buckwheat cakes, or flapjacks, 'corn cakes,' or biscuits, flour biscuits, etc., etc." For dinner he began with "a small plate of soup," followed by "roast beef, boiled turkey with oyster sauce, boiled ham, roast duck, no gravys except what is in the dish, which to me is a great deprivation, puddings, tarts, and apples."[39]

•   •   •

ONE OF THE most ghastly events that occurred in Washington in the mid-1830s involved the attempted assassination of the President of the United States—and it happened in the Capitol itself. On January 30, 1835, President Jackson was leaving the funeral services for Representative Warren R. Davis of South Carolina held in the House chamber. He had reached the entrance of the Rotunda of the east portico of the Capitol when a thirty-year-old man, his face virtually hidden by a thick black beard, stepped out from the shadows, pointed a pistol directly at Jackson's heart and squeezed the trigger. An explosion reverberated around the Rotunda, but the gun had misfired. The cap of the pistol discharged but failed to ignite the powder in the barrel. The madman produced a second gun, which he held ready-cocked in his left hand. Again he took dead aim at the President and pulled the trigger. Another stupendous explosion, but once more the gun misfired. Jackson lunged at his assailant, brandishing his cane, but the would-be assassin, Richard Lawrence, an unemployed housepainter, was seized by onlookers and carted off to prison. Tried and found not guilty by reason of insanity, Lawrence was committed to an asylum.

The first attempted assassination of a President took place at the entrance of the small rotunda near the east portico on January 30, 1835.

Violence had obviously escalated in political life beyond anything previously imagined. It was, remarked the *New York Evening Post,* "a sign of the times."[40]

Another appalling incident involving members of the House took place in 1838 when Jonathan Cilley, a representative from Maine, fought a duel with William Graves of Kentucky and was killed.[41] What added to the horror was the knowledge that no real animosity existed between the two men. It seems that a Washington correspondent for Colonel James Watson Webb's newspaper, the *New York Courier and Enquirer,* had charged an unnamed congressman with corruption. Cilley chose to ridicule the charge, claiming it came from a corrupt and partisan editor. In a handwritten note, Webb demanded an explanation and asked Graves to deliver it for him. Cilley refused to accept it, insisting that Webb was no gentleman. Graves took offense with the implication that he, too, was no gentleman and challenged Cilley to a duel. The challenge was accepted and Cilley insisted on rifles. He was supposedly an expert marksman.[42]

The two men met on February 24 at Bladensburg near the capital. As customary, both men fired two rounds. Neither man injured the other, and that should have ended the duel. But Henry A. Wise, a fiery, rabidly proslavery representative from Virginia who served as Graves's second, talked both of them into undertaking a third round. This time Graves inflicted a mortal wound on his opponent in what seemed to many like barbaric slaughter. It "is looked upon by most people here," wrote Fairfield to his wife, "as a deliberate murder." Cilley "is represented by all as being as brave a man as ever walked. His conduct on the ground is said to have been beyond all praise by those acquainted with and acknowledging the validity of the laws of the duello." The incident shocked the entire nation. Wise was investigated by a House committee for his role in the killing, but it did not find him guilty of abusing Cilley's rights as a member of Congress.[43]

So shaken and angered was the entire Washington community that the Senate passed a bill outlawing dueling in the District of Columbia. John Quincy Adams led the fight for the measure in the House. It became law on February 20, 1839.

THE MARKEDLY DRAMATIC shift in the membership of the House included other changes less violent. The clerk, in his annual report of 1827, noted the employment of young boys as pages to run errands and deliver messages. Generally these boys were orphans or sons of acquaintances of members. The practice of employing them probably started much earlier, even as early as the 1st Congress. Initially no more than two or three pages were appointed, but the number slowly mounted until by 1839 there were eighteen.[44]

Another important change was the appearance of a new political party. During the debates over removal of the bank deposits, the Senate, under

Clay's leadership, censured Jackson for acting contrary to the wishes of Congress. The President protested the action as unconstitutional, since the House initiates any such action against the executive. He insisted on his prerogatives as head of the government. The President, he declared, "is the direct representative of the American people." He is "elected by the people and responsible to them."[45]

Those who abominated Jackson's methods and claims of primacy, along with National Republicans, Federalists, states' righters, and some nullifiers, among others, allied themselves in the formation of a new party with a new name. They called themselves Whigs, supposedly in imitation of their revolutionary forebears who contended against the Crown.

AGAIN JACKSON DEMONSTRATED his aggressive leadership in his handling of the crisis that resulted when South Carolina nullified the tariff laws of 1832 and 1828. On December 10, 1832, following his reelection, the President issued a proclamation to the people of South Carolina in which he warned them against attempting secession. "Disunion by armed force is treason," he declared. "The power to amend a law of the United States assumed by one State, is *incompatible with the existence of the Union*."[46] He subsequently asked Congress for a Force Bill authorizing him to use the military to collect import duties in South Carolina.

In an effort to conciliate the South and work out a compromise, the House Ways and Means Committee prepared a bill that would dramatically reduce tariff duties over a two-year period. But the bill ran into stiff opposition from protectionists. At this juncture Clay proposed a measure in the Senate that would reduce the rates to the level recommended by the Ways and Means Committee but do it over a ten-year period. He convinced Senator Calhoun to support this compromise and his spokesman in the House, Representative Robert P. Letcher, moved its substitution to the original House bill. This Compromise Tariff of 1833 passed both houses and Jackson signed it on March 4, 1833, along with the Force Bill, thus ending the nullification crisis, although not the belief of many southerners that secession was a viable option when fundamental state rights were violated.

THE SECTIONAL ISSUE between a free North and a slave South intensified during the 1830s and 1840s. A powerful abolitionist movement developed during the Jacksonian era, and it was only one of dozens of reform programs that surfaced at that time. Organizations appeared to advance the cause of women's rights, labor, temperance, peace, strict observance of the Sabbath and reform of penal and mental institutions. But the antislavery movement was unquestionably the most important and most potent.

Abolitionism had been present for decades, particularly among some religious groups, such as the Quakers. But with the intellectual and religious excitement generated by the Second Great Awakening over the preceding thirty and more years, along with the massacre of slaves in the Denmark Vesey conspiracy of 1822 and the Nat Turner rebellion in 1831,* the movement became militant and produced an army of reformers determined to extinguish slavery in the United States.

Petitions flooded the Congress, demanding that some action be taken, such as terminating slavery in the District of Columbia and in the territories. But most of these petitions were simply tabled and forgotten. Southern Congressmen demanded that all discussion of slavery in whatever form be silenced. After all, the Constitution recognized the existence of the "peculiar institution" and the right of each slaveholding state to count three-fifths of its slaves as part of their population when deciding representation in the lower house. Nevertheless, the right of petition was fundamental to American liberty, insisted John Quincy Adams in response, and must be preserved.

The battle over the issue began in the House on December 16, 1835, when Representative James H. Hammond of South Carolina moved that the petitions not be received. The Speaker, James K. Polk of Tennessee, permitted several members to argue in favor of such a gag and then shut off further debate on the subject.

A six-week shouting match ensued. Adams tried to gain the floor to argue his case while several southerners sought to block his efforts. "Am I gagged, or am I not?" he screamed at the chair. Shouts of "Order!" "Order!" echoed around the chamber.[47] The matter was finally turned over to a special committee under the chairmanship of Representative Henry L. Pinckney of South Carolina, which brought back a report on May 18, 1836, that was instantly labeled "the gag resolution." The report stated that "all petitions, memorials, resolutions, propositions or papers relating in any way or to any extent whatsoever to the subject of slavery or the abolition of slavery shall, without being either printed or referred, be laid upon the table and that no further action whatever shall be had thereon."[48]

Two other resolutions accompanied the report. The first declared that Congress had no authority over slavery in the states. It was adopted, 182 to 9. The second stated that any interference with slavery in the District of Columbia was "inexpedient." It, too, passed, 132 to 45. As for the gag resolution itself, the measure won approval on May 26 by a vote of 147 to 68.

---

*Denmark Vesey led a small army of followers in a general revolt in Charleston, South Carolina, to escape their servitude. Five companies of militia crushed the rebellion and thirty-five slaves were hanged. Nat Turner and nearly one hundred slaves virtually wiped out a white community as they hunted for weapons to make good their escape to freedom. But white men retaliated in a bloody massacre. Probably several hundred blacks were summarily executed.

When Adams's name was called, he angrily stood his ground. "I hold the resolution to be a direct violation of the Constitution of the United States, of the rules of this House, and of the rights of my constituents."[49]

Year after year the attack against these resolutions was renewed. Speaker Polk decreed that they expired with each Congress and had to be reinstated. That ruling allowed Adams, among others, to rave and rant against the violation of the right of petition. Frequently, Adams lost control of himself and he started shouting and bickering and abusing his colleagues.

"Expel him!" "Expel him!" cried southerners. "What, are we to sit here and endure such insults?" they called to the Speaker. "We demand that you shut the mouth of that old harlequin."

At one point Adams had the effrontery to submit a petition from constituents in Massachusetts who asked Congress to adopt a measure by which the United States could be "peaceably" dissolved. He said the time had not yet come for such action and asked that the petition be referred to a committee with instructions to report a reply stating the reasons it should not be granted.[50]

And that did it. Representative Thomas Gilmer of Virginia demanded that Adams be censured for presenting such a despicable petition. But that was not good enough for southern members. They held a caucus and agreed to drop the censure motion and substitute one that charged Adams with committing treason for daring to offer such a petition. Thomas Marshall of Kentucky, the nephew of the late chief justice, John Marshall, was chosen to introduce the motion.

Adams demanded a trial since he had been accused of a high crime. This provided him with extended floor time to rail against the slavocracy, who, he said, sought nothing less than crushing "the liberties of the free people of the Union." He even demanded that the clerk read the opening paragraphs of the Declaration of Independence. "Read them, sir, and let the House listen."[51]

He savaged individual colleagues, referring to them as "slave mongers" and "beef-witted blunderheads." As for Marshall, Adams called him an ignoramus and an alcoholic who should go home and study law and "learn a little of the rights of the citizens." He labeled Henry A. Wise a criminal for his role in the Cilley-Graves duel, a man who dared to enter the House "with his hands and face dripping with the blood of murder, the blotches of which were yet hanging upon him."

It was wild. Wise responded in "a most solemn and lugubrious manner," and used "the most acrimonious and insulting language towards Mr. Adams," accusing him of "treading on the grave of . . . his father, and with being a vampire."[52]

But Adams gave as good as he got, and Wise did himself more harm than good. Then, after two weeks of vilifying the South for its attempts to destroy the right of habeas corpus, trial by jury, freedom of speech and the

Henry A. Wise's hands and face were "dripping with the blood of murder," charged John Quincy Adams on the floor of the House, because of his involvement in the duel between Jonathan Cilley and William Graves that ended in Cilley's death.

press, to say nothing about the right of petition, Adams finally decided the House was sick to death of the subject and allowed the resolution calling for a trial to come to a vote. On February 4, 1842, it was defeated 105 to 80.[53]

The interminable length of some of the speeches during this fracas induced Representative John C. Clark of New York to introduce the "one-hour rule," which was promptly passed. It had become necessary, as one commentator said, "to assume the power to stop the expenditure of too much wind."[54]

Adams's triumph marked the beginning of the end of the gag. But another two years were necessary to kill it outright. Session after session the New Englander tried to block passage of the resolution, and each year the vote against him steadily dwindled. Northern representatives, especially Democrats, felt the mounting pressure of their constituents, who made known their belief that the gag contradicted the basic concepts of American liberty. Finally, on December 3, 1844, the resolution was rescinded by a vote of 108 to 80. "Blessed, forever blessed, be the name of God," exclaimed the exultant Adams.[55]

As reported in many newspapers around the country, the net result of this unseemly conflict was the decline of the prestige of the House, and of Congress generally.[56]

THE DEMOCRATS ELECTED Martin Van Buren to succeed Andrew Jackson in 1836. Unfortunately for him, a severe economic depression occurred a month after he had been sworn into office. It was part of a worldwide recession but was particularly severe in the United States, lasting well into the 1840s. Naturally the Whigs had little trouble ousting Van Buren in the election of 1840 and replacing him with General William H. Harrison, who had the reputation of defeating Indians at the Battle of Tippecanoe. His running mate, John Tyler, had been a Democrat but split with Jackson over the nullification controversy. Both houses of Congress were also captured by the Whigs in this election.

Sadly, Harrison died a month after his inauguration and Tyler assumed the full powers of the presidency, despite real concern that his Democratic background would annul Whig plans to create another national bank and raise tariff rates.

And that is exactly what happened. Tyler vetoed the legislation the Whig leadership put before him, and at length he was expelled from the party. Anxious to win Democratic support in the next election, and convinced that Texas, which had won its independence from Mexico in 1836, should be added to the Union, Tyler proposed a treaty annexing Texas. But the Senate shot it down.

Instead of embracing Tyler and naming him for a second term, the Democrats nominated James K. Polk for the presidency in 1844 on a platform calling for the reannexation of Texas (it was presumed that Texas was really part of the Louisiana Purchase) and the reoccupation of the Oregon Country. The Northwest Territory was jointly occupied by Britain and the United States from the forty-second parallel to 54° 40′, the southern boundary of Russian Alaska. "Fifty-four Forty or Fight," was the jingoistic slogan of the Democratic campaign, and it attracted many voters. The spirit of "Manifest Destiny" resounded around the country, a belief that the United States had a right given by "Providence" to "overspread" and possess the entire continent and thereby provide liberty and self-government for all its inhabitants. According to this theory, Texas belonged in the Union.

It was during this presidential campaign that Samuel F. B. Morse received a $30,000 appropriation to run telegraph wires from Washington to Baltimore for a long-distance test of his invention. Telegraph reports from the Democratic National Convention meeting in Baltimore were received, detailing what was happening at the convention, and Morse wrote them down and posted them in the Capitol Rotunda. Newspapers quickly recognized the potential of Morse's invention and initiated what would become in time the wire services to report the proceedings of Congress. The *Baltimore American* paid Morse a penny a word to write up an account of the activities in Congress. It marked the beginning of a new relationship between representatives and senators and the press.[57]

In the 1844 election, the Whigs nominated Henry Clay, who opposed territorial expansion, knowing it would provoke a war with Mexico over

Texas. Polk narrowly defeated Clay, whereupon the incumbent President, John Tyler, capitalized on the Democrat's victory and proposed a joint resolution by both houses of Congress admitting Texas as a slave state into the Union. A simple majority from two houses was infinitely easier to obtain than a two-thirds majority from one. That was the reasoning behind this ploy. The joint resolution was introduced in the House of Representatives as a legislative measure at the start of the new session. Despite protests that this procedure violated the Constitution, since the Senate enjoyed the exclusive privilege of ratifying treaties, the resolution passed both the House and the Senate. Tyler signed it on March 1, 1845, just days before he was scheduled to leave office. Texas ratified the annexation on July 4 and joined the Union on December 29, 1845.

As for the Northwest Territory, President Polk was far more interested in California than Oregon and so he willingly agreed to a treaty with Britain on June 18, 1846, to split the disputed territory at the forty-ninth parallel, with the United States annexing the lower half. Once England had been neutralized, Polk offered to purchase California from Mexico, an offer immediately rejected.

Although the mounting tension regularly produced violent reaction and angry words in the House during the heated debate on Texas and the Northwest Territory, every so often incidents would occur that would break the tension and put the members in a better humor. For example, Representative William Sawyer of Ohio would leave his seat regularly at one o'clock in the afternoon, go to a window with a recess, open a bundle wrapped in newspaper and pull out a sausage for lunch. He used a bandanna pocket handkerchief as a napkin. Having satisfied his hunger, he would brush away the crumbs, dispose of the newspaper and return to his seat.

The *New York Tribune* reported Sawyer's daily ritual, much to the amusement of the nation. Sawyer's rustic manners—he supposedly came from "some backwoods benighted region in Ohio"—and outspoken views on weighty topics frequently caused other representatives to double up with laughter. On one such occasion he spoke to the question of the distribution of appointments in the states and territories. As a man who believed in the axiom "To the victor belong the spoils," he said that the Democrats had a right to office, having won the last election. "They had at great expense and trouble," he pontificated, "—very great expense and trouble elected Mr. Polk."

The other members started snickering. And what did they find, he continued, but 730 clerks holding office in Washington and 235 of them were Whigs. "Yes, sir," he declared, "bold, daring Whigs!"

"How do you know they are Whigs?" shouted a member.

"Don't I know a *Whig* from a *Democrat* as far as I can see him?" Sawyer shot back. At that remark, the House exploded "in a roar."

"A Whig always dresses up fine, or better than Democrats do," he went on, "and looks like he thought he knew more and was a great deal better than a Democrat: they ain't plain folks like we are." That produced "Roars of laughter from all sides, and the galleries."[58]

No doubt about it, the democratization of the chamber was complete. Representatives with "rustic manners" from some of the most "benighted" and "uncivilized" regions of the country now sat in the People's House. And they were there to stay.

WHEN MEXICO REFUSED to sell California, President Polk ordered General Zachary Taylor to cross the Texas border and advance to the Rio Grande, thereby invading what Mexico regarded as its territory, but which was disputed by the United States. The Mexican army attacked the invaders and sixteen American lives were lost, which gave Polk the excuse to go to Congress, declare that "Mexico has . . . shed American blood upon American soil" and ask that it "recognize the existence of war."[59] He and several Democratic leaders on the House Military Affairs Committee had previously worked out a bill appropriating $10 million and authorizing the President to call for fifty thousand volunteers. A number of Whigs protested. Not only was this an act of outright aggression, they argued, but they were being asked to vote on providing volunteers before war had been declared. The Democrats quickly settled that problem by attaching a preamble to the measure stating that war already existed by virtue of an act of the Republic of Mexico. That wording took the place of a formal declaration, and on May 11, the measure passed the House by a vote of 174 to 14. The Whigs added their support, lest the record show them as hostile to supplying reinforcements needed by the army. The Senate concurred, 40 to 2, and Polk signed it on May 13, 1846.

The Mexican War constitutes a dark page in the history of this country, but without question the American people then believed that Texas and the rest of the Northwest Territory rightfully belonged to the United States, and that once annexed the inhabitants in these areas would enjoy the blessings of liberty and democracy. But, as many congressmen realized, the war could bring on controversial problems for the country and possibly lead to civil war.

The country was still changing. The Jacksonian era with its emphasis on political and social reform, democratic improvement and westward expansion was giving way to Manifest Destiny, heightened political partisanship, sectional rivalry and escalating conflicts in Congress. Shortly after Polk's inauguration, Andrew Jackson died on June 8, 1845, at his home outside Nashville. Most of his important contemporaries would soon follow and the nation would be bereft of the statesmen who always found the compromises to fend off threats of secession and bloody conflict.

•　　•　　•

AFTER RETURNING TO Massachusetts following the adjournment of the House, John Quincy Adams suffered a small stroke on November 20 that left him temporarily paralyzed on his right side. But to the amazement of his family and doctors he recovered and insisted on resuming his duties as an elected member of the House of Representatives. When he appeared at the doorway of the House chamber, Representative Hunt of New York was speaking. Hunt halted his address in midsentence. All eyes turned to the doorway. "The members present rose spontaneously as Mr. Adams entered." Several of them, including southerners such as Isaac Holmes of South Carolina, rushed forward and took Adams by the arm and escorted him to his seat. Other members gathered around the venerable man, congratulating him on his return. In a feeble voice, Adams "briefly tendered his heartfelt thanks."

This small incident, commented Nathan Sargent, the sergeant at arms, demonstrated that though members can rave and rant at one another "yet, down, down beneath the surface agitated by the storms of politics, those emotions and sympathies" that ennoble human nature "remain undisturbed, only requiring proper occasions to call them into action." The clerk, Benjamin Brown French, agreed. "Mr. Adams . . . has many failings, but he is a great & a good man notwithstanding them all."[60]

The 30th Congress convened on the first Monday of December 1847, with the Whigs holding a majority of seats. Robert C. Winthrop of Massa-

The brilliant career of John Quincy Adams ended with his tragic death in the House from a stroke.

chusetts was elected Speaker. Among the new members was a tall, gangling representative from Illinois named Abraham Lincoln. He was known, said one, more for his storytelling and hearty laugh than he was for his oratory or participation in the business of the House. But he did deliver one memorable speech about the President's demand for a declaration of war against Mexico. Polk had no right, Lincoln declared, to send General Taylor into what he, the President, regarded as American soil but which in fact was Mexican territory. "Allow the President to invade a neighboring nation, whenever he shall deem it necessary to repel an invasion . . . and you allow him to make war at pleasure."[61] Otherwise, the Illinois representative was hardly noticed.

Once more John Quincy Adams attended the 30th Congress, and his very presence seemed to cloak the room with dignity and distinction and an aura of statesmanship. On February 21, 1848, he rose from his seat to speak, several petitions clutched in his hand. Suddenly he faltered and toppled forward. Fortunately a colleague caught him in time and prevented him from collapsing to the floor.

"Mr. Adams is dying!" screamed a voice in the chamber. The House was in "great commotion . . . every countenance expressing intense anxiety." Several more members rushed to provide assistance and Adams was carried to a sofa, then to the Rotunda and finally to the Speaker's room.[62]

Adams lived another two days, dying at 7:15 p.m. on February 23, 1848. Funeral ceremonies were held in the House, and the silver-mounted coffin bore an inscription written by Daniel Webster to the effect that this extraordinary man had served his country for half a century and enjoyed its highest honors.

His generation, the generation that dramatically assisted the growth of the nation, the generation of Jackson, Adams, Clay, Webster, Calhoun, Benton and any number of other distinguished statesmen, was slowly passing from the scene. And who could replace them? Who could find the solutions to the nation's problems and prevent possible secession and civil war?

7

The Struggle to Save the Union,
1846–1860

It was Saturday, August 8, 1846, and Congress planned to adjourn on Monday. At this late hour, President Polk decided to ask the House for an appropriation of $2 million with which to negotiate a treaty with Mexico. Hopefully, the treaty would involve a "cession of territory." For this anticipated territory, he said, "we ought to pay them a fair equivalent."[1]

Members of the House were annoyed at this last-minute request, just as they were about to take off for home, but agreed to hold an evening session to consider the measure. The heat and humidity in the chamber were oppressive and ice water and fans were in constant demand. What added to the annoyance and discomfort was the manner in which the administration had behaved over the past several months, ramming one bill after another through Congress "with little regard for the feelings of rank-and-file members." To wit: tariff reduction, the Oregon treaty, recognition of hostilities with Mexico, bills for supporting the war and a veto of a river and harbors measure that was loaded with pork "so dear to many congressmen." And it had all been accomplished by "cracking the whip" and invoking rigid party discipline.[2]

Now Polk talked of territorial expansion, an issue that was sure to provoke heated controversy since it would no doubt involve the question of slavery. But that hardly slowed the Democratic floor leaders from demanding immediate action, even as Congress prepared to adjourn. So the House reluctantly agreed to consider the proposed appropriation after supper that evening.

On returning from dinner, some of the members were inebriated, which did not bode well for any debate that might ensue. They formed themselves into a Committee of the Whole and adopted a rule that limited debate to two hours and the speaking time for each member to ten minutes. By now they were disgruntled, and the heat and humidity had turned their annoyance into anger.[3]

Hugh White, a New York Whig, initiated the furor by charging the administration with a damnable plot to seize territory in order to expand slavery, and he was supported by Robert C. Winthrop of Massachusetts. Two Democrats defended the President, but more support was needed and the chairman had to ponder very carefully who would speak next. At that point David Wilmot of Pennsylvania, a freshman member, asked to be recognized. An impetuous, ruddy-complexioned, disheveled and tobacco-chewing young fellow, he was about to precipitate, in a single stroke, a major brouhaha in the House that would split both major parties along sectional lines.

The chairman stared at Wilmot. Since time was limited, he no doubt hesitated to recognize the fledgling congressman. Still, Wilmot had a perfect record of supporting the President, including the pullback from the 54°40′ Oregon boundary, and especially the tariff revision in which all the other Pennsylvania members had voted against the administration. The chair hesitated only a moment and then recognized "the gentleman from Pennsylvania." Wilmot had ten minutes.

The young man rose and proceeded in the time allotted to him to send shock waves reverberating across the chamber. He offered a "Proviso" to the $2 million appropriation bill, "that, as an express and fundamental condition to the acquisition of any territory from the Republic of Mexico . . . neither slavery nor involuntary servitude shall ever exist in any part of said territory." He insisted that he did not oppose slavery where it already existed, such as Texas. But free territory—which is what existed in Mexico—was another matter. "God forbid that we should be the means of planting this institution upon it."[4]

The House erupted. By his action Wilmot not only provoked a battle royal in the chamber over the issue, but had initiated a revolt against the President. Administration congressmen loitering in the hallway outside crowded back into the room. In no time three members from the cabinet arrived. William W. Wick, an Indiana Democrat, offered a substitute amendment that invoked the Missouri Compromise line of 36°30′ to any new territory acquired from Mexico, but this was defeated, 89 to 54.

Southerners then moved to table the proviso, which would kill it. A roll call ensued, and it produced a startling and momentous change. A division developed, not between Whigs and Democrats, but between northerners and southerners. Seventy-four southerners and four northerners agreed to table; ninety-one northerners and three southerners voted in opposition. Holding to its rule of two hours for debate, the House finally passed the Wilmot Proviso, 85 to 80, with every negative vote, except three, coming from the slave states. The bill then went to the Senate, where southerners had greater voting strength. The proviso died in the upper house.[5]

The nation fretted over what might happen next, but some newspapers, like the *Boston Whig,* correctly noted what it all meant. "As if by magic, it [the proviso] brought to a head the great question which is about to divide the American people."[6] Like the gag resolution, it would be introduced each new session, and each time the House would approve it and the Senate kill it. The Wilmot Proviso, in the words of one historian, "utterly shattered both the Whigs and Democrats along sectional lines from 1846 to 1850."[7]

When Congress reconvened in December 1846, Polk again requested an appropriation to acquire Mexican territory and recommended that Oregon be organized as a territory. Only this time he wanted $3 million instead of the $2 million that he failed to get in August. He also summoned Wilmot to the White House and got him to promise not to reintroduce his proviso. Wilmot agreed, although he warned that he would vote for it if someone else introduced it.[8]

And someone else did. On January 4, 1847, Representative Preston King of New York proposed an attachment to the $3 million bill that included the proviso. Then, to really ignite passions, the House Committee on Territories reported an Oregon bill that excluded slavery. Southern members vehemently objected, not because they had any desire to introduce slavery into Oregon but because the bill contained the "principle of congressional exclusion," which could keep slaves from other areas if Congress so directed. Furthermore, southerners demanded a reciprocal arrangement for territory in the Southwest. If Oregon was to be free, another territory had to be open to slavery. Equal balance between the North and South had been an accepted political principle for decades. Thus the question of slavery in Oregon, which realistically would not happen, nevertheless became a bargaining chip in the ongoing legislative contest between the two sections.

Southerners offered a solution. Acting at Calhoun's urging, Armistead Burt of South Carolina suggested an amendment to the Oregon bill that stated that the territory should be free, "inasmuch as the whole of the said territory lies north of 36°30'," that is, the line stipulated in the Missouri Compromise. But the House rejected Burt's amendment on a strictly sectional vote, 113 to 82.[9] Then, on February 15, it once again passed the Wilmot Proviso as an attachment to the $3 million bill, which the Senate promptly rejected. Even so, Congress enacted the bill without the proviso in order to provide the money the President needed to negotiate with Mexico.[10]

The situation grew worse with each passing month. Neither side would yield. Columbus Delano of Ohio lashed out at southerners, promising an end to their accursed and inhuman institution. "We will establish a cordon of free states that shall surround you, and then we will light up the fires of liberty on every side until they melt your present chains and render all your people free," he shouted.[11]

Southerners roared back. Henry Hilliard of Alabama, James A. Seddon of Virginia, Henry Bedinger of Virginia, Robert Roberts of Mississippi and Barnwell Rhett and Andrew P. Butler of South Carolina all promised to shatter the Union and secede if slavery was denied them in any way by congressional action.[12]

With the Mexican War winding down with each passing month, the House had reached an impasse over devising a plan for the territories which the United States anticipated acquiring. American arms had scored one military victory after another in swift succession. In the Battle of Buena Vista in February 1847, General Zachary Taylor and his untried army defeated a much larger Mexican force under Santa Anna, the president of Mexico, and virtually ended the war in northern Mexico. At the same time, General Winfield Scott, at the head of an army of ten thousand men, landed at Veracruz and marched to Mexico City. He captured the capital in September 1847. Finally, General Stephen Kearny, with a force of less than two thousand, swept across New Mexico, proclaiming it part of the United States, and then reached San Diego in California on December 12, 1847, where he established a provisional government.

Meanwhile, the President sent Nicholas Trist, a clerk in the State Department, on a secret mission to Mexico to arrange a treaty of peace. Recalled midway in his negotiations, Trist disregarded his instructions and completed the Treaty of Guadalupe Hidalgo, by which Mexico accepted the Rio Grande as the Texas border and ceded New Mexico and California to the United States in return for $15 million. In addition, the United States would assume claims of American citizens against Mexico of up to $3.25 million.

Some in Congress and the cabinet hoped to swallow all or a good part of Mexico proper, but Henry Clay advised Polk to accept the Trist treaty and bring the abominable war to an end. Polk agreed, won immediate ratification from the Senate and signed the document on March 10, 1848.[13]

Manifest Destiny had brought the country to a new era in its history, one that elicited pride in the expansion of the nation—most particularly when the discovery of gold in California in January 1848 sent a torrent of prospectors pouring into the region—but one that created a series of crises during the next decade that threatened to tear the Union apart.

With an upcoming presidential election in the fall, Polk opted to retire after one term. In his place the Democrats nominated Lewis Cass, former territorial governor of Michigan and member of Jackson's cabinet, who supported the doctrine of popular sovereignty, or squatters sovereignty, which contended that local government in the territories should decide the question of slavery. As his running mate, they chose William O. Butler. Some dissident Democrats split off from the party and held a convention at which they nominated Van Buren and endorsed the Wilmot Proviso. The Liberty Party, which favored abolition, joined these dissenters and met at Buffalo, where they formed the Free-Soil Party, which nominated Van Buren for President and Charles Francis Adams, the son of John Quincy Adams, for Vice President on a platform of "free soil, free speech, free labor, and free men."[14]

Once more Henry Clay sought the Whig nomination, but the convention decided to try another victorious general and named Zachary Taylor to head the ticket, along with Millard Fillmore as his running mate. In a very close contest, Taylor defeated the other candidates by taking 163 electoral votes to 127 for Cass. Van Buren received no electoral votes but deprived Cass of enough popular votes to give New York to Taylor and with it the election. Had either New York or Pennsylvania voted for Cass, he would have won.

Clearly, the old issues of tariff, bank and internal improvements over which Whigs and Democrats had fought during the Jacksonian era had faded away. The single issue of slavery in the territories replaced them, and it sliced across both parties.

When the 30th Congress convened on December 6, 1847, Senator John C. Calhoun made a heroic effort to ally southern Whigs with southern Democrats. Some sixty-nine southern congressmen met in caucus on the evening of December 22 in the Senate chamber to devise a strategy whereby the right of slaveholders to introduce their "peculiar institution" into New Mexico and California would be protected. It was understood that President Taylor planned to bring California and New Mexico into the Union as states and thereby preclude (hopefully) any fight over the issue. The caucus met for three sessions, during which the members hammered away at their "constitutional" right to take their property anywhere in the territories. In addition, they wanted an improved law that would counter northern efforts to prevent the recapture of runaway slaves; and they opposed any attempt to end the slave trade in the District of Columbia.

These sessions were expected to unite southerners and provide a substantial voting bloc in Congress. Calhoun served as spokesman for the caucus and wrote an "Address" which the members were asked to sign. A number of southern Whigs had various objections to the document, so only forty-eight members added their signature.[15] The movement to bring about a voting bloc had obviously failed.

Further attacks on the southern position continued on December 13, when John G. Palfrey of Massachusetts introduced a bill for the abolition of slavery in the District of Columbia. It was defeated, 82 to 69. At the same time, the House adopted a motion instructing its Committee on Territories to apply the Wilmot Proviso to both New Mexico and California. The vote was 106 to 80. Then, in April 1849, President Taylor sent Thomas Butler King, a Georgian, to California, with instructions to encourage efforts by the local authorities to apply for statehood.[16]

But the likelihood of obtaining swift agreement on admitting California and New Mexico as states in the Union rapidly disappeared when the 31st Congress convened on December 3, 1849. Two days earlier, on Saturday, December 1, a caucus of Whigs had been held. Georgia's Robert Toombs, "the stormy petrel, often grand as a declaimer, and always intolerant, dogmatic and extreme," and Alexander Stephens, of "fragile frame, and delicate sensibilities," who looked like a boy grown prematurely old, led the southern members.[17] They tried to convince their northern colleagues not to impose the Wilmot Proviso on the Mexican settlement or attempt to end the slave trade in the District of Columbia. But northern Whigs refused, so Toombs, Stephens and most of the other southern Whigs walked out of the caucus, swearing to block the election of any northern Whig to a leadership position who would not repudiate the Wilmot Proviso. The rump caucus ended with an overwhelming vote of support for the Massachusetts Whig Robert Winthrop in the election of Speaker. He was a much respected and scholarly Boston patrician who had served with distinction as Speaker during the previous Congress. But he had only a slim chance of attracting any southern votes.[18]

The crisis flared into the open when the House convened and attempted to organize itself. There were 112 Democrats, 105 Whigs and 13 Free-Soilers in the House, and it immediately became obvious that more than half of the members were freshmen. The New York delegation, for example, included 22 first-term representatives out of a 34-man aggregate. And they were young. The average age was forty-three and only 2 members in the entire House were over sixty-two.[19] All of which—since many of them were fire-breathing hotheads—guaranteed trouble.

It came instantly. No sooner had they convened than the House quarreled over naming a Speaker, since that officer would appoint committee members and thereby control the legislative agenda. Neither major party had a controlling majority, and the outcome of the election depended on the swing votes of independents and Free-Soilers. The contest for the office of Speaker included eleven candidates, and the balloting turned long and ugly.

Some of the major participants in the struggle included such Democrats as Howell Cobb of Georgia, Linn Boyd of Kentucky, John A. McClernand of Illinois and Thomas Bayly of Virginia. Among Whigs who took an active part in the ensuing debates, besides Winthrop, Toombs and Stephens, were Thaddeus Stevens of Pennsylvania, Horace Mann of Massachusetts and Thomas L. Clingman of North Carolina. The Free-Soilers were led by Joshua R. Giddings of Ohio, Preston King of New York and Joseph M. Root of Ohio.

At one point, Toombs became so irate that he resorted to threats. "I . . . avow before this House and country," he stormed, "and in the presence of the living God, that if by your legislation you seek to drive us from the territories of California and New Mexico . . . and to abolish slavery in the District of Columbia, thereby attempting to fix a national degradation upon the States of this Confederacy, *I am for disunion* and . . . I will devote all I am and all I have on earth to its consummation."[20]

Other Whigs like Thaddeus Stevens sneered at the threat. They had heard it all before. But Alexander H. Stephens jumped to his feet and reiterated it. "I tell this House that every word uttered by my colleague meets my hearty response. . . . I would rather that the southern country should perish . . . than submit for one instant to degradation."[21]

It was disgraceful. In its entire history the House of Representatives had never been so unruly and chaotic. Never before had it run out of control. The clerk, Thomas Jefferson Campbell, who presided, could not keep order. Frequently the chamber rang with cries of "order, order, order" from every quarter, including the gallery.

And so, on December 3, a three-week endurance contest to elect a Speaker began. On the first ballot Howell Cobb received 103 votes, while Robert Winthrop garnered 96. There were also scattered votes (by Free-Soilers, for example) for other less likely candidates, including David Wilmot. No candidate had the necessary majority of votes cast and the House proceeded to a second, a third and then a fourth ballot without success. Day followed day, week followed week as the representatives tried to resolve the impasse. Every night the northern Whigs caucused and reaffirmed their commitment to Winthrop, while southerners promised to prevent his election at all costs. During the day the members shouted and ranted at one another, and on one occasion a fistfight broke out. It was approaching bedlam.[22]

During the heated exchanges William Duer of New York called Richard K. Meade of Virginia a "disunionist."

"It is false," cried Meade in a loud and angry voice.

"You are a liar, sir," responded Duer. Whereupon Meade rushed at Duer to strike him, but their friends promptly surrounded the two men in an effort to keep them apart.

"Had a bomb exploded in the hall," wrote the sergeant at arms, Nathan Sargent, "there could not have been greater excitement."[23]

Members rushed from their desks. It was a melee. Sargent picked up the mace and descended on the crowd.

"Take away the mace," the members shouted, "it has no authority here." But the very presence of the brandished mace helped to restore quiet and order.[24]

Meade sent Duer a formal challenge to settle the matter, but again their friends intervened and a duel was fortunately avoided. For someone like William Yancey of Alabama, "most daring of the firebrands in the 1840s, 'a duel was only a pleasant morning recreation.' "[25]

By this time a sizable number of House members carried a weapon invented by Henry Deringer, a Philadelphia gunsmith, that was small enough to fit in a man's pocket. Every member felt obliged to protect himself against the likelihood of personal injury.

On the forty-first ballot some thirty different candidates received votes for Speaker. Finally, after fifty-nine futile attempts to name a Speaker, Frederick P. Stanton of Tennessee, a Democrat, suggested on Saturday, December 22, that if they continued to fail to elect a Speaker after three more attempts, the House agree to allow a plurality vote to determine the winner.

That had never happened before. The Speaker had always been elected by a majority vote. But the exhausted members readily agreed to the change, and when, on the sixty-third ballot, Cobb received 102 votes to Winthrop's 99, he was declared the new Speaker.[26]

Having selected a minority Speaker, the House then set about completing its organizational structure. By comparison it took only twenty votes to name a clerk, fourteen for a doorkeeper, eight for a sergeant at arms and three for a chaplain.[27] Southerners demanded assurances that these men pass muster on the question of slavery.

It was a triumph for the southern Whigs in derailing northern efforts to elevate Winthrop, but it boded ill for the future of the Whig Party. The Democrats now controlled both houses of Congress, but could they legislate effectively in view of the existing divisions within the House? Having demonstrated their voting strength, the southerners promised to bring legislation to a complete standstill by dilatory motions, roll calls, attempts at filibustering and long-drawn-out harangues, whatever the rules allowed. They intended to block appropriations and any other measure until they had satisfaction about the question of slavery.

The nation seemed headed for disruption and chaos. And it got worse with each passing day. As the situation deteriorated, many congressmen turned to the aging Henry Clay, who had just been reelected to the Senate after an absence of seven years, in the hope that he "may be able to calm the raging elements." And he did not fail them. On January 29, 1850, he proposed in the Senate a series of eight resolutions that he believed would address each of the issues involved in the territorial and slavery questions and would be satisfactory to both North and South. The eight included admission of California without reference to slavery; territorial governments for New Mexico and Utah based on popular sovereignty; settlement of the Texas boundary and assumption by the United States of the Texas debt on condition that Texas relinquish all claim to any part of New Mexico; the "inexpediency" of abolishing slavery in the District of Columbia without the consent of the people living in the district but the "expedience" of abolishing the slave trade; passage of a more effective fugitive slave law; and the denial of congressional authority to interfere in the interstate slave trade.[28]

The imagination, daring and sweep of this compromise plan staggered his colleagues and the nation at large. It now appeared that an agreeable settlement had been devised that could prevent secession and civil war. "Henry Clay may never reap the reward of his devotion to the United States, to the Union, and to the constitution," declared the *New York Herald,* "but posterity will do him justice."[29]

Legislative leadership had obviously moved to the Senate. By its failure to conduct its affairs in an intelligent and civilized manner, the reputation of the House fell dramatically with the general public. But Clay's heroic effort to find a solution to the crisis did help lower the level of agitation and tumult in the House. Cobb and a number of Democratic leaders, including John A. McClernand and Linn Boyd, chairman of the Committee on Territories who often chaired the Committee of the Whole, and Thomas H. Bayly, chairman of Ways and Means, were particularly active in quieting the fears and concerns of the other members. But their efforts were almost derailed when a Free-Soiler, James D. Doty of Wisconsin, proposed that California be admitted as a state without any legislation attached regarding the other territories, a motion that infuriated southerners, who promised a long and drawn-out fight on the floor. Any solution to their problems required a quid pro quo. Otherwise southerners were prepared to exit the Union. "Do us justice," demanded Clingman, "and we continue to stand with you; attempt to trample on us, and we part company."[30]

Speaker Cobb then held a meeting in his house with select members, including Toombs and Stephens, Boyd and McClernand, where they crafted an agreement calling for the organization of the New Mexico and Utah territories on the basis of popular sovereignty with the understanding that California would be admitted as a free state and slavery retained in the District of Columbia. The very fact that Toombs and Stephens were willing to meet with Cobb and the other Democrats to find a solution to their impasse was very encouraging.[31]

For the next several months the Senate held the nation's attention as

During the tumultuous years leading to the Civil War, Howell Cobb had the dubious distinction of winning election as Speaker without a majority vote.

the great men of the age spoke to the crisis. It was arguably the most celebrated debate in congressional history. Clay appealed for mutual concessions, which was the only basis for compromise, he said. But John C. Calhoun condemned the North and demanded the restoration of southern rights through a constitutional amendment. He could not deliver his speech because of illness, so Senator James M. Mason of Virginia read it for him. "Disunion is the only alternative that is left us," he threatened. Shortly thereafter, on March 31, 1850, he died.[32]

Daniel Webster delivered his justly famous "Seventh of March" speech: "I wish to speak today not as a Massachuetts man, not as a Northern man, but as an American. . . . I speak today for the preservation of the Union. Hear me for my cause."[33]

Then, on July 9, President Taylor, who opposed the immediate territorial organization of New Mexico and Utah, died suddenly and was succeeded by Millard Fillmore, who supported Clay's compromise. There were sighs of relief. The change boded well for a peaceful resolution of the crisis.

Until the unexpected happened. Instead of allowing eight separate bills to be introduced, Clay agreed to a single package, an Omnibus Bill, that contained each individual proposal. He should have known better, given his experience in winning passage of the Missouri Compromise. Since the Omnibus Bill was a single measure and gave senators no choice but to say yea or nay (or abstain) for the entire bill, it went down to defeat on July 31.

A disheartened Clay left the capital in an effort to regain his strength and health. Meanwhile, Senator Stephen A. Douglas of Illinois unraveled the Omnibus Bill and arranged to bring each measure up for a separate vote. He recognized that because feelings ran so high, congressmen could not be expected to vote affirmatively across the board. Combining the proposals into one bill united the opponents of each measure. By separating them, members had the option of voting for one and against another. Fortunately, it turned out that a majority existed for each part of the compromise, and they passed.[34]

In the House, the Democratic leadership tried to steer the debate toward quick acceptance of the bills. Over a five-month period, 111 representatives spoke in hour-long harangues, not one of which could compare with the eloquence and statesmanship of those in the upper house. Webster described their efforts with scalding accuracy. "It is a strange and a melancholy fact, that not one single national speech has been made in the House of Representatives this session. Every man speaks to defend himself, and to gratify his own constituents. That is all."[35]

A major problem in obtaining House approval for the compromise was the Texas boundary and debt, which involved Texas bonds and the bondholders' lobby. It was repeatedly pointed out that payment of the $10 million debt would "make splendid fortunes in little time" by taking money "from the pockets of the people" and giving it to "stock-jobbers" and "gamblers in Texas script."[36] Fortunately a possible solution was put forward on August 28, when Chairman Linn Boyd proposed that the bill on the Texas debt and boundary be combined with a measure to establish the territorial organization of New Mexico. It was an effort to test the sense of the House on the doctrine of popular sovereignty in the territories. "We have . . . been listening to speeches for nine long months," he lamented. "I am astonished at the patience with which our constituents have borne our procrastination. I think we have talked enough—in God's name let us act."[37]

The vote was called on September 6. If the measure passed there was hope for the rest of the compromise proposals; if it failed any compromise was doomed.

"It was an exciting time, and much confusion prevailed," wrote a reporter for the New York Herald on September 7. As the clerk began calling the roll, the members hushed. Silence. "Seldom have we known so much quiet as then," said the reporter. When the roll call ended members rose from their desks and crowded around the clerk's table. Disorder returned and Cobb rapped for silence so he could announce the result. Then he began.

"Ayes 107," he said. He stopped. He waited to allow a latecomer who had just arrived to add his vote, after which he declared in a loud voice, "Yeas 108, nays 98."

The House broke out in loud cheers and earsplitting whistles, "the most peculiar and attractive of which was a sort of unpremeditated allegro whistle, which the *[Globe]* Reporter does not remember to have heard before, certainly never in the House of Representatives."[38]

Boyd's "little omnibus," as the combined bill was called, had passed, and the news electrified Washington, which celebrated through the night of Saturday, September 7. Processions, bonfires, cannon salutes, noisemakers of every description, speeches and serenades took place all over the city. There was almost universal celebration. "Hail Liberty and Union, and Domestic Peace!" trumpeted the *National Intelligencer*. "Hail the return of Government from its long aberration back to its just sphere of action and usefulness." On September 9, the bill to admit California as a free state passed, 97 to 85, and the Utah territorial bill followed by the same count. Finally, the Fugitive Slave Law was enacted on September 12 by 109 to 76, which completed the settlement between the opposing groups.[39]

Two days after California's admission as the thirty-first state in the Union, two representatives from the state took their seats in the House of Representatives.

At one point, Congressman David S. Kaufman of Texas looked up over the main entrance to the House chamber to stare at the statue of Clio, the muse of history, who holds a pen and is seemingly taking notes of the events occurring on the floor below. "Oh!" he sighed, ". . . may our action be such that she will be enabled, out of the events of this session to fill the brightest page of human history—that which records the triumph of a free people over themselves, their passions, and their prejudices."[40]

This Compromise of 1850 postponed secession and civil war by ten years. And those ten years—thanks in large measure to the genius of Henry Clay—allowed the North to further industrialize its resources and "find" Abraham Lincoln to lead the nation during its greatest national crisis.

Members of Congress were overjoyed at escaping the tumult of Washington. They returned home to "mingle with their constituents and ascertain the feelings of the people" about what had occurred in the capital over the past several months. There was resentment and growing opposition in the North to the Fugitive Slave law, and many threatened to block its execution. But, on the whole, people seemed overjoyed that conflict had been avoided and peace restored, so they turned "a deaf ear to croakers and prophets" of doom.[41]

As though to confirm this spirit of compromise, the next session of Congress was relatively calm. The two major parties held their national conventions, at which the Democrats nominated Franklin Pierce of New Hampshire and William R. King of Alabama for the offices of President and Vice President, while the Whigs chose General Winfield Scott of Virginia and William A. Graham of North Carolina. The Free-Soilers, on the other hand, named John P. Hale of New Hampshire and George W. Julian of Indiana. Because so many Free-Soilers were former Whigs, General Scott lost a great number of popular votes and only captured four states in the general election: Massachusetts, Vermont, Kentucky and Tennessee. It was obvious that there was little enthusiasm for the candidates of the Whig Party; more important, the struggles of the past several years had wounded the party badly.

To make matters worse, Henry Clay died on June 29, 1852, followed by Daniel Webster on October 24. Their wise counsel was missed when, in December 1853, Senator Augustus C. Dodge of Iowa introduced a bill to organize the Nebraska Territory without mentioning slavery. Since it was part of the Louisiana Purchase and north of the 36°30′ line as established by the Missouri Compromise, it was understood that slavery was prohibited. The bill was referred to the Committee on Territories chaired by Senator Stephen A. Douglas of Illinois. But Senator David R. Atchison of Missouri, a slave state, had promised his constituents that he would obtain the repeal of the Missouri Compromise. So he pressured Douglas to add such a provision to the bill. For his part, Douglas wished to report a measure that left it to the people of the Nebraska Territory to decide the slavery question on the basis of popular sovereignty.

Further consultations ensued. Atchison conferred with the President and his cabinet, as well as Chairman Douglas and members of his committee, and they finally agreed on a bill to split the territory in two and organized Nebraska for the northern area and Kansas for the southern. In addition, the Missouri Compromise was declared "inoperative."

All hell broke loose. The bill meant that the vast area that had once been closed to slavery was now open to its extension, a possibility that drove many northern congressmen to uncontrolled anger. In the Senate, Charles Sumner of Massachusetts and Salmon Portland Chase of Ohio denounced the measure as a "gross violation of a sacred pledge" and a "criminal betrayal of precious rights." It was nothing more than "an atrocious plot" by slaveholders to spread their abominable institution throughout the United States.[42]

In the House, a Nebraska bill was also introduced, which had the active support of representatives from Iowa, Missouri and Illinois who wanted to facilitate the building of a railroad through the northern tier of states that would eventually reach the Pacific Ocean. The bill not only organized Nebraska, but also extinguished Indian titles to the land. And it passed the House, 107 to 49.[43]

Senator Douglas, who had invested heavily in real estate in Illinois and Michigan, also championed the northern railroad scheme, while southern-

ers countered by insisting on a more southerly route through already existing states and organized territories. Recognizing that the Missouri
Compromise barred slaveholders from the northern area, representatives
from the South supported an amendment to the Nebraska bill that specifically repealed that portion of the compromise that drew a boundary line at
36°30'. Also, by dividing the territory—Kansas to the west of Missouri and
Nebraska to the west of Iowa and Minnesota—it was clearly intended that
Kansas would be slave and Nebraska free. The Nebraska measure was no
longer a railroad bill.

Despite the concerted opposition of Chase, Sumner and others, the
Kansas-Nebraska Act passed the Senate by a 37 to 14 vote on March 3, 1854.
But in the House the battle was fiercer and more drawn out. The members
refused to send the bill to the Committee on Territories and instead referred it to the Committee of the Whole, where it was buried along with
several dozen other bills. Nevertheless, the Pierce administration forces,
directed by Senator Douglas, amassed enough votes in the House during
March and April to table everything ahead of the Kansas-Nebraska bill.
Roll call after roll call disposed of these intervening measures until the territory bill finally emerged.

The ensuing struggle over the measure continued for two weeks with
Georgia Whig Alexander H. Stephens serving as the administration's floor
manager. "It is time that this measure was brought to a final vote," he cried.
"It has been under consideration before Congress for the last five months. It
has been discussed in the Senate; it has been discussed in the House; it has
been discussed before the country, and every man, I doubt not, has made
up his mind on the subject. Why should we longer delay?" With a healthy
application of "whip & spur," he succeeded in gaining passage of the measure on May 22 by a vote of 113 to 100, and President Pierce signed it eight
days later. "If I had not been here the Bill would never have been got
through," Stephens boasted. "I took the reins in my own hand and drove
with whip & spur until we got the 'wagon' out of the mud." In the vote
northern Democrats were evenly divided, while an overwhelming number
of southern Democrats and a dozen southern Whigs supported the measure.[44]

It was a frightful mistake. The Compromise of 1850 had brought a degree of peace to the nation. Now the Kansas-Nebraska Act shattered it, raising, in the words of Senator Douglas, "a hell of a storm." Why did Congress
do it? Why did the administration support the measure? For a railroad to
be built across the northern tier of states? True, that was a motivating factor, and any number of congressmen, including Douglas, had invested
heavily in real estate in the surrounding states. Greed is always a powerful
engine in American politics. And some presumed that repealing the Missouri Compromise line would have little impact on the slavery question

since the territory was considered geographically unsuited for the importation of slaves. Foolish men thought they could enrich themselves at public expense and get away with it.

Douglas claimed full responsibility. "I passed the Kansas-Nebraska Act myself," he later bragged. "I had the authority and power of a dictator throughout the whole controversy in both houses. The speeches were nothing. It was the marshalling and directing of men, and guarding from attacks, and with a ceaseless vigilance preventing surprise."[45]

The Kansas-Nebraska Act was a gross miscalculation. And the nation paid a heavy price for it.

Party loyalty evaporated. Sectional loyalty replaced it. The solid South demonstrated what it could do to protect its interests in the lower chamber against an overwhelming majority in the North. The bill passed because a southern Whig, Alexander H. Stephens, mustered a bipartisan coalition and rammed it through the House.

The bill also played a vital role in realigning the major parties. On February 28, 1854, a number of Free-Soilers, northern Whigs and antislavery Democrats met in Ripon, Wisconsin, and recommended the formation of a new party to be called "Republican." Months later, after passage of the Kansas-Nebraska Act, a meeting on July 6 in Jackson, Michigan, formally adopted the new name and demanded the repeal of the Kansas-Nebraska and Fugitive Slave Acts and the abolition of slavery in the District of Columbia.[46] This new party would soon reflect what was happening in the nation at large.

THE POPULATION IN the country had shifted dramatically. At the start of the new government under the Constitution in 1789, most Americans were predominantly British in origin with a small mixture of other European nations, and virtually all of them were native born. From just a few million in 1800, the population in 1850 had reached 25 million, of which one-fifth were African-American slaves. But by the mid-1850s, immigration from Germany and Ireland (following the potato famine between 1846 and 1850) soared and averaged about half a million a year. By 1860, of a total population of 31 million, about 4,100,000 were foreign-born and 4,400,000 were Negro. Suddenly native-born Americans became conscious of the large number of foreigners in their midst and many of them resented it, particularly when it involved employment and politics.[47] In addition, most of these aliens were Roman Catholic. This nativist surge finally produced an anti-immigrant, anti-Catholic, and antislavery party called the American, or Known-Nothing, Party, from the practice of members responding with "I know nothing" because, in part, they wished to hide their obvious prejudices.[48]

Amazingly, both the Republican and the American parties scored huge victories in the fall elections of 1854. Know-Nothings won 43 seats in the House, Republicans captured 108 and Democrats took 83. Of the 42 northern Democrats who voted for the Kansas-Nebraska Act, only 7 were reelected. It was an electoral earthquake.

The election was won by Know-Nothings, not by Republicans, insisted Senator Douglas. The anti-Nebraska movement, he argued, became "a crucible into which they [Know-Nothings] poured Abolitionism, Maine liquor-lawism,[49] and what there was left of Northern Whiggism, and then the Protestant feeling against the Catholic, and the native feeling against the foreigner."[50]

The rise of the Know-Nothing and Republican parties signaled the beginning of the end of the Whig Party, which was hemorrhaging at both ends. In the North, Whigs were deserting to the Know-Nothing and Republican parties, in the south, to the Democratic Party. Northern Democrats who were anti-Nebraska were also abandoning their party.[51]

With Know-Nothings holding the balance of power between the Republicans and Democrats in Congress, a titanic battle erupted in December 1855 over the election of the Speaker for the 34th Congress. The chamber resounded with long, acrimonious speeches in which threats and near fist-fights were a regular occurrence. And members continued arming themselves with knives and pistols to protect themselves from sudden attacks. The contest for Speaker lasted nine weeks, and not until the 133rd ballot was Nathaniel P. Banks, a Know-Nothing and a Free-Soiler from Massachusetts, elected by a plurality vote of 103 to 100 over William Aiken of South Carolina.

The strength of the American or Know-Nothing Party resulted from its wide appeal. Not only was it a nativist and an anti-immigrant party, but it reached out to abolitionists and followers of the temperance movement as well. The following year, the party scored additional electoral triumphs, causing many to predict that it could capture the presidency in 1856. But many Americans were genuinely shocked by the extreme political drift of the nation. "How can anyone who abhors the oppression of negroes be in favor of degrading classes of white people?" asked Abraham Lincoln. "As a nation, we began by declaring that *'all men are created equal.'* . . . When the Know-Nothings get control, it will read 'All men are created equal, except negroes, *and foreigners, and catholics.'* "[52]

Fortunately, the Know-Nothings as a viable party disappeared almost as quickly as they had arisen. At a national council meeting of the party in Philadelphia in June 1855, southern delegates won acceptance of a resolution that indirectly endorsed the Kansas-Nebraska Act, for it declared that existing laws must be supported as a final solution to the slavery question. The adoption of this resolution emptied the council meeting of virtually all its delegates from the free states, with the exception of California, New

York, New Jersey and Pennsylvania.[53] When the party convened to nominate Millard Fillmore as its presidential candidate in the 1856 election, southern delegates, with the aid of New Yorkers, voted down a resolution in favor of the restoration of the Missouri Compromise. Fifty northern delegates from eight states walked out, reassembled in a separate meeting, and issued a call for another convention of northern Know-Nothings in June. The remaining delegates nominated Fillmore for president, but he ran a poor third with only 8 electoral votes (Maryland), behind the Democrat, James Buchanan, who garnered 174 votes and the Republican, John C. Frémont, who won 114. Frémont captured eleven states and 1,340,000 popular votes to 1,833,000 for Buchanan. It was a remarkable showing for the young Republican Party. Had Pennsylvania and either Illinois or Indiana switched their votes, Frémont would have entered the White House.[54]

Meanwhile, violence broke out in the Kansas Territory between pro- and antislavery forces and generated a local civil war known as "Bleeding Kansas." To investigate this developing catastrophe, Speaker Banks appointed a three-man committee, consisting of one proslavery representative, Mordecai Oliver of Missouri, and two antislavery representatives, John Sherman of Ohio and William A. Howard of Michigan. The committee later reported that Kansas, in its present condition, could not hold a free election without a new census, impartial judges and the presence of U.S. troops at every polling place.

The violence in Kansas was soon repeated in the nation's Capitol. Congressmen were fully armed. In fact, it was said that Linus Comins, a representative from Massachusetts, carried a rifle disguised as a walking cane. Other congressmen would point to him and say, "There goes the gentleman with a walking gun!"[55]

Then, on May 19, 1856, at one o'clock in the afternoon, the tall, elegant and arrogant senator from Massachusetts, Charles Sumner, delivered a powerful and mesmerizing speech in the upper house entitled "The Crime Against Kansas," in which he accused "hirelings picked from the drunken spew and vomit of an uneasy civilization" of invading Kansas, where they illegally imposed a proslavery legislature upon the citizens by force and violence.[56]

It was not enough for him to speak generally and critically about the South. No, he needed someone to personify that "rotten society," so he chose the scholarly, kindly, sixty-two-year-old senator from South Carolina, Andrew Pickens Butler. He mocked Butler's speech impediment and intelligence. "Butler," he sneered, "cannot open his mouth but out there flies a blunder."[57] But what could one expect? He was a native of South Carolina, Sumner continued, a state notable for its lack of learning and culture. On and on he went in one of the most abusive speeches ever delivered in Congress.

A violent reaction followed immediately. Representative Preston S. Brooks, a young, handsome nephew of the pilloried Butler, wrote to his brother that "I felt it to be my duty to relieve Butler and avenge the insult to my state."[58] He asked a colleague from South Carolina, Laurence Keitt, to accompany him and ward off any bystander who might try to stop him from punishing Sumner, and on May 22 the two men walked over to the near-empty Senate shortly after the noon adjournment and found Sumner sitting at his desk, franking copies of his "Crime Against Kansas" speech.

"Mr. Sumner," Brooks barked in a threatening voice, "I have read your speech twice over carefully. It is a libel on South Carolina and Mr. Butler, who is a relative of mine."[59] And with that remark he raised a large and heavy gutta-percha cane he had purchased for the purpose and struck Sumner over the head.

Worse, he did not stop. Again and again he raised the cane and repeated blow after blow after blow. Sumner vainly tried to escape. But his chair was pulled close to the desk and the rug underneath prevented him from pushing it out and standing up. So, with one mighty heave, he raised himself bodily, and in doing so tore the desk from its moorings. The legs of the desk had been screwed to the floor. Once free of confinement, Sumner

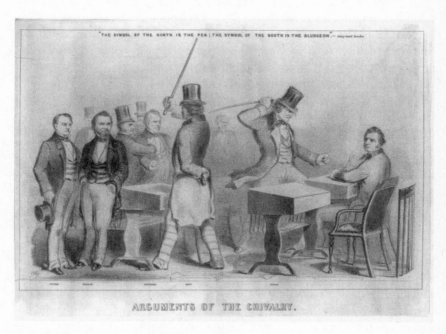

Representative Preston Brooks savagely attacked Senator Charles Sumner with a heavy cane for his insulting speech against the South, South Carolina and its senior senator, Andrew Butler.

rose to his full height and then toppled forward and fell to the floor, blood streaming from his head and face, while Brooks still rained blows about his head and shoulders until the cane snapped in two. "Every lick went where I intended," Brooks later bragged; ". . . towards the last he bellowed like a calf. I wore my cane out completely but saved the Head which is gold. The fragments of the stick are begged for as *sacred relicts.*"[60]

Bystanders rushed to aide the stricken man and led him to an ante-room where Dr. Cornelius Boyle dressed his wounds. "I could not believe that a thing like this was possible," muttered Sumner, as he lost consciousness.[61]

The reaction to "Bully" Brooks's assault was instantaneous. Members of the House wanted him expelled, but by the count of 121 yeas to 95 nays they failed to achieve a required two-thirds vote. All but one southerner voted against expulsion.

On July 14, Brooks rose in the House and said that his attack on Sumner was a "personal affair" and that he meant no disrespect to the House or Senate, but that his actions were compelled by his regard and affection for his uncle and South Carolina. "And now, Mr. Speaker, I announce to you and to this House, that I am no longer a member of the Thirty-Fourth Congress."[62] With that, he walked proudly out of the chamber as the gallery saluted him with cheers and applause. A hero at home, he was overwhelmingly reelected by his constituents and returned triumphantly to the House on August 1, 1856. But five months later he died of a liver ailment at the age of thirty-seven. Said Charles Sumner after his recovery, "Poor fellow, he was the unconscious agent of a malign power."[63]

Although the temper in Congress had sunk to a new low with members beating one another senseless and failing to resolve the great issues dividing the country, they had no trouble at all in finding enough agreement to vote themselves a salary raise from $8 per day, as passed in 1818, to $3,000 a year. No outcry from the electorate forced a repudiation of what had earlier been called a Salary Grab; perhaps they were distracted by more threatening matters.

During this period of crisis one of the worst Presidents in the nation's history assumed the office of chief executive: James Buchanan. In delivering his inaugural address as President, he made the truly stupid mistake of assuring the public that the Supreme Court was about to hand down a decision that would settle the problem of slavery in the territories once and for all. The question immediately arose as to how he knew beforehand what the court would decide. Sure enough, two days later, Chief Justice Roger B. Taney delivered the Dred Scott decision that declared the Missouri Compromise unconstitutional (it had already been repealed by the Kansas-Nebraska Act) and denied Congress the power to prohibit slavery in the territories. But the decision solved nothing, and the reputation of the court around the country plunged to the lowest point in its entire history.

Meanwhile, a rigged proslavery convention was held in Lecompton, Kansas, in which a constitution was written that protected slavery and denied to the electorate the right to ratify or reject it. Voters were given the choice of accepting slavery or forbidding the further introduction of slavery into the state. Either way Kansas would allow slavery.

Despite the fraud involved, Buchanan asked Congress to admit Kansas with the Lecompton Constitution, and his action unleashed a three-month brawl in Congress, most especially in the House. Late-night sessions were frequent, and wild, free-for-all shouting matches a daily occurrence. At one point Laurence M. Keitt of South Carolina angrily labeled Galusha Grow of Pennsylvania "a black Republican puppy." To which Grow responded, "No Negro-driver shall crack his whip over me!"

A melee ensued. Fifty or more representatives rushed at one another. They wrestled, shoved and punched one another as the Speaker, James L. Orr of South Carolina, pleaded for order.

Members "stewing and sweating in their sleep" suddenly came awake and began "striking out" wildly. Newspaper reporters in the "side galleries," thinking "they were in a vast oyster saloon in a state of drunken demoralization, went to cracking smutty jokes and pelting each other with spit balls." At this point the sergeant at arms grabbed the mace and "waved his spread eagle" over the heads of the members, shouting for everyone to return to his seat.[64]

The madness finally turned to comedy. John F. "Bowie-Knife" Potter[65] of Wisconsin reached for the hair of William Barksdale of Mississippi and pulled off his wig. "I've scalped him," cried the startled Potter, which set the whole house laughing. And that ended the melee.[66]

This wrestling and punching match was perhaps the largest such free-for-all in the history of the House. It set a record.[67]

Joint conferees agreed on a new bill, which provided for another vote by the electorate on the Lecompton Constitution, and it passed both houses. On August 2, 1858, Kansas voters rejected the constitution, and Kansas remained a territory with slavery as dictated by the Dred Scott decision. Not until secession and the departure of southerners from Congress were northerners able to admit Kansas as a free state.

WITH THE COUNTRY rapidly expanding in size, especially after the Mexican War and the admission of California as a state following the Compromise of 1850, it was decided that the Capitol had to be enlarged to handle all the new members. There were many complaints about the lack of space and, of course, the dreadful acoustics in the House. So, on September 30,

1850, legislation was enacted to authorize the expansion of the building by adding new wings to both the north and south ends of the Capitol. Thomas U. Walter, the favorite of the House of Representatives, was named chief architect to operate under the aegis of the Interior Department, and the cornerstone was laid on July 4, 1851, with more celebratory speeches, salutes, parades and processions than Washington had ever witnessed before.[68]

A few months later, on December 24, a disastrous fire caused by a defective chimney flue broke out in the Library of Congress and resulted in the loss of thirty-five thousand volumes, or 65 percent of the library's holdings. Destroyed were two-thirds of the books purchased from Thomas Jefferson in 1815, Gilbert Stuart's portraits of the first five Presidents, busts of George Washington, Jefferson and Lafayette, as well as prints, manuscripts, maps and official documents. The room was nothing but a burned-out shell once the fire was extinguished, after which Walter was asked to propose a new interior. Displaying great ingenuity, he designed an incombustible cast-iron room without any wood at all. It was immediately approved and the reconstruction was completed on July 1, 1853.[69] It was located at the extreme end of a small gallery off the Rotunda. A sliding door on noiseless wheels opened into a "softly carpeted room—grand, long and high—whose glass ceiling, veined by cornicing, fluting, and garlands," seemed "bright like burnished gold."[70]

In short order there were criticisms about the progress of the extension of the north and south wings, and Secretary of War Jefferson Davis, the most influential member of Franklin Pierce's cabinet, had the project transferred to the War Department. He assigned Captain Montgomery C. Meigs of the Corps of Engineers to oversee the operation, who, together with Walter, revised the floor plans of the two wings. Now both legislative chambers were located at the center of each wing, which deprived them of natural lighting from windows but which Meigs felt would improve acoustics and allow for better circulation of air by the installation of multiple doors on all sides of the chambers. This central location would also permit the use of corridors on every side, which could be cordoned off from the public to allow easier access for members. One of the main complaints by congressmen with respect to their present quarters was the difficulty of getting into their chambers without struggling through hordes of lobbyists and tourists crowding near the single entrance.

On February 20, 1855, Meigs submitted plans to the House Committee on Public Buildings for the construction of a gigantic fireproof iron dome designed by Thomas U. Walter from studies he had done of the domes of St. Paul's, the Pantheon and St. Peter's. It was to be built over the Rotunda in place of the existing Bulfinch dome, and on March 3, 1855, the President approved an appropriation of $100,000 for its construction. The Bulfinch

During the Civil War, the continued construction of the Capitol dome—a symbol of the Union—could be seen by Confederates across the Potomac River.

dome was demolished by the end of November 1855, and a temporary roof installed over the Rotunda.[71]

A contract was also awarded to J. W. Thompson & Brothers on June 15, 1855, to install plumbing for running water and gas for illumination in the new wings. The introduction of gas lighting was precipitated by the crash of a cut-glass chandelier in the House chamber on December 18, 1840. This massive fixture of seventy-eight oil lamps weighed over seven thousand pounds and burned whale oil. The oil not only added to the weight of the chandelier, but also, if ignited, could cause a major fire, such as had occurred in the Library of Congress. Fortunately no one was injured in the accident, but several desks were badly damaged.[72] It reminded members that a very dangerous contraption hung over their heads and needed to be replaced. In addition, it was believed that gas would be cheaper and more efficient, and produce a cleaner, brighter light. So in 1847, when James Crutchett successfully conducted experiments in producing gas from cottonseed oil on the Capitol grounds, Congress agreed to convert to this new form of illumination. A three-inch gas main was laid under the floors to supply the gas,[73] and exquisite chandeliers were hung from the vaulted ceilings of offices, hallways and committee rooms.[74]

The lighting in the Rotunda required 1,083 jets, which were installed in 1865 and could be ignited simultaneously, thanks to an invention of Samuel Gardinier. An electrical current activated magnets and wires used in the operation. By throwing a few remote switches one person could light hundreds of lamps. This invention was the first application of electricity in the Capitol. Later the Edison Company placed 650 electric lights in the north wing and 200 in the south wing. By the end of the century more than 1,150 lights had been installed.[75]

Because of the lack of a sufficient and readily available water supply, the fire in the library burned out of control—water had to be thrown through the library's windows to try to douse the flames—and gutted the room. To rectify this problem, a four-inch cast-iron water main was installed in the Capitol on June 15, 1855, under corridor floors. The pipe supplied water to drinking fountains, washbasins and committee and cloakrooms. Water closets were connected to iron waste pipes leading to a main sewer. Thus, by the middle of the 1850s, plumbing, ventilation, lighting and heating were modernized.[76]

The expansion of the Capitol created space for additional committee rooms, and this in turn led to the hiring of staff members to serve the committees. By 1860, each committee had at least one clerk to record its work and prepare documents and bills for submission to the entire House. At first they were hired for the duration of the session. Later they became permanent, and their number swelled as the business of Congress increased over the next few decades. Individual members were also allowed one clerk at a salary of $100 per month. Almost immediately they became indispensable. "One wonders now how they once did without them," wrote one journalist, "they release the members from so many burdens and so much tedious work."[77]

Shortly after the 35th Congress assembled, Meigs informed the secretary of war that the new House chamber was ready for occupancy. On December 13, 1857, the Reverend George Cummins preached before a crowd of two thousand, and on December 16 the House members convened in their new chamber for the first time. There were 262 carved-oak desks designed by Walter with matching oak chairs and removable cushions to permit cane seats in the summer. Flanking the Speaker's rostrum were large portraits of George Washington and the Marquis de Lafayette,[78] both of which hung in the old chamber. In the corner was a depiction of the surrender of Cornwallis by Constantino Brumidi, which was intended to be the first in a series of historical paintings for the wall panels. Best of all, the acoustics proved to be infinitely better than in the old hall.[79]

The former House chamber remained vacant until 1864, when Congress invited each state to contribute two statues of its prominent citizens for a permanent display. Thus the old room became the new Statuary Hall, located directly south of the Rotunda.

• • •

WASHINGTON ITSELF CONTINUED to change. Once the opening session of Congress approached, reported Mary Jane McLane, "our city gives notice . . . by the usual premonitory symptoms. The streets and the people have an air of *fete* and expectancy. Shop windows display more than their customary attractions. . . . Hotels have their reinforcements of waiters and runners . . . while long lines of posted play-bills show that all the amusement of the 'season' have commenced." Omnibuses ran along Pennsylvania Avenue "for the convenience of Senators, Congressmen, and others on their way to the Capitol," but these streetcars, pulled by mules, very often got stuck in huge mud-holes after a rainy spell. The food market, claimed Sara Pryor, wife of Representative Roger Pryor of Virginia, "was abundantly supplied with the finest game and fish from the Eastern shore of Maryland and Virginia, and the waters of the Potomac. Brant, ruddy duck, canvasback duck, sora, oysters, and terrapin were within the reach of any housekeeper. Oysters, to be opened at a moment's notice, were planted on the cellar floors, and fed with salt water."[80]

But a dreadful murder occurred in Washington in 1857 that shocked the nation. Representative Daniel E. Sickles from New York learned that his wife was carrying on an affair with Philip Barton Key, the district attorney for the District of Columbia. On a bright, Sunday morning, Sickles left his house on Lafayette Square, spotted Key on the street and "without warning, drew a pistol and shot him down like a dog." Sickles surrendered himself and was imprisoned, "where he enjoyed the comforts of the keeper's room." After all, he was a congressman. He also "received the visits of many friends." His defense argued his innocence by reason of temporary insanity, and since he was a particular friend of President Buchanan, the attorney general did little to prosecute the case. Sickles was acquitted by a jury of his peers who did not offer a reason for their decision, "and his friends gave him a round of supper parties."[81]

THE SQUABBLING OVER Kansas continued. And southerners were further incensed when a book published in 1857 by a native North Carolinian, Hinton R. Helper, entitled *The Impending Crisis of the South and How to Meet It*, was endorsed by sixty-eight House Republicans, and a hundred thousand copies were distributed as campaign material. The book argued from statistics that slavery had impoverished many southern whites and that the peculiar institution was detrimental to their economic welfare. Southerners in the House swore to block any of the sixty-eight members from holding high elective office or important chairmanships.

In the summer of 1858, Abraham Lincoln challenged Stephen A. Douglas to a series of debates in which Lincoln asked the senator to reconcile the doctrine of popular sovereignty with the Dred Scott decision. Douglas's

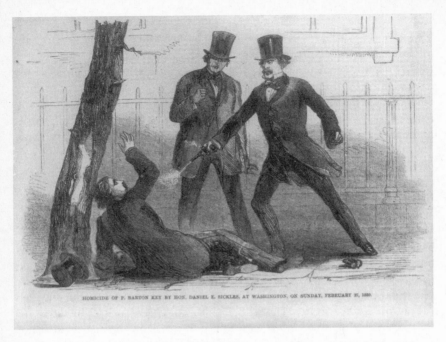

HOMICIDE OF P. BARTON KEY BY HON. DANIEL E. SICKLES, AT WASHINGTON, ON SUNDAY, FEBRUARY 27, 1859.

As a congressman, Daniel Sickles received favored treatment in jail despite having murdered Philip Barton Key.

reply at Freeport, Illinois, that slavery could not "exist a day or an hour anywhere, unless it is supported by local police regulations," infuriated southerners, especially since Douglas was the leading Democratic contender for the presidency in 1860. They refused to support a candidate who held this view. The debate helped lift Lincoln to national attention.[82]

John Brown's raid at Harpers Ferry in mid-October 1859 and his subsequent trial and execution, along with four of his sons, intensified the quarreling and spread alarm throughout the southern states. Moreover, it set the stage for another battle when the 36th Congress convened on December 5, three days after Brown was hanged. There were 109 Republicans; 88 Democrats who stood with the Buchanan administration; 13 anti-Lecompton Democrats; and 27 Know-Nothings, most of whom were southerners. Since no party enjoyed a majority, the Know-Nothings held the balance of power.

On the first vote for Speaker, Thomas S. Bocock of Virginia, the choice of the Democratic caucus, led the field with 86 votes, followed by the Republican, John Sherman of Ohio, with 66; Galusha Grow of Pennsylvania, also a Republican, with 43; and Alexander R. Boteler of Virginia, a Know-Nothing, with 14. Grow withdrew after the first ballot, Bocock after the eleventh. Consequently the Republicans concentrated their entire strength upon Sherman, who was opposed by two Know-Nothings, Emerson Etheridge of Tennessee and William N. H. Smith of North Carolina, and an assortment of Democrats: John S. Millson of Virginia, Charles L. Scott of California, Andrew J. Hamilton of Texas and John A. McClernand of Illinois.[83]

Because John Sherman was one of the sixty-eight who had endorsed *The Impending Crisis of the South,* southerners rejected him out of hand, arguing that he was unfit. John S. Millson of Virginia declared that "one who consciously, deliberately, and of purpose lent his name and influence to the propagation of such writings is not only not fit to be speaker, but is not fit to live." Laurence M. Keitt of South Carolina shouted that "the South here asks nothing but its rights . . . I would have no more: but, as God is my judge, as one of its representatives, I would shatter this republic from turret to foundation-stone before I would take one tittle less." Thaddeus Stevens, as usual, sneered a response that southerners had made the same threat over and over because they "found weak and recreant tremblers in the North who have been affected by it, and who have acted from these intimidations."[84]

As the oratory intensified, pandemonium broke out. The House was in an uproar. The clerk, elected by the previous Congress, lost any semblance of control. Members darted up and down the aisles while "two or three of the smallest pages—sweet little fellows in white jackets and cambric collars—had taken advantage of the general confusion, and were amusing themselves with great glee—one on a tin trumpet . . . on which he was performing with more delight to himself than to his hearers."[85]

And so it began all over again. Day after weary day of balloting and arguing and shouting and threatening. Because Senator William H. Seward of New York, the leading contender for the Republican presidential nomination in 1860, had given a speech in Rochester declaring that "an irrepressible conflict" existed in which the United States would either become entirely slaveholding or entirely free, he came in for considerable lambasting during the House debate, and was charged with assisting John Brown's raid. To the wild applause of southern Democrats, Martin J. Crawford of Georgia stormed: "We will never submit to the inauguration of a Black Republican President. I speak the sentiment of every Democrat on this floor from the State of Georgia."[86]

The verbal exchanges grew hotter with each passing day. When John B. Haskin of New York rose to speak, he became so emotional and angry in his remarks and so agitated in his physical exertions that a pistol fell out of the breast pocket of his coat. Luckily it did not discharge. But several members were positive that he had deliberately drawn the weapon with the intention of using it and rushed forward to disarm him.[87]

Again pandemonium. And everyone knew that members on both sides, along with their friends in the galleries, were fully armed with revolvers and bowie knives.

The rancor on the floor of the House infected social relationships like never before. "Our social lives," recorded Sara Pryor, "were now strictly drawn between North and South. Names were dropped from visiting lists, occasions avoided on which we might expect to meet members of the party antagonistic to our own."[88]

By mid-January, Sherman had garnered 112 votes and came within three votes of election. No effort was made to accept a plurality vote because members knew that southerners would filibuster against it. On January 27, William Smith of North Carolina received 112 votes, and Sherman's vote on the same ballot slipped to 106. The House then adjourned from Friday to Monday, January 30. When it reconvened, Sherman withdrew his name, and the Republicans nominated William Pennington of New Jersey, a complete nonentity. Three days later and after five more ballots, the contest finally ended. On February 1, the forty-fourth trial, Pennington received a majority of 117 votes, the exact number necessary for election.[89] He proved to be totally unfit to preside over the House, much less control it, and did exactly what he was told by Republican party leaders. Without comment or question, he even accepted the complete list of committee appointees dictated by Sherman. His constituents promptly voted him out of office at the next election.[90]

With a Speaker like Pennington and a President like Buchanan and the Congress in disarray, the country was headed for total disaster. When the Democrats held their convention in Charleston on April 23 to choose Buchanan's replacement, the southerners demanded protection of slavery in the territories as the price of their continued participation in the party. This was unacceptable to northerners who supported Stephen A. Douglas. As a result, the delegates from eight southern states walked out of the convention. The party split, with northerners meeting in Baltimore on June 18 and nominating Douglas and Herschel V. Johnson of Georgia for Vice President, while southerners, who also met in Baltimore on June 28, nominated John C. Breckinridge of Kentucky and Joseph Lane of Oregon.

The Republicans convened in Chicago on May 16 and on the third ballot named Abraham Lincoln and Hannibal Hamlin of Maine as their candidates. They rejected Seward, whose "irrepressible conflict" speech had frightened the electorate. A fourth candidate, John Bell of Tennessee, was chosen by remnants of the Whig and American (Know-Nothing) parties at Baltimore who declared themselves the Constitutional Union Party. Edward Everett of Massachusetts was named the candidate for Vice President.

U. S. HOUSE OF REPRESENTATIVES.

The House chamber as it looked after the north and south wings were added to the Capitol.

The catastrophic split of the Democratic Party virtually guaranteed Lincoln's election. He carried eighteen free states; Breckinridge captured eleven slave states; Bell won three border states; and Douglas won one state and scattered votes from a second state. Lincoln received 180 electoral votes, a clear majority, and that victory precipitated secession and civil war.

8

The Civil War, 1860–1865

I T WAS A ghastly winter. In the months following the election of Abraham Lincoln as President, one deplorable event succeeded another. "In the whole history of the American people," James G. Blaine of Maine later wrote, "there is no epoch which recalls so much that is worthy of regret and so little that gratifies pride."[1]

The mood among Congressmen as they reassembled in early December 1860 for their lame-duck session reflected the apprehension and fear felt by most Americans. Southern representatives spoke openly of secession, and their northern colleagues countered by threatening military action. The House convened on December 3, sat through a roll call and heard a spirited invocation by their chaplain. That evening Representative Clement L. Vallandigham, a Democrat from Ohio who had recently chaired the national Democratic campaign committee for Stephen A. Douglas, wrote his wife and told her that "I have just witnessed the assembling of the last Congress of the *United* States at its last session. It was a solemn scene."

Indeed. The breakup of the Union appeared imminent, and Vallandigham characterized the day in the House as one of "tribulation and anguish."[2]

As soon as word reached Charleston, South Carolina, that the "black Republican" had been elected President, the legislature summoned a state convention, which met on December 20, 1860, and formally dissolved the connection between South Carolina and the other states comprising the United States of America. This action was soon imitated by other southern states. Mississippi seceded on January 9, 1861, Florida on January 10, Alabama on January 11, Georgia on January 19, Louisiana on January 26 and Texas on February 1. These states ultimately joined together to form the Confederate States of America. They held a convention in Montgomery, Alabama, on February 8, where their representatives drew up a constitution and established a provisional government. Closely resembling the U.S. Constitution, the Confederate document contained notable differences, including a recognition of the independent and sovereign character of each state. The following day Jefferson Davis was elected provisional President of the Confederacy and Alexander H. Stephens Vice President.

During the lame-duck session in the House from December 3, 1860, to March 3, 1861, the victorious Republicans had not yet taken control, but they exercised considerable influence in turning back several Democratic efforts at compromise or settlement. They met such attempts with "sneers and skepticism." There was a move to create a special committee of thirty-three representatives (one member from each state) to study political conditions around the country and submit recommendations that would maintain the integrity of the Union and avoid civil war. Democrats particularly dreaded the possibility of conflict. "War is disunion," cried Stephen A. Douglas, "war is final, eternal separation."[3] In the House, Samuel S. Cox of Ohio swore that Democrats would never "thrust Republican wrongs down the throats of the South at the point of a bayonet. . . . Let the cry of the democracy be, COMPROMISE OR PEACEABLE SEPARATION."[4]

But nothing prepared the members for the horrendous scene of representatives from the seceded states taking their leave from the House of Representatives, an institution most of them loved and revered. For the most part these "departing brothers" did not indulge in individual addresses, although a few did, and their remarks were rancorous. The first to leave, of course, were the South Carolina members on December 24, 1860. "In a brief card[5] before the House by Speaker Pennington," they announced that since the people of their state had "in their sovereign capacity resumed the powers delegated by them to the Federal Government of the United States, their connection with the House of Representatives was thereby dissolved." They "desired to take leave of those with whom they had been associated in common agency, with mutual regard and respect for the rights of each other." They "cherished the hope" that in future relations they might "better enjoy the peace and harmony essential to the happiness of a free and enlightened people."[6]

The other members from seceded states retired from the House in the order in which their states had departed. "There was no defiance, no indulgence of bravado." The Mississippi delegation regretted the "necessity" that had impelled their state to adopt secession but declared the action had met "their unqualified approval." The card was obviously written by Lucius

Q. C. Lamar, declared Blaine, "and accurately described his emotions." Lamar looked back "with tender regret to the Union whose destiny he had wished to share and under the protection of whose broader nationality he had hoped to live and to die." A few members of other departing delegations fired off bitter reproaches, especially against the Republican Party, "but the large majority confined themselves to the simpler form of the card."[7]

"The wives, daughters and other female connections of Southern members, were in the galleries constantly to cheer by their presence and smiles the fervid efforts of these secession orators." In glancing over the names of these departing colleagues, S. S. Cox could not "but regret that so much of genius, energy, and goodness have been misled to their own ruin and that of their States."[8]

With the departure of the southerners—all told, thirty-three men[9] resigned in this first wave—their desks and chairs in the House were also removed and throughout the war years that followed, the space created became a constant reminder of their absence to the remaining representatives. As Cox said, enormous talent was lost.

It was an agony to see these men leave the House. More than seventy years had passed since the first House convened and sixty-five men set about constructing a Union based on the Constitution. And now it was dissolving. There were tears shed on the floor and in the gallery.

A peace convention was undertaken to save the Union, and delegates from northern, southern and border states met behind closed doors in Washington on February 4, 1861, with John Tyler, the former President, presiding. But they failed to work out an acceptable agreement. Another attempt to prevent secession came on February 28, when Congress considered a joint resolution to amend the Constitution and guarantee slavery in the states where it already existed. But some sixty-five Republicans opposed it, led by Thaddeus Stevens. He was sustained by John Bingham of Ohio, Roscoe Conkling of New York, Owen Lovejoy of Illinois, Galusha A. Grow of Pennsylvania and Elihu B. Washburne of Illinois. Even so, a number of other Republicans supported the resolution, such as John Sherman of Ohio, Schuyler Colfax of Indiana, Thomas Corwin of Ohio, Charles Francis Adams of Massachusetts and Justin Morrill of Vermont. Despite its intensely controversial provision, the amendment passed the House, 133 to 65, and the Senate, 24 to 12, but the states failed to ratify it.[10]

Buchanan closed out his presidency with words of regret about the disruption of the Union and lamented his inability to do anything about it. The well-meaning but inept Speaker, William Pennington of New Jersey, addressed the House on March 2, 1861, noting the sad departure of their southern colleagues: "No lover of his country can witness such an exhibition without feelings of the deepest anxiety. . . . As a member of the Union,

I declare my conviction that no tenable ground has been assigned for a dissolution of the ties which bind every American citizen to his country; and impartial history will so decide."[11]

In his inaugural address on Monday, March 4, 1861, President Lincoln tried to assure the South that he had no intention of interfering with slavery in the states where it presently existed. And he repeated what President Jackson had declared about the indivisibility of the Union. No state, he insisted, may assume the right to separate itself from the others.[12] But this statement contradicted what he had said as a one-term member of the House of Representatives back in 1848. "Any people, anywhere, being inclined and having the power," he contended from the House floor, "have the right to rise up, and shake off the existing government, and form a new one that suits them better. This is a most valuable—a most sacred right—a right which we hope and believe, is to liberate the world."[13]

He thought differently in 1861 as he tried desperately to hold the Union together. As President, he had no choice but to enforce the laws, and that duty included maintaining federal property within the seceded states. His decision to provision Fort Sumter in Charleston harbor prompted the Confederates to attack the fort and force its surrender on April 12. And thus began the Civil War.

On April 15, Lincoln summoned the 37th Congress to meet in special session on July 4, and he called for 75,000 volunteers to defend the Union. In the absence of Congress, he exercised his powers as commander in chief and expanded the military, authorized the purchase of armament and suspended the writ of habeas corpus in Florida and Maryland. He also directed the states to increase the size of their militias to help in the struggle. By the summer of 1861, the Union had 186,000 men under arms. Similarly, President Davis summoned southerners to defend their homeland and within a few months some 112,000 recruits responded to his call.

Once fighting broke out, four states of the upper South joined the original seven states of the lower South and seceded from the Union: Virginia on April 17, Arkansas on May 6, Tennessee on May 7 and North Carolina on May 20. Normally, Virginia would send fourteen representatives to the House, Arkansas two and North Carolina eight. Tennessee usually sent ten, but in 1861 only three members were elected from the strongly loyal districts of the state, and they took their seats at various times in 1861, 1862 and 1863. Four other slave states—Delaware, Maryland, Kentucky and Missouri—remained loyal to the Union, despite strong sentiment for the Confederacy in sections of those states and determined efforts by some to provoke secession.

When Virginia seceded, the Confederate government moved its capital to Richmond. In short order rebel soldiers began to appear within sight of Washington.

Terror gripped the city. At any moment the rebels might cross the

Potomac River and seize the nation's capital. It was a frightening and very real possibility. Fortunately, a rush call for help brought five companies of soldiers from Pennsylvania, comprising a force of 476 "unarmed and ununiformed" officers and men.[14] They arrived in Washington at six o'clock on the evening of April 18, 1861. One young soldier, Curtis Clay Pollock, a nineteen-year-old private in Captain James Wren's Washington Artillerists, wrote to his mother about their experience in Baltimore. At the time, Maryland teetered toward secession, and sympathetic demonstrations for the Confederacy occurred regularly. "We were met by an immense crowd and the whole force of the city police (about 200). We had two miles to go to the depot where the Washington train started from. We were hissed and hooted and called all manner of hard names and the people were hurrahing for Jeff Davis and the Confederacy. It would have taken very little to raise a row but we had no arms and we did not say anything to them."[15] Bricks, rocks and other missiles were hurled at them, and several soldiers were injured. When they reached Washington, to their great delight, they found the streets crowded with people who cheered their arrival. They marched straight to the Capitol, mounted the steps and found quarters among the many rooms and corridors of the newly built House chamber in the south wing.

Another soldier, with the unlikely name of Nicholas Biddle, was struck on the head with a rock thrown by a secessionist in Baltimore.[16] When he reached the Rotunda of the Capitol he removed his cap, exposing a blood-soaked handkerchief. As he marched to the House chamber he left behind a trail of blood spots on the floor. He was immediately hailed as "the first man to spill blood for the Union in the war."[17]

After these soldiers found their quarters, they were marched to the basement of the Capitol to receive the new Springfield rifles. To their amazement, President Lincoln, Secretary of State William H. Seward and Secretary of War Simon Cameron were present during this operation, and Lincoln personally walked down the lines and shook hands with all the company members.[18] The following day the Massachusetts Sixth Regiment, the first fully equipped unit to respond to Lincoln's call for troops, marched into town and took over the Senate chamber. These troops were joined a week later by the New York Seventh Regiment. Thousands of barrels of flour, seized at Georgetown, were placed in the windows and corridors of the Capitol as a barricade. The basement of the building provided space for kitchens and ad hoc cooking areas to feed this occupying army, and the men bedded down temporarily in both chambers of Congress, the corridors and the galleries.[19]

"Several thousand more troops arrived yesterday," Thomas Walter, the architect of the Capitol, wrote his wife; "—the city swarms with them; they say there are 30,000 here—There are 4,000 in the Capitol, with all their

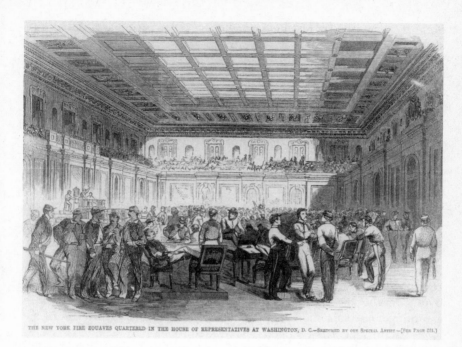

THE NEW YORK FIRE ZOUAVES QUARTERED IN THE HOUSE OF REPRESENTATIVES AT WASHINGTON, D. C.—SKETCHED BY OUR SPECIAL ARTIST.—[SEE PAGE 201.]

With the outbreak of the Civil War and the threat of invasion of the capital by Confederate forces in Virginia, Union soldiers were quartered in the halls of Congress.

provisions, ammunition, and baggage, and the smell is awful—The building is like one grand water closet—every hole and corner is defiled—one of the Capitol police says there are cart loads of ____ in the dark corners. Mr. Denham says in one of the water closets rooms where he made an attempt to step in, some 200 at least must have used the floor. . . . It is sad to see the defacement of the building every where. These are nasty things to talk to a lady about, but ladies ought to know what vile uses the most elegant things are devoted to in times of war."[20]

SINCE ALL ATTENTION in Washington was focused on the prosecution of the war, there was little interest or enthusiasm in continuing the building program of the Capitol—especially the dome, which was incomplete. The architect, Thomas Walter, hoped to see the work continued but Montgomery Meigs ordered a shutdown. And Secretary of War Simon Cameron informed the construction company of Janes, Fowler, Kurtland & Company on May 17, 1861, that further payment for the dome was suspended until the country's finances improved. Since a small fortune in building materials lay scattered around the construction site, the idea of abandoning tons of iron to the vagaries of weather and scavengers seemed ludicrous. The company therefore decided on its own to continue the construction with the hope that Congress would eventually pay for the work once it was completed and the war brought to a successful end.

But Lincoln interceded. On April 16, 1862, he directed the resumption of construction of the dome and transferred oversight of the building from the overburdened War Department to the Department of the Interior, by which order Walter regained his authority to supervise the project. It was a significant gesture during the height of the Civil War, and perhaps the President sensed the importance of and need for completing this gigantic structure. After all, its imposing presence could be seen clear across the Potomac in Virginia so that civilian and military Confederates could view this symbol of the Union to which they once belonged.

THE SPECIAL SESSION of the 37th Congress summoned by the President convened on July 4, 1861, a bright and sunny day. With most representatives from the seceded states gone, the Republicans had little difficulty in assuming control. Democrats were in a distinct minority. The clerk of the House, John W. Forney, rapped the crowded room to order, and the chaplain, the Reverend Thomas H. Stockton, delivered a prayer asking God to correct the "erroneous views" of their departed brethren. Then the clerk read President Lincoln's message to Congress, in which he defended his actions in suspending the writ of habeas corpus. Although he felt he had the right to expand his powers under the Constitution, he assured the members "that nothing has been done beyond the constitutional competency of Congress," and he expressed confidence that the legislature would "ratify" the extraordinary measures he had taken.[21]

Representative Clement Vallandigham carried on a prolonged and futile fight against Lincoln's acts of "usurpation," and ten days later introduced seven resolutions censuring the President for the suppression of freedom of speech and the press, the suspension of the writ of habeas corpus and the establishment of a naval blockade, among others, but by voice vote the House quickly dispatched the resolutions by laying them on the table.[22]

After hearing the President's message, the House chose Emerson Etheridge of Tennessee as the new clerk, "in compliment to his fidelity and courage as a Union man" from a state that had seceded, and elected Galusha A. Grow of Pennsylvania as Speaker, thereby ending "any hope of sectional reconciliation."[23] Radical in his views about slavery, Grow was a six-foot two-inch combative shaft of determination, as well as witty, energetic and a highly skilled parliamentarian. To an overflowing crowd of spectators in the galleries who roared approval throughout his opening address as Speaker, he cried, "No flag alien to the sources of the Mississippi

The notorious copperhead, Clement Vallandigham, persisted in attacking President Lincoln on the House floor for suspending habeas corpus and free speech.

River will ever float permanently over its mouth till its waters are crimsoned in human gore; and no one foot of American soil can ever be wrenched from the jurisdiction of the Constitution of the United States until it is baptised in fire and blood. If the republic is to be dismembered and the sun of liberty must go out in endless night, let it set amid the roar of cannon and the din of battle, when there is no longer an arm to strike or a heart to bleed in its cause."[24]

Speaker Grow promptly filled the committees with party stalwarts, most notably, Thaddeus Stevens of Pennsylvania, who was appointed chairman of the Ways and Means Committee, and Elihu Washburne, named chairman of the Committee on Commerce. Five days later, Stevens reported out a bill authorizing the secretary of the treasury, Salmon P. Chase, to borrow $250 million over the next twelve months. To obtain almost immediate approval for the bill, he asked for and obtained a suspension of the rules and the limiting of debate to only one hour. Before the special session adjourned on August 6, it passed sixty-six bills, all but four of which related to the war. This record of productivity would continue into the second and third sessions of the 37th Congress.[25]

Stevens quickly emerged as the most powerful member of the House, not only because of his chairmanship of Ways and Means and control of all budgetary matters, which automatically made him the party's floor manager, but also because of the skill and deftness with which he maneuvered quick passage of vital legislation. Clubfooted, stern-faced, topped by an ill-fitting and unattractive black wig, he looked frightening, almost sinister. Never "tender-hearted, winning or conciliatory," as Noah Brooks, a newspaper man, wrote, Stevens was "argumentative, sardonic, and grim."[26] "He had the reputation," agreed James G. Blaine, "of being somewhat unscrupulous as to political methods, somewhat careless in personal conduct, somewhat lax in personal morals; but to the one great object of his life, the destruction of slavery and the elevation of the slave, he was supremely devoted." His wit and sharp and vicious tongue were his most potent weapons. Much like John Randolph at the beginning of the century, Stevens terrorized colleagues; but "Randolph in his braggart prime," declared Perley Poore, "was never so imperiously insulting as was Mr. Stevens toward those whose political action he controlled."

Clearly, as Poore reported, Stevens "was the despotic ruler of the House."[27] Conscious of his own lack of financial knowledge, Stevens delegated considerable responsibility in his committee to capable colleagues. He relied most especially on Elbridge G. Spaulding of New York, a banker, who headed the banking subcommittee, and Justin Morrill of Vermont, who handled tariff matters.[28]

A superb parliamentarian, Stevens commanded the floor whenever he chose; he limited debate on legislation; and he called for a vote as soon as he decided enough had been said. After all, he argued, it was wartime and appropriation bills had to be enacted swiftly so that the military could be properly financed. Under his direction, the army was reorganized, the navy enlarged, direct taxes levied, and the tariff revised. Although Stevens differed with Lincoln on several issues—ending slavery, for example, or finding more aggressive generals to defeat the Confederacy—he did work effectively with the administration, especially Secretary of the Treasury Salmon Chase, to provide whatever the President needed to prosecute the war.

In addition to Stevens, there were a number of other able Republican representatives, including Elihu B. Washburne of Illinois; Sam Hooper, Alexander H. Rice and John B. Allen of Massachusetts; Roscoe Conkling of New York; and William D. Kelley of Pennsylvania. And, of course, Grow

Thaddeus Stevens could be as mean as he looks here when debating slaveholders or fighting for the rights of freedmen and the underprivileged.

was a potent force in all House affairs. On the Democratic side there were John J. Crittenden, the veteran of Kentucky, and Clement I. Vallandigham and S. S. Cox of Ohio. They struggled long and hard to block critical Republican initiatives that they felt impinged on liberty.

LIKE LINCOLN, MANY members of Congress believed the war could be swiftly fought and won. One sudden and unexpected blow against the rebel capital in Virginia might bring a quick end to the fighting. So, yielding to pressure, the President agreed to order Major General Irvin McDowell, who had thirty thousand men in Washington, to march toward Richmond, even though these troops had not yet been properly organized or trained. Moreover, the three-month term of enlistment was about to expire for many of these soldiers, so they were anxious to leave the capital and return home.

The event became a celebration of sorts. Washingtonians decided to trail behind the army and watch them annihilate the rebels. They were joined by congressmen and journalists and visitors. But what they witnessed came as a rude shock. On July 21, the Union army met the Confederate force of about twenty-two thousand commanded by General Pierre Beauregard at Manassas Junction, a little town on Bull Run, or creek, about thirty-five miles southwest of Washington. At first they seemed to carry the day. But Confederate reinforcements arrived and the Union troops were thoroughly routed. The shattered, disorganized and ill-trained army rushed headlong back to the capital, colliding with panic-stricken civilians who witnessed the devastating disaster and were attempting to get out of harm's way as fast as possible.[29]

After another defeat on October 21 at Ball's Bluff, close to Washington, some of the most extreme Republicans, known as Radical Republicans, led by Senators Benjamin Wade of Ohio and Zachariah Chandler of Michigan and Representative Thaddeus Stevens, demanded an implacable, uncompromising prosecution of the war against the rebellious South and an end to slavery. As a result, the Joint Committee on the Conduct of the War, approved on December 9, 1861, a week after the 37th Congress convened for its first regular session, was given broad investigatory power to send for persons and papers and sit during sessions of both houses of Congress. It was composed of three senators (Chandler, Wade and Andrew Johnson, a Unionist Democrat from Tennessee)[30] and four representatives chosen by Speaker Grow (George W. Julian of Indiana, Daniel W. Gooch of Massachusetts, John Covode of Pennsylvania and Moses Odell, a Democrat from New York), chaired by Wade and dominated by Radical Republicans. None of these men had military experience and all shared a distrust, if not a disdain, of the military.[31]

The committee investigated the War Department for allegations of fraud and incompetence, delved into government security, including rumors that Mary Lincoln was a Confederate spy, and harassed the President over his reluctance to support immediate emancipation and his failure to bring the war to a speedy and successful end. It was "a mischievous organization, which assumed dictatorial powers. Summoning generals before them, and having a phonographer to record every word uttered, they would propound very comprehensive questions," such as "what do you know about war?" Some of these generals "scolded and carped and criticised and caviled, told half truths and solid lies, and the August and astute Committee listened with open ears."[32] In the course of its history it issued eight volumes of reports on military defeats and provided documentation that severely damaged the military reputation of General George B. McClellan, whom the committee thoroughly loathed.[33] The members of the joint committee met with Lincoln and his cabinet on January 6, 1862, only to learn "that neither the President nor his advisors seemed to have any definite information respecting the management of the war, or the failure of our forces to make any forward movement."[34]

And thus began once again a struggle between the legislature and the executive to control national policy. There were strong, determined and purposeful men in both the House and Senate intent on having an important voice in deciding important issues; and there was a strong, determined and purposeful man in the White House who resisted such interference. Each side felt it had the right and duty to prosecute the war in a particular manner. Each side came to feel that the other side was a hindrance in ending the war successfully and saving the Union.

With the cost of the war rising to nearly $2 million a day, the House passed the legal tender bill on February 6, 1862, authorizing the issuance of "greenbacks" as legal tender, the first paper currency ever issued by the national government. Andrew Jackson must have turned in his grave. The Senate gave its approval on February 25. Then, on April 16, Congress abolished slavery in the District of Columbia with compensation to those who would free their slaves. In the House, Stevens adroitly pushed through a resolution disallowing amendments and limiting debate to one minute. As Elihu Washburne explained, "If gentlemen of the other side offer amendments, let us hear them, and then vote them down." The bill passed the House, 92 to 38, on April 11, supported by all the Republicans and a handful of northern Democrats and border-state Unionists.[35]

Thus, at long last, and after decades of angry debate and violence, the Congress had finally broken the southern slave system. And Republicans rejoiced. "A few of the radical members indulged in excessive and quite undignified manifestations of this delight," sneered one critic, "hurrahing in the corridors, and seizing every negro they met and overwhelming them with congratulations."[36] Others hoped that Lincoln would veto the measure. Indeed the President rather disliked any emancipation legislation to affect the district without the approval of the residents. He also feared that the legislation had been rushed through Congress to force him to take a stand on the question. But, after a short delay, he did sign the bill on April 16. Later Congress abolished slavery in the territories without compensation.

The following month, on May 20, 1862, the Homestead Act was passed, by which 160 acres of public land were given to those who would reside on and farm the land for five years. This act made it possible for some twenty-five thousand settlers to stake claims to more than 3 million acres of land before the war ended. Likewise, the Morrill Land Grant College Act passed on June 17, providing 30,000 acres to each member of Congress to finance public agricultural and mechanical colleges within the states and territories. The U.S. Internal Revenue Act of 1862, passed on July 1, established taxes on just about everything imaginable, most of which did not survive the war. But the Bureau of Internal Revenue, created by this act, did become a permanent fixture in the government. Also on that date, President Lincoln signed the Pacific Railroad Act, which granted land and funds to corporations to organize and build what would become a transcontinental railroad from Omaha, Nebraska, to Sacramento, California.

The summer of 1862 witnessed a series of major defeats for the Union army. The Seven Days battle brought an end to the Virginia Peninsula campaign. At the Second Battle of Bull Run in late August, the Union army suffered another humiliating rout and beat a hasty and confused retreat to Washington, whereupon General Robert E. Lee led his Confederate forces across the Potomac River into northern territory. And although the struggle at Murfreesboro, Tennessee, provided a Union victory, it was the deadliest battle of the war with casualties running to twenty thousand on both sides.

There was genuine fear that these military disasters and the loss of so many lives could result in a Democratic victory at the polls in the 1862 midterm election. Besides, Lincoln's failure to emancipate the slaves brought heightened demands that he do something about it. Radicals were particularly vociferous. Lincoln was "nothing better than a wet rag," stormed William Lloyd Garrison, who found the President's policies "stumbling, halting, prevaricating, irresolute."[37] More moderate Republicans preferred to stand behind Lincoln, support his efforts to end the war and let him decide in good time on emancipation.

In the ongoing political struggle, slavery had become the defining issue. War Democrats accepted the goal of Union through military means, yet they opposed emancipation. If they favored emancipation they usually switched parties and joined the Republicans. Peace Democrats, on the other hand, argued for reunion through negotiation but like the War Democrats denounced emancipation. Anti-abolitionists to a man, they blamed the Republicans for provoking the South into seceding.[38]

By this time Lincoln had decided to free the slaves. Although the military fighting at Antietam Creek in Maryland on September 17 ended in a draw, General Lee pulled back to Virginia, allowing the administration to claim victory. With this "victory," Lincoln issued a preliminary Emancipation Proclamation in which he would free all slaves as of January 1, 1863, in Confederate areas still in rebellion against the United States. "I wish it were a better time," he told his cabinet. "I wish that we were in a better condition. The action of the army against the rebels has not been quite what I should have best liked."[39] Even so, he claimed victory, which allowed him to go forward and issue the Emancipation Proclamation. Two days after the preliminary proclamation he announced that at his discretion the writ of habeas corpus could be suspended anywhere in the United States.

Nevertheless, the election of 1862 did indeed produce sizable Democratic gains in Congress. They picked up 28 seats and now had an aggregate of 72 in the House. But the Republicans, who had lost several seats, still retained control with a total of 86, augmented by the presence of 25 members of the Unionist party. Still, frightened Republicans regarded the election as "a great, sweeping revolution of public sentiment."[40]

Since the spring of 1862, Union military forces had controlled two of the four congressional districts in Louisiana. As a result, Benjamin F. Flanders and Michael Hahn presented their credentials of election to the House on December 19 and 22, 1862, respectively. By a House resolution of February 17, 1863, they were permitted to take their seats. Hahn claimed his seat on February 17, and Flanders on February 23.

Encouraged by the electoral results, the Peace Democrats began a systematic attack on the administration and its policies, particularly over the suspension of habeas corpus and the jailing of dissenters. On the House floor they howled their opposition to this "imperial military despotism." Clement Vallandigham, in a fiery speech on February 23, denounced Lincoln's tyrannical rule. As a staunch patriot, "undismayed, unseduced, unterrified, and heedless of the miserable cry of disloyalty," he insisted that he was morally justified in pillorying the President and all his works.[41]

Called "Copperheads" by their opponents because they wore "copperpenny" badges to signify their conciliatory attitude toward the South, these Peace Democrats actively engaged in antiadministration activities that eventually discredited their cause. When the Confederates inflicted one of the worst Union defeats of the war at Fredericksburg, Virginia, on December 13, 1862, these Copperheads demanded to know how much longer such butchery would go on.

Immediately after the Emancipation Proclamation took effect on Janu-

ary 1, 1863, Stevens managed the passage of a bill in the House for the re-
cruitment of 150,000 black soldiers. In responding to his critics who worried
about arming black men, he thundered, "Yes, there is a God . . . , an avenging God, who is now punishing the sins of this nation for the wicked wrongs
which for centuries we have inflicted upon a blameless race and which
many of you wish to make perpetual. I will say to my colleagues, and to
those who believe in divine retribution, what I have before said; 'Hasten to
do justice and stay the sword of the avenging angel.' "[42]

To assist and direct the war effort, Congress passed the Conscription
Act on March 3, 1863, the final day of the 37th Congress, by which all men
between the ages of twenty and thirty-five were subject to a draft. But it
exempted those who paid a commutation fee of $300 or hired a substitute
to enlist for three years. Conscription had never been an American choice
in providing troops to fight a war, at least not without strong vocal opposition. And such opposition exploded in the draft riots in New York City in
July 1863, violence that actually masked a race riot.[43]

To add to the dismay of those who feared government suppression of
individual rights, Thaddeus Stevens introduced a habeas corpus bill in the
House, giving the President the authority, at his discretion, to suspend the
writ for the duration of the war. It passed in March 1863. Over the next
several years there were military arrests and repeated violations of constitutional rights.

Vallandigham, who had failed to win reelection in 1862, gave a political speech in Mount Vernon, Ohio, on May 1, 1863, in which he contended
that the war could have been concluded by negotiation but that the administration needlessly prolonged the bloodshed in order to liberate blacks and
enslave whites. Accused of advocating resistance to the Lincoln administration and expressing sympathy for the enemy, he was arrested, denied the
privilege of habeas corpus, tried by a military commission and found guilty
of disloyal opinions. He was sentenced to prison for the duration of the war
under General Order No. 38. But Lincoln commuted the sentence and ordered Vallandigham escorted to the Confederacy.

Although Confederate arms won a stunning victory over Union forces
that were twice their size at the Battle of Chancellorville in early May 1863,
the war began to turn against them. General Ulysses S. Grant captured
Vicksburg, Mississippi, in July, slicing the Confederacy in two, and Lee's
invasion of the North was turned back at Gettysburg, Pennsylvania. Most
important, as it subsequently turned out, Lincoln had at last found in Ulysses
S. Grant a general who could win battles and bring the war to an end.[44]

IN THE HOUSE there were the usual political battles, but also, strangely, a
wedding in the spring of 1863. Miss Elida Ramsey and Mr. John Fowler were
members of the choir that "led the singing in the House of Representatives

for the religious services held in the House during the old war days." As far as anyone knew, it was "the only bridal ceremony ever conducted within the walls of the legislative chamber."[45]

The wedding was a bright note in an otherwise gloomy, war-weary Capitol. The building itself was, at the time, undergoing extensive changes. Despite the war and its enormous financial drain, Thaddeus Stevens regularly permitted bills to go forward to pay for the completion of the majestic dome of the Capitol. Progress had been slow because of engineering difficulties, especially in making certain the old Rotunda could support the massive weight of the new dome. Furthermore, Walter had redesigned the structure in 1859 to provide for both an inner and outer dome, and the inner one allowed him to conceal the extensive ironworks and supporting masonry of the outer dome and provide an enlarged "eye" to a gigantic canopy suspended between the two domes that stretched sixty-five feet in diameter.

Then he invited Constantino Brumidi, who migrated to this country in 1855 after a career in Rome working at the Vatican and several Roman palaces, to paint a fresco on the eye of the concave canopy. Brumidi started painting the fresco as soon as the dome had been completed, and finished it eleven months later. Entitled *The Apotheosis of Washington*, the fresco depicts the first President rising into the heavens, surrounded by figures representing Liberty and Victory. A rainbow arches under his feet, and he is flanked by thirteen females representing the thirteen original states. Six scenes with figures representing agriculture, mechanics, commerce, science, war and marine decorate the perimeter of the canopy. These figures are up to 15 feet tall in order to allow anyone on the floor to identify them. A master of illusion, Brumidi was able to give the impression of three-dimensional figures floating in space on an area that covers 4,664 square feet, 180 feet above the floor.[46]

To complete this magnificent structure it was decided to erect an enormous statue representing Freedom at the top of the outer dome. Thomas Crawford, an American sculptor working in Rome, was commissioned in 1855 to provide the figure. What he produced was a nineteen-foot six-inch classical bronze female figure in flowing robes with her right hand resting on the hilt of a sheathed sword and her left hand holding a laurel wreath and a U.S. shield with thirteen stripes. She wears a crested Roman helmet,[47] encircled with stars, and composed of an eagle's head, feathers and talons like a Native American headdress. The figure stands on a cast-iron globe with the words *E Pluribus Unum* inscribed upon it.

The final section of the *Statue of Freedom* was bolted into place on top of the new Capitol dome on December 2, 1863. There was little ceremony to mark the occasion, which is exactly what Walter wanted. After consulting with the War Department, he agreed to have a battery of artillery at the

The Apotheosis of Washington, *the fresco painted on the inner dome of the Rotunda by Constantino Brumidi.*

Capitol fire a thirty-five-round salute, one for each state. At a quarter past twelve, with the statue securely anchored on its pedestal, Charles F. Thomas, the Capitol's chief machinist, raised an American flag over its head and the booming artillery announced the triumphant conclusion of a magnificent work of classical grandeur.[48] By its imposing size and beauty, the completed Capitol seemed to proclaim to the world the permanence of the American Union.

Walter told his wife, "I have succeeded in putting on the head of the statue without accident. Her ladyship looks placid and beautiful—much better than I expected. There was an immense crowd to witness the operation, and everything was done with propriety and dignity."[49]

THE GLORY OF the new dome was also viewed by the members of the 38th Congress when they convened on December 7, 1863. They felt emotionally uplifted by the imposing structure. Then, unexpectedly, House members found themselves "in a state of Revolution"—a political revolution, reported Republican Henry L. Dawes of Massachusetts to his wife. Throughout the war, party lines in many states regularly fluctuated. Among Democrats there was a split between those who supported the war and those who demanded peace. Border-state Unionists were divided between those who favored and those who condemned Lincoln. And Republicans separated into Radicals and Moderates depending on their goals and loyalty toward the administration.

The House in the 38th Congress reflected these splits, and rumors started flying that the acting clerk, Emerson Etheridge of Tennessee, a southern Unionist, would attempt to take advantage of the situation and execute a coup by invalidating the credentials of several Republican congressmen to form a coalition of Democrats and border-state Unionists who would then organize and control the House.[50]

Republicans had enacted a bill on March 3, 1863, the last day of the 37th Congress, that directed the clerk to place on the roll only the names of those individuals whose credentials proved "they were regularly elected in accordance with the laws of their States respectively, or the laws of the United States." Their object, of course, was to deny the seating of "bogus members," as they called anyone elected from rebel states. But the act failed to bar those members from Union-controlled areas of the Confederacy.[51] This seeming oversight may have occurred so that Republicans could admit such representatives from the South as necessary in case their votes were needed to keep the House under their control.

The rumors that Etheridge would attempt to use this statute to bring about a coalition of Democrats and border-state Unionists alerted Republicans to take action, and they held a caucus on Sunday, December 6, the day before the House convened. At the caucus it was decided that if Etheridge excluded Republican members-elect, Thaddeus Stevens would make a motion to place Elihu Washburne of Illinois in the chair as Speaker pro tem. Once Washburne mounted the chair, the regular organization of the House would ensue and Republican certificates of election recognized. A committee was also formed at the caucus, consisting of Stevens, Henry Winter Davis of Maryland, Frederick A. Pike of Maine, freshman James A. Garfield of Ohio and Henry L. Dawes of Massachusetts, to counteract the attempted coup. Later that day, Dawes and Pike visited Etheridge in the hope of dissuading him from his intended action. The clerk tried to allay their fears but their suspicions remained. Meanwhile, President Lincoln summoned Schuyler Colfax of Indiana, the Republican nominee for Speaker in place of Galusha Grow, who had been defeated in the 1862 election, to the White House and instructed him "to be sure to have all our men there. . . . Let our men organize the House."[52]

The House session began before galleries packed with people waiting to see what Etheridge would do. And he did not disappoint them. He rose and announced that he would call the roll of those members "whose credentials show that they have been regularly elected in accordance with the laws of the States respectively, and with the laws of the United States." Whereupon he excluded sixteen Republican representatives from the border states of Maryland, Missouri and West Virginia (which had seceded from the Confederate state of Virginia on June 11, 1861, and was admitted to the Union on June 20, 1863), and the states of Kansas (admitted January 29, 1861) and Oregon (admitted February 14, 1859). Then, to the shock of some, he read the names of three representatives from Louisiana elected by a conservative faction in that state.[53]

Stevens rose from his seat. "If the Clerk has concluded the reading of the list which he proposes to read, I ask that, for the information of the House, he will now read the names which he has omitted to call."

Etheridge turned and stared at Stevens. "The Clerk asks first to be indulged in reading the names of the Delegates from the Territories."[54]

"Certainly," Stevens responded.

When that formality ended, Stevens repeated his request. Etheridge insisted that the credentials of those individuals whose names he had not called, in his opinion, "did not show what they ought to have shown, according to the act of the 3rd of March, 1863." A Democrat then asked that the act in question be read. The clerk obliged, "looking half defiantly to the Administration side" of the House. The climax to this contest came when Dawes proposed that the names of the excluded Maryland members be read. A Democrat protested that the motion was out of order and moved that it be tabled. Then Etheridge made a colossal mistake in carrying out his "Revolution." He ruled that the motion was in order, and he did so with the intention of giving Cox and his Democratic allies the opportunity to show the overwhelming voting strength of the Democratic-border-state coalition.[55]

But Cox failed to deliver. The vote to table Dawes's motion was defeated, 94 to 74. Curiously, the victory for the Republicans was provided by five Democrats and six border-state Unionists who voted with the majority, clearly demonstrating the superior organizing skills of the Republicans. Then, in swift succession, the names of the excluded members were read and the roll call completed, followed by the election of Schuyler Colfax as Speaker by a wide margin over S. S. Cox and two other conservative candidates, and Edward McPherson as clerk over Etheridge, who received all the opposition votes.[56]

It was a close call. Republicans were not about to lose control of the House, and they breathed a sigh of relief when Colfax mounted the Speaker's rostrum.

Schuyler Colfax! At this stage of his career Colfax was generally popular with his colleagues, brimming over with affability and graciousness, and always ready to help "friend or foe alike."[57] But his excellent traits did not last long. He proved to be an incompetent presiding officer, and was later described by his critics as a "miserable popinjay, charlatan, and small potato demagogue."[58] He soon revealed to all, both members of the House and the American people, that he was a scoundrel and a crook.

WITH THE CONTINUED success of Union forces on the battlefield during the spring and summer of 1863—Vicksburg, May 18–July 4, 1863; Gettysburg, July 1–3, 1863; and Chattanooga, August 21, 1863—Lincoln issued a Proclamation of Amnesty and Reconstruction on December 8, 1863. This proclamation proposed that when 10 percent of those persons in the seceded states who voted in the presidential election of 1860 swore an oath of loyalty to the United States, they might then form a government without slavery, which he would recognize, and reestablish themselves within the Union. This relatively mild plan of reconstruction of the seceded states met with stiff opposition from Radical Republicans, who firmly believed that Congress must administer the restitution of the Union, not the President.

And they made their opinions public when the 38th Congress assembled. Once the House and Senate completed their respective organizations, the battle with the executive branch was renewed, only this time the Radicals swore they would have much more control of reconstruction than they presently exercised in fighting the war.

As Speaker, Schuyler Colfax was accused of presiding "in rather a slap-dash-knock-'em-down-auctioneer style."

In other legislative areas the Republicans turned out a raft of important measures. Stevens's Ways and Means Committee proposed to raise the tariff to an average of 47 percent and to impose taxes of 5 percent on incomes starting at $600 and rising to 10 percent on incomes over $5,000. It also called for excise taxes (the first since Jefferson ended them) on a long list of products. All these recommendations were approved. The National Banking Act, initially passed in March 1863, was expanded and required national banks to invest one-third of their capital in U.S. securities. It was not a national banking system, as such, but a device to raise money to finance the war.

Many of the measures recommended by Ways and Means favored the nation's wealthiest. The war generated a rapid expansion of the North's industrial might. Fierce competition developed among industrialists, bankers, manufacturers, investors and farmers in a wide array of endeavors, such as railroads, steel, oil, meat packing, textiles, flour mills and munitions. They also competed to gain favor in Congress, especially in the awarding of contracts and land grants. Lobbyists were increasingly employed to serve the interests of these entrepreneurs and found many congressmen of both parties only too happy to cooperate in "sweetheart arrangements" for a financial consideration. Since the Republican Party controlled Congress, that party became "an increasingly corrupt instrument."[59] Bribes and secret deals were not uncommon, and conflict of interest was rampant.

There were a number of "field-days" in the House during the 38th Congress when attempts were made to censure or expel some of the more fiery Copperheads. On one occasion Speaker Colfax left the chair and, amid "a profound silence" in the chamber, offered a resolution to expel Alexander Long of Ohio, who said he favored acknowledging the independence of the Confederacy. While debate over this expulsion proceeded, another Peace Democrat, Benjamin G. Harris of Maryland, announced his agreement with Long and said that peace could only be achieved by recognizing the rebel states. "There was a general outcry from the Union members," reported one journalist, whereupon Harris shouted, "The South asks you to let them alone; but no, you say you will bring them into subjection; that is not yet done, and God Almighty grant that it may never be; I trust you will never subjugate the South."

Instantly, the House collapsed into the "wildest confusion," with a score of members shouting for recognition. Finally, the stentorian voice of Elihu Washburne of Illinois could be heard demanding Harris's expulsion. So now there were two such motions. Then came a third. Fernando Wood of New York, who had succeeded to the leadership of the Peace Democrats in the 38th Congress after Vallandigham's defeat, said that if Long were expelled, he should go with him, as he endorsed every word that the Ohio representative had uttered. At this, Washburne, "pale with rage," shook his fist at Wood and shouted, "We'll put you out, too."

But the two-thirds vote necessary for expulsion could not be obtained, so Long and Harris were merely censured by a vote of 93 to 18.[60]

Elsewhere in the country the real war continued its relentless pace. With the victory at Vicksburg, General Grant was shifted to the east and took up command of Union forces in Virginia. On May 5, 1864, he began his monthlong Wilderness campaign. At about the same time, General William T. Sherman set out with a hundred thousand troops from Chattanooga and began his invasion of Georgia, heading for Atlanta.

AS THE WAR began its long-drawn-out conclusion, another presidential election intervened. There was no question that the Republicans, including the most radical, would renominate Lincoln at their convention in Baltimore on June 7, 1864, but some were offended by the fact that Andrew Johnson, the loyalist military governor of Tennessee, was selected for Vice President on a National Union ticket in an effort to appeal to Democrats and symbolize the restoration of the Union. The Democratic Party, meeting in Chicago in late August, nominated the popular General George B. McClellan for President and George H. Pendleton of Ohio for Vice President.

The ongoing destruction of the Confederacy made it clear to Radical Republicans in both the House and Senate that a plan had to be enacted by Congress to restore the Union or forfeit all direction of reconstruction to the President. And they made their position absolutely clear on July 4, 1864, the last day of the congressional session, by maneuvering passage of the Wade-Davis bill. Representative Henry Winter Davis of Maryland, author of the bill along with Senator Ben Wade of Ohio, stated the position of the Radicals with great precision. "Until . . . Congress recognize a state government organized under its auspices," Davis thundered, "there is no government in the rebel states except the authority of Congress."[61] Lincoln, of course, presumed and acted upon the belief that he could direct reconstruction and had in fact already recognized Louisiana and Arkansas as being restored to the Union under his 10 percent plan. But when representatives from those two states appeared in Congress they were denied their seats.

Davis, throughout the debate over the Wade-Davis bill, regularly consulted with Stevens. "I called in the committee of Ways and Means room to see old Stevens," he wrote on one occasion. "Grim, savage, sarcastic, mordant as ever—living on brandy & opium to subdue perpetual pain & mocking at the powers that be in the most spicy way."[62]

Mordant or not, Stevens was an invaluable ally in gaining passage of the Wade-Davis bill in the House on May 4, 1864, by a vote of 73 to 49. The measure required that a majority—not 10 percent—of the electorate swear to past and present loyalty before they could form a government. It also demanded the abolishment of slavery, and decreed that no one could vote

Representative Henry Winter Davis of Maryland argued for a radical reconstruction of the South following the Civil War and sought to block Lincoln's more moderate efforts.

who held a state or Confederate office or carried arms against the United States.

After the bill passed Congress, Lincoln pocket vetoed it, stating in a proclamation that he was not committed to any single plan of reconstruction. He also denied that Congress had the authority to abolish slavery in the states. The Radicals responded by issuing the "Wade-Davis Manifesto," asserting the absolute authority of Congress in dealing with the rebellious states and instructing Lincoln to execute the laws of the country, not legislate them. His job was to put down rebellion, the document declared. Leave political reorganization to Congress.

Lincoln's political position was strengthened by the capture of Atlanta by General William T. Sherman and his Union forces on September 1, 1864, and he won reelection in November. The National Union Party had successfully brought together in support of Lincoln an electorate committed to the preservation of the United States as envisioned by the Founders. It was no mean achievement.

When Congress reconvened in December, the President asked the House to join the Senate in passing the 13th Amendment to the Constitution, which would end slavery throughout the United States. The Senate had passed it on April 8, the previous spring, by a vote of 38 to 6, which had been accompanied by a "faint rumble of applause."

How different in the House. When the vote on the amendment was called on January 31, 1865, in response to Lincoln's request, the galleries, corridors and lobbies were jammed. In the chamber sat Chief Justice Salmon P. Chase and Associate Justices Noah Swayne, Samuel Miller, Samuel Nelson and Stephen Field. There were also dozens of senators, several members of the cabinet and many ministers from foreign countries.

The roll call began, and as the clerk slowly read each name, groups of members gathered around anyone keeping a tally. A number of Copperheads surrounded Pendleton, and the expressions on their faces appeared "gloomy, black, and sour." When any member who was known to oppose the amendment changed his mind and voted "aye," a "clatter of applause, irrepressible and spontaneous, swept through the House." When the roll call ended, Speaker Colfax announced the result. His voice trembled as he cried out, "On the passage of the Joint Resolution to amend the Constitution of the United States the ayes have 119, the noes have 56. The constitutional majority of two-thirds having voted in the affirmative, the Joint Resolution has passed."

Suddenly the House burst into a storm of joyful shouts. "Strong men embraced each other with tears. The galleries and aisles were bristling with standing, cheering crowds. The air was stirred with a cloud of women's handkerchiefs waving and floating; hands were shaking; men threw their arms about each other's necks, and cheer after cheer, and burst after burst followed." Fully ten minutes elapsed before the House quieted and allowed Ebon C. Ingersoll of Illinois to move an adjournment "in honor of the sublime and immortal event."[63]

Of the 119 members who voted for the amendment, 10 were Democrats. And those 10 were essential to the final victory. Without them there would not have been a two-thirds majority as stipulated in the Constitution.

Outside the chamber cannons thundered a salute on Capitol Hill, announcing to one and all that slavery no longer existed in the United States, provided of course that three-fourths of the states agreed.[64]

Two weeks later something extraordinary happened. Since 1827 blacks had been officially banned from the House chamber. Then, on Sunday, Feb-

Unlike the Senate, the House celebrated the passage of the 13th Amendment to the Constitution, which abolished slavery, with loud cheers and applause.

ruary 12, 1865, an African-American preacher by the name of Henry Highland Garnet addressed a vast concourse of listeners. It was the first time in the history of the House of Representatives that a black man had spoken publicly, and his eloquence, according to the press, "thrilled" his audience. He begged Congress to extend freedom for black people, extend it from emancipation to full citizenship. "Emancipate," he cried. "Enfranchise. Educate, and give the blessings of the Gospel to every American citizen."[65]

To add to the jubilation, the House also decisively defeated a reintroduced Wade-Davis bill. And that action had great meaning. Clearly, Lincoln would continue to direct reconstruction, an intention articulated in his second inaugural on March 4, 1865, when he said, "With malice toward none, and charity for all . . . let us . . . bind up the nation's wounds."[66]

The day before the end of the 38th Congress, the House instituted an important change in its rules. Because of the tremendous workload placed on the Ways and Means Committee, and the worsening health of its chairman, Thaddeus Stevens, who wished relief, the House, on March 2, 1865, revised its rules and split the committee into three segments: Appropriations, Banking and Currency, and Ways and Means (revenue). Speaker Colfax named Justin Morrill to chair Ways and Means, and Theodore Pomeroy of New York to chair Banking and Currency. Stevens took over Appropriations.[67]

• • •

FINALLY, THE WAR ended. The killing stopped. At its conclusion, Washington was "delirious with gladness when General Grant came marching home" after accepting the surrender of General Robert E. Lee at Appomattox Court House. April 13 was a "day of general rejoicing. . . . The stars and stripes waved over the public and many of the private buildings. . . . As night came on . . . bonfires blazed in the streets, and fireworks lit up the sky. In the forts and camps around the city blazed huge bonfires, while the heavy siege guns thundered their joyful approval of peace."[68]

Then tragedy struck. The following day, April 14, 1865, at Ford's Theater, President Lincoln was assassinated by John Wilkes Booth. He had saved the Union, only to die before completing the task of reconstruction. Vice President Andrew Johnson succeeded him.

After lying in state at the White House for four days, the remains of the dead President were transferred to the Rotunda of the Capitol, escorted by an imposing military and civic procession. "The day was observed throughout the Union as one of fasting, humiliation and prayer." Lincoln had acquired such a complete "ascendancy over the public mind in the Loyal States," reported James G. Blaine, "that any policy matured and announced by him would have been accepted by the vast majority of his countrymen. But the same degree of faith could not attach to Mr. Johnson; although after the first shock of the assassination had subsided, there was a general revival of trust, or at least of hope, that the great work which had been so faithfully prosecuted for four years would be faithfully carried forward."[69]

With Johnson in the presidential office, Radical Republicans celebrated. He had been a member of the Joint Committee on the Conduct of the War, and no one had been more vociferous in his criticism of secessionists and those in the North who sympathized with them. Members of the joint committee exulted in the knowledge that their former colleague had achieved the presidency, and they invited him to attend their remaining meetings. Most Radicals convinced themselves that they could control him, and they returned home in a happy frame of mind when Congress adjourned on April 15.

But they could not have been more mistaken. With the final capitulation of all Confederate forces, President Johnson issued two proclamations providing for the reestablishment of loyal governments in the seceded states. Without summoning Congress into special session to assist in the process, he appointed provisional governors to call state conventions that were expected to nullify their secession ordinances, repudiate their Confederate debt and ratify the 13th Amendment. He granted amnesty to all except leading civil and military officers of the Confederacy and those owning more than $20,000 worth of property. Those exempted could apply directly to him for individual pardons. And only those with amnesty or pardons could participate in reconstructing the state.

It seemed obvious that Johnson was intent on completing reconstruction himself prior to the first meeting of the 39th Congress scheduled to convene in December, and that action only enraged the Radicals who were determined to have Congress dictate and direct the process.

From Philadelphia, Thaddeus Stevens wrote to Johnson: "I hope I may be excused for putting briefs on paper that I intended to say to you orally. Reconstruction is a delicate question. . . . It is a question for the Legislative power exclusively. . . . Better call an extra session than to allow many to think that the executive was approaching usurpation."[70] He also attempted to convince Johnson to abandon the wholesale pardoning of former rebels.

Stevens soon decided to confront the President face-to-face and tell him bluntly to back off. On November 29 he had a long interview with Johnson and assured him that the rank and file of the Union Party in Pennsylvania and most other northern states opposed the President's plan of reconstruction. If he, Johnson, persisted in executing his policy, warned Stevens, he could expect no support from Republicans in Congress.

Despite the congressman's arrogance in presuming to tell the President what he should or should not do, Johnson controlled his temper. Still, he would not yield. Instead, he appealed for harmony, arguing that the Union must be restored, that the country needed to be quieted as quickly as possible. But his words fell on deaf ears.

As he left the White House, Stevens knew that he must summon his Radical Republican friends to a caucus to plan their strategy to halt any further move by the President to reconstruct the South.[71]

A titanic collision was about to take shape between the executive and the legislative branches of the government, a collision that would disfigure the nation for generations to come.

9

Reconstruction, 1865–1877

ETURNING TO CONGRESS for the start of the 39th Congress in early December, 1865, the Union-Republicans were "in no mood to accept unconditionally the reconstruction policy that had been developed by the executive department of the Government." Even so, they had arrived at no "consensus" about an alternate plan. Most of them were simply "determined not to act precipitately on the reconstruction question, but to delay."[1]

Delay. That idea had already developed in the mind of Thaddeus Stevens when he summoned a secret caucus in Washington on Friday, December 1, of about twenty-five or thirty "of the most extreme radicals in Congress." His purpose in calling them together was to arrive at some "mutual understanding" of what they should do when the southerners appeared in the House to claim their seats. At the meeting Stevens recounted his interview with Johnson, assuring his colleagues that the President was "wedded to his own plan of reconstruction," and that they must act together "in spite of the President" and, if necessary, "to break entirely with him."

But these Radicals, most of whom now favored a complete transformation of southern society, not just emancipation, worried about what action the Senate might take. They feared that the upper chamber would admit the southern members from Johnson's reconstructed states when they appeared in Congress. To get around that danger the Radicals agreed to form a joint committee of Congress "to whom everything relating to the southern delegations and the treatment of the rebel states, should be referred"; and the resolution, they agreed, should include a provision that would prevent one house from admitting southern representatives without the consent of the other. It was then decided at this caucus that Stevens would present the resolution to the full Republican meeting scheduled for the next evening, December 2, 1865.[2]

When the Republican Conference assembled, all the Radicals were present, and one of them, Justin S. Morrill of Vermont, was elected chairman. A committee of seven, with Stevens as chair, was then appointed to consider what should be done about the southerners chosen to serve in Congress. In the committee Stevens promptly presented the resolution adopted the previous evening, but the more moderate members of the group failed to grasp its full significance and so the resolution was approved unanimously. Later the moderates realized their mistake. But it was too late. "The Union party in the House of Representatives had unanimously committed itself to the program of the radicals."[3]

Although the Union-Republican Party held a three-to-one majority over the Democrats in the House as Congress convened, 136 Republicans to 38 Democrats, both moderates and Radicals were concerned about representation in the House now that the slaves had been emancipated. The counting of persons in a census would enhance southern voting in both the House and the Electoral College by a considerable number now that the three-fifths of the slave population stipulation in the Constitution no longer applied. An alliance between the Democrats and the southerners might give them control of Congress.

So the seating of southerners in the 39th Congress became a matter of real concern, a concern that could be easily resolved by the clerk of the House, Edward McPherson. *Harper's New Monthly Magazine,* which was published prior to the opening of Congress, stated that "by law, the clerk of the preceding House of Representatives is to make out the roll of persons elected to that body, and only those whose names are on that roll can act until the House has been organized." Furthermore, Congress on July 2, 1862, had "prescribed that every member should take an oath containing this clause: 'I do solemnly swear that I have never voluntarily borne arms against the United States . . . ; that I have voluntarily given no aid, countenance, counsel, or encouragement to persons engaged in armed hostility thereto: . . . that I have never yielded a voluntary support to any pretended Government, Authority, Power, or Constitution, within the United States, hostile or inimical thereto.' " Surely no southerner from a seceded state could take that oath, the magazine commented. Moreover, it continued, would McPherson exercise his legal right of deciding upon the validity of the credentials submitted by southerners?[4]

Other newspapers conjectured about what the clerk might do, and it was generally expected that he would omit the names of the southern members-elect from the roll. To do otherwise would have effected a "*coup d'etat*." McPherson himself felt that the House itself must decide upon their claims, not the clerk.[5]

Without question it would be a dramatic scene when the southerners appeared in the chamber to claim their right to participate in the business of the House. President Johnson hoped that at least Horace Maynard, a loyal Unionist member from Tennessee, would be seated and thereby provide the precedent for seating all the other southern claimants.[6]

On Monday, December 4, 1865, the 39th Congress convened. It was a bright, balmy day and a huge crowd gathered at the Capitol to watch the historic proceedings. "There is no mistaking the Republican side of the House: there is such a placid, self-satisfied look upon the faces of the members, as much as to say, 'We have got it all in our own hands,' " reported Emily Edson Briggs, writing under the pen name "Olivia" for the *Philadelphia Press*.[7]

As the Republican members entered the chamber they were visibly annoyed to discover a scattering of southerners in the room from the supposedly reconstructed states of Louisiana, North Carolina and Tennessee who were ready to resume their positions as members of the House of Representatives, as if nothing had happened over the past four years. Resentment was rife. Further poisoning the atmosphere was the fact that new southern governments formed under the Johnson plan had established "black codes" by which freed slaves were denied their rights as freedmen and frequently bound to white masters to work without pay as though they were still slaves.

Stevens had already decided that the clerk, who would preside over the House until a Speaker was elected, would block the seating of any of these men from the seceded states by excluding them from the roll. And although McPherson had studied law in Stevens's office, owed his present position to Stevens's influence and regarded the Pennsylvania congressman as his mentor and idol, he had already determined on his own that the House must decide the question of who gets seated.[8]

The session got under way, and McPherson started the roll call. When he skipped over the name of Horace Maynard, who was present in the chamber, Maynard called out: "Mr. Clerk, I beg to say that in calling the roll of the members . . ."

That was as far as he got.

McPherson stopped reading. "The clerk will be compelled to object to any interruption of the call of the roll," he pontificated. Then he resumed reading the names on the roll.

"Does the Clerk decline to hear me?" Maynard angrily responded.

"I decline to have any interruption of the call of the roll."[9]

Maynard quieted for the moment. At the conclusion of the roll call,

Justin Morrill moved to elect the Speaker. Maynard interrupted again and his words registered his pent-up fury. He demanded that his name be added to the roll.

Shouts reverberated around the room. An uproar ensued. At this point Stevens jumped in and called for order, while the clerk declared he would not recognize any gentleman not on his list. According to the clerk's understanding, Tennessee was not yet back in the Union.

Now Democratic representative James Brooks of New York intervened. If Tennessee was not in the Union, he argued, how could Andrew Johnson be President? McPherson replied that he could explain his reasons, but Stevens waved him aside by stating that "it is not necessary. We know it all." Brooks pointed out that a Republican Congress had permitted two representatives from Louisiana to vote for Speaker the previous year. But now the names of the Louisiana delegation were excluded from the rolls. "Why this inconsistency of action?" he demanded.

Boos and catcalls echoed around the chamber. After more shouting and cries for order, the House chose to get on with its business and proceeded to reelect Schuyler Colfax as Speaker over James Brooks, 139 to 36, despite the fact that Colfax had already made an unenviable reputation for himself. He "presided in rather a slap-dash-knock-'em-down-auctioneer style, greatly at variance with the decorous dignity of his predecessors."[10]

Although Johnson declared the Union restored in his first message to Congress on December 4, Stevens asked for unanimous consent in the House for a resolution, as decided in caucus, for the establishment of a House-Senate Joint Committee of Fifteen on Reconstruction to report on whether the rebel states should be represented in Congress.[11] Failing to receive unanimous consent, Stevens moved a suspension of the rules, which carried. Under the operation of the previous question, debate was blocked and the resolution approved. Accordingly, the joint committee was created, consisting of nine members from the House and six from the Senate. And one important provision was included. Until the committee issued its report and was acted upon by Congress, "no member shall be received into either House from any of the said so-called confederate States."[12]

It only remained for the southerners to exit the chamber. They rose from their seats and quietly left the room.

On December 14, the Speaker chose a number of Radicals to sit on the joint committee with Stevens at their head, but not until December 21 did the president pro tem name the six Senate members.[13] On the whole, however, the committee was largely moderate in composition and chaired by Senator William P. Fessenden of Maine.[14] In the ensuing months, it heard testimony from an assortment of witnesses condemning Johnson's amnesty policy and claiming that if representatives from the South were readmitted "the condition of the freedmen would be very little better than that of the slaves."[15]

In a long, closely argued speech before the House on December 18, Thaddeus Stevens insisted that the Confederate states be treated as "conquered provinces," and that only Congress, with the approval of the President, should work out the terms by which the rebel states could be readmitted to the Union. "We have turned over, or are about to turn loose, four million slaves without a hut to shelter them or a cent in their pockets. The infernal laws of slavery have prevented them from acquiring an education, understanding the commonest laws of contract, or of managing the ordinary business of life. This Congress is bound to provide for them until they can take care of themselves. . . . If we fail in this great duty now, when we have the power, we shall deserve and receive the execration of history and of all future ages."[16]

In dealing with the South, Congress confronted a section of the country that lay in ruins: plantations devastated, billions of dollars in human "chattel" wiped out, transportation wrecked and its once great cities, such as Atlanta, in shambles. Confederate soldiers returned home to find their houses burned, farms destroyed and their families living in near destitution. Because of these conditions, Stevens hoped to bring about a redistribution of land in order to break up the power structure of the planter aristocracy and provide freedmen with enough land from the "forfeited estates of the enemy" to support themselves. But Congress would not sanction such a "radical" action and overwhelmingly defeated it.[17] Instead, in February 1866, it passed a bill that enlarged the Freedmen's Bureau, giving it judicial powers to protect former slaves against discrimination. First created on March 3, 1865, the Freedmen's Bureau had done admirable work in caring for southern refugees, both black and white. This new bill extended the bureau indefinitely and was intended to apply to freedmen in all parts of the country without antagonizing the President. It was sponsored by moderates, such as Fessenden and Lyman Trumbull of Illinois, chairman of the Senate Judiciary Committee, who felt they could work with the President to counteract the black codes. To the surprise of Congress, Johnson subsequently vetoed the measure on the grounds that Congress had no right to legislate such a question with eleven states unrepresented. It was a gigantic patronage scheme, he insisted, that was totally unaffordable. Congress had never felt obliged to provide economic relief or purchase land for "our own people." Such aid, he claimed, would imply that blacks did not have to work for a living. The House promptly overrode his veto, 109 to 40, but the Senate sustained it when five Republican members reversed their positions.[18]

Moderates were shocked and dismayed by the President's action. And, at this point, they held a controlling hand in the House, not the Radicals. Subsequently, Trumbull offered a bill "which embodied the moderates' position" and granted civil rights to all persons born in the United States, except Indians. It passed both houses on April 9, 1866, with virtually every Republican voting to approve it. The measure spelled out rights to be "enjoyed equally without regard to race," such as making contracts, bringing lawsuits and enjoying "security of person and property." It authorized federal officers to bring suit against violators, with trials held in federal courts. And it made "all persons who deprived a citizen of civil rights liable to fine or imprisonment." But, as Trumbull made explicitly clear, it did not grant blacks political rights.[19]

This Civil Rights Act was "the first statutory definition of the rights of American citizenship" and "reflected how ideas once considered Radical had been adopted by the party's mainstream." It was not limited to the South, but applied to the North as well, where discriminatory laws had been enacted and still remained in force.[20]

Johnson vetoed the bill. He argued that it violated "all our experience as a people" and constituted "a stride toward centralization, and the concentration of all legislative powers in the national Government."[21] And the veto message was blatantly racist in tone. He doubted blacks could qualify for citizenship and argued that states had the right to discriminate on the basis of race.

The veto utterly outraged the majority in both houses. It alienated all the moderates who wanted to cooperate with him. "The veto of the Freedmen's Bureau Bill," declared the *New York Herald* on March 28, 1866, "was but the distant thunder announcing the approaching storm. The veto [of the Civil Rights Act] was the storm itself. . . . It is a declaration of war." On April 9, 1866, the House repassed the measure, overriding the veto, and the announcement of the vote "was received with an outburst of applause, in which members of the House, as well as the throng of spectators, heartily joined, and which did not subside for some moments."[22] The Senate also repassed the bill to the delight of both moderates and Radicals. "It is now manifest," cried Trumbull on the Senate floor, that the President "will approve no measure" that would protect "the freedmen in their liberty and their property."[23] It was the first major piece of legislation in American history that was enacted over the objections of the President.

Clearly, many Republicans, especially Radicals, meant to define and protect the rights of citizens by exercising broad national powers. Without hesitation, they swept aside concerns about states' rights and federalism if they interfered with the national effort to safeguard those rights.[24] Equality before the law would be protected by the national government. The states were simply disregarded, their powers reduced. Men like James G. Blaine of Maine and John A. Bingham of Ohio, who had opposed foisting a social revolution upon the South and did not believe an open break with the President was necessary or wise, now supported the principle of civil equality for former slaves. And when Johnson vetoed the Civil Rights Act he forfeited their support. In a slow but steady movement, they drifted over to the side of the Radicals.

According to a leading Reconstruction historian, the President's rejection of this bill was "the most disastrous miscalculation of his political career." If he "aimed to isolate the Radicals and build up a new political coalition around himself, he could not have failed more miserably. Moderates now concluded that Johnson's policies 'would wreck the Republican party.' They also believed the Civil Rights Bill, as Sherman put it, was 'clearly right.' "[25]

It was a revolutionary turn of events and boded ill for Lincoln's policy of "malice toward none."

Still, the questionable constitutionality of the Civil Rights Act prompted the joint committee to propose the 14th Amendment, which defined citizenship to include black males and forbade any state from limiting the rights of citizens without due process of law. It also nullified the three-fifths clause of the Constitution, thereby increasing southern representation in the House (when those states were readmitted) by twelve seats. One clause excluded those from voting in national elections until 1870 who had voluntarily aided the Confederacy.

Stevens opened debate in the House on the amendment in early May 1866, arguing that it established the principle that state laws "shall operate *equally* upon all." Although the final approval of the amendment on June 13 included changes introduced in the Senate, such as eliminating the clause calling for the disenfranchisement of those who had fought for the Confederacy, Radicals like Stevens accepted these changes, however reluctantly. "Do you inquire why . . . I accept so imperfect a proposition? I answer, because I live among men and not among angels."[26]

Such leading suffragists as Susan B. Anthony and Elizabeth Cady Stanton denounced the amendment because its second section regarding the voting process in state and federal elections specifically introduced the word "male" into the Constitution. Limiting male voting would reduce a state's representation in the House; suffrage restrictions based on gender would not.

Suffragists felt betrayed. They could no longer trust men in seeking their own rights, they complained. They now realized they must create an independent suffragist movement if they were ever to achieve equality.[27] In 1869, Elizabeth Cady Stanton and Susan B. Anthony formed the National Woman Suffrage Association, which only admitted women; but the American Woman Suffrage Association welcomed both men and women. In 1890, the two groups merged under Stanton's leadership and became the National American Woman Suffrage Association. Their fight for suffrage equality now began in earnest.

The 14th Amendment to the Constitution has given rise to many interpretations of its elusive wording. What needs to be remembered is that the measure was reworked many times in committee and on the floor of both houses in order to find language upon which all Republicans—Radicals and moderates—could unite, language that would provide "strong federal action to protect the freedmen's rights."

But one thing is certain. Clearly, in the words of John A. Bingham of Ohio, "the powers of the States have been limited and the powers of Congress extended," by the amendment.[28]

Republican-controlled Tennessee ratified the amendment on July 19, 1866, and was immediately restored to the Union, "but without an explicit Congressional acknowledgment that this established a binding precedent."[29] Eight representatives, including Horace Maynard, took their seats during the next few days or later in December. The other southern states hoped that the approaching congressional election in 1866 would constitute a repudiation of what they regarded as a Radical agenda and provide the election of a more moderate Congress that would devise a quicker and milder form of Reconstruction. They therefore rejected the amendment, three unanimously, two others with only a single contrary vote. As a result, ratification of the 14th Amendment was subsequently made a condition for readmission into the Union. The contradiction involved in demanding that the South ratify an amendment before being readmitted did not trouble these congressmen in the least. They shrugged off the fact that if a state can ratify an amendment, it is already in the Union.

THE SITUATION IN the South worsened when race riots occurred in Memphis and New Orleans in the spring and summer of 1866. In Memphis, a three-day assault on blacks by white mobs, resulting from an altercation between white and black drivers of horse-drawn hacks on May 1, left forty-eight persons dead, all but two of them black, five black women raped and many churches, schools and homes pillaged or destroyed by fire.[30] Twelve weeks later, in New Orleans, the streets erupted in rioting on the opening day of a constitutional convention that had been called to enfranchise blacks. An indiscriminate massacre of black convention delegates occurred in the convention hall, despite the hoisting of white flags of surrender. The incident discredited presidential Reconstruction, even though Lincoln, not Johnson, had established the state government in Louisiana. Memphis and New Orleans proved to many northerners that the South was unregenerate, and it strengthened the claims of Radicals that southern states were not ready to be readmitted to full membership in the Union.

In an effort to plead his case to northerners, President Johnson undertook a speaking tour of Philadelphia and New York, then swung north around New York to Cleveland and St. Louis on August 28. He was accompanied by General Grant, Gideon Welles, the secretary of the navy, and

Admiral David Farragut. Dubbed "the swing around the circle" to further the cause of moderation, the tour proved disastrous. Johnson was baited, mocked and scorned. In St. Louis he sounded wild, certainly unpresidential. "I have been traduced, I have been slandered, I have been maligned. I have been called Judas Iscariot," he ranted. ". . . Who has been my Christ that I have played the Judas role? Was it Thad Stevens?"[31]

Not surprisingly, the fall election resulted in a complete Democratic rout. Republicans now controlled two-thirds of both houses in the next Congress, enough under most circumstances to override a veto. "The President has no power to control or influence anybody," jeered Senator James W. Grimes of Iowa, "and legislation will be carried on entirely regardless of his opinions or wishes."[32]

"It is now our turn to act," commented Representative James A. Garfield of Ohio. The southern states "would not co-operate with us in rebuilding what they destroyed. We must remove the rubbish, and build from the bottom."[33]

And action came almost immediately. By this time most moderates had come to accept the Radical insistence that some form of military rule for the South was necessary. In the words of George Julian of Indiana, what the South needed was not oaths of loyalty that invited men to commit perjury, but "*government,* the strong arm of power, outstretched from the central authority here in Washington."[34]

On January 3, 1867, Stevens introduced the First Reconstruction Act, which when much amended in the House and Senate became known as the Military Reconstruction Act. It divided the South into five military districts and gave each commander broad powers under martial law to preserve order, protect blacks and advance political Reconstruction. In a moving speech he reminded his colleagues of the treatment meted out to freedmen and loyal Union men in the South. Action was necessary, he declared, "to protect those people from the barbarians who are now daily murdering them; who are murdering the loyal whites daily and daily putting into secret graves not only hundreds but thousands of the colored people of that country."[35] John A. Bingham, the most forceful spokesman for the moderate position, argued against such an extreme measure and accused Stevens of trying to rush the bill through the House. He offered an amendment that would permit the restoration of any state once it ratified the 14th Amendment and guaranteed black suffrage, to which another moderate Republican, James G. Blaine, added that states should be permitted to disfranchise those who had participated in the rebellion. During a day of high drama, on February 13, 1867, Blaine moved to recommit the military Reconstruction bill to the joint committee, but, in a masterful speech, Stevens beat back the challenge and the motion to recommit was defeated. He pleaded with the young members of the House to rise to the occasion "without bickering, without small criticisms" and advance "the great cause of humanity and universal liberty."[36] It was one of the few speeches ever delivered in Congress, said one, "that have resulted in the changing of votes."[37] The bill carried by a count of 105 to 55. Johnson, of course, vetoed it, but on March 2, 1867, Congress overrode his veto.

On the same day, Congress also enacted the Army Appropriation Act, which decreed that the President must issue all military orders through the General of the Army, Ulysses S. Grant, whose headquarters could not be moved from Washington without Senate approval, thus limiting Johnson's authority as commander in chief. This was followed by enactment, over the President's veto, of the Tenure of Office Act, which prohibited the President from removing officials approved by the Senate without first obtaining senatorial consent.

Johnson also vetoed the enabling act that would bring Nebraska into the Union in the belief that it would further strengthen Republican control of Congress. The House overrode the veto in March by a vote of 120 to 44, the Senate by 31 to 9. It was the only time in American history that a state was admitted to the Union over a presidential veto.

Contempt for the President had reached such a level that on January 22, 1867, Congress decreed that the 40th and all succeeding Congresses would meet immediately upon the adjournment of the preceding one, thereby keeping Congress in almost continuous session. What this action did in effect was grant Congress the right to call itself into special session, a prerogative previously exercised only by the President. "Though the President is Commander-in-Chief," proclaimed Stevens, "Congress is his commander; and God willing, he shall obey. He and his minions shall learn that this is not a Government of kings and satraps, but a Government of the people, and that Congress is the people."[38]

Thus, the 40th Congress convened moments after the 39th Congress expired at noon on March 4, 1867, and it was immediately realized that an enabling act was necessary if the Reconstruction measures were to be properly implemented and become operative. Accordingly, the Supplementary Reconstruction Act was passed on March 23, 1867, and vetoed by Johnson the same day. The President's veto was again overridden by Congress. This act authorized military commanders to enroll qualified voters, including blacks, and hold elections for constitutional conventions to establish new state governments that would guarantee black suffrage and ratify the 14th Amendment. Congress itself would decide when to end military rule and when to accept the representatives elected in the southern states.

Starting on June 20, 1867, Johnson took it upon himself to interfere with military Reconstruction by issuing a set of orders regarding the registering of voters and the treatment of civilian officials. Whereupon Congress passed another Reconstruction act specifically contradicting every point of the President's June 20 orders. He, in turn, vetoed the measure, which both houses overrode the same day.[39]

ON AUGUST 12, 1867, while Congress stood in recess following two special sessions, Johnson suspended Secretary of War Edwin Stanton, a holdover from the Lincoln administration who had opposed Johnson's June 20 order, and appointed General Grant to replace him ad interim. Determined to remove every officer who was particularly ardent in enforcing the Reconstruction Acts, the President also dismissed General Philip H. Sheridan from command of the Louisiana-Texas military district and General Daniel Sickles from the South Carolina military district. Before he was through, he had removed all but one of the military commanders in the South. If nothing else, these actions proved to the American people that he was hellbent on undermining the Reconstruction laws enacted by Congress.

After the House returned for a third special session, the Judiciary Committee, on November 20, recommended impeachment of the President by the narrow vote of 5 to 4. But, on December 7, 1867, the House rejected the recommendation, 108 to 57, when two minority reports insisted that there was no evidence that the President had committed a high crime or misdemeanor as stipulated in the Constitution.

That would have been the end of it, except that Johnson unwisely resumed his quarrel with Congress. First, in compliance with the Tenure of Office Act, he submitted to the Senate his reasons for suspending Stanton, which the upper house rejected, 36 to 6, in January 1868. Then he removed General John Pope from command and asked Congress to vote a resolution of thanks to General Winfield S. Hancock, who had replaced General Sheridan, and who disapproved of the Reconstruction Acts and had issued a military order affirming the supremacy of civil government over military rule.[40] At the same time, Radicals had persuaded Grant to turn over his office to Stanton, who resumed his position. Then, in a fit of defiance, the President dismissed Stanton a second time on February 21, 1868, accused Grant of treachery and appointed Adjutant General Lorenzo Thomas to take his place ad interim. Stanton immediately notified the Radicals in Congress of the President's action and received a one-word order in response from Senator Charles Sumner: "Stick." Stanton promptly barricaded himself in his office.[41]

That same day, Representative John Covode of Pennsylvania offered a motion that "Andrew Johnson, President of the United States, be impeached for high crimes and misdemeanors in office."[42] The motion was referred to the Joint Committee on Reconstruction, which recommended impeachment. Stevens, looking more feeble than usual, wanted the House to proceed immediately to a vote on the question, but many members wished to speak to the issue, and so a prolonged debate ensued with most Radicals reciting the President's past misdeeds and disregarding the charges that would constitute "high crimes and misdemeanors."

Wild rumors circulated that the President had summoned thousands of armed men from Maryland to protect him. The House seethed with anticipation. A "vast, excited and expectant throng" swarmed into the galleries and many spectators fought to gain entrance to the floor to fill the aisles and spaces outside the circle of desks and in front of the rostrum. At any moment some expected to see soldiers bursting through the chamber's doors to drive out the assembled representatives.[43]

None appeared, and the debate grew heated. At one point, on February 22, Democrat James Brooks of New York denounced what he called the Republicans' attempted political coup and likened it to the Reign of Terror in the French Revolution. He noticed the date—Washington's birthday—the memory of whom, he said, should inspire us to devotion to the public good, yet "you propose to depose the President of the United States and to substitute a President of your own, the present President of the Senate [Benjamin Wade] in his stead."[44] At that time the line of succession passed from the Vice President to the president pro tem of the Senate.

On Monday, February 24, 1868, at five o'clock in the afternoon, by a vote of 126 to 47, the House approved impeachment. All the Republicans voted aye, with sixteen absent and not voting; all but one Democrat voted nay. A committee of seven was then appointed to prepare the articles of impeachment. The seven included Thaddeus Stevens, John Bingham of Ohio, George Boutwell of Massachusetts, George W. Julian of Indiana, John A. Logan of Illinois, James F. Wilson of Iowa and Hamilton Ward of New York.

On March 2, 1868, at four o'clock in the afternoon, nine articles of impeachment were reported to the House and adopted seriatim. These included Johnson's alleged violations of the Tenure of Office Act and Command of the Army Act and his attempt at a conspiracy "by intimidation and threats" to prevent Stanton from holding office in violation of the Constitution.[45] During the voting, a number of senators crowded into the chamber and, along with a group of Radicals, privately pleaded with the members to approve impeachment. Although ill and soon to die, Stevens directed these efforts. On the floor, in one of his last speeches, the gravely ill old man insisted that never was such a great malefactor so gently treated as Andrew Johnson. "Why, I'll take the man's record, his speeches, and his acts before any impartial jury you can get together, and I'll make them pronounce him either a knave or a fool, without the least trouble."[46]

To prosecute the case before the Senate, the House next elected by ballot seven managers, individuals already selected for nomination in a caucus held the previous Saturday evening. The seven included Bingham, who led with 114 votes out of 118 cast, then General Benjamin F. Butler, [47] Boutwell, Wilson Williams, Logan and Stevens, who received the least number of

This formidable group of House members prosecuted the impeachment charges against President Andrew Johnson. From right to left: Benjamin Butler, James F. Wilson, Thaddeus Stevens, George S. Boutwell, Thomas Williams, John A. Logan and John A. Bingham.

votes, 105. At the first meeting of the managers, Boutwell was chosen chairman over Bingham by the votes of Stevens, Logan and Butler. Bingham had the support of Wilson and Williams. When the result was announced, Bingham felt slighted and showed his disappointment by indicating that he planned to resign from the group. To prevent Bingham's departure, Boutwell, at the next meeting, resigned as chairman, and nominated Bingham to take his place. "It seemed to be important," Boutwell later wrote, "that the entire force of the House of Representatives should be directed to one object: the conviction of the accused. Beyond this, Mr. Bingham and Mr. Wilson had been opposed to the impeachment of Mr. Johnson when the attempt was first made in the House of Representatives. I thought it important to combine the strength that they represented in support of the proceeding in which we were then engaged."[48]

The following day, March 3, the House adopted two additional charges: one based on "certain violent utterances of the President" and a final catch-all called the omnibus article. On March 4, the House resolved itself into the Committee of the Whole and followed the managers to the Senate chamber, where the articles of impeachment were read. All the representatives then withdrew, and the Senate decreed that the trial would begin at one o'clock the following afternoon.[49]

It began on schedule with the chief justice of the United States, Salmon P. Chase, presiding. Outside the Capitol an enormous crowd gathered, "pleading, swearing for admittance—offering untold sums for a little insignificant bit of pasteboard. . . . A ticket is the only open sesame" that would allow attendance to the proceedings. "The Senate chamber, always chilly in comparison with the warm, leaping blood of the House, is now wrapped in judicial robes of coldest grey," wrote Emily Briggs.[50]

After the chief justice arrived and the Senate formed itself into a judicial body, members of the House were announced. They filed into the room led by Elihu B. Washburne, chairman of the Committee of the Whole. Next, the team of prosecutors arrived in a procession. Thaddeus Stevens by this time was so ill that two officers of the House, David Reese and John Chauncey, had to lift him into a large armchair and carry him from his lodgings across the public grounds, up the broad Capitol stairs and into the Senate chamber.

In a loud voice, the sergeant at arms called out, "Andrew Johnson," three times, but the accused was not present. Johnson was defended by his attorney general, Henry Stanbery, who resigned his position to represent him, and four distinguished lawyers, including William M. Evarts and Benjamin R. Curtis, a justice of the Supreme Court.

Stanbery started off by reading a communication from Johnson to the chief justice asking for a forty-day postponement in order to prepare and answer the charges brought against him. "Forty days!" bellowed Ben Butler, "as long as it took God to destroy the world by flood!"[51] But the court permitted a delay, albeit a shorter one, and not until March 30 did the actual trial begin.

Butler led off with a three-hour harangue. The lead prosecutor because he was the most experienced trial lawyer, he performed so wretchedly that he virtually made acquittal a certainty. It was as though he presumed the senators would vote for conviction no matter the evidence, and therefore there was no need to argue convincingly and make a strong case. In addition, he was personally disliked by a number of senators. In fact, according to one reporter, "No man in this broad land is so fearfully hated as Benjamin F. Butler."[52]

Be that as it may, Butler lambasted Johnson with senseless arguments. In an attempt "to bring into disgrace and contempt the Congress of the United States, and to destroy confidence in and to excite odium against Congress and its laws," Butler contended, "he, Andrew Johnson, President of the United States, made divers speeches set out therein, whereby he brought the office of President into contempt, ridicule and disgrace. . . ."

Bingham, in a three-day marathon, asked the senators to consider whether the President might "judicially construe the Constitution for himself, and judicially determine finally for himself whether the laws, which by your Constitution are declared to be supreme, are not, after all, null and void and of no effect, and not to be executed, because it suits the pleasure of his highness, Andrew Johnson, first king of the people of the United States, in imitation of George III, to suspend their execution." Here was a prime example of rhetoric run amuck without real substance to prove the charges.

George Boutwell, one of the most persistent and determined leaders of the impeachment process, orated rather than argued. "Never in the history of any free government," he growled, "has there been so base, so gross, so unjustifiable an attempt upon the part of the executive, whether Emperor, King, or President, to destroy the just authority of another department of the government." Again, commented constitutional lawyers, assertion of wrongdoing was no substitute for evidence.

Stevens spoke standing at the desk of the secretary of the Senate, but he was so feeble that he asked permission to sit down. After reading from his prepared statement for half an hour his voice failed and he turned his manuscript over to Butler, who intoned the final pages. "How can he escape the just vengeance of the law?" Stevens asked. How can any senator "vote for his acquittal on the ground of its unconstitutionality?" To do so would create a "track of infamy which must mark his name, and that of his posterity! Nothing is therefore more certain than that it requires no gift of prophecy to predict the fate of this unhappy victim."[53]

When the prosecution ended its case, the crowded galleries erupted into noisy and disorderly acts of approval. "Men and women rose to their feet cheering, clapping hands and waving handkerchiefs." The chief justice called for order and was answered with laughter, hisses and boos, whereupon he ordered the galleries cleared.[54]

The defense argued the constitutional question and sought to prove that Johnson had not committed an impeachable crime. Justice Curtis demonstrated that Lincoln had appointed Stanton, not Johnson, and therefore the Tenure of Office Act did not apply. He also convinced the senators that impeachment was a judicial, not a political, proceeding. For the sake of the Constitution, he pleaded, politics must not determine the outcome of their collective vote.[55]

On May 16, the members of the court voted on the eleventh article (the omnibus, the most comprehensive one) and Johnson escaped removal from office by the count of 35 in favor and 19 against, just one vote shy of the two-thirds necessary for conviction. The nineteen included seven Republicans and twelve Democrats. Senator Edmund G. Ross of Kansas, a Radical no less, displayed courage and conviction by casting his vote for acquittal. Two more ballots on the second and third articles were taken on May 26 and produced the same result, whereupon the Senate adjourned as a court of impeachment.[56]

"What was the verdict?" screamed Stevens, still held aloft by his bearers. Told the result, he lifted his arms into the air and shouted, "The country is going to the devil."[57] He was carried away through a crowd of bystanders.

The verdict on removal resulted most probably because of how Senator James W. Grimes of Iowa, among others, felt about the evidence and proofs of guilt presented by the prosecution. The court, he declared, had been asked to decide based solely on politics. "I can not agree to destroy the harmonious working of the Constitution for the sake of getting rid of an

The tally sheet showing votes by individual senators on the impeachment of President Johnson.

unacceptable President. Whatever may be my opinion of the incumbent, I can not consent to trifle with the high office he holds. I can do nothing which, by implication, may be construed into an approval of impeachment as a part of future political machinery."[58]

Here was another turning point in the relationship between Congress and the chief executive. Where Lincoln exercised enormous presidential powers during the war years, Johnson lost them in his struggle to control Reconstruction. And this loss "tipped the balance of power from the presidency to the Congress." For the rest of the century, Presidents who followed Johnson failed to challenge congressional dominance—which is the way it ought to be, declared John Sherman, speaking for many leading Republicans: the executive "should be subordinate to the legislative branch," just as the Founders intended.[59]

Johnson served out the remainder of his term in office without further controversy.

On May 16, several days after the first vote on impeachment, the Republican national nominating convention met in Chicago and chose General Ulysses S. Grant as its presidential candidate on the first ballot and the Radical Speaker of the House, Schuyler Colfax, for the second slot. The platform condemned Johnson and endorsed the congressional program of Reconstruction. At their convention in July, the Democrats nominated Horatio Seymour, former governor of New York, and Francis P. Blair of Missouri. Seymour's record of opposition to the war and sympathy for the draft rioters in New York in 1863, along with Blair's racism and opposition to the Reconstruction Acts, made this a particularly weak ticket. Worse, they conducted one of the most blatantly racist campaigns in American history.[60]

Six of the former Confederate states were readmitted to the Union after they had complied with the conditions imposed by Congress; and with their approval, the 14th Amendment won ratification on July 28, 1868. The six included Arkansas (June 22), Florida (June 25), North Carolina (July 4), Louisiana (July 9), South Carolina (July 9) and Alabama (July 13). And their representatives showed up in Congress almost immediately: four from Arkansas taking their seats on June 24; one from Florida on July 1; seven from North Carolina on July 6 and 20; five from Louisiana on July 18; four from South Carolina on July 18 and 25; and six from Alabama on July 21 and 22.

On August 11, 1868, Thaddeus Stevens died at the age of seventy-six. His body lay in state in the Capitol Rotunda for a day, attracting a huge crowd of mourners. Both hated and admired, he had spent his life trying to win equality for all citizens, especially African-Americans, and aid the poor and oppressed. One of the most unique, controversial, determined and complicated leaders in the entire history of the House of Representatives, he was typical of many congressmen, before and after, who were miserable human beings and yet devoted and brilliant legislators.

Grant defeated Seymour on November 3 by capturing twenty-six out of thirty-four states and winning 214 electoral votes to his opponent's 80. A large black vote in the reconstructed southern states decided this lopsided election. The Republicans conducted their campaign by waving "the bloody shirt" as a reminder of the recent rebellion. It proved very effective.

The second session of the 40th Congress closed on November 10, 1868, after 345 days, but the third session convened less than a month later on December 7, a clear indication that the legislature meant to retain absolute control over the operation of the government and prevent the executive from exercising any direction or influence whatsoever. Then, on February 26, 1869, Congress passed the 15th Amendment to the Constitution, which forbade any state from denying a citizen the right to vote because of race, color or previous condition of servitude, something Stevens had been fighting for during the final years of his life. All unreconstructed states had to ratify this amendment before they would be readmitted to the Union. Ratification came in March 1870.

Virginia was restored to the Union on January 26, 1870, Mississippi on February 23 and Texas on March 30. Virginia's eight representatives took their seats between January 27 and February 1; Mississippi's five on February 23 and April 8; and Texas's four on March 31. Georgia had been restored on July 21, 1868, but its representatives were not seated on March 5, 1869. It was readmitted on July 15, 1870, and its six members took their seats in January 1871.

NORTHERNERS BEGAN TO tire of Reconstruction following passage of the 15th Amendment. They had more important things on their mind, like business and the economy. In April 1869, Henry Adams, grandson of John Quincy Adams, declared that Reconstruction had "lost much of its old prominence in politics."[61]

Hiram R. Revels, an African-American Republican from Mississippi, won election to the Senate to fill the unexpired term of Jefferson Davis. He was a Methodist-Episcopal minister and had served as chaplain of a black regiment during the Civil War. He took his seat on February 25, 1870, after attempts to disqualify him failed.

The first African-American to successfully win election to the House, Joseph H. Rainey, a Republican from South Carolina, was sworn in on December 12, 1870. A barber who labored on a Confederate blockade runner, he became the first black man to preside in the House when Speaker James G. Blaine of Maine turned the gavel over to him in May 1874. Other African-Americans who joined the House included Benjamin S. Turner of Alabama,

Republican Joseph H. Rainey, from South Carolina, the first African-American elected to the House, was sworn in on December 12, 1870.

Robert C. De Large and Robert B. Elliott from South Carolina, Josiah T. Walls of Florida and Jefferson F. Long of Georgia. Needless to add, all these men were Republicans. A total of sixteen African-Americans served in Congress during Reconstruction, and many of them had been free before the war began. But they suffered undisguised hostility from some white members of Congress and encountered innumerable problems living in a segregated capital. Whether by design or accident, they were assigned seats very near the door, perhaps so they could beat a hasty exit if trouble erupted in the chamber over their presence. Virtually all of them served only one or two terms.[62]

　　According to one observer, the social life in the capital was "revolution-ized" after the arrival of African-American legislators. Not only could blacks be seen in the House and Senate, but in the courts as well. "There are colored lawyers, doctors, and professors in full business at the national

THE FIRST COLORED SENATOR AND REPRESENTATIVES,
In the 41ˢᵗ and 42ⁿᵈ Congress of the United States.

This group of African-American senators and representatives served in the 41st and 42nd Congresses. Hiram R. Revels is the first man on the left, and Joseph Rainey is second from the right.

capital." Back in 1858, just prior to the Civil War, "a white man could not safely advocate ordinary justice to a black man," reported John Forney, the clerk of the House. "He was subjected to inconceivable obloquy, not alone in the Legislatures, but in society." Southerners were models of politeness "till their peculiar institution was touched. Then the mask was dropped, and arrogance expelled all courtesy." Now, in the 1870s, "you do not see men inflamed by bad whiskey seeking quarrels with their associates. . . . The bowie-knife, the pistol, the bludgeon, lie buried in the grave with secession and State rights."[63]

If northerners felt that the 15th Amendment ended Reconstruction and secured suffrage for blacks throughout the country, they did not understand that although the amendment forbade depriving any citizen of the right to vote on racial grounds, it did not forbid states from enacting literacy, educational and property tests that whites would later invoke to restore "home rule" and end what they called "Black Reconstruction."

One of the most effective means of preventing African-Americans from voting was intimidation. The Ku Klux Klan, founded in Pulaski, Tennessee, in 1866, with ex-Confederate general Nathan Bedford Forrest as the first Grand Wizard, had the specific intent of reestablishing white supremacy and, through violence and lawlessness, striking terror throughout the Negro community and keeping blacks from the polls. Klan beatings and lynchings became daily events, especially on election days, and one scholar has estimated that approximately four hundred hangings of blacks occurred between 1868 and 1871.[64]

Although it is true that northern public opinion had grown weary of Reconstruction, the emergence and growth of the KKK convinced a large number of northerners that southerners were still rebels and deserved the continued intrusion of federal troops and federal law in the operation of their states. Accordingly, the 41st Congress, which convened its first session on March 4, 1869, passed three Enforcement Acts in 1870–1871, the first two of which prohibited the use of force or intimidation to limit voting and established federal supervisors for registration. It also authorized the use of federal courts to prosecute violators of the laws. The third Enforcement Act, also known as the Ku Klux Klan Act, empowered the President to both employ military force to suppress those who would deprive citizens of their political rights and suspend the writ of habeas corpus in rebellious states when necessary. Democrats rather regarded these laws as "Force Acts" and doubted their legitimacy. Twenty years later, when the Democratic Party controlled both the White House and Congress, it repealed most of them.[65]

On May 22, 1872, Congress enacted the General Amnesty Act, which ended the disability to hold office from all but the most prominent ex-Confederates. The Grant administration itself slowly moved away from employing federal troops and courts to protect African-Americans and their white friends. As a result, white supremacy gradually took hold in several of the former Confederate states and they were "redeemed" from Republican rule.

Native Americans were also denied their rights. The government and settlers removed the Indians from their lands and herded them into reservations. From the beginning of the Republic, whenever Indian land was needed treaties were negotiated by the President and ratified by the Senate, as though the tribes were independent, sovereign nations. No longer. The House finally refused to fund treaties with Indians over which it had no authority. The appropriation bill for the fiscal year 1872, approved on March 3, 1871, included a clause that said that "hereafter no Indian nation or tribe within the territory of the United States shall be acknowledged or recognized as an independent nation, tribe, or power with whom the United States may contract by treaty."[66] That meant Congress could direct Indians any way it wished. Now Indians could be preyed on at will. And they were.

THE ACT OF January 22, 1867, mandating that Congress meet immediately upon the adjournment of the preceding one, was repealed during the 42nd

Congress, thereby returning to the President the authority to call Congress into special session. When the 43rd Congress convened on December 1, 1873, who should appear but the ex-Confederate Vice President, Alexander H. Stephens of Georgia. He had won a special election following the death of his predecessor. When he rose to address the House on December 11, James G. Garfield was awestruck. "Reduced almost to a skeleton," recorded Garfield, he was "lifted to his feet by friends and supporting himself on his crutches and wearing a black cap and gloves, made a remarkable speech. . . . I have never seen so much intellectual power exhibited from so fragile and feeble a form."[67]

Stephens was soon followed by a veritable army of ex-Confederates. Some in Congress were appalled; some were hopeful that it was the beginning of a healing process between North and South. As a result of the many scandals revealed in the second Grant administration (1873–1877), the

Alexander H. Stephens, former Vice President of the Confederacy, was reelected to the House, where he argued against passage of the Civil Rights Act of 1875 because, he said, it was unconstitutional.

mounting northern indifference to the problems of Reconstruction and an economic depression that descended on the nation in 1873, Republicans lost many northern House seats in the 1874 election, and Democrats won over two-thirds of the southern contests. Something like six Confederate cabinet officers, fifty-eight members of the Confederate Congress and nine Confederate army officers won seats. When the 44th Congress convened, there would be 181 Democrats to 107 Republicans in the House.

However, the lame-duck session of the 43rd Congress completed its efforts to protect African-Americans from white curtailment of their rights. In 1875 it finally passed the Civil Rights Act, which prohibited racial discrimination in public accommodations, public transportation and jury selection. All seven black members of Congress spoke during the debate "with vigor and eloquence." Several of them related the indignities and insults they endured in the past, such as Rainey being tossed out of a Virginia streetcar, Richard H. Cain and Robert B. Elliott being denied access to a North Carolina restaurant and James T. Rapier being turned away by hotels at every stopping point between Montgomery and Washington.[68]

"Why is it that colored members of Congress cannot enjoy the same immunities that are accorded to white members?" asked Rainey on the floor of the House on December 19, 1873. "Why cannot we stop at hotels here without meeting opposition? Why cannot we go into restaurants without being insulted? We are here enacting laws for the country and casting votes upon important questions, we have been sent here by the suffrages of the people, and why cannot we enjoy the same benefits that are accorded to our white colleagues on this floor?"

Alexander H. Stephens delivered a major speech against the civil rights bill when debate resumed on January 5, 1874, contending that it would transform the country into a "centralized empire." His opposition, he declared, "springs from no prejudice, in the slightest degree against any man, woman or child within the limits of the United States, on account of race or color or previous condition of servitude." It springs, rather, from "the want of the necessary power, under the Constitution," and is therefore "exceedingly injudicious and unwise. . . . Better leave all such matters to the States," he argued.[69]

He was answered by a black colleague, Robert B. Elliott, who gave a notable speech on January 6, 1874, that attracted national attention. He said he had "high personal regard" for Stephens because of his mental prowess and long experience in public affairs. "But in this discussion I cannot and I will not forget that the welfare and rights of my whole race in this country are involved. When, therefore, the honorable gentleman from Georgia lends his voice and influence to defeat this measure, I do not shrink from saying that it is not from him that the American House of Representatives should take lessons in matters touching human rights. . . . When the gentleman was seeking to break up the Union of these States" and announced "the birth of a government which rested on human slavery as its corner stone," he "ruthlessly spurned and trampled on" the black race. Now free blackmen were present in the House chamber "to meet him in debate, and to demand that the rights which are enjoyed by their former oppressors . . . shall be accorded to those who even in the darkness of slavery kept their allegiance true to freedom and the Union."[70]

The Republicans decided to put off a final vote of the civil rights bill until after the 1874 election. But that election ended in a debacle for the ruling party. Whereupon Ben Butler, the manager of the civil rights bill in the House, dropped a controversial clause mandating integrated schools, and Speaker James G. Blaine and James Garfield, chairman of the Appropriations Committee, both of whom favored a civil rights bill and opposed further intervention in the South, worked out a scheme to "overcome the legislative in-fighting" among Republicans over Reconstruction, and allowed passage of the bill.[71] On February 4, 1875, by a vote of 162 to 100, with 27 members not voting, the lame-duck House passed the Civil Rights Act of 1875. The Senate concurred, and President Grant signed the bill on March 1.

THAT ACTION, AND the ratification of the 13th, 14th and 15th Amendments to the Constitution, brought about a constitutional revolution in the country that extended equality under the law to millions.[72] It remained only to extend these privileges to all persons regardless of gender.

And women did not keep silent on the issue. They had been badgering Congress for some time to extend the voting rights. Victoria Woodhull, a well-known spiritualist, an advocate of free love and the first woman to open a brokerage firm on Wall Street, submitted a memorial to Congress on December 19, 1870, declaring that women already had voting rights under the 14th and 15th Amendments. They had been permitted to vote in Wyoming in November 1870, and some women, notably Susan B. Anthony and Virginia Minor, sought unsuccessfully to win the right to vote through court action.[73] Now Woodhull asked to address the Judiciary Committee to make her case. Despite past repeated requests by women, not one of them had ever spoken directly to a congressional committee. But Woodhull was not to be denied. There is no telling how she convinced Ben Butler to "open [the] committee for me," but "he did." On January 11, 1871, Victoria Woodhull became the first woman to address a congressional committee and present her memorial. Only two members of the Judiciary Committee, Butler and Judge Loughridge of Iowa, supported the idea of granting women the right to vote, and they were in a distinct minority. John Bingham of Ohio wrote the committee's majority opinion and stated that the issue was the prerogative of the courts and the states, not the Congress. He recommended that the memorial be laid on the table, and the members agreed. Woodhull then requested permission to hold a public meeting in the House chamber to discuss the issue, but that, too, was rejected on February 6, with only forty-two House members voting in favor. Still, the issue would not go away. Like it or not, Congress had not heard the last of the demand that voting rights be extended to women.[74]

THE ISSUE DID not command national attention when the Republican National Convention met in Cincinnati on June 16, 1876, and nominated Rutherford B. Hayes of Ohio for President and William A. Wheeler of New York for Vice President. The scandals revealed during the Grant administration and the financial panic that occurred in 1873 did not bode well for the Republicans. So the Republicans searched for someone who appeared untainted by corruption. Hardly known outside of Ohio, Hayes enjoyed an "unblemished reputation" whose "chief excellence" was "his intuitive perception of what at the moment is practically attainable."[75] So he was chosen.

The Democrats, meeting in St. Louis in late June, nominated one of the richest corporate lawyers in America, Samuel J. Tilden of New York, who had helped prosecute and break up the Tweed Ring. They named Thomas A. Hendricks of Indiana as his running mate. The November election came as another rude shock for Republicans. Tilden not only received over 250,000 more popular votes than his rival, but he also won the electoral votes of such northern states as New York, New Jersey, Connecticut and Indiana for a total of 184.[76] He also carried the South, except in such lingering Republican enclaves as Florida, Louisiana and South Carolina. "So much fraud and intimidation took place in the disputed states," argues one historian, "that no one may ever know who really won those elections."[77] Two sets of electoral returns were reported from each of those three states, one favoring Tilden, the other Hayes. The Oregon electoral count was also in dispute. Of all these disputed votes, Tilden needed only one of them to win the presidency. Hayes needed them all.

"It now appears that we were defeated by the combined power of rebellion, Catholicism and whiskey, a trinity very hard to conquer," sniffed James A. Garfield.[78] Hayes himself agreed that he had lost the election. "I am of opinion that the Democrats have carried the country and elected Tilden," he told a group of reporters. "We must I now think prepare ourselves to accept the inevitable," he wrote in his diary. "I do it with composure and cheerfulness"[79]

But the Democrats, and Tilden in particular, failed to assert any leadership or provide the members of Congress with a "decisive and consistent course of action." They failed to undertake a public appeal for the justice of their cause; they failed to encourage southerners to protest what was de-

clared in dispute; and they failed to make any effort to ask Hayes to con-
cede. In fact, by their failures, they encouraged the opposition to pursue a
course by which they could win the election.[80]

On December 7, 1876, three days after the second session of the 44th
Congress convened, Representative George W. McCrary of Iowa, a Republican, introduced a resolution in the Democratically controlled House call-
ing for the appointment of a special committee to prepare a solution by
which the crisis could be resolved. With the approval of the Judiciary Committee, the House adopted the resolution without debate. Accordingly,
Democratic Speaker Samuel J. Randall, elected on December 4, chose
Henry B. Payne of Ohio to head the House committee, consisting of such
Democrats as Eppa Hunton of Virginia, Abram S. Hewitt of New York and
William M. Springer of Illinois, and such Republicans as McCrary of Iowa,
George F. Hoar of Massachusetts and George Willard of Michigan. On De-
cember 15, the Senate passed without opposition the appointment of a sim-
ilar committee.[81]

After much discussion, the committees of the Republican Senate and
the Democratic House finally agreed to set up an Electoral Commission
consisting of five members from each house and five justices of the Supreme
Court, who would hear evidence and render a decision as to which electoral
returns to count. Since the Republicans and Democrats each placed fourteen members on the commission, the fifteenth member would determine
the outcome of the election, and he was expected to be Justice David Davis
of the Supreme Court, an independent. Unfortunately, that ideal solution
was foiled when the Illinois legislature elected Davis to the U.S. Senate on
January 25, 1877. He was replaced on the commission by Justice Joseph P.
Bradley, a Republican.[82]

On February 1, the two houses of Congress convened in the House of
Representatives to count the electoral ballots as required by the Constitution. A mob crowded into the galleries, and the diplomatic corps came out
in force. At one o'clock in the afternoon the members of the Senate marched
into the chamber in "solemn procession," led by the president pro tem,
Thomas W. Ferry of Michigan. They were preceded by Captain Bassett, who
carried two mahogany boxes filled with electoral ballots. "In a theatrical
bass voice," Ferry called the members to order. Then he opened one of the
boxes and drew out an envelope with the Alabama returns. It was read to
the members. State followed state alphabetically until Florida was reached.
At that point, Dudley Field of New York rose and objected to the counting.
There were two sets of returns from Florida. Which ones to count? That was
now up to the Electoral Commission. The returns of all the disputed states
were then turned over to the Electoral Commission. After that, the senators
marched out of the chamber, carrying with them the empty locked boxes.
Both houses adjourned to await the verdict of the commission.

For the next four days, before a crowded audience in the old Senate chamber, then the home of the Supreme Court, the commission met and heard the arguments of the Republican and Democratic attorneys. But they faced the same dilemma that bedeviled the Congress—namely, the constitutional right of the tribunal to go beyond the evidence contained in the certificates and examine the validity of the charges of fraud and illegality. On February 6, the commission went into a closed-door seven-hour executive session.

The session continued the next day. Then, at 2:13 p.m. Justice Bradley, who had indicated a preference for Tilden, rose and read a statement. He declared his opposition to hearing "extrinsic evidence." That meant that there would be no examination of charges of fraud and corruption in any of the disputed states. It seemed clear that Bradley had been successfully pressured by Republican leaders and industrial lobbyists to vote for Hayes. At 4:00 p.m. the decision was publicly announced, and that ended any hope of a Tilden victory. On succeeding days all the disputed returns were awarded to Hayes by a vote of 8 to 7, along strict party lines.[83]

Insisting they had been robbed, the Democrats threatened a filibuster in the House to delay the formal (and constitutional) requirement of counting the ballots. The very fact that the commission refused to investigate the alleged fraud provided indisputable proof, the Democrats contended, that the commission's vote was the result of connivance and corruption.

The Senate voted to accept the commission's decision, but on February 12, the House rejected it, 168 to 103, with 19 abstentions. The threat of a filibuster became real as the House quarreled and debated and called for a new election. Amid deafening confusion, some of which was organized, the Democratic Speaker, Samuel J. Randall of Pennsylvania, tried to maintain order by overruling any motion or any person who tried to divert the House from resolving the crisis.

As inauguration day—March 4, 1877—approached there was concern that Grant's term would end and the executive office would be vacant. The House passed a bill establishing a line of succession from the president pro tem of the Senate to the Speaker of the House to the secretary of state, but the Senate simply ignored it. Meanwhile promises, commitments, bargains, deals and all manner of schemes were concocted to end the threat of filibuster and declare Hayes the new President. A lobby headed by Thomas A. Scott, president of the Pennsylvania Railroad, and Iowa congressman Grenville M. Dodge, chief engineer of the Union Pacific, convinced southern congressmen that the only way the Texas & Pacific Railroad would be built from East Texas to the Pacific coast depended on a Republican victory. In addition, promises were made that the Hayes administration would withdraw all federal troops from the South, appoint at least one southerner to the cabinet and provide a share of federal patronage, and make available sufficient funds for the rebuilding of the South's shattered economy.

On Saturday, February 24, 1877, after an emotional speech by Abram S. Hewitt of New York, one of Tilden's staunchest supporters, the Republicans caught a hint in his words and manner that the Democrats might be willing to accept Hayes. Serious negotiations between the two parties then began. A meeting was held on the evening of February 26 at Wormley's Hotel[84] between a small group of congressmen from both houses, who worked out the details of what has been called the "Compromise of 1877."[85]

So a deal was struck, the filibuster dissolved and on Friday, March 2, at 4:00 a.m. Rutherford B. Hayes was declared the new President with an electoral count of 185 to Tilden's 184. The President-elect rode into Washington that very day in a private railroad car provided by Thomas A. Scott. On Saturday, President Grant held a dinner party in the White House for his successor and, at his request, Chief Justice Morrison R. Waite administered the oath of office privately to Hayes in the Red Room, since March 4 was a Sunday. The public inauguration took place on March 5, without incident, and on that day the new President fulfilled the first part of the bargain by appointing David M. Key of Tennessee to be postmaster general. A month later—over ten years since the Civil War had ended—Hayes withdrew the last federal troops from the South, bringing Reconstruction to a close.

10

The Gilded Age, 1869–1895

MARK TWAIN COAUTHORED a book with Charles Dudley Warner in 1873 entitled *The Gilded Age: A Tale of Today,* which depicted an American society riddled with corruption. Senator Abner Dilworthy and Colonel Beriah Sellers, its main characters, are involved in a railroad bribery scheme, which includes the government. The novel was indeed a "tale of today" because it typified business operations following the Civil War. And the title of the book, *The Gilded Age,* has been used by historians to characterize the entire era of American history from the Grant administration to the end of the nineteenth century.[1]

Long before Rutherford B. Hayes won the presidency, the Gilded Age had begun. It reached its apogee during the administration of Ulysses S. Grant. Big business had so corrupted the electoral process during and after the Civil War that money had become the fastest and best method of acquiring access to government and its power.

Henry Adams, an historian of note, reminisced about government in the Gilded Age and described it as "poor in purpose and barren in results. One might search the whole list of Congress, Judiciary, and Executive during the twenty-five years 1870–1895," he lamented, "and find little but damaged reputations."[2]

It is an exaggeration, of course. But not by much. The remarkable industrialization of the nation from 1860 to 1890 resulted in large measure from direct or indirect government support. The expansion of the railroad in this period from thirty thousand miles of track to two hundred thousand involved massive public assistance, especially in the form of land grants. Higher tariffs stimulated such industries as steel, copper and wool, and federal banking and monetary policies attracted both foreign and domestic investors. Businesses that needed tariff protection or political favors of one kind or another, or land grants, inevitably offered loans or bribes or financial support to preferred congressmen. And these congressmen were all too quick to accept what they liked to think were "gifts" in recognition of their status and importance. Chairmen of special committees were always a target of such beneficence. Even men whose integrity was recognized and respected had no problem engaging in activities that today would be regarded as conflict of interest. Railroads regularly rewarded congressmen with cash, free passes and stock. Representative Grenville Dodge of Iowa, for example, served as chief engineer of the Union Pacific Railroad from 1866 to 1870, coinciding with the years he was a Republican congressman in the 40th Congress (March 1867 to March 1869). Jay Cooke, the so-called financier of the Civil War, held a mortgage on Speaker James G. Blaine's Washington home and regularly conferred favors on select congressmen. Sooner or later the scandals were bound to splatter into public view, and it was during the 1870s that the worst of them came to light.

THE NOTORIOUS CRÉDIT Mobilier scandal rocked the nation. Exposed by Charles A. Dana's *New York Sun* on September 4, 1872, this scandal involved the Vice President and former Speaker Schuyler Colfax, along with Henry Wilson of Massachusetts, who succeeded Colfax as Grant's vice presidential running mate in the election of 1872, Secretary of the Treasury George S. Boutwell, a former representative and a prosecutor in the impeachment trial of Andrew Johnson, and twelve other members of Congress, among them James A. Garfield, chairman of Appropriations; Henry L. Dawes, chairman of Ways and Means; William D. ("Pig Iron") Kelley, chairman of Civil Service; John A. Bingham, chairman of the Judiciary Committee; and Glenn W. Scofield, chairman of the Naval Committee.

Crédit Mobilier was a dummy construction company formed by the Union Pacific Railroad to provide profits from the building of the railroad, and Republican Oakes Ames of Massachusetts sold its stock to select congressmen who would use their political influence to benefit the company. It was alleged that in appreciation for the stock, the recipients helped defeat legislation that would have regulated the Union Pacific's railroad rates.[3]

Despite these allegations (they came late in the campaign), President Grant and his running mate, Henry Wilson, won the election in the fall of 1872 over the Liberal Republican ticket of Horace Greeley, the editor of the *New York Tribune* who, in 1848, had served a short and undistinguished term in the House of Representatives, and B. Gratz Brown. The Liberal Republican faction developed within Republican ranks in 1871 and attracted a number of reform-minded Democrats. It was led by the German-born senator Carl Schurz, a former Union general. A varied and disparate group, the Liberal Republicans crusaded for civil service reform and tariff reductions, and against further federal intervention in the South.

Tariff reform became a leading problem toward the end of the century. Republicans tended to be protectionists—that is, those who wanted to keep out foreign competition—and they supported higher tariff rates, which, however much they assisted American manufactures, usually resulted in higher prices at home for many basic goods. They also provided additional revenue for the government, which sometimes resulted in a surplus in the Treasury and consequently encouraged large "pork barrel" projects by congressmen. Most Democrats, but not all, tended to be antiprotectionists and fought to reduce the surplus. Many of them, but again not all, favored an across-the-board reduction of tariff rates.

Greeley also ran on a platform that advocated a return to specie (gold and silver) payments in place of paper (greenbacks). This hard-money-versus-soft-money controversy became another major issue in the late-nineteenth century. Inflationists (soft-money advocates) argued in favor of paper in order to increase the amount of money in circulation, while anti-inflationists (hard-money supporters) demanded a strong currency, which meant the circulating medium must be backed by specie. Generalizations are always risky, but by and large Democrats tended to favor soft money and Republicans hard money

The Democratic Party chose to endorse Greeley and Brown, rather than nominate a separate ticket, and the Prohibition Party named James Black and John Russell as its candidates. Once again the Republicans "waved the bloody shirt," linking the Liberal Republicans with unreconstructed southern rebels. Greeley proved to be an ineffectual candidate and died a few weeks after the election.

Once Congress reconvened in December 1872, the Crédit Mobilier scandal had to be faced squarely, and the Speaker, James G. Blaine, who disclaimed any involvement in the affair, appointed a select committee of five, chaired by Luke P. Poland, a Republican from Vermont, to investigate.[4] Every individual mentioned in the scandal appeared before the committee and tried to exonerate himself. Ames defended his actions through a written statement read by his counsel, denying that he had ever attempted to bribe a member of Congress. All he did was sell stock to the members as a sound investment.[5] What was so wrong in that? It was business, nothing more.

On February 18, 1873, the committee reported that Ames was "guilty of selling to members of Congress shares of stock in the Crédit Mobilier of America, for prices much below the true value of such stock, with *the* intent thereby to influence the votes and decisions of such members in matters to be brought before Congress for action." The report also contended that Charles H. Neilson, the son-in-law of Representative James Brooks of New York, had received from Ames fifty shares of stock in Crédit Mobilier "for the use and benefit of said Brooks," knowing that it was intended "to influence the votes and decisions of said Brooks as a member of the House" and "as a Government director of the Union Pacific Railroad Company." The committee then recommended the expulsion of Ames and Brooks from the House of Representatives, but they exonerated all the others who had been mentioned in the scandal. It concluded that "these others" might have been "indiscreet" but were not guilty of criminal intent. In fact most of these participants had returned the stock as soon as the scandal broke and denied making a financial killing. Garfield, for example, netted a profit of only $329.[6]

The committee took particular delight in nailing James Brooks, a Democratic leader and a constant critic of Republican policies during the Civil War and Reconstruction. Now it could repay him for all the trouble he had caused. It recommended that he be "absolutely" condemned for using his position as a director of the Union Pacific and member of the House to procure Crédit Mobilier stock for himself and his family, "whose interests depended directly upon the legislation of Congress."[7]

On February 27, 1873, the House, by a vote of 115 to 110, with 15 abstentions, "absolutely" condemned Ames; and followed it with a similar condemnation of Brooks by a vote of 174 to 32. The striking difference in the vote is indicative of the thirst for revenge among Republicans. In the voting, several of those mentioned in the scandal abstained, including Bingham, Dawes, Garfield, Kelley and Scofield.

During the voting, Ames and Brooks sat at their places, their faces deathlike masks. They knew what was coming and felt the disgrace very deeply. When the decision was announced, a strange and unbelievable scene followed. Republican members who had just voted to condemn Ames rushed up to him and asked his pardon. "We know you are innocent," they babbled, "but we had to do it in order to satisfy our constituents."[8]

Only in Congress!

The two men were not expelled, but their terms were due to end momentarily and they both died shortly thereafter. The others implicated managed to survive the scandal, except Schuyler Colfax, who had contradicted himself so often in his testimony that the public turned against him and his career ended in disgrace.

SADLY, THE CRÉDIT Mobilier scandal was just one in a long catalog of corrupt behavior by government officials. Hardly a government office resisted the temptation to put its hand in the till. Within a week of condemning Ames and Brooks, Congress joined the plundering by voting itself a 40 percent salary increase from $5,000 to $7,500 in the "Salary Grab" Act of

March 1873. And this boost in pay was awarded retroactively. In a rider to an appropriations bill, each member received a $5,000 bonus.[9]

But the windfall did not last. The violent reaction of an outraged public forced Congress to repeal the law on January 20, 1874. "We witnessed the humiliating spectacle of twenty-five different members rushing in with a bill to repeal the salary clause," wrote James Garfield, chairman of the Appropriations Committee and the chief floor manager for the House bill, "when everybody knew that one was enough. Of course this was done merely to exhibit to the public eye an appearance of zeal."[10]

The question of congressional salaries has, from time to time, caused a popular uproar. In the beginning, the salaries were fixed at a per diem rate, and when, in 1816, there was an effort to move to a yearly salary, the public reacted so violently that Congress repealed the act and returned to a per diem rate. Not until August 16, 1856, at the height of the slavery conflict that led to the Civil War, did the Congress finally agree to fix salaries at $3,000 per annum. And there was no public outcry. Then, on July 28, 1866, again without a public disturbance, Congress gave itself a $2,000 raise and agreed to a $5,000 salary. After the Salary Grab of 1873, it would take thirty-three years before Congress would again risk another pay raise.

The truth of the matter is that congressmen were grossly underpaid.[11] The price of living in Washington had escalated in the previous decade. According to one reporter, it cost well-to-do members of Congress about $2,000 a month to live in the capital, "but they live high and entertain lavishly." A representative who had a wife and children to support would rent rooms in a boardinghouse and could get through the month on about $150, or $1,500 for the year. "But even this cast a big hole in his income" because of the cost of food and clothing and many incidental expenses. "I have talked with hundreds of members about their expenses here," this journalist reported, "and they all have told me the same story; that is, if they could not make some money, or at least a little money, on the outside, there would always be a balance on the wrong side of the ledger."[12]

And so some congressmen stole to make ends meet.

HOWEVER, THERE WERE a number of important pieces of legislation enacted throughout the period. To start, the Public Credit Act passed in 1869 promised to discharge all government obligations to public creditors and redeem war bonds in coin or its equivalent as a means of strengthening public credit. The Judiciary Act of 1869 established the Justice Department, and the Patent and Copy Right Act of 1870 protected the rights of creative individuals, including artists, inventors and scientists. And the Territory of the District of Columbia Act, approved in 1871, established the territory of the district with a presidentially appointed governor and secretary, and a two-house legislature in which the lower house was popularly elected.

The consequences of the involvement of congressional leaders with big business was bad enough for the Republican Party, but the onset of the Panic of 1873, an economic depression that lasted until 1879, proved devastating. The panic was triggered by the overexpansion in commerce, industry and agriculture, plus the wild speculation in railroads, and the failure of the Jay Cooke banking firm. It generated widespread distress. The stock market collapsed, 3 million workers lost their jobs over the next five years, mills and factories shut their doors, banks closed, farm prices dropped and one in four railroads defaulted on their bonds.[13] And how did Congress react? It released millions of dollars in greenbacks. Earlier, in February 1873, toward the close of the 42nd Congress before the panic struck, it had passed the Coinage Act—later savaged as "the Crime of '73"—which eliminated the silver dollar from circulation and made gold the only coin to be minted. Then, when the depression exploded in September, soft-money advocates condemned the "Crime" and demanded that Congress increase the money supply to combat the economic suffering by minting silver dollars at a ratio to gold of 16 to 1. The recent discovery of silver in the mines of Nevada, Colorado and Utah, they argued, provided the easy means of achieving this goal.

Not surprisingly, the Republican Party suffered a major electoral defeat in the midterm election of 1874. Their majority of 110 seats in the House changed to a 60-seat majority for the Democrats, who would now have 181 members to the Republicans 107. The Senate, however, remained safely Republican.[14] But this Democratic victory began a long period of divided government wherein many bills initiated in one house died in the other.

After the election, the Republican lame-duck session of the 43rd Congress enacted the Specie Resumption Act, which directed the replacement of greenbacks with gold coin after January 1, 1879. It also raised the tariff to generate needed revenue. This was the same lame-duck session that passed the Civil Rights Act of 1875.

Blaine, the outgoing Speaker, had, during his six-year tenure, inaugurated several important changes in the conduct of House business. He referred to the Speaker's list of those who desired to speak on the floor and recognized only those who favored the bills he supported, which was a major step in increasing his power. But, although he was extremely partisan, he respected the rights of the minority. For example, he was unwilling to block their tactics of obstructionism, such as calling for roll calls or quorum calls or other parliamentary maneuvers. For this reason he was respected by both Republicans and Democrats. On one occasion when Ben Butler of Massachusetts attempted to sneak a bill through the House to force the southern states to permit blacks to vote, Blaine presided "in full evening dress," having been summoned from a dinner party, to defeat Butler's scheme. The session lasted from 7:30 in the evening until 4:00 the following afternoon and, according to one report, Blaine never once left his post, except for a moment during the calling of the roll, which could not be interrupted by any member. Food and refreshments were brought to his desk to help sustain him, and Butler's Force Bill was rejected. "Never during his whole service as Speaker of the House," declared the *New York Tribune* of February 26, 1875, "has Mr. Blaine displayed to better advantage his exceptional ability as a parliamentarian and presiding officer, or his power to dispose instantly of the most perplexing questions." When Blaine retired from the chair a week later and was voted the thanks of the House, "the applause from both sides of the aisle was thunderous and in waves."[15]

THE 44TH CONGRESS convened on December 6, 1875, and House Democrats, thirsting for blood upon their return to power following a sixteen-year sojourn in the wilderness, initiated upward of fifty committee investigations into every operation of the now beleaguered Grant administration. They brought many scandals to light. The President's private secretary, General Orville E. Babcock, allegedly directed a "Whiskey Ring," in which the government was defrauded of millions of dollars in taxes through the sale of whiskey bearing forged revenue stamps. The ring was exposed by the *St. Louis Democrat* in the spring of 1875 and resulted in the indictment of over two hundred individuals, many in the Treasury Department. Babcock was also indicted but escaped imprisonment through the intervention of the President.[16]

The secretary of war, William W. Belknap, was impeached by the House on March 2, 1876, for accepting bribes for the sale of trading posts in the Indian Territory. He resigned to avoid trial.[17]

Not only the Treasury and War Departments dabbled in embezzlement and fraud, but the Freedmen's Bureau, the Navy Department, the Interior Department, the Post Office and the attorney general's office helped themselves to whatever largess they could identify, resulting in many indictments, resignations and, on occasion, convictions. Even James G. Blaine, now House minority leader, and the front-running Republican contender for the Republican presidential nomination in 1876, was accused of having used his position as Speaker to offer worthless bonds as collateral for a loan of $64,000 he had received from the Union Pacific Railroad and which he had never been asked to repay. Supposedly, he used his influence as Speaker to provide the railroad with a land grant. To investigate the charges, a subcommittee of the House Judiciary Committee interviewed a man by the name of James Mulligan, who claimed he had letters proving the accusations against Blaine. These letters were written to Warren Fisher, one of the contractors of the Little Rock & Fort Smith Railroad, who had authorized Blaine to sell securities in the railroad and receive his commission in bonds. Mulligan was Fisher's bookkeeper and formerly employed by Blaine's brother-in-law, Jacob Stanwood. Mulligan and Stanwood quarreled and Blaine was called in to arbitrate the dispute. Of course, Blaine decided in favor of his brother-in-law, whereupon Mulligan severed his relationship with Stanwood. Then, when the value of the bonds plummeted because of the railroad's financial problems, Thomas A. Scott, president of the Union Pacific Railroad, bought the bonds from Blaine at an inflated price, and the Speaker pushed through legislation to benefit Scott's railroad.[18]

On the morning Mulligan was scheduled to testify before the subcommittee, he was intercepted at his hotel by Blaine, who talked him into surrendering the letters. According to Mulligan, Blaine "abjectly begged for the letters," declaring that if the committee got hold of them "it would ruin him for life." He "prayed . . . and implored me to think of his six children and his wife." He said he even "contemplated suicide." Finally, he asked Mulligan if he would like a consulship. None of this importuning worked, so Blaine asked if he could examine the letters, promising to give them back. Foolishly, Mulligan agreed, whereupon Blaine reneged on his promise, thrust the letters into his pocket and strode out of the room.[19]

Blaine told a different story, claiming that "my offering him a consulship and about my being ruined and all that sort of thing, is mere fancy." Furthermore, he said, he made no promise about returning the letters because "they were strictly private letters which Mulligan had no right to have" and had "no more connection or relationship with the examination now going on before the Judiciary Committee than the man in the moon."[20]

Rather than turn the letters over to the Judiciary Committee, Blaine decided to give a dramatic performance in the House on June 5, 1876, citing personal privilege, in which he would read the supposed proofs of his guilt. Known for his debating skill, to say nothing of his audacity, he believed his only hope of getting off scot-free was to go on the offensive. Besides, it was only days before the Republican presidential nominating convention met, and Blaine, as the leading contender, had to exonerate himself or risk losing the nomination.[21]

The galleries were packed with eager spectators waiting for this glamorous man to show his mettle. Scores of visitors defied the doorkeepers and jammed their way to the floor of the House. All eyes were riveted on Blaine. Tall, imperious, self-confident, verbally agile, a gambler with an explosive temper, he was a master of the dramatic art, and proceeded to give a sensational performance.

Blaine rose from his place, drew himself up to his full height and gained recognition. In a slow, measured tone of voice, he began his speech. Suddenly, he thrust his hand into the breast pocket of his coat, drew out a packet of letters and held them up for all to see. Then he brought the packet down on his desk with a loud smack. In a voice soaring with emotion he cried, "I am not afraid to show the letters. Thank God Almighty! I am not ashamed to show them. There they are," he bellowed, as he pointed to the pile. "There is the very original package. And with some sense of humiliation, with a mortification which I do not pretend to conceal, with a sense of outrage which I trust any man in my position would feel, I invite the confidence of 44,000,000 of my fellow countrymen, while I read those letters from this desk."[22]

Naturally he edited what he read, leaving out what some might consider incriminating evidence. But his performance was flawless. To a very large extent he modeled his political style after Henry Clay. His voice rose in pitch, his arms swung in every direction and his fingers pointed to emphasize his meaning. His audience, unaware that this was an act, marveled at his histrionics. As he commented on what was written, interpreting as he went along, the crowd regularly broke into cheers. He convinced one and all of his innocence.

He ended on a triumphant note. He knew that Josiah Caldwell, another promoter of the Little Rock & Fort Smith Railroad, had sent a telegram to J. Proctor Knott of Kentucky, the fiercely partisan Democratic chairman of the Judiciary Committee, apparently clearing Blaine of any wrongdoing. But Knott had not revealed this evidence, nor told anyone about it. Knowing this, Blaine ended his speech by turning toward Knott and forcing him to admit that he had concealed Caldwell's telegram. That telegram, Blaine trumpeted, "completely and absolutely exonerated me from this charge, and you have suppressed it."[23]

The audience gasped. Blaine had demolished his accusers. The tumult from the floor and galleries drowned out the chair's efforts to restore order. It was a scene of wild jubilation. "I have been a long time in congress," declared James A. Garfield, "and never saw such a scene in the house."[24]

For the moment, the accused walked out of the chamber completely exonerated. Several weeks later Robert G. Ingersoll of Pennsylvania nominated Blaine for President at the Republican Convention in Cincinnati, dubbing him "a plumed knight" who "marched down the halls of the American Congress and threw his shining lance full and fair against the brazen forehead of the defamers of his country and maligners of his honor."[25]

It is a pity what happened to James G. Blaine. He was a man of extraordinary abilities. His colleagues admired and respected him because of his statesmanlike handling of his duties as Speaker. Champ Clark, a future Democratic Speaker, said that "a more brilliant man never figured in American politics than James Gillespie Blaine. His friends are fond of comparing him to Henry Clay, and indeed the two careers are filled with startling parallels." Both Blaine and Clay desperately wanted to be President. Both would have made distinguished chief executives, judging by what they accomplished as public servants. Both failed to win the confidence and trust of the American people. Both are tragic heroes.[26]

BUT THE GILDED Age was not all moral depravity. There were brighter moments, including the efforts to make Washington a more livable city, even though those efforts wallowed in corruption because President Grant appointed his cronies to key positions, and they brought on a disaster that bankrupted the district. Newspapers had long complained that the capital was a place where "the rents are high, the food is bad, the dust is disgusting, and mud is deep, and the morals are deplorable." Some suggested moving the capital farther west, possibly to Chicago or St. Louis. Alerted to the danger that could threaten their livelihood, district businessmen took action. A group of 150 influential citizens petitioned Congress to establish a territorial government and initiate local control. The Territory of the District of Columbia Act resulted, and Grant immediately started paying off political debts by exercising his appointive powers. He named Henry Cooke, the brother of the financier Jay Cooke, as territorial governor, and placed another crony, Alexander Shepherd, on the Board of Public Works.[27]

Give the devil his due. Shepherd, over a period of time, transformed the city from a "slovenly and comfortless sleepy old town" into a "great and beautiful metropolis." Old buildings were demolished, every street was paved, disease-infested canals were drained and filled in, aqueducts were built, railroad tracks were torn up, sewers were covered over and sixty thousand trees were planted. The entire city was graded: the low places were filled in and the elevations were lowered. Some ninety miles of streets were paved with wood or asphalt and "are kept as clean as your parlor floor," wrote one visitor. The street cleaner "rides a great machine whose roller is covered with hundreds of stiff little twigs, arranged in a spiral. As the horses pull the machine along, the roller turns, and the broomlike twigs sweep the dust and dirt off to the side where they are gathered up and carted away."

In addition, this visitor continued, Washington had "the most reasonable streetcar system in the United States. There are two-cent, three-cent and five-cent fares. . . . There are hundreds of horsecars, and the transfer system is such that you can go all over the city for one fare, or at the farthest for two."[28] These cars ran every five minutes "in place of the solitary stage" that used to plod "its slow way between Georgetown and the Capital."[29]

Where streets and avenues crossed, traffic "circles" with central fountains were constructed, and the circles were soon named after Civil War heroes, such as John Logan, Philip Sheridan, Winfield Scott and Samuel Du Pont.

"Splendid mansions" already lined Vermont, Massachusetts and Connecticut Avenues. "The French, Spanish, English and other foreign governments have bought on and near these avenues for the purpose of building on them handsome houses for their separate legations."[30]

Parks were designed and ornamented with shrubs, trees, flowers and fountains. Frederick Law Olmsted, the distinguished landscape architect responsible for New York's Central Park, was hired to create a plan for the improvement of the grounds around the Capitol. He designed the terraces that circle the north, south and west sides of the structure. These terraces serve as a kind of pedestal on which the building sits. In addition, public monuments were erected to honor the nation's past heroes. "The old provincial Southern city is no more," reported the *New York Independent.* "From its foundations has risen another city, neither Southern nor Northern but national, cosmopolitan."[31]

It cost a great deal of money to bring about this transformation, a lot of which was siphoned off by Grant's cronies, in particular Shepherd and the "henchmen of those members of Congress whose votes secured him liberal appropriations." Over $2 million was spent on the beautification and another $9 million in debts were authorized. Despite the contribution by Congress of $5 million, the district collapsed into bankruptcy in the summer of 1873. The First Bank of Washington closed and its president, Henry Cooke, resigned as governor of the district. Congress investigated and, after hearing testimony of bribery and assorted forms of thievery, dissolved the territorial government. Shepherd fled to Mexico.[32]

This sparkling, tree-lined city had grown from a population of less than 61,000 during the early Jacksonian period to 150,000 during the Gilded Age. And the increase in wealth had been even greater. The number of churches during that time increased from twenty-four to over two hundred. There were no worthwhile public schools for white children in the 1820s and it was forbidden by law to instruct black children. By the 1880s there were 26,696 pupils in white schools, instructed by hundreds of teachers, and something like 11,640 black children enrolled in colored schools. During the Jacksonian era, streets were lighted at night by the moon—or not at all if it was a cloudy evening. By the Gilded Age, streets were illuminated by gas and electricity.[33]

In the past, especially the 1840s, few members of Congress brought their families to Washington; now, in the 1870s, more than half of them did so. Because they no longer messed together in boardinghouses, the listing of "Members in Messes," which had been regularly printed in the *Congressional Directory,* was eliminated.[34] The building of hotels and private residences accelerated and Washington began to look like a thriving city.

Two decades earlier, business in the district was mainly conducted on two streets: Pennsylvania Avenue and Seventh Street. Now G Street and New York Avenue were entirely occupied by stores and offices, and F Street "is the shopping street of the city." By the end of the century a congressman exiting from the Capitol could hop on "an electric car which whirls him up the avenue to the Willard [Hotel], nearly a mile, in seven minutes."[35]

The changes in Washington reflected the many dramatic developments in the country. Technological advances in agriculture produced more than enough crops to feed the nation and a number of foreign nations as well. The telegraph reached across the continent, as did the railroad. The telephone and typewriter were introduced, and a cable was successfully laid across the Atlantic Ocean. The Edison Electric Illuminating Company built the first electric plant in New York City in 1882. A few years later the American Bell Telephone Company, which owned the telephone patents, reorganized itself to become the American Telephone and Telegraph Company. Immigration swelled, and cities grew in number and size.

It needs to be remembered that while these developments transformed American life, Congress was deeply engaged in enacting Reconstruction legislation. Both these major events—Reconstruction and the industrialization of America—occurred simultaneously. As a consequence, northern states were constantly distracted from the problems of Reconstruction and the need for reform. Instead, they focused on the engines of moneymaking and those modern improvements that were refashioning society. As the Republican governor of South Carolina noted, "The North is *tired* of the Southern question."[36]

A particularly bright note occurred during the final days of the Grant administration, when the country celebrated the centennial year of the Republic. It was another splendid reminder of the greatness achieved in the country over the past one hundred years. At precisely twelve o'clock on July 4, church bells struck and fire alarm bells sounded once, then seven times, then seven times again, and finally six times to denote "1776," which was followed by a similar peal to mark the current year—"1876." At the same moment, the *Statue of Freedom* atop the Capitol dome was lighted by electricity and shone brilliantly over the entire city. Thirty-seven pieces of artillery at the armory boomed a national salute, "and there was general ringing of bells, large and small, with firing of pistols and blowing of horns."[37]

THE YEAR 1876 also witnessed a presidential election, an election that culminated in Hayes's victory and what seemed to many to be just another example of the widespread corruption within the government that was so prevalent during this Gilded Age. But Washington was not alone. Scandals abounded throughout the United States. The Tweed Ring in New York City, for example, stole money on a monumental scale. William Marcy Tweed, the boss of Tammany Hall, the city's Democratic machine, and his cohorts seized the municipal treasury and made off with somewhere between $100 and $200 million through kickbacks, fake vouchers, padded bills and other fraudulent devices. The cartoons of Thomas Nast in *Harper's Weekly* helped expose the corruption. Tweed himself was ultimately arrested and convicted. He died in prison, although many others in the ring escaped to Europe with their plunder.

And corruption flourished throughout the South, where the rebuilding of a shattered society provided the opportunity for carpetbaggers, scallywags and the criminal-minded to take advantage of the many building contracts and bids for social services that had become available to cheat, bribe, steal, raise taxes and increase state debts.

The Democratic leader of the House, Samuel J. Randall of Pennsylvania, was elected Speaker at the start of the second session of the 44th Congress on December 4, 1876, succeeding Michael C. Kerr of Indiana, a Democrat, who had died the previous August. Like Speaker Blaine, the very forceful, able, forty-nine-year-old Randall recognized those on the floor who supported legislation in which he was interested. He made committee assignments the same way. He headed a five-man committee that revised the rules of the House, which greatly strengthened the power of the Speaker. The Rules Committee, a select committee, had been relatively negligible for much of the nineteenth century.[38] Randall and his committee undertook a massive overhaul of House rules by reducing their number from 166 to 44, elevating the Rules Committee to that of a standing committee and designating the Speaker as chairman with the authority to appoint the chairmen and members of all standing and select committees. Furthermore, future rule changes had to be referred to the Rules Committee itself.

Other committees also increased their authority. As Woodrow Wilson noted in his book *Congressional Government: A Study of American Politics,* "the House sits . . . to sanction the conclusions of the committees. . . . It leg-

Speaker Samuel J. Randall undertook a massive overhaul of House rules, which greatly strengthened his authority.

islates in its committee-rooms . . . so that it is not far from the truth to say that Congress in session is Congress on public exhibition, whilst Congress in its committees is Congress at work."[39] Since the House was now dominated by inflationists, Richard P. Bland of Missouri introduced a bill calling for the free and unlimited coinage of silver at the ratio of 16 to 1. But the Senate modified it and stipulated that the treasury secretary must purchase not less than $2 million or more than $4 million worth of silver per month. Eastern financiers and their supporters in the Senate opposed the unlimited feature of Bland's bill because of the danger of runaway inflation and accepted this compromise on February 28, 1878. But when President Hayes vetoed it, Congress passed it over his veto, 196 to 73 in the House, and 46 to 19 in the Senate.

Another area of conflict between the executive and Congress involved patronage. Civil service reform was badly needed. Senator Roscoe Conkling of New York derisively referred to it as "snivel service." "During the last twenty-five years," James Garfield recorded, "it has been understood, by the Congress and the people, that offices are to be obtained by the aid of senators and representatives, who thus become the dispensers, sometimes the brokers of patronage." For all intents and purposes, he continued, the Tenure of Office Act "has virtually resulted in the usurpation, by the senate, of a large share of the appointing power." This measure "has resulted in seriously crippling the just powers of the executive, and has placed in the hands of senators and representatives a power most corrupting and dangerous."[40]

Hayes challenged one of the most powerful figures in Congress, Senator Roscoe Conkling, the leader of the "Stalwart" (Radical) faction of the Republican Party, by ordering an investigation of the notoriously corrupt patronage system operating in the New York Custom House, the political power base of the Conkling organization. Chester A. Arthur was its collector and Alonzo B. Cornell its naval officer. President Grant had given control of the patronage of the Custom House to Conkling, but Hayes was determined to end it. The President therefore fired both Arthur and Cornell and with the help of Democrats secured Senate confirmation of their replacements. This victory by Hayes crippled the Conkling machine and diminished Stalwart influence in the Senate.

An even more serious struggle developed between the House and the President. Democrats, who controlled the House, were determined to annul several Reconstruction measures that were still operative in the South, such as requiring a test oath for jury duty, authorizing armed forces to protect voters at the polls and establishing election laws to protect national elections from fraud. In the 45th Congress, Republicans still dominated the Senate, so there was little the Democrats in the House could do except perhaps to block the annual appropriations for the army. The Democratic leadership finally came up with a better plan by which they could force the

President to accept their demands. They decided to attach riders to appropriation bills. In effect, they said to him that if you want supplies, you must acquiesce to our demands.

On the final night of the 45th Congress, about two hours after midnight, Garfield, speaking for the President and his party, offered a compromise. "I made a speech of fifteen minutes," he said, and was greeted by a clamorous shout of refusal by the Democrats.[41] Finally, Congress passed the army appropriation bill, but it carried a rider that prohibited, among other things, the use of federal troops or armed civilians to keep the peace at the polls where congressional elections were involved. Hayes struck back with a veto. "The new doctrine, if maintained," he wrote in his message of April 29, 1879, "will result in a consolidation of unchecked and despotic power in the House of Representatives. A bare majority of the House will become the Government. The Executive will no longer be what the Framers of the Constitution intended—an equal and independent branch of the Government."[42]

The Democrats tried again with a bill to prohibit federal force at elections except on application from the state, and once more Hayes vetoed. A third, then a fourth, then a fifth and even a sixth attempt was put forth but each time Hayes stood his ground, and the Democrats could not override. It was a major victory for the chief executive, who finally forced the House to reluctantly approve the appropriation acts without imposing its will on the President. Actually the Democrats never wished to curtail executive power. They simply wanted the total end of federal interference in southern elections.[43]

Throughout this struggle Hayes had the strong support of James Garfield, who, at various times, feared the President might weaken in his resolve to stand firm. "I spent an hour with the President yesterday on the veto," Garfield wrote his wife. "I think I have never had so much intellectual and personal influence over him as now. He is fully in line with his party."[44]

HAVING PLEDGED NOT to seek a second term at the time he accepted nomination in 1876, Hayes stepped aside in 1880. In this ongoing struggle within the Republican Party between Conkling's Stalwart faction and the "Half Breed" (supposedly not "real Republicans") faction, led by James G. Blaine, over the issues of spoils and civil-service reform, the Half Breeds threw their support at the Republican nominating convention to a "dark horse," James A. Garfield. After thirty-six ballots, the party finally chose Garfield to head the ticket. A former college president and war hero who loved to read classical literature in the original languages, Garfield stood six feet tall and exuded massive physical strength. In addition, "he was handsome, a soldier, widely read, eloquent of speech, and charming of manner."[45] And he had served the party and the President well as House leader. He proved to be the perfect presidential candidate. As a sop to the Stalwart faction, and a means of securing New York's electoral vote, the Republicans nominated Conkling's chief lieutenant, Chester A. Arthur, for Vice President. By satisfying (to an extent) both factions, the party came together in support of the ticket.

The Democrats put up Civil War general Winfield Scott Hancock and William H. English, but its platform hardly differed from that of the Republicans, except for their insistence on a tariff for revenue only, not protection. By 1878, the Greenback Party had emerged with a platform advocating free coinage of silver, woman suffrage, federal regulation of interstate commerce and a graduated income tax. It nominated James Weaver for President in the election of 1880.

With the return of prosperity and the large financial support provided the Republican Party by private industry, to say nothing of his personal attractiveness, Garfield won the election, the first candidate to go directly from the House of Representatives to the White House. In addition, it was the first election in which electors were chosen by popular vote in every state. Garfield received 214 electoral and 4,449,053 popular votes to 115 electoral and 4,442,035 popular votes for Hancock. The popular vote proved to be very close. The Democrat carried the South, something that would persist for nearly a hundred years. If nothing else, Garfield's victory demonstrated that the Republican Party could capture the presidency without the southern black vote. And the Republicans won control of the House for the first time since 1874. There were 152 Republicans to 130 Democrats in the 47th Congress.[46]

Since the new census showed the population of the country had reached 50.2 million, the number of seats in the House of Representatives was increased from 293 to 332—and it kept expanding each decade. By the end of the century, representatives numbered 386 and senators 76. The South particularly benefited from this increase, and formed a solid block of Democratic strength. By virtue of intimidation and discriminatory laws regarding suffrage, southern states virtually nullified the 15th Amendment with respect to black voting rights. Democratic rule—which meant white rule— returned in force and made the "Solid South" possible.

Once President Garfield had been inaugurated on March 4, 1881, he clashed with the Stalwarts over control of patronage; and he further alienated them by appointing Blaine as his secretary of state. But his assassination by a disgruntled and unstable office seeker, Charles J. Guiteau, who contended that he wanted the Stalwart, Chester Arthur, as President, helped destroy the Stalwart faction. Shot on July 2, 1881, at the Washington railroad station, Garfield lingered for more than two months before dying on September 19.

THE ASSASSINATION OF Garfield in 1881, plus the victory of the Democrats at the polls in the fall election of 1882, prompted the lame-duck Congress, with President Arthur's strong endorsement, to enact the Pendleton Civil Service Reform Act on January 16, 1883. In the House the vote was 155 to 47.[47] The act established a permanent three-man Civil Service Commission to hold competitive examinations and make appointments based on merit. Of some one hundred thousand government positions, approximately fourteen thousand of them were filled by examination during Arthur's term in office. It was a good start, but further reform of civil service was needed if the patronage system was ever to be controlled.[48]

Earlier, on May 6, 1882, Congress passed the Chinese Exclusion Act, which suspended for a ten-year period the immigration of Chinese laborers, who were blamed for high unemployment and low wages in California. It was the first time immigration into this country was restricted based on nationality.[49] And the tariff commission, created on May 15, 1882, authorized the presidential appointment of a nine-man group to recommend revision of tariff rates. On December 4, the commission brought forth a substantial list of tariff reductions.

With the Democrats in control of the House when the 48th Congress convened on December 3, 1883, they engaged in a bitter contest for the Speakership between John G. Carlisle of Kentucky, a man who had led the fight against the demands by protectionists for higher tariff rates, and Samuel J. Randall of Pennsylvania, whose state demanded tariff protection and expected Randall to safeguard its interests. Carlisle set up his campaign headquarters in the Metropolitan Hotel, while Randall, "surrounded by a group of Philadelphia business men," chose the Ebbitt House. Betting at the Willard Hotel was $500 to $350 that Randall would win because of the strong financial backing he received from business interests.

When the Democratic Caucus convened on December 1, it chose Carlisle, to the surprise of many. "The South and West elected Carlisle tonight," reported the *Louisville Courier-Journal,* "on a principle. . . . It is the tariff." The party stands "for the reform of abuses, and for the rights of the people against monopolists of all kinds."[50] It was the first time since the Civil War that protectionists had failed to elect one of their supporters to the office of Speaker. In the House election that followed, the vote for Speaker was 190 for Carlisle to 113 for J. Warren Keifer.

And the Kentuckian was determined to lower tariff rates. After all, the surplus for the fiscal years 1881 was over $100 million, largely due to the tariff. Carlisle favored a tariff for revenue only, not as a means of keeping foreign products from competing with American goods.[51] Randall was turned aside because he had favored protection. On the last day of the Republican-led lame-duck session back on March 3, 1883, Abram S. Hewitt of New York got into a shouting match with Randall in one of the House cloakrooms. "I shall not be dictated to," cried Randall. To which Hewitt thundered, "You will find your days numbered next December in the Democratic caucus." And Hewitt's prediction proved to be true. Randall was defeated for the Speakership. As compensation, since he had provided such heroic work against the Civil Rights Act and the Force Bills, and as a gesture toward party harmony, he was appointed chairman of the Appropriations Committee by Carlisle.[52]

As Speaker, Carlisle expanded the power of the Rules Committee by initiating the practice of appointing the chairmen of Ways and Means and Appropriations to sit as regular members of this committee. Indeed, his committee appointments and his control of recognition on the floor furthered his ability to impose his will on the House. He frequently turned to a member and asked, "For what purpose does the gentleman rise?" and then refused recognition if he disagreed with whatever the member had in mind. He could be tough and autocratic when it came to floor recognition.

Carlisle was forty-nine years of age, with bushy eyebrows, gray-blue eyes and brown hair. He was clean-shaven, unlike so many of his bearded colleagues during the years of the Civil War and Reconstruction. He surrounded himself with capable administrators, according to most observers, and he had a wonderful faculty for grasping and settling a question almost before it was raised.[53]

As Speaker of the House during the 48th, 49th and 50th Congresses, John G. Carlisle labored unsuccessfully to lower the tariff.

Unfortunately, during his long six-year tenure as Speaker for the 48th, 49th and 50th Congresses, he was unable to do the one thing he desperately wanted to accomplish: lower the tariff. The protectionists knew how to thwart him. They resorted to what was known as "the disappearing quorum." Someone would question the presence of a quorum. The roll would be called and members would not answer when the clerk read their names. Although physically present in the chamber, they would be recorded as absent. Enough absent voters arranged by either party (but usually the minority party) could halt the business of the House. The quorum had disappeared. So the sergeant at arms and his assistants would go out and search the city for real absentees and would physically drag them into the chamber. But when their names were called they would sit mute and not respond. And there was nothing Carlisle could do about it. Frustrated, he was forced to admit that "the chair knows of no process by which a member of the House can be compelled to vote."[54]

One tariff bill was introduced that asked for only a 20 percent reduction to be applied horizontally to all duties on manufactured articles. But Randall and his followers shot it down. Several other such attempts at tariff reform got nowhere, much to the delight of the Republicans as they watched the Democrats devour one another.

If the tariff question divided Democrats, Republicans split over civil-service reform. Independent Republicans who placed this reform above party loyalty were dubbed Mugwumps, because they were seen as fence-sitters with their "mugs" on one side of the fence and their "wumps" on the other. Some of the more prominent Mugwumps included E. L. Godkin, Carl Schurz, George William Curtis and Charles Francis Adams, Jr. They took offense when the 1884 Republican National Convention nominated Blaine for President and John A. Logan for Vice President. They felt Blaine did not support reform, and, what was worse, he was tainted with scandal and corruption. Characterizing themselves as individuals who acted on principle and not blind loyalty to party, they advocated further civil-service reform, the elimination of corrupt machine politics, and the restoration of fairness and decency in political discourse, a plea heard frequently in the future. So the Mugwumps supported the Democratic candidate, Grover Cleveland, a reform mayor of Buffalo and governor of New York, and Thomas A. Hendricks. Cleveland alone among the candidates was recognized as a reformer who would fight the monopolists and their greedy purposes. It was a hotly contested campaign in which newspapers had finally gotten hold of the Mulligan letters and published them, prompting the Democrats to sing out, "Blaine, Blaine, James G. Blaine, the Continental Liar from the State of Maine." Republicans responded by accusing Cleveland of fathering an illegitimate child, and they sang, "Ma, ma, where's my Pa? Gone to the White House, Ha, Ha, Ha."[55]

But what really hurt Blaine was the remark by the Reverend Samuel D. Burchard, leader of a group of clergymen, that the Democratic Party was the party of "Rum, Romanism and Rebellion." This was said in Blaine's presence at a meeting in a New York City hotel, and the candidate failed to disavow the characterization. It cost him many votes in New York among Catholic Irish-Americans—and with it the election. Republican officials appealed to Roscoe Conkling to help Blaine, but Conkling responded, "No, thank you. I don't engage in criminal practice."[56]

It was a very close election. Cleveland won 4,911,017 popular and 219 electoral votes to Blaine's 4,848,334 popular and 182 electoral votes. Cleveland was the first Democratic President since James Buchanan. And although the Republicans gained nearly two dozen additional seats in the House of Representatives, the Democrats retained control.

But real authority in Congress had shifted to a select group of men. In

James G. Blaine's brilliant defense of his conduct on the House floor during the investigation of the Mulligan affair earned him the title of the "white plumed knight."

the House, the fact that the Speaker chose committee members solidified his power; and committee chairmen, usually rising to their positions through seniority, gained enormous command in shepherding individual bills directed to their care to final passage. In December 1885, the House agreed to shift authority over appropriations away from the Appropriations Committee, which, under Randall, had been tightfisted in allocating funds to individual committees. For example, money required by the Army, the Navy, Indian affairs, the post office, and diplomatic affairs that normally came from the Appropriations Committee was now determined by the individual committees (army, navy, Indian affairs, etc.) that handled these matters. Another reason for limiting the authority of the Appropriations Committee was that its chairman, Randall, "broke away from the main body of Democrats on the tariff," and as further punishment, but "not desiring to demote him," Democrats decided to "shear him of a large part of his power by giving authority to half a dozen other committees to report appropriations bills."[57]

Thus, a collection of committee chairmen and the Speaker virtually ran the House. For an individual member, this consolidation of control meant that if he did not occupy a seat on one of the leading committees, he had "little, if any, opportunity to accomplish anything, much less distinguish himself," commented one journalist. ". . . [And] the member of the House who is unfortunate enough to belong to the minority has no show whatever in legislation. He is absolutely cut off from everything but his vote, and that counts for nothing in final results."[58] Moreover, voting by the members invariably followed the party line. This era reaffirmed the importance of parties and the necessity of each representative accepting the direction of the party leadership.

THE CONSOLIDATION OF power in Congress reflected the consolidation of financial power taking place in the United States at that time. Monopolies and trusts were created to eliminate competition. In 1882 the Standard Oil Company formed a trust with a number of affiliated oil producers and refiners to create a company that controlled 90 percent of all the oil produced and refined in the United States. Investment bankers financed consolidations in utilities, railroad and industrial enterprises. The number of state-chartered trust companies rose to near three hundred, with investments hovering around a quarter of a billion dollars. The rapaciousness of these moguls earned them the inelegant title of "Robber Barons," and these barons were not above using their money to corrupt congressmen to obtain the kind of legislation that would help their industries get richer and more powerful or prevent legislation that would control or regulate them. Hard cash was the coin of the realm, and unless a candidate was a millionaire, or sponsored by one, it was virtually impossible during the Gilded Age to be elected by state legislatures to the U.S. Senate.

Corporations used lobbyists extensively to work their will in Congress. Former congressmen who hovered about the Capitol "like birds of prey," and journalists who were paid so little by their newspapers that they were obliged "to prostitute their pens"—these were the so-called impoverished ones employed by businessmen to influence legislation. Sam Ward was known as the "King of the Lobby" because of his extravagant wining and dining of congressmen to advance the interests of the corporations and foreign governments who were his clients. But perhaps the most adroit lobbyists belonged to "the gentle sex." "Women make excellent lobbyists," declared one contemporary, "as they are more plausible than men, and cannot be shaken off as rudely."[59] Some of the ladies were widows or daughters of former congressmen. "They were retained with instructions to exert their influence with designated Congressmen." If they failed to win their vote for or against a particular bill, these ladies endeavored to keep them away from the House when the bill was voted upon. To aid them in this work, "pleasant parlors" were provided them "with works of art and bric-a-brac donated by admirers." A supper was

THE SPIDER-LOBBYIST AT HOME.

Lobbyists have always played a role in congressional history, and none more effectively than the "spider lobbyists" during the Gilded Age.

usually served. A cold game pie, broiled oysters, mixed salad and champagne or Burgundy might constitute the fare. "Who can blame a Congressman," wrote Perley Poore, "for leaving the bad cooking of his hotel or boarding-house . . . to walk into the parlor web which the cunning spider-lobbyist weaves for him?"[60]

What had happened to the democracy bequeathed by the Jacksonians? Universal manhood suffrage had been achieved, but political machines in the cities chose candidates for office and arranged their election, and African-American males in the South found themselves excluded from the polls. More and more immigrants flooded into the country and became easy targets not only for political bosses seeking to build mass electorates, but also industrial tycoons who operated sweatshops and rarely paid a living wage.

In general this was a low point in American politics. And the venality of this age was physically reflected in Congress. The conduct of members in the House was a disgrace and imitated the vulgarity of the times. Visitors in the galleries were shocked to see their representatives sprawled in their chairs, feet on their desks, spitting tobacco juice on the carpets as they aimed for spittoons. Few paid any attention to the business at hand. The Speaker frequently pounded his gavel and demanded that the members give their attention to whoever had the floor. But the general hubbub continued without interruption. Representatives who had been recognized rattled on about anything and nothing, which increased the noise level and the size of the *Congressional Record* but little else.

"Do Congressmen smoke during the session," asked one man rhetorically. "Why bless you, yes. I have seen ladies grow sick in the galleries from the vile odor of the tobacco that rises from the two-for-five-cent cigars in the mouths of the so-called gentlemen below. The Congressmen smoke in their very seats . . . they chew, too! Every desk has a spittoon of pink and gold china beside it to catch the filth. . . . It costs at least four hundred dollars a year to take care of the spittoons for the House, even though your average Congressman often disregards his spittoon and spits on the floor."[61]

Besides spittoons, nine immense bathtubs were purchased and located in the basement under the House at a cost of $175 each, and at least fifty members took a bath every day "at the expense of Uncle Sam. . . . Senators and Supreme Court Justices are reported to use these Capitol baths as often as the Representatives." One congressman got caught in a tub during a crucial vote and a page hurriedly fetched him. "Holding a blanket tightly around his dripping form, the Congressman made his way to the floor of the House, where his vote was counted just as though he had been clothed in the more conventional manner."[62]

At the start of a new session during the Gilded Age, House members frequently found "bouquets of flowers [and] gifts of admirers" waiting for them and brought to their seats. Their individual seats were known to all lobbyists. Members had obtained their seats by drawing lots, except for the dean of the House, the oldest member in terms of service. "He is the only one who has the right to a choice of seats."[63]

How Congress had changed! Long gone were the great days when a Clay or Webster or Stevens could give a speech and influence votes by their oratory. Now votes were not decided in the chamber but in smoke-filled rooms in or out of the Capitol.

In this new industrial age, the electorate became more vocal and insistent in demanding government control of business. And they could not be silenced. Complaints about railroad abuses, such as rebates, railroad pools and discriminatory rates, grew louder and stronger with each passing year and resulted in a congressional probe that finally produced federal regulation of interstate commerce. The House passed the Interstate Commerce Act by a vote of 219 to 41, the Senate by 43 to 15, and President Cleveland signed it in early February 1887. This act prohibited discriminatory rates, rebates and a higher charge for a short haul over a long haul. Railroads had to post their rates and not change them without giving adequate notice. The act also established a five-member Interstate Commerce Commission (ICC), the nation's first regulatory agency. The commission was authorized to investigate railroad management and subpoena company records.

But the cleverness of the railroads' lawyers in finding loopholes in the law (a standard practice to this day), combined with the power and influence of their lobbyists and several decisions by the Supreme Court that favored the railroads, all but rendered the ICC virtually powerless.

Five days after passage of the ICC, the 49th Congress enacted the Dawes General Allotment Act, or Severalty Act, on February 8, 1887. This bill ended Indian tribal identities and initiated the distribution of tribal lands (severalty) in the amount of 160 acres to heads of Indian families and 80 acres to each adult single person. It was felt that life for Indians on reservations hindered their assimilation into American life. Any excess land not allotted to Native Americans—approximately two-thirds of the total— would be made available to non-Indian homesteaders with the proceeds directed toward financing Indian education and health care. Several Indian tribes protested. "Our people have not asked for or authorized this," argued delegates from the Cherokee, Creek and Choctaw nations. "Our own laws regulate a system of land tenure suited to our condition." Over the objections of several congressmen, who called the bill a means of despoiling the Indians, the bill won approval. Both the ICC and the Dawes Act, like most of the important legislation during the Gilded Age, passed Congress without any real involvement of the President.[64]

An interesting side note to the Indian question is the fact that Charles Curtis of Kansas, a Republican, is credited with being the first Native American elected to the House in 1892. He was the son of a quarter-blood Kansa (Kaw) woman and a white father. He served on public lands and expenditures committees and as chairman of the Committee on Indian Affairs. He was a strong advocate of the government's allotment program for Native Americans. He sponsored the Curtis Act of 1898, which abolished tribal courts, and helped advance Oklahoma's statehood. He later won election to the Senate.[65]

One particularly happy development during this period involved the work of Secretary of the Navy William C. Whitney, who assisted the emergence of the United States as a naval colossus. At the end of the Civil War the American Navy, with its fleet of decaying wooden ships, ranked twelfth among the world's naval powers. A naval commission recommended the building of steel warships in 1881, and on March 3, 1883, Congress authorized the building of three such ships, and later extended that number. Secretary Whitney provided innovative leadership not only in reorganizing his department and getting rid of the wooden warships, but he also began an intense program of building or authorizing the construction of almost two dozen new vessels outfitted with the latest improvements in naval armament. His untiring efforts also helped advance the nation's steel industry. Before he was done, a fleet of steel battleships and cruisers had been built. By the end of the century, the nation ranked third among the world's naval powers.

Of the sixteen Congresses that met from the end of the Civil War to the end of the nineteenth century, Democrats in the House held a majority in eight of them—the 44th, 45th, 46th, 48th, 49th, 50th, 52nd and 53rd—and the Republicans controlled eight: 39th, 40th, 41st, 42nd, 43rd, 47th, 51st and 54th. However, Republicans had greater electoral success in the Senate and the presidency. For the first half of this period, the House concentrated on issues involving the Reconstruction of the South and civil rights; during the second half, it switched to economic problems like the tariff and soft money versus hard money. By and large Democrats remained true to the Jeffersonian creed of economy and limited government, while Republicans tended to direct the government in favor of a system of protective tariffs, the funding of public works and reliance on gold-backed currency.

Although several of the Speakers during this period—Blaine (1869–1875), Randall (1876–1881) and Carlisle (1883–1889)—had a measure of talent in directing the affairs of the House, not one of them during the Gilded Age had the strength of purpose and the commanding presence to bring about a revitalized House that could shape national policy and pass legislation demanded by the electorate. Despite the fact that Presidents failed to challenge congressional dominance, this generation, it seemed, could not produce a Henry Clay and enact what the people needed in the way of reform. As a consequence, innumerable bills, running into the thousands, died in committee. As a matter of fact, over eleven thousand measures perished with the conclusion of the 1884–1885 session of the 48th Congress.

Unfortunately, complained Henry Adams, "Congress is inefficient, and shows itself more and more incompetent, as at present constituted, to wield the enormous powers that are forced upon it." The workload was also part of the problem. "The business of a member of Congress," claimed James Garfield prior to his election as President, "must have more than quadrupled during the last twenty years." Veterans and widows applying for pensions, manufacturers urging higher tariff rates and especially heads of corporations demanding tax relief or special consideration for their companies due to the changes brought on by the rise of big business took up most of a congressman's time. "New powers, new duties, new responsibilities, new burdens of every sort," declared Adams, "are incessantly crowding upon the government."[66] In addition, many new members were novices, elected as a result of scandal, and they were not equal to the task of acting like legislators.

The 50th Congress, which convened on December 5, 1887, set a record as the most "feeble" Congress in American history. On January 8, 1888, the *Washington Post* published an editorial entitled "Slowly Doing Nothing." It claimed that the "system of rules is the primary cause of the wonderful inertia of this unwieldy and self-shackled body. . . . In stalling legislation and keeping everybody else from doing anything, a few members are all powerful."

Even more disturbing was the failure of House members to engage in the kind of debates that typified the antebellum period. The heated give-and-take of representatives during the 1830s, 1840s and 1850s in arguing over national issues did not engage members in the Gilded Age. Oratorical contests such as those between Clay and Randolph, Adams and Wise, Webster and Calhoun and others were "as rare . . . as a real tournament of medieval times." The oratorical splendor of the Jacksonian era was a thing of the past.[67]

With a mounting surplus in the Treasury that only encouraged "pork-barrel" projects, President Cleveland used his veto power 414 times—mostly on pensions, one-fourth of which were probably fraudulent, according to one historian[68]—compared with 205 vetoes by all of his predecessors combined; and he pleaded for a reduction in the tariff, a main source of the surplus. But he succeeded only in alienating factions within his own Democratic Party. In the presidential election of 1888, he was defeated by Benjamin Harrison, and with the inauguration of the Harrison administration the House of Representatives at last found the first of a series of Speakers who would take control and direct the course of legislative history into the twentieth century.

It would begin the era of the modern Speaker.

11

"Czar" Reed and "Uncle Joe" Cannon, 1888–1910

THE HOUSE WAS about to receive its master. Many members felt that House operations needed reform, and some of them believed they knew the man who could bring it about. Then, with the election of the 51st Congress in November 1888, which returned the Republicans to power in the House, 173 to 156, the master arrived.

Thomas Brackett Reed was elected a Republican representative in 1876. Born in Portland, Maine, he attended Bowdoin College and served in the state legislature. He was a tall, heavy-set man, standing six feet three inches and weighing over 250 pounds, with a round face and high forehead. He physically dominated any room he entered. He walked with a lurching motion as though aboard a ship rocking in the sea. "He was one of the few men in public life at whom strangers on the street turned to stare. He had a massive two-story head, thatched with thin, flossy, flaxen hair, a scant mustache, and a lily-white complexion. . . . He had a clear, strong, resonant voice, with a distinctive down-east twang, which filled the great hall of the House and could be heard above any uproar." But it was high pitched and, to some ears, raspy, emitting an unpleasant nasally sound. Quick witted, ferociously intelligent and sharp tongued, he loved to deflate windbags with a stinging retort. To a fellow Republican he once remarked, "You are too big a fool to lead and you haven't got sense enough to follow." Yet Reed could be charming and personally attractive—which was his usual deportment. "His ways were frank and open," wrote Mark Twain. "His was a nature that invited affection—compelled it, in fact—and met it halfway. Hence he was 'Tom' to most of his friends, and to half the nation." Henry Cabot Lodge of Massachusetts agreed, declaring, "No more agreeable companion ever lived."[1]

As chairman of the Rules Committee in 1882, Reed had made his first important move in forcing the House to attend to business and not allow a willful minority to obstruct it. On May 20, the House was obliged to consider a disputed election from South Carolina. Clearly, the Republican claimant would be seated, so the Democratic minority in the House decided to block all action by introducing either motions to adjourn or other dilatory motions. This went on for seven days until on Saturday, May 27, Reed was recognized to submit a privileged report from his committee. Democrats objected, but the Speaker at that time, J. Warren Keifer, ruled them out of order. The gist of the report instructed the Speaker not to allow endless motions for adjournment. As Reed said, "Whenever it is imposed upon Congress to accomplish a certain work, it is the duty of the Speaker . . . to see that no factious opposition prevents the House from doing its duty. He must brush away all unlawful combinations to misuse the rules and must hold the House strictly to its work."[2]

The Democrats protested but Reed stood his ground, and the amendment to Rule XVI, which effectively stopped filibustering in election disputes, was accordingly adopted.

Control of his committee, along with his towering intellect, diligent attention to the work at hand and his personal attractiveness, vaulted Reed to a leadership position in the Republican Party. Thus it came as no surprise that when Benjamin Harrison was elected President in November 1888, and the Republicans won control of both the House and Senate, Thomas B. Reed was elected Speaker of the 51st Congress. Still, it did not come easily. The Republicans had a small majority in the House and held a caucus to choose their leader. Several other candidates, including William McKinley and Joseph Cannon, were considered because a number of members worried that Reed's sharp tongue might prove offensive and because he represented Maine, a politically unimportant state. But Henry Cabot Lodge and several other New Englanders put up a stiff fight for Reed's election by the caucus. On the second ballot, he received 85 votes to McKinley's 38 and Cannon's 19. Reed then went on to beat the Democrat, John Carlisle, by twelve votes.[3]

Reed had already made clear how the House would be run under his direction. In an article in the *Century Magazine* he announced that dilatory motions to delay or block the business of the House should be barred. "The rules of this House," he said, "are not for the purpose of protecting the rights of the minority, but to promote the orderly conduct of the business of the House."[4]

Federal Hall, the site of the first Congress of the United States under the Constitution.

For ten years after the government moved to Philadelphia, Congress met in this county courthouse just a short distance from Independence Hall.

*The pristine city of Washington in all its bucolic and mosquito-infested charm
before its transformation into the governing center of the nation.*

A famous painting of a night session of the House by Samuel F. B. Morse, better known as the inventor of the telegraph.

The Bulfinch dome of the Capitol in Washington before the extended north and south wings were added.

The Electoral Commission that decided the Tilden-Hayes presidential election. Notice the presence of women on the floor.

The 100th Congress as seen from the Democratic end of the chamber.

*The Capitol today as seen from Independence Avenue with the south wing,
where the House of Representatives meets, in the foreground.*

Straight off, Reed appointed William McKinley of Ohio to head Ways and Means. McKinley had built a reputation as a man of principle and a staunch advocate of tariff protection. An excellent speaker and a congenial colleague, he was a favorite among Republicans. Next, Reed appointed Joseph G. Cannon of Illinois to chair the Appropriations Committee. Cannon was the complete opposite of McKinley. A man of crude manners and profane speech, he rose steadily by dint of his party loyalty and diligent committee work. Short, with white hair, chin whiskers and the inevitable stump of a cigar pronged between his teeth, Cannon was personally popular and was affectionately known as "Uncle Joe."[5]

To climax his plan to bring order and discipline to the House, Reed then appointed McKinley and Cannon to the five-man Rules Committee, where the three of them constituted a majority. Since the rules had to be revised or reenacted with every new Congress, Reed, as chairman, together with McKinley and Cannon, drafted a new set, one of which would constitute a veritable "revolution." They agreed that the traditional method of determining a quorum, practiced since the 1st Congress—by counting only

Thomas Brackett "Czar" Reed of Maine, clearly among the three or four great Speakers of the House.

those who voted and not those who were actually present in the room—had to be terminated.

The dramatic showdown came on January 29, 1890, when the House turned to consider a contested election in West Virginia. Naturally, the Republicans had every intention of seating the Republican claimant. The Democrats, just as naturally, were determined to block him. Once Charles F. Crisp of Georgia moved for consideration of the action, the new Reed strategy came immediately into play. As the vote was taken, all the Democrats sat silently in their seats when their names were called, but all 173 Republicans responded.[6]

Reed then made his move. He felt he was on firm constitutional grounds and could only hope that all the Republicans would support him in what he was about to do. If they did not, he would resign.

Reed turned to the Clerk. "The Chair directs the Clerk," he said in a firm but calm voice, "to record the following names of members present and refusing to vote." The Republicans burst into applause. Then Reed began to call the names of the Democrats who were present and not voting. Charles Crisp of Georgia, minority leader on the Elections Committee, jumped up and raced down the lobby directly in front of the Speaker, shouting, "I appeal from the decision of the Chair." Whereupon the Democrats applauded wildly.[7]

Bedlam ensued. The Democrats screamed objections while Republicans shouted and whistled their approval. The House became a deafening mass of individuals yelling, laughing, clapping, pounding their desks and stamping on the floor.

William Breckenridge of Kentucky, "a giant in frame and with a voice of thunder," bellowed, "I deny the power of the Speaker, and denounce it as revolutionary." "For some minutes there was pandemonium with a hundred men in front of the Speaker's desk, shaking their fists at the man in the chair," recalled Joseph Cannon, a few years later, "and drowning one another's voice in their defiance."[8]

Reed remained calm throughout the uproar. James B. McCreary of Kentucky finally caught Reed's attention when his name was called. "I deny your right, Mr. Speaker," he shrieked, "to count me as present, and I desire to read from the parliamentary law on that subject."

Unruffled, Reed stared at McCreary in disbelief. "The Chair," he responded, "is making a statement of the fact that the gentleman from Kentucky is present. Does he deny it?"

Republicans guffawed. And, as the House began to quiet down, Reed explained that the Constitution clearly states that members may be compelled—yes, compelled—to attend to provide a quorum. If something other than attendance was necessary, he continued, the Constitution would have provided it. "The Chair thereupon rules that there is a quorum present within the meaning of the Constitution."[9]

With that announcement both the House and galleries rose to their feet, cheering or booing, and it took fifteen minutes before some semblance of order was restored.

"Mr. Speaker," Crisp protested, "I appeal to your fairness as a man," and, turning to his Republican colleagues, continued, "gentlemen, I appeal to your fairness as men, to give us simply an opportunity to reply to the arguments which the Speaker has seen proper to make. Are you afraid to hear the rulings that have been made in this House for a hundred years?"[10]

And so the battle was joined, and it continued for the remainder of the day. That night Reed met with Cannon and McKinley to devise strategy for the coming days. Reed informed them that he would allow the debate to proceed for as long as the Democrats wanted to talk. He would "give the Democrats all the rope they wanted, as the more they had the more they would get themselves entangled."[11]

The debate continued for three days. It was one of the most tumultuous scenes in the entire history of the House. Roll call after roll call produced similar results: Democrats did not answer; Reed pronounced them present; then he declared a quorum. Carlisle and Crisp led the Democrats in demanding a continuation of the traditional policy of counting, while Cannon, "as a

This cartoon depicts Reed's success in bowling over the opposition to his new rules, which helped expedite House business.

member of the Rules Committee, and as perhaps a more experienced parliamentarian than McKinley," led the Speaker's defense on the floor.

"I denounce you," shouted Richard Bland of Missouri at the Speaker, "as the worst tyrant that ever ruled over a deliberative body." Again and again Democrats called Reed a despot and czar, and in short order the name "Czar Reed" stuck to him. At one point, as Democrats threatened to leave the chamber, the Speaker ordered the doors locked. The angered representatives then tried hiding under their desks to avoid being seen and counted.[12]

Sheer lunacy. Still Reed would not back down. Finally, the Republicans were able to muster a quorum without the Democrats—even bringing two members in on stretchers—and Reed's ruling was approved. The battle ended. The Speaker had triumphed, and he now had a new name: Czar Reed.

And he had every intention of exercising his increased powers to make certain the House attended to business. As he said earlier, "The best system is to have one party govern and the other party watch, and on general principles I think it would be better for us to govern and the Democrats to watch."[13]

And govern he did. Besides ruling that everyone present in the chamber would be counted for a quorum, Reed also refused to entertain motions he regarded as dilatory. That was an important reform in forcing the House to attend to business. Furthermore, he declared that the Rules Committee would control the calendar and decide which bills would come before the entire House. Measures not approved by the leadership would be placed at the end of the calendar, where they would most likely die a quiet death. In addition, Reed created a "morning hour" at which time committees would report bills to be voted on. Finally, the Committee of the Whole, used frequently to facilitate consideration of bills, would require only one hundred members to constitute a quorum. As such, these new rules now provided the Speaker with increased authority and tighter control of the operations of the House, which he chose to share with a select number of party leaders. This centralized structure and strong leadership continued for the next twenty years, even after Reed resigned.

Reed's diligence—he read the many reports and documents that came before him and patiently listened to the concerns of his colleagues—added to his authority. His style, his manner and his work habits inaugurated the era of the modern Speaker. Part of what came to personify the modern Speaker was the way in which Reed lived, in and out of the House. He roomed modestly in the Shoreham Hotel, where he held small dinner parties. He was much sought after in society and had a reputation for lively conversation. His wit and verbal agility made him a formidable leader and a favorite among Washington hostesses. On one occasion he boarded a Washington street car with Robert R. Hitt of Illinois, his trusted lieutenant. Hitt handed the conductor a large bill that the conductor was unable to change. Reed intervened and paid the fare, then he turned to Hitt and said: "Do you work this racket on the conductors as a regular thing?" On another occasion a member was delayed in getting to Washington because of a "flood on the railroad," so he telegraphed Reed, saying "Washout on line. Can't Come." His vote was important, so Reed telegraphed him back, "Buy another shirt and come on next train."[14] He was a "source of pure delight," said one writer. "To laugh with him was a joy, to be laughed at another matter."[15]

It was no laughing matter when a correspondent of the *Louisville Times,* Charles E. Kincaid, approached former congressman William Preston Taulbee of Kentucky on the east staircase in the House wing of the Capitol and shot him in the head on February 28, 1890. Blood, "gushing in a steady stream," stained the marble stairs as Taulbee staggered down the few remaining steps to the landing before collapsing. A powerfully built man, he had served in the House in the 49th and 50th Congresses and was known as a "ready talker." Thirty-nine years of age, he was "more frequently on his feet than any other young member. He had an immensely powerful voice, and in the tumults which sometimes occurred in the House it could always be heard above the din."

The dispute between the two men went back many months when Kincaid wrote an article in his newspaper accusing the congressman of involvement in a Patent Office scandal. When Taulbee later spotted the journalist in the House, he grabbed him by the lapel of his coat, hauled him into the corridor and pulled his nose. The thirty-four-year-old Kincaid was a small, slightly built individual, suffering from a nervous ailment. He struggled to free himself.

"I am in no condition for a physical contest with you," he stammered. "I am unarmed."

"Then you had better be," Taulbee roared.

The reporter took the advice, obtained a gun and around 1:30 p.m. shot the former congressman on the right side of the right eye. A crowd surrounded the wounded man and rushed him to Providence Hospital, where he died on March 11.[16] Kincaid was arrested by the Capitol police, tried and found not guilty on the grounds of self-defense.

The bloodstains on the marble staircase proved to be a constant reminder of what could happen within the walls of the Capitol, and it troubled many congressmen. They could only hope that Reed's strong leadership in the House would be sufficient to prevent a similar occurrence in the future.

TRADITIONALLY, REPUBLICANS SUPPORTED higher tariff rates to protect American industries and agricultural products. In April 1890, William McKinley dutifully reported from the Ways and Means Committee a bill that raised duties on almost every import that competed with American products. Such non-American items as coffee, tea and spices were placed on the free list, along with raw sugar. But American producers of raw sugar in Louisiana were given a bounty of two cents a pound so that they could compete with the sugar coming from Cuba and Hawaii.[17] On average, the rates were raised 49.5 percent. During the debate, Richard W. Townshend of Illinois tried to argue against protection, but he complained that he could not get five minutes into his speech when Republicans would cry, "Vote, vote, and seek to put me down."

Reed looked askance. "It is because you make the same speech every time," he responded in a flat voice. "It is not the speech we complain of so much as the monotony of the thing; we want a change." The Republicans burst into laughter, and the bill sailed through the House on May 21, 1890, by a vote of 164 to 142.[18]

It was a different story in the Senate. There senators from the silver-mining western states promised to defeat the tariff bill unless a more acceptable coinage act for silver was enacted. They called for the free and unlimited coinage of silver at the ratio of 16 to 1 with gold. In 1890 the ratio was around 20 to 1 on the market. In addition, southern senators threatened to join their western colleagues if a proposed "Force Bill," which would protect black voters in the south, was enacted. The Force Bill provided that when one hundred voters in any district applied for an investigation, federal officials would inspect and verify the votes cast in a federal election. Southerners argued that such a bill was intended to restore "Negro rule" in their region.

Fearful that the McKinley Tariff would fail, the Republicans dropped the Force Bill and suggested a compromise on silver. The Sherman Silver Purchase Act, which proved acceptable to westerners, required the U.S. Treasury to purchase 4.5 million ounces of silver a month at market price—more than twice what was bought under the Bland-Allison Act and estimated to be the total U.S. production of silver—and pay for it with legal tender notes redeemable in gold or silver. The act passed on July 4, 1890, whereupon the Senate enacted the McKinley Tariff, and Harrison signed it on October 1, 1890. Very quickly, the tariff was seen as a tax on the poor to benefit rich industries. And it proved lethal to many Republican congressmen.[19]

One interesting provision of the McKinley Tariff, introduced by the Senate, was the imposition of reciprocal tariff agreements by which the President could raise duties to meet discrimination by foreign nations and sign trade conventions without asking for congressional approval. McKinley himself strongly opposed reciprocity, but the House, with the President's active endorsement, approved it.

It was a major victory for the Harrison administration. The President had persuaded Congress to alter one of its most jealously guarded prerogatives, namely, the process of levying taxes.[20]

Of even greater moment at the time was the need for federal legislation to curb the growth of monopolies in basic industries, such as oil, sugar and beef. The public feared that monopolies would stifle competition among small and middle-sized companies and allow monopolists to overcharge for their products. Some twenty-seven states and territories had already passed antitrust legislation, but this did not satisfy the public. They demanded federal action. Although the Republican Party was reluctant to initiate such a bill, it recognized the political necessity of bending to popular will. In July 1890, the Sherman Anti-Trust Act passed, which declared that "every contract, combination in the form of trust or otherwise, or conspiracy in restraint of trade . . . is hereby declared to be illegal."[21]

The inherent weakness of the new antitrust law was its ambiguity and failure to define such words as "trust," "restraint" and "combination." It was not clear whether labor unions and railroads were to be regarded as similar to business corporations. As a result the law was not vigorously enforced and trusts and combinations continued to be formed under other names.

By this time Republican control in the House was so complete that the 51st Congress proved to be one of the most productive of the entire century. It passed 611 bills, many of which were important, including the admission to the Union of North and South Dakota, Montana, Washington, Idaho and Wyoming, and the establishment of a territorial government in Oklahoma. A great number of appropriations for such matters as internal improvements, pensions, expanded copyright coverage, a new immigration law and naval construction were also enacted. The pork barrel swelled. The extent of Congress's generosity reached $1 billion.

One billion dollars! That figure shocked many Americans, who criticized this "Billion-Dollar Congress." But Reed allegedly responded to the criticism by acknowledging that "it is a billion dollar country."[22] Still, there was so much bitterness in the country over Congress's prodigality and over the unpopularity of the McKinley Tariff that the Democrats won a landslide victory in the congressional election of 1890. The House now had a staggering Democratic majority of 231 to 88 Republicans. Both William McKinley and Joseph Cannon were defeated for reelection to the 52nd Congress. But Republicans retained control of the Senate, 47 to 39, because of the many hold-overs who were not up for re-election. Thus a divided Congress virtually guaranteed the end of significant legislation for the next two years.[23]

When the lame-duck Congress ended on March 3, 1891, it was the general practice for the House to pass a resolution on the last day thanking the Speaker for his impartiality. It was a formality. The resolution was normally adopted unanimously, reported Joseph Cannon in his *Memoirs*, and the House would break up "in a friendly spirit, often with general singing and schoolboy antics."

Not now. "When it came time for the offering of the usual resolution, no Democrat could be found who would sponsor it, so bitter were they against Tom Reed. In the end, I offered the resolution," declared Cannon, "which was adopted by a strict party vote."[24]

Among Democrats, there was a protracted battle for nomination to the Speakership between Charles Crisp of Georgia, Roger Q. Mills of Texas, and William M. Springer of Illinois. Thirty ballots were required before Crisp was finally chosen. Born in Sheffield, England, of naturalized English-American parents who settled in Georgia, Crisp served in the Civil War, was captured at Spotsyvlania, studied law after the war and was elected to the 48th Congress in 1882. He went on to win a decisive victory for Speaker over Reed, 228 to 83. Indeed, there were so many Democrats in the 52nd Congress that seventy-five of them had to be seated on the Republican side of the House.[25]

As Speaker, Crisp tried to lessen the force of Reed's "revolutionary" Rules in an effort to widen distribution of power and responsibility. He did not appoint the chairmen of Ways and Means and Appropriations to the Rules Committee. Nor did Reed's quorum rule particularly concern him because of the overwhelming majority enjoyed by the Democrats. Still, when Reed, now minority leader, and the Republicans repeatedly brought the House to a complete halt by dilatory motions and endless roll calls, Crisp was obliged to reintroduce the Reed Rules, thereby vindicating what Reed had done earlier.

The first session of the 52nd Congress accomplished little, but at least the level of oratory improved considerably with the likes of Reed, William Jennings Bryan, a freshman member, Bourke Cockran, Henry Cabot Lodge and William Wilson participating in House debates.

CONDITIONS AROUND THE country reflected the bitterness in the House. The Haymarket Massacre in Chicago in May 1886, for example, occurred when labor rallies triggered fierce clashes with the police and ended with the hanging of four anarchist labor leaders. This was followed by the violent strike at the Carnegie Steel plant in Homestead, Pennsylvania, in July 1892, and the wild Pullman strike in Illinois in 1894, called when George Pullman, the inventor of the Pullman railroad car, fired one-third of his factory workers and cut salaries, necessitating federal intervention. All these events publicized the growing economic distress faced by the laboring poor. Labor unions such as the American Federation of Labor organized the protests to publicize the misery.

Agriculture, too, suffered an economic slump in the 1890s and generated alliances that created the People's Party, better known as the Populist Party. The Populists elected fourteen members to the House in 1890 and held a presidential nominating convention in Omaha, Nebraska, for the

1892 election. They named James Weaver of Iowa for President and James G. Field of Virginia for Vice President. Their platform called for the free and unlimited coinage of silver at the ratio of 16 to 1, government ownership of all transportation and communication facilities, a graduated income tax, the direct election of senators, adoption of a secret ballot, a shorter day for industrial workers and the right to effect legislation through initiative and referendum procedures. The party's leaders included Ignatius Donnelly, Mary Elizabeth Lease, "Sockless Jerry" Simpson and Senator James Kyle of South Dakota.

The economic conditions brought on by the rise of big business, the growth of monopolies and the plight of laborers and farmers emphasized the grim fact that the United States had developed into a nation divided by class on the basis of wealth. And the injustices resulting from those conditions not only produced the Populist Party but later generated the Progressive Movement, by which the oppressed found the courage to speak out and protest living conditions and demand relief. They sought better wages and hours, women and child labor laws, and legislation dealing with safety and health conditions of factories.[26]

The Republicans nominated Harrison for a second term, along with Whitelaw Reed of New York, while the Democrats turned once again to Grover Cleveland. The former President and his running mate, Adlai E. Stevenson of Illinois, were decisively elected. The Populists garnered over a million popular votes and 23 electoral votes and won 8 seats in the House. The Democratic majority in the House was reduced to 220 to 126 for Republicans, but now, for the first time since the Civil War, the party controlled both houses of Congress and the presidency. Crisp was reelected Speaker and found flowers waiting for him. But there were no flowers on Reed's desk. "Oh," he responded when his attention was directed to this oversight, "it is because I am nobody's darling."[27]

The country suffered a severe economic depression in 1893 triggered by the McKinley Tariff, which had reduced U.S. revenues, and by the run on the gold reserves caused by Britain's unloading of American securities. Five hundred banks closed, more than fifteen hundred businesses failed, 30 percent of the railroad system collapsed and unemployment soared.[28] The depression lasted for the entire four years of Cleveland's second administration. To stop the hemorrhaging of gold, Cleveland summoned Congress into special session to convene on August 7, 1893, and asked that the Sherman Silver Purchase Act be repealed. The House voted for repeal by a margin of 239 to 108 on August 28, and the Senate followed two months later.[29]

But the depression only got worse. In April 1894, an "army" of unemployed, led by Jacob S. Coxey of Ohio, a Populist, marched on Washington and demanded jobs and an increase in the money supply. Coxey and several other leaders were arrested and the "army" was forced to disband, but the march by "Coxey's Army" further publicized conditions among the working poor and encouraged them to organize and fight for their rights.

In the House, William Jennings Bryan of Nebraska and Richard ("Silver Dick") Bland of Missouri, the leaders of the silver bloc, wrote an "Appeal of Silver Democrats" and demanded currency inflation through the free and unlimited coinage of silver at the ratio of 16 to 1. By expanding the amount of currency in circulation, resting on silver dollars and not paper, they argued, prices would rise and the purchasing power of dollars would be stabilized. But the "Appeal" was signed by only a minority of Democrats.[30]

The Democrats did try to repeal the McKinley Tariff and substitute one that would lower rates. William L. Wilson of West Virginia, chairman of the Ways and Means Committee, introduced a bill that significantly lowered the level of duties and increased a number of articles on the free list, such as sugar, coal, iron ore, wool and lumber. The bill also included a 2 percent flat rate on personal and corporate incomes over $4,000, a provision crafted by Bryan, presumably to offset the loss of revenue caused by a lower tariff. In a forceful and dramatic speech on the floor, Wilson concluded his presentation by stating that "this is not a battle over percentages, over this or that tariff schedule, it is a battle for human freedom." The House burst into wild applause as he ended his speech.[31]

Debate on the bill consumed much of January 1894, during which Reed and Bourke Cockran engaged in a spirited clash of arguments, for and against the reductions. Reed spoke for two hours. He dubbed the Wilson bill "odious," one that pretended to give protection without providing it and would certainly aggravate the depression that enveloped the country. He insisted that a protective tariff promoted the diversification of industry, "raised the level of civilization" and encouraged invention. When he concluded his speech, he immediately exited the chamber, accompanied by a tremendous ovation from fellow Republicans. A page had a huge floral tribute to deliver from admirers but was obliged to place it on an empty desk.[32]

Nevertheless, it was Wilson's stirring and emotional appeal that won the day. And when the bill carried by a vote of 204 to 140, on February 1, several colleagues, including Bryan, lifted Wilson on their shoulders and paraded him around the chamber while Democrats cheered, joined by visitors in the galleries.[33]

But the Senate made mincemeat of the reform efforts of the House by adding 634 amendments that raised the level of rates and returned many items on the proposed free list, such as sugar, iron ore and coal, to the duty list. A number of protectionist Democrats, led by Arthur P. Gorman of Maryland, aided the emasculation of the Wilson bill and called down on themselves the wrath of President Cleveland; but his wrath only strengthened their determination to ensure the higher rates when the bill came before the joint conference committee. The Wilson-Gorman Tariff passed Congress on August 27, 1894, without Cleveland's signature.

That did not end the matter. The Supreme Court, in the 1895 case *Pollock v. Farmers Loan and Trust Company,* sliced away the income-tax provision, declaring it a direct tax and therefore unconstitutional since a direct tax had to be apportioned according to the population of each state. The first peacetime attempt to tax incomes as well as securities and corporate profit, this income tax necessitated a constitutional amendment.

The continuing economic depression brought about another political upheaval in the 1894 midterm elections when the Republicans captured 245 House and 44 Senate seats to 104 and 39 for the Democrats. "The Democratic mortality will be so great next Fall," predicted Thomas B. Reed, "that their dead will be buried in trenches and marked 'unknown.' "[34] On December 2, 1895, he was returned to the Speaker's chair, and his rules were adopted with little dissent by the 54th Congress. The reelected Joseph Cannon regained leadership of the Appropriations Committee, a position he held until 1903, when he mounted the rostrum as Speaker. As a consequence, the centralization and consolidation of power in the House continued during the last two years of President Cleveland's administration.[35]

The continued depletion of the gold reserves in the U.S. Treasury forced John G. Carlisle, the secretary of the treasury and a former Speaker of the House, to seek a loan through the issuance of bonds. He worked out a $62 million loan with a banking group headed by J. Pierpont Morgan and August Belmont in which 3.5 million ounces of gold would be purchased with bonds, half the gold to come from abroad. For their efforts, the bankers probably reaped a profit of $1.5 million.

The maintenance of the gold standard became a leading issue in the presidential election of 1896. Under the skillful management of Marcus A. Hanna, a Cleveland mining and shipping magnate, the Republican Party at its convention in St. Louis in mid-June nominated William McKinley for President and Garret A. Hobart of New Jersey for Vice President on a platform that affirmed the party's commitment to the single gold standard, a high protective tariff and an aggressive foreign policy.

The Democrats met on July 8 in Chicago and adopted a platform calling for the free and unlimited coinage of silver at the ratio of 16 to 1, as well as end to both protective tariffs and the use of injunctions against labor. It also condemned the Supreme Court's ruling against the income tax. During the convention William Jennings Bryan gave a speech that electrified his audience. "We are fighting in the defense of our homes, our families, and posterity," he cried. ". . . Having behind us the producing masses of this nation and the world . . . we will answer their demand for a gold standard by saying to them: You shall not press upon the brow of labor this crown of thorns, you shall not crucify mankind upon a cross of gold."[36]

His audience exploded. They screamed their approval and nominated him as their presidential candidate, along with Arthur Sewall of Maine for Vice President. But the "Battle of the Standards"—that is, the gold standard versus the silver—split both major parties, with silver Republicans deserting their party and gold Democrats deserting theirs. The Populist Party narrowly endorsed Bryan, but chose the fiery Thomas E. Watson of Georgia for Vice President. Unfortunately, the acceptance of Bryan, rather than putting forward their own candidate, demoralized the Populist Party, which ceased to function thereafter as an effective political organization.

Although Bryan, the "Great Commoner," as he was called, traveled thousands of miles and spoke to enthusiastic crowds in twenty-nine states during a fourteen-week campaign, he lost the election to the highly financed and superbly managed Republican organization. Bryan was condemned as a radical who would destroy the basic institutions of the American government, and workers were told not to report back to work if Bryan was elected. McKinley conducted his campaign from the "front porch" of his Canton, Ohio, home while Hanna convinced industrialists to contribute to a war chest that rose to over $16 million. Between these campaign funds and the negative campaign waged against Bryan, McKinley won the election with 271 electoral and over 7 million popular votes to Bryan's 176 electoral and 6.5 million popular votes. The Republican Party also retained control of both houses of Congress.[37]

ONCE AGAIN, REED reigned as Speaker of the 55th Congress. In 1897, for the very first time, he designated a member, James A. Tawney of Minnesota, to serve as a "whip" to keep track of how Republicans felt about particular issues to be debated in the chamber and make certain they voted as directed by the leadership. The term came from the English phrase "whipper-in," the person on a fox hunt charged with keeping the dogs close to the pack. Tawney served as whip until 1905, when he was appointed chair of the Appropriations Committee. The Democrats created the whip position for their party in 1901.[38]

With the government under solid Republican control, Congress responded to McKinley's call in his first inaugural address for an even higher tariff to offset the multimillion-dollar deficit facing him. Nelson Dingley, Jr., chairman of the Ways and Means Committee in the House, introduced an appropriate bill that Reed steered through the lower chamber in less than two weeks. The vote, 205 to 122, demonstrated the strength of Republican rule, and on July 24, 1897, the Dingley Tariff became law with hardly any discussion of its many provisions. Reed's strong-arm tactics would come into play again and again by the majority party. The tariff raised protective rates to the highest level in U.S. history and remained in effect for twelve years, longer than any other tariff in the nineteenth century.

But the absolute authority of the Speaker now came under increasing attack. The word "czar" was continually hurled at Reed. Populist senator William V. Allen of Nebraska was particularly sharp in his criticism. "We have a horrid example before us constantly like a nightmare, in another end of the Capitol building," he thundered on February 10, 1898, "where one man transacts the business of 357, which absolutely paralyzes one branch of Congress, a thing which, to my way of thinking is an absolute, positive, inexcusable, bold, and open disgrace to the American people. . . . Forty-five States of this Union, with their Representatives numbering 356, all held metaphorically speaking, by the throat as a highwayman would treat you when he wanted you to deliver your money. Your legislation may pass if it meets his stamp of approval, and it is rejected if it does not."[39]

But there were other voices that approved Reed's tactics and iron-rod control of party discipline. On January 21, 1897, the *Nation* ran an article under the title "Our Ruler, the Speaker" in which it noted the many times Reed had ruled against the consideration of bills he regarded as detrimental to the nation's welfare. They were bad bills, the article insisted, and needed to be blocked. "We are bound to say" that what the Speaker "prevents Congress from doing is a cause for rejoicing. The presumption is that the thing Congress wants to do is a bad thing. If we could only be sure of always having a benevolent tyrant as Speaker, the system would not be a bad one."[40]

OF PARTICULAR SIGNIFICANCE at this time, and something that had long been desired, was the removal of the Library of Congress from its "iron room" in the Capitol to a new building a short distance away. The library had outgrown its cramped space, particularly after passage of the Copyright Act of 1870, which required the library to acquire two copies of every book published. A flood of published works descended on the iron room. Within a year the number of new publications in the building rose from approximately 20,000 to 246,000. At first it was proposed that the west front of the Capitol be extended to accommodate the collection, but the librarian, Ainsworth Rand Spofford, argued for a separate building altogether, one capable, in time, of holding millions of volumes.[41]

Despite the inconvenience of not having documents and books close at hand, Congress had finally agreed with Spofford and appropriated half a million dollars in 1886 for the construction of a new Italian Renaissance library on East Capitol Street, following a design submitted by the Washington firm of Smithmeyer & Pelz from twenty-seven competitive entries. The building, completed in 1897, was constructed during a time of acute economic distress. In the summer and fall of that year, some eight hundred tons of books, documents, maps, manuscripts of history, music and drama, photographs, paintings, prints and other related materials were transported to the magnificent new structure, later called the Jefferson Building. Horse

The "iron room" of the Library of Congress in the Capitol bulged with books following passage of the Copyright Act of 1870, which required the library to acquire two copies of every book published.

carts, wheelbarrows and many other makeshift vehicles were called into service. On November 1, the building was open for public inspection and, on Thanksgiving, some five thousand visitors crowded through the splendidly decorated rooms to view the collection. The murals, sculpture, bronze doors, and decorative painting were and remain (thanks to recent efforts at restoration) breathtakingly beautiful.[42]

In 1897, electric lights replaced gas in the ceilings of the two chambers of Congress. Electric lights had already been installed in the cloakrooms, lobbies and stairways in 1885, and the success of this initiative prompted the House to extend electric lighting in its chamber with the addition of two hundred electric lamps.

A significant alteration in House membership had also occurred by this time. From the 1st Congress in 1789 onward, representatives rarely remained in office beyond two or three terms. There was a constant turnover. But by the end of the century members were staying for longer periods, and the number of newcomers elected to the House had declined to 30 percent. At the opening of the 57th Congress in 1901, two-thirds of the House were returning members. As a result, senior representatives began insisting on their right to hold membership in the most important committees, such as Rules, Ways and Means, and Appropriations. Seniority, then,

The visually magnificent reading room of the newly built Library of Congress.

became the norm by which positions on committees were assigned, and the recognition of this right determined a good deal of future legislation as the nation moved into the twentieth century and the new millennium. Chairmen became absolute rulers of their committees and frequently had a voice in selecting the other members of their committees. In 1904, the *Congressional Digest* changed its listing of members from an alphabetical order to one of continuous service, a clear indication that seniority now provided an important degree of rank among the members.

By the turn of the century office space had become a problem. Chairmen of committees had rooms assigned to them in the Capitol, but the other members had to fend for themselves, usually using their boardinghouses or renting a cheap room to conduct their business. Originally members had desks from which to work, but, in 1857, when the new House chamber of the Capitol was occupied, the desks were removed and curved benches were installed in their place. But this arrangement proved unsatisfactory. The benches were eliminated and the desks and chairs restored in 1860.[43]

The working conditions in the House had become so impossible by 1900 that Congress authorized the architect of the Capitol to draw up plans to provide suitable space for the members to conduct their business, and, in

1903, appropriated the funds to begin construction. In December 1907, the first House office building was completed, consisting of 397 offices and 14 committee rooms. It faced Independence Avenue, and was occupied by the 60th Congress.[44]

As for staff, the representatives during the nineteenth century did without help or hired assistants on their own. A few hundred employees who maintained the Capitol and provided security and postal services or ran errands constituted the entire workforce. In 1840, an additional hundred or so clerks, messengers and janitors were hired, a number that kept slowly expanding toward the end of the century. But the enormous increase in the staff did not occur until later in the twentieth century.

And the 59th Congress finally gave itself a salary raise. After thirty-three years, members dared to risk the displeasure of their constituents by increasing their salary from $5,000 to $7,500. To prevent public outrage, this compensation act would not become effective until after the next Congress had convened.

AS THE NATION grew in power and financial strength it veered once again toward a policy of Manifest Destiny, a policy of territorial expansion. In 1867, William Seward, the secretary of state under Lincoln and Johnson, had negotiated a treaty with Russia to acquire Alaska for $7.2 million. There was a great deal of opposition in the country to what was called "Seward's Folly" because of the high cost of the purchase, but the discovery of gold and later oil and gas more than justified the acquisition of this enormous territory.

The expansion of the nation continued with the annexation of the Hawaiian Islands in July 1898. American merchants, planters and missionaries had established economic and cultural interest in and connections with the islands in the 1830s, but in a successful revolt they deposed the reigning monarch, Queen Liliuokalani, in 1893, and established a government that sustained itself until Congress passed a joint-resolution in the McKinley administration in 1898 annexing the islands, despite the stiff objections of anti-imperialist Republicans, including Reed, and a great number of Democrats. Many realized that these islands could provide refueling bases and naval facilities. Two years later Congress granted Hawaii territorial status.[45]

The growing imperialistic impulse in the United States, the nation's pride in its wealth and military strength, the sense that it had a mission to spread freedom and democracy around the globe, combined with its humanitarian regard for the suffering of those under dictatorial rule, brought about a collision with Spain over conditions in Cuba, where rebels had begun an insurrection to free the island from Spanish rule. The revolution was brought about in part by a failed economy on account of the Wilson-Gorman Tariff, which reimposed a duty on raw sugar. Spain's iron-fisted response in crushing the rebellion evoked sympathetic outcries of protest in the United States. American "yellow journalist" newspapers, such as William Randolph Hearst's *New York Journal* and Joseph Pulitzer's *New York World,* recorded incidents of alleged Spanish atrocities against Cubans. Responding to the country's mood, the House and Senate passed a concurrent resolution in February 1896 favoring recognition of Cuban belligerency. The situation markedly worsened when the USS *Maine,* on a friendly visit to Havana, was sunk by an explosion on February 15, 1898; 260 officers and sailors perished. It was generally supposed that the crime had been perpetrated by Spanish officials.

Joseph Cannon, chairman of the Appropriations Committee, was summoned to the White House on Saturday evening, February 19, following the sinking. He found McKinley pacing the floor and looking very grave. "I am afraid we are going to have war," the President said, "and we have not powder and shot enough for the first round."

Cannon responded by suggesting an appropriation of $50 million, but McKinley said he was reluctant to ask Congress for it, fearing it would be seen as a sign that he had decided to go to war. Cannon offered to take on the burden himself by introducing the bill and winning its passage. Without notifying Speaker Reed, who strongly opposed a war, the chairman presented the appropriation measure on March 9 and gave a short speech in which he said the money was a sort of insurance policy by which American national honor would be protected. Joseph W. Bailey of Texas, the Democratic minority leader, agreed. "It ought to be understood in Spain and it ought to be understood in every country on the globe," he said on the floor, "that while this great country sincerely desires to be at peace, it is prepared for war, if war becomes inevitable."

Cannon himself opposed going to war with Spain—he had actually remarked that "many of the gentlemen who are loudly shouting for war are agonizing to shed their blood in selling supplies to the government"—but he believed that war was inevitable and that "common sense demanded that preparation be furthered before the jingoes got completely out of hand."[46]

Congress unanimously voted $50 million for national defense. On leaving the Capitol on the evening in which the bill passed the House, Cannon ran into Reed.

"Joe, why in hell did you do that?" declared Reed, annoyed that he had not been informed beforehand of Cannon's intended action.

"Tom, I have always been your friend," Cannon replied, "and you have been mine. The Speaker ought to be consulted on all matters of importance. I did not come to you because I knew you would be against what I was going to do, and as I intended to introduce this bill anyhow, I decided not to put you in that position."

The two men continued walking together. At length Reed muttered, "I suppose you did the right thing."[47]

The House erupted with shouts and applause when Bailey took the floor on March 30, 1898, and introduced a resolution to recognize Cuban independence. Reed had difficulty holding the Republicans from approving the resolution until a committee attended the President and informed him that the House would not wait beyond April 4 for a reply from Spain regarding the sinking of the *Maine* or for decisive presidential action. McKinley received word that Spain was preparing a satisfactory response, but he was caught up in the war fever and sent a message to Congress that barely mentioned the report he had received and called for "forcible intervention" in Cuba. While both houses considered a joint resolution as to what action to take, members of the House and visitors in the galleries sang patriotic songs well into the morning.

At 3:00 a.m. on April 19, the resolution to recognize Cuban independence passed the House by a vote of 325 to 19. It also passed the Senate. This resolution demanded the immediate withdrawal of Spain from Cuba and authorized the President to employ military force if necessary to carry it out. The Teller Amendment to the resolution, introduced in January 1898, stated that the United States had no desire to annex Cuba but would leave control of the island to its people once peace had been established.

McKinley signed the resolution on April 20, whereupon Spain broke diplomatic relations with the United States the next day and declared war on April 24. The House responded with its own declaration of war on April 25 by a vote of 311 to 6, making it retroactive to April 21. Reed voted with the minority. "I envy you the luxury of your vote," he remarked. "I was where I could not do it."[48] The Senate voted its declaration, 42 to 35.

Reed had done everything in his considerable power to block action on declaring war, but in the end he failed. Then, less than three months later, on July 7, 1898, Hawaii was formally annexed. Again the Speaker tried to sidetrack the annexation resolution in the Rules Committee since he felt strongly that the imperialistic thrust of the nation was a violation of its traditional foreign policy and would jeopardize the nation's unity by overextending its responsibility. But a petition circulated among the members called for a vote on the resolution, and there was nothing Reed could do to halt this steamroller. When, at last, the resolution did come before the House it passed overwhelmingly, 209 to 91, on June 15. Reed was ill at the time and absent when the vote was taken. Representative John Dalzell of Pennsylvania rose and declared that he was authorized to say that the Speaker would have voted no if present.[49]

The Spanish-American War provided the United States with a series of naval and land victories in Cuba and the Philippines. A young, wealthy, powerful and emerging giant had taken on a poor, weak and decrepit ancient and brought her to her knees. Spain sued for peace late in July and, at the Treaty of Paris on December 10, 1898, ceded Puerto Rico and Guam to the United States as a war indemnity, along with the Philippines, in return for $20 million. And Cuban sovereignty was recognized.[50]

One of the most unique features of the House of Representatives under the Constitution is the fact that delegates from the territories can participate, and have participated, in important debates in the lower chamber, despite the fact that they have no vote. Today there is one delegate from each of the territories: Puerto Rico, Guam, American Samoa and the Virgin Islands. Earlier, the many territories of the United States sent nonvoting delegates to the House, including the first Hispanic, Joseph Hernandez, a delegate to the 17th Congress, from Florida. He served from September 22, 1822, to March 1823. But the first Hispanic elected to the House proper was Romualdo Pacheco, a Republican from California. He served three terms, starting in 1877. By the mid-1990s, there were seventeen Hispanics in the House—and their number keeps growing.[51]

In signing the Treaty of Paris, ending the Spanish-American War, the United States had foolishly and needlessly embarked on an imperialistic course that divided the nation. By thrusting itself into Asian affairs, where it had little real interest or concern, the country was courting catastrophe—and it came at Pearl Harbor in 1941.

The Senate ratified the treaty with two votes more than the required two-thirds, but the Philippine people rose in revolt against the United States. They had expected independence and, under the leadership of Emilio Aguinaldo, they fought to win it. The United States was obliged to send in troops to put down the insurrection, a policy that seemed to contradict the basic ideals of freedom on which the American Republic was founded. McKinley appointed a commission, headed by William Howard Taft, a federal circuit court judge, to establish a government in the Philippines.

Reed had opposed the war, the annexation of Hawaii and what he regarded as American tyranny over the Philippine people. American imperialism made him gag. "I have tried," he said, "perhaps not always successfully, to make the acts of my public life accord with my conscience, and I cannot now do this thing." He attempted to explain his position to his Republican colleagues, but most of them turned a deaf ear. "The best government of which a people is capable is a government which they establish for themselves," he declared. "With all its imperfections, with all its shortcomings, it is always better adapted to them than any other government, even though invented by wiser men." Later, Amos J. Cummings of New York noticed the Speaker lumbering toward the Capitol, "silent and alone." Poor man, he thought, "he has no intimate associates."[52]

"Reed is terribly bitter," wrote Theodore Roosevelt, governor of New York, to Henry Cabot Lodge on December 20, 1898, "saying all sorts of ugly things about the administration and its policy in private talks, so I keep out of his way, for I am fond of him and I confess that his attitude is painful and disappointing to me beyond words."[53]

Feeling the way he did, the Speaker could no long remain in Congress. On September 4, 1899, two months before the opening of the 56th Congress, Thomas Brackett Reed resigned his Speakership and his seat in the House of Representatives.

But he had another reason for leaving. At the age of sixty, with a family to support, "he deemed it a duty he owed to them to quit politics, practice his profession, and make something for them to live on when he was gone." So he opened a successful law office in New York City and "by his ability and by the aid of influential friends he succeeded in accumulating a hundred thousand dollars or more." He lived only three years after retiring from Congress, dying on December 7, 1902, and he left his fortune to his widow and daughter.[54] Without question he was one of the greatest, most innovative and most important Speakers in the history of the Congress.

He was replaced as Speaker by a nonentity: David B. Henderson of Iowa, a tall, one-legged veteran of the Civil War and a former chairman of the Judiciary Committee, who served two terms.

SIX MONTHS AFTER Reed resigned, Congress passed the Currency or Gold Standard Act on March 14, 1900, an important measure by which gold became the standard unit of value and placed all U.S. money on a parity with gold. It marked the end of a two-decade struggle over the silver question. Then, the following November, the nation reelected McKinley as President, along with a forty-two-year-old Rough Rider from the Spanish-American War, Theodore Roosevelt, as Vice President, a selection that Mark Hanna, the skillful manager of McKinley's 1896 campaign, strongly opposed. The Democrats nominated William Jennings Bryan on a platform of anti-imperialism, antitrust and free silver.

Both houses remained in Republican control after the election, and just prior to McKinley's inauguration for his second term, Representative George H. White, a North Carolina Republican and an African-American, gave his last speech in the House on January 31, 1901. Earlier, in 1900, he had introduced a bill making lynching a federal crime punishable by death, but it was ignored in the Judiciary Committee. It signaled the start of the long struggle in Congress to enact federal antilynching legislation. Since Reconstruction there had been sixteen black Representatives from the South, but White, as his farewell, predicted that someday other blacks from his region would sit in Congress. Unfortunately, not until the 1970s did his prediction materialize with the election to the House of such distinguished individuals as Barbara Jordan of Texas and Andrew Jackson Young of Georgia. However, Oscar De Priest, a black Representative from Illinois, served from 1929 to

1935. In the entire history of the House he was the first African-American to be sent to Congress from a northern state. Since De Priest's election almost two dozen African-Americans from the North have served in the House.[55]

ON SEPTEMBER 6, 1901, just six months into his second term and two months before the 57th Congress was due to convene, President McKinley was shot by Leon Czolgosz, an anarchist, at the Pan-American Exposition in Buffalo, New York. He died on September 14. Although Theodore Roosevelt tried to reassure the nation by promising to "continue, absolutely unbroken, the policy of President McKinley," he was known to champion progressive causes such as child labor laws, food and drug regulation, conservation, railroad reform and trust-busting. Any number of party leaders were concerned about what he might do. "Now look," cried Mark Hanna, "that damned cowboy is President of the United States."[56]

And they had good reason to be concerned, as the nation soon discovered. Populists and all manner of social reformers from the East and the West joined Roosevelt under the banner of Progressivism, a movement to further popular government and progressive legislation dealing with such matters as women and child labor, wages and hours, and safety and health conditions in factories. Using the "bully pulpit," as he termed his position in the White House, the new President won popular support for needed reforms, especially trust reform, which was occasioned by the continued trend in business toward consolidation. The formation of the U.S. Steel Company, the first billion-dollar corporation, and the Northern Securities Company, a railroad holding company, launched Roosevelt's crusade against industrial abuses. At his request, Congress passed the Expedition Act on February, 11, 1903, to expedite federal prosecution of antitrust suits by giving them precedence in circuit court proceedings. Passage of a bill on February, 14, 1903, creating the Department of Labor and Commerce (which included a Bureau of Corporation with authority to investigate and subpoena testimony on activities by corporations involved in interstate commerce), went a long way toward enhancing Roosevelt's campaign to curb trust formation. So, too, did the enactment of the Elkins Act on February 19, 1903, which sought to eliminate rebates on freight charges and regulate shipping, and the Hepburn Act that reinforced the power of the Interstate Commerce Commission to set railroad rates. Committed to conservation, Roosevelt also sought passage of the Newlands Act, passed on June 17, 1902, which directed the proceeds from the sale of arid and semi-arid lands in the west to be used for the construction of dams and other reclamation projects. This act has often been compared to the Homestead Act in shaping the development of western America.[57]

An important milestone in the history of the House was reached with the election of Joseph Cannon as Speaker in November 1903. Straight off, he pronounced his basic creed: "I believe in consultin' the boys, findin' out what most of 'em want, and then goin' ahead and doin' it. The Speaker is the servant, not the master, of the House."[58] But the truth was quite the opposite. Actually, Joseph Cannon considered himself the absolute ruler of the House of Representatives and was determined to maintain the status quo. During House debates on measures brought forward by his Appropriations Committee, he had proved his mettle. "His delivery was slashing, sledge-hammery, full of fire and fury," reported C. W. Thompson, a *New York Times* reporter.[59] He despised all reform, whether it came from his own party or the opposition. President Roosevelt was an aberration, as far as he was concerned, and it was jokingly reported that when God created the world, if a decision had to be made as to whether civilization should be brought out of chaos, Cannon would have voted for chaos.

A gregarious, friendly, personable man, a cigar securely anchored between his teeth, Joseph G. Cannon was born in North Carolina, but his family moved to Indiana, where he studied law and opened a practice. He moved to Illinois in 1858, met Abraham Lincoln, served as the state's attorney and won election to Congress in 1870 when the new census raised

Speaker Joseph ("Uncle Joe") Cannon with his ubiquitous cigar.

the number of representatives from Illinois from nine to fourteen. Except for two defeats, he served fifty years in the House. A tough-minded fiscal conservative, he showed talent as an administrator and was appointed chair of the Appropriations Committee. "You may think my business is to make appropriations," he reportedly said, "but it is not. It is to prevent their being made."[60]

Elected Speaker at the age of sixty-seven, he was the "oldest and longest-serving representative ever to be elected."[61] He ruled as Speaker from the 58th through the 61st Congresses and he held in his hands, reported George Norris, a Republican from Nebraska, "the political life of virtually every member." He rewarded the faithful, and punished the disloyal. "I doubt," said Norris, "if any Speaker in the history of Congress was as ruthless as Joe Cannon sometimes was."[62] He disciplined those who failed him by changing their committee assignments, including chairmen. Or he postponed committee appointments for months if it served his purpose. As chair of the Rules Committee, he dictated what action would come before the House. Under normal conditions, and when it suited his purposes, he followed the seniority system in appointing chairmen; otherwise he disregarded it.

One of his chief complaints against his predecessor, Speaker Henderson, was the fact that he allowed the House to become subservient to the Senate. On his election, Cannon promised that he would reassert House leadership and "battle the domineering Senate."[63] Good to his word, he defended the rights and privileges of the House against the President and the Senate—especially the chief executive, since that office had now become very active in advancing legislation—and won the admiration and respect of his colleagues, who called him "Uncle Joe." As Speaker, he said he would head the Republican party in the House, and make its will absolute. "Results cannot be had except by a majority, and in the House of Representatives a majority, being responsible, should have full power and should exercise that power."[64] "Inevitably," reported Norris, "members knew they would be pleading on bended knee before the Speaker for favors to perpetuate themselves in office."[65] Yet many complained. "We are no less Republican because we would be free members of Congress," snapped John M. Nelson of Wisconsin. "We do not need to be kept on leading strings." When one constituent asked his representative for a copy of the House rules, the member sent him a picture of Uncle Joe Cannon.[66]

The Speaker normally operated through a small group of like-minded men, consisting of Soreno E. Payne of New York, chair of Ways and Means and the majority leader;[67] John Dalzell of Pennsylvania, a member of both the Rules and Ways and Means Committees; James A. Tawney of Minnesota, the party whip and later chair of the Appropriations Committee; James R. Mann of Illinois, a masterful parliamentarian and Uncle Joe's watchdog; and Nicholas Longworth of Ohio, the very talented and urbane son-in-law of Theodore Roosevelt.[68] "Nowhere in the land is any body of men ruled with so despotic a hand by so small a governing body," wrote one journalist.[69]

The Speaker was not a legislator but a parliamentarian. In point of fact, he introduced only one bill during his entire career in the House, and that happened in 1874 when he sponsored legislation for postal reform. A convivial, hail fellow who enjoyed the company of his colleagues, he loved to play poker and drink good whiskey.[70]

Alice Roosevelt Longworth, daughter of the President and wife of the future Speaker, Nicholas Longworth, remembered a poker game at the home of John Dwight, at that time the Republican whip. She was warned by William Howard Taft not to get between Cannon and a spittoon. "I thought he was joking," she said. "I had not the faintest idea that one encountered spittoons anywhere except in hotels, trains, and the Capitol." But it was no joke. When Cannon sat down at the poker table he demanded a spittoon. Sorry, he was told by the host, there was none in the house. Would an umbrella stand do? Of course, Cannon replied. "It was put beside him and he used it freely and frequently throughout the evening," Alice reported.[71]

The host, John Dwight, provided other benefits for the Speaker. He was said to have developed many of the "modern techniques of an effective whip." He could frequently be seen, "whip's book in hand," checking out the whereabouts of the members. He could always tell the Speaker how many members could be rounded up immediately, and how many more could be corralled within twelve or twenty-four hours. He would inform representatives when they might expect a vote on any given bill and warn them against missing it.[72]

President Roosevelt recognized Cannon's power in the House and tried to work with him. He had already served two years as President when Uncle Joe became Speaker. Realizing at once that Cannon was not another David Henderson who could be expected to automatically execute the requests of the White House, Roosevelt regularly solicited the Speaker's advice.[73] They met several times a week, sometimes daily, but the two men were at such opposite ends of the political spectrum that their relationship never developed into anything legislatively productive. Cannon was the first Speaker since the Civil War to meet with the President regularly, now that the chief executive was taking an active part in influencing Congress. Increasingly, with the emergence of the Progressive movement throughout the country, the House split between those who favored reform and were called "Insurgents" and those like Cannon who resisted change and were known as "Stalwarts." Roosevelt was once encouraged to "lay down on Uncle Joe," to which he replied, "It will be a good deal like laying down on a hedgehog."[74]

•   •   •

NOT UNTIL ROOSEVELT was elected President in his own right in 1904 did he feel comfortable about pressing for additional social and economic reforms. In his first message to Congress after his election he proposed a number of measures regarding child labor, slum clearance, and the strengthening of investigative agencies. He enjoyed limited success with the passage on June 30, 1906, of the Meat Inspection Act and the Pure Food and Drug Act. But it took publication of Upton Sinclair's book, *The Jungle,* which exposed the filthy conditions in the meat-packing houses, to overcome opposition to the Meat Inspection Act in the House Agriculture Committee, chaired by the conservative New York Republican, James Wadsworth, and allow the bill to come to the House floor for a vote. This act required sanitary conditions and federal inspection of meatpacking facilities involved in interstate commerce. The Pure Food and Drug Act forbade the manufacture and sale of adulterated or fraudulently labeled food and drugs sold in interstate commerce.

In one sense, Roosevelt was only keeping abreast of a larger (Progressive) movement within the country which demanded an end to the abuses of greedy corporations and machine politics. Several states initiated such reforms as the direct primary, the initiative and the referendum to allow the electorate a greater role in government. Writers such as Sinclair, Ida Tarbell, Henry Demarest Lloyd, Lincoln Steffens and others exposed the widespread corruption within business and cities and governments. Roosevelt called them "Muckrakers,"[75] but these reformers made the country aware of the evils in society and the need to terminate them. Stalwarts in the House and Senate resisted any attempts by the Insurgents to enact corrective legislation, contending that any interference with business was unconstitutional and likely to be struck down by the courts. They even warned that Roosevelt's attacks on big business could cause a financial panic, and indeed one occurred in 1907. Cannon was especially effective in preventing legislation to provide inheritance and income taxes, the extension of workers' compensation, and the enactment of an eight-hour workday. Although the rules had not changed essentially, he and his cohorts on the Rules Committee had learned how to employ them to control, direct or limit legislation. "The three members who constitute a majority of that committee," declared the then minority leader, Joseph Bailey of Texas, had "become a legislative triumvirate," deciding what "business the House must transact" but also what it may not.[76] It even controlled which amendments would or would not be allowed. Worse, no change in the rules could come to the floor except through a report from the committee itself.

Cannon's exercise of the Speaker's powers was far different from Reed's. Where Reed sought to end obstructionism so that the House could address the increased size of the legislative workload, Cannon sought to curtail the proper business of the House in order to maintain the status quo. Where Reed used his intellectual prowess to assert control, Cannon "just smiled, unbuttoned his vest, loosened his trousers and with his folksy, good fellow approach" beat back all opposition by a negative ruling and then called on the majority to uphold his decision.

Thus, much of Roosevelt's program of reform was either killed outright in committee, amended to disfigurement or simply ignored by the Cannon-controlled House. Not since the days of Andrew Johnson were a President's proposals met with such obstructionism. The electorate resented this behavior, and Uncle Joe became the target of considerable criticism. "Cannonism" entered the vocabulary, meaning congressional intransigence. It was even reported that the Speaker refused to receive a presidential message and had locked the doors of the chamber when the message arrived. Legislation "did not take place in congressional chambers," declared the *New York Times* on December 13, 1908, "but in Uncle Joe Cannon's little red room across the hall."[77]

It was slow, but already forces were shaping up in the House to curtail the Speaker's power. Just as the second session of the 60th Congress was about to end in mid-January 1909, the House Insurgents introduced several resolutions that called for ending the Speaker's authority to appoint committees and their members. They also demanded the creation of a Calendar Tuesday, which would allow the members to act on legislation approved in committee but opposed by the leadership and not cleared by the Rules Committee. Cannon and his Republican Stalwarts countered with a compromise that established Calendar Wednesday, but which permitted the majority (not two-thirds as proposed by the Insurgents) to set the day aside. Calendar Wednesday was adopted on March 1, 1909, and provided for the alphabetical calling of the roll of the standing committees every Wednesday. Legislation might be brought to the floor by a committee when its name was called.[78] It was a promising effort to curtail Cannon's tyranny, but unfortunately it proved ineffective. One or two committee reports might consume the entire day. It was, grumbled Norris, "a homeopathic dose of nothingness."[79]

The Insurgents knew they had to go further in their plans, and their numbers steadily increased with each new election, thanks to the continued rise of Progressivism, the support of President Roosevelt and the success of the Muckrakers in revealing corruption within business and government. The *Baltimore Sun* claimed that Cannon was "the very embodiment of all the sinister interest and malign influences that have brooded over this land and exacted toil from every hearthstone."[80] Republicans generally came to realize that Cannonism had to end. On March 17, 1910, the process began.

George Norris, the very able Republican from Nebraska and a leader of

George Norris led the House forces that stripped Speaker Cannon of his absolute power.

the Insurgents, rose to propose a resolution he said was privileged by the Constitution.[81] The day before, the Speaker had ruled that a vote on a resolution concerning the census could be held because the Constitution mandated a census and therefore the resolution was constitutionally privileged. Norris immediately spotted his opportunity. By claiming his resolution was privileged, since the Constitution decreed that each house may determine its own rules, he could prevent the resolution from being referred to the Rules Committee.

"It was the hour for which I had been waiting patiently," Norris said. "I had in my pocket a resolution to change the rules of the House." It had been there so long it was tattered and frayed. He pulled it out and waited.[82]

Cannon thought a moment. Then he permitted Norris to read his resolution. It was a moment that would spell the end of Cannonism.

Norris paused briefly. Then he proceeded to read his resolution. It proposed that the Rules Committee be increased to fifteen members and reflect geographic distribution, and that it select its own chairman. In addition— and this was a serious blow to Cannon—the Speaker would not be eligible to serve on the committee. John Dalzell, a Stalwart Republican from Pennsylvania, realized what had happened and immediately raised a point of order on the grounds that the resolution was not privileged. It took a long twenty-six-hour debate and a great deal of emotional exchange to thrash out the matter, but on March 19, the Speaker ruled in favor of the Dalzell point of order.

In the interim Norris conferred during the night with Representative James Beauchamp "Champ" Clark of Missouri, the Democratic floor leader, and Oscar Underwood of Alabama, Clark's close parliamentary officer and long recognized as one of the best parliamentarians in the House. To Norris's surprise and consternation, they told him they did not like his method of selecting the Rules Committee. "I was stunned," reported Norris. Obviously "they were expecting confidently to control the House in the next election, and they wanted to acquire the great power for a Speaker of their own choice which we were endeavoring to take away from Joe Cannon."[83] Nevertheless, in order to win Democratic votes for his proposal, Norris realized he had to consent to their demand, namely, that the members of the Rules Committee be selected by the entire House. He agreed to amend his resolution. A compromise had been reached.

Norris reported back to the other Insurgents, who at first resisted the Democratic demand but then accepted the fact that without Democratic votes the likelihood of changing the Rules Committee was next to impossible. They capitulated. Thus when Cannon ruled that Norris's resolution was not privileged, the Democrats appealed the ruling and by a vote of 182 to 162 the House overruled the Speaker, sending shock waves through the ranks of the Stalwarts. Norris dutifully offered changes to his proposal. He eliminated the geographic representation and reduced the numbers on the Rules Committee from fifteen to ten members who would be elected by the entire House membership, not appointed by the Speaker.

"It was a continuous rough-and-tumble on the floor," reported Alice Longworth. "Uncle Joe, who so recently had been regarded with fear, respect, and even some degree of affection, was greeted with jeers and cat-

James Beauchamp "Champ" Clark conspired with George Norris to defeat "Uncle Joe" Cannon and became Speaker himself following the mid-term election of 1910.

calls. As events suited or displeased them, the opposing sides cheered, clapped, and thumped on the desks and floor, and exchanged rough personalities. Members who had sneaked home to get a little sleep were corralled by the Sergeant-at-Arms to make a quorum. Nick [Longworth] was one who was routed out at five in the morning and taken to the House."[84]

The representatives then proceeded to debate the resolutions, and to the chagrin of Cannon and his henchmen the House, adopted them by the vote of 191 to 156, with 150 Democrats joining 43 Republicans to create the result.[85]

At last the House had regained its authority. The Speaker had been stripped of his absolute power.

12

The Speaker Eclipsed and Revived, 1910–1928

POOR "UNCLE JOE." It was quite a fall. "Cannonism was dead," he admitted, "dead as a doornail, dead as a last year's birdnest, dead as a defeated presidential candidate (and is there anything deader than that?), dead as an exploded campaign sensation."[1] But he took the defeat with good grace. "I'll just keep on speaking and praying," he declared.[2]

And because of Cannonism, the Republicans suffered a devastating electoral defeat in November 1910. On March 5, 1911, Uncle Joe turned over the Speaker's gavel to Champ Clark of Missouri. To make matters worse, the former tyrant was defeated for reelection to Congress in 1912 when Woodrow Wilson won the White House. But at the age of seventy-eight, the old man bounced back in 1914 and won reelection to the House three more times before retiring for good in 1923 at the age of eighty-seven. Three years later he died.

In the 1912 election, Republicans split and Wilson won the presidency over Theodore Roosevelt, who ran on a Bull Moose ticket (he said he felt as strong as a bull moose) favoring progressive reforms, and William Howard Taft, who was seeking reelection on the traditional Republican ticket and ran behind Roosevelt. Eugene V. Debs, the Socialist candidate, received almost a million popular votes.

Just prior to Wilson's election, the number of representatives in Congress was fixed at its present cap of 435. After the last census in 1910 the number was set at 433, but in 1912, with the addition of one representative each from the new states of Arizona and New Mexico, the figure rose to 435. And because of the size of the increased membership, the desks in the chamber were removed and replaced by rows of chairs arranged in a semi-circular configuration facing the podium. On January 10, 1913, money was appropriated to purchase 450 chairs and two tables on a new floor. This change provided more spacious aisles and ended the practice of Representatives having to draw lots for seat assignments. It also reduced the noise level in the chamber. No longer would desk drawers be slammed shut. And it was cleaner, too, because the avalanche of paper on desks and on the floor was markedly reduced.[3]

Democratic representative Cordell Hull of Tennessee arrived in the House at the beginning of the century, an ambitious young man with aspirations of making a name for himself in Congress, especially since Democrats were bent on reforming governmental operations. Straight off, Hull was told that "unless a new member specialized he would get nowhere in Congress, and if he did so he might or might not get somewhere. I decided to specialize in revenue, tariff, and other forms of taxation, economics and finance. I noticed there were few serious students of these subjects, whereas so-called dry statistics were as interesting to me as a 'dime novel.' "[4]

With men like Hull, who would later serve so brilliantly as secretary of state in the administration of Franklin Delano Roosevelt, the Democrats felt they could now proceed to build on the reforms of 1910. "Now at long last we had power," said Hull, "and with it a chance to put into effect some of the ideas we cherished."[5] They stripped their Speaker of the right to decide membership on House committees. The appointing authority was turned over to the Ways and Means Committee with their selections to be approved by the Democratic Caucus. "We did not want even a Democratic Speaker to have the authority Cannon had exercised.," said Hull.[6] Oscar W. Underwood of Alabama was chosen to head Ways and Means, and the members of that committee became a Committee on Committees

Cordell Hull, a leading Democratic House reformer in the early twentieth century, made a specialty of legislation dealing with tariffs and taxation.

and actually exercised the authority of recommending to the Caucus the Democratic assignments of other committees and their chairmen. In effect, the power of the Speaker shifted to Underwood who, because of his position, also served as the majority leader both in name and in fact.[7]

Underwood was able, though not brilliant, according to Hull. He "possessed common sense and was always on the alert. By his personality he kept everyone united and in good humor." He was "universally conceded to be a splendid statesman and the most capable floor leader within anyone's memory. He never lost his temper."[8] By virtue of his several offices—chair of Ways and Means and the Committee on Committees and majority leader—Underwood became the most powerful officer in the House. He believed in party government in which the decisions reached in the Democratic Caucus were binding on its members. And each member of the Caucus was permitted to express his opinion before the final vote was taken. "Let 'em talk," said Underwood. "Let 'em have it all out here. Then there will be no kick afterward."[9] In this way he ensured united action on the floor of the House. To prevent discord, he generally based his appointments to standing committees on seniority, arguing "that any other course would lead to turmoil."[10] Since seniority was the deciding factor, the chairmen of these committees were increasingly southerners, as Underwood knew only too well, being a southerner himself. In the 62nd Congress, for example, thirty-nine of the fifty-six standing committee chairmen came from the South, and they retained their positions over long periods of time. The power of the South in Congress therefore rose to a height that was all out of proportion to the number of citizens living in that area. What ultimately resulted was the increase of influence and authority by committee chairmen, a situation that would soon breed tyranny and necessitate reform. The Caucus also allowed the minority party to decide its own committee assignments, a practice that has been standard ever since.[11]

"We then went to work—night and day and Sunday—with enthusiasm," reported Hull. Chairmen were removed if they failed to pass muster. "Edward Pou of North Carolina was removed from the Ways and Means Committee and Claude Kitchin, from the same State, substituted for the reason that Pou had once voted for a tariff on lumber."[12] Thus, much of the early success of Woodrow Wilson's legislative program was due in large measure to a united party that Underwood had created in the House, and the enthusiasm and determination of its members to advance the President's reform efforts. But in 1915, Underwood left the House and moved to the Senate, whereupon Claude Kitchin replaced him as majority leader. Unfortunately, Kitchin disagreed with Wilson on several issues, most importantly on foreign policy, and these disagreements fragmented the once-solid Democratic House.[13]

As the consequence of an investigation by a subcommittee on Banking and Currency, chaired by Arsene Pujo of Louisiana, in which such luminaries as J. Pierpont Morgan and other prominent bankers testified to the monopolistic practices that consolidated the control of private money in the hands of a few New York and Boston banks, the Federal Reserve Act was enacted in 1913. This legislation, shepherded through the House by Carter Glass of Virginia, chairman of the Banking and Currency Committee, "a gentlemanly but irascible little man weighing about one hundred pounds,"[14] established twelve regional banks, each owned by private member banks and authorized to issue Federal reserve notes to member banks. A Federal Reserve Board controlled this decentralized system, and its seven members were appointed by the President with the consent of the Senate. The Board was authorized to raise or lower the discount rate of the member banks, thereby enabling it to direct the availability of credit in the nation. This action created not only a new and sound currency, but it also effectively terminated the control of credit and money throughout the country by a few Wall Street banking firms.

Responding to the increased demands for reform during the Progressive era, Congress agreed to two important amendments to the Constitution. The first was the 16th Amendment, approved by the House on July 12, 1909, by which an income tax was legalized. The amendment received Senate support and won adoption in February 1913. Just a few months later the 17th Amendment, approved by both houses in May 1912, and providing for the popular election of senators, was ratified on April 8, 1913. It has been argued that the 16th Amendment was the most powerful addition to federal authority in the entire twentieth century. And the 17th Amendment markedly enhanced the democratization of the government.

One of the first things President Wilson did on taking office was call the Congress into special session to reform the tariff. Indeed, so determined was he to accomplish his program of free enterprise and put an end to special privileges that encouraged the formation of monopolies—a program called the New Freedom—that he kept Congress in continuous session for a year and a half, something previously unheard of, even during the Civil War and early Reconstruction.[15] He reinforced his intentions by appearing personally before both houses of Congress on April 8, 1913, an action that revived the practices of Presidents Washington and Adams. He told the members that he wished to act as a partner in their legislative endeavors, not "a mere department of the Government hailing Congress from some isolated island of jealous power."[16] And because so many Democratic House members were newly elected freshmen with no legislative experience in Congress—114 of them had been chosen for the first time—they enthusiastically cooperated with the President to enact his New Freedom program into law.

Prior to his departure for the Senate, Underwood reported a new tariff proposal from his Ways and Means Committee that sharply lowered the rates from the average 40 percent ad valorum rates of the Payne-Aldrich Tariff of 1909 to about 29 percent, with many items placed on the free list. To compensate for the loss of revenue, the Underwood bill included a graduated income tax drafted by Cordell Hull. The young Tennessean favored a flat-rate income tax but yielded to the arguments put forward by John ("Cactus Jack")[17] Nance Garner of Texas for graduated rates.[18] To make certain the bill would win approval, Underwood announced to his colleagues that committee assignments would be delayed until the tariff had passed, a not so subtle warning that a vote against the bill would jeopardize a member's chances for an important committee position.

In the Senate, lobbyists tried to emasculate the measure, but an investigation into their activities, and the revelation of involvement by senators in companies affected by the tariff, brought about the passage of the Underwood-Simmons Tariff on October 3, 1913, which reduced rates on nearly a thousand basic items, such as wool, sugar, iron ore, leather, hemp, wood, coal and many foodstuffs. President Wilson helped achieve passage of the bill by publicly denouncing the "insidious" lobby that sought to defeat "the interest of the public for [its] private profit."[19] This tariff also levied a 1 percent tax on incomes above $2,000 with a $1,000 exemption for married men, and a graduated tax of 1 to 6 percent on incomes from $20,000 to $500,000.[20] In addition, the President was empowered to negotiate reciprocal trade agreements with foreign nations.

To reign in the unfair trade practices of many corporations, Representative Henry D. Clayton of Alabama, chairman of the House Judiciary Committee, introduced a bill which strengthened the Sherman Anti-Trust Act by including practices not covered by the earlier legislation, such as price discrimination, interlocking directorates and the acquisition of stocks in other companies to lessen competition. The Clayton Antitrust Act passed both houses in October, 1914, just weeks after the passage of the Federal Trade Commission Act. The latter act, introduced in the House by Democratic representative Raymond B. Stevens of New Hampshire, aimed to prevent unfair practices in interstate commerce. It abolished the Bureau of Corporations and replaced it with the Federal Trade Commission, consisting of five members who received annual reports from corporations and had authority to issue cease and desist orders—subject to judicial review—to halt business practices it deemed to be unfair or in restraint of trade.[21]

IN WINNING PASSAGE of much of his New Freedom initiative, Wilson adopted the old Jeffersonian practice of working directly and personally with members of Congress, especially committee chairmen. He encouraged loyalists to serve as his liaison with the House, but he operated surreptitiously and discreetly so neither the public nor Congress were consciously aware of his methods. He was his own chief lobbyist. It was said that he often waited in elevators to meet with particular congressmen whose help he needed.

At one point Wilson almost lost control of Congress when, following the outbreak of World War I in Europe on August 4, 1914, a German submarine torpedoed the USS *Lusitania* on May 7, 1915, and 128 American lives were lost. Then Germany announced that its U-boats would attack unarmed merchantmen without warning, whereupon Wilson refused to warn American citizens against traveling on such vessels in an attempt to uphold the rights of neutrals. He cautioned Americans against doing anything that would violate U.S. neutrality. Consequently, the House Foreign Affairs Committee acted on its own initiative and adopted a resolution, introduced by A. Jeff McLemore of Texas, advising Americans to avoid traveling on unarmed ships. To Wilson this was a direct challenge to his leadership and an attempt by the House to formulate foreign policy. A similar resolution in the Senate introduced by Thomas P. Gore of Oklahoma brought the matter to a head. To block this action, the President brought considerable pressure on Congress through his liaison men, especially "Cactus Jack" Garner of Texas, a member of the Ways and Means Committee, who twice a week (and sometimes more often if necessary) surreptitiously took public transportation to the White House, entered the building through a side door and was immediately ushered into the Oval Office.[22] Together they devised a strategy by which Wilson succeeded in having the Senate resolution tabled on March 3, 1916, by a vote of 68 to 14, and the House resolution tabled on March 7 by a vote of 276 to 142.[23]

But Wilson had to contend with Claude Kitchin, the majority leader, who repeatedly accused the President of pursuing a policy that jeopardized America's neutrality in the European war. Kitchin stacked the military and naval affairs committees with like-minded southern conservatives who bottled up the administration's defense initiatives. A great many other Democrats in both houses agreed with Kitchin, and it soon became apparent that they verged on open revolt against Wilson's leadership.

Recognizing the military weakness of the United States as the war in Europe grew more dangerous, the Senate introduced a bill that would create a "Continental army" of 261,000 and a regular peacetime force of 250,000 officers and men. It also increased the size of the National Guard and established a reserve officers' training corps in schools and colleges. Peace-minded Democrats, led by Kitchin, adamantly opposed the idea of a Continental army and struck it from the bill. There followed many stormy sessions between the two houses and between Congress and the President. Several conferences were held in which Wilson denounced interference from Congress, especially within his own party, arguing that it would undermine his authority at home and discredit him abroad. They in turn warned him that his policies were leading the nation into war.[24]

As finally enacted on June 3, 1916, the National Defense Act expanded the regular army to 175,000 men and, over the next five years, increased its size to 223,000 and authorized the enlargement of the National Guard to 450,000. It also established the Reserve Officers Training Corps at colleges and universities. But Wilson's idea of a national volunteer Continental army was scrapped on the insistence of Kitchin, who controlled the Military Affairs Committee. In addition, the measure established the Council of National Defense to prepare for possible mobilization, and it appropriated $315 million for naval construction and expansion.[25]

Concerned about the need to strengthen his farm policy and thereby his bid for reelection in 1916, Wilson signed the Federal Farm Loan Act in July 1916, which divided the country into twelve districts under the supervision of the Federal Farm Loan Board, consisting of the secretary of the treasury and four members. A Farm Loan Bank was established in each district that could provide farmers with long-term, low-interest credit. Also, he signed the Keating-Owen Child Labor Act on September 1, 1916, which forbade the sale in interstate commerce of products made by children under sixteen.

The presidential election of 1916 turned out to be a very close race. The Republicans nominated Supreme Court Justice Charles Evans Hughes, who had once served as governor of New York. The Progressives sought to nominate Roosevelt once again, but he declined and threw his support to Hughes. The Democrats naturally chose Wilson for a second term on a platform that emphasized peace. "He kept us out of war," they contended.[26]

Not until late returns put California in the Wilson column did it become certain that the President had won reelection. The electoral vote was 277 for Wilson and 254 for Hughes. The Democrats retained control of the Senate but lost the House. There was practically an even split between the two major parties, with the Republicans taking 216 seats and the Democrats 210. It meant that the Progressives and Independents held the balance of power. With the help of the Independents, the Democrats were able to organize the House and reelect Champ Clark as Speaker.

Among the new members was Republican Jeannette Rankin of Montana, a thirty-six-year-old suffragette and social worker. Although the Constitution had not yet been amended to give women the vote, many states had already done so. And Rankin was among the freshmen representatives of the 65th Congress. "I feel tremendous responsibility," she told a *New York Times* reporter. "As Representative of the state of Montana, I shall represent to the best of my ability the men, women, and children of my state. But . . . I feel it is my special duty to express also the point of view of women

and to make clear that the women of the country are coming to a full realization of the fact that Congress is a body which deals with their problems."[27]

When Rankin was sworn in on April 2, 1917, she strode down the aisle
of the chamber, arm in arm with her Montana colleague, John Evans, looking neither to the left nor right, while the room rang with the cheers and
applause of her fellow suffragettes and other friends and relatives seated in
the gallery. "She wore a well-made dark-blue silk and chiffon suit, with
open neck, and wide white crepe collar and cuffs;" reported Ellen Maury
Slayden, the wife of a Texas congressman; "her skirt was a modest walking
length, and she walked well and unselfconsciously. Her hair is a common-
place brown and arranged in a rather too spreading pompadour shadowing
her face. She carried a bouquet of yellow and purple flowers, given her at the
suffrage breakfast." As she reached her seat she was immediately surrounded by other representatives who shook her hand, congratulated her
and wished her a long and successful career.[28]

The roll call began, and when the clerk called Rankin's name the House
rose and cheered. She rose, too, and bowed to the members "with entire
self-possession."[29]

WITH CONGRESS NOW in session, Wilson offered a proposal for ending
the war in Europe without victory, one without annexations and one that
would include an international organization dedicated to keeping the
peace. Then events took a sudden turn. In an attempt to win a quick victory,
Germany unleashed a program of unrestricted submarine warfare early in
1917, even though it risked U.S. entry into the war. The President broke
diplomatic relations with Germany and asked Congress for authority to
arm merchant ships and wage what would be in effect an undeclared naval
war. Both houses approved arming merchant ships but baulked at authorizing a naval war. At that point Wilson revealed the intercepted note written
by Arthur Zimmermann, the German foreign secretary, to the German
minister in Mexico in which it was promised that Texas, New Mexico and
Arizona would be returned to Mexico if Mexico declared war against the
United States. Release of the note produced a hysteria that changed many
peace activists into warmongers.

With the sinking of several American ships by German submarines,
Wilson summoned a special session of the 65th Congress to convene on
April 2, 1917. On that day, at 8:30 p.m., the President appeared before a joint
session and asked for a declaration of war. He characterized the unrestricted
submarine attacks as "warfare against mankind." It is a "fearful thing," he
continued, "to lead this great peaceful people into war. . . . But the right is
more precious than peace, and we shall fight for the things which we have
always carried nearest our hearts. . . ."[30] The Senate responded quickly and

two days later, on April 4, 1917, by a vote of 82 to 6, passed the war resolution.

But the House witnessed a prolonged debate that lasted through the night. It was April 6—which happened to be Good Friday—and the galleries were electrified when Kitchin rose and delivered an emotionally powerful speech. Wearing a blue business suit, a high white vest and a black string tie, he read from five sheets of typed manuscript. "Mr. Chairman," he cried in his slightly husky voice, "in view of the many assumptions of loyalty and patriotism on the part of some of those who favor the resolution [to declare war], and insinuations by them of cowardice and disloyalty on the part of those who oppose it, offshoots, doubtless, of a passionate moment, let me at once remind the House that it takes neither moral nor physical courage to declare a war for others to fight. . . . This nation is the last hope of peace on earth, good will toward men. . . . I am unwilling by my vote today for this nation to throw away the only remaining compass to which the world can look for guidance in the paths of right and truth, of justice and humanity, and to leave only force and blood to chart hereafter the path for mankind to read."[31]

As Kitchin returned to his seat, the entire House rose and applauded. Many disagreed with him, but they respected him for following his conscience. Speaker Clark informed the House that however regrettable it was to differ with the President, particularly when he was the head of one's own party, nevertheless each branch of the government had its own role and responsibilities. The President "has his functions to perform and, as far as I have been able to observe, he is not bashful about performing them. The House and Senate have their functions to perform, and, if we are men, we will perform them." Any member who violates his convictions because they run counter to those of the President "is not fit to sit in the House or the Senate."[32]

The clerk then began to read the first roll call on the resolution to declare war. When he got to Jeannette Rankin, she did not respond when her name was called. "There was a hush," she wrote, "and I didn't say a word." She knew that she did not have to vote until the second roll call. She sat in her seat, pondering her vote.

Suddenly a familiar figure stood before her. Uncle Joe Cannon, the former Speaker, looked solemnly at her and offered advice. "Little woman," he said, "you cannot afford not to vote. You represent the womanhood of the country in the American Congress. I shall not advise you how to vote, but you should vote one way or another—as your conscience dictates."[33] Then he walked away.

There was a "breathless silence" during the second roll call when Rankin's name was called. She rose to her feet and in a firm voice declared that she wanted to "stand by my country, but I cannot vote for war. I vote no." The *New York Times* said she was "in a state bordering on frenzy, weeping copiously during the roll call." But by the time she voted she was composed. "I had wept so much that week," she remembered, "that my tears were all gone by the time the vote came."[34] The final tally was 373 in favor, 50 against and 9 not voting.

Near dawn, the House adjourned, and almost the entire membership crowded around Kitchin, many with tears in their eyes.[35] They had been deeply moved by his passionate appeal for peace. At 1:18 p.m., Wilson signed the resolution and the United States entered World War I.

RANKIN'S ACTION IN voting against war certainly did not help the many organizations of women who had been demanding the suffrage for decades. Granting a woman the right to vote would weaken the ability of the country to go to war and threaten the very foundation of the Republic, argued some. But a new organization, the National Woman's Party, took the lead in badgering Congress to pass an amendment to the Constitution outlawing the denial of the vote because of gender.

At the same time that women petitioned for the suffrage they also teamed up with the Women's Christian Temperance Union and the Anti-Saloon League to demand the outlawing of liquor, thereby taking full advantage of the anti-German sentiment in the country since many distillers and brewers were of German descent. Congress adopted the 18th Amendment[36] to the Constitution on December 18, 1917, prohibiting the manufacture, transportation and sale of alcoholic liquors. It was ratified on January 29, 1919, but repealed by the adoption of the 21st Amendment in 1933.

Women continued their fight for the vote, and petitions by the hundreds flooded into Congress. On January 10, 1918, the House of Representatives passed a resolution, 274 to 136, setting forth the 19th Amendment, which provided women's suffrage. But the Senate did not concur. Not until 1919 did Congress finally endorse a joint resolution amending the Constitution which forbade "denying or abridging" the right to vote to anyone on account of sex. The House passed the resolution on May 21, 1919, by a vote of 304 to 89, with 200 Republicans, 102 Democrats, 1 Prohibitionist, and 1 Independent voting "aye," and 19 Republicans and 70 Democrats voting "no." The Senate agreed on June 4, 1919, fifty years after the first woman suffrage measure was introduced in the House. The amendment was ratified on August 26, 1920, in time for a presidential election.

One reason for the eventual success of the 19th Amendment was the support President Wilson provided. After all, he said, if women are partners in the war against Germany, surely they deserve to share in the blessings of a free nation. "Shall we admit them only to a partnership of suffering and sacrifice and toil," he said, "and not to a partnership of privilege and right?"[37]

During the next decade and a half, following the ratification of the 19th Amendment, twenty women trooped into the House as members. In 1922, Alice Robertson of Oklahoma became the first woman to preside over the lower chamber, and a year later, Mae Ella Nolan of California rose in rank to chair the Committee on Expenditures in the Post Office Department. Mary Norton of New Jersey chaired four House committees during her twenty-five years as a member. When a colleague referred to her as a "lady," Norton retorted, "I'm no lady. I'm a Member of Congress, and I'll proceed on that basis."[38] Most of these women were well-educated and came from upper middle class families. More than half attended college. While they lacked electoral experience, they had played active roles in party politics and even served as lobbyists. Several of them were widows who won election to the seats held by their recently deceased husbands. At least two of them had distinguished fathers: Ruth Bryan Owen was the daughter of William Jennings Bryan, and Ruth McCormick was the daughter of Mark Hanna. McCormick headed the Republican Women's National Executive Committee. Their ranks were small in the beginning but would steadily swell for the remainder of the century.[39]

IN PROSECUTING THE war, the Congress not only authorized loans and bonds to finance the conflict but passed the Selective Service Act on May 18, 1917, which called for the registration for military service of all men between the ages of eighteen and forty-five. There was a heated debate in both houses over its constitutionality, and Speaker Champ Clark even surrendered the chair to oppose the bill. Of the more than 24 million men registered during the war, almost 3 million were called to service in the army. Congress also passed the Espionage Act in 1917, establishing fines and imprisonment to prevent disloyal activities. It allowed the postmaster

Following the ratification of the 19th Amendment, a number of women entered Congress, among them Representative Mary Norton of New Jersey, who chaired four House committees during her twenty-five-year tenure.

general to exclude from the mails any materials deemed seditious or treasonable. The constitutionality of the act was upheld in 1919 by the Supreme Court in *Schenck v. United States.*

Not until the late spring of 1918 did U.S. military forces in large numbers join the Allies at the front. Meanwhile, Germany had signed a peace treaty with the new Soviet government and then launched in May an all-out offensive against the western Allies. Wilson had already begun planning for the aftermath of war, and early in 1918, he came before Congress and outlined his Fourteen Points as the basis for a just and lasting peace, once Germany was defeated. His proposal called for freedom of the seas, open covenants openly arrived at, restoration of national boundaries, establishment of an independent Poland, the formation of a League of Nations and others. These points, he argued, were the "only possible program" for peace. Unfortunately, he did not consult with the Republican opposition in the Senate in formulating his program, and then he proceeded to ask the electorate to return a Democratic Congress in the 1918 midterm election in order to prevent Europe from interpreting a defeat of his party as a "repudiation of my leadership." His request and presumption offended the electorate, who responded by sending a majority of Republicans to both houses of Congress. In the House the Republicans numbered 237 to the Democrats' 191, and 7 Independents; in the Senate it was an almost even split with 48 Republicans, 47 Democrats and 1 Independent. Meanwhile the war in Europe ended with the defeat of the German army and an armistice was signed on November 11, 1918.

Wilson traveled to France to attend the Versailles Peace Conference, which would officially end the war. But the overthrow of the Czarist regime in Russia and the inauguration of the Bolshevik Revolution unleashed a wave of isolationist sentiment across the United States. This Red Scare, as it was called, produced a patriotic fervor that resulted in scattered assaults on the civil liberties of individuals and a near hysterical fear of Communist infiltration into the United States.

Meanwhile the House Republicans struggled over who should lead the party now that they held the majority. James Mann of Illinois, the minority leader for the past four years and Cannon's close associate, was supported by the conservatives for the position of Speaker. The more reform-minded Republicans, worried over the possibility of a return to Cannonism and the harm it could do the party in the presidential election of 1920, backed Frederick Gillett of Massachusetts. Mann's candidacy was totally spiked when an investigation revealed that the meatpacking companies had provided him with gifts and other financial "goodies." To which the Gillett men rallied with the cry, "Can, can the Packers' Mann." That finished Mann, and Gillett was chosen Speaker.

But Mann proposed the creation of a Committee on Committees

composed of one member from each state and assigned the duty of naming the majority leader, whip, committee chairmen, and members of the Steering Committee. The subsequent adoption of this proposal gave control of the House organization to the conservatives, and although the reformers had won the Speakership, the Old Guard, as it was called, retained mastery of the party.

The first thing the Committee on Committees did was appoint Mann as majority leader. But he declined and the post was turned over to Frank Mondell of Wyoming, a loyal supporter of both Cannon and Mann, and "a man with no obvious leadership qualities." Even so, Mondell was a more powerful House figure than the Speaker, Frederick Gillett.[40]

When the third session of the 65th Congress ended on March 3, 1919, "a rag bag of exhausted, frowzy legislators . . . [had] what the old door-keeper called a 'social session.' " It was not uncommon. One member stood in front of the rostrum and led the members in singing a variety of songs while the Marine Band played "full tilt." "I could not help being filled with malicious amusement," chortled Alice Longworth. "Yet the whole scene was reassuring—the carefree, good-natured, informal untidy crowd—it was so completely American."[41]

A DISAPPOINTED WILSON returned from France where the delegates to the Versailles Peace Conference had emasculated his Fourteen Points. To retain the idea of a League of Nations he had agreed to compromises in the final treaty that negated all possibility of a just and lasting peace. Among other things, the treaty saddled Germany with sole blame for the war and demanded an impossible $56 billion in reparations. It virtually invited a retaliation in the future.

The United States was in no mood to involve itself in European affairs that would surely jeopardize the traditional foreign policy of neutrality, and this hostile mood reinforced those in the Senate who were determined to block ratification of the Versailles Treaty. Led by Senator Henry Cabot Lodge of Massachusetts, now chairman of the Senate Foreign Relations Committee, who contended that the treaty jeopardized American sovereignty, the opponents of the treaty tied it up in committee for six weeks in order to arouse public opinion against ratification. Many Senators were also incensed that Wilson failed to invite a congressional delegation to accompany him to Paris. To counter these tactics, the President took his case directly to the electorate in September 1919, traveling nearly ten thousand miles and giving dozens of speeches. In poor health, he finally collapsed after attending a rally in Pueblo, Colorado. Stricken by a massive stroke on October 2, he could no longer continue the fight. Meanwhile, Lodge offered fourteen reservations to the treaty, but they were defeated. Then, a motion by Democrats to ratify the treaty without reservations also went down to defeat, 53 to 38.

That night the "irreconcilables," as the extreme isolationists were called, celebrated their victory at the home of Nicholas Longworth, where the wife of Senator Warren G. Harding of Ohio—he was a Lodge supporter and a member of the Senate Foreign Relations Committee—cooked scrambled eggs for the triumphant guests. The "Duchess," as Mrs. Harding was called, also tended bar. When Harding or Longworth or any other guest wanted another drink they would call out, "Duchess, you are lying down on your job," and Mrs. Harding would "obediently get up and mix a whiskey and soda for them."[42]

Warren G. Harding rose to notorious fame when the Republican National Convention met in Chicago in June 1920, and the delegates, lacking an outstanding candidate, eventually chose him to head the ticket after he assured the leadership that he had not been involved in any scandal or improper behavior. Handsome, silver haired and intellectually vapid, he skillfully managed to hide his numerous extramarital shenanigans. His genius, according to John D. Hicks, "lay not so much in his ability to conceal his thought as in the absence of any serious thought to reveal."[43] For Vice President, the convention settled on Calvin Coolidge of Massachusetts, whose outstanding achievement as governor of his state, according to conservatives, was breaking a strike by Boston policemen.

Democrats also floundered in naming a ticket. After forty-four ballots, the exhausted delegates in desperation finally selected James M. Cox, the governor of Ohio, along with Franklin D. Roosevelt of New York, who had served as assistant secretary of the navy in Wilson's administration.

Although Cox and Roosevelt tried to make the election a referendum on the League, the American people were tired of global problems and were entranced by Harding's "back to normalcy" and "America First" appeals. As a result, the election turned into a landslide for the Republicans. They won the presidency, 404 electoral votes to 127, and both houses of Congress. In the House the membership numbered 300 Republicans and 132 Democrats, and in the Senate 59 Republicans and 37 Democrats. Even Champ Clark, the outgoing Speaker, was defeated, along with Cordell Hull and Henry Rainey. Claude Kitchin of North Carolina became the Democratic party leader, but ill health forced him to leave Washington for a rest in 1921, and he appointed J. Finis Garrett of Tennessee as floor leader over John Nance Garner of Texas, with whom he had had several disagreements. Not until Garrett left the House in 1928 to run for the Senate was "Cactus Jack" able to resume his climb toward the Speakership.

THE NATION HAD changed—profoundly. What came as something of a shock was the news that the census of 1920 documented the fact that most Americans now lived in or near cities. The generally held notion that this country was populated mainly by farmers, living in small communities and displaying all the virtues of agrarian life, received a rude awakening. Americans in the 1920s were mainly city folk and their manner and style of living reflected the change. The long, trailing dresses that women wore heretofore were slowly being shortened. Large, plumed hats that required pins to keep them in place were no longer fashionable and had been replaced by smaller, more comfortable ones.

The most important exception to this generalization about the urbanization of the country was the south. It looked no "different than it had at the end of Reconstruction in the 1870s." Southerners planted and harvested as they had for decades, and suffered chronic agricultural depression. It was a hard life made worse by the grinding poverty inflicted on African-Americans on account of racial bigotry and discrimination. As a result, a half million blacks migrated from their rural communities to the industrial north following the Great War. And that number continued to rise throughout the 1920s until another million of them had deserted the south to find employment in the factories and packing houses of the north.[44]

With the enactment of the Volstead Act on January 16, 1920, passed over Wilson's veto and intended to implement the 18th Amendment, Prohibition became law, but Americans hardly abandoned their drinking habits. To obtain liquor they relied on bootleggers to keep them well supplied or made it themselves in their bathtubs. This acceptance of illegal activities produced a corrupting attitude throughout the country and encouraged a carefree disregard for the law.

Even lawmakers violated the law. "Outside of the official houses Prohibition in Washington was ignored from the start," reported Alice Longworth. "When it first came in we grumbled, shrugged our shoulders, decided to use the stock we had, and when that was gone turn our attention to wine making and distilling in the home, thinking that undoubtedly supplies would trickle in from one source or another. I don't think that we foresaw in the slightest degree the great bootlegging industry that was to develop, the complete and organized violation of law and order. . . . We bought pounds of grapes and experimented with wine making, and I recollect that we had a small still with which our butler managed to concoct a very passable gin from oranges."[45] Because of the profits involved in the illegal transportation of liquor from foreign countries, like Canada, criminals were attracted to the business. Organized crime became rampant with the Mafia controlling much of the gambling, bootlegging and prostitution in the cities.

Congress's official and exclusive bootlegger was George L. Cassiday, whom the press dubbed "The Man in the Green Hat," presumably because he was wearing a light-green felt hat when he was arrested. He plied his trade during the presidential administrations of Harding, Coolidge (the peak of his operation) and Hoover. A friend first introduced him to two southern representatives, both of whom had voted for Prohibition, who needed a supplier, and from those acquaintances he went from customer to customer and was soon supplying virtually the entire House of Representatives. The greatest demand was for rye, Scotch, bourbon "and all sorts of imported and bonded liquors," he said during an interrogation. "I recall one member in particular who was perhaps the largest consumer of liquor of any variety that I ever met in or out of Congress. . . . This representative was one of the party leaders in the House and one of the ablest debaters in either branch of Congress. He was a 'bottle-a-day' man. I have seen him many times take a regular-sized water glass, full to the brim, and drink it to the last drop."[46]

One day a midwestern representative said to him, "George, did it ever occur to you it would be easier to bring supplies into the building in larger lots and distribute it from a base of operations from the inside?" That idea certainly made sense, so Cassiday began storing and cutting liquor for the use of members in the House Office Building itself. One of his "good customers" gave him a key to a room in the building. "I found that on days when I wasn't too busy with deliveries I could bring in a couple of suitcases full and get it into the room without being bothered." He usually gained access at night by one of the side entrances, just as the House adjourned, and therefore he went unnoticed because of the many people passing in and out of the building. It got so that the place "seemed like home to me. I knew every nook and corner in it. The fact that the Capitol police and the door guards were appointed by members of Congress seemed to assure me of protection in getting into the building. Once inside I was always sure of a hearty welcome in the offices which I visited in a day's rounds."

Of the delegations from the then forty-eight states in the House, "I would give it as a conservative estimate that my list included members from

George L. Cassiday, the "man in the green hat," was the bootlegger for House members and operated out of a room in the House Office Building.

a good majority of the states." Finally, after being arrested several times, the last on October 31, 1929, Cassiday was sentenced by the District Court to one year and nine months in prison.[47]

Ordinary citizens frequented "speakeasies" where they could purchase illegal liquor provided they would "speak easy." In these dark, crowded places young women, called flappers, could be seen dancing the Charleston. They wore short dresses, cut their hair short, and smoked cigarettes. Having lost husbands, brothers and boyfriends in the war, and parents during the influenza outbreak of 1918–1919, they exhibited a carefree wildness and independence that represented an entirely new version of the American woman. They had the vote and a sense of freedom that encouraged sometimes outrageous behavior.

Interestingly, the women members of the House of Representatives were divided on the question of Prohibition. Some advocated temperance, but not all. Moreover, they did not vote as a bloc, which party leaders feared. They failed to put forward an agenda of "women's issues." That failure came as a relief to male members who assumed they would act together and try to initiate legislation on "trivial" causes. Some males took offense by the very presence of these newcomers and regularly criticized them for one fault or another. Katherine Langley of Kentucky irritated any number of

With the coming of women's suffrage, Alice Robertson of Oklahoma, Mae Ella Nolan of California and Winnifred Huck of Illinois were among the first House members to invade what had previously been an all-male club.

colleagues because of her dress and general appearance. "She offends the squeamish by her unstinted display of gypsy colors on the floor," reported one journalist, "and the conspicuousness with which she dresses her bushy blue-black hair."[48] Women had invaded what had been for over a hundred years an exclusive men's club and they were resented.[49]

But some of the women charmed their colleagues. Florence Prag Kahn, for example, bowled them over. Witty and fiercely intelligent without making a show of it, Kahn succeeded her late husband, Julius, and was sometimes asked to preside over particularly heated debates in the House because of her ability to maintain control. A Republican from California, she was the first woman to win a seat on the powerful Appropriations Committee. When asked why she was so popular, she candidly replied, "Sex appeal."[50]

Langley and Kahn represented what came to be called the Jazz Age that followed World War I. The title derived from the new popular music that had migrated north from New Orleans when thousands of African-American southerners relocated in the big cities like Chicago. Jazz captured the tempo of the times, a sense of rootlessness in which the music had no basic key and performers could improvise as they departed from and returned to the basic melody.

The ten-year period following the end of World War I, known as the Roaring Twenties, was also distinguished by an economy that seemed unstoppable in its growth and strength. In addition, it was a period when the Ku Klux Klan renewed its hold on bigots throughout the south and then spread northward and established itself in many northern states.

The Red Scare with its fear of communism and foreign influence in American life led to the arrest of hundreds of individuals suspected of subversive activities, particularly after an unsuccessful assassination attempt on the life of the U.S. attorney general, A. Mitchell Palmer, on June 2, 1919. Few questioned the legality of such arrests. Even the courts seemed indifferent to upholding the law where communists were concerned, so widespread was the fear of foreign radicals. This disdain for the rules of society and scorn for conventional behavior spread to every section of the country and corruption seeped into local, state and national governments.

IN WASHINGTON, PRESIDENT Harding would become a symbol of corrupt government because of his own immoral behavior and the many scandals that permeated his administration. When he first came to the capital as a senator, he and Longworth found they had much in common: "booze," gambling and sex.[51] Then, in 1921, two naval oil reserves at Teapot Dome in Wyoming and Elk Hills in California were transferred from the Navy Department to the Interior Department and subsequently leased to private oil companies. This transfer was investigated by a group of Democratic and several Republican senators when the House refused to look into the

matter. The Teapot Dome scandal was the most notorious of the many misdeeds committed during the Harding administration. Over the next few
years the Senate Committee on Public Lands unearthed bribery and corruption in a number of executive departments.

As for responsibility by the United States in global affairs, Harding announced in his inaugural address that this country would "seek no part in
directing the destinies of the world," which killed any hope of the country
joining the League of Nations.[52] The disheartened and gravely ill Wilson
pronounced Harding's remark as a retreat into "sullen and selfish isolation
which is deeply ignoble because manifestly cowardly and dishonorable."[53]
On March 19, 1920, a resolution of ratification of the Treaty of Peace with
Germany was defeated in the Senate. Not until July 2, 1921, did a congressional joint resolution officially end this nation's war with Germany and
Austria-Hungary.

Immediately on taking office, Harding called Congress into special
session on April 11, 1921, and asked them to lower taxes and raise the tariff.
Frederick H. Gillett of Massachusetts was again elected Speaker, but an
eight-member Republican Steering Committee, chaired by the majority
leader, Frank W. Mondell, controlled much of the business of the House.
This committee met virtually every day with the Speaker and the chairman
of the Rules Committee. Together they decided which bills would come
before the House, and they effectively blocked any legislation not in accord
with their conservative thinking.

Some Representatives complained. One member of the Rules Committee wanted several resolutions he had written down taken to the floor. The
chair, Philip P. Campbell of Kansas, read them and thrust them into his
pocket. Just a minute, the member blurted. This committee decides what
goes to the floor, not you. Whereupon Campbell responded, "You can go to
hell. It makes no difference what a majority of you decided. If it meets with
my disapproval, it shall not be done. I am the committee, in me repose absolute obstructive powers."[54]

Such arrogance and contempt for the rights of individual members was
a throwback to the worst practices of Cannonism, but the chairman spoke
the truth. Since the Speaker had been stripped of much of his authority, and
Frank Mondell, the majority leader, proved incompetent, real power resided with committee chairmen, especially those of the most important
standing committees. These individuals arranged the agenda of their committees, appointed the subcommittees and assigned them specific tasks,
and decided which pending bills would be considered and ultimately
brought to the entire House. In effect they achieved absolute control of the
legislative process.

Because the House had no strong individual in a position of leadership,
it was overshadowed by the Senate. Most legislation during the Harding

administration was initiated by the upper house, and even bills emanating from the House were usually rewritten when they reached the Senate. Mondell frequently opposed measures put forward by the President, including a tax cut, and found it impossible to work effectively with the administration. According to the *New York Sun,* Harding was obliged to go to Representative Nicholas Longworth of Ohio for help to get his program considered by the House.

THE ISOLATIONISM AND xenophobia that had seeped through the vitals of the country finally found expression in the passage of the First Immigration Quota Act on May 19, 1921, limiting the number of immigrants to be admitted each year. According to this law, the number of aliens of any nationality was not to exceed 3 percent of the number of persons of that nationality listed in the 1910 census. It also set a limit of 357,803 immigrants per year. "Above all, the policy now adopted meant that in a generation the foreign-born would cease to be a major factor in American history."[55] But history dictated otherwise.

Seeking to bring more efficient management to the country's financial affairs, Congress passed the National Budget and Accounting Act on June 10, 1921, which created a Budget Bureau in the Treasury Department to regulate and supervise the expenditures of the national government. In addition, the General Accounting Office was established under a comptroller general to monitor and audit the government's accounts.

In response to the President's requests, and without any real help from the majority leader, Congress approved the Fordney-McCumber Tariff, which raised rates on both agricultural and industrial products, with special protection given to the sugar and textile companies. The income tax was also lowered in the Revenue Act of 1921. Only nine Republican members in the House voted against it. The vote was 274 to 125.

BUT THERE WAS some movement toward economic and social improvement. Progressives of both parties, including Senators Robert La Follette of Wisconsin, George Norris of Nebraska, William E. Borah of Idaho and Burton K. Wheeler of Montana, and Representatives Victor Berger of Wisconsin, a Socialist who had been twice expelled from the House, Fiorello La Guardia of New York and John M. Nelson of Wisconsin, held a conference in Chicago in May 1923. They agreed on a program of reform which would provide farm relief, a child labor limitation, lower railroad rates, limits on the power of injunctions which were used to halt labor strikes, restoration of excess profits taxes and freedom for the Philippines, among others, none of which could pass muster as far as the Rules Committee was concerned. Representative Nelson became the spokesman for the Progressive group, although La Guardia was a frequent and lively agitator.

On August 2, 1923, Harding suddenly and unexpectedly died of a heart attack in San Francisco just as the scandals of his administration were about to flare into public view. Calvin Coolidge immediately succeeded him, taking the oath at 2:47 on the morning of August 3. One of the first things he wanted to do was amend the Immigration Act to limit more drastically the entrance of certain nationalities deemed unworthy of entering the United States.

When the 68th Congress convened in December 1923, Nicholas Longworth had announced his candidacy for majority leader of the Republican Party and was elected by a voice vote. Mondell was no longer in the way since he had conveniently decided to run for the Senate in 1922, a contest he lost. But the Progressives held up the election of Gillett for Speaker for two days and eight ballots until they reached an agreement with Longworth about reform. Nelson, La Guardia and Roy O. Woodruff, Republican from Michigan, met with the majority leader and got him to promise a full debate on revision of the Rules and give Nelson a seat on the Rules Committee.[56] Afterward, Democrat Henry T. Rainey of Illinois congratulated Longworth for having steered safely "between the Scylla of progressive Republicanism . . . and the Charybdis of conservative Republicanism. . . . There is not a scratch on the ship. The paint is absolutely intact."[57]

With the defeat, death, retirement and removal to the Senate of several Old Guard members, such as Cannon, Mondell and Mann, the House Republican Party lost much of its fierce conservatism. Now, the members set about liberalizing their Rules, and the debate lasted five days. The discharge rule was one important change. Under the new rule a bill could be brought to the floor for action by means of a petition signed by only 150 House members. In addition, the rule forbidding members from offering amendments to revenue and tariff bills that were not "germane" was eliminated. The rules were also altered to prevent what was called a "pocket veto" by the chairman of the committee. Representative Thomas Blanton complained that Chairman Campbell had "kept the rule in his pocket and choked the will of Congress and laughed at us when we insisted that he obey the rules as a servant of this House, and we were absolutely helpless."[58] Chairman Snell, who succeeded Campbell, assured the House that the new rule "absolutely does away with any possibility of a pocket veto by the chairman of the committee and fully protects the committee if the person authorized to call up a resolution does not do so within the prescribed time."[59]

The House got into a lively debate over the change of the Immigration Act that Coolidge had suggested in his first message to Congress. And the debate reflected the isolationism and xenophobia that permeated the country in postwar America. La Guardia strongly opposed extending the restrictions, and he was contradicted by several firebrands. "We have too many aliens in this country," bawled Representative Elton Watkins of Oregon; ". . . we want more of the American stock."

But "is not this country made up of immigrants no matter what period of history you take?" La Guardia shot back. Certain members, he continued, take pride that their ancestors arrived on the *Mayflower* but they need to remember that "the distinguished navigator of the race of my ancestors came to this continent two hundred years before yours landed at Plymouth Rock."[60]

Representative J. N. Tincher of Kansas decided to take on La Guardia. "I think this chamber here is a place where we ought to think, act and do real Americanism," he cried. By allowing more immigrants into the country the day may come when a representative in this House will have to say " 'Mr. Speaker' in Italian or some other language." La Guardia just shook his head in disbelief.[61]

Finally, Albert Johnson, chair of the House Immigration Committee, introduced a bill lowering the quota of each nationality to be admitted to the United States to 2 percent based on the 1890 census. Moreover, only 150,000 immigrants would be admitted each year and Japanese citizens were excluded altogether. After a long debate, the House passed the measure 323 to 71 on April 12, 1924. With the approval of the Senate, the Immigration Quota Act became law on May 26.[62]

Interestingly, this Congress also enacted the Indian Citizenship Act on June 2, 1924, by which Native Americans became citizens of the United States. It had taken generations to achieve, but the native population, in one respect, had finally been recognized as equal members of the American society, although discrimination continued unabated.

Less than a year later, congressmen gave themselves a healthy increase in salary. They raised the amount from $7,500, which had been passed in 1907, to $10,000.

The Republican organization disregarded the growing discontent within its ranks and nominated Coolidge in 1924. The insurgent Republicans formed a new Progressive Party and endorsed Robert La Follette of Wisconsin, attracting all manner of political exotics, including Socialists, Bull Moosers, and Single Taxers. They argued for the nationalization of the railroads, public development of hydroelectric facilities, and the right of Congress to override decisions of the Supreme Court.[63]

It was a rare opportunity for the Democrats to take advantage of the Republican upheaval, but they, too, lacked unity and purpose. Democrats battled among themselves over issues and candidates. Northern city Democrats, who represented the foreign born, Jews and Catholics, demanded the condemnation of the Ku Klux Klan, but southern Democrats, controlled to a large extent by the KKK, fought the proposal. Northerners wanted repeal of the 18th Amendment, but rural and southern delegates, dominated by religious fundamentalists, successfully blocked it. After a long struggle, principally between Governor Alfred E. Smith of New York, a Catholic, a "wet" on Prohibition, and a chieftain of the New York City political machine, Tammany Hall, and the former secretary of the treasury William G. McAdoo, who supported southern drys, the Democrats, in desperation, and after 103 ballots, nominated John Davis, a New York lawyer allied with banking and industrial interests.

An important innovation occurred during this presidential election. For the first time the conventions were broadcast over a new communications medium: radio. Such ratio stations as WEAF and WJZ in New York and WCAP in Washington, together with a network of sixteen stations in twelve cities, carried these events. Because politicians were not used to speaking into a stationary microphone and normally prowled back and forth across a stage, the networks erected railings around the microphone. Some politicians had a natural flare for this new medium, others did not. Franklin D. Roosevelt had a marvelous radio voice, and his nomination of Governor Al Smith, wherein he hailed the candidate as "the Happy Warrior of the political battlefield," electrified the audience and proved to be the highlight of the Democratic convention.[64] But William Jennings Bryan, an old-style orator, could not be confined and he wandered around the platform. As a result much of his speech was lost.

The introduction of broadcasting and its tremendous impact on the political scene resulted in passage of the Radio Control Act on February 23, 1927, which created the Federal Radio Commission (later changed to the Federal Communications Commission) of five members appointed by the President with power to regulate radio stations and issue and revoke licenses to operate the stations. Later, with the invention of television, the authority of the FCC was extended to cover this new medium.

The campaign of 1924, as well as the conventions, was also broadcast. And America listened. Al Smith's nasal, New York accent proved to be a liability. Coolidge gave only occasional speeches but he did provide a final talk before the campaign ended that was carried coast to coast by a record twenty-six stations. Obviously the new medium had changed—and would continue to change—politics and campaigns. The old style of florid speechmaking did not carry well, nor did oratory of limited thought. Now politicians like Roosevelt, who had a warm, personal style that conveyed conviction and intelligence to his audience, won favor with the public and advanced their careers.

Americans seemed satisfied with a Republican administration that gave them balanced budgets and two tax cuts in four years. The electorate was generally prosperous with only western farmers a source of discontent since they were mired in the Depression.[65] Thus, few were surprised when the Republicans won a stunning victory at the polls, although only 52 percent of those eligible to vote did so. Coolidge garnered over 15 million votes to 8 million for Davis and almost 5 million for La Follette. The Republicans increased their majority in the House by capturing 247 seats to 183 for the Democrats; in the Senate the count was 54 to 40 in favor of the Republicans.[66]

Longworth was disturbed at the number of insurgents who called themselves Republicans but followed a Progressive Party platform that departed sharply from the orthodox Republican faith. And he meant to do something about it. When Congress reconvened after the election, he read the insurgents out of the party. "Of the 247 Republicans [elected to the House]," he complained, "at least twelve openly supported the third-party candidate. . . . Some of them even went so far as to leave their states and campaign against Republican candidates for Congress and in favor of Democratic candidates. These men cannot and ought not to be classed as Republicans in the next Congress."[67] He therefore barred them from the Republican Conference and deprived them of committee assignments. He replaced John Nelson on the Rules Committee and removed James A. Frear from Ways and Means. He insisted he was not punishing them but simply instructing them on their responsibilities as Republicans. He said he hoped their exile would be temporary. A strong believer in party discipline, he had every intention of restoring Republican unity in the operation of the House.[68]

At last, after many years, the House had a competent leader. Longworth proved to be a very strong and influential manager of the business of the House. When particular issues took extra time he convened the House early in the morning. If necessary he scheduled night sessions and sent the sergeant at arms out to restaurants and speakeasies to round up members and escort them back to the House. "No one seemed to mind," said one reporter. "He drove the members with such good humor that even the dreaded night sessions became evenings of merriment. It was not unusual for members to form impromptu barber shop quartets to entertain colleagues while waiting for the sergeant-at-arms to round up the absentees."[69]

Longworth rose to the challenge of furnishing direction and purpose to House business and in time restored its dominance in legislative affairs. His manner was benign and his strategy marked by wisdom and experience. He exercised his authority with grace and tact. He exhibited firmness, parliamentary adroitness, personal benevolence and good humor. He was especially attentive to the needs of the rank and file, not just those in positions of authority. He reached out to all, inviting members to join him at his special table in the House restaurant, something never done before. Even John Nance Garner of Texas, who became minority leader in the 71st Congress, joined him at the table. The two men frequently met and became good friends. By posting the legislative schedule each week Longworth ended another source of Democratic annoyance, that of keeping the schedule secret from the minority.[70]

When several female representatives complained that they had no lavatory or room to relax, he immediately responded to their needs and made an appropriate room available to them. Today the women occupy the old Speaker's office where John Quincy Adams died. Longworth also changed the form of address when referring to female members of Congress from "the gentle lady," which was considered condescending, to "the gentle-woman."

He reformed the *Congressional Record* by forbidding the insertion of undelivered speeches or the insertion of extraneous material. The *Record* had become a hodgepodge of nonsensical matter that had little to do with House business or legislation. And he resumed meeting with the President on a regular basis to map out party strategy, a practice that had ended with Theodore Roosevelt's administration.

Most important of all, he encouraged and promoted civility among House members, which enhanced morale and resulted in a noticeable increase in bipartisanship. Even the quality of debate seemed to improve under his leadership.[71]

Longworth assumed charge of the Steering Committee and the Committee on Committees and placed reliable Republicans on the Rules Committee. He strongly believed that the Speaker should be a man of authority and power and he had every intention of restoring the position to what it had been before 1910. "Regardless of the rules," he contended, "the speakership always will be what the Speaker makes it."[72]

Longworth won the Republican nomination for Speaker at a secret caucus in February 1925, nine months before the new Congress would convene. He won the position over Martin Madden, chairman of the Appropriations Committee. John Q. Tilson of Connecticut was chosen majority leader, an election engineered by James Begg of Ohio, Longworth's most trusted lieutenant. Tilson was an able parliamentarian, but unimaginative, and a man who did not question the Speaker's leadership. He worked well with Longworth and together they proved to be a most formidable leadership team.[73]

At the opening of the 69th Congress in December, 1925, Longworth won election as Speaker on the first ballot in the House by the vote of 229 to 173 for the Democratic leader, Finis J. Garrett of Tennessee. And Longworth brought with him all the authority he formally exercised as majority leader. He had no intention of abdicating any portion of it, and the House went along with him. He, together with Tilson, Begg and Bertrand Snell of New York, chairman of the Rules Committee, formed the inner circle of advisors, and as such were known as the Big Four because they wielded the greatest influence in the House, thus replacing the Steering Committee as the Republican party's chief policy-making body.[74]

When this 69th Congress opened, Longworth appeared dressed to the nines. He wore a tailor-made morning coat, a spiffy dress shirt, and patent leather shoes with brown spats. He was quite a sight. And he radiated self-possession and commanding dignity. "I want to effectively assist you," he told his colleagues upon his election as Speaker, "in bringing about universal recognition of the fact that this House, closer as it is to the people than any similar body and more directly responsive to their will, is in truth, as it ought to be, the great dominant legislative assembly of the world." He left no doubt that he intended to be both Speaker and principal leader of the House. "I promise you," he declared, "that there will be no such thing as favoritism in the treatment by the Chair of either parties or individuals. . . . I believe it to be the duty of the Speaker . . . to assist . . . the enactment of legislation in accordance with the declared principles and politics of his party."[75]

Without question Longworth meant to be a strict party leader, and for the next six years, 1925–1931, he acted out this role. The rules were changed, such as the 150-signature discharge petition, which he had opposed. Now it would take a majority of the membership to bring a bill to the floor. Democrat Edward Pou of North Carolina said that he did not expect that "the steamroller would be put into action so soon." The new rule, added Charles Crisp of Georgia, son of the former Speaker, "hermetically seals the door against any bill ever coming out of a committee when the Steering Committee or the majority leaders desire to kill the bill without putting the members of the House on record on the measure."[76] With the help of Tilson, Begg and Snell, Longworth restored much of the Speaker's authority that had been lost with the defeat of Uncle Joe Cannon.

Longworth also brought in a new parliamentarian, Lewis Deschler from Ohio, "whose encyclopedic knowledge and impartiality would eventually make him a legend in the House."[77] Deschler held the office for the next fifty years, providing each Speaker he served with expert advice on House rules and procedures. Sam Rayburn, a future Speaker, often included him in his private conversations with party leaders.

Thanks to Longworth, the House passed Coolidge's two most important requests, namely, another tax reduction and ratification of the European debt settlements. The Senate could not match his skill, leading one newspaper to marvel that under Longworth "the House has become the dominant body."[78] Senator Henry Cabot Lodge agreed. "The prestige of the House grew amazingly in recent years, and the major credit therefore unquestionably belongs to Mr. Longworth . . . Time and again in the last few years it has been the House which led the way toward sound legislation. . . . It

The incomparable Alice Roosevelt Longworth together with her spouse, the Speaker of the House, Nicholas Longworth.

is unmistakably to the House that the country has learned to look for legislative leadership."[79]

However, this paragon had disturbing weaknesses. Hyperactive sexually, he invited dangerous situations. And drunken poker parties figured high in Longworth's list of personal pleasures. A heavy drinker, if not an alcoholic, he frequently used the Henry Clay Room (or the "Board of Education,"[80] as it was unofficially called) to instruct freshmen members on how to vote on a particular bill and engage in drinking bouts with his cronies, especially "Cactus Jack" Garner, "one of the most determined boozers the Capitol has ever known," according to the House doorkeeper, William "Fishbait" Miller. At 5:00 p.m. Garner would signal Longworth with the words "Let's cut this stuff out, it's time to strike a blow for liberty," and off they would go to the hideaway.[81]

A deeply flawed man of questionable character, Nicholas Longworth was nonetheless one of the great Speakers of the House of Representatives.

13

The Great Depression, the New Deal and the Outbreak of War, 1928–1941

THE COUNTRY DANCED and celebrated the "Roaring Twenties." There was money to be made, and everybody seemed to be making it, one way or another.

Not the farmers. They continued to experience economic depression, and their dire situation should have been a warning to the rest of the nation of the disaster about to happen. They appealed to the government for immediate help but little was forthcoming.

One of the more unique developments in the 1920s was the appearance of voting blocs in Congress on issues that frequently crossed party lines. It began just before World War I when the Anti-Saloon League helped create a national demand for prohibition. Not since the Civil War had a single issue coalesced individuals from several parties and resulted in a constitutional amendment.

Perhaps the most noteworthy group in Congress, arguing for a special interest in the 1920s, was the farm bloc. There were any number of farm organizations already in existence—National Grange, American Farm Bureau Federation, Farmers National Council, among others—and as farm prices went into a long decline following World War I, these organizations demanded subsidies that would underwrite the unloading of farm surpluses overseas. Western and midwestern representatives in Congress, both Republican and Democrat, appreciated the voting strength of these organizations and did not dare oppose their demands. The legislation enacted was twice vetoed by Coolidge on the ground that the bills constituted price fixing for a special interest.

But the lingering farm depression that threatened to spread to the commercial and industrial sections of the nation could not be dismissed so easily. In the presidential election of 1928, Herbert Hoover, the Republican candidate, pledged to provide relief for farmers. The Democrats chose Al Smith, a Catholic and Tammany Hall leader, as their presidential candidate, and he was soundly defeated in the fall election. Hoover and his running mate, Charles Curtis, won a popular plurality of more than 6 million votes over Smith and his vice presidential candidate, Joseph T. Robinson. The Republican ticket captured forty states and 444 electoral votes, while the Democrats took just eight states and 87 electoral votes. The Republicans also made great gains in the House. They had 267 seats in the 71st Congress to 167 for the Democrats. Longworth had a one-hundred-seat majority with which to legislate. There was real fear at the time that the Democrats would follow the Whigs into oblivion.[1]

This election also brought Republican Oscar S. De Priest of Illinois to the House, the first black Representative ever from outside the south. He served from 1929 to 1935. Born in Alabama to former slaves, he grew up in Kansas and later moved to Chicago, where he became the first black alderman. His arrival in Washington challenged the strict segregation that pervaded every aspect of Washington life, and several southerners said they would not accept offices adjacent to De Priest's. In 1931, he introduced a bill that would provide pensions to ex-slaves over the age of seventy-five, and he unsuccessfully attempted to desegregate the House restaurant.

The Negro restaurant was located in the basement next to the kitchen. The other public restaurant served only whites. Said Representative Charles L. Underwood of Massachusetts, "As a rule, the colored people prefer to attend their own churches, their own schools, and their own restaurants . . . and my experience has always been that they're happy in that attitude." Extremely unhappy about the Jim Crow restaurant in the Capitol, De Priest, on January 23, 1934, introduced a resolution on the House floor to end this discrimination but he failed, proving once again how racially segregated Washington really was, and how determined to stay that way. De Priest himself was defeated for reelection in the Democratic landslide of 1934.[2]

HOOVER CALLED A special session of the 71st Congress on April 15, 1929, to enact legislation that would bring relief to farmers. He suggested raising the tariff on imported agricultural products as one possible solution. Long-

Oscar De Priest repeatedly tried and failed to integrate the House dining room for members. African-American members were expected to eat next to the kitchen located in the basement of the Capitol.

worth had no trouble winning passage of the Smoot-Hawley Tariff in the House, 264 to 147, but the Senate introduced so many amendments (some twelve hundred) that it took over a year to finally win passage of the bill. On June 17, 1930, the President signed this tariff, which raised import duties on farm products to 45 percent, the highest it had ever been, which provided special protection for textile products, sugar, cotton and citrus fruit. So high was the tariff barrier that twenty-six foreign countries instantly retaliated by raising their own tariff rates, and American exports went into a steep decline.

This tariff was a total disaster, and it was the last time Congress set tariff rates.

As further help to farmers, Congress passed the Agricultural Marketing Act in June 1929 which set up the Federal Farm Board, which had eight members, and the office of the secretary of agriculture. It provided for a revolving fund of $500 million for low interest loans to agricultural cooperatives to enable them to build warehouses and sell surplus crops in an "orderly" way.[3]

Congress also responded to a presidential request and passed a combined census-reapportionment bill, which established a permanent system for reapportioning the 435 House seats after each census. Following the

1930 census, a tremendous shift in representation took place, reflecting the country's continuing urbanization. Twenty-one states lost a total of twenty-seven seats while California doubled its representation, and Texas, Michigan, Ohio, New York and New Jersey also gained seats.

THEN, STARTING ON October 23, 1929, the nation suffered a devastating blow when the stock market crashed and within one terrible month something like $30 billion in the market value of listed stocks was wiped out. The Great Depression began. It lasted approximately ten years. Unemployment ran high, the price of goods collapsed, businesses went bankrupt.

Hoover immediately called for a relief program that would provide federal leadership for voluntary efforts at the state and local levels. He also requested appropriations of $100 to $150 million for a public works program. But the electorate was losing confidence in the Republican Party and in the November election of 1930 handed the Democrats, for the first time since 1919, a very thin majority in the House, 220 Democrats to 214 Republicans. It was no landslide—at least not yet.

When the 71st Congress came to an end at noon on March 4, 1931, Speaker Longworth rose from his chair, his gavel firmly grasped in his hand as he approached the rostrum. Suddenly the House members rose to their feet and broke out into a thunderous applause. "Several prolonged rebel yells" from the Democratic side added to the tumult. It was a unique and deeply felt tribute to Nicholas Longworth.

And when the House finally adjourned, many members were reluctant to leave the chamber. Someone wheeled in an old piano and the representatives gathered around it and began singing sentimental ballads. Then Cliff Woodrum of Virginia started crooning "Carry Me Back to Old Virginny," and Longworth joined in. The decade of the Roaring Twenties ended in the House of Representatives with a celebration in song.

The Speaker died the following month. He went to visit friends in South Carolina, where he contracted pneumonia and died on April 9, 1931. His body was carried back to Cincinnati in a funeral train packed with his friends. Among many things, commented one newspaper, he proved that leadership in the House depended "not on the rules but on the man."[4] Amen.

AS THE DEPRESSION deepened there were any number of congressmen who believed with Andrew Mellon, the secretary of the treasury, that somehow the normal operations of the business cycle would bring about an upturn in economic conditions. It was just a matter of time. "Let the slump liquidate itself," Mellon snapped in a burst of Social Darwinism. "Liquidate labor, liquidate stocks, liquidate the farmers. . . . People will work harder, live a more moral life. Values will be adjusted, and enterprising people will pick up the wrecks from less competent people."[5]

So Congress did nothing to address the depression. What could they do? They really had no answers. Besides, the leadership, especially in the Senate, was still fundamentally conservative and fearful of change. But as the 72nd Congress prepared to convene, a number of Progressive Republicans in the House, led by Fiorello La Guardia, demanded revisions of the Rules to permit bills to be discharged from committees when 100 members voted in favor, rather than the 218 then required. The Democratic majority fixed the figure at 145 representatives, which was one-third of the entire membership. The Democrats then elected John Nance Garner as Speaker, the sixty-two-year-old Texan who had served in the House for twenty-eight years.

In his message to Congress on December 8, 1931, Hoover emphasized the need to improve the credit and financial structure of the country, suggesting the formation of an "emergency reconstruction corporation" that would lend money to financial institutions, the railroads and agricultural credit agencies.[6] When the administration spokesmen in the House introduced a bill to establish the Reconstruction Finance Corporation, La Guardia objected, calling it a "millionaire's dole."[7] What was needed, he insisted, was a national system of unemployment insurance. After all, employers kept their machinery well oiled, housed and insured against theft and fire, while the operators of the machinery were ignored. Nonetheless, on January 22, 1932, Congress passed the Reconstruction Finance Corporation, which created a government lending agency with a capital of $500 million and with authority to borrow up to an additional $1.5 billion. The agency issued tax-exempt bonds and extended credit to banks, corporations and railroads. It did not assist small businesses or individuals who faced the loss of their homes, but it did prevent most of the nation's large banks from going bankrupt. The Glass-Steagall Act, passed on February 27, 1932, permitted the Federal Reserve Banks to sell $750 million from the government's gold supply to meet the continuing foreign withdrawals. And the Federal Home Loan Bank Act made capital available to building and loan associations.[8]

Meanwhile Senator George W. Norris and Representative La Guardia sponsored the Norris-La Guardia Act, which recognized labor's right to unionize, limited the power of federal courts to issue injunctions against labor's right to organize and outlawed "yellow dog" contracts, which obliged workers to promise not to join a union. It was approved on March 23, 1932.[9]

Still the depression deepened. A fight in the House over a sales tax on manufactured goods proposed by the administration ended in defeat for the bill when members realized how harmful it would be to consumers who would bear the burden of the tax. Even so, a number of Democrats in the House favored a sales tax, insisting that balancing the budget was the best way to combat the depression. However, under the direction of Representative Robert "Muley" Doughton of North Carolina, rebellious Democrats joined La Guardia and his Progressive Republicans to kill the bill. In its place they substituted taxes on income and real estate.

The economic desperation suffered by countless citizens in 1932 produced the "Bonus March" on Washington, when from twelve thousand to fifteen thousand unemployed war veterans descended on the capital and demanded immediate payment in cash of the bonus passed in 1924 over Coolidge's veto to recompense veterans for their low-paying service during the late war—but not payable until 1945—while nonveterans enjoyed full employment and high wages. They sang war songs and carried placards that read, "Cheered in '17, Jeered in '32."[10] They built a shantytown on Anacostia Flats just outside the capital. When a riot resulted in the deaths of two persons, Hoover summoned the army to maintain order. General Douglas MacArthur, then chief of staff, dispersed the veterans with tear gas and burned the shantytown.

The efforts of the Progressives in Congress to initiate legislation that

The "Bonus March" occurred during the Great Depression in late July 1932, when thousands of unemployed veterans of World War I descended on Washington to demand the bonus promised in 1924 to be paid immediately, rather than in 1945.

would provide federal money for public works and relief for the starving unemployed were rebuffed by the President, who insisted that the government should balance the budget and not provide an enormous pork barrel. A proposed $900 million for public works, he said, "is an unexampled raid on the public treasury." Nonetheless, led by Speaker Garner, the Democrats in the House, with the assistance of Progressive Republicans, again led by La Guardia, passed a $2 billion relief measure for the unemployed. A similar bill sponsored by Robert Wagner of New York passed the Senate, but the President vetoed it. He opposed its public works feature and especially a provision that would allow the Reconstruction Finance Corporation to make loans to individuals and small businesses. He also vetoed a bill proposed by George Norris for the construction of a hydroelectric facility at Muscle Shoals on the Tennessee River in northern Alabama. Hoover regarded the measure as a gigantic centralization of banking and finance which would put the government into private business. In short, it was socialistic.[11]

Before Congress adjourned in the summer of 1932 it did pass an Emergency Relief and Construction Act and the Federal Home Loan Bank Act to grant assistance, relief and home mortgages to needy individuals and businesses.

Meanwhile, the Democrats held their national nominating convention in Chicago in June, 1932, which turned into a battle between the forces of Al Smith, supported by Tammany Hall, and Governor Franklin D. Roosevelt of New York, who had won reelection in 1930 by the largest majority ever received by a gubernatorial candidate in the state's history. He had suffered an attack of polio in 1921 but had achieved partial recovery by 1928.

The fight in Congress over the sales tax convinced Progressive Democrats at the convention that they had to turn aside the conservative party leadership and choose a liberal presidential candidate such as Roosevelt. Smith had a solid bloc of anti-Roosevelt supporters, but on the fourth ballot "Cactus Jack" Garner, a strong favorite son of Texas and the South, threw his support to Roosevelt in return for the nomination as Vice President. The deal had the benefit of removing the conservative Garner from the important position of Speaker. He was replaced in the 73rd Congress by Henry T. Rainey of Illinois. Once nominated, Roosevelt boarded an airplane and flew to the convention to accept the nomination, pledging "a new deal for the American people."[12]

It is worth noting that the introduction of airplanes as the result of the Wright brothers' historic flight in 1903 and their subsequent employment during World War I led to the creation of a bureau within the Commerce Department to oversee the safety of civil aviation and the licensing of pilots and aircraft. Another important invention in the late nineteenth century, the gasoline-powered automobile, radically changed the lives of Americans

Democrats eased out John ("Cactus Jack") Garner as Speaker of the House by nominating him for Vice President in the 1932 presidential election.

in every section of the country. These two important inventions were, in a sense, the beginning of a long train of other discoveries in the twentieth century that would transform the nation and dramatically magnify its global power and influence.

Unbelievably, both parties during the presidential campaign of 1932 seemed more concerned over Prohibition than unemployment. "Here we are," jeered John Dewey, "in the midst of the greatest crisis since the Civil War and the only thing the two national parties seem to want to debate is booze."[13]

The election of 1932 completely reversed the political fortunes of the two parties. Roosevelt garnered nearly 23 million popular and 472 electoral votes. The Democrats also elected majorities of 311 to the Republicans' 116 seats in the House and 60 to 35 in the Senate. Of the Democrats elected, 131 were freshmen, thirsting for leadership.

One of the first things the lame-duck House did when it reconvened in early December was vote, 272 to 144, for repeal of the 18th Amendment. Of the 100 negative Republican votes, 70 came from lame-duck members, and of the 44 negative Democratic votes, 11 were also lame ducks.

The 21st Amendment, repealing the 18th Amendment, was passed by Congress on February 3, 1933, and ratified on December 5, 1933. Earlier, under the sponsorship of George Norris, the 20th Amendment to the Constitution was passed on March 2, 1932, and ratified on February 6, 1933. This amendment directed that henceforth the members of Congress elected in November would take office on January 3 and the President and Vice President on January 20 instead of March 4, thus shortening lame-duck sessions.

This final gathering of the 72nd Congress had the distinction of failing to produce a single important piece of economic legislation. And the failure severely damaged the reputation of Congress. Industrial construction had plunged from $949 million to a disastrous $74 million. Three years into the depression, the conditions in the country had worsened appreciably. Runs on banks, with depositors attempting to withdraw their money, occurred daily, and 5,504 banks closed from 1930 through February 1933.

THE INAUGURATION OF Franklin Delano Roosevelt on March 4, 1933—the last time a President would be sworn into office four months after election—came at a time in which the depression had generated wild talk about the need for dictatorial direction of the government and the economy. "A genial and lighthearted dictator might be a relief," commented one publication, "from the pompous futility of such a Congress as we have recently had."[14] In Germany, such a dictator had already appeared, but he was hardly "genial and lighthearted." Adolf Hitler was chosen chancellor in January 1933. But Roosevelt in his inaugural address assured the American people that "the only thing we have to fear is fear itself."[15]

His first action on becoming President was to shut down all banks in the country for four days. Next he summoned Congress into special session on March 9, a session that continued until June 15. While members of the House were still finding their way into the chamber on the appointed day, the Speaker started reading the only copy available of the administration's Emergency Banking Relief bill, which contained last-minute corrections written in pencil. It was one of Roosevelt's major legislative measures, and after thirty-eight minutes of supporting speeches the bill passed the House sight unseen by a unanimous voice vote. Within four hours of the first day of the session, Congress had enacted a banking bill that authorized the secretary of the treasury to investigate the condition of all banks in the country and permit them to reopen if sound. The measure also declared illegal the ownership of gold and instructed the treasury secretary to call in all gold and gold certificates. By midsummer three-fourths of all banks in the United States had resumed normal operations. Confidence slowly returned, and the runs on banks virtually ceased.

Once the new Congress began business, there were so many Democrats in the House that many of them had to find seats on what had traditionally been the Republican side of the chamber. "A few years ago," joked one

Democrat to Republican House leader Bertrand Snell of New York, "you had to use the whole house for your caucus—now you can hold it in a phone booth." Worse, the Republicans were disorganized, dispirited and quite fearful of Roosevelt's popularity with the electorate. Said one Democrat: "The Republican side . . . looked pitiful—mostly empty seats as they had been well thinned out in the previous election. The few remaining members were afraid to squawk."[16]

The Democratic majority in the House was led by the Speaker, Henry T. Rainey of Illinois, and the majority leader, Joseph W. Byrns of Tennessee. But Rainey proved to be a very ineffective leader, and FDR simply used him to convey his instructions. A steering committee was established, consisting of the Speaker, the majority leader, the whip, the chairs of Ways and Means and Rules and fifteen regional representatives, but the real authority in the House emanated from Roosevelt and operated through the Rules Committee. Bills were sent down (often concocted hurriedly by a "Brain Trust" of Columbia University professors, including Adolf A. Berle, Jr., Raymond Moley and Rexford G. Tugwell),[17] and the Rules Committee then made certain that nothing got in the way of their enactment. The displacement of party leadership in Congress by the chief executive was possible because of the crisis facing the country, the need for quick and effective action and the extraordinary popularity of the President. As he had said in his inaugural, the nation demanded action, and action he would provide.[18]

The economic crisis had reached major proportions when Roosevelt took office. Fourteen million individuals were out of work, industry seemed paralyzed, thousands of banks had closed and Americans rushed to withdraw whatever savings they had accumulated. In a history-making special session of Congress the new administration laid the foundation of the New Deal in the first hundred days. Roosevelt himself had no strong commitment to a particular economic program but was willing to experiment to find the way to combat the depression. When conventional methods failed, he quickly sought others. But one thing he did believe: government should lead the way in directing the American economy.

And the overwhelming majorities the administration enjoyed in Congress helped him speed the process of recovery. At the Democratic Caucus held on March 11, Congressman Clifton Woodrum of Virginia warned members that when the President received a copy of the *Congressional Record* in the morning he will look over the roll call that would bind the Caucus to support the President's economy bills, "and from that he will know whether or not the Members of his own party were willing to go along with him in his great fight to save the country."[19]

One of the things Roosevelt asked for was an amendment of the Volstead Act prohibiting the manufacture and sale of liquor. The 21st Amendment was still being ratified by the states and would not receive final approval until December 1933, but the President asked Congress to redeem a party pledge and end Prohibition by legalizing beer. There were many protests, of course, but even some dry congressmen supported the measure. Impatient for quick action, a number of representatives began chanting, "Vote—vote—we want beer," and within a week both houses had passed a beer bill legalizing the manufacture and sale of wine and beer of 3.2 percent alcoholic content. The President signed it on March 22.

DURING THESE TURBULENT times the House wanted and needed strong direction, and one of the men to emerge as a leader was Sam Rayburn of Texas. He had served as chair of the Interstate and Foreign Commerce Committee during the 72nd Congress, and although poorly educated he proved to be a formidable competitor in the many legislative battles that broke out during the next few months and years. The Interstate and Foreign Commerce Committee was one of the most important in the House, just behind Rules, Ways and Means and Appropriations. Its jurisdiction included everything from exports to railroads, dams, merchant marine, the Panama Canal and food and drug regulation. An intensely loyal advocate of New Deal legislation and concerned about the hastily drafted bills by Roosevelt's Brain Trust, Rayburn rewrote many of these bills so that they could pass muster in his committee and the other committees to which they were sent. He had help from two brilliant young New Deal lawyers, Thomas G. Corcoran and Benjamin V. Cohen, who knew their way around the House and provided the language necessary to get these bills approved.

Rayburn himself coauthored several major bills during these one hundred days. On some of the measures he worked "for three weeks, day and night," and it exhausted him, reported Cohen. "He had hearings all morning, was on the floor all afternoon. There was a constant stream of people wanting to see him, and he had to see most of them. Then he conferred with Tom and me, often at night, sometimes at breakfast."[20] He was a "a short, heavy-set, jowly man with a bald head that really shone." He was very sensitive about his baldness, remarked Thomas "Tip" O'Neill, a future Speaker, which may explain "why he often wore a black hat." In the many floor fights he waged, this tough Texan proved his mettle and importance to the administration.[21]

In short order over the following weeks, the Civilian Conservation Corps (CCC), the Agricultural Adjustment Act (AAA), the Tennessee Valley Authority (TVA), the Federal Securities Act, the National Employment System, the Gold Standard Repeal Act, the Banking Act of 1933 and the National Industrial Recovery Act were approved. These measures authorized employment of a quarter of a million jobless male citizens between the ages of 18 and 25; created the AAA to control surplus crops so

*Sam Rayburn, known af-
fectionately as "Mr. Sam,"
served longer as Speaker
than any of his predeces-
sors.*

as to increase farm prices; established the TVA, an independent public
agency to build dams and power plants and develop rural electrification;
removed the United States from the gold standard and made all contracts
and private obligations payable in legal tender; created the Federal Deposit
Insurance Corporation (FDIC) to guarantee the safety of individual bank
deposits up to $5,000; and empowered the President to prescribe fair trade
codes for industries. The National Industrial Recovery Act (NIRA) also
established the Public Works Administration to stimulate the economy by
constructing huge public works, and it guaranteed the right of workers to
organize and bargain collectively through representatives of their own
choosing.

Several of these laws, in particular the NIRA, were drawn under closed
rules in which only amendments from Ways and Means were permitted.
This was done in order to cut down the amount of time for floor debate and
prevent amendments that would emasculate the bill, a decision approved
by the Rules Committee, although hotly contested. Joseph Martin of Massachusetts, a Republican, complained that only a "select few," therefore,
would decide the ideas to go into the bill rather then "the views of 435 congressional districts."[22] Nevertheless the NIRA passed the House 326 to 75.

In the summer of 1932, the Congress had reduced members' salaries from $10,000 to $9,000. Now on March 20, 1933, they were lowered even further, to $8,500.

When the special session ended on June 16, 1933, it had legislated the most extraordinary series of economic reforms in the nation's history. It committed the nation to a program of government-industry cooperation; helped farmers; assumed responsibility for the welfare of millions of unemployed; pledged to help individuals keep their homes and farms; guaranteed bank deposits; and initiated a vast public works program.[23]

Despite the efforts of the administration and the Congress to alleviate financial suffering, the income of most Americans by the end of 1933 had declined by half. Some nine thousand banks and eighty-six thousand businesses had failed. A million or more individuals had been evicted from their homes when they could not meet mortgage payments or pay the rent. As a consequence, they slept in parks, doorways and open fields if the weather permitted. A farmer received 10 cents for a bushel of oats, several cents below what it had cost him to raise the crop. Food and clothing were very inexpensive, but few had the money to buy these necessities.[24] Approximately 20 million Americans needed some form of federal relief to stay alive.

In order to win approval for several money bills, Edward Pou, chair of the House Rules Committee, brought out a rule by which no amendments to appropriations bills would be permitted if they conflicted with the Economy Act passed on March 20, 1933, a measure designed to balance the budget and save hundreds of millions of dollars of normal expenditures. Many Democrats refused to go along, siding with the minority leader, Bertrand H. Snell, who called it the "most vicious" rule ever proposed. Still, Chairman Pou managed to get it approved but by the narrow vote of 197 to 192. The new rule did prove to be efficient in producing legislation, and committees worked all day and night to grind out the unending number of new measures forwarded to them. Said one Republican Congressman from Tennessee: "I have seen the Congress of the United States absolutely abdicate its authority to the Executive. I have seen a dictatorship spring up which must have made the noses of Herr Hitler, Stalin, Mussolini and Mustapha Kemal of Turkey turn green with envy."[25]

The administration went so far as to propose a Reciprocal Trade Agreement Act that allowed the President to raise or lower existing tariff rates up to 50 percent for countries that would reciprocate with similar concessions. Republicans howled their objections, claiming it violated the Constitution. When presented to the House, the bill was amended to limit the President's negotiating power to three years and to terminate any agreement after three years. The act passed the House 274 to 111 on March 29, 1934, with only two Republicans voting for it, and the Senate agreed two months later. FDR signed it on June 12. By this legislation Congress had once again delegated to the executive its authority over rate setting, a power it had jealously guarded for 150 years.[26]

During this session Congress also established the Federal Farm Mortgage Corporation to provide refinancing of farm debts at favorable terms, the Securities and Exchange Commission, designed to prevent price manipulation of stocks and curb speculation, and the Federal Communications Commission to regulate radio, cable and telegraph transmissions.

In the midterm elections the Democrats increased their majorities in both houses of Congress. Traditionally the party in power loses seats, and many expected it to happen in 1934. But the results came as a shock to Republicans. In the House there were now 322 Democrats, 103 Republicans and 10 Independents; in the Senate, 69 Democrats, 25 Republicans and 2 Independents. The gain in the House was particularly encouraging for Democrats. For the Republicans it was a disaster. "Never in the history of the Republican Party had its percentage of the House seats fallen so low."[27]

BEFORE THE FIRST session of the 74th Congress convened, Speaker Rainey died of a heart attack, and Rayburn challenged the majority leader for the Speakership but was turned back. Joseph W. Byrns of Tennessee, as chairman of both the Appropriations Committee and the Democratic Congressional Campaign Committee, had considerable clout on his side, along with the tradition of seniority as majority leader, and he soundly upended the upstart. William B. Bankhead, chairman of the Rules Committee, became majority leader.

A liberal bloc in the House, called the "Young Turks," also emerged, composed mostly of Democrats and led by Maury Maverick of Texas, the grandson of Samuel A. Maverick, the Texas rancher who refused to brand his cattle and in so doing made "maverick" a synonym for anyone who is unorthodox in his thinking or behavior. Congressman Maury Maverick also coined a notable word, "gobbledygook," to describe bureaucratic jargon. The Young Turks met every week in a second-rate restaurant to plot strategy, but they never achieved real influence in the House and after a few years disbanded. Maverick himself was defeated for reelection in 1938.[28]

In his annual message to Congress in 1935, FDR outlined a program of social reform that historians have come to call the Second New Deal, the chief beneficiaries of which would be labor and small farmers. Perhaps the most radical of the President's proposals—certainly the most innovative— was the Social Security Act passed on August 14. The bill established a federal-state system of unemployment compensation and old-age pensions, thus transferring to the federal government functions that once had been the responsibility of families and of state and local governments. Some members of Congress had doubts about this measure because it imposed a tax on employee wages and employer payrolls beginning January 1, 1937, but would not begin to pay retirement benefits until 1942, a date later advanced to 1940 by amendments in 1939. Also important was passage of the Banking Act of 1935, the only fundamental revision of the Federal Reserve Act since its inception. By this act a new board of governors had direct and complete control over interest rates, reserve requirements and the open market operations of the Federal Reserve Banks.[29]

The National Labor Relations Act (Wagner Act) placed the government in support of the right of labor to bargain collectively, and it required employers to permit the unionization of their companies peacefully. This was one of the most radical of New Deal bills and yet it moved through Congress with little opposition. In addition, the Holding Company Act broke up large electric power holding companies and placed the financial operations of these companies under the supervision of the Securities and Exchange Commission (SEC). The bill was introduced in the House by Sam Rayburn and passed over the bitter resistance of the power companies. There were at least six hundred utility lobbyists badgering every one of the 531 members of the House and Senate. "I knew," Rayburn later remarked, "that if I ever was going to be Speaker I just had to succeed" in getting this bill passed, "and by God, I would rather have died than to have failed."[30] He succeeded and the legislation ultimately abolished holding companies.

Despite Roosevelt's many victories in Congress, resistance to his authority was beginning to build. The Supreme Court struck down essential elements of the New Deal, including the National Industrial Recovery, Agricultural Adjustment, and Bituminous Coal Conservation Acts. The bituminous measure, or "little NRA," as it was called, set up a board to oversee the coal industry regarding price-fixing, production quotas and labor regulations. On Black Monday, May 27, 1935, the court, in the case *Schechter Poultry Corp. v. United States,* declared unanimously that the industry code provisions of the NIRA were unconstitutional on the grounds that they amounted to an improper delegation of power by Congress to private industry. The following January, in the case *United States v. Butler,* the court invalidated the agricultural law that authorized payments to farmers for keeping land out of production. It ruled that the measure was an invasion of state power over intrastate commerce. And in the bituminous coal case the court decided in May 1936 that the law was an improper regulation of manufacturing.[31]

Another setback for FDR was the active and successful efforts of the new chairman of the Rules Committee, John J. O'Connor of New York, to frustrate Roosevelt's efforts to move bills quickly past his committee and get action on the House floor. A Tammany Democrat, aggressive and unpopular but lodged in the committee because of his seniority, O'Connor frequently persuaded his committee to resist FDR's pressure to hurry measures to the floor.

Still, Roosevelt's popularity with the electorate continued strong, and he won another landslide victory against Alfred M. Landon of Kansas in November 1936 when he captured 60.4 percent of the popular vote and every state but Maine and Vermont. FDR carried with him a slew of Democrats running for federal and state offices. In the House there was an overwhelming majority of 333 seats compared to 89 for the Republicans.

The previous June, Speaker Byrns had died, the first Speaker to pass away while the House was in session. No further business could be conducted until a new Speaker was elected, and so, without opposition, William Bankhead was chosen to succeed him on June 4, and Sam Rayburn was named majority leader over O'Connor. FDR had stepped in to arrange Rayburn's election, not only because he was a loyal follower but also because he was an efficient expediter of New Deal measures, particularly in winning passage of the Holding Company Act. The President succeeded in blocking O'Connor's reach for a higher position of leadership, but he furthered the resentment in Congress over his ever-expanding interference in legislative affairs.

A split within the Democratic party began to develop along regional and ideological lines when the 75th Congress convened on January 5, 1937, and a new conservative bipartisan coalition emerged among southern Democrats and northern Republicans. Unfortunately, Rayburn proved to be a less than successful majority leader, and it only encouraged Roosevelt to contact committee chairmen directly to get his legislation through the House. Floor leadership was simply not Rayburn's style. He found the sometimes necessary wheeling and dealing distasteful. Although an excellent debater and hardworking legislator, he had trouble keeping increasingly rebellious Democrats in line, most especially those who resented FDR's intrusion in House affairs. Besides, Rayburn's unshakable loyalty to Roosevelt weakened his influence with many of his colleagues. Then he was given the impossible task of convincing Democrats to agree with the President's foolish plan to remake the Supreme Court.

Roosevelt called in the Democratic leaders of both houses on February 5, 1937, and informed them of the message he planned to send to Congress requesting authority to appoint a new judge for each federal judge who had served on the court for at least ten years and did not retire six months after reaching the age of seventy. Among the nine members of the Supreme Court (the "nine old men," they were called by critics), six justices had passed the age of seventy. Clearly FDR was striking back at the court for invalidating the NIRA, the AAA and the Bituminous Coal Acts.[32]

Roosevelt's audacity amazed and shocked many in the House. Speaker Bankhead was appalled. He turned to Representative Lindsay Warren of North Carolina and in an exasperated tone said, "Lindsay, wouldn't you have thought that the President would have told his own party leaders what he was going to do?" And then, answering his own question, he said: "He didn't because he knew that all hell would break loose."[33]

The inviolability of the court had long been acknowledged. Its lofty position in standing above politics and partisanship was generally accepted and understood by the American people. But FDR saw only its conservative mentality and apparent opposition to social and economic reform. Convincing the Congress of the justice and necessity of his "court-packing" plan would be herculean, and the President turned to the majority leader for assistance. Clearly Rayburn was not up to the task, but Roosevelt's interference had the effect of further alienating many House members and strengthening the opposition coalition that had begun to form.

Those representatives and senators who opposed many of Roosevelt's programs but kept quiet for fear of reprisals from their constituents now had a perfect excuse to break with the President, certain the electorate would resist any tampering with the court. Representative Hatton Summers of Texas, chairman of the House Judiciary Committee, declared, "Boys, here's where I cash in my chips."[34]

The public attack on the court was an example of poor judgment and bad timing by FDR inasmuch as the court, in March 1937, had already begun to indicate an understanding and sympathy with some of the purposes of the New Deal, and it approved a number of important pieces of legislation. A state minimum wage bill was upheld, thereby encouraging the administration to sponsor a federal minimum wage and maximum hours bill that would also set child labor standards. In addition, the justices also approved the National Labor Relations Act, the Social Security Act and the Farm Mortgage Corporation. It had become an entirely different court. Apparently the justices also studied the electoral returns.

FDR backed off from his attempt to pack the court, and a bill was then passed that included some minor reforms of the federal courts but forbade any change in their membership. Subsequent retirements and deaths allowed the President to create a court that looked increasingly more favorably on congressional intervention into economic problems.

However, FDR continued to have problems with certain members of the House. Five southern Democrats and four Republicans on the Rules Committee, chaired by O'Connor, blocked a wage and hours bill from reaching the floor of the House. They even thwarted a hearing on the measure. The failure of the court-packing scheme and the action by the Rules Committee had one salutary effect: they helped restore a better balance between the executive and legislative branches. No longer could the President expect Congress to accede to his every wish—with or without consultation. A proper respect for the prerogatives of the House and Senate was necessary if the President expected to win approval for his more controversial measures.

One important success was passage of the National Housing Act on September 1, 1937. Senator Wagner had been trying for years to get it passed, but it was defeated in the House. Here is one instance where the President's support proved decisive. Henry Steagall, chairman of the Housing committee, considered the measure financially reckless and socialistic, but out of a sense of party loyalty agreed to allow the bill to be reported out of committee. At this point Roosevelt worked his vaunted political magic on several members and it finally passed. The Wagner-Steagall Housing Act created the United States Housing Authority as a public corporation under the Department of the Interior, and made available $500 million in loans for low-cost housing. By 1941 the authority had provided funds for the building of over 500 low-rent housing projects that contained 161,000 apartments at a cost of $767,526,000.

BECAUSE OF THE dangerous developments that had occurred in Europe, in large measure resulting from economic crises, the President considered calling for some sort of collective security such as Wilson had proposed with the League of Nations. With such dictators as Stalin in the Soviet Union, Hitler in Germany and Mussolini in Italy endangering world peace—for example, Hitler and Mussolini provided military aid to the fascist army of General Francisco Franco, who had launched a civil war against the Republican government of Spain, while Stalin supported the loyalists in Spain—the need for some action that would "quarantine" nations that threatened international stability seemed to FDR to be imperative. But a strong element of isolationism still permeated the United States, and any talk of collaborative action with Europe brought an immediate and angry response from a concerned electorate. The great fear was the threat of communism and radical ideas infiltrating into this country and undermining basic American ideals. For the moment, then, FDR focused his attention on the military unpreparedness of the United States, and he asked Congress to appropriate a billion dollars for defense and the building of a two-ocean navy.

Roosevelt called Congress back into special session in November 1937 to consider unfinished business, particularly the wage and hours bill. But again the Rules Committee barred any action. Controlled by a majority coalition of southern Democrats, led by Edward Eugene Cox of Georgia, a fiery antilabor critic, and Howard W. Smith of Virginia, a frail, soft-spoken country lawyer who wore pince-nez eyeglasses and wing collars, and conservative Republicans, consisting of Joseph W. Martin of Massachusetts, Carl E. Mapes of Michigan, J. Will Taylor of Tennessee and Donald H. McLean of New Jersey, and chaired by John J. O'Connor, the Rules Committee pretty much brought House action on a number of administration bills to a near-complete halt.[35]

A reorganization measure that would permit the President to "reshuffle agencies" in the interest of efficiency was introduced, but some House members "genuinely feared a Roosevelt despotism." Hamilton Fish of New York asked, "Why should Congress continue to surrender and abdicate its legislative functions to the Chief Executive and leave itself with no more legislative authority than [Mahatma] Gandhi has clothing?" On April 8 the House defeated the bill, 204 to 196, with 108 Democrats deserting the President. "One of the greatest defections in history, it marked the worst rebuff Roosevelt was to suffer in the House."[36]

At this point Roosevelt set to work and skillfully drew his forces together in Congress. He had help from a sharp recession that occurred in 1938 and, as a consequence, he was able to get most of the measures he wanted enacted into law. In the House, Mary T. Norton of New Jersey, chair of the Labor Committee and a zealot in matters of labor, filed a discharge petition to force the Rules Committee into bringing the wage and hours bill to the floor. She readily acquired the 218 signatures necessary for a discharge. The highly influential Eugene Cox led the opposition and frequently lost control of himself. On one occasion he started a fistfight on the floor; on another he pulled the hair of a hostile member. "I warn John L. Lewis [head of the United Mine Workers] and his Communistic cohorts," he raged, "that no second-hand 'carpetbag expedition' in the Southland, under the banner of Soviet Russia . . . will be tolerated."[37]

To win votes for the discharge, party leaders passed the word that they would not support the farm bill, yet to be considered, if farm representatives did not sign the petition. When the vote was taken nearly 80 percent of the House Democrats voted in favor of discharge and the bill came to the floor. On June 25, 1938, the Fair Labor Standards Act (or Wage and Hours Act) passed in the House by a vote of 314 to 97. In addition to prohibiting child labor, it established a minimum wage of 25 cents an hour to be increased to 40 cents an hour after seven years, and a maximum work week of forty-four hours for the first year and forty hours thereafter. Almost a million workers immediately benefited financially from this law. On the same day, the Food, Drug and Cosmetic Act was approved, which widened the scope of the Pure Food and Drug Act of 1906. It required manufacturers of foods, drugs and cosmetics to list the ingredients on their product labels and prohibited false and misleading advertising.

The Agricultural Adjustment Act of 1938 replaced the Soil Conservation Act, which Congress had adopted in 1936 after the Supreme Court struck down the first AAA. The legislation provided soil-conservation payments to farmers and permitted keeping farm surpluses off the market. Billions of dollars were also made available to the WPA to launch a huge public works program in cooperation with the states.

·　　·　　·

BECAUSE OF THE continued fear of foreign influence, the House, by a vote of 191 to 41, set up a committee on May 26, 1938, to investigate "the extent, character, and objects of un-American propaganda activities in the United States." The committee was headed by Martin Dies, Jr., Democrat from Texas, a rabid xenophobe, labor critic and anti–New Dealer, whose clownish antics when he first entered Congress earned him the dubious title of leader of the House "Demagogues Club," a group of younger members who pledged to vote for any appropriation bill and against any tax measure. Dies defined Americanism as simply the recognition that "Americans derived their fundamental and inherent rights not from society or government but from 'Almighty God.' " At another time he claimed that the Roosevelt administration was staffed by "Communists, Socialists, and the 'ordinary garden variety crackpots.' " Secretary of the Interior Harold Ickes retorted that Dies was the "outstanding zany of American political history."[38]

The original resolution in the House that created the Dies Committee to investigate un-American activities limited the probe to eight months, but continued concern by Americans about the country's safety convinced the representatives to extend the committee each year until 1945 when it was renamed the House Committee on Un-American Activities and became a standing committee.

The hearings of the Dies Committee began in the summer of 1938, ignored the threat of fascism and concentrated on communist infiltration into the country. Witnesses made many unsupported accusations and the accused rarely had the right of rebuttal. During the first few days of the hearings, something like 640 organizations, 483 newspapers and 280 labor unions were cited as having communist connections.[39]

THE EVER-INCREASING OPPOSITION of some Democrats to Roosevelt's New Deal prompted the President to attempt a "purge" from Congress of the most objectionable members in the midterm election of 1938. During the primary elections he supported their opponents. But the attempted purge, like his court packing, was a political mistake and failed to bring about the results he expected. In the November election the Democrats lost 71 seats while the Republicans gained 80. The Democrats still held a majority in the House, 262 to 169, with 4 Independents, but the conservative coalition retained their stranglehold over the Rules Committee The only real victory FDR obtained was the defeat of the Rules Committee chairman, John J. O'Connor. The Republicans, now led by the astute Joseph W. Martin, Jr., of Massachusetts, frequently teamed up with Democratic conservatives to block further New Deal initiatives. Martin developed strong ties to Eugene Cox, who exercised real power in the Rules Committee.

"It did not take us long," announced Martin, "to put the fear of God into the Democratic leadership. I instituted new discipline in our ranks.

Joseph Martin, on the right, was generally admired by members of both political parties, and most likely for that reason lost his leadership position within the Republican Party. He's shaking hands with Sam Rayburn.

One of the forms it took was an elaborate new whip organization that I established, basing it on a system of key men representing each section of the country. It was their responsibility to know how the members in the House from their section stood on every issue and to get them to the floor when a vote was coming up. By telephone and by fast footwork these whips were able within a matter of minutes to assemble practically our full membership." Proudly, Martin declared that "nineteen times in a row we defeated the Democrats" on various issues.[40]

Supporters of the President in the House now faced a greatly strengthened Republican–Democratic–conservative coalition and a Republican Party that had been revived as a national power. Worse, since FDR was not expected to run for a third term in 1940, members of Congress no longer feared his power at the polls to cause them harm nor control of the patronage by which he could command their loyalty.

During the winter and spring of 1938–1939, Congress began to challenge FDR and halt his further expansion of the New Deal. The House cut the administration requests for additional relief appropriations, defeated a housing bill and abolished a profits tax. But it passed the Hatch Act, which forbade federal employees from engaging in political activity. "For God sakes," several House members told the President's press secretary, "don't send us any more controversial legislation."[41] Clearly the House meant to reassert itself as an independent institution, not a rubber stamp for the President.

BUT EVENTS IN Europe changed everything. Chancellor Hitler denounced the Versailles Peace Treaty and began to rearm Germany while Britain and France looked the other way. He then sent his troops into the demilitarized German Rhineland, concluded a military alliance with Italy and Japan, occupied Austria, signed the Nazi-Soviet pact with Stalin and threatened to invade Czechoslovakia if that country did not surrender the Sudetenland to Germany. Meanwhile, Hitler's Italian ally, Benito Mussolini, launched an attack on Ethiopia.

Had Britain and France acted boldly as these events unfolded they might have put a stop to this mounting danger that would bring about another world war. But their unwillingness to risk a possible conflict with a rearmed Germany allowed the situation to deteriorate. In Congress there was a feeling that America's priority lay in providing economic recovery here at home. Any involvement in European affairs was regarded as dangerous to our interests and institutions. There were organized peace efforts throughout the country aimed at making certain the nation's leaders knew that the electorate opposed war and any entanglement with Europe. The spirit of isolationism soared.

When Hitler invaded Poland on September 1, 1939, and war was declared against Germany by Britain and France, Roosevelt called Congress into special session on September 21. He asked that the arms embargo of the Neutrality Act of 1937, which forbade the sale of U.S. armaments to belligerents, be repealed, thus permitting Britain and France to purchase arms and munitions in the United States. Meanwhile, the Soviet Union invaded Poland on September 17 as part of the agreement Stalin had signed with Hitler, and then attacked Finland on November 30. Two weeks later it was expelled from the League of Nations. To the surprise of many, the Soviet Union found Finland impossible to subdue, and so a peace treaty between the two nations was signed on March 12, 1940. The danger of this spreading war had become acute, and Congress acted swiftly in acceding to Roosevelt's request and passed the Neutrality Act of 1939.[42]

There followed a quiet period during which Hitler prepared for a spring offensive. The newspapers called it the "phony war." Then, on April 10, 1940, Germany launched a blitzkrieg or lightning war, in which tanks, dive bombers, airborne troops and motorized infantry invaded and overran Denmark, Norway, Holland, Belgium, Luxembourg and France. British troops were evacuated from Dunkirk, France, in late May, and Italy declared war against France and Great Britain. Paris fell on June 16 and the Germans occupied all of northern and western France. In England the prime minister, Neville Chamberlain, resigned and was succeeded by Winston Churchill.

THE SUDDEN DEATH on September 15, 1940, of the Speaker of the House of Representatives, William Bankhead, opened the way for the election of one of the most important modern Speakers in the history of the office, Sam Rayburn. Bankhead had been ill for quite some time, and frequently absented himself from Congress. As majority leader, Rayburn took his place and presided over the House, winning the respect and admiration of his colleagues for his skill in conducting business. More important, he was determined to win back the independence of the House and "not yield to the executive any more of its constitutional prerogatives."[43] He won a number of concessions from the White House, such as a promise to pull no more surprises like the court-packing scheme and an agreement to meet weekly with the congressional leadership, something that has since become regular practice. FDR also consented to Rayburn's request that the number of White House lobbyists be reduced and that all administration business with the House be conducted through the Speaker's office, not through individual committee chairmen, which had been FDR's practice.

With Speaker Bankhead's death, no business could transpire in the House until a new Speaker was elected. The very next day his flower-draped coffin rested in the well of the House when the members filed into the chamber. The clerk, South Trimble, presided. John McCormack of Massachusetts rose and nominated Rayburn to replace Bankhead. Trimble then turned and looked at the minority leader, Joseph Martin, who shook his head to indicate he had no nomination to make, and Rayburn was elected by acclamation. After the oath was administered the new Speaker began the funeral rites. President Roosevelt sat directly in front of the coffin while members of the Senate, the cabinet, the Supreme Court and the diplomatic corps took whatever empty seats were available. Rayburn and Martin delivered the eulogies. A choir from St. Margaret's Episcopal Church sang while invited guests watched from the galleries.

Rayburn designated McCormack to be majority leader, and the two men proved to be a very effective team: Rayburn established goals and direction while McCormack kept the majority united, carefully implementing the legislative strategy devised in Rayburn's Board of Education, a hideaway first used by Speaker Longworth on the first floor of the Capitol that had now become a meeting place for Democratic potentates. The forceful leadership in the House restored much of the authority lost during the tenure of Rainey and Bankhead and greatly improved morale among its members.

And strong leadership in the House was necessary as the danger to peace in this country increased. Probably a large majority of Americans loathed Hitler, but they were deeply divided over the best course the United States should follow. There quickly developed an organization known as America First that resisted any effort to interfere in Europe. In the House the "great majority" of Republicans were isolationists, especially members from the Midwest. On the other side were the internationalists, who argued that a Europe dominated by Hitler would threaten the peace and safety of the United States. Throughout the spring and summer of 1940 these two sides carried on a bitter debate. "To have tried to align the body of Republican Representatives behind Roosevelt's foreign policies," minority leader Joe Martin explained, ". . . would have torn the Republican organization to tatters."[44]

President Roosevelt placed himself clearly at the head of the internationalists group and called for a vast expansion of defense expenditures. He asked for an appropriation of $1.2 billion for defense spending and signed the first Revenue Act of 1940, raising the federal debt limit to $4 billion. During the summer Congress appropriated $9.25 billion to prepare the country for possible war and, in response to the President's request, passed the first peacetime Selective Service Act (or draft) in American history. This act provided for the registration of all men between the ages of twenty-one and thirty-five for a one-year training period. It generated some 1.2 million troops and eight hundred thousand reservists.

In September the President transferred fifty old but still serviceable destroyers to Britain so that the Royal Navy could hunt and destroy U-boats and convoy merchant ships across the oceans. In return, the United States received the use of eight naval bases from Newfoundland to British Guiana. Isolationists cited this exchange and the Selective Service Act as proof that Roosevelt was intent on committing the nation to war.

Since 1940 was a presidential election year, both parties came out in favor of increased aid to Great Britain. The Republicans had expected to nominate a strong anti-interventionist, such as Senators Robert A. Taft of Ohio or Arthur H. Vandenberg of Michigan, but the country panicked over the collapse of France to German military might and the convention decided to nominate a less-controversial candidate, Wendell Willkie of New York. FDR let it be known that he would accept a nomination for a third term, even though such a move flaunted a tradition against more than two terms that began with George Washington. Leaders of the party expected to place a new man in nomination, but the majority of delegates wanted Roosevelt, and he was unanimously chosen on the first ballot.[45]

During the campaign there hardly seemed any difference between the two candidates with respect to domestic and foreign policies. When Willkie argued that Roosevelt was leading the country into war, the Democrats campaigned on a slogan that FDR had "kept us out of war." In reply to the Republican attack, Roosevelt insisted he would not send American troops into any foreign wars.

In the election, Willkie won 45 percent of the popular vote, but he carried only ten states with 82 electoral votes, while FDR garnered a plurality of nearly 5 million votes (down from 11 million in 1936) and 449 electoral votes. The Democrats slightly increased their majority in the House by winning 267 seats against 162 for Republicans and 6 Independents.

IN EARLY DECEMBER, FDR received a letter from Churchill expressing urgent need for munitions, airplanes and other supplies to carry on the war and explaining that Britain lacked the adequate dollars to pay for them. England desperately required American help to keep open the North Atlantic supply lines in the face of mounting attacks by German submarines. Roosevelt solved the problem by devising a lend-lease program. In a press conference, and then a "fireside chat" by radio, he explained to the American people the absolute need to lend or lease to Britain the equipment and supplies necessary for victory over the forces of fascism. "We must be the great arsenal of democracy," he declared.[46] He also appealed to Congress for support of those nations who were fighting in defense of what he called the Four Freedoms: freedom of speech, freedom of religion, freedom from want and freedom from fear.

The House chamber was undergoing a massive renovation when FDR gave his State of the Union address on January 6, 1941. Steel girders and I-beams were visible to everyone in the room. "It looked for all the world like a building shored up against bombs."[47] It was a fitting setting for a speech that caused many in the audience to think carefully and long about what role Congress would play in the ever-deepening crisis.

The lend-lease bill was submitted to the House on January 10, 1941, by majority leader McCormack and received a full and open debate. Passage of the measure meant nothing less than full-scale American commitment to the defeat of Germany. Isolationists condemned the bill as a death trap for the Republic. Nevertheless, the Senate passed the bill on March 8, and three days later the House approved it by a vote of 317 to 71. The measure allowed any nation whose defense the President deemed vital to American interests to receive arms and munitions and any other supplies and equipment by sale, transfer, exchange or lease. The value of these defense articles was not to exceed $1.3 billion.

Although Roosevelt was still anxious to keep the United States out of war, he was certainly willing to do everything possible to ensure Germany's defeat. Even when U-boats attacked and sank American destroyers with a loss of American lives he did not ask Congress for a declaration of war. And when Germany invaded the Soviet Union on June 21, 1941, he immediately assured the Soviets that they would receive lend-lease assistance as soon as possible.

AFTER THE FALL of France, the Japanese continued their aggression toward China and seized northern Indochina. Fearful that Japan would attack Siberia or the East Indies, Roosevelt issued a sharp warning on July 26, 1941, renouncing the Japanese-American Commercial Treaty of 1911 and stopping the shipment of oil, scrap iron, steel and rubber to Japan.

With the world situation worsening, Roosevelt decided that the one-year enlistment under the Selective Service needed to be extended "until such time as may be necessary in the interests of national defense," and he asked Congress to enact his request. But many Democrats objected, including internationalists. They regarded the twelve-month service period as a "moral contract" with the draftees, and they were not about to break it. Even Speaker Rayburn opposed it, but he felt obliged to support the President. "Things are changing fast and matters are becoming more complicated and dangerous every day," he said.[48] He advised FDR that he might be able to squeeze through the House a twelve-month extension, but certainly not what the President originally requested. How about the Senate's eighteen-month extension? Was that doable? No, replied Rayburn, not without at least twenty Republicans switching over and offsetting the desertion of sixty Democrats who had pledged to vote against any extension. Moreover, he said, it would take the determined effort of the Speaker to corral a majority.[49]

At a final meeting between Rayburn, Majority Leader McCormack and Andrew J. May, chairman of the Military Affairs Committee, who would manage the bill on the floor, it was decided to opt for an eighteen-month extension. The Speaker then spent what little time remained before Joint Resolution 290 on extension was presented to the House, doing what he could to drum up support. He put himself on the line. "I need your vote," he told members privately. "I wish you'd stand by me because it means a lot to me." Several representatives later admitted that they switched from opposing to supporting the resolution for "Mr. Sam."[50]

On August 10, shortly after 10:00 a.m., the House resolved itself into a Committee of the Whole to debate the joint resolution. The galleries were jammed with uniformed draftees who wanted to be released and expected the House to provide it. "Every House member could feel their stares." Lyndon Johnson of Texas, a member of the Military Affairs Committee, took the floor and spoke in favor of the bill, arguing that "if we vote down this proposal, we will vote to send two-thirds of our present army home [when] it is just reaching a point where it is approaching adequacy." Republicans hammered away at this violation of a pledge given draftees under the original measure. Everett Dirksen of Illinois called it "this crowning infamy." And so when the members had exhausted their arguments, pro and con, the vote was taken and showed 203 in favor and 202 opposed.

The Speaker suddenly felt calm. He had achieved his goal. But before he could announce the vote, Dewey Short of Missouri, who led the opposition, rose and asked for a recapitulation of the vote. He really wanted another vote—a vote to reconsider—but instead simply asked for a validation of the already completed vote.

Rayburn tensed. "Does the gentleman desire that before the vote is announced?" he responded.

Not realizing he was stepping into a trap, Short offered no objection.

"On this roll call," Rayburn declared, "203 members have voted aye, 202 members nay, and the bill is passed." And with that announcement, the tally was frozen.

Short then repeated his request, not realizing that it involved a purely mechanical operation to make sure every member's vote was recorded correctly. Under House rules no vote could be changed, and any member who had failed to respond on the first or second roll call could not vote on recapitulation.

It turned out that when the roll was called again every vote had been recorded properly.

"There is no correction of the vote," said Rayburn in a firm voice. "The vote stands, and the bill is passed. Without objection, a motion to reconsider is laid on the table."

Shades of Henry Clay!

Suddenly, Short and the other opponents realized what the Speaker had done. They shouted their objections. "Point of order," they cried.

"I wanted to move to reconsider the vote by which the bill was passed," explained Short, not recapitulate. Too late.

"The gentleman . . . is not eligible to make that motion," Rayburn responded.

Another opposing member, H. Carl Anderson of Minnesota, questioned whether the Speaker had announced that a motion to reconsider was laid on the table.

"The Chair has stated twice that he did make that statement," Rayburn shot back.

"I'm sorry to have to differ with you, Mr. Speaker."

The Speaker's face turned red. "The Chair does not intend to have his word questioned by the gentleman from Minnesota—or anyone else."

And that ended it. The powerful leadership of the Speaker had achieved something essential for the welfare of the nation. War in Asia loomed, and to disband the army in August of 1941 would have sacrificed the nation's defense and ability to respond if attacked. Pearl Harbor lay only four months away. The following day's newspapers rang with announcements of what had happened. A headline in the *Cleveland Press* read, "Rayburn Wields an Iron Fist on House to Jam through Draft Extension Bill."[51]

THE JAPANESE, MEANWHILE, were incensed by Roosevelt's renouncing the Japanese-American commercial treaty of 1911 and stopping the shipment of oil, scrap iron, steel and rubber to Japan. General Hideki Tojo and other Japanese militarists regarded it as a hostile act, and when Tojo became premier, replacing Prince Konoye, he began making plans to attack the United States. On November 20, 1941, a carrier strike force under the command of Admiral Isoruku Yamamoto set sail from Japan and headed toward Hawaii, maintaining radio silence.

On Sunday morning, December 7, 1941, three waves of attack bombers from the carriers struck the American naval base at Pearl Harbor. Taken completely by surprise, the Americans suffered crippling losses. Some nineteen ships were sunk or disabled, including eight battleships. Over two thousand American soldiers and sailors died in the onslaught.[52]

Roosevelt had just finished lunch when Secretary of War Stimson informed him of the attack. The President immediately summoned the leaders of Congress to meet him that evening. The next day he addressed a joint session of Congress. Supported on the arm of his son, James, he mounted the rostrum as the assembled members of Congress, the cabinet, the Supreme Court, and the foreign diplomatic corps cheered and applauded.

Suddenly Rayburn rapped his gavel and the crowd grew silent. After the introduction the President began to speak. "Yesterday," he began, "December 7, 1941—a day that will live in infamy—the United States of America was suddenly and deliberately attacked by naval and air forces of the Empire of Japan. . . . I ask that Congress declare that since the unprovoked and dastardly attack by Japan on Sunday, December seventh, a state of war has existed between the United States and the Japanese Empire."[53]

The joint session ended at 12:40 p.m. The Senate returned to its chamber and within minutes voted 80 to 0 for war. In the House Rayburn recognized the majority leader, John McCormack, who was designated to offer the war resolution.

"Mr. Speaker," cried Jeannette Rankin of Montana, "I object."

She had voted against war in 1917 and was defeated when she made a bid for the Senate. Now she was back in Congress after twenty-two years and was still a dedicated pacifist.

"There can be no objection," Rayburn shot back at her. Then he signaled McCormack to get on with the resolution.

The first woman member of the House, Jeannette Rankin, hastened to the Republican cloak room for protection after voting against a declaration of war against Japan following the attack on Pearl Harbor in 1941.

The resolution was read.

The members were unwilling to listen to lengthy speeches, and McCormack allotted only twenty seconds to speak on behalf of the resolution calling for a declaration of war. "This is the time for action," he said.

"Vote! Vote!" screamed House members.

The chair recognized the minority leader, who asked for unanimous approval of the resolution. An isolationist, Representative Hamilton Fish, Jr., of New York urged his fellow isolationists to join him in support of war. "The time for debate is past," he declared. "The time for action has come."

"Mr. Speaker! Mr. Speaker," shouted Rankin, determined to express her opposition to any declaration of war.

"Sit down, sister," bellowed one member.

Not to be dismissed so easily, Rankin roared at the top of her lungs, "I rise to a point of order."

Rayburn ignored her and directed the clerk to call the roll.

The final vote was not unexpected: The resolution passed overwhelmingly, 388 to 1.

Anger at Rankin was so intense that after the vote she rushed to the cloakroom at the rear of the chamber, where she stayed until the police could arrive and escort her safely to her office in the House Office Building.

The resolutions from both houses of Congress were hurried to the White House, where FDR signed them at 4:10 p.m. Now the United States was officially at war. Three days later Congress declared war against Germany and Italy, and this time Rankin voted "present."[54]

14

The Hot and Cold Wars, 1941–1952

THE NATION ENTERED a period of global war, followed by a period of the threat of global annihilation. There was real concern that civilization on the planet could be wiped out. And American politics entered an era of sudden shifts and surprising developments.

THE DECLARATION OF war in 1941 against Japan, Germany and Italy necessarily increased the President's involvement in and control of foreign and military policy, and Congress moved swiftly to enact the laws necessary for the prosecution of the war. It authorized huge powers to the President. On December 16, 1941, the First War Powers Act was approved, followed on March 27, 1942, by the Second War Powers Act, which allowed the President to "make such redistribution of functions among executive agencies as he may deem necessary"—in short, to reorganize the government as he saw fit.[1] Earlier, the Revenue Act of 1941 raised all major taxes and brought in revenues of $13 billion, the largest single revenue bill in the nation's history up to that time.

The Women's Army Auxiliary Corps Act, sponsored by Edith Nourse Rogers of Massachusetts, passed on May 14, 1942, and created up to 150,000 noncombatant positions (mostly nurses) for women within the U.S. Army. Her proposal, she told her colleagues, "gives women a chance to volunteer to serve their country in a patriotic way." Almost 350,000 women served in the WAACs and similar groups in other military branches.[2]

President Roosevelt appointed Donald M. Nelson to head the War

Production Board, which had authority to mobilize the nation's resources to prosecute the war. Price controls and rationing were established, along with the offices of economic stabilization, scientific research, censorship, war information and strategic services.

The anger, outrage and thirst for revenge by Americans over Pearl Harbor was reflected in their overwhelming demand that the nation's war effort be concentrated against Japan. Fearful that FDR favored pursuing the war in Europe first, rather than Asia, a group of representatives and senators from California, Oregon and Washington joined other public officials, pressure groups and newspapers and publicly complained that the West Coast of the United States was vulnerable to invasion and demanded that Japanese aliens and Japanese-Americans be removed to the interior. Roosevelt responded in February and March 1942 by authorizing the secretary of war to designate restricted military zones from which "unacceptable" individuals would be excluded. Over a hundred thousand persons of Japanese descent, including Japanese-American citizens, living along the West Coast and in Arizona were removed to detention camps in the interior. In some respects the operation resembled the removal of Native Americans in the early nineteenth century under Presidents Jackson and Van Buren, except, in this later instance, many of the victims were American citizens. On March 21, 1942, the House and the Senate put their legislative stamp of approval on this action. Without debate, both houses unanimously passed a bill making it a crime to violate military orders in restricted military zones, thus becoming an accomplice to this massive violation of the basic rights of American citizens. Even the Supreme Court upheld the action as a means of ensuring national security.[3]

But the war in Europe also needed attention. During the past year, Hungary and Romania had joined the Axis Powers—Germany, Italy and Japan—and Italy had invaded Greece. With German military assistance, Italy had forced Greece to surrender on April 27, 1941. England sustained constant and heavy bombing, while the German army, beginning on June 22, 1941, drove deep into the Soviet Union, and laid siege to Leningrad. Worse, the not yet generally known systematic extermination of Jews had begun in the gas chambers of Auschwitz, Poland. Meanwhile, following the Pearl Harbor horror, the Japanese attacked British and American territories in Asia, capturing Guam, Hong Kong, Singapore and the Philippines. Within six months of declaring war, Japan controlled the western half of the Pacific Ocean and expanded its territorial conquests to more than a million square miles in southeast Asia.[4]

THE WAR PROMPTED the development of a frightening but crucial weapon: the atomic bomb. The Manhattan Project, under the direction of Brigadier General Leslie R. Groves, was established to secretly build it. The minority leader, Joseph Martin of Massachusetts, remembered that one morning during the war he was summoned by Rayburn to a meeting with Secretary of War Henry L. Stimson, General George C. Marshall, the chief of staff of the Army, and John McCormack. At the meeting Stimson and Marshall announced that the United States was engaged "in a crash program to develop the atomic bomb before the Germans perfected one." Marshall went into detail about the designs of the bomb, and Stimson warned that if the Germans "got the weapon first, they might win the war overnight."

Then came the blow. They needed "an additional $1,600,000,000 to manufacture the bomb. Because of the overriding necessity for secrecy, they made the unique request that the money be provided without a trace of evidence as to how it would be spent."[5] Actually, the three bombs produced by the Manhattan Project cost in excess of $2 billion, with the money hidden in several appropriations bills under the guise of engineering and related operations. Only a select number of congressmen shared the secret, including Rayburn, McCormack, Martin and the majority and minority leaders of the Senate. The first such bomb exploded on July 16, 1945, in a test at Alamogordo, New Mexico.

The cost of the war ran into the billions, and Secretary of the Treasury Henry Morgenthau appeared before a packed room of the House Ways and Means Committee in March 1942 to ask for $56 billion for defense, out of a total budget of $59 billion. "War is never cheap," admitted the secretary, "but . . . it is a million times cheaper to win than to lose." He recommended increases in individual income, corporate and excise taxes. At one point a national sales tax was suggested, but the public reacted so vehemently against it that the idea was dropped.[6]

The Revenue Act of 1942, as written, was "the largest tax bill ever undertaken in the history of our Government," commented Robert L. Doughton of North Carolina, chairman of Ways and Means. It increased excise profits tax rates from 60 to 90 percent, and income tax rates from 4 to 6 percent. The Senate added a Victory Tax of 5 percent on those with a gross income over $624.[7]

This act not only was the largest tax bill in history up to that time but also was an important measure in the evolution of federal taxation. In order to collect money from a wider span of Americans, the measure lowered exemption levels to the point where they produced millions of new taxpayers. In fact, the act has been described as the income tax that transformed a "class tax" into a "mass tax."

A SYSTEMATIC ASSAULT on the administration by Republicans and anti–New Deal Democrats was launched following the midterm election of 1942. By and large Americans were dissatisfied with the progress of the war and the direction of domestic affairs. They resented the price, wage and rent controls, rationing and the forty-hour workweek. Farmers complained about the loss of farm labor to the city, the lack of farm machinery and the ceilings on farm prices.[8] Americans also resented the fact that Congress very surreptitiously voted itself a generous retirement package, the first in congressional history, which was attached to a civil service bill. At the same time that the American people were asked to make sacrifices, congressmen were exempting themselves. For years Americans had been asked to send "Bundles to Britain" to aid the suffering people in England; now, to show their outrage, they began sending "Bundles to Congress," consisting of old clothes. And although the measure was quickly repealed (389 to 7 in the House, 75 to 5 in the Senate), Congress continued to show its concern for its own needs and welfare. For example, the rationing of gasoline during the war allowed exemptions. With an "X card" a person could purchase unlimited amounts of gasoline. Naturally a number of congressmen applied for the card, proving once more, according to critics, that they were not prepared to make the sacrifices they asked of average citizens. So virulent was public reaction that the guilty congressmen returned their X cards.

Electorate dissatisfaction with conditions in the country, combined with the retirement and X card revelations, brought congressional prestige to a new low. As a consequence, the Democrats lost 45 seats and Republicans gained 47 in the 1942 election. In the Senate, Democrats surrendered nine seats but continued in the majority with 57 against 38 for the Republicans and 1 Independent. Democrats also retained control of the House, 222 to 209, with 4 Independents, but the number of conservatives had been increased sufficiently to encourage an even greater push against New Deal operations. In the Rules Committee the two southern members regularly voted with the four Republican members to block administration measures from reaching the floor. In a real sense this coalition of Republicans and southern Democrats constituted the House majority during the 1943 and 1944 congressional sessions.

Because of the huge expenses involved in the war, Republicans and anti–New Deal Democrats argued that there should be corresponding cuts in nonmilitary spending. So they targeted a number of New Deal agencies for elimination. First to go in 1943 was the Civilian Conservation Corps, followed by the Works Progress Administration, the National Youth Administration and the National Resources Planning Board, which formulated many of the New Deal programs. These anti–New Dealers also wanted to reduce the appropriations for the Civilian Defense, War Information and Price Administration offices, insisting that these agencies were involved in social and economic reforms rather than the war effort.[9]

Eugene Cox demanded that the new Congress recapture its delegated powers. "Government by bureaucrats must be broken," he growled, "and broken now."[10] Following Eugene Cox's lead, Howard W. Smith of Virginia, an extremely conservative member of the Rules Committee, chaired an investigating committee to find instances where executive agencies acted beyond the scope of their authority. "What I propose to do," he admitted, "is have the committee call up and put [members of these agencies] on the carpet, ask them to point out the law by which they acted. If they can't point to the authority at law, we are going to ask them, 'well, where the hell then did you get the authority' . . ."[11]

DURING THE WAR years there was a proliferation of congressional investigating committees. The most prominent was Senator Harry Truman's Special Committee to Investigate the National Defense Program. In the House, John H. Tolan's House Committee on Interstate Migration widened its activities to include production problems. Then there were committees to investigate small business, gasoline and fuel-oil shortages and military and naval affairs. A good dozen committees concerned themselves with manpower policy, rubber production and agricultural needs. Many of these committees overlapped in their jurisdictions, which obviously resulted in the duplication of effort. And, in the hearings, there was a good deal of sniping at the administration for failures or oversights or miscalculations.[12]

For the United States and its allies, the war took a turn for the better with the first major defeat of the Japanese naval forces. An enormous fleet of Japanese warships under the command of Admiral Yamamoto headed for Midway Island, a base of strategic importance because of its location a thousand miles northwest of the Hawaiian Islands. For the United States, the capture of Midway would have been catastrophic. Fortunately, American experts had broken the Japanese code, and the fleet under Admiral Chester Nimitz was laying in wait. In a furious battle that lasted from June 3 to June 6, 1942, torpedo bombers from the U.S. aircraft carriers *Yorktown, Hornet* and *Enterprise* decimated the Japanese fleet, sinking four aircraft carriers and destroying 275 airplanes. Yamamoto ordered what remained of his fleet to return home. This decisive battle of the Pacific stopped the forward movement of the Japanese eastward, rescued Hawaii from possible invasion and restored the balance of naval power in the Pacific.

In January 1943, Roosevelt met with Churchill in Casablanca, and the two leaders agreed that "unconditional surrender" by Germany was their goal. They also decided that Allied forces would invade Sicily, an operation that began in July with Dwight D. Eisenhower as supreme commander of Allied forces. Two months later the successful Allied forces invaded Italy at Salerno and Taranto. The Italian government surrendered and withdrew from the war.[13]

Back home, the hard-driving, aggressive head of the United Mine

Workers, John L. Lewis, called a strike of four hundred thousand coal miners for higher wages, defying the President's executive order of April 1943 to keep wages and prices stable. When the workers turned a deaf ear to the President's request and the War Labor Board's order to return to work, Congress passed the Smith-Connally Anti-Strike Act on June 25, 1943, making it illegal to strike in any war industry. In addition, those unions in companies not involved in the war effort must observe a thirty-day cooling-off period before initiating a strike. Roosevelt vetoed the bill, but Congress easily passed it over his veto, 244 to 108 in the House, and 65 to 25 in the Senate.

There was considerable antilabor sentiment in the House, led by Howard Smith, who very cleverly managed to shift the antistrike bill from the prounion Labor Committee to the Military Affairs Committee, whose chairman, Andrew J. May of Kentucky, narrowly survived a reelection challenge from the CIO. Then Smith outmaneuvered the pro-labor forces in the House to win passage of the measure.

By this time, nearly two years after Pearl Harbor, the American people had clearly moved away from isolationism. The need to undertake efforts which would help secure a durable peace brought about the conversion of many former isolationists in Congress (such as Senator Arthur Vandenberg of Michigan) to the importance of bipartisan support for the establishment of a United Nations once the war ended. In the Senate, resolutions favoring such an international organization were introduced by Tom Connally of Texas, chairman of the Senate Foreign Relations Committee, and, in the House, by J. William Fulbright of Arkansas, a freshman Democrat. On September 21, 1943, the House overwhelmingly approved the Fulbright Resolution by a vote of 360 to 29, and on November 5, the Senate followed suit with the Connally Resolution.

Meanwhile FDR, Churchill and Stalin, the so-called Big Three, met in Tehran, Iran, on November 28, 1943, to plan the invasion of western Europe and the destruction of Nazi Germany. The Russians had launched a counteroffensive that would in the next few months lift the siege of Leningrad, recapture Stalingrad and drive the Germans out of Russia. Now, at the Tehran Conference, Stalin reaffirmed his commitment to enter the war against Japan, and the three leaders agreed to establish an international union to keep the peace when the war ended.[14]

On returning home, Roosevelt found the House in an uproar over the Treasury Department's request for an additional $10.4 billion to finance the war and control inflation. Members of the Ways and Means Committee accused the President of suggesting a tax that they insisted would wipe out the middle class and jeopardize the solvency of countless businesses. Instead, they introduced and the House passed a revenue bill that would raise about $2.1 billion in additional revenue that Roosevelt quickly rejected. He vetoed it on February 22, 1944, saying it was "not a tax bill but a tax relief bill, providing relief not for the needy but for the greedy." This was the first time a President had vetoed a revenue bill.

Both houses rejected the President's position. The veto was condemned in the words of Alben Barkley of Kentucky, the Senate majority leader, as an "assault upon the legislative integrity of every member of Congress."[15] On February 24, by a vote of 299 to 95 in the House, and on February 25, by a vote of 72 to 14 in the Senate, they overrode the veto. It was the first revenue act in American history to become law over a presidential veto.

This revenue act was the last of the wartime tax laws, all of which substantially increased the number of taxpayers throughout the country. During World War I approximately 13 percent of workers paid income taxes, a percentage that declined to 7.1 percent in succeeding years. By the end of World War II the percentage ballooned to 64.1, and it has remained above 60 percent to the present.[16]

With another presidential contest approaching, polls indicated that most servicemen would vote Democratic. Not surprisingly, Roosevelt and his advisers requested a voting act that would authorize absentee voting for members of the armed forces. However, Republicans and southerners feared that if a large number of servicemen and -women exercised the suffrage, they could, to the detriment of the Republican party, decide both local and national elections. So Senators Robert A. Taft of Ohio, a Republican, and James O. Eastland of Mississippi, a Democrat, campaigned vigorously against the administration's plan and successfully substituted the Soldiers Vote Act, which effectively prevented southern African-Americans from voting. The bill authorized absentee voting but forbade any action that would subvert state voting laws, such as those in the South that blocked blacks from exercising their rights as citizens.

However, Congress did pass the Servicemen's Readjustment Act of 1944, better known as the G.I. Bill of Rights, authorizing the Veterans Administration to assist veterans of World War II in readjusting to civilian life by providing loans, academic training, medical assistance and employment programs. So successful was the program that within ten years more than half of all World War II veterans had taken advantage of one or more of the benefits provided by the bill.[17]

Meanwhile the war in Europe entered a new phase. At dawn on June 6, 1944, some 176,000 Allied troops aboard 4,000 landing craft, supported by 600 warships and an air cover of 10,500 planes, crossed the English Channel in Operation Overlord and landed along a fifty-nine-mile stretch of the Normandy coastline, surprising the Germans, who expected the invasion to come at Calais. By the end of the day the Allied troops had secured a foothold on the continent and began what would be the recapture of Europe.

During the summer of 1944, the Democrats renominated Roosevelt for an unprecedented fourth term as President. The much appreciated and respected Harry Truman was chosen to run for Vice President. Truman had done a superb job handling the Senate committee investigating the National Defense Program. He was a serious student of American history and did not wish his committee to be guilty of the blunders and stupid interference committed during the Civil War by the Joint Committee on the Conduct of the War.

The Republicans nominated Thomas E. Dewey of New York, an outstanding prosecuting attorney and an internationalist, for President, along with John W. Bricker of Ohio for Vice President. Dewey did not attack Roosevelt's policy or conduct of the war but implied that FDR was a tired and sick old man, which he was. Nevertheless the public reelected Roosevelt, although his plurality was much reduced from previous elections. Congress remained in Democratic hands; in fact the Democrats gained twenty-one additional seats in the House.

In the Pacific the early successes of the Japanese, especially the capture of the Philippines, were halted as American marines captured Guadalcanal and the Solomon and Marshall Islands and reoccupied Guam. In October 1944, American forces under General Douglas MacArthur returned to the Philippines, and the naval battle of Leyte Gulf resulted in the decisive defeat of the Japanese and totally destroyed Japan's naval might.

THE AMERICAN PEOPLE could finally begin to see and hope for a conclusion to a war that had required many sacrifices. They endured many deprivations—especially food and fuel shortages—and always the sudden agony of a notice informing them that a loved one had been killed. But they suffered whatever they were asked to do in the knowledge that the nation was combating evil in the world and helping people of many continents win back their freedom.

With the return of Congress on December 21, 1944, for the start of the 79th Congress, the pro- and antiadministration forces were nearly equal. Determined once again to assert its authority and its position as a coequal branch of government, the House terminated many wartime agencies and transferred some activities to private business. With an eye toward reforming many legislative problems, Congress established a Joint Committee on the Organization of Congress shortly after the first of the year with Senator La Follette as chair and Representative Mike Monroney of Oklahoma as vice chair and composed of six members from each house, equally divided between Democrats and Republicans. Extensive hearings were held in which many members of Congress testified. But the committee's final report took years to complete.

Meanwhile, as Allied forces drove across Europe and Germany was subjected to constant air raids (British bombers virtually destroyed the unprotected city of Dresden, killing between one hundred thousand and three hundred thousand people), Roosevelt, Churchill and Stalin met at Yalta February 4–11, 1945, to plan the shape of Europe and the division of Germany after the war.

Two months later, on April 12, 1945, FDR died of a cerebral hemorrhage in Warm Springs, Georgia. That day Speaker Rayburn had invited Vice President Truman to join him "downstairs," his word for the well-known and frequently used Board of Education. Truman had just arrived when he received a message to call the White House. He poured himself a drink and then phoned Steve Early, the President's press secretary, who told him to come immediately to the executive mansion.

Truman paled. "Jesus Christ and General Jackson," he blurted, and rushed to the White House, where Eleanor Roosevelt put her hand on his shoulder and said. "Harry, the President is dead."[18]

The end for FDR came just as Russian forces were about to launch an assault on Berlin and American forces had captured Iwo Jima and invaded Okinawa.

BY THIS TIME the Board of Education had become a regular hangout for Democratic leaders where important legislative business transpired. It was also a place to instruct freshmen representatives on what was expected of them. According to Representative Carl Albert of Oklahoma, who was elected to the 80th Congress in 1946, Rayburn offered sage advice to newcomers. "Mostly, he stressed that a congressman should never forget his district. Answer every letter you get, he told me, particularly the ones handwritten in pencil on Big Chief tablet paper. He said when a person like that writes you, he really needs help. If you help him, he will never forget it, and he will be your friend for life."[19] Another young Representative, Jim Wright of Texas, agreed. "Jim," said Rayburn, "there are two things that are most important for your success: the people that you choose to help you in your office. Pick carefully, and be sure that they are people who understand the importance of the opinions of your constituents, the needs of your constituents, and the things they ask you to do. . . . The other thing is selecting the committee that you want to serve on."[20]

The Reverend Adam Clayton Powell, the combative, quarrelsome representative from Harlem, in New York, remembered his initial meeting with Mr. Sam. The Speaker looked straight at Powell and said, "Adam, everybody down here expects you to come with a bomb in both hands. Now don't do that, Adam. Oh, I know all about you and I know that you can't be quiet very long, but don't throw those bombs. Just see how things operate here. Take your time. Freshmen members of Congress are supposed not to be heard and not even to be seen too much . . . get reelected a few more times, then start moving. But for God's sake, Adam, don't throw those bombs."

Adam Clayton Powell began his career in the House as a champion of civil rights.

When Rayburn finally ended his lecture, Powell, who was not about to be intimidated by any southern white man, responded, "Mr. Speaker, I've got a bomb in each hand, and I'm going to throw them right away."

Rayburn doubled over and "almost died laughing." Afterward the two men became "close friends" and frequently conversed about religion. Powell claims he talked the Speaker into joining the church.[21]

At the end of each day's session in the House, Rayburn invariably invited a select few to join him "downstairs" and, in the words of "Cactus Jack" Garner, "strike a blow for liberty." The regulars included Lyndon Johnson of Texas, Eugene Cox of Georgia and John W. W. Patman of Texas. A rather unusual member was the House Parliamentarian, Lewis Deschler, who began his tenure under Longworth and remained in his position until 1975 when Carl Albert served as Speaker. He knew the rules of the House so well that not one of the Speakers he served ever had a ruling overturned. During his many years as Speaker, Rayburn found him indispensable.

The Board of Education was a surprisingly small room that measured twelve by twenty feet with a high, ornately decorated ceiling. Framed and signed photographs, political cartoons and a few portraits decorated the walls. A large refrigerator, camouflaged in a veneer box, stood at one end of the room and a large matching desk at the other end where Rayburn, who always sat at his desk, kept the liquor. On a table nearby was the usual "bottle of Virginia Gentleman bourbon, some water, and a bucket of ice." Mostly overstuffed chairs in leather were scattered around the room, and a long black leather couch with red pillows lined one wall. "In the Board of Education the boys would have a few pops, and Mr. Sam would hold forth on legislation, the various committee chairmen, history, world politics, and sports." Sometimes a few Republicans were invited if they could help with legislation.[22]

FOUR DAYS AFTER Roosevelt's death, on Monday afternoon, April 16, 1945, Truman delivered his first address as President to a joint session of Congress. He was so overwhelmed by the situation that he mounted the rostrum and immediately started to read from his prepared text. "Just a minute, Harry," Rayburn interrupted, "let me introduce you," forgetting for the moment that he had told Truman earlier, "You are not 'Harry' to me anymore."[23] Then Rayburn looked solemnly at the members of Congress and dutifully intoned the words, "The President of the United States."

The new President promised to defend the ideals proclaimed by FDR and he asked for the support of all Americans. "The armies of liberation are bringing to an end Hitler's ghastly threat to dominate the world. Tokyo rocks under the weight of our bombs. . . . I want the entire world to know that this direction must and will remain—*unchanged* and *unhampered!*"[24]

Truman directed that the plans for a meeting in San Francisco to write a charter for the United Nations go forward, and he hosted the conference. At approximately the same time, in late April, Mussolini was captured and hanged by Italian partisans, and Hitler killed himself in his bunker in Berlin.

On August 8, Russia declared war against Japan and invaded Manchuria. When the United States, Great Britain and China demanded that Japan surrender unconditionally and the demand was rejected, the United States dropped an atomic bomb on the military base and city of Hiroshima on August 6, killing or injuring over 160,000. Three days later a second atomic bomb was dropped on Nagasaki, wiping out the city. On August 14, the Japanese accepted unconditional surrender but were permitted to retain their emperor, subject to the orders of the supreme commander of the Allied forces in the Far East, General Douglas MacArthur.[25]

The Senate ratified the United Nations Charter by a vote of 89 to 2 on July 28, 1945, which committed the nation to a policy of internationalism, and the United Nations officially began its operation on October 24, 1945, with Eleanor Roosevelt as a member of the U.S. delegation.

WHEN THE 79TH Congress first met in January 1945, the division between the southern–conservative–Republican coalition and liberal followers of the President had become sharply defined, making legislation more difficult to achieve. For example, Martin Dies announced his intention to resign at the end of 1944, whereupon the leadership of the House decided it was time to quietly terminate the Dies Committee. But the extremely conservative Representative from Mississippi, John E. Rankin, had other ideas. He moved that the Dies Committee be renamed the Committee on Un-American Activities and made a standing committee. His amendment was defeated, however, in an "anonymous" vote, 146 against and 136 in favor. So he asked for a "public" vote, knowing that many members of the House would hesitate before voting publicly against an anticommunist measure. As a result, the amendment passed, 207 to 188.

The new committee under Democratic chairmen avoided controversy; but when the Republicans gained control of the House in the 80th Congress, the chairman of the House Un-American Activities Committee, J. Parnell Thomas of New Jersey, conducted hearings in October 1947 into the motion-picture industry and made almost daily headlines in the newspapers. A long line of movie stars and studio magnets were asked to name members of the Communist Party, and ten accused screenwriters and producers were questioned about their affiliation with subversive organizations. These "Hollywood Ten," as they were called, challenged the right of the committee to ask about their political beliefs and refused to answer. Each was convicted of contempt of Congress and put on a blacklist, thereby denying them employment. Eventually the blacklist expanded to include performers in radio and television. Ronald Reagan, president of the Screen Actors Guild, testified before the committee and agreed that the labor problems in the movie industry had been fomented by Communists. "In opposing those people, the best thing to do is make democracy work," he said. "In the Screen Actors Guild we make it work by insuring everyone a vote and by keeping everyone informed. I believe that, as Thomas Jefferson put it, if all the American people know all of the facts they will never make a mistake."[26]

Later in August 1948, Richard Nixon, a freshman member of the committee, launched a celebrated investigation of Whittaker Chambers, an editor of *Time* magazine, in which Chambers accused Alger Hiss, formerly of the State Department, of allegedly providing him with secret government documents, a charge Hiss denied. The committee could not determine which of the two men was lying, but Hiss was later convicted of perjury.[27]

Fear of Communism and its possible spread into the free world intensified in the United States following the conclusion of World War II. The Soviet Union dominated and controlled Eastern Europe. Indeed, it occupied the territory surrounding the city of Berlin, a city divided territorially among the four powers: France, England, Russia and the United States. In a speech in Fulton, Missouri, on March 15, 1946, Winston Churchill stated that "from Stettin in the Baltic to Trieste in the Adriatic, an Iron Curtain has descended across the Continent."[28]

The Western powers continued to call for the establishment of governments elected by the people in Eastern Europe, but the Soviets had no intention of allowing the creation of new, possibly hostile governments along their border. When it became obvious that Russia would not agree to settling the German question, the western powers took steps to unify their three zones while the Russians began to establish an East German government. Then, on July 24, 1948, Stalin attempted to drive the western powers out of Berlin by cutting off all traffic into the city. Truman responded by airlifting supplies to Berlin. From July 1948 to September 1949, with the cooperation of Britain and France, something like 2.5 million tons of fuel, food and other goods were flown into the city around the clock.[29]

A Cold War, as opposed to a hot one, now existed between the free world and the Soviet Union. The world had become an increasingly dangerous place, especially when, on September 24, 1949, it was revealed that the Soviets had exploded their first atomic bomb. Truman subsequently announced that the United States would undertake the development of an even more powerful weapon, the hydrogen bomb. The annihilation of civilization had become a real possibility.

With the new, awesome and frightening power of atomic energy now at the disposal of the United States, the Congress passed the Atomic Energy Act on August 1, 1946, transferring authority over atomic energy from the War Department to a civilian committee of five appointed by the President. Overseeing the activities of this Atomic Energy Commission was a Joint Commission of Atomic Energy, consisting of nine members from the House, appointed by the Speaker, and nine members from the Senate, appointed by the President of the Senate. The committee would deal with problems relating to the use, development and control of atomic energy.

The United States also signed the twelve-nation (Canada, Britain, France, Belgium, Luxembourg, the Netherlands, Italy, Spain, Portugal, Denmark, Norway and Iceland) North Atlantic Treaty, which the Senate ratified on July 21, 1949, in which it was agreed that an attack on any one of them would be considered as an attack upon all, requiring whatever action necessary to secure the safety of each member nation. This treaty also established the North Atlantic Treaty Organization (NATO), headed by a council, to draw up plans for the defense of the group. Later, in 1952, Greece and Turkey joined NATO. It was the first time the United States committed itself to a peacetime European alliance.

AT LONG LAST the Joint Committee on the Organization of the Congress, established in 1944, submitted its report and recommendations in March 1946. Consequently, the two houses passed the Legislative Reorganization Act on August 2, 1946. It was a sweeping bill to reorganize both branches of Congress. It reduced the number of standing committees in both chambers and redefined their jurisdictions. In the House the number was reduced from forty-eight to nineteen and in the Senate from thirty-three to fifteen.[30] It also provided members with increased staff and money to run their offices. Other provisions sought to improve the flow of legislation between the two houses and between the legislature and the executive branches. One important addition to this bill was the requirement that lobbyists register and report their expenditures to the clerk of the House.[31]

Best of all, as far as the members were concerned, the bill increased their salaries from $10,000 to $12,500 and retained an existing $2,500 nontaxable expense allowance for each representative and senator. Members were also included in the Civil Service Retirement Act and became eligible for benefits on reaching the age of sixty-two after a minimum of six years of service.

Overall, however, the report was a disappointment. It did not address some of the worst problems in Congress, such as the power of the Rules Committee in the House, selection of committee chairs by seniority and the use of the filibuster in the Senate.

Chairmen of all committees, and especially the Rules Committee, had such enormous power to impose their will on their colleagues that the failure of the Reorganization Act of 1946 to address the problem particularly disappointed Speaker Rayburn and the more liberal members of the House. The problem of the Rules Committee needed attention because the interests of the Democratic leadership could be nullified when the conservative southern Democrats on the Committee—notably Howard W. Smith of Virginia and Eugene Cox of Georgia—teamed with Republicans to block action on bills they disliked. The conservative coalition at times even tried to outmaneuver the chairman, Adolph Sabath of Illinois, who replaced John O'Connor after the latter's defeat in 1940. Because the Rules Committee had no written procedures, the chairman had broad discretion on setting the agenda, calling up bills, and deciding on when to put an issue to a vote.

Cox subsequently decided on a plan to reduce the chairman's influence on the committee. He and his conservative colleagues abhorred a bill Sabath favored. So he notified the chairman that he planned to introduce a resolution allowing members of the committee to call up a bill even if the chairman objected. This was a direct attack on Sabath's authority and prestige. The chairman begged Cox to reconsider. He had a bad heart and this resolution could finish him.

"Mr. Cox, this will kill me, if you pass this resolution," he cried. "The humiliation! It will kill me."

Cox shook his head. "I don't care," he snarled. "You have delayed this too long."

At that, Sabath suddenly pitched forward, slumped out of his chair and fell to the floor in a heap.

Chairman Adolph Sabath once feigned a heart attack to maintain his control of the Rules Committee.

"Oh my God," Cox exclaimed, "I've killed him!"

The other members in the room rushed to Sabath's side, lifted him off the floor and carried him into the adjoining room and laid him on a large leather couch. Then they hurried out to find medical help. Clarence Brown of Ohio stayed behind to watch over the stricken chairman.

When things quieted, Sabath stirred. He turned his head and opened one eye to see who was present.

"Why you old rascal," blurted Brown, "there's nothing wrong with you."

Sabath just smiled. "Well," he said, "Mr. Cox didn't get his resolution, did he?"[32]

When the first reorganization bill reached the lower chamber, the Speaker sat on it for six weeks. He did not like those parts of the measure that created majority and minority policy committees, nor did he like the idea of a legislative–executive council that would strengthen relations with the executive branch through regular meetings with the President. Both these parts infringed on his own power as Speaker, and not until the Senate agreed to strike these provisions did Rayburn send the measure to committee. The bill, as finally approved both in committee and Rules, passed the House by a vote of 229 to 61. In sum, despite its defects, the Legislative Reorganization Act of 1946 "significantly altered the organization of Congress and its committees," even though it left the Rules Committee "virtually untouched." Which meant that Rules no longer served as "an arm of the majority party leadership" but had become "an independent base of power in the House."[33]

The private feud between Sabath and Cox did not end in committee. It also exploded on the floor of the House during a debate on a housing bill in June 1949. Sabath had control of the time allotted for the debate and gave a spirited speech in defense of the measure. Cox disagreed. The bill "openly and boldly" proposed "socialism to be our new national policy," he growled. He asked Sabath to allow him ten minutes to make his speech, but Sabath said he could not spare that much time.

"Liar!" shouted the fiery, sixty-nine-year-old Georgian. He insisted that the white-haired, eighty-three-year-old Sabath had promised him ten minutes. Whereupon he stepped up and punched Sabath in the face and knocked his glasses to the floor. He later dismissed the incident with the offhanded remark that "I just sort of brushed him on the cheek."

But the stocky, five-foot-four-inch Sabath reacted vehemently. He wheeled and hit the Georgian with a "sharp right and left to the stomach," according to reporters in the gallery. The sergeant at arms and Representative James Delaney from New York quickly separated the two men.

Later the two pugilists settled their disagreement and posed for newspapermen with their arms around each other's shoulders. "I have a genuine affection for Adolph," gushed Cox. "He's a fine old man. I really love him."[34]

The conservative bent of the Rules Committee was also reflected in the growing number of Republicans and southern Democrats in the House who now insisted that American businessmen and farmers would be better off and more productive if freed from crippling government-sponsored regulations. However, Truman wanted to maintain price controls in order to hold the line against inflationary pressures until production could match demand. With the war over and veterans returning, the American people created a tremendous demand for many "luxuries" denied them over the last five years, such as automobiles, appliances, homes and rationed meat. Moreover, labor demanded increased wages.

A railroad strike threatened to paralyze the country, forcing Truman to seize the railroads on May 17, 1946. Then he asked Congress to grant him the power to declare a state of national emergency whenever a strike in a vital industry under federal control threatened national security. The strikers would be drafted into the army, workers would lose seniority and the leaders would be fined and jailed. The House passed the bill, but the Senate killed it after the strikers returned to work.

At this juncture John L. Lewis led his United Mine Workers out on strike for higher wages and improved working conditions, whereupon the President seized the mines. A new contract was signed that conceded most of Lewis's demands, but both he and the union were fined for defying a federal judge's injunction against the strike.[35]

The midterm elections of 1946 proved devastating for the Democrats because there was widespread discontent with conditions in the country. Rising prices, the shortage of essential commodities like meat, anger toward organized labor and perceived infiltration of labor unions by Communists fed this discontent and led to a landslide victory by the Republicans.

PATRONAGE

G.O.P.

IT AIN'T
FUNNY!
SUPPOSE YOU
HADN'T TOUCHED
A DECK IN
20 YEARS!

In the midterm election of 1946, Republicans won control of both houses of Congress for the first time since 1928.

"Had enough? Vote Republican!" was their campaign slogan. And the electorate did exactly that, awarding control of both houses of Congress to the Republican Party for the first time since 1928. They had taken 246 seats in the House to 188 for the Democrats, and 51 seats to 45 in the Senate. Among the newly elected members were two future Presidents: John F. Kennedy and Richard Nixon. Joseph Martin of Massachusetts was chosen Speaker and Rayburn became minority leader.

For the first time, the proceedings of the House were telecast, and as the vote was taken for Speaker of the 80th Congress on January 3, 1947, close-ups showed viewers the bandage on the tally clerk's finger. Television would soon become a powerful force in the political world.

A more congenial attitude among members developed in the late 1940s with the establishment of a number of clubs. The Marching and Chowder Club, founded in 1947 by a group of young Republicans, including Richard M. Nixon of California, limited membership to sixteen. They met weekly on Wednesday afternoon, generally in a member's office, and discussed current issues over drinks. Other long familiar clubs included the S.O.S. Club and the Acorn Club. Earlier, Fiorello La Guardia and John J. Boylan of New York formed a bipartisan La Guardia–Boylan Spaghetti Association and hosted regular spaghetti dinners for members. Nicholas Longworth had conducted a Sunday Morning Marching Club that took a two-hour walk through Rock Creek Park. And the Tantalus Club consisted of new

House members who pledged to support every bill which any one of them sponsored. It was their way of defending themselves against "arrogant" seniors.[36]

In an effort to improve relations with the Republican Congress, Truman willingly shed many of the wartime powers he had inherited and continued to meet with the leaders in deciding on policy and measures to be brought before both houses. He also requested passage of his presidential succession bill in which the Speaker first and the president pro tem second would succeed the President and Vice President upon their deaths, followed by the secretary of state and other cabinet members according to rank. Republicans, now that they constituted the majority party, heartily endorsed the bill. They even applauded Truman on his "commendable lack of partisanship." The House voted for the succession measure, 365 to 11, and the Senate concurred, 50 to 35, and it became law on July 18, 1947.

The anger toward labor unions again surfaced in Congress with the passage in June 1947 of the Taft-Hartley Act over Truman's veto. In the House, Howard W. Smith, a longtime and rabid foe of organized labor, along with other conservatives from both parties, drew up provisions that were included in a bill submitted by Fred A. Hartley, Jr., of New Jersey, chair of the Labor Committee. They met in either Smith's congressional office or a small Rules Committee room close to the House floor, where they devised their plans. Adolph Sabath of Illinois termed their proposal "the most vicious, restrictive and destructive anti-labor bill ever brought before this House." As finally passed, the Taft-Hartley Act outlawed the closed shop in which only union members could be hired by employers; forbade secondary boycotts and jurisdictional strikes; allowed employers to sue unions for damages caused by strikes; and required cooling-off periods and temporary injunctions to be issued by the President when national health and safety were endangered.[37]

The Congress also passed the National Security Act of July 26, 1947, creating the National Security Council to advise the President and Congress, and the Central Intelligence Agency (CIA) to take command of the nation's intelligence operation. Furthermore, it combined the Departments of the Army, Navy and Air Force in a single Department of Defense with Joint Chiefs of Staff, and its secretary was given cabinet status. It also set up subcabinet departments for the Army, Navy and Air Force.

The Rules Committee during the 80th Congress acted more in harmony with the Republican leadership than it had under Democratic rule. With Smith, Cox and other (usually southern) Democratic conservatives voting with the Republicans on many issues, Speaker Martin was able to exercise a firmer control of what was sent to the floor.

The situation in Europe had deteriorated to such an extent that the Western powers and the Soviet Union had come to an uneasy truce over the division of the continent. When the Russians demanded that Turkey cede territory and permit them to build naval bases in the Bosporus, and supported a Communist attempt to take over the government of Greece, Truman went before a joint session of Congress on March 12, 1947, and asked for an appropriation of $400 million for economic and military aid to Turkey and Greece. In announcing what was called the Truman Doctrine he said that the foreign policy of the United States must "support free peoples who are resisting attempted subjugation by armed minorities or by outside pressure."[38] The speech defined the Communist threat as a global danger, and became the future rationale for U.S. military intervention in both Europe and Southeast Asia.

Although there was initially strong opposition in Congress to the request, Senator Vandenberg overcame it with a proposal that the aid would be withdrawn as soon as the Security Council of the United Nations gave evidence of its willingness and ability to act. The appropriation was then approved by large majorities in both houses of Congress in May 1947.

The aid enabled Turkey to withstand Russian pressure; and the Greek civil war ended in 1949.

Further buttressing of protection for free people in Europe came with the Marshall Plan, enunciated by Secretary of State George C. Marshall in a speech at Harvard University on June 5, 1947, in which he said the United States was prepared to help European nations to rebuild their economies. France, Britain, Italy and Germany verged on bankruptcy after the war, and there was a clear danger of a Communist takeover of France and Italy.

Some $22.4 billion was deemed necessary to avert a continental disaster, and Congress debated the European Recovery Program for ten months before finally agreeing. The seizure of Czechoslovakia by the Communists in February 1948 provided the initiative for passage of the program. In March 1948, both houses gave their consent and Truman signed the measure on April 3, 1948.[39]

The pent-up anger against FDR personally and his New Deal generally found expression in this 80th Congress by the passage on March 24, 1947, of the 22nd Amendment to the Constitution, limiting the tenure of future Presidents to two terms. It was ratified on February 26, 1951.

The decline of Truman's popularity throughout the country and the internal disorder of the Democratic party gave the Republicans great hope that they might take over both the Congress and the presidency in the election of 1948. Southerners were angry over the fact that Truman had appointed a Civil Rights Committee in 1946 and had urged Congress to enact the committee's recommendations to root out racial discrimination. In addition leftists who hoped for cooperation with the Soviet Union denounced Truman's Cold War policies as certain to lead to a third world war.

The Democratic National Nominating Convention met in Philadelphia on July 12, 1948, and nominated Truman for President and Alben Barkley, the Senate majority leader, for Vice President, although many delegates believed they would be defeated. Late in the evening, Truman finally appeared and gave a rousing campaign speech in which he promised to call Congress into special session to address some of the nation's most pressing problems.

A bitter and prolonged floor fight broke out over the civil rights plank of the party platform. This plank demanded a permanent civil rights commission and federal legislation outlawing lynching and poll taxes. When the plank was adopted, thirty-five members of the Mississippi and Alabama delegations walked out of the convention, waving the battle flag of the Confederacy. Dixiecrats from thirteen southern states organized the States' Rights Democratic Party and held their own convention on July 17 in Birmingham, where they nominated Governor J. Strom Thurmond of South Carolina for President and Governor Fielding Wright of Mississippi for Vice President. They did not expect to win the presidency, but they did hope to force the election into the House of Representatives, where they could engage in trade-offs to achieve their objectives.[40]

Five days later, leftist Democrats held their convention in Philadelphia and formed the Progressive Party. They nominated Henry A. Wallace, former secretary of commerce, who had been dismissed by Truman in 1946, for President, and Senator Glen Taylor of Idaho for Vice President. Their platform called for the nationalization of certain basic industries along with friendship with the Soviet Union.

With this split of the Democratic Party into three segments, many thought Truman faced certain defeat. The Republicans, in their glee, met in Philadelphia. While some supported Senator Robert Taft, others hoped to persuade General Eisenhower to accept the nomination. But on the third ballot, Thomas Dewey was again chosen, along with Governor Earl Warren of California.

So certain was Dewey of election that he conducted a very leisurely campaign, while Truman went on a whistle-stop tour by railroad in which he gave 351 speeches to an estimated 12,000,000 people. He called the 80th Congress back into special session on July 26, and invited them to at least carry out the civil rights promises that both major parties had adopted. But it did not honor his request, whereupon he dubbed it the "do-nothing Congress."

"Give 'em hell," the crowds roared at Truman as he listed the failings of the legislature. He blamed poor economic conditions on the Republican-dominated Congress, which had rejected his program for aid to farmers and had passed the Taft-Hartley bill over his veto.

To the utter surprise of the entire nation, Harry Truman won an overwhelming victory over Dewey, 303 electoral votes to 189 for Dewey and 39 for Thurmond. In the popular vote Truman received 24,105,812 to Dewey's 21,970,065, Thurmond's 1,169,063, and Wallace's 1,157,172. What is more, the Democrats regained control of Congress, winning a majority of 93 seats in the House and 12 in the Senate. The count was 263 Democrats in the House and 171 Republicans, along with 1 Progressive Party member, Vito Marcantonio; in the Senate there were 54 Democrats to 42 Republicans.

The reasons for this sudden reversal were not difficult to find. The Taft-Hartley Act convinced labor in the big cities that the Republicans did not welcome their support. The Democrats also attracted midwestern farm votes by advocating the retention of price support at 90 percent of parity while the Republicans mentioned only "flexible" price support. The rebellion by leftists against the President convinced Americans that the Truman administration was not soft on communism as Republicans tried to insinuate. And the revolt of southerners provided proof to African-Americans that the Democratic Party was not dominated by racist bigots. Truman had managed to hold together the basic elements that comprised the New Deal coalition. More than anything else, the fact that the country enjoyed peace and prosperity as never before benefited the Democratic Party. And finally, Republicans, starting with Dewey, took the American people for granted—which is always a mistake in politics.

When the 81st Congress convened on January 3, 1949, Sam Rayburn again resumed the Speaker's chair, and although the Democratic party enjoyed a healthy majority dominated by liberals intent on assisting the administration in furthering social and economic reforms, it faced the implacable opposition of the conservative-dominated Rules Committee. To resolve the problem at a caucus, the Democrats voted 176 to 48 to adopt the Twenty-One-Day rule proposed in a letter sent by Herman Eberharter of Pennsylvania, a northern liberal, to all the newly elected members of the House. The object of his proposal was to deprive the Rules Committee "of its broad powers to block consideration of, or to demand changes in, legislation. . . ." According to the proposed Twenty-one-Day Rule, the chairman of any House committee could bring a bill passed by his committee to the House floor for action if the Rules Committee failed to act on it within twenty-one calendar days of the chairman's request for a special rule.[41]

On the first day of the first session of the 81st Congress the House adopted the Twenty-one Day Rule by a procedural vote of 275 to 143. As expected, Eugene Cox attempted to win repeal of the rule. He did so to prevent debate over a controversial civil rights bill. During the debate on the repeal resolution, the Rules Committee chairman, Adolph Sabath, informed the House that "there is an unfortunate condition that exists in the Rules Committee because ... three members of the Committee on Rules elected as Democrats on the Democratic ticket but are Democrats in name only, unfortunately vote and gang up with the Republicans, leaving me, the chairman and the other real Democrats on the committee in a minority." There were, he continued, at least thirty-three petitions filed to take advantage of the Twenty-one Day Rule that would be blocked if the rule were repealed.[42] Forthwith, Cox's resolution to repeal the rule was rejected by the House, 183 to 236, with many Republicans siding with the Democratic majority because they did not want to be seen as opposing civil rights legislation. The rule was used eight times during this Congress to obtain passage of bills bottled up in the Rules Committee, such bills as statehood-enabling acts for Alaska and Hawaii, an anti–poll-tax measure, establishment of the National Science Foundation, and a rivers and harbors bill.

As it turned out, this rule change was essential in carrying out the program that Harry Truman, in his inauguration address on January 20, 1949, called the Fair Deal. His ideas basically broadened some of the social and economic aspects of the New Deal. He sought increases in unemployment compensation and the minimum wage, national medical insurance, extension of the Social Security system, civil rights legislation, federal aid to education and higher taxes on corporations, among others. And Congress obliged him. It raised the minimum wage from 40 to 75 cents an hour, extended Social Security to 10 million new beneficiaries, passed a housing act for low-income families, expanded water-control, irrigation and hydroelectric facilities of the Reclamation Bureau and enacted the Agricultural Act of 1949, which set agricultural price supports at 90 percent of parity.

Unfortunately, bipartisan support for some of the President's program eroded after 1949 as another "red scare" spread across the nation. A number of leading Republican congressmen, including Senator Robert Taft of Ohio, attempted to reap political gain by attacking the patriotism and impugning the loyalty of the Truman administration and the Democratic Party. When General Chiang Kai-shek's Nationalist government in China was defeated by Communist rebels under Mao Tse-tung, the Republicans blamed Truman for the disaster. In Congress, House Republican Walter H. Judd of Minnesota and Senate Republican William Knowland of California accused the administration of virtually handing China to the rebels. The reason, they insisted, was the fact that the State Department and Foreign Service were honeycombed with communists.

To exacerbate the fear of an expanding Communist world, there followed the shock of new revelations of subversion at home. Alger Hiss, who had held an important post in the State Department and had been accused of turning over secret government documents to a former Soviet courier, was convicted of perjury. Julius and Ethel Rosenberg were tried, convicted and executed for helping the Soviets build their atomic bomb. Several thousand federal employees resigned or were discharged because the FBI or the Civil Service Commission considered them bad security risks.

Adding to the red scare was the announcement on February 9, 1950, by Senator Joseph R. McCarthy of Wisconsin, speaking at a Republican Women's Club at the McClure Hotel in Wheeling, West Virginia, that he held in his hand a list with the names of 205 card-carrying Communists in the State Department. He later went on to accuse a number of political leaders, including General George Marshall, of treason. As chairman of a Senate investigating committee, he recklessly and falsely accused both Republicans and Democrats of un-American activities. His investigation of the Army led the Senate, by a vote of 67 to 22, to condemn him on December 2, 1953, for "conduct that tends to bring the Senate into dishonor and disrepute." Before he was done and called to account, "McCarthyism" had became synonymous with demagoguery and false accusation.[43]

Passage of the McCarran Internal Security Act of 1950 and the McCarran-Walter Immigration and Nationality Act of 1952 sought to address the problem of Communist infiltration into the United States and were passed over Truman's veto. The security act required Communist organizations to register with the attorney general and provide membership lists and financial statements. The immigration bill continued the national origins quota system and provided for the exclusion and deportation of aliens with unacceptable political views, especially from southern and Eastern Europe. However, it did rectify an old injustice by permitting the annual admission of two thousand Asians on a quota basis.

The Cold War heated up considerably when on June 25, 1950, North Korea attacked the Republic of South Korea. The U.N. condemned the invasion and summoned its members to go to South Korea's rescue. Without consulting Congress, Truman immediately authorized the use of American armed forces in Korea, while the U.N. placed the troops of fifteen other member nations under U.S. command, headed by General Douglas MacArthur.

When China informed the west that if U.S. or U.N. forces crossed the thirty-eighth parallel in Korea, the People's Republic of China would dispatch troops into North Korea to defend it, few leaders in the west took the warning seriously. As a result, MacArthur's offensive in November to drive the North Koreans behind the border into Manchuria brought over a million Chinese troops streaming down the peninsula, and they drove the Americans back to the thirty-eighth parallel.

A war with China was unthinkable. As General Omar Bradley, chairman of the Joint Chiefs, declared, a war with China "would be the wrong war, at the wrong place, at the wrong time and with the wrong enemy."

Simultaneously, Congress was in the throes of a heated debate over whether American troops should be sent to bolster the defense of Europe. Congress, especially the Senate, was attempting to assert its authority in the matter of foreign policy, and while it did agree to send four divisions of troops to Europe, it succeeded in passing a resolution warning Truman against sending additional troops to Europe without congressional approval. The President simply ignored the warning.

Fearful of a war with China, the administration ordered MacArthur to limit his activity to the defense of the Republic of Korea. But the general disagreed with the order. In an action that directly challenged the administration's foreign policy, he sent a letter to Joseph Martin in which he wrote, "We must win. There is no substitute for victory." The letter was read in the House, to the delight of many Republicans. Truman replied by relieving MacArthur of his command. It was "a simple matter of whether or not in this country civilian control of the military was paramount." He could do nothing else and still be President of the United States, he said.[44]

On November 1, 1950, two Puerto Rican nationalists, Oscar Collazo and Griselio Torresola, attempted to assassinate Truman at Blair House, where the President was residing during the renovation of the White House. Torresola was killed in the attempt, but Collazo was captured, tried and sentenced to death for killing a guard. However, on July 24, 1952, the same day that he signed an act passed by Congress making Puerto Rico a self-governing commonwealth of the United States, Truman commuted Collazo's sentence to life imprisonment.

FOR THE PAST two years the House and Senate chambers had been undergoing extensive remodeling. From July to December 1949 and again from July to December 1950 workmen accomplished the reconstruction. Not since 1857 had the House been subject to overall renovation. The present roofs in both houses with their skylights and iron trusses were replaced with reinforced concrete slabs and steel beams. Shatterproof glass in the center of the ceiling was installed and illuminated from above, which provided a greater amount of light. "Noiseless" seats replaced the old seats in the galleries. In addition, the acoustics and air-conditioning were improved, and best of all—so the members said—new chairs were set in place on the House floor.

A line of eleven silver stars, representing the eleven states that had ratified the Constitution when the House first met in 1789, were set in marble and installed above the Speaker's chair. But what about North Carolina and Rhode Island, which subsequently ratified the Constitution? To keep peace and satisfy a number of complaining representatives, two additional stars were installed.

The House Appropriations Committee voted $2,274,500 to remodel the House. During the periods of construction the Senate returned to the old Supreme Court room on the floor below and the House moved into the large Ways and Means Committee room in the Longworth Building, which had only recently been constructed. This was the fifth move of the legislative branch since the Congress first relocated in Washington back in 1800.

The renovations completed, the dedication took place on January 1, 1951. It was the first time the Congress had met on New Year's Day. Some wags called it the "hangover" session of the lame-duck 81st Congress.[45]

THE BITTERNESS TOWARD the Truman administration and the unexpected defeat of their presidential candidate in 1948 encouraged many Republicans to support Eugene Cox when, on the first day of the first session of the 82nd Congress on January 3, 1951, he once again moved the repeal of the Twenty-One-Day rule. Republican Charles Halleck of Indiana, the majority leader of the 80th Congress, supported the repeal, arguing that the Rules Committee needed to screen out "unwise, unsound, ill-timed, spendthrift and socialistic measures." Sabath reminded the House that the "unholy alliance" of southern Democrats and conservative Republicans would "tear down the rights of every member of the House," but his warning went unheeded and 152 Republicans joined 91 Democrats to repeal the Twenty-One-Day rule by a vote of 243 to 180.[46]

Moreover, with the presidential election of 1952 approaching, the Republicans felt once again that they could wrest control of the government from the Democrats. Americans had grown tired of the Korean War, which continued despite the fact that peace talks had begun the year before. In addition, the McCarthy attacks had convinced many Americans that the Truman administration was incapable of protecting the country from internal subversion. And evidence of corruption by some members of the administration drove Truman's rating in the opinion polls to unprecedented lows. Then, in their efforts to block the conservative and anti–New Dealer Robert Taft from the nomination, moderate Republicans—such as Henry Cabot Lodge, the grandson of Woodrow Wilson's nemesis, Thomas Dewey, Earl Warren and others—persuaded General Dwight Eisenhower to run for President. He received the nomination on the first ballot at the Republican convention in Chicago in early July 1952. Senator Richard Nixon of California was chosen for Vice President, having gained national attention through his efforts to expose Alger Hiss.

Truman chose not to run for reelection, and the Democratic convention selected Governor Adlai E. Stevenson of Illinois, along with Senator John Sparkman of Alabama. The popular Eisenhower, a genuine war hero who promised to go to Korea and help bring the war to an end, won an overwhelming victory by a vote of 442 electoral ballots to 89 for Stevenson. He even carried four southern states: Tennessee, Virginia, Florida and

Texas. The Republicans also captured both houses of Congress by narrow margins: one vote in the Senate and eight in the House. The Republicans took 221 seats in the House against 213 for the Democrats. In the Senate the Republicans had 48 votes and the Democrats 47.

The long twenty-year control of at least one or more of the three branches of government by the Democratic Party had come to an end. With such a razor-edged majority, the Republican Party could not dismantle the New Deal, even if it so desired, but it hoped to halt any effort to keep it from expanding.

15

The Gatekeeper and the Fight for Civil Rights, 1953–1961

With both the executive and legislative branches now in Republican hands, and with a President who was immensely popular with the electorate, the possibility for energetic, effective and dynamic leadership in national and international affairs seemed very likely. But Eisenhower believed that too much power had been exercised by his predecessors and therefore did not try to establish control over Congress or provide a clear vision of where he felt the country should go. He believed that leadership consisted of reconciling different opinions on important issues, not constructing programs and guiding Congress to their enactment. Quarrels over party policies and patronage frankly bored him. He much preferred to play golf with businessmen. Consequently, the Republican majorities from 1953 to 1955 never established real command of Congress. And after 1955 the Democrats regained control of both houses and won increasing majorities with each election.

The Republican party desperately needed rebuilding, especially in Congress, and throughout Eisenhower's presidency it remained bitterly divided between conservatives and moderates, isolationists and internationalists. But the American people truly needed and wanted a period of quietude after the long turbulent years of depression and war. This, Eisenhower provided. He steered the government through a series of crises without resorting to violence and war. And he committed himself and his party to many of the social and economic reforms established during the years of the New Deal and the Fair Deal, such as the extension of social security, public housing and aid to education. He followed a policy of economic conservatism and social liberalism. He characterized himself as "liberal on human issues, conservative on economic ones."[1] Most particularly, he opposed governmental development where private utilities could do the work, not excluding atomic and power facilities.

When the 83rd Congress convened on January 3, 1953, Joseph W. Martin of Massachusetts was chosen Speaker, and Charles Halleck of Indiana the majority leader. Halleck also became the President's principal ally and spokesman in the House. The new chair of the Rules Committee was Leo E. Allen of Illinois.

As a skilled diplomat and political realist, Eisenhower understood the necessity of cooperating with the Democratic leadership, since conservative Republicans could not be counted on to support his more moderate proposals. These conservatives, hell-bent on lowering taxes and cutting expenditures, rather than Eisenhower's priority of balancing the budget, followed the lead of the seventy-eight-year-old Daniel Reed of New York, the feisty old-guard Chairman of the Ways and Means Committee, who at one point railed that he would drive through a tax cut "no matter what Eisenhower, or [Treasury Secretary George M.] Humphrey or anyone else had to say about it."[2] In his State of the Union address, Eisenhower had declared, "Reduction of taxes will be justified only as we show we can succeed in bringing the budget under control. . . . Until we can determine the extent to which expenditures can be reduced, it would not be wise to reduce our revenues."[3]

Reed caused the Eisenhower administration so much trouble that his critics dubbed him the "Neanderthal man." He could work himself into a rage over tax reduction at the slightest provocation, and it took the determined leadership of Speaker Martin and Majority Leader Halleck to prevent an open rupture within the party. When Reed tried to bring to the floor a tax reduction bill, Martin asked Leo Allen, the chair of the Rules Committee, to keep it locked up. In another action, a six-month extension of the excess profit tax of 1950, scheduled to expire in mid-1953, and requested by the administration, won passage when Martin threatened to bypass the Ways and Means Committee by invoking a little-known House procedure whereby the Rules Committee could grant a rule on a bill still in committee. Minority leader Rayburn had the wit to advise his members to steer clear of Republican infighting. He recognized that Eisenhower would need the support of congressional Democrats and they would benefit from the collaboration.[4]

Of particular importance was the passage of a bill expanding the Social Security system. On January 14, 1954, the President recommended the additional coverage of 10.5 million workers with increased monthly benefits.

What had become the "third rail" of American politics (touching it could cause political death) roused little controversy in Congress, and on September 1, Eisenhower signed the Social Security Amendments of 1954.[5] Also important was passage of the Wiley-Dondero bill on May 3, 1954, authorizing the construction with Canada of a twenty-seven-foot-deep channel between Montreal and Lake Erie. The project was completed in June 1959 and made possible the navigation of ships from Montreal to Lake Superior, except during the winter.

One of Eisenhower's first initiatives was to remove price and wage controls imposed during the Korean War. As promised during the campaign, he went to Korea to see what he could do to bring about a truce. And six months after taking office he fulfilled his pledge to end that war. On July 27, 1953, the United States, North and South Korea, and the People's Republic of China signed an armistice agreement that recognized the thirty-eighth parallel as the dividing border between North and South Korea.

Still, the communist threat remained. The ruthless suppression of freedom in eastern Europe by the Soviets, especially in putting down rebellion in East Berlin and Hungary, encouraged the House to respond favorably to the administration's request for additional funds to strengthen the military. With the considerable help of Carl Vinson of Georgia, chair of the Armed Services Committee when the Democrats regained control of the House after 1955, Eisenhower was able to increase defense budgets to unprecedented heights. The rise of what he called the military-industrial complex was expected to prepare the nation for any possible threat to its safety. In what was termed the Eisenhower Doctrine, Congress authorized the President to extend military and economic aid to guard the Middle East from communist expansion. Then, when communists led by Fidel Castro captured Cuba, the threat to American liberty became a frightening possibility. And the development of a hydrogen bomb—far more terrible than the atomic bomb—by both the United States and Russia worsened fears that the planet could be blown up at any time by an escalation of the Cold War.

With regard to legislation, both the House and Senate were very much influenced by world events. Isolationism was a thing of the past. Within two years of Eisenhower's inauguration, two-thirds of national expenditures went for national security.

BUT CONGRESS WAS badly shaken on March 1, 1954, when the kind of violence that regularly erupted in Europe suddenly occurred in the chamber of the House of Representatives. A group of Puerto Rican nationalists entered the Ladies Gallery, where no ticket was required for admittance. A security guard asked if they had any cameras, which were barred, but failed to check for guns. None of the would-be assassins expected to leave the Capitol alive.

It was 2:20 p.m. and the House was in the midst of voting on a bill authorizing the continuation of a program for admitting Mexican farm laborers for temporary employment into this country. Lolita Lebron, a Harvard-educated radical, led a group of three followers: Rafael Cancel Miranda, Irvin Flores and Andrew Figueroa Cordero. They rose from the back row of the gallery as Lebron screamed, *"Viva Puerto Rico libre,"* and waved a Puerto Rican flag. Then the three peppered the floor with twenty-nine shots from Lugers and an automatic pistol. One of the bullets struck the desk of Charles Halleck, the majority leader.

Speaker Martin said he had just finished counting the ayes—there were 168—and was about to call for the no votes "when I heard the first two or three cracks. I looked up to see what was going on and I moved back against the wall."

As shots rang out, representatives bolted for the doors while some members ducked behind chairs and others simply dropped to the floor. Several members were struck by bullets as the nationalists kept firing. Ben F. Jensen, Republican from Iowa, raced toward one door and was hit from behind in the right shoulder. He stumbled through the door and fell to the floor. "Oh my God," he groaned, "he got me in the back."

Representative Alvin M. Bentley, Republican from Michigan, was the most severely wounded. Bullets struck him in the chest and abdomen. He slumped to the floor, just a few feet from the Speaker's rostrum, blood staining his shirt.

Representative James Van Zandt, Republican from Pennsylvania, crawled into the cloakroom and from there exited the chamber and raced up the stairs to the gallery. With the help of spectators and security guards he overpowered the would-be assassins, and they were taken into custody. They were later tried and sent to prison, where they remained until President Jimmy Carter granted them clemency in 1979.

In all, five Congressmen were wounded. Besides Jensen and Bentley, there were George H. Fallon, Democrat from Maryland, who was hit in the right hip; Kenneth A. Roberts, Democrat from Alabama, who took a bullet in his left knee; and Clifford Davis, Democrat from Tennessee, who received a bullet in the right calf. Fortunately, all five men recovered, although Bentley "was never really the same," said one witness.

Because most of the shots were directed toward the opposite side of the chamber, rather than directly below, they failed to kill anyone, which may have been intentional. At least that is what Lebron said at her trial.

The following day the House held its regular session and some two hundred members showed up. This was an unusually large midsession turnout and meant to convey an encouraging message to the country. Naturally numerous bills were introduced to increase security in the chamber, including one to install bulletproof glass between the gallery and the floor.

No action was taken. Instead, a bill made it a felony punishable by a $10,000 fine and 10 years in prison for an unauthorized person to carry a weapon into the Capitol or on its grounds. Metal detectors were not installed in the Capitol until the 1970s after a bomb exploded in a Senate restroom. The governor of Puerto Rico, Luis Munoz Marin, sent a cablegram to the House in which he said that everyone in Puerto Rico was shocked by the "savage and unbelievable lunacy" of the attack. He called it "completely unrepresentative" of the feelings of Puerto Ricans.[6]

IN THE MIDTERM elections of 1954, the violence in Southeast Asia resulted, in part, in a dramatic comeback by Democrats. Communist nationals in Indochina had been waging a struggle for independence against the French since 1946. Now, with the conclusion of the Korean War, the Chinese increased aid to these nationals. At a foreign ministers conference in Geneva in May 1954, agreement was reached to divide Indochina into two parts, like Korea. On October 11, 1954, the Viet Minh captured control of the northern half of what would now be called Vietnam and a non-Communist government assumed charge of the southern half. And, in one of his last acts as President, Eisenhower sent 3,500 troops to bolster the non-Communist southern portion of Vietnam.

The Congress also passed the Communist Control Act of 1954, declaring that the U.S. Communist party "should be outlawed" and assigned penalties under the Internal Security Act. In his initial State of the Union address, Eisenhower had declared that the immigration policy of the United States did "in fact discriminate," and he asked Congress to enact a new law that would "guard our legitimate interests and be faithful to our basic ideas of freedom and fairness to all." In response, Congress passed the Refugee Relief Act on August 7, 1953, authorizing the admittance of 209,000 refugees.[7] Furthermore, the U.S. signed a pact on September 8, 1954, creating a Southeast Asia Treaty Organization (SEATO), which pledged joint action if any member nation (the United States, Britain, France, Australia, New Zealand, Pakistan, Thailand and the Philippines) was attacked, and it provided special protection for Cambodia, Laos, and South Vietnam.

The success of the Democrats in the 1954 midterm election because of a recession and the inability of the Republicans to cope with it gave them a thin margin of control of both houses of Congress. In the House, they won 232 seats to the Republicans' 203; in the Senate, the number was 48 Democrats to 47 Republicans and one Independent. Rayburn and McCormack resumed their offices and Carl Albert was chosen majority whip. Eisenhower, a skillful backroom trader, felt he had to work with the Democratic leadership to achieve his goals, and Rayburn in the House and Lyndon B. Johnson, majority leader in the Senate, went along and adopted a policy of accommodation with the administration.[8]

• • •

CARL ALBERT CAME to the House in 1946 from a district in Oklahoma that was adjacent to Rayburn's district in Texas. Well educated, he displayed enough talent to catch Rayburn's eye, and when he was invited to join him and a small group of representatives in the Board of Education, he said, "I knew that I was on my way" up the ladder of party leadership. Even so, in all the time he worked with Rayburn and visited him in Texas, Albert never called him "Sam." It was always "Mr. Rayburn."[9]

Over several years Albert learned a great deal about how the House operated, and he mastered the different procedures rather quickly. Of necessity, he learned how to be an effective whip. First, he said, he had to know every one of the Democratic members and "what made each of them tick, what made each of them vote." For any given bill he had to know what the largest number of Democrats would support and "what instruments could increase those numbers, if necessary, one by one." In addition, he had to "predict how scores of votes—major and minor, procedural and substantive— would turn out. I had to do all that so that the Democratic leadership could define and could pass a legislative program." Finally, he had to make every effort to persuade members to change their vote when the leadership so decreed.

At first, Albert said, the Democratic Caucus assigned fifteen regional whips to assist the whip. That was back in 1933. Then the number of regional whips was increased to eighteen, each one of whom was assigned a dozen members to get to know and keep tabs on. "The regional-whip system," Albert admitted, "was essential to our operations. Before major votes, we used it to conduct formal polls. . . . Armed with that information, we knew what was likely to happen even before a floor fight would begin."[10]

Scheduling became an important function of the whip. The regional whips conducted weekly polls to see which members would be away from the Capitol over the next several days. "That allowed us to set the week's calendar with the most critical votes coming when we could expect maxi-

Carl Albert was undoubtedly the best-educated Speaker in U.S. history. He expanded the Speaker's visibility around the globe.

mum support." During the days of those important votes, Albert had the regional whips check their attendance polls against the first quorum call. "If a member whom we had expected had not answered the call, I got on the phone and tracked him down. Just before the vote was to be taken, the regional whips, the Capitol switchboard, and I went to work again, calling every member's office and thereby getting our people on the floor in fifteen minutes' time."

Albert realized that with only a twenty-nine-seat majority no whip or majority leader could expect to push through a controversial issue. "Any significant issue would open fissures that would doom the question and divide the party. On top of that, we were working with the first Republican president since the Great Depression."[11]

Another thing Albert and all other newcomers to the House learned was the ease with which members could "sit on the fence." What their constituents never knew was that "real action in the House is not necessarily on the bills, but on the amendments. Under the rules at that time members voting on amendments would walk down one of two aisles . . . depending on whether they were voting yea or nay. When they reached the front of the line, they were tapped on the shoulder by a teller—a fellow representative who was counting the votes. The final count would be recorded, but unless you were watching from the gallery and could recognize individual members from behind, it was almost impossible to know how—or even if—an individual member had voted." It proved easy for a member to duck a vote when he made promises to both sides and even lie about it "because there was no way anybody could check."[12]

For the most part Democrats in 1955 were willing to work with the popular Eisenhower unless, of course, he attempted to dismantle the New Deal reforms. In fact the Democrats supported 121 of the administration's first 164 initiatives. Because of his military experience they were particularly willing to acknowledge Eisenhower's leadership in foreign affairs. World War II had taught most legislators about the need for strong executive leadership. It was understood that partisanship, in the words of Carl Albert, "ended at America's shores."[13]

One young representative marveled at the cordiality he encountered on entering Congress. "One's overwhelming first impression as a Member of Congress," wrote Clem Miller, Democrat from California, "is the aura of friendliness that surrounds the life of a congressman. No wonder that 'few die and none resign.' Almost everyone is unfailingly polite and courteous. Window washers, clerks, senators—it cuts all ways. We live in a cocoon of good feeling. . . . The freshman congressman is being constantly made aware of the necessity, even the imperative of getting along with his fellow congressmen. Congress is a large body. To accomplish anything, the procedure must be formalized—obeisance must be paid to tradition and seniority."[14]

Another young member of the House was Thomas P. ("Tip") O'Neill, Democrat from Massachusetts, who later described living in Washington in the 1950s. "I needed a cheap place to live," he wrote, ". . . so I teamed up with Eddie Boland, my old state house pal, and we found ourselves an efficiency apartment at 1500 Massachusetts Avenue, Northwest. We slept on a couple of couches and paid a total of sixty-seven dollars a month in rent." It was a very small apartment, so they later "traded up" to a one-bedroom apartment in the same building that rented for $87. Now they had a living room and a kitchen, although they never once cooked a meal on the premises. They ate at restaurants every night with friends and colleagues, and O'Neill played poker on Wednesday at the University Club. On any given night there might be two or three dozen congressmen at the Club. After dinner they played cards, which was, said O'Neill, "a great way to meet some of my colleagues and to learn what was going on in their districts all over the country. . . . Over the months I got to know them all, Democrats and Republicans alike. There were no [political] parties and no factions in that room. There was only fellowship." It was a happy time.[15]

Still there was controversy, not that it affected the comradeship that existed off the floor. One of the most controversial issues to arise during this era was civil rights. On winning election to the House, Adam Clayton Powell, Jr., of New York, promised his constituents to work night and day to bring about the abolition of the poll tax and the end of segregated transportation. He also pledged to make lynching a federal crime.[16] Forthwith, he devised the Powell amendment, which he attached to a wide range of bills. It required that no federal funds be advanced if discrimination was practiced or involved in any way. "The bombs Mr. Sam had advised me against [when they first met] were beginning to drop, drop, drop upon the marble of men's conscience." As early as June 4, 1946, Powell was able to successfully attach to Public Law 396, the school lunch program, his Powell amendment. Thereafter, whenever he saw an opportunity, be it measures involving education, the military, construction, transportation, whatever, he would introduce his amendment. Unfortunately, it became a kind of "kiss of death" to any bill that carried his attachment. Southerners with their conservative allies saw to that.

The greatest obstacle to any civil rights legislation was Howard W. Smith. As chairman of the Rules Committee he stood ready to defeat any attempt to bring legislation to the House floor that he disapproved, especially civil rights. A future Speaker described him as "a taciturn man who used to wear rimless glasses and an old-fashioned wing collar. He was also an arrogant son of a bitch, and an ultraconservative who was no more a Democrat than the man in the moon."[17] In part, Smith's power resulted from his thorough knowledge of House rules and how to use them. He was the smartest man and the most able legislator "that I ever saw in Con-

From his position of power as chairman of the Rules Committee, Howard Smith fought every effort to implement civil rights legislation.

gress," said Carl Albert, excepting Sam Rayburn. And unlike Eugene Cox, who had an uncontrollable temper, Smith was the soul of gentlemanly grace and conduct. He was the kind of man, remembered Albert, "who could drape an arm around your shoulder while his free hand was cutting out your heart." "He'd cut your head off if he wanted you out of the way."[18] Clare E. Hoffman, Republican from Michigan, once described Judge Smith as "one of the wisest, foxiest, smoothest, soundest operators that ever came to Congress in my time." To others he was just a vile and detestable dinosaur.[19]

Three times a week, at 10:30 a.m., Judge Smith convened the Rules Committee in a small room just off the House floor. Nothing unexpected happened at these meetings. They were all "prearranged." The Judge made sure of that.

But the committee, in and of itself, exercised enormous authority, even without an authoritarian at its head. It had the right to send down reports on rules and have the reports take precedence over everything else. By and large a bill from any other committee had to be given a rule before it could advance to the floor. And that rule could determine how it was debated, the time allotted for debate, the number and types of amendments, if permitted, to be allowed, and sometimes the exact wording of permissible amendments. A bill that received an open rule cleared the way for unlimited amendments.[20]

There were only four means by which a measure could be brought to the floor without a rule: by suspending the ordinary procedure with a two-thirds vote; by employing the Calendar Wednesday method, mandating same-day action on a bill; by placing a bill on the Consent Calendar and thereby having it called to the floor on the first and third Mondays of each month; and by winning approval for a discharge petition. But each one of these techniques was rarely successful. A discharge petition required a two-thirds vote of the entire House. Carl Albert stated that from 1923 to 1959 some 797 discharge petitions had been filed but only one bill (the wage and hours bill of 1938) ever became law. As for the Consent Calendar procedure, a single objection from one of the 435 members would block it. And Calendar Wednesday required the Speaker to call on committees in alphabetical order, which meant that the Agricultural or Appropriations chairmen, in cooperation with the Rules Committee chair, could consume the entire day before bills from the Judiciary, Veterans' Affairs, or Ways and Means could be heard. Thus, for all intents and purposes, the Rules Committee controlled the fate of legislation.[21]

As head gatekeeper in control of the flow of legislation to the House floor, Smith counted on the four Republicans on the committee to side with him, along with the Democrat, William M. Colmer of Mississippi. The other Democrats, Homer Thornberry of Texas, Richard Bolling of Missouri, and Tip O'Neill of Massachusetts, had ties to Rayburn and/or McCormack and invariably voted against the chairman.

But Congress could not go on indefinitely refusing to address important issues, such as civil rights, housing and education. Truman had failed to win civil rights legislation from Congress and so was forced to use his executive powers to fight Jim Crow laws. Eisenhower continued this policy, if halfheartedly, but only Congress had the power to initiate legislation that would strengthen civil rights laws already on the books. In the meantime, the Supreme Court, with Earl Warren as Chief Justice, ruled on May 17, 1954, in the landmark case *Brown v. Board of Education of Topeka,* that compulsory racial segregation in public schools was a violation of the 14th Amendment's guarantee of equal rights to all citizens. The following year the court went further and instructed all federal district courts to require local authorities to move with "all deliberate speed" toward the desegregation of all public schools. Also, in 1955, Rosa Parks refused to relinquish her seat to a white man in a Montgomery, Alabama, public bus, and her action touched off a year-long bus boycott in that city led by the Reverend Dr. Martin Luther King, Jr. There followed a series of bombings of black churches and homes that ignited national horror at what was happening in the South.

Not surprisingly, a liberal Democrat, Congressman Richard Bolling of Missouri, decided to try again to get Congress to act. In January 1956, he went to Speaker Rayburn and asked for his support for a voting rights bill that would end the disenfranchisement of African-Americans in the south. He knew that for such legislation to have any chance of passage it would need the active support of the Speaker from Texas. He chose voting rights instead of school desegregation because it was less susceptible "to inflammatory opposition by racists."[22] He took his case to Rayburn, he later declared, "not so much because of his influence in the House itself but because of his prestige and influence among Southerners in both the House and Senate."[23] Moreover, through Rayburn, it was hoped that the support of the Senate majority leader, Lyndon B. Johnson, could be obtained so that a Senate filibuster could be prevented. Bolling knew that although the House had passed five anti-poll-tax measures from 1942 to 1947, the Senate had failed to act on them or blocked them with filibusters. In the 1950s the Senate also killed the creation of a fair employment practices commission and a U.S. commission on civil rights.

Bolling laid out his proposal in great detail. Rayburn just listened. Finally, he interrupted the young congressman and said, "I'm not against the right to vote. Every citizen should have that." But he made no commitment.[24]

The Eisenhower administration also decided to initiate civil rights legislation in the hope of winning back the support of African-Americans, support the Republican Party had enjoyed since Reconstruction and lost with the election of FDR. Therefore, the President instructed his attorney general, Herbert Brownell, to draft a suitable bill. The resulting effort was a rather comprehensive measure and included a provision which gave the attorney general the unprecedented power of enforcing civil rights in housing, restaurants, theaters, hotels and voting. Eisenhower did not approve such broad authority for the attorney general and asked him to cut it back and then submit it to Congress as a Justice Department bill, not a White House measure.

Richard Bolling was one of the leading reformers in the House who championed voting rights legislation.

Although other members of the House intended to propose legislation dealing with civil rights, including Emanuel Celler of New York, chairman of the Judiciary Committee, which had jurisdiction over such legislation, it was agreed among liberal Democrats that Republicans were more likely to support a bill if it came from the Eisenhower Justice Department, thereby making it bipartisan, rather than one hatched by the opposition alone. Bolling also decided that since it would be impossible to get congressional approval for any legislation before the approaching presidential election of 1956, the best thing for liberals to do was to get something debated in the House and then campaign on the issue in the fall. After the election they could then reintroduce the bill, win passage and send it to the Senate early in 1957.[25]

Bolling, who by this time was seen as Rayburn's point man on the Rules Committee, explained his strategy to the Speaker, recommending that he inform Senator Johnson what the liberals in Congress expected to happen. Of course there would be a problem getting any such bill through the Rules Committee, but the current mood in the nation for civil rights seemed so strong that even the tough-minded and powerful chairman, Judge Smith, would be unable to resist it.

Meanwhile, southern senators, outraged by the Supreme Court's Brown decision, prepared "A Declaration of Constitutional Principles" in which they argued, among many things, that "parents should not be deprived by government of the right to direct the lives and education of their own children." Called the "Southern Manifesto" by the press, it was signed by nineteen Senators and eighty-one representatives from the eleven states of the Old Confederacy.[26] On March 12, 1956, Judge Smith laid the manifesto before the House and denounced the *Brown* decision. But unlike the Senate, the House did not raise the rebel yell or carry on a protracted debate. It simply inserted the Manifesto in the record.[27]

Instead, the members of the House looked to a bill, HR 627, to achieve their goal of strengthening civil rights, a bill reported out on April 25, 1956, by the Judiciary Committee, where it had been written on the basis of the recommendations submitted by the Justice Department. This bill established the six-man bipartisan Commission on Civil Rights to investigate allegations of discrimination on account of "color, race, religion, national origin or sex, and illegal voting." It also authorized the attorney general to "institute civil action . . . in U.S. district courts whenever persons have engaged . . . in any acts of civil rights offenses." A minority of seven southerners on the committee denounced the bill and insisted it would "bring new and novel principles" into play that would constitute a "constant threat to any state or local government. . . . To empower the Attorney General in the name of the U.S. to institute civil actions . . . before state remedies have been exhausted would devastate the principles of states' rights."[28]

The bill went to the Rules Committee, where Smith delayed holding hearings as long as possible. Finally, Representative James Roosevelt of California, the eldest son of the late President, filed a discharge petition on June 5 to take the civil rights bill out of the control of the Rules Committee and bring it straight to the House.

To prevent this action, Smith reluctantly initiated hearings on June 20. The following day Representative William M. Colmer noticed that the committee lacked a quorum and raised a point of order. The judge counted only five members present, instead of the necessary seven, and he abruptly adjourned the meeting. Further meetings, he said, were subject to his call, but he added, "I'm not interested in calling a meeting."[29]

House Republicans recognized their uncomfortable position. They realized that it was not in their interest to be seen as opposing civil rights. The minority leader, Joseph Martin, pointed this out repeatedly, both publicly and privately. He claimed that the five Republican members of Rules favored the bill. Therefore, if at least two Democrats on the committee joined them, the bill would receive a rule. He pressured the Republican members of the Rules Committee to vote to give the bill a rule. The next day, by an 8 to 3 vote, the committee, called by Smith, requested that hearings begin immediately. On June 27, again by a vote of 8 to 3, the committee provided an open rule that brought HR 627 to the floor. Debate on the bill commenced on July 16.

During the House debate, Chairman Celler of the Judiciary Committee declared that "we can no longer accept the moth-eaten argument of 'separate but equal' as pronounced by the Supreme Court in *Plessy vs Ferguson* (1896). The innermost demand of the Negro people is recognition of equal human dignity." But Thomas G. Abernathy, Democrat from Mississippi, insisted that "discrimination . . . is something which every man has a right to practice." And Representative Bruce Alger of Texas, a

*Another and very important advo-
cate of voting rights legislation was
Emanuel Celler, chairman of the Judiciary Committee.*

Republican, commented, "once you yield to the federal government the
right to tamper with state law pertaining to voting, you have already lost
your freedom, no matter what the phrasing."

Joseph Martin rose on July 19 and reminded his fellow Republicans of
something he felt was obvious. "I want to tell the Republicans in this House
if they follow the southern democracy in the defeat of this bill, they will
seriously regret it. . . . This bill has been jockeyed into the position where
the one group who will be blamed for [its] defeat, if it is defeated, is the
Republican party. I just want to point out to the Republicans not to fall into
this trap."[30]

In mobilizing opposition to the bill, Smith schemed to introduce crippling amendments that would emasculate it. And he had the conservative
coalition to back him up. According to one member, this is what he planned:
as the civil rights bill moved to a critical stage, a conservative Democrat
would telephone a "hard core" of about fifteen members[31] to say: "Okay, we
got a bill coming up. Let's all get together and see what we're going to do on
it." They then would meet in one of their offices with Judge Smith "in charge.
He was the man we all looked to for leadership." Together they would plot
their strategy.[32]

As it actually developed, the group held a caucus and proceeded to examine every line of the measure, pausing at unacceptable sections to discuss how to handle them. The entire operation was "somewhat like a
religion, with the Judge being the chief missionary."[33] Once a consensus

was reached, the "hard core" members agreed to contact other representatives in their state delegations. Following that, they contacted Republican conservatives, led by Charles Halleck of Indiana, a disagreeable, abrasive individual who had ingratiated himself with many southern Democrats, usually by drinking bourbon with them. They would try to discern how much support they could expect from the Republicans and make their plans accordingly.

On the liberal side of civil rights, the leaders included Bolling, Emanuel Celler, James Roosevelt and Charles Diggs among Democrats, and Jacob Javits and Kenneth Keating of New York and Hugh Scott of Pennsylvania among Republicans.

Since liberals were notorious for their absentee record in the House, Smith thought he knew how to cripple the bill with amendments. But first he demanded frequent half-hour quorum calls, sometimes as many as thirty in a single day. Then he assigned sixteen representatives to introduce twenty amendments. On the final day of discussion for the amendments, after which a vote would be taken, he set one hour for the debate. Southern supporters of the amendments rose one after the other to claim a portion of the allotted debating time. However, instead of using the time to speak, each one simply yielded back their time, thus shortening the debate and bringing the amendments to a vote a good deal earlier than expected. With the liberals missing, the crippling amendments were certain to pass.[34]

Rayburn recognized what was happening. He immediately surrendered the gavel and went looking for Bolling. He found him in the corridor heading for the Democratic cloakroom. In a commanding voice he said, "You'd better get your boys here quickly."[35]

In an instant Bolling knew what the Speaker meant. He also "knew then for the first time that I had been correct in believing that Rayburn would be a supporter of the civil rights bill to guarantee voting rights to Negroes." He looked at Rayburn's face and he realized also that he had better move quickly. "I started running, just as fast as I could run."[36]

Indeed, Rayburn, like a number of other congressmen who initially opposed such legislation, had agonized over segregation and racial inequality and finally agreed with the Supreme Court's Brown decision that segregation was wrong. "If you had been on that Court," Rayburn declared, "you'd have voted exactly as they voted—if you were an honest man." Naturally he was torn. He represented a district in Texas that was strongly pro-segregation. But he always despised those in Congress who were, as he said, "afraid of their districts."[37]

Carl Albert had the same problem as Rayburn, since his district abutted the Speaker's. He asked for advice. "Carl," responded Rayburn, "under the Constitution, every man has a right to vote. You can defend that position before any audience in this country."[38]

Jim Wright of Texas remembered standing behind the rail of the House having a smoke with a colleague, "as we used to do in the old days," when a page came up to him and said, "Mr. Wright, the Speaker wants to see you." So "I went up to the podium. I remember precisely all these years later, almost fifty years . . . what Mr. Rayburn said exactly. He said, 'Jim, I think you want to go for this bill. I know you're receiving a whole manner of secretive letters, threatening you with all sorts of retribution. But I think you're a big enough man to overcome that. And I know you'll be proud in future years that you did.' "[39]

Alert to the real danger that faced the bill, Bolling summoned the whips of the fledgling liberal House Democratic Study Group (DSG) and they rounded up their supporters, who came dashing into the House chamber. The crippling amendments were defeated, one by one, and HR 627 passed the House on July 23, 1956, by a vote of 279 to 126. There were 168 Republicans who voted for it and 24 who voted against, and 111 Democrats voted yes and 102 no.

As understood beforehand, there was no time for the Senate to act before adjournment—a filibuster would have surely occurred—but members of the House on both sides of the aisle could go to the country in the November elections and declare that they had passed civil rights legislation.

The importance of the House Democratic Study Group cannot be emphasized too strongly in the ongoing struggle to safeguard civil rights. Originally led by Representative Eugene J. McCarthy of Minnesota, a number of progressive Democrats banded together in 1956 to win support for not only civil rights but also housing, labor, medical care, and education. Approximately eighty of them read a "liberal manifesto" into the *Congressional Record* in 1957, calling for strong Democratic leadership to overcome the conservative coalition that dominated the House through the seniority system. They intended to establish a record with which to challenge Republicans in the next national election. Not surprisingly, Speaker Rayburn opposed the establishment of the DSG as a direct challenge to his leadership in the House.[40] Carl Albert kept his distance. "My position as whip," he later wrote, "ruled out any personal participating," something many liberals held against him when he ran for the Speakership later on.[41]

Toward the end of the 1959 session, reported Albert, six liberals called a meeting of northern and western Democrats to discuss "imperative issues of concern" and forty representatives showed up. It was like a revival, he said, in which member after member rose "to confess his own failure or frustration and to signify his own willingness to work for the common good." Soon the revival turned into an organized religion. Calling themselves the Democratic Study Group as a liberal response to the conservatism of seniors and southern Democrats, their numbers swelled to 125. They elected Lee Metcalf of Montana as chairman of their organization and surrounded him with experienced assistants, including vice chairmen John Blatnik of Minnesota, Frank Coffin of Maine, William Green of Pennsylvania and James Roosevelt of California, along with Frank Thompson of New Jersey as secretary. At one point, Sam Rayburn was heard muttering to himself that if these smart young kids wanted to take him on, he would "tear them to pieces."[42] Actually they wanted to cooperate with the Speaker and help him, not take him on. It was the conservative power structure of the House they wanted to challenge. But they disapproved of Rayburn's style of arranging informal coalitions between southern conservatives and northern liberals.

Richard Bolling of Missouri, "a regular at the Board of Education" who "became something of a protégé of Speaker Rayburn" and "was a steady champion of liberal causes," served as a link for the DSG with the Democratic leadership. The DSG frequently turned to him "as a source of important counsel," as they continued their fight for social equality.[43]

Although a civil rights law had not been enacted, the House did pass and the Senate agreed to several other important pieces of legislation. On June 29, 1956, the Highway Act was passed, which authorized over $30 billion for construction of a 41,000-mile interstate superhighway program over the next thirteen years. This was the largest public works project ever attempted, and it effectively reshaped the physical geography of the United States. Congress also approved water conservation bills, school and hospital construction bills and a health bill that supported medical research.[44]

A month after the enactment of the Highway Act, President Eisenhower signed a joint resolution passed by Congress declaring the U.S. national motto to be "In God We Trust."

Despite the fact that he had suffered a serious heart attack, Eisenhower decided to run for a second term. On October 11, 1956, Democrat Adam Clayton Powell, Jr., of New York endorsed Eisenhower because of his civil rights stand, as did many other black leaders and voters. They gave notice that their support for either party would depend on their records, particularly in the field of civil rights.[45]

Once again Stevenson carried the Democratic banner and was badly defeated when Eisenhower took all but seven southern states. Interestingly, Democratic majorities were elected in both houses of Congress. In the House the Democrats had 234 seats to 201 for the Republicans, a gain of four seats. Eisenhower became the first candidate to win the presidency since the election of 1848 whose party failed to carry either house. But then, said Carl Albert, "everyone knew that the general's famous battle jacket had no coattails at all."[46]

In the House there were three groups of Democrats: one group represented the last of the old-time big-city machines whose members were mostly northern and eastern. Their ethnic and working-class constituencies regularly chalked up huge majorities at the polls. A machine boss like Tom O'Brien of Chicago, said Albert, could sit silently on the House floor "and with the slightest nod of his head decide the fate of many a bill; he did not have to say a word to do it." A second group comprised a relatively small but very vocal liberal contingent who liked to get up and speak at the slightest provocation. Usually northern, western and young, such as Eugene McCarthy of Minnesota and Lee Metcalf of Montana, they formed the DSG and advocated strengthening civil rights legislation and increasing social security. Most of them were mavericks, "unwilling to scar their convictions with the branding iron of compromise." The third group, and probably the most important because of their number, were southerners. Some sixteen southern states provided more Democrats than all the other states combined. They elected 134 of the 234 Democrats in the House. Once elected, these representatives were returned every two years, election after election, and, as a result, they held some of the most important committee chairmanships. In 1956, eight of the fifteen members of the Ways and Means Committee were senior southern Democrats. Thus, their hold in the House "was a hold upon the lever that governed the country."[47]

During his tenure as chairman of the Armed Services Committee, Carl Vinson determined virtually every penny spent by the Army, Navy, Air Force and Marines.

Lyndon Johnson liked to tell a story about when he was in the House and served on the Armed Services Committee, chaired by Carl Vinson of Georgia, a particularly strong minded individual who ran the committee "with no tolerance at all for interference." On one occasion Johnson tried to ask an admiral a question during a hearing, whereupon Vinson slammed his gavel down on the desk and declared the question out of order. Now Johnson was not the man to be bullied this easily. He protested that after serving three terms in the House he ought to be allowed to "ask a simple question." Vinson paused for a moment and then said, "All right, but just one."[48]

Together with Senator Richard Russell of the Senate Armed Services Committee—also from Georgia—Vinson determined every penny to be spent by the Army, the Navy, the Air Force and the Marines of the United States, along with the exact location and appropriation of every military base in every congressional district in the country. He exercised a tight-fisted control of the committee. When the Military Affairs Committee and the Naval Affairs Committee were merged to form the Armed Services Committee in 1946, Vinson asserted his authority as chairman by abolishing all subcommittees, dividing the committee into three groups and reserving to himself the right to assign bills to any one of the three. Since he decided who would introduce important bills to the House, it became the "lever he used to keep the thirty-seven members of the committee in line." Moreover, said Carl Albert, "his great expertise, his awesome intelligence, his fierce willpower—these allowed him to make the most of it."[49]

It was even worse with the Rules Committee. When the members revolted against "Uncle Joe" Cannon, barred him from membership on this committee, and decided that its members would be appointed and its chairman chosen like those of any other committee, they not only made it independent of the Speaker but independent of the members themselves. The committee then became the prize that any strong-willed group outside the elected leadership could seize. The group who won it, said Albert, "were

Clarence Cannon chaired the Appropriations Committee and fought every effort of the Senate to initiate legislation involving the expenditure of federal funds.

those brilliant practitioners of congressional politics. They were the southern Democrats."[50] And that group was sworn to prevent any civil rights legislation as violations of states' rights, be it federal aid bills for school construction or public housing. If Adam Clayton Powell tacked on an antisegregation amendment to a bill, as he frequently did, that bill was blocked. "In practice, then, that one committee could serve not as a traffic light but as an execution chamber."[51]

After his reelection, President Eisenhower urged Congress in his January 1957 State of the Union address to pass the civil rights bill as approved by the House. With the administration and the Democratic House leadership of the 85th Congress fully behind the bill, Rayburn set about winning swift House passage. The bill, once more, went to the Judiciary Committee, and it was reported out on April 1, 1957. There was no roll call taken in the committee on the final vote, according to Chairman Celler, but the margin was approximately three-fifths to two-fifths. The southern members succeeded in stripping the attorney general of authority to bring suit for damages on behalf of alleged victims of discrimination. But they left intact his authority to sue for an injunction in such cases.[52]

This was now HR 6127, and it went to the Rules Committee, which met on April 8. Bolling insisted the committee hold immediate hearings and clear the bill for full House action. He also told the House of a rumor circulating on the Hill that the conservative coalition planned to delay any decision on civil rights until next year so that the differences among Democrats—southerners versus liberals—could be put on record during a midterm election year.

Despite Smith's urging to postpone action, the committee voted him down, and the Judge scheduled hearings to begin after the Easter recess, a month away. The bill was so threatening to the south that Smith conferred secretly and regularly in his office with other southern Congressmen from both houses.

Hearings began on May 2, with Smith employing one tactic after another to delay action as long as he could. To maneuver around him, the Democratic leadership wanted the committee to call for a special meeting so that the bill could get to the floor, an action necessitating the approval of seven of its members. The Democrats agreed, except for Colmer and Smith, but not the Republicans. The seventh vote was lacking. Only when the leadership of the Republican party decided to apply pressure did Hugh Scott of Pennsylvania provide the seventh vote. The meeting was held and on May 21 the four northern Democrats and four northern Republicans voted 8 to 4 to give the bill an open ruling, which allowed it to go to the House. The rule also permitted four days of debate and unlimited amendments. On June 5, the House, by a roll call vote of 291 to 117, agreed to adopt the open rule on the bill.

But Smith had one more trick up his sleeve. His purpose was to force the bill back to the Judiciary Committee so that the entire process would have to be repeated. He and Colmer persuaded New York Republican William Miller, who had supported the 1956 civil rights bill, to propose recommittal. In return, the two southerners promised to block passage of a federal waterpower bill for Niagara Falls which would hurt several private utilities that supported Miller.

Smith rose on a point of order. As chairman of the Rules Committee he had failed, as was customary, to notify the parliamentarian and the Speaker beforehand about the requirement that every change in the bill to existing law be specified. The bill must be returned to committee. But the trick failed. Rayburn declared that the so-called changes were not changes at all but additions to existing law. Had Smith succeeded in his plan, the bill would have been rerouted through the Rules Committee and surely would have died that session.

The southern strategy for defeating the bill now rested on adding amendments that would *strengthen* its protection of civil rights and thereby render it unacceptable in the Senate. But Bolling believed that if the bill had enough sacrificial provisions that the Senate could attack and eliminate—which would later allow them to explain to their constituents that the bill in its final form was much weaker than the House version—then an effective bill could get through. In which case, said Bolling, southern Senators "could soothe their inflamed segregationist constituencies and possibly feel satisfied enough to refrain from a filibuster."[53]

Again southerners got a freshman Republican from the north to offer an amendment requiring a trial by jury in civil rights contempt cases.[54] This would guarantee that no one in the South would ever be convicted, since white jurors would be the necessary peers of the defendants on trial. Representative Adam Clayton Powell argued that there could be no effective civil rights bill "if the amendment—trial by jury—is in it, and no one knows this better than the gentlemen of the South."[55]

The amendment failed, and HR 6127 passed on June 18, 1957, by a roll call vote of 286 to 126, with Republicans almost unanimously in favor, 168 to 19, and the Democrats almost evenly split, 118 to 107. In substance the bill matched that of the measure passed in 1956. Passage was due mainly to the solid support of Republicans, and most especially the work of Joseph Martin, Hugh Scott of Pennsylvania and Leo E. Allen of Illinois, the ranking Republican on the Rules Committee, and the DSG.

Judge Smith was furious and denounced both political parties for conspiring "to win votes of the negro race by getting the credit of this assault upon the white race."[56] On July 25, 1957, he made one last effort to kill the civil rights bill, but it passed by a roll call vote of 208 to 203.

The measure then went to the Senate, where Lyndon B. Johnson, the majority leader, played a crucial role in winning passage. First, he had to prevent an *organized* filibuster, and he did that by assuring his colleagues that he would hold around-the-clock sessions if one was attempted. Many southerners were reluctant to filibuster because it might lead to strengthening cloture* procedures for ending filibusters permanently. And that they could never abide. They also recognized the widespread support for civil rights legislation, particularly now that the Eisenhower administration was strongly behind it. Then Johnson worked out a deal with his fellow southerners. He labored "tirelessly from faction to faction . . . quietly, almost in secret." By amending HR 6127 and stripping it of the most offensive features he believed that what remained might be reasonably acceptable to many of his southern associates. What he did was craft an amendment requiring a jury trial in cases of voting rights, and he deleted the section which gave the attorney general power to institute suits in school desegregation cases. In other words only one provision of the civil rights bill would be enacted: voting, with a jury trial attached. The other parts were too distasteful for southerners to swallow. Naturally southerners would vote against the bill but would also decline staging a filibuster. Richard Russell of Georgia warned of a possible danger in the unamended measure. In a notable speech he gave on the Senate floor on July 2, he expressed the fears of most of his southern colleagues when he said that under the unamended act, the President, or anyone designated by him, could employ the military to enforce judicial rulings as they did during Reconstruction. Southern entrepreneurs who operated separate dining establishments and places of amusement who refused to conform to an injunction issued by the courts "could be jailed . . . and kept in jail until they either rotted or until they conformed to the edict to integrate their place of business."[57]

Thanks to Johnson and Russell, the amended version of the measure was adopted by the Senate, 52 to 38, and returned to the House in August. It went forthwith to the Rules Committee, where the gatekeeper, Howard W. Smith, was waiting to lock it up and throw away the key. Although by this time the administration and a large contingent of congressmen were demanding immediate action, Smith took it upon himself to disappear and therefore prevent a committee meeting. One rumor insisted that he had gone back to his farm in Virginia "to check on a burned barn." That prompted Leo Allen, senior Republican on the Rules Committee, to remark that he "knew Judge Smith was opposed to the civil rights bill. But I didn't think he would commit arson to defeat it."[58]

Actually, Smith told the committee's legal counsel, T. M. Carruthers, "I

---

*A parliamentary device to end a filibuster. At the time, to invoke cloture required the approval by two-thirds of Senate members present and voting.

am going away for several days, but I'm not going to tell you where I'm going so then you won't have to lie because I know Mr. Rayburn will be calling
you before I get out of town to see where I am." Later he admitted he had
gone to North Carolina to visit his daughter and her family, who were on
vacation. "Things were pretty hot up here, I'll admit that," he chuckled,
"and they were sort of getting under my skin and everybody else had had a
vacation—I hadn't had any and I just up and left here. . . . [It was] a lot of
good fun."[59]

Ten days later Smith returned, and before he was prepared to consider
releasing the bill from his committee, he set about negotiating a deal with
Speaker Rayburn. He would send forth the weakened civil rights bill in
exchange for the Speaker's agreement to kill several pending bills providing
federal aid to various projects. And so the deal was struck.

Much as they hated the amended bill, members of the House recognized that the Senate version was the only bill that could realistically get
through the Congress—whereupon opposition crumbled. On August 27, by
a vote of 279 to 97, the House approved the Senate bill but instituted one
change that Senator Johnson had offered, namely that judges might try minor voting rights offenses without a jury.

The bill then went back to the Senate, where Strom Thurmond waged a
one-man filibuster that lasted twenty-four hours and eighteen minutes, the
longest filibuster in Senate history. But it was another lost cause. Not another southerner joined him. When Thurmond finally ended his marathon
speech and sat down, the Senate passed the revised bill on August 29 by a
vote of 60 to 15. President Eisenhower signed it into law on September 9,
1957.[60]

The Civil Rights Act of 1957 created a Civil Rights Division in the Department of Justice and set up a Commission on Civil Rights. It empowered
the attorney general to seek court injunctions against those who attempted
to deprive citizens of their voting rights. Those accused would be tried by a
jury of their peers. It was a weak bill and proved to be all but useless. Discriminatory election practices continued in the south unabated. Those registrars accused of violating the law were found not guilty by all-white juries.
In addition, the number of registered black voters did not increase significantly over the next several years. Still, Congress had at last enacted a civil
rights bill, the first such since 1875. And, as Johnson said very graphically,
"Once you break the virginity, it'll be easier the next time."[61]

Five days before the President signed the bill, the first outright defiance
of the Supreme Court ruling in the Brown case occurred on September 3 in
Little Rock, Arkansas, when the governor, Orval E. Faubus, called out the
National Guard in an attempt to prevent the integration of the high school.
Much as Eisenhower deplored the Brown decision, he could not allow defi-
ance of national authority to go unchecked, so he federalized the National

Guard and dispatched regular army troops to reopen the school and keep order. The very thing Senator Russell feared in the unamended Civil Rights Act had occurred. Even without the dreaded sections of the bill, the President had used his authority as commander in chief to compel obedience to a court order. It was now obvious that the rights of African-Americans would be protected by the federal government, employing military force if necessary. It was also obvious that discrimination based on race in whatever form was legally over.

Judge Smith tried to limit the Supreme Court's power to strike down state laws under the doctrine of federal legislative preemption.* He introduced a bill known as HR 3 that would counteract, he said, the "symptom of a dangerous disease that threatened to destroy completely the sovereignty of the states." The bill was first reported by the House Judiciary Committee on July 3, 1956, and passed by the House two weeks later but ultimately died in the Senate.[62]

It would take several more years before a more effective civil rights bill would be passed. But as a result of the 1957 Civil Rights Act, the initial opposition to the admission of Hawaii as a new state in the Union dissipated. That opposition was based on the fear by southerners of admitting a state with a majority of non-Caucasians and the likelihood of their representatives in the House and Senate favoring civil rights legislation. There was also concern that admission would upset the political balance in Congress. But when Alaska was admitted on July 7, 1958, the opposition to Hawaii faded. It joined the Union as a state on August 21, 1959.

A new Civil Rights Act, which provided criminal penalties for bombings or other actions which attempted to obstruct court orders was passed in 1960. But it was not a major advance against racial discrimination. It was more an expression of "responsible moderation," advocated by Johnson, one he believed would be a victory for "fair play" and "common sense."[63] The 23rd Amendment to the Constitution was also passed and ratified in 1961, by which citizens of the District of Columbia (predominantly African-American) were granted the right to vote for President and Vice President.

IN LATE 1958, thanks to the determined efforts of Speaker Rayburn, the extension of the east front of the Capitol was begun. The weight of the dome on the portico and the crumbling exterior sandstone necessitated this repair and reconstruction, despite the objections of preservationists who regarded the east front as having enormous historic importance, starting

---

*This doctrine is based on the fact that the Constitution is the supreme law of the land. State law in conflict with it is invalid. HR 3 would limit this federal right of preemption under certain circumstances.

with the inauguration of President Andrew Jackson, and therefore should not be desecrated. Still, the danger of falling masonry and the visible cracks in the exterior that had been patched with cement convinced Rayburn to take the lead in winning approval for the extension. The money was appropriated in 1955, but the Speaker suffered bitter criticism for his efforts to get the rebuilding started.

The east front was extended by 33 feet, thereby allowing 90 additional rooms to be constructed. By faithfully replicating in marble the design of the original portico, the setting of this historic site was preserved. This reconstruction of the east front and the repair of the dome was completed in time for the inauguration of President John F. Kennedy on January 20, 1961.[64]

IN THE MEANTIME, a new potential threat to the country's security suddenly developed. The race into space with Russia began when the Soviet Union launched its first satellite, Sputnik, in the fall of 1957. Congress responded with the passage of the National Aeronautic and Space Act of 1958 that created a civilian authority to direct the nation's scientific efforts to explore space. Military projects, however, remained with the Department of Defense.

When John F. Kennedy won the presidency over Richard Nixon in 1960 by just over 118,000 popular votes, he became an ardent advocate of space exploration. He also intended to institute a program that would "get the country moving again" and would start off by asking for an expanded housing program, federal aid to education and a higher minimum wage. These bills had been introduced in the House over the past two years, and each one, according to Carl Albert, "died a graceless death in the Rules Committee at the hands of Judge Smith and his gang of five."[65]

In the House, at the start of the first session of the 87th Congress on January 3, 1961, there were 263 Democrats and 174 Republicans. The Senate had 64 Democrats and 36 Republicans. Rayburn was Speaker and McCormack majority leader, but Joseph Martin had been ousted as minority leader by Charles Halleck at the beginning of the 86th Congress in January 1959, mostly because of the disastrous midterm election of 1958 when Republicans lost forty-seven seats in the House and the Democrats gained forty-nine. Besides, Martin was seen by his Republican colleagues as lacking in aggressiveness and having too close a relationship with Rayburn. It was reported that Rayburn was once asked to campaign against Martin in Massachusetts. "Speak against Martin," Rayburn snapped. "Hell, if I lived up there, I'd vote for him."[66] So Martin was replaced with Halleck, who was known as a "gut-fighter."

Under the circumstances the Democratic leadership in the House then asked itself, "Could we meet our obligations to the House and the nation" and legislate President Kennedy's program "with an independent and hostile Rules Committee?" To address the problem and answer the question, Rayburn asked Smith on December 31, 1960, to come to his office, where he informed him that he intended to enlarge the Rules Committee by three members. After all, he declared, the new President had a right to have his program considered by the House. The three new members would include two Democrats and one Republican. But such a change in a committee required the approval of the entire House and he therefore wanted Smith to introduce the appropriate resolution in order to avoid a floor fight.

Not surprisingly, Smith rejected the suggestion flat out. He said he stood ready to combat any move to alter the committee or "its ability to block any legislation that he felt would bring ruin to America—by building schoolrooms, for example."[67]

Rayburn probably expected such a response. So he thanked Smith for coming and the Judge left. Later that day Rayburn called another meeting in his office that included McCormack, Albert, Bolling, Lew Deschler, the House parliamentarian, and a few Texas congressmen. He related his meeting with Smith and repeated his insistence that the President's program must have a fair opportunity for success.

But he was reminded that one other means of changing the committee was possible. William Colmer, the Mississippi Democrat who regularly voted with Republicans on the committee to form a conservative majority, had not supported the Democratic presidential ticket and could be removed from Rules and replaced by a loyal Democrat. In the past, the Republican caucus had punished Republicans who supported Roosevelt's Bull Moose campaign in 1912 and Robert La Follette's Progressive candidacy in 1924 by stripping them of their seniority and replacing them on important committees. Such a move required the action of only the Democratic Caucus that Rayburn controlled and not the entire House. It was up to Rayburn to decide.

President Kennedy tried to help, and learned an important lesson in the process. He met with the congressional leadership and, after dispensing with some routine business, turned to the subject on everyone's mind. "Now, I'd like to talk about the Rules Committee," he announced.

Suddenly, the flat of Rayburn's hand hit the table with a resounding smack. It was like a gunshot. "No, sir," he shouted. "That is House business, and the House of Representatives will decide that. The White House has no business there at all."[68]

Everyone in the room froze. They were shocked. No one moved or said a word. Kennedy realized his mistake and quickly moved on to another topic.

But every House member soon learned how their Speaker had stood up to the President and reasserted their rights.

Having made up his mind on the strategy to follow, Rayburn called in a group of liberal Democrats on January 2, 1961, and informed them that Judge Smith had refused to allow the expansion of his committee and that therefore he, the Speaker, would recommend to the Democratic Caucus that William Colmer be removed from Rules and replaced with a loyal Democrat. He gave them this information, knowing it would be leaked immediately to the press. But that was part of his plan.

Southerners, naturally, were outraged. The Judge even offered to release the first five Kennedy proposals if Rayburn would back off. But the Speaker refused, pointing out that the President would undoubtedly have a lot more than five bills to offer. As a matter of fact, in the three years of his presidency, Kennedy sent down 1,034 recommendations.[69]

Moderate Democrats begged for a compromise. They did not want to "have to choose between Howard and Sam." So the "Swamp Fox," as he was sometimes called, Carl Vinson of Georgia, the tough chairman of the Armed Services Committee, went to the Speaker and suggested that Rayburn drop the idea of purging Colmer in return for enlarging the Rules Committee by three members. "That was exactly where Mr. Rayburn had started," snickered Carl Albert, "and, I suspect, exactly where he wanted it decided. The purge threat had served to make the expansion seem moderate."[70]

And so the fight was taken to the Caucus. Rayburn worked diligently to round up support for expansion. "He monitored, directed, and coordinated all of our efforts," said the whip. He called in a lot of IOUs, and with others he said simply, "The question under discussion is a simple one. Are you for the Speaker or are you for that old man from Virginia." The old man from Virginia was actually two years younger than Rayburn. Freshmen Representatives knew instinctively that opposing the Speaker was not an intelligent way to start a House career.

To no one's surprise, the House Democratic Caucus meeting on January 17 approved by a voice vote the proposal to enlarge the committee. The Republican Conference six days later voted overwhelmingly against it. Charles Halleck angrily argued with those he believed to be wavering. Meanwhile, Vice President Johnson "cruised the Capitol corridors like a one-man enforcer." He pinned one Congressman against a wall and said, "If Sam Rayburn is hurt, his blood will be on your hands."[71]

Precisely at noon, January 31, 1961, "Mr. Sam" entered the chamber and mounted the steps to the Speaker's rostrum amid a thunderous round of applause from the members on seeing the bald head and glowing face of the presiding officer. Every seat in the chamber was filled, the galleries crowded with visitors seated on steps and standing against the walls. The room rocked with shouts and foot stamping. No Speaker had been given a standing ovation in the 172 years Congress had been in existence. But on

that day, "for the first time ever, this Speaker entered to a standing ovation."[72]

Rayburn gaveled for order. H. R. Gross of Iowa, a "Republican gadfly,"
demanded a roll call, after which the battle began. A resolution was offered
to increase the Rules Committee to fifteen and, when Judge Smith rose to
speak, an absolute hush enveloped the room. In the course of his remarks
he pledged to "cooperate with the Democratic leadership of the House of
Representatives just as long and just as far as my conscience will permit
me."[73]

At that the House erupted in laughter which shocked and angered the
old man. He stood quietly for a moment and then lashed back. "Some of
these gentlemen who are laughing maybe do not understand what a conscience is. They are entitled to that code, and I think I am entitled to
mine."

Halleck added his fear that "the floodgates will be let down" if the resolution passed "and we will be overwhelmed with bad legislation."

Then the Speaker rose from his seat, turned the gavel over to Albert,
and slowly descended to the well to address the House amid another burst
of applause and cheers, mostly by Democrats. He unfolded a sheet of paper
and began to read. "Whether you vote with me today or not, I want to say
that I appreciate your uniform kindness and courtesy that has been displayed toward me." He looked at his colleagues and, in the opinion of many,
received back the warmth of their admiration and affection.

"This issue, in my mind, is a simple one," he continued. "We have
elected to the Presidency a new leader. He is going to have a program that
he thinks will be in the interest of and for the benefit of the American
people. . . . I think this House should be allowed on great measures to work
its will, and it cannot work its will if the Committee on Rules is so constituted as not to allow the House to pass on those things. . . . Let us move this
program. Let us be sure we can move it. And the only way that we can be
sure . . . in my opinion, my beloved colleagues, is to adopt this resolution
today."[74]

When he finished he returned to the rostrum, retrieved the gavel,
slammed it to the table and said, "The Clerk will call the roll." The entire
chamber tensed as the vote proceeded. The first three answered no, followed by the next two who shouted aye. Back and forth it went. Sometimes
one or the other side would advance by two or three votes; sometimes the
vote was tied. When the clerk reached Jim Wright of Texas, Mr. Sam led by
one with twelve left to vote.

When the tally ended, the clerk handed his card to the Speaker. Rayburn glanced at it and then announced, "On this vote, there being 217 ayes
and 212 noes, the resolution is adopted."

The House went wild. The cries, shouts, applause and foot stamping was deafening. Of the 217 majority, 195 were Democrats, including 47 southerners led by Carl Vinson, and 22 Republicans. Those opposed amounted to 64 Democrats, all but one of them southerners, and 148 Republicans. When asked why he, a southerner, favored the change, Carl Vinson responded: "Now the way I look at that proposal, we weren't voting to pack the Rules Committee. It was already packed, and I was in favor of unpacking it"[75]

Amid the cheers and shouts, those who had lost sat glumly in their seats. Judge Smith showed no expression and slowly walked out of the chamber. When asked by reporters why he had lost, he responded, "We didn't have the votes." He accepted "defeat gracelessly," said Carl Albert. For one thing he refused to provide the three new members of his committee with chairs similar to those used by the others. He provided straight-back chairs on which spectators sat. When the member from Alabama, Carl Elliott, received a chair from his constituents that was larger and fancier than the chairman's with a brass plate affixed and Elliott's name inscribed on it, Smith finally gave in and ordered the purchase of three more chairs identical with those of the other members. In a real sense Smith's defeat signaled the end of the obstructionist power of the Rules Committee.

"Howard Smith was a gentleman of conscience and a legislator of brilliance," reported Albert, "but in the end he was just a mean old man."[76]

16

The Great Society, Voting Rights and Vietnam, 1961–1969

THE DECADE OF the 1960s was a period of unimaginable violence. The nation suffered one of the most staggering jolts to the body politic when a young, handsome and vibrant President was assassinated, followed not much later by the assassination of his younger brother who was campaigning for President. Then an outstanding leader of the civil rights movement was assassinated. City streets were bloodied with the fallen victims of racial prejudice and hatred.

THE DECADE OPENED with the death of a beloved Speaker. Sam Rayburn commemorated his 16 years and 273 days as Speaker on Monday, June 12, 1961, and the House had duly honored him. "At high noon on June 12," he told one reporter, "I will have been Speaker twice as long as anybody else," doubling Henry Clay's service record of 356½ days. [1]

By prearrangement Rayburn relinquished the chair to Charles Halleck, the minority leader, following the roll call which showed that 344 members were present. The majority leader, John McCormack, rose and offered a resolution which the clerk read. "Resolved, That the House of Representatives hereby extends its heartiest congratulations to its beloved Speaker . . . [and] expresses its deep appreciation . . . for his impartiality, integrity and outstanding parliamentary skill in presiding over this House." McCormack read a letter from President Kennedy, which said in part: "immeasurable is the respect, esteem, and affection which all of us who have served with you hold for you today."

Then a parade of representatives added to the encomiums, starting with Joseph Martin, who congratulated Rayburn for his "unfailing fairness and courtesy to the Members on both sides of the aisle." The minority whip, Leslie C. Arends of Illinois, said that the Speaker "always recognized and defended the rights of the minority." Ben F. Jensen of Iowa pointed out that Rayburn cared for new members and was "fair, reasonable, courteous and helpful" to them. "For that we love him." What was truly remarkable was that all acknowledged the civility that characterized House proceedings under Rayburn's control, even during the most heated debates.

When the words of admiration and affection by the members ended, Rayburn rose to speak. With tears in his eyes he carefully stepped down from the rostrum and faced the smiling faces of his colleagues.

"Members of the House of Representatives," he began, "if I were given to emotional outbursts, a smoldering emotion would break forth in me now, because I am one who has deep emotions and am appreciative of friendships and the loyalties of other people as I trust I have demonstrated through the years my love and my loyalty to friends, to causes and to my country. . . . The House of Representatives is, has been, and if you and I have our way will continue to be, the greatest legislative forum upon the earth. We have kept it that way and I trust those who follow us will know the history of our institutions and keep this Government free."[2]

Many in the audience noted how physically fit Rayburn looked, despite his seventy-nine years. On a recent trip to his home in Bonham, Texas, he was given a thorough checkup by his personal physician.

"You'll live to be 106," the doctor assured him.

"I'll settle for 104," Rayburn told a friend. "It's because I'm having my way."[3]

Speaker Sam Rayburn died of cancer five months later at his home on November 16, 1961. "He's the greatest of all the Speakers I've ever known," declared Jim Wright. He "was kind of heart. He wanted to be helpful to his colleagues." And he was unique.[4]

Three months later the House and Senate held a similar ceremony for Carl Hayden, Democrat from Arizona, because he was the first person to serve for fifty years as a member of Congress. The eighty-four-year-old senator began his congressional career in the House on February 19, 1912, and later moved to the Senate. He retired on October 14, 1968.

The careers of these men demonstrated how far things had changed in the House. In the beginning most representatives served only a few terms and moved on. By the late twentieth century, congressmen made a career of serving in Washington.

•   •   •

THESE CELEBRATIONS BRIEFLY turned attention away from increased
tension on account of the space race between the United States and the
Soviet Union and the continued fears in America over Russian expansion.
Although President Kennedy asked for an increase of $126 million to the
$1.1 billion Eisenhower had requested for NASA, the House Science and
Astronautics Committee thought the amount should be higher, but was
told by the head of NASA that this country's space program was "not keyed
to an all-out crash basis to provide maximum rocket lift at the earliest possible moment."[5] Nevertheless, the committee added another $127 million to
the President's request. The wisdom of this increased appropriation seemed
apparent when the Russians put the first man, Yuri Gagarin, in space on
April 12, 1961. Not until May 5 did Alan Shepard, Jr., complete a suborbital,
three-hundred-mile flight, aboard a Redstone rocket. Twenty days later
President Kennedy addressed a special joint-session of Congress and declared that "this nation should commit itself to achieving the goal, before
this decade is out, of landing a man on the moon and returning him safely
to earth."[6] Then, on February 2, 1962, John Glenn orbited the earth three
times in four hours. Not until July 1969 did Neil Armstrong and Edwin
Aldrin succeed in reaching the moon aboard a gigantic Saturn rocket and
walk on its surface, as television viewers around the world watched. They
planted an American flag on the site and left a plaque that read "We came
in peace for all mankind."

But the space race was only one segment of the U.S-Soviet rivalry. On
December 2, 1961, three weeks after the death of Sam Rayburn, Fidel Castro disclosed in a national broadcast speech that he was a Marxist and that
Cuba would adopt a communist system. The revelation gravely disturbed
many Americans because the island was just a scant ninety miles from the
coastline of Florida. American property on the island was seized and Castro became an ally of Russia. Before leaving office, Eisenhower had approved a plan for the invasion of Cuba by anti-Castro Cubans trained and
supplied by American arms and money and protected by U.S. aircraft. But
it was President Kennedy—on the advice of his military and intelligence
officials who assured him that Castro did not possess sufficient forces to
repulse an invasion and that the Cuban people would join the revolt—who
gave approval for the invasion to begin on April 17, 1961. Neither assumption proved to be correct, and the invasion at the Bay of Pigs resulted in
total disaster. Kennedy refused to provide air cover and as a result over a
thousand invaders were captured, tried and sentenced to thirty years in
prison. Moreover, Premier Khrushchev threatened to assist Cuba if the
United States did not back off.

The situation worsened dramatically when the Soviets built missile
sites on the island capable of launching nuclear bombs against the United

States. In a televised speech to the nation on October 22, 1962, President Kennedy demanded that the Soviets dismantle the bases and withdraw the missiles. Pending compliance, the President imposed a "quarantine" on Cuba in which U.S. warships would stop and search all ships bound for the island, regardless of nationality, and turn back any carrying military weapons. Fortunately, six days later, Khrushchev ordered the removal of the missile bases, and the likelihood of nuclear war between the two countries was averted.

A year earlier another crisis had arisen on August 13, 1961, when the Soviet-dominated East German government, in defiance of international agreements, closed its border crossings in Berlin. This was immediately followed by the building of the Berlin Wall, an action that separated East and West Berlin for the next twenty-eight years.

THESE EVENTS SEVERELY tested Kennedy's mettle and revealed his inexperience in the conduct of foreign affairs. His relations with Congress also proved deficient in that he was unable to establish his leadership in legislative matters. A young, seemingly vigorous man, who hid his many medical problems from public knowledge, he spoke boldly and called for measures that would combat tyranny, poverty, disease and war. And although the Senate seemed eager to enact the President's "New Frontier" initiative, the House made clear its determination to decide which of Kennedy's several proposals would become law. This renewed intention by the House of becoming the decisive agent in the formulation of national policy—since it was the body closest to the people—resulted, to a large extent, from the continuing commitment to conservative ideas embodied by southern Democrats and northern Republicans.

The President's first defeat at the hands of the House of Representatives came with his proposal for an ambitious federal-aid-to-education bill of $5.6 billion to strengthen and equalize educational opportunities. The money would go toward building schools, raising teachers' salaries and establishing scholarships for needy undergraduate students in colleges and universities. It was just the kind of proposal that drove Judge Smith into a tantrum. He sent a press release to southern newspapers denouncing the measure. "This is not a bill to aid education," he ranted. "It is a bill to aid the NAACP, to complete the subjugation of the Southern states and control the direction and conditions under which our youth is to be educated."[7]

The Catholic bishops asked to share in this educational bonanza, but Kennedy—himself a Catholic—refused, convinced it was unconstitutional. The bishops argued that giving federal aid solely to public schools was discriminatory and defeated the very purpose of improving education throughout the country. The House Education and Labor Committee, under the chairmanship of Adam Clayton Powell, Jr., stepped in and reported an education bill for public school construction and teachers' salaries on June 1, 1961, but a number of Catholics in the House—there were eighty-eight of them at the time—wanted to hold it up until a vote could be held on the extension of the National Defense Education Act (NDEA), which included loans for private schools. The issue of religion, which Kennedy had hoped to avoid, became a controlling factor in this contest, an issue that would rise many times in the future whenever aid to education was proposed.

The Rules Committee, whose membership had been permanently increased to fifteen, then agreed to withhold action on the public school measure until it received a bill to extend the NDEA. Voting to withhold action were five Republicans, two southern Democrats (Smith and Colmer) and two northern Catholic Democrats (James J. Delaney and Thomas P. "Tip" O'Neill).

Chairman Powell worried that the public school bill was so burdened with controversy that it might have to be postponed for a year. "Someone's got to blow the whistle" on the warring factions, he declared, "someone beyond the Committee and the Congress."[8] Obviously that meant the President, but Kennedy was so preoccupied with the crises in foreign affairs that he could exert no real leadership or help.

Once the NDEA bill arrived in the Rules Committee, hearings were held and on July 18, 1961, by a vote of 8 to 7, the committee agreed to table both the education and NDEA bill along with a college measure to support scholarships. Voting to table were five Republicans, two southern Democrats and one northern Catholic Democrat, Delaney. Tip O'Neill voted against tabling. A month later Chairman Powell brought forward a public school aid bill that attempted a compromise. He circumvented the Rules Committee by introducing it on Calendar Wednesday, but the House voted it down, 170 to 242. All else having failed, Powell asked for an extension of the NDEA for two years and this passed the House on September 6 by a vote of 378 to 32. Suspension of the rules by a two-thirds vote permitted the bill to come directly to the House. Kennedy signed it "with extreme reluctance" on October 3.[9]

The failure of the school-aid bill resulted from three factors: southern opposition, the introduction of the religious issue, and the lack of leadership, either in the lower chamber or the White House. Since 1950 three attempts had been made to enact a general school aid bill and all of them had failed.

Howard Smith also railed against Kennedy's use of "back-door spending," that is borrowing from the Treasury in order to finance particular executive agencies. It was a convenient way for agencies to bypass the Appropriations Committees of the House and Senate and exercise greater control over government finances. This practice began in 1932 when Congress authorized the Reconstruction Finance Corporation to borrow money from the Treasury for its lending operation. The money came from the sale of government bonds to the public. Over the years the Treasury had advanced $26.6 billion to the RFC and received $13.6 billion in repayment, the balance of which was written off at the direction of Congress. The present dispute broke out over a depressed-area bill in which a conference committee of the two houses retained the Senate's provision for borrowing $300 million from the Treasury, again bypassing the Appropriations Committees of Congress. In the House, the chairman of the Appropriations Committee, Clarence Cannon, Democrat from Missouri, pounced on it. "Let us vote down this conference report with this silly backdoor shenanigan put in by the Senate. It is financial duplicity. It is fiscal insanity." Smith agreed. "If you establish this precedent you might as well abolish the Appropriations Committee and spend it all through the back door."[10]

In 1961 backdoor spending accounted for $19.6 billion for housing, veterans, foreign relations and agricultural needs. Critics like Smith and Cannon insisted such "shenanigans" violated the Constitution, increased the debt ceiling (the national debt stood at $290 billion) and undermined the American dollar. It would lead to Communism if continued, ranted Cannon.[11]

The fact that it was the Senate's provision that had caused this furor only aggravated a growing dispute that had been going on for several years between the two houses of Congress. Since the Constitution specified that all revenue bills must originate in the House, an argument arose over whether the Senate had the right to initiate appropriations bills, or add funds to House-enacted appropriation measures, or even approve those turned down by the House. The Senate contended that just because appropriations bills originate in the House, that fact did not exclude the upper house from enacting their own appropriations measures. After all, Article 1, Section 7 of the Constitution states that while the House originates revenue bills, the Senate "may propose or concur with Amendments as on other Bills."

Also at issue was where conference committees on appropriations of the House and Senate should meet, and if so who should preside. Carl Hayden, Democrat from Arizona, the eighty-four-year-old chairman of the Senate Appropriations Committee, and the eighty-three-year-old Cannon argued for their respective rights. The dispute became a kind of turf battle, with neither octogenarian willing to give way.

Cannon was very set in his ways, and Carl Albert said it was extremely frustrating dealing with him. The power of the purse, continued Albert, "came awfully close to being *his* power of the purse."[12] Yet Cannon was a bit of a loner and as such never exercised the influence in the House that Howard Smith or Carl Vinson did. Behind his back his colleagues called the pinched-face Cannon the "Mole." When someone accused him of being two-faced, he retorted, "If I had another face, don't you think I'd use it?"[13]

In many ways Carl Hayden was just like him. On April 10, 1962, the House Appropriations Committee adopted a resolution calling for a rotation between the House and Senate sides of the Capitol as sites for the joint conferences. The Senate Appropriations Committee responded with a proposal that half of all appropriations bills originate in the upper house, a proposal that was immediately rejected. As a result, final approval of a number of bills was stalled over the next several months while the two committees tried to iron out their differences. Meanwhile government agencies were running out of money and all appropriations for the fiscal year beginning July 1 were bottled up.[14]

Following the death of Sam Rayburn, the Democrats had elected John W. McCormack their new Speaker in the Democratic Caucus on January 3, 1962. Carl Albert had become majority leader and Hale Boggs of Louisiana the party whip. The Republicans again chose Halleck as minority leader and Leslie C. Arends of Illinois as whip.

As majority leader, McCormack had been "very feisty . . . and an able, gifted debater." But "he mellowed" on becoming Speaker. "They all mellowed when they became Speaker," said Bob Michel of Illinois. "They realized they're the Speaker of the whole House, not just one party."[15] In an effort to reconcile the warring committees, Speaker McCormack suggested that seven members from each committee meet in the Old Supreme Court Chamber. That room seemed to provide neutral ground, since it almost, but not quite, stood halfway between the two houses. Unfortunately, McCormack lacked the political skills of Rayburn to accomplish his goal and his suggestion died aborning. In addition, Cannon wanted the chairmanship of the joint conference committee meetings to be rotated. This was necessary, said Cannon, because the chairman "frequently decides what the compromise will be and that puts us at a great disadvantage. Every bill we have passed for years has been increased by the Senate. They put in every thing they can think of just because some Senator wants it for his state. If we could preside at conferences half of the time, maybe we could cut out half of these increases."[16]

The Senate responded by passing a bill adding over $140 million more to an already approved House appropriations bill and requested that the House agree to it so as to preclude the necessity of a joint conference meeting. The House committee promptly refused the recommendation and instead reported a "continuing resolution," which for one month permitted government agencies to meet their financial obligations for the coming fiscal year. Both houses agreed to it. But that meant Congress had to pass additional continuing resolutions each month to keep the government operating, which it did for August, September and October. At one point, on October 10, 1962, the House adopted a resolution on a roll call vote, 245 to 1, rebuking the Senate for its "infringement on the privileges of this House." Senator Russell sneered at the House's "fantastic interpretations of the Constitution" and offered to debate the question. Senator Wayne Morse of Oregon, a former professor of constitutional law, chided the House for attempting to turn the Senate into "an American House of Lords."[17] The two quarreling committees then set up special five-man teams to resolve the impasse. Russell and Representative Albert Thomas of Texas headed their respective teams and agreed to the creation of a joint committee to examine all the disputed questions and make recommendations at the beginning of the next Congress.

Cannon was particularly critical of the Democratic leadership for failing to support him in his efforts to protect the rights of the House. "Daily we were importuned by the Speaker to yield to the Senate to surrender the prerogatives of the House," he declared on the last official day of the 87th Congress, October 13, 1962. As for our leaders, he went on, "I honor the offices they hold but I cannot endorse the quality of leadership. I have sat under 10 Speakers but I have never seen such biased and inept leadership." As one of its last acts before adjournment, the Senate, by voice vote, adopted a resolution asserting its "coequal power with the House to originate appropriations bills."[18]

Cannon's remarks were a stinging rebuke of McCormack but many members totally agreed. All of which initiated talk that a new and more aggressive Speaker was needed to conduct the affairs of the House. McCormack was regarded by many as uneducated. He had not attended high school. As a youth he read law books at night while working during the day as a $4-a-week office boy for a law firm. In 1913 he passed the Massachusetts bar examination, served in the U.S. Army during World War I, was later elected to the state legislature, and went to the House of Representatives in 1928.

As for the appropriations feud, the House delivered a savage blow to the pride, dignity and prestige of the Senate by passing a supplemental appropriations bill, which included provisions that eliminated the backdoor spending on several programs already in operation, programs the Senate was still debating. Once the supplemental bill passed, the House adjourned for the year, giving the Senate the choice of accepting the bill as it stood or refusing it and thereby terminating the funding of the existing programs.

The Senate was furious. The House had violated what the Senate members regarded as the usual courtesy one house extended toward the other. "We have taken a shellacking," fumed majority leader Senator Mike Mansfield of Montana, "and I think it is outrageous." The minority leader, Everett Dirksen of Illinois, agreed. The action of the House was an "affront to the Senate," one that should not be tolerated. Still, what choice did they have? Reluctantly and angrily, the Senate approved what the House had passed.[19]

Carl Albert managed to find a compromise regarding the place where the conference committee should meet. He and the Capitol architects pored over the building's blueprints and found one location, Room 101 of the East Front extension, that was exactly halfway between the Senate and House wings. Thus, with time and the death of Clarence Cannon on May 14, 1964, the feud between the two chambers slowly petered out. Cannon was replaced as chairman by George H. Mahon of Texas, who had chaired the defense subcommittee since 1949. Senator Hayden chose not to run for re-election in 1968, and with the passing of these two antagonists the bitter and somewhat ridiculous dispute came to an end. Hayden died in 1972.

ANOTHER PROBLEM AND one that would continue for the President was the obstructionism of Howard Smith. So, at the beginning of the session, President Kennedy invited the "gatekeeper" to the White House to discuss his forthcoming program. He outlined his New Frontier proposals and pushed for the creation of a new urban affairs department. Polite as ever, Smith said he had "certain fixed ideas that I could not yield," but after forty-five minutes he agreed to let the House hear an urban affairs bill. Not that it did any good. By the time the 87th Congress adjourned, the conservative coalition had squashed the bill, along with other measures that would create Medicare, provide college aid, and outlaw literacy tests as a device to block blacks from voting.[20]

Of the many programs that President Kennedy hoped to inaugurate as part of his New Frontier initiatives, the establishment of a Peace Corps was one of the first he created by executive order. He won congressional support by virtue of the Peace Corps Act, September 22, 1961, in which $40 million for fiscal 1962 was provided for a group of Americans to work abroad and bring badly needed skills to underdeveloped countries. But the need at home in several areas was also great, particularly among African-Americans. Still Kennedy let it be known that civil rights was not a top priority for his administration. Most likely he needed southern support for his other programs, such as education and housing, and did not wish to provoke them into siding with the opposition.

Events would change his mind. Freedom Riders, intent on assisting African-Americans in the south, were attacked in Alabama and their bus burned by an angry mob. When race riots broke out, the governor was obliged to declare martial law to restore order. The violence escalated as the nation once again became incensed by southern intransigence. But the incident had the salutary effect of providing the sole important action taken by the 87th Congress with respect to civil rights: passage of the 24th Amendment to the Constitution outlawing poll taxes as a requirement for voting. At the time, five states—Virginia, Texas, Alabama, Arkansas and Mississippi—charged a poll tax. The House passed the amendment on August 27, 1962, and it was ratified on January 23, 1964.

Ratification undoubtedly occurred because of the continuing and mounting evidence of violations in the south of voting and desegregation laws. Violence resulted with sit-in protests by civil rights activists who were determined to desegregate lunch counters, hotels, movie theaters, trains and buses. Americans watched as these scenes of anger and frustration and fury were played out and televised around the country. On October 1, 1962, the most important clash of federal–state authority since the Civil War occurred when James Meredith, a twenty-nine-year-old African-American, attempted to register at the University of Mississippi. Governor Ross Barnett tried to prevent the enrollment, and when rioting occurred President Kennedy was obliged to send federal troops to restore order and see that Meredith was enrolled.[21]

The Reverend Dr. Martin Luther King, Jr., and his Southern Christian Leadership Conference initiated nonviolent demonstrations on April 3, 1963, in Birmingham, Alabama, the one city that rigidly controlled the tradition of segregation. "If we can crack Birmingham," declared King, "I am convinced we can crack the South. Birmingham is a symbol of segregation for the entire South."[22] The police commissioner, T. Eugene "Bull" Connor, was prepared to meet these nonviolent demonstrations with force. Once the demonstrations began in the spring of 1963, the police clubbed, arrested and jailed over two thousand African-Americans in Birmingham.

In the House on May 8, Chairman Emanuel Celler opened hearings on civil rights legislation before his Judiciary Committee. "Police clubs and bludgeons, fire hoses and dogs have been used on defenseless school children who were marching and singing hymns," he contended.[23] The motel where King was staying and the home of his brother were bombed, causing the black population to explode in violence. Rocks were thrown and vicious dogs and hoses were turned on the rioters. Kennedy sent in troops and at long last recognized his responsibility to take legislative leadership. Following the rioting, some 127 civil rights bills were introduced in the House. "The cause of desegregation must cease to be a Negro movement, blessed by white politicians from the Northern states," wrote Walter Lippmann in the *Washington Post* on May 28. "It must become a national movement to enforce national laws, led and directed by the National Government."

The country had descended into mayhem and unimaginable turmoil. City streets became the arena for bloody encounters between protesters and local police.

Republican Senators met and agreed that they must take action to realize the equality of rights and opportunities guaranteed by the 14th and 15th Amendments. And on the House floor, the debate centered on proposed legislation to ensure civil rights for all citizens which was regularly interrupted by southern representatives demanding quorum calls.

When Governor George Wallace of Alabama stood in the door to block two black students from registering at the University of Alabama on June 11, 1963, Kennedy federalized Alabama's National Guard and forced Wallace to step aside. He then addressed the nation and said that he would ask the Congress to make a commitment "it has not fully made in this century to the proposition that race has no place in American life or law."[24] The next day, Medgar Evers, the Mississippi civil rights activist, was shot in the back while standing at his own front door. On June 19, 1963, in a special message, Kennedy followed through with the boldest proposal to advance civil rights that had ever been put forward by any President.[25]

With pressure building to address one of the great social ills of the nation, over two hundred thousand black and white activists marched from the Washington Monument to the Lincoln Memorial in Washington on August 28, 1963, where they heard Martin Luther King, Jr., deliver his famous "I have a dream" speech. It was the largest public demonstration ever held in the nation's capital.

But passage of a comprehensive civil rights bill required considerable planning and the implementing of a strategy that could counteract the coalition between southern Democratic Congressmen and northern Republican conservatives. On January 8, 1963, the day before the opening of the 88th Congress, the leadership of the Republican party in the House had been successfully challenged by a group of younger men who felt they should have a larger role in the party's leadership. Newly elected Donald Rumsfeld of Illinois remembered that Robert Griffin of Michigan called him and said, "Don, we want to organize the freshmen Republican Congressmen to support Jerry Ford. He's going to run for Conference Chairman against Charles G. Hoeven of Iowa."[26] Rumsfeld agreed to help and round up supporters. "We went to work and got Gerald Ford elected." These "Young Turks," as they were dubbed, especially resented Charlie Halleck, who was a tough, frequently irascible leader, but they realized that his political skills were too formidable to overcome.

Gerald R. Ford of Michigan was a soft-spoken and extremely amiable young man, a former Big Ten football player whose "prime qualification was that he had few enemies in the House." In engineering their scheme, the Young Turks kept their plotting secret and on the day the Conference met they sprang their coup and elected Ford by a vote of 86 to 78. The Conference then went on to reelect Halleck and Arends to their leadership positions. The disgruntled Hoevens told newsmen that he was "the scapegoat and fall-guy" of liberal Republicans who were determined to take over the leadership. "You'd better be careful," he warned Halleck. Ford has "just taken my job and the next thing you know he'll be after yours."[27]

On August 28, 1963, more than two hundred thousand black and white activists marched from the Washington Monument to the Lincoln Memorial in Washington, where Martin Luther King, Jr., delivered his famous "I have a dream" speech.

Tip O'Neill rather liked Ford. "He was the All-American nice guy. After 5 o'clock, we were the best of friends. Jerry understood, as I did, that democracy works best when the opponents flail away at each other in public, then sit down in a room and work it out."[28]

Since both Halleck and Ford were considered too conservative to help convince Republicans to support the Kennedy civil rights bill, the administration turned to William McCulloch of Ohio, senior Republican on the House Judiciary Committee, who had a record of support for moderate civil rights bills. But McCulloch insisted on two conditions: first, that the House refuse any change to the bill that the Senate might impose, as had happened in 1957; and second, the administration would give Republicans equal credit for passing the civil rights bill.

The agreement was struck and the Judiciary Committee then concluded lengthy hearings and brought forward a bipartisan omnibus civil rights bill on October 29, 1963, that even exceeded the administration's requests in that it authorized the Justice Department to bring suit to desegregate public facilities, and it broadened the power of the Civil Rights Commission. It also established an Equal Employment Opportunity Commission that included most companies and labor unions.

"When I got to the House," remembered Donald Rumsfeld, "the civil rights movement was kind of coming along. And I would go to meetings with a group of Republican Congressmen who would meet with the civil rights leaders. . . . The country really doesn't know it . . . but in fact, there were many more Republicans who voted for the civil rights legislation than Democrats, in both the House and Senate. The critical people were Everett Dirksen in the Senate and Gerald Ford and Bill McCulloch, the ranking member on the Judiciary Committee."[29]

THEN, IN THE midst of this forward movement on civil rights, the nation was jolted by the shocking assassination of President Kennedy in Dallas, Texas, on Friday, November 22, 1963. The temper, mood and political atmosphere in the country underwent a profound change. Kennedy's body was flown back to Washington, where it lay in state in the White House before being moved to the Rotunda of the Capitol and placed on a catafalque that had been used for President Lincoln. Throughout the night and the next morning, thousands of mourners silently filed past the coffin. Heads of state and foreign dignitaries from around the world arrived to pay their respects to the dead President. The brief ceremony included short eulogies by Senate majority leader Mike Mansfield, Speaker of the House John McCormack, and Chief Justice Earl Warren.[30]

The nation wept. It was numb. Who could believe such a tragedy? A man so young, so promising, so beloved. The violence in the United States had reached disastrous proportions. President Lyndon Baines Johnson, who had been sworn into office aboard the airplane that brought Kennedy and his wife back to the capital, addressed Congress on November 27 and said that no eulogy "could more eloquently honor President Kennedy's memory than the earliest possible passage of the civil rights bill for which he fought so long."[31] He later announced that the Speaker, who was next in line to the presidency, would be kept informed on national security matters and invited to attend National Security Council meetings.

One of the major pillars of Kennedy's legislative program, the Clean Air Act of 1963, passed Congress on December 17. It seemed to signify a desire by the members of both houses to show how devastated everyone felt about his death.

In his first State of the Union address at the opening of the second session of the 88th Congress on January 8, 1964, President Johnson declared the beginning of a "War on Poverty" in the United States. And again he pleaded for passage of the civil rights bill.[32] As promised, the Rules Committee began hearings on the bill and voted, 11 to 4, on January 30, 1964, to send it to the floor under an open rule and allot ten hours of debate. Six Democrats and five Republicans voted to clear the bill. The four dissenting votes naturally came from the southern members.

Southern Democrats held a closed-door caucus to devise the strategy to kill or emasculate the bill. Colmer chaired the meeting. It was decided not to attempt delaying tactics for fear of antagonizing their conservative Republican colleagues, but to concentrate their efforts mainly on the public accommodations and employment provisions in the bill, along with the section dealing with the cutting off of federal funds.

During the House debate, Clarence J. Brown of Ohio, the ranking Republican on the Rules Committee, appealed to members to "conduct this debate on so high a plane that we can at least say to our children and grandchildren, we participated in one of the great debates of modern American history and we did it as statesmen and not as quarreling individuals." The arch-conservative William Colmer urged Republicans to remember that "power would be given not only to the President and to the Attorney General, but more than that, given to every bureaucrat in the executive department to cut off all federal aid from your hometown, from your county, and from your state."[33]

But another southern Representative, Charles L. Weltner of Georgia, said that members from his section of the country had a choice of voting "no" and thereby taking a stand "with tradition, safety and futility," or follow another path. "I believe a greater cause can be served. Change, swift and certain, is upon us, and we in the South face some difficult decisions. We can offer resistance and defiance, with their harvest of strife and tumult. . . . Or we can acknowledge the measure as the law of the land. . . . I will add my voice to those who seek reasoned and conciliatory adjustment to a new reality; and finally, I would urge that we at home now move on to the unfinished task of building a new South. We must not remain forever bound to another lost cause."[34]

Die-hard conservatives like Howard Smith called the bill a "monstrosity" and even tried to kill it, he thought, by adding a ban on sex discrimination. A fellow southerner, Carl Elliott of Alabama, declared that "Smith didn't give a damn about women's rights, black rights, equality. He was trying to knock off votes either then or down the line because there was always a hard core of men who didn't favor women's rights."[35] Another southerner, Jamie L. Whitten of Mississippi, noticed "the agreement between the Republican leadership over here and the Democratic leadership over there to pass through this House every last bad provision that is in this bill, of which there are hundreds."

But Smith's amendment was strongly supported by several congresswomen, including Martha Griffiths, a Democrat from Michigan and the first woman on the Ways and Means Committee, Katharine St. George, a Republican from New York and a member of the Rules Committee, Catherine Dean May, a Republican from Washington, and Edna Kelly, a Democrat from Brooklyn. They demanded equal treatment for women, condemned job discrimination against women, and swore that the amendment would not rescind protective labor laws in the states. "Some men in some areas of the country might support legislation which would discriminate against women," declared James Russell Tuten of Georgia, "but never let it be said that a southern gentleman would vote against such legislation." And most of the southern gentlemen in the chamber agreed with him. When the amendment was approved, 168 to 133, a woman in the gallery cheered and was quickly expelled from the room.[36]

After many hours of intense debate the House passed the civil rights bill on Monday, February 10, 1964, by a 290 to 130 roll call vote, and it won approval without a single major amendment that would weaken the measure. Ninety-four amendments were rejected. Of the 256 Democrats, 152 voted for and 96 against the measure; of the 177 Republicans, 138 voted for and 34 against. It was later observed that southerners seemed to have little stomach for the struggle and a number of them voted for the bill. At no time did they show a trace of the indignation that marked the 1963 contest, and they abandoned any attempt to delay the debate.

Naturally, the Senate launched a filibuster on March 30—Mansfield lacked Johnson's leadership skills to prevent it—which ended on June 10 with a cloture vote. It was the first cloture vote in history to succeed on a civil rights filibuster. Then, on June 19, exactly one year after President Kennedy submitted it to Congress, the civil rights bill passed the Senate by a vote of 73 to 27. A number of amendments had been necessary to secure passage, and the House agreed to the changes by a two to one margin. Before admitting defeat, however, Smith denounced the bill on the floor as a return to Reconstruction. "Already the second invasion of carpetbaggers of the Southland has begun. Hordes of beatniks, misfits, and agitators from the North with the admitted aid of the Communists, are streaming into the Southland on mischief bent, backed and defended by other hordes of Federal marshals, Federal agents, and Federal power." Smith concluded by muttering, "God save the United States of America."[37]

The House hurriedly sent the bill to Johnson who signed it only a few hours after its passage. The signing ceremony was televised at 6:45 p.m. from the East Room of the White House in the presence of members of Congress, cabinet members, foreign ambassadors and leaders of the civil rights movement.[38] Johnson called on all Americans "to join in this effort to bring justice and hope to all our people."[39]

The Civil Rights Act of 1964 was the most far-reaching civil rights legislation enacted since Reconstruction. It went far beyond what Kennedy originally proposed. It forbade discrimination on account of race in most places of public accommodation; attempted to protect the right of blacks to vote; banned discrimination on account of race or sex by employers, employment agencies and labor unions; created an Equal Employment Opportunities Commission; prohibited discrimination in the use of federal funds by states and other local authorities; empowered the attorney general to initiate cases to speed the desegregation of schools; and created a Community Relations Service to help individuals and officials deal with racial problems at the local level.[40]

The successful passage of this Civil Rights Act resulted mainly from two factors: the widespread feeling around the country that the denial of basic liberties for African-Americans and the violent suppression of their attempts to achieve them had to end, and the outpouring of grief over the assassination of President Kennedy that demanded a halt to the civil unrest permeating the entire country.

President Johnson saluted this 88th Congress on what it had achieved. "This has been a year without precedent in the history of relations between the Executive and the Legislative Branches of our Government," he declared at a White House gathering on August 10. "This session of Congress has enacted more major legislation, met more national needs, disposed of more national issues than any other session of this century or the last."[41]

THE POLITICAL WORLD changed in 1964 and it led to the most significant flurry of legislation since the New Deal. Lyndon Johnson won a landslide presidential victory over Republican Barry Goldwater of Arizona, who had voted against the Civil Rights Act. Johnson took 44 states and the District of Columbia for a total of 486 electoral votes to his opponent's 6 states and 52 electoral votes. Goldwater carried the Deep South: Alabama, Georgia, Louisiana, Mississippi and South Carolina. Furthermore, the Democrats increased their control of Congress with 295 seats in the House and 68 in the Senate, compared to the Republicans' 140 House and 32 Senate seats. The Democrats picked up 48 seats previously held by Republicans and lost only 10 of their own. "There were so many Democrats," declared Donald Rumsfeld, "that they had to sit on the Republican side of the aisle."[42] But five new Republican representatives from Alabama and one each from Georgia and Mississippi were elected to the House, the first Republicans elected to Congress since Reconstruction. More would follow in future elections.

The electoral disaster of 1964 for the Republicans convinced many of them that their leadership needed overhauling. Halleck was deemed too old, too forbidding, too irascible. He drank too much, and lacked initiative. John V. Lindsay and Charles Goodell of New York, Robert Griffin from Michigan, Donald Rumsfeld of Illinois and Thomas B. Curtis of Missouri, among others, agreed that a House Republican Conference should be called to address the problem. Curtis "was kind of the intellectual leader of that group," commented Rumsfeld, ". . . a very thoughtful man, a real student, a teacher and a leader." But Rumsfeld was the organizer. As they looked around the 140 Republicans in their efforts to find a substitute for Halleck, "we kind of unanimously agreed that he [Ford] was the one person that conceivably could eke out a victory over Charles Halleck" and "make a better minority leader." He "was liked, a responsible legislator, a person who knew the budget and appropriations process very well, and had friends on both sides of the aisle. He was younger and had some energy. We thought he'd represent the party in a way that would enable us to maybe become a majority party some day. We didn't feel that way about Charlie Halleck, despite his many talents and skills. So we went to work and talked Gerry Ford into doing it."[43]

At first Ford hesitated, but then he realized that as minority leader he had "a real chance to become Speaker someday—a personal goal ever since I came to Washington," he admitted.[44] He therefore consented.

Ford tried to phone Halleck, who was vacationing in Florida, to tell him of his decision to run against him but failed. So he sent him a telegram; and he dispatched telegrams to his colleagues and friends in the House. The strategy of his supporters, most probably devised by Rumsfeld, involved telephoning as many House members as possible and asking for their help before Halleck returned to Washington. Party leaders such as Richard Nixon and Barry Goldwater were informed and asked to remain neutral. "We worked hard on it," Rumsfeld recalled. "I spent probably as much time on it as anybody and ended up really as one of two or three people who kind of managed the thing." The other two were Charles Goodell and Tom Curtis. "And, of course, history was changed."[45]

The contest between the two men was not about ideologies. Both were

The genial Jerry Ford had one ambition: to become Speaker of the House. Instead he became President of the United States.

conservative and had similar voting records. Rather it was a battle between two different personalities and leadership styles. On Monday, January 4, 1965, the opening day of the 89th Congress, the Republican Conference convened in the Ways and Means Committee room of the Longworth Building. A secret ballot was held, and after two rounds it was announced that Ford had defeated Halleck by a vote of 73 to 67. "It was very close," said Rumsfeld, "and I guess we guessed right. He was the person who could win, and he did."[46] Ford was now the new minority leader, and Melvin Laird of Wisconsin replaced him as the GOP Conference chairman. "It was a beauty contest," snorted Halleck, "and I never figured I'd win one of those."[47]

FORD REMEMBERED THAT when he first came to the House he was told by Earl Michener of Michigan, a senior member, that he could choose one of two alternatives. He could spend most of his time in his office taking care of the needs of his constituents, or he could spend his time on the floor of the House listening to his colleagues, learning parliamentary procedures and getting to know the other members personally. "Since I had a good staff to handle constituent problems," Ford later wrote, "I elected to spend time on the floor. That's how I got to know Richard Nixon."[48]

Obviously the Republican members of the House opted for a new style of leadership, one less willing to exploit a Republican–Southern coalition. More particularly, there was "a wonderful group of young folks," named "Rumsfeld's Raiders" because he "was more of the activist, the one who organized them. We then would work with the leadership and try to come up with things that would be useful. . . . We were trying to get some reforms in the House, so that we'd have a little more influence, effect, control, or some more staffing. And Tom Curtis was the guru behind all of that."[49] In addition, Ford worked hard as minority leader and regularly toured the country to campaign for Republican candidates.

At their caucus on January 2, 1968, House Democrats did something quite extraordinary. By a secret vote of 157 to 115, they censured two southern members, John Bell Williams of Mississippi and Albert W. Watson of South Carolina, for publicly supporting the Republican presidential candidate in the election of 1964. Moreover, they stripped them of their seniority. It was the first time since 1911 that Democrats had taken such action. Watson switched to the Republican Party and later won reelection to the House, the first Republican from South Carolina to do so since Reconstruction.[50]

THE FIRST SESSION of the remarkable 89th Congress convened on January 4, 1965, with McCormack as Speaker, Albert as majority leader, Hale Boggs as majority whip, Ford as minority leader and Leslie C. Arends as minority whip. They would soon produce an enviable record of social reforms.

In his State of the Union address that evening, President Johnson called for a program to achieve a "Great Society." Taking advantage of his political strength in Congress, and exercising extraordinary leadership skills, he broke the logjam that had prevented passage of a number of measures that would enhance the lives of Americans in every region of the country. Medicare for the elderly financed through the Social Security system and Medicaid for the needy won passage on July 30, 1965. Social Security benefits were increased by 7 percent, and widows sixty-two years of age became eligible for benefits. But the enactment of two education bills constituted what many considered the major success of the first session of the 89th Congress.

The Education Act of 1965 provided $1.3 billion in direct aid to public schools, sidestepping the religious issue by including aid to parochial school children in a number of "shared services." And the Higher Education Act of 1965 appropriated $650 million for scholarships for needy students attending colleges and universities. The Immigration Act of 1965 fundamentally changed the immigration policy of the United States by doing away with quotas, putting all nations on an equal footing and limiting admission to 170,000 annually with a maximum of 20,000 from any one nation. The Water and Air Quality Acts were also enacted, along with a Housing and Urban Development Act that provided federal assistance for the construction of low-rent public housing and urban renewal. The Food Stamp Act authorized the federal government, in cooperation with state governments, to provide stamps by which the poor might purchase food. And the Economic Opportunity Act created an office to administer ten programs to confront the many causes of poverty in the country. To win passage of this latter bill in the House, and overcome southern opposition, the administration agreed to permit state governors to veto all community action projects.[51]

Much of the credit for this extraordinary legislative achievement belonged to Johnson himself. "Lyndon Johnson," wrote Tip O'Neill, "worked more closely with the Congress and followed the details of legislation more carefully than any other president I've seen. He left nothing to chance. . . . When it came to politics, that man knew all the tricks. . . . When it came to dealing with Congress, he was the best I'd ever seen. . . . And what a talker! That man could talk a bone away from a dog."[52]

And a significant amount of credit must go to Wilbur Mills, the chairman of the Ways and Means Committee, who helped provide the money necessary to carry forward these social reforms. Mills had gained his power through his extraordinary knowledge of the tax code and his ability to lucidly explain the most complicated money bills to his colleagues on the House floor. Moreover, when he assumed the chairmanship of his committee he abolished all its subcommittees, thus increasing his own authority and control over every aspect of Ways and Means responsibilities.[53] But more than anything else, he was an expert on building a consensus within his committee, of winning bipartisan support before moving any bill to the floor. Medicare is one example. Earlier, he had blocked Johnson's efforts to provide mandatory medical insurance for the elderly because he knew he did not have the votes in the House to win passage. It would be an exercise in futility, he lectured. But following the election of 1964 and the influx of Democratic representatives and senators, Mills recognized that an even more ambitious bill than the one Johnson had advocated could win approval. Thanks to him, the enlarged bill, as passed and signed by the President on July 30, 1965, included low-cost insurance to cover doctors' bills as well as hospital costs for all persons over sixty-five. Medicare has been a godsend to the elderly.

With the failure of efforts to improve voter registration for blacks in the south, Martin Luther King, Jr., fresh from his Nobel Prize triumph in Oslo, launched a voting-rights offensive in Selma, Alabama, on January 18, 1965. In that city, only 2.1 percent of the registered voters were listed as African-American, despite the fact that town was 57.6 percent black.[54] "We plan to triple the number of registered Negro voters in Alabama for the 1966 Congressional elections," declared King, "then we plan to purge Alabama of all Congressmen who have stood in the way of Negroes . . . A state that denies people education cannot demand literacy tests as a qualification for voting."[55] On "Bloody Sunday," March 7, some six hundred civil rights activists headed out of Selma and got only as far as the Edmund Pettus Bridge, where they were attacked by state and local police and driven back to Selma. The leaders sued for court protection to hold another march—a fifty-four-mile Freedom March from Selma to the state capital in Montgomery. Federal district court judge Frank M. Johnson, Jr., ruled in their favor. On Sunday, March 21, some 3,200 marchers set out for Montgomery, walking 12 miles a day and sleeping in the fields. On Thursday, March 25, they reached the capital, some 25,000 strong. Again, rioting occurred, with state troopers and mounted policemen brandishing night sticks, firearms and tear gas. A horrified nation watched on television as screaming, bloody marchers fled from their attackers.

More demonstrations occurred in Washington with round-the-clock pickets posted at the White House, the Capitol, and the Justice Department. Sit-ins blocked traffic on Pennsylvania Avenue during the rush hour. All of these demonstrators demanded congressional action.[56]

Again the nation was forced to confront its history of strife and violence. A country that liked to see itself as compassionate and generous toward the less fortunate had to face the fact that bigoted rednecks could regularly sully that image worldwide.

Eight days after "Bloody Sunday," President Johnson addressed an extraordinary, televised night session of the two houses of Congress and urged passage of stronger voting rights legislation. "It is not just Negroes," he said, "but it is all of us, who must overcome the crippling legacy of bigotry and injustice. And we *shall* overcome." Emanuel Celler, the dean of the House since Carl Vinson's recent retirement and chairman of the Judiciary Committee, began hearings on March 18, at which time he demanded that the trickery and legalisms and coercion that blocked the voting rights of blacks in the south "must be smashed and banished."[57] By June 1, a bill was ready, but it could not reach the floor. It was locked for five weeks in the Rules Committee under Chairman Smith's watchful eye. Cellers initiated proceedings to have the bill dislodged under the twenty-one day rule, which had been readopted at the beginning of the 89th Congress. This threat probably persuaded the Rules Committee to grant an open rule on July 1 by which ten hours of debate were authorized for the bill and amendments.[58]

Debate began on July 6 with Cellers praising what his committee had concocted and Smith denouncing it as an unconstitutional "vendetta" against the south, a bill "dripping in venom."[59] After many hours of verbal wrangling, the final version of the bill passed the House on August 3, 1965, by a vote of 328 to 74, with 37 southern Democrats voting aye. Two days later President Johnson signed the Voting Rights Act of 1965 in the same room in the Capitol that Lincoln had used to free slaves conscripted into the Confederate army. LBJ assured a television audience that the measure was a "triumph for freedom as huge as any victory that has ever been won on the battlefield." By this act, he declared, "we strike away the last major shackle of those fierce and ancient bonds" that had bound African-Americans to slavery since their arrival on this continent.[60]

The act suspended literacy and other tests for voting and authorized federal supervision of registration in those districts that had used such tests. Registrars were assigned to Alabama, Georgia, Louisiana, Mississippi, North Carolina, South Carolina and Virginia, and within five months African-American registration in the south increased 40 percent. In Judge Smith's home state of Virginia black registration jumped from 38.3 to 59.8 percent during the period from 1964 to 1969.[61] It was a major triumph for an already successful administration.

OF THE SEVENTY-ONE Democratic freshmen in 1965, sixty-seven of them voted for Johnson's Great Society measures, including urban mass transit, clean air and water pollution programs, immigration reform and the new Department of Housing and Urban Development. They were anxious to assist in the many social reforms the President requested, but, as they soon learned, Congress had its own traditions and procedures and they needed to be respected. One of the new Democratic members of this 89th Congress was Tom Foley of Washington, a man who would rise swiftly to party lead-

Shirley Chisholm, standing to the far right, and Ron Dellums, standing in the center of the back row, were among the members of the black caucus of the House that was formed in 1969.

ership. He later remembered the advice he was given at an orientation session for new Democratic members. It came from Michael Kirwan of Ohio, who, as a "powerful member of the Committee on Appropriations," was known as "Mr. Public Works" because "you couldn't get a footbridge built in the United States without Mike's approval." In any event, Mike's advice was simple and direct. He said "he wanted to warn us about the single greatest danger that could occur to a new Member of Congress entering his or her congressional service." And what was that danger? All in the room "leaned forward to hear" the deathless wisdom about to be imparted to them. Then, in sepulchral tones, Kirwan declared "that the danger was thinking for yourselves! Avoid that, he said, at all costs. Avoid thinking for yourselves. You must follow the subcommittee chairman, follow the committee chairman. Support the chairman of the Democratic Caucus. Follow the majority whip. Support the majority leader. And especially, above all, support, defend and follow the Speaker." At the moment Foley, like many others in the room, was "outraged," but years later when he himself became Speaker he laughingly thought that Kirwan was right after all.[62]

As a matter of fact, new members needed to recognize that the House was hierarchical and run by an oligarchy. It has its "own traditions, customs

and rules." To get ahead and succeed as a legislator in 1965, according to senior congressmen, a member must "work hard," "specialize," do their home-
work, "be in attendance on the floor," keep silent until "you know what you
are talking about," "follow your committees," "learn parliamentary procedure" and "be courteous to your colleagues."[63]

Foley claims that luck also played an important role in his steady ad-
vance to party leadership. More times than not, luck can determine the
success or failure of a congressman's career and the outcome of legislation.
And something truly important was driven home to Foley at the start of his
tenure. He remembered what was said to him as a freshman member of the
Agriculture Committee by its chairman, Harold Cooley of North Carolina.
"I want to welcome you to the Agriculture Committee," Cooley began.
"But, I also want to make it clear that I hate and detest to hear freshmen
members of this committee interrupting senior members when they are
speaking. By asking questions or asking them to yield or any other disruptive activity, you freshmen members will find, if you only remain silent and
attentive, you may learn enough to make a constructive contribution to our
committee. In the meantime, observe the decorum of the committee which
puts senior members, in all circumstances, preference over freshmen."[64]

Although the way of doing business in committees remained relatively fixed and traditional, their personnel kept changing. One of the
most significant was the defeat in 1966 of Judge Howard W. Smith, who
lost in the July 12 primary election to George Rawlings by 364 votes. In
the campaign, Rawlings lashed Smith for his record against housing, education, civil rights, Medicare and the antipoverty programs. Thanks to
the Voting Rights Act of 1965, African-Americans in the district had registered and voted in record numbers. To many it seemed like an appropriate way to bring to an end the political career of the gatekeeper. Ironically,
Rawlings himself lost the election to William L. Scott, a conservative Republican, who had the active support of Ford and the National Republican Committee.

ALTHOUGH FORD COULD do little to sidetrack the President's Great Society program, a new issue developed that would ultimately drive Johnson
from office: Vietnam. The war between the Communist North Vietnamese
against the non-Communist South Vietnamese intensified; more and more
the government of South Vietnam needed American economic and military aid to survive. At the very beginning of his administration, Johnson
committed himself to providing that aid. By the summer of 1964 some
twenty-one thousand American servicemen were stationed in Vietnam as
advisers, but the need for additional troops kept growing.

On August 4, 1964, two U.S. destroyers were attacked in the Gulf of
Tonkin. President Johnson ordered retaliatory air strikes and asked Con-

gress to approve his action. On August 7, 1964, Congress passed the Gulf of Tonkin Resolution, one of the most fateful and controversial in U.S. history. The House passed it by a vote of 414 to 0, and the Senate, 88 to 2. Johnson signed it on August 10. The attack was overblown by the administration and used as a pretext for entering the war with congressional approval, just like the sinking of the USS *Maine*. This resolution allowed the President as commander in chief to take all necessary steps to repel any armed attack against U.S. forces and prevent further aggression in Vietnam.[65]

Despite U.S. aid and a two-phase plan to bomb North Vietnam, the situation in South Vietnam grew steadily worse as one civilian government followed another in a series of coups that weakened the effort to bring the war to an end. By the beginning of 1965, Johnson began committing combat forces to Vietnam to serve as fighting personnel and not merely as advisers. On July 28, 1965, he increased troops from 75,000 to 125,000, and the first major ground battle of the war involving Americans took place on August 18, 1965, on the Van Tuong peninsula.

On May 6, 1965, Congress approved the necessary military funds to fight the war requested by Secretary of Defense Robert S. McNamara, by a vote of 407 to 7 in the House and 88 to 3 in the Senate, amounting to $700 million. The seven House members who voted against it were northern and western Democrats, two of them freshman. "What we are being asked to do," declared George E. Brown of California, "is approve a policy of the Administration in waging war in Viet Nam. This I cannot do."[66] Democrat Wayne Morse of Oregon commented, "I say sadly and solemnly, but out of deep conviction, that today my Government stands before the world drunk with military power" and has laid the foundation for "intense Asiatic hatred."[67]

At the same time, students in various colleges and universities, starting with the University of California, Berkeley, staged demonstrations and sit-ins, protesting the war. They burned their draft cards. The Pentagon informed the President that success in Vietnam could only come with the increase of troops from 120,000 to a "minimum essential force" of 550,500.[68]

And the cost of the war kept mounting. One request for additional funds followed another. To offset this expense, Republicans set out to cut almost every item of the President's domestic program. Inflation soared, and economists around the country called for a general tax increase, which Johnson rejected. The closest the House came to voting on the administration's Vietnam policy was the March 1966 roll call vote, which went 389 to 3, on supplemental funds for military spending, most of it intended for conducting the Vietnam war. The three dissenting votes came from Phillip Burton of California, John Conyers, Jr., of Michigan and William F. Ryan of New York.

The mounting concern over Vietnam had political repercussions. The results of the 1966 congressional elections came as quite a shock to Democrats. Minority leader Ford's untiring campaign efforts helped his party gain forty-seven seats in the House, a rather encouraging recovery from the Goldwater debacle of 1964. This success greatly strengthened Ford's position as party leader and won him national attention and respect. What alarmed Democrats was not only the loss of so many seats but also the gains made in the south by the Republican party. For the first time since Reconstruction, Republican senators and representatives were elected from districts that had traditionally been Democratic. The once solid South for the Democratic Party was solid no longer.

How had it happened, wondered Carl Albert? After all, the 89th Congress had an approval rating of 71 percent. What had gone wrong? The Voting Rights Act might explain southern defections, but what of the others? "Our major accomplishments—Medicare, aid to education, tax reform, and voting rights—earned favorable ratings of 82, 92 and 95 percent, respectively," Albert marveled. "Never in my lifetime had Congress been so highly regarded, and rightly so." Why such a debacle?

It was Vietnam that made the difference. Those ratings came before "war spending began to overheat the economy and send inflation soaring; before the terrible riots in Chicago, Atlanta, Cleveland and New York City; before the disruptive demonstrations on college campuses." And, most especially, before the bad nightly news that came from Vietnam listing the numbers of dead and wounded Americans. The congressional elections took place after these disasters and gave the Republicans more new seats than anyone expected. "That broke the back of the Great Society right there," declared Albert. "Thus fortified, they proceeded to turn back new initiatives and reduce old ones to sepulchers haunted with dead promises of what might have been."[69]

AND THE FIGHTING in Vietnam intensified. The Communist People's Republic of China promised in August 1967 to aid North Vietnam, at the same time it shot down American planes violating its airspace. More American troops were poured into the war zone; the number of soldiers rose to 535,000. Something like a hundred thousand tons of explosives per month were dropped on North Vietnam. On October 12, a bipartisan group of thirty House members sent Johnson a letter urging him to halt the bombing of North Vietnam. Over a week later tens of thousands of antiwar protesters marched in Washington. Still the war raged on. Because it cost $2 billion a month to continue the fighting, Johnson was forced to reduce expenditures on domestic programs designed to alleviate poverty and urban conflict. Inflation continued to skyrocket and brought more demands for a tax increase.

Johnson pressed the Congress for such an increase in order to protect

In October 1967 tens of thousands of antiwar protesters marched in Washington to demonstrate their opposition to the Vietnam War.

his Great Society. But Ways and Means chairman Wilbur Mills refused to support any increase until significant cuts were made to domestic spending. He finally handed the President an ultimatum: choose between guns and butter, war and domestic spending. In return for a tax increase, Johnson agreed to significantly weakening the Great Society, with a $6 billion spending cut of the domestic programs.[70]

ALTHOUGH THESE CUTS severely undermined the Great Society program, there were other recent measures initiated by Congress that benefitted the public at large. In the summer of 1966 the Freedom of Information Act passed, by which the government and its agencies were required to make available to citizens upon request all federal documents and records, except those in special exempt categories. The National Traffic and Motor Vehicle Safety Act and Highway Safety Act became law in September 1966, which established safety standards and required states to set up federally approved safety programs. Also enacted was the Fair Packaging and Labeling Act, on November 3, 1966. There was even consideration of legislation for congressional reform! The Joint Committee on the Reorganization of Congress recommended a list of reforms, and while the Senate acted on them, the House did not. But a reckoning was soon to develop.

At long last the Rules Committee agreed to a few necessary changes. Since Howard Smith had been defeated, the chairmanship would normally pass to William M. Colmer by virtue of his seniority, but to win that appointment Colmer was forced to agree to the first written set of rules for the committee. These rules included various ways in which a majority of the members could call a meeting in the absence of the chairman and call additional meetings if necessary. No longer could the chairman refuse to summon a meeting or prevent one by absenting himself. The "effect of these reforms was to make the Rules Committee more cooperative with the leadership."[71]

Other committees made changes. The House Banking and Currency Committee reorganized itself and stripped the chairman, Wright Patman of Texas, of his power to appoint special committees and subcommittees. And the Agriculture Committee gave minority members more involvement in the functioning of the committee, and agreed to make public all roll call votes taken in closed sessions.

A major change in the way the House would conduct its affairs in the future was the creation of a 10-member bipartisan Select Committee on Standards and Conduct (Ethics Committee), authorized to draft a code of conduct for members.[72] The need for such a committee arose with the investigation by the Special Subcommittee on Contracts of the House Administration Committee, chaired by Wayne Hays of Ohio, of Adam Clayton Powell and his alleged misuse of funds from the Education and Labor Committee, which he chaired.[73]

Frustration over the Vietnam War, rioting in the nation's urban ghettos, and rising government spending provided a troubling background for the opening of the first session of the 90th Congress on January 10, 1967. All elected representatives, except Adam Clayton Powell, were sworn in. On a motion by Lionel Van Deerling of California, Powell was directed to "stand aside" because of his alleged misuse of government funds. The House voted to exclude Powell pending an investigation and report by a special committee chaired by Emanuel Celler. That report, which recommended that Powell be seated but stripped of his seniority and be required to pay Congress $40,000, came on March 1. The House rejected it, and after four and half hours of debate the decision was made to exclude Powell from membership in the 90th Congress. Powell then filed suit in the federal district court challenging the decision. It was the first such challenge in American political history. At the same time, he won reelection in 1968, taking 80.6 percent of the vote, no doubt precipitated by the anger of his mostly black constituents, who were outraged by the action taken against him by his predominantly white colleagues. He was seated in the 91st Congress. But he was fined $25,000 by the House and lost his seniority. However, on June 16, 1969, the Supreme Court ruled by a vote of 7 to 1 that he had been unconstitutionally excluded from the House, since conditions of membership only included age, citizenship and inhabitancy. It left to the lower courts the questions of the fine and his seniority. By this time, perhaps weary of batting his head against a stone wall, perhaps resentful of having to live for weeks at a time in such a totally segregated city as Washington, Powell appeared infrequently in the House—his record of 5 percent roll call attendance provided proof—and he had become one of the least effective and influential members of Congress. As Representative Arch Moore of West Virginia said, the seating of Powell meant only that he would have a key to a suite of offices in one of the House buildings. Even his constituents finally turned against him. He was defeated in a primary contest by Charles B. Rangel and died shortly thereafter.[74]

On March 14, 1968, the House Standards of Official Conduct (Ethics) Committee finally came forward with its Code of Conduct. Melvin Price, a Democrat from Illinois and chair of the committee, reported a resolution amending House Rules to provide a code requiring limited financial disclosure of outside income by representatives and top employees. The resolution also directed that the committee be made permanent with investigative and enforcement powers. On a roll call vote it passed 406 to 1, with Peter H. B. Frelinghuysen, Republican from New Jersey, casting the single nay vote. He said the disclosure rule was meaningless and unclear.[75]

The following year the members of both houses, for the first time in 180 years of congressional history, made limited disclosures of their financial holdings. Representatives were required to report their interests in any firm doing business with the federal government or subject to federal regulatory agencies in which ownership exceeded $5,000. They also must report any professional activities from which they received $1,000 or more. Members of both houses were required to file confidential financial reports in sealed envelopes, which would not be available to the public. The House reports could be opened only upon a majority vote of the House Committee on Standards of Official Conduct.[76]

The House also tried and failed to initiate further reforms. Thomas B. Curtis, a Republican from Missouri, claimed that the House had become "an organization where 'wheeling and dealing' instead of honest study and honest debate determine decisions that it makes." He attributed this failing to the growth of committees into "little centers of power in the area of their assigned jurisdictions" where senior members "make decisions in lieu of the other members of the committees and of Congress itself," something that had been true for decades. Such "narrow mindedness on the part of the chairmen and senior members of the . . . standing committees of the House of Representatives," he argued, "fits in aptly with the efforts of groups outside the Congress who wish to manipulate the decision-making process. These groups assist the senior members of the committee to maintain their vested interests in controlling the subject matter of their committee's jurisdiction and in their efforts to mutually protect each other's jurisdictions and the process itself."[77]

But there were any number of reform-minded Republicans and Democrats who were determined to institute changes in committee procedures and broaden minority rights, and on June 20, 1968, a bill was introduced by Ray J. Madden, a Democrat from Indiana, that attempted a compromise of sorts between the reformers and those riveted to the existing power structure. The bill streamlined procedures regarding appropriations measures and lightened the ever-increasing workload of members. It also provided a professional staff for minority committee members. But it did not address the most controversial areas—namely, the seniority system and House and Senate floor rules. Speaker McCormack favored the bill, and had he had the skill of Rayburn to gather support, it might have passed. But the Rules Committee, by unanimous vote, deferred action and that put an end—temporarily—to reform.[78]

Clearly, the House was undergoing a transformation. The traditional ways of doing business had started to yield to the reforming efforts of young liberals. Speakers Rayburn and McCormack exercised extreme caution in dealing with chairmen and dreaded any challenge to the southern members of the Democratic Party, or "crunchers," as Richard Bolling of Missouri called them, that might drive them into the arms of the Republicans. But by the 1960s the newer members of the House were intent on democratizing the institution through the diffusion of power among a wider group of members and opening up "procedures to public scrutiny." The impetus for change came from the DSG, led by such liberals as Bolling, John Brademas of Indiana, Morris Udall of Arizona, Frank Thompson of New Jersey, Henry Reuss of Wisconsin, Donald Fraser of Minnesota, Phillip Burton and Chet Holifield of California, and James O'Hara of Michigan.[79]

With each passing month, the attention of the country and the Congress turned more and more to the Vietnam conflict. In January 1968, the Vietcong launched a major attack, called the Tet Offensive after the Vietnamese holiday on which it occurred, against every important South Vietnamese city and town, and even shelled the American embassy in Saigon. This disaster was followed by the capture of the USS *Pueblo*, an intelligence ship loaded with spying equipment, by the North Koreans off their coast. Johnson realized the danger of tangling with the North Koreans and backed away from contesting the seizure.[80]

When Senator Eugene McCarthy of Minnesota announced his candidacy for the Democratic presidential nomination on a peace platform, thousands of young Americans flocked to his standard. Robert Kennedy, the brother of the late President and now a senator from New York, also announced his candidacy. Johnson realized his unpopularity had risen so high that his reelection was out of the question, so he withdrew from the race in a televised address to the nation on March 31, 1968. He also announced the end of bombing of North Vietnam in the hope that it would lead to a negotiated settlement.[81]

Then the violent American past erupted once more on April 4, 1968, with the assassination of Dr. Martin Luther King, Jr., in Memphis by James Earl Ray. It triggered further violence when rioting occurred in more than one hundred cities, including Washington, D.C.[82] The fear generated by the civil unrest never seemed to end. The nation faced the fact that its streets at home and the streets in Vietnam were bloodied because of the presence of Americans intent on killing to settle opposing social and political viewpoints.

1968 proved to be a very bloody year. Violence struck once again during the primary elections for the presidential nominations when Robert Kennedy was assassinated in California on June 5, 1968, by a mentally deranged Jordanian immigrant, Sirhan Sirhan. Two such untoward tragedies in a single family seemed unbelievable. Again, the nation mourned.

More violence followed. The Democratic convention in Chicago, held August 26–29, became a battleground between Chicago's police and angry Vietnam protesters. The International Amphitheater, where the convention was held, was ringed by security forces, a barbed-wire fence and security checkpoints. The country's radicalized youth sang "We Shall Overcome," the civil rights anthem, while being peppered with tear gas by the police. Television cameras recorded the riot for the "edification" of the entire nation. Police used clubs indiscriminately, and bystanders, cameramen and members of the press were assaulted. It was a "police riot," according to a later investigation. But the delegates at the convention did decide on a presidential ticket. They selected Hubert Humphrey, the Vice President under Johnson, and Senator Edmund S. Muskie of Maine for their ticket. The Republicans, meeting in Miami, chose Richard Nixon and Spiro Agnew, the governor of Maryland, on August 8.

Most probably the "police riot" in Chicago helped win the election for Nixon in a very close contest. In fact it was one of the closest elections in U.S. history. Nixon won 43.4 percent of the popular vote (31,004,304) to Humphrey's 42.7 percent (30,691,699). The margin of difference was .01 percent of the popular vote. George C. Wallace, the former governor of Alabama and the candidate of the American Independent Party, a southern conservative organization, garnered 9,787,691 popular votes. But Nixon won 301 electoral votes from 32 states to Humphrey's 191 from 14 states and Wallace's 46 electoral votes from five southern states.[83]

Not until the following day was it known whether anyone had an electoral majority, raising the distinct possibility that the election might revert to the House of Representatives with all its potential political horrors. So alarming did that possibility seem to many representatives that on September 18, 1969, the House passed a constitutional amendment by a 338 to 70 roll call vote that would abolish the Electoral College—something that had been unsuccessfully attempted many times, almost from the beginning of the Republic—and provided for direct popular election of the President and Vice President. Opposition to this measure came largely from southern Democrats. However, the Senate refused to act on the bill and it died.

This election also produced the first seating of a black woman in the House: Shirley Chisholm, a Democrat from New York. She served seven terms in Congress and frequently spoke out for civil rights and women's rights and against the Vietnam War. A courageous, strong-willed and assertive woman—she later ran for President—Chisholm protested when assigned to the Agriculture Committee, which had little relevance to her urban constituents, and was promptly switched to the Veterans Affairs Committee.

Congress remained in the hands of the Democrats, despite Nixon's victory. There were 243 Democratic and 192 Republican Representatives in the House and 58 Democratic and 42 Republican Senators. Morris Udall of Arizona decided to challenge McCormack's leadership, insisting that while he had genuine affection and respect for the Speaker there was an "overriding need for new direction and new leadership in the House."[84] In an interview he gave in January 1962, Udall had come out strongly against McCormack, declaring, "It's easy to see why he's so unpopular in spite of the fact that he has a progressive record, is fairly able, and works like hell.

Shirley Chisholm was the first African-American woman to win election to the House of Representatives.

He's standoffish, high-handed, not warm at all. He's blunt and brusque, doesn't mix with the boys or go out and get drunk with them." Perhaps the "main thing people have against him," Udall continued, "is his total lack of tact and finesse. Just about everybody I have talked with, especially among the younger men, said they'd have voted for anybody running against Mc-Cormack."[85]

Actually, the Speaker was generally liked "but rarely feared." He lacked effective and forceful leadership, especially in regard to liberal legislation, and seemed to represent the old order of conducting House business. Several times in the past there had been calls for McCormack to withdraw, both by members and the press.[86] The best known indictment of the Speaker came from a 1965 book, *House Out of Order,* by Richard Bolling of Missouri. Three years later, Bolling listed McCormack's failings in another book, *Power in the House.* They included lack of regularity in scheduling, a lack of forceful leadership on behalf of liberal legislation, an inability to anticipate trouble before it was too late to do anything about it and an unwillingness to take control of important committees by appointing capable Democrats to them.

Udall begged McCormack to resign and urged Majority Leader Carl Albert to take his place.[87] This revolt by some members was given greater urgency when the *Washington Post* printed an editorial on January 17, 1967, in which it suggested that the Speaker "step down gracefully before further disarray within the House detracts from his long record of legislative service."

Albert, of course, had no intention of declaring his candidacy, and Udall was no match for McCormack. In fact, Udall declared that his challenge was intended to be "symbolic" and a signal to other candidates to come forward. In a secret ballot in the House Democratic Caucus on January 2, 1969, the members nominated McCormack to serve as Speaker, 178 to 58. But those 58 votes "indicated a large element of discontent with McCormack's leadership."[88] The House of Representatives was about to undergo rapid change.

17

Scandal, Watergate and Reform, 1969–1980

PUBLIC DISAFFECTION WITH the nation's Vietnam policy continued to worsen, and criticism in Congress became more vocal in 1969 with increased demands that U.S. troops be withdrawn and that a definite timetable be devised to bring the war to an end. Congressional supporters of the administration's policy argued for a sixty-day moratorium on criticism so that the President could have breathing space in which to negotiate a settlement.[1] During the debate in the House, Representative Andrew Jacobs, a Democrat from Indiana, insisted on October 14, 1969, that critics were not trying to stir hatred for the President, that criticism during wartime was legitimate and appropriate. "The Americans who have died in Vietnam will not have died in vain," he declared, "if their deaths have taught the United States to mind its own business and to lead the world by its example."[2]

All during the debates, the galleries were filled with many antiwar students who regularly rotated with students waiting in line outside. When the House adjourned for the day, hundreds of these students gathered on the front steps of the Capitol and sang "We Shall Overcome." Beginning on October 15, 1969, a million or more Americans participated in antiwar demonstrations, and over 50 members of Congress took an active part in the protests.[3]

On November 3, in a television address, President Nixon revealed that he had "initiated a plan which will end this war" and achieve a "peace with justice" in Vietnam. Ten days later he visited both houses of Congress, which happened to coincide with a three-day antiwar rally in Washington that attracted a quarter of a million protesters. By a roll call vote of 334 to 55, the House passed a resolution on December 2 supporting the President's efforts to win a peaceful settlement of the war. It was the first major policy declaration by the House since the Gulf of Tonkin Resolution of August 1964.

When it was reported in the *New York Times* on November 17, 1969, by Seymour Hersh, an independent investigator, that American troops were responsible for the massacre of more than a hundred Vietnamese civilians in the village of My Lai in the Quang Ngai province of South Vietnam in March 1968, a horrified Congress instituted an investigation. Both the House and Senate Armed Services Committees held closed-door hearings, out of which came recommendations for amending the Uniform Code of Military Justice. Several individuals, among them Lieutenant William Calley, were court-martialed. In March 1971, Calley was convicted of premeditated murder of at least twenty-two Vietnam citizens and sentenced to life imprisonment. But his sentence was later reduced, and he was released after serving only three and a half years. His commanding officer, Captain Ernest Medina, whom Calley claimed had ordered him to kill the civilians, was also tried but found not guilty.[4]

THE HOUSE WAS saddened that same fall over a scandal that suddenly arose in the office of Speaker McCormack. The scandal developed because of a suit initiated by the Securities and Exchange Commission (SEC) against the Parvin Dohrmann Company, a development enterprise, for allegedly manipulating the price of the company's stock and for deceiving the public about its manipulation. The company was informed that the trading of its stock would be suspended. Anxious to have the suspension lifted, the chairman and trustees of the company retained Nathan Voloshen, a congressional lobbyist, to help them secure the lifting of the suspension from the SEC. Voloshen allegedly used the prestige of the Speaker's office illegally by working through Dr. Martin Sweig, a forty-eight-year-old administrative assistant and secretary for House Speaker John W. McCormack. It also came to light that Voloshen and Sweig were under investigation by two federal grand juries, one involving Victor Frenkil, a contractor, who attempted to employ threats and political influence to squeeze an additional $5 million from the government, on top of the $11.7 million he had already received for constructing an underground parking facility for the Rayburn House office building. "He reportedly went to a select group of lawmakers for the kind of pressure that helps swing deals."[5]

In October 1969, McCormack placed Sweig on leave of absence without pay. Meanwhile *Life* magazine published an article on October 23 arguing that the Speaker's office had been used as a "power base" by Voloshen and

Sweig. It claimed that evidence existed that "McCormack was more than naively involved in whatever took place in his office." *Life* also stated that Voloshen "made free use of the official prestige, including the name, the stationary, the chair, the telephone of McCormack," and had Sweig's "full compliance." Worse, the magazine reported that it had "uncovered literally dozens of fixed cases, near fixes and plain shakedowns emanating from Voloshen's power base in the Speaker's office."

Jack Anderson of the *Washington Star* also alleged that Sweig could imitate McCormack's Boston accent and often posed as the Speaker in telephone conversations, even fooling President Johnson on one occasion.

On October 24, McCormack held a news conference and insisted that he had no knowledge of influence peddling from his office. He denied the allegations of *Life* magazine and announced that he would seek reelection to the House in 1970 and reelection as Speaker. "Whether I'm here any more depends on the people of my district. They know me. They know that my life—personal and private—is an open book."[6]

The media had a field day in reporting the problems the Speaker encountered in running the House and its legislative processes. Although McCormack was never directly linked to any crime, his assistant, Sweig, and Voloshen were indicted and charged with conspiracy and perjury be-

John McCormack was the last Speaker to serve in the House without having a high school diploma.

fore the grand jury. Voloshen pleaded guilty to conspiracy in using the Speaker's office to defraud agencies of the federal government. He was fined $10,000 and given a one-year suspended prison sentence. Sweig was tried for conspiracy and seven counts of perjury. A jury found him guilty of one count of perjury and acquitted him of the other charges. He was sentenced to thirty months in jail and fined $2,000. During the trial McCormack testified that he had no knowledge of Sweig's activities, admitting that he was "not an inquiring fellow," a remark that further damaged his reputation.[7]

In the House, a resolution expressing a lack of confidence in McCormack's leadership was proposed by Jerome R. Waldie, Democrat from California, on January 19, 1970, but it was tabled by a vote of 192 to 23. As Gerald Ford said, McCormack was not as successful as Rayburn "in cracking the whip over independent Democrats. He was just too decent a man to stifle those who disagreed with him."[8] Many House members had no real quarrel with McCormack personally, except that they regarded him as "a man of the past." The struggle was not so much a question of age versus youth but rather whether there would be a real break from "the old guard establishment as personified by Speaker McCormack."[9]

Still the pressure kept mounting. Finally, on May 20, 1970, the seventy-nine-year-old McCormack announced that he would retire at the conclusion of the 91st Congress. Many of his colleagues rightly noted that his retirement would mark the end of an era. Lyndon Johnson was the last President to be born in a log cabin, and McCormack would be the last Speaker who did not attend high school. It was a sad conclusion to an otherwise notable and very respectable career.

With McCormack's retirement certain, the tide of reform which he had resisted was unleashed, "and the House of Representatives embarked upon a period of change unlike anything witnessed since the revolt against Joe Cannon."[10]

The need for reform was accelerated by the regular revelations of improper conduct by members of Congress. In the summer of 1970 it was reported that the Ford Motor Company had a habit, over the past ten years, of leasing insured Lincoln Continental sedans to special members of Congress for $750 a year. There were nineteen such members, all but two of them chairmen or ranking minority members of committees involved with auto safety, public works, highway matters or taxes. There were at least four criminal statutes that forbade members from accepting such gratuities. In addition, there were the usual illegal campaign contributions from corporations that allegedly went to such luminaries as Gerald R. Ford, Hale Boggs, Leslie C. Arends and others, as well as instances of conflict of interest.[11]

Meanwhile, the *Wall Street Journal* published an article in which John C. Watts, Democrat of Kentucky, and former Democratic Representative A. Sydney Herlong, Jr., of Florida, were cited as having been members of the tax-writing Ways and Means Committee when they received loans of $37,937 to cover the purchase of $50,000 worth of bonds in the West Virginia Turnpike. This prime example of apparent conflict of interest, however, was not pursued by the House Ethics Committee.

Conflict of interest had always been a problem with Congress. But by 1970 it was gargantuan. It was estimated that there were ninety-seven bankers who were members of the House, and a good dozen of them sat on the Banking Committee. A few months earlier it was proposed that this committee investigate the activities of bank lobbyists, but in a secret session the proposal was voted down. "You're just trying to embarrass Sy!" cried one member. Obviously, said the *New York Times,* "Good old Sy is Congressman Seymour Halpern, the New York Republican" who, the *Wall Street Journal* reported, had been the "lucky beneficiary of more than $100,000 in relatively unsecured loans from half a dozen banks."

One day, several members of the House were "sitting around grumping about how misunderstood" they were by the public and how quick people were to complain about congressional dishonesty. "Why," said one, "some people even seem to think that a salary of $42,500, retirement pay of up to $18,000 a year, cheap hospitalization, free junkets, cheap insurance and an assortment of other goodies should be reward enough; these radicals think, in other words, that politicians shouldn't take money on the side." But "if I didn't have an outside income at forty-two five I couldn't stay in the House." He said he had a wife, a mother-in-law and three children to support.[12]

True, congressmen had never been paid a livable salary, right from the beginning. In effect, they were asked to make a sacrifice to serve the people's needs. Most stayed only a session or two before leaving to earn a more profitable income from the private sector. But when sessions grew longer and lasted most of the year and congressmen began making a career in the legislature, it became obligatory that their salaries reflect these changes. Otherwise, they must look elsewhere where temptations abound.

Wayne Hays of Ohio, chairman of the powerful House Administration Committee—"among the top junketeers in the House and perhaps best known in some circles as the member who took the House restaurant headwaiter on one of his junkets to Paris"—agreed that the dangers of graft or bribery were ever present. But forget about increasing the responsibilities of the Ethics Committee, he said. "Nobody comes before his constituents more often than a Congressman, which is every two years. And if they think you are doing something shady, they won't send you back. It's just that simple."[13]

Representative Thomas F. Johnson of Maryland was finally carted off to jail in 1970 after being convicted, eight years earlier, of unlawfully pocketing $17,500 for trying to help a savings-and-loan officer escape federal prosecution. Worse, *Life* magazine alleged that Congressman Cornelius Gallagher of New Jersey had ties to the Mafia. Gallagher pleaded guilty to seven counts of perjury, conspiracy and tax evasion and was sentenced to two years in prison and fined $10,000. And Bertram L. Podell, Democrat from New York, was indicted by a federal grand jury on charges of conspiracy, bribery, perjury and conflict of interest. He pleaded guilty to the conspiracy and conflict of interest charges but denied accepting a bribe. No wonder, cried Omar Burleson of Texas, that the electorate judges Congress to be nothing but "a bunch of bums."[14]

On December 31, 1971, John Dowdy, Democrat of Texas, was convicted of conspiracy, perjury and accepting a bribe. He swore he never received a $25,000 payment to block a federal investigation of a home improvement company in 1965. The House Ethics Committee spent six weeks investigating Dowdy's transgressions and reported a resolution directing him to refrain from voting in the House and participating in committee business. This was the first attempt by this committee to initiate action against a member, but the Rules Committee did not report the resolution and Dowdy voted three times by proxy in the House Committee of the District of Columbia, despite his promise to the new Speaker, Carl Albert, to abide by the resolution of the Ethics Committee.[15]

Still, it should be remembered that throughout the history of the House, the great majority of Congressmen were at least as honest and honorable as their constituents, if not more so. In fact, during the first seventy years of the twentieth century, just twenty-two members had been indicted for serious crimes and only fourteen were convicted.[16]

The Senate had its share of scandals as well, although not as many as those in the House. It censured Thomas Dodd of Connecticut for mishandling campaign funds, and Senator Russell B. Long of Louisiana, who chaired the Finance Committee, was accused of conflict of interest since his family's fortune came from oil and gas production and he stood as a "citadel guarding the oil depletion allowance." Between 1964 and 1969, over $300,000 of his income was tax free, thanks to the depletion allowance for those years.[17]

If the scandals of this era seem no worse than those of the past, it was a reminder once again that political power invites corruption; it invites the dispersal of money to entice the weak, the corrupt and the arrogant who think they can escape detection. It was a reminder of what Andrew Jackson declared in his bank veto in 1832: that the greedy are ever ready to use congressional influence to line their pockets and that the government must be an honest broker to all the citizens of this country.

MEANWHILE, THE WAR in Vietnam intensified. In an effort to clear out Communist sanctuaries along the Cambodian boarder with South Vietnam, President Nixon ordered American troops to invade and destroy these sanctuaries in April 1970. The invasion of Cambodia, along with the expansion of American involvement in a war in Laos, the country that bordered

Cambodia to the north, only protracted the war, despite Nixon's announcement that he would start withdrawing U.S. troops from Vietnam. In late December 1970, Congress repealed the Gulf of Tonkin Resolution and the President signed it on January 13, 1971.[18]

Then on June 13, 1970, the *New York Times* published the Pentagon Papers. These were classified documents that detailed decisions leading to U.S. involvement in Vietnam. They had been obtained from Daniel Ellsberg, a former Defense Department employee, and their publication further eroded public confidence in the war and the administration's handling of it.

The war, the mounting number of scandals and the imminent departure of Speaker McCormack finally prompted northern liberals of the majority party to launch a major assault against "the old guard establishment." And their initial vehicle was the Democratic Caucus, which had been virtually dormant for the past half century. The caucus usually met once a year, just before Congress assembled, to settle organizational matters. It was a sleeping giant, since it had power over committee assignments and could adopt rules that would affect House governance. Both Rayburn and McCormack had resisted summoning the caucus because it might weaken their authority, but McCormack was persuaded during his last Congress to support holding a monthly meeting of the caucus. This, in turn, led to the formation of an Organization, Study and Review Committee, chaired by Julia Butler Hansen of Washington, to study the problem of legislative reform and make recommendations. "The committee proved to be the catalyst for the adoption of the Legislative Reorganization Act of 1970."[19] That act passed the House by the lopsided vote of 326 to 19 on September 17. The Senate followed along, and on October 26 it became law.

The Legislative Reorganization Act addressed the problem of committee rules and procedures. It required all committee roll call and House Committee of the Whole votes to be made public. It implemented electronic voting and permitted television and radio coverage of House hearings with the approval of a majority of committee members. It authorized recorded teller votes and limited (but did not end) proxy voting. It established an Office of House Legislative Counsel and a Joint Committee on Congressional Operations to recommend further improvements in the operations and organization of Congress. And it empowered committees to function despite recalcitrant chairmen.

By the beginning of the 91st Congress there were 21 House committees and 145 subcommittees. Although the Legislative Reorganization Act did not end the committee system or the power of chairmen to direct their committees (especially in selecting subcommittees and the chairs of the subcommittees), it did end the era "when powerful committee chairs and other senior members could forestall structural and procedural changes that appeared to undermine their authority."[20]

Passage of the bill climaxed a five-year struggle to democratize House operations, led in the main by members of the DSG, now chaired by Phillip Burton of California, a heavy-drinking, foul-mouthed womanizer who was nevertheless an energetic and effective legislator, a staunch liberal and environmentalist, and a man who regularly indulged in hardball political tactics to achieve his reform goals. Frequently compared to Lyndon Johnson in his drive for power, Burton once bragged that he could round up a hundred votes "to have dog shit declared the national food."[21] Never once did he take a bribe or a gift from a corporation or lobbyist. He was one of the more memorable members of the House, with outsized appetites and passions.

The DSG was particularly eager to end secrecy in the House, and the Legislative Reorganization Act did help to achieve that goal by allowing recorded teller votes.[22] However, it did nothing about terminating the seniority system. In the minds of many reformers, Congress needed to find a more intelligent system of selecting chairmen.

With McCormack's announcement that he would retire from the House at the end of the 91st Congress, there was little doubt that the popular, five-foot-four-inch former Rhodes scholar, Carl Albert, would take his place as Speaker in January 1971, although Dan Rostenkowski, Democrat from Illinois and chairman of the Democratic Caucus, and Richard J. Daley, the mayor of Chicago, opposed him because of several feuds going back to the Democratic National Convention of 1968. When asked why he opposed Albert's election, Rostenkowski responded, "That is not true. I never opposed Carl Albert. Daley did." Then, when Illinois representatives Frank Annunzio, Mel Price and Morgan Murphy pledged to Albert, Daley called Rostenkowski into his office and made him "get Annunzio and Morgan Murphy to tell Carl Albert that they're withholding their endorsement."

Naturally Annunzio, Murphy and Mel Price did not tell Albert that it

Phillip Burton's rage for reform probably prevented him from winning election to the Democratic leadership.

was Daley who ordered them to withhold their endorsement. "It was Rosten-kowski. . . . Well, Albert never forgave me for that," Rostenkowski claimed. ". . . And it was not my fault."

"I liked Carl Albert," Rostenkowski later remarked. "I thought he was a brilliant guy," but he "was a little man in a big man's world. Although he was honest and sincere, he just didn't measure up. And his judgment was not as good as it should have been."[23]

Besides, he was a product of the old regime. Like Rayburn, he believed that the Speaker was an insider who operated within the system to make it work. He was sympathetic to the aims of the DSG, but he distanced himself from their specific proposals. He believed in the committee system and did not wish to terminate the role of seniority. He believed that the House could only work effectively if those in "positions of responsibility had sufficient power." Like McCormack, he was a transitional figure, destined to guide the House from the old order to the new.[24]

In his private life, Albert had a drinking problem, and it sometimes caused embarrassment, especially during social occasions attended by important guests and foreign dignitaries. It diminished his standing among many members.

Mayor Daley wanted Hale Boggs as Speaker and Rostenkowski as majority leader. But Rostenkowski had the good sense to realize that his chances were slim and he dropped out of contention. In the Democratic Caucus, Albert won 220 votes to 20 for John Conyers of Michigan, an African-American who challenged Albert when he failed to support an effort to strip three Mississippi Democrats of their seniority.

The real race in the Democratic Caucus involved the position of majority leader. Hale Boggs of Louisiana was the favorite, but there were four other contenders: B. F. Sisk of California, James O'Hara of Michigan, Wayne Hays of Ohio and Morris Udall of Arizona, who was Boggs's leading opponent. The Arizona representative was a "true liberal," said Tip O'Neill, and very popular because he was responsible for a system of automatic pay raises in Congress. "If there is one thing that congressmen really love," O'Neill explained, "it's a pay raise. But if there's one thing they really hate, it's having to vote for a pay raise. Under Udall's plan, they would receive pay raises automatically—without having to cast a vote that would be unpopular at home."[25]

A few days before the Caucus vote, O'Neill ran into Rostenkowski at a local restaurant.

"We gave you a screwing today," Rostenkowski laughed. Danny had met with the five announced candidates and they had agreed that if O'Neill did not declare his candidacy for majority leader he could not run.

"I'm not running," Tip replied. "I'm with Boggs."

"Don't give me that," Rostenkowski responded. "We know you're trying to sneak in through the back door."

True, a number of members wanted O'Neill to run and hoped that if there was a deadlock in the Caucus the members would turn to him. But he wisely saw "that this wasn't my year." Besides, he had pledged to support Boggs, a southern liberal, even regarding civil rights. And, as things turned out, "it was Danny who got the screwing" because the next morning there was a vote to select the chairman for the Democratic Caucus and Rostenkowski was running for reelection and did not expect any opposition, having served in this position for four years. But to his surprise and consternation, the Texas delegation nominated their colleague, Olin Teague, a popular war hero and chairman of the Veterans' Affairs Committee. And even though Teague announced to the assembled Caucus that he was not a candidate, they elected him anyway. "I got defeated by Tiger Teague, who voted for me," exclaimed Rostenkowski. "I saw him vote for me."[26] The liberals among Democrats voted against Rostenkowski because of his ties to Mayor Daley, who was a pariah because of the 1968 convention in Chicago, and many of Albert's friends voted against him because of the feud. The vote in the Caucus was 155 to 91 in favor of Teague. "I got my brains knocked out," Rostenkowski admitted.[27]

In the balloting for majority leader, Hays and O'Hara dropped out and Boggs was chosen with 140 votes to 88 for Udall and 17 for Sisk. Although Boggs had a progressive record, he was able to obtain the votes of many southern conservatives on the basis of personal friendships.

There were rumors that Rostenkowski would be appointed whip in return for his support of Boggs, but again he was turned aside. Boggs asked Albert three times to make Rostenkowski the whip and three times he was refused. Tip O'Neill won the position. O'Neill was chosen largely in the hope that he would serve as a link to the liberal faction of the party. His opposition to the continuation of the Vietnam War, his support of Eugene McCarthy for President in 1968, and his advocacy of the immediate removal of troops from Vietnam established his credentials among liberals. "I haven't found any members of the Democratic Study Group who don't feel they now have a voice in the leadership," commented O'Neill.[28]

Although the new leadership was not exactly what the liberals had hoped to achieve—Udall was their candidate—they did manage to strike at the conservative coalition and put a sizable dent in the seniority system.[29] The members accepted the recommendations of the Organization, Study and Review Committee in which committee chairs could be selected by criteria other than seniority. Administrative ability might now be recognized as a prime factor in any selection. What helped produce this change was acceptance by the Caucus of a resolution declaring that if ten Democrats challenged nominations from the Committee on Committees, then the Caucus must conduct an open vote on these nominations.[30]

On the Republican side, the Conference agreed to allow all their members the right to vote on nominations for ranking members of each House committee. It also stipulated that the chosen ranking member of each committee would be selected by vote, not simply on the basis of seniority. As expected, it again elected Ford and Arends as minority leader and whip, respectively.[31]

The anger generated around the country over the continuation of the Vietnam War came close to home a few months later when on March 1, 1971, a bomb exploded in a restroom in the Capitol half an hour after a telephone call warned of the action as a protest against U.S. involvement in Laos. The repairs cost $200,000 and resulted—finally—in increased security measures throughout the Capitol Building.

On November 30, 1971, the House passed the Federal Election Campaign Act by a roll call vote of 372 to 23. It was designed to regulate political campaign spending by presidential contenders and candidates for Congress. It placed limits on political campaign expenditures and required disclosure of campaign contributions. Among other things it reduced the amount a candidate or family members could contribute to his or her campaign: $50,000 for President or Vice President, $35,000 for Senator, and $25,000 for Representative. After a conference to resolve differences with the bill passed by the Senate, the House approved it on January 19 by a vote of 334 to 20. The Senate had already approved it on December 14, and Nixon signed it on February 7, 1972. "We have a crackerjack bill here," laughed John B. Anderson of Illinois. "It will stop millionaires from buying Senate seats and the Presidency. It brings this television monster under control."[32]

In a separate action in March 1972, Congress passed and sent to the states for ratification an equal rights amendment (ERA) to the Constitution. Martha Griffiths forced the bill's discharge from the Judiciary Committee, where it had languished for nearly twenty years because of Chairman Celler's opposition. Leading the floor fight, Griffiths insisted that women were discriminated against in employment, property rights, divorce proceedings, pensions and inheritance. Bella Abzug, the feisty member from New York, condemned the fact that women were even denied seats on some of the most important House committees, such as the Armed Services and Foreign Affairs Committees, the "very committees which make the decisions that send our children and youths off to war in Asia." Emanuel Celler argued that sex discrimination should be corrected by specific statutes, not a constitutional amendment. But his argument failed to convince his colleagues and the House approved the proposed ERA by a vote of 354 to 24. This amendment stated that equality of rights must not be denied or abridged by the states or the United States on account of sex. But the amendment failed to obtain the necessary approval by three-fourths of the states.[33]

The President scored an important breakthrough in foreign affairs

Martha Griffiths of Michigan forced the Judiciary Committee to discharge the Equal Rights Amendment to the Constitution; it had languished there for nearly twenty years.

when, in February 1972, he visited Communist China and agreed to a joint communiqué on the need for greater interaction between the two countries. Only a well-known anticommunist like Nixon could have gotten away with this historic diplomatic triumph. Then, after extended negotiations, an agreement was signed in Paris on January 27, 1973, between North and South Vietnam, and between the U.S. and the Vietcong's Provisional Revolutionary Government of South Vietnam, to end the Vietnam War. Not unexpectedly, the fragile South Vietnam government soon collapsed, the country was overrun by the Vietcong and the remaining Americans in the country had to be hurriedly evacuated by helicopter. It was a soul-searing defeat for the American nation.

THEN WATERGATE OCCURRED. It was one of the worst tragedies in the history of the nation, and it began to unfold on June 17, 1972, when five men were caught at 2:30 a.m. while attempting to burglarize the offices of the Democratic National Committee in the Watergate, an apartment-hotel complex in Washington adjacent to the Potomac River. It soon developed that these men had connections with the White House and the Republican National Committee to Reelect President Nixon and were obviously attempting to gain information that could be used in the forthcoming election. This burglary soon escalated to engulf and destroy the Nixon administration. The irony is that Nixon and his running mate, Spiro Agnew, overwhelmed the Democratic ticket of Senator George

McGovern and R. Sargent Shriver in the 1972 election, winning 520 electoral votes to 17.

Despite their staggering electoral loss of the presidency, Democrats increased their majorities in Congress: in the Senate by two seats; in the House, their majority stood at 244 to 191 for the Republicans. And a number of women joined the House of Representatives as a result of this election. They included Pat Schroeder, Barbara Jordan, Elizabeth Holtzman, Yvonne Burke, Marjorie Holt, and, following the deaths of their husbands in plane crashes, Cardiss Collins and Corinne Claiborne "Lindy" Boggs.

After his landslide victory—he had the third highest electoral total in American history—Nixon continued his practice of impounding funds for programs passed by Congress that he did not approve. He tried and failed to get Congress to give him authority to decide where spending cuts should be made. So he simply blocked execution of the appropriations. Speaker Albert warned that the constitutional balance of power between the executive and legislative branches was being eroded, and Claude Pepper of Florida urged the House to join the Senate in protesting this outright and improper encroachment on the legislative branch by the executive.[34]

At the Democratic Caucus on January 2, 1973, Albert was easily nominated for another term as Speaker, and O'Neill, who had been the whip, was elevated to majority leader, owing to the untimely death of Hale Boggs in an airplane accident in Alaska. The question then arose as to whether O'Neill would appoint the new whip, as previous majority leaders had done, or have the Caucus members make the selection, inasmuch as the whip joins the party leadership and presumably moves up the ladder and eventually becomes Speaker. The job should be elective, chorused the liberals, led by Phillip Burton, who planned to run for the office himself since he had lost the confidence of Tip O'Neill and knew he could never get it by appointment. Burton lobbied 85 percent of his colleagues and even won over Carl Albert, who did not realize that Burton's plan to further democratize party operations directly undercut Tip's prerogative. The Speaker soon found out.

"You can't do that," O'Neill shouted at Albert. "He's a revolutionary. He's crazy. We can't work with him on a leadership team."[35]

So when the Caucus convened on January 2, O'Neill declared that he favored the traditional method, then called a recess before the vote on the motion could be taken. During the recess, he lobbied Burton's southern supporters, convincing five of them to switch sides. They not only generally liked O'Neill but also believed that he would appoint John J. McFall of California to the post, a man who was more conservative than most other candidates. Burton's reach for power was thus cut short by nine votes in the Caucus, and Tip's right to appoint the whip was sustained.[36] O'Neill named McFall as whip on January 6, 1973.[37]

The Democratic liberals then initiated a frontal assault on the seniority system by demanding that committee chairmanships be assigned by a majority vote in the Caucus and that all balloting be conducted by secret ballot. Conservatives and seniors immediately protested and insisted on an open vote. "If I'm going to be stabbed in the back," shouted Chet Holifield, chair of the Government Operations Committee, "then I want it to be done openly."

At that point O'Neill offered a compromise. He proposed that the voting be taken by secret ballot if 20 percent of the Caucus members demanded it. O'Neill's suggestion passed by the vote of 117 to 58. "I don't think any reformer could have gotten the same thing passed," remarked David Cohen of Common Cause. "It was a good move. I think O'Neill knew that unless the chairmen were made accountable, the leadership would have no leverage."[38]

"The seniority system—for sixty-two years the path to legislative domination—died that day," declared Speaker Albert. ". . . From that moment on every chairman knew that power flowed not from personal longevity but from the entire Democratic membership."[39] Chairmen did, of course, remain powerful, but they were now subject to the approval of their colleagues. The House was slowly evolving into a more democratically operated institution.

However, in the process of selecting chairmen in 1973 under this new system, something remarkable happened. The Caucus members proceeded to elect the same men who would have won the chairmanships if the system had remained unchanged. Not until 1975 did the Caucus exercise its right to oust sitting chairs by replacing three of them. "I am wildly happy at what we've done," enthused Phillip Burton. "We're finally getting somewhere."[40]

The next month the Caucus required all House committee hearings to be open unless they dealt with matters of national security or personal matters. A majority vote of the committee members was necessary to close the hearings. The Caucus also modified the way in which bills come to the floor under a rule that disallows amendments. This was a direct attack on Wilbur Mills, the autocratic and very conservative chairman of Ways and Means, who argued that bills from his committee were so complex that amendments would distort and weaken them. The Caucus also established a new Democratic Steering and Policy Committee on February 22 to determine both party policy on legislative matters and nominate all standing committee chairmen for Caucus approval. By 1974 it made Democratic committee assignments for all committees, except Rules, which was appointed by the Speaker.[41] Carl Albert regarded this latter action as "the most significant reform of his speakership." It "effectively made the Rules Committee an arm of the Speaker."[42]

The Republicans, meanwhile, were not inactive. In 1973 a group of conservatives in the party, led by Sam Steiger of Arizona and Edward Derwinski and Philip Crane of Illinois, among others, founded the Republican Study Committee, modeled after the DSG, to advance a conservative social and economic agenda with particular focus on legislative activity, academic outreach, electoral involvement and House relationships with the executive branch of government. By 1981 approximately 150 House Republicans had joined this committee, and it was recognized as the "conservative conscience" of the party.

On January 31, 1973, the full House agreed by a vote of 282 to 91 to create a select committee, chaired by Richard Bolling, to review the committee structure of the House and recommend which committees should be eliminated, what new ones should be created, the function of subcommittees, and the rules for committee procedures. Five Democrats and five Republicans constituted the committee, and this bipartisan approach won the support of the leadership of both parties. The final report of the committee when submitted on March 19, 1974, called for a "complete restructuring that touched on twenty of our twenty-one committees."[43]

The Bolling Report was referred to the Democratic Caucus for endorsement, but despite the pressure of the House leadership, the Caucus voted 111 to 95 to sidetrack the plan and send it to Julia Butler Hansen's Committee on Organization, Study and Review. The reforms suggested in the Bolling Report were much too extensive to win widespread support, and required too many sacrifices from the members. So it was handed over to the Hansen Committee. This was "a deliberate act to kill it," claimed a spokesman for the liberal Americans for Democratic Action, concocted by Phillip Burton and executed by a secret ballot, most probably because of the intense rivalry between Bolling and Burton.[44]

The reform of procedures and rules recommended by the Hansen Committee were adopted in the House by a vote of 203 to 165 on October 8, 1974. It was supported by 70 percent of Democrats, whereas 65 percent of Republicans preferred the Bolling proposal.[45] The reforms enacted called for the end of proxy voting in committees, allowed the leadership to organize each new Congress before they convened, gave the Speaker more latitude in assigning bills to committees, required all committees to have at least four subcommittees and provided the minority party with control over one-third of the committee staffs.[46]

It was a major defeat for the Speaker, who was sympathetic toward the reformers' aims but probably realized that he had encouraged Bolling too much and that the resulting proposal was far more than House members could stomach. Further reform would take time.

Meanwhile, Congress had become increasingly concerned over the President's exercise of his authority as commander in chief to engage this country in foreign wars without the consent of the legislature. It finally decided to act, despite threats of a presidential veto. In 1973 it passed the War Powers Resolution, which required the chief executive to consult with Congress before committing troops in any hostilities. It further required the termination of military engagements within sixty days unless Congress declares war or authorizes a continuation of the military engagement. Nixon vetoed the resolution on grounds that it violated his constitutional obligations, but on November 7, 1973, the House overrode his veto by 284 to 135, just four votes over the two-thirds majority required by the Constitution. Hours later the Senate added its insistence on the bill's passage by a vote of 75 to 18. The War Powers Act became law without the President's signature and has been regularly bypassed or ignored by subsequent chief executives.

Because of strong presidential "interference" in determining budgetary matters, Congress passed the Budget and Impoundment Control Act, which sought to give the legislature greater control over spending and budgeting, on July 12, 1974. The act created House and Senate Budget Committees to determine overall spending, appropriations and tax measures. It also established a Congressional Budget Office to provide technical assistance, but not until February 24, 1975—mostly out of concern that the office be nonpartisan—was Alice M. Rivlin, an economist, sworn in as director. In addition, procedures were set up by which impounding could be overridden.

Charles Johnson, who joined the Office of the Parliamentarian in May 1964 and later became the House parliamentarian, commented on "the incredibly accelerated pace of the change" that occurred in the House over the last thirty years of the twentieth century. The "variety of institutional changes," he said, was startling: ". . . the breakdown of the seniority system, open voting in the Committee of the Whole, the advent of television, the Budget Act, the War Powers Act—all these statutes that set in place various procedures vis-à-vis the executive branch, all of these trends began and accelerated in the '70s."[47]

The House had evolved into a new and more open, modern and democratic institution, with further changes yet to come.

THE NATION WAS jolted back to the question of corruption in government when Spiro Agnew was indicted on the charge of accepting payoffs from construction company executives while governor of Maryland and while Vice President. On September 25, 1973, Agnew had a meeting with Speaker Albert and requested a House impeachment investigation, citing the precedent of Vice President John C. Calhoun, who had demanded and received such an investigation when he was charged with bribery in 1826.

The request placed Albert in a very delicate situation in view of his position in the line of presidential succession. So he summoned the Democratic and Republican leadership to his office, along with the chairman of the Judiciary Committee, Peter Rodino of New Jersey, and the ranking Republican, Edward Hutchinson of California, and invited their recommendation. Gerald Ford spoke in favor of the request, while Tip O'Neill opposed it. Already there was talk of impeaching the President over the Watergate break-in and therefore any action against him seemed less likely if Agnew was under investigation. O'Neill preferred to have the House go after the President, not the Vice President, and he had been trying for some time to initiate it, considering the incriminating evidence that had been mounting against Nixon for many months.

The parliamentarian, Lewis Deschler, known to be conservative, prepared a recommendation based on precedent and constitutional law in which he argued in favor of granting Agnew's request. But Tip countered with the political argument. He saw the Vice President as an "embattled politician seeking a way out of the criminal justice system."[48] Let the courts handle Agnew, he protested.

He convinced Albert. On September 26 the Speaker announced that the request was denied. The House would not institute an impeachment investigation. The Democrats would save that option for the man in the Oval Office.

Consequently, on October 10, 1973, Spiro Agnew pleaded no contest to a single charge of income-tax evasion as part of a plea bargain and resigned his office as Vice President of the United States.

The 25th Amendment to the Constitution provided that the President nominate a replacement. Nixon chose Gerald R. Ford, the minority leader of the House. Before doing so, he first queried Ford about his future political ambitions. Ford assured him that he had no plans regarding the presidential election in 1976. "Just because I'd be serving as Vice President for the remainder of his term didn't mean I'd expect to be the Presidential nominee in 1976."

"Well, that's good," responded Nixon, "because John Connally [of Texas] is my choice for 1976. He'd be excellent."

"That's no problem as far as I'm concerned," Ford assured the President.[49]

So he was appointed, and the Senate confirmed him on November 27 by a vote of 92 to 3, and the House did the same on December 6 by a vote of 387 to 5. He never really wanted such a high office. His ambition stopped at the office of Speaker, which he never achieved. "As has happened so often in my life I received a break," he admitted. His breaks had begun with his first assignment to a major House committee when he arrived in Congress, and they continued regularly until he finally sat in the White House.[50]

The Republican Conference chose John J. Rhodes of Arizona to succeed Ford as minority leader when both Arends and Anderson decided against running for the position. A conservative like Ford, Rhodes had chaired the House Republican Policy Committee and served on the Appropriations Committee.

THE SCANDAL TOUCHING the Vice President could not compare to the ever-unfolding Watergate scandal. Nixon denied any connection to the break-in, but a massive cover-up was instituted in the White House to protect the would-be burglars. Perjury, obstruction of justice and bribery were just a few of the crimes the White House allegedly committed. The burglars were tried by the chief judge of the U.S. District Court of the District of Columbia, John J. Sirica, and five of the accused pleaded guilty and two were found guilty by a jury. During the trial, information surfaced that forced the resignations on April 30, 1973, of two close advisers of the President, H. R. Haldeman and John R. Ehrlichman, as well as the Attorney General Richard Kleindienst, who was replaced by Secretary of Defense Elliot Richardson.

To add to the Watergate scandal, Representative William O. Mills, Republican from Maryland, committed suicide on May 24, 1973, when it was revealed that he failed to report a $25,000 campaign contribution from Nixon's reelection finance committee. He was the third member of Congress since January 1, 1946, to commit suicide and the fourteenth member to meet a violent death.[51]

Early in 1973, the Senate had voted to investigate presidential campaign activities and created a committee headed by Senator Sam J. Ervin, Jr., of North Carolina. This Senate Watergate Committee commenced public hearings on May 17, and its televised proceedings attracted national attention. During testimony to the committee from June 25 to 29, John Dean, the President's former counsel who had been recently fired, revealed that Nixon had been party to the cover-up, and Alexander Butterfield, a former presidential aide, disclosed on July 16 that since 1971 the President had tape-recorded all his conversations in the White House and the Executive Office Building. The committee and Judge Sirica ordered that the tapes be turned over to the special prosecutor, Archibald Cox, who had been appointed by Attorney General Richardson in May. On July 23, Nixon refused, citing executive privilege. These subpoenas, he said, constituted "such a massive invasion of presidential conversations that the institution of the presidency itself would be fatally compromised" if he complied.[52] But Judge Sirica, on August 29, ordered that nine tapes be turned over to him for private review.

Nixon then offered a compromise in which written summaries of the tapes, verified by Senator John C. Stennis of Mississippi, would be provided. Cox rejected it. Whereupon the President ordered both Attorney General Richardson and Deputy Attorney General William D. Ruckelshaus to dismiss Cox, and both refused and resigned. Solicitor General Robert H. Bork became the acting attorney general, and he fired Cox during this so-called Saturday night massacre of October 20, 1973. Texas trial lawyer Leon Jaworski was then appointed special prosecutor, replacing Cox.

Under pressure, Nixon agreed to comply with the subpoena and released some of the tapes on October 2. A month later, on November 21, a gap of eighteen and a half minutes was discovered, which experts later decided was caused by multiple erasures. This gap involved a conversation between Nixon and Haldeman on June 20, 1972.

Although many House members refused to even think about impeaching the President, sixteen impeachment resolutions, sponsored by eighty-four members, were introduced in the House. These were referred to the Judiciary Committee. Ironically, Nixon might have escaped impeachment if the eighty-four-year-old Emanuel Celler, Chairman of the Judiciary Committee, had not been defeated in a primary Democratic nomination for the 93rd Congress in 1972, by Elizabeth Holtzman, an attorney. Her election by only six hundred votes was momentous because she became a member of the Judiciary Committee that was now chaired by Peter Rodino. "If Celler had remained as chairman, Nixon could have served out his entire second term," declared Tip O'Neill. Celler would have insisted either that "the charges against Nixon were too weak to be taken seriously or that the whole issue was beyond the scope of his committee." He was a stubborn, arrogant old man and nobody could get him to move—not Rayburn, not McCormack and "certainly not Carl Albert. If the impeachment process had gone to the Judiciary Committee under Manny Celler, it would have died there."[53]

The committee began closed preliminary hearings on October 30, 1973. One million dollars was appropriated for the investigation, and a staff of one hundred persons was assembled, including forty-five lawyers. There were six major categories in the investigation: Watergate break-in and cover-up, personal finances, political use of government agencies, domestic surveillance, impoundment of funds and campaign fund abuses. Although the impeachment of Andrew Johnson had been conducted by a select committee, the Speaker decided that Nixon's impeachment should be handled by the entire Judiciary Committee of thirty-eight members under Peter Rodino, a quiet man, said Albert, of quiet talents.[54]

The reason for assigning the full committee to this task and not a select committee was the recognition that it would provide the public with a lesson in how Congress operated. During his thirty years as a member of the House, Albert had heard many complaints against the Congress: the slowness of members in their deliberations, the inefficiency of its procedures, the arrogance of its anonymous old men, the mediocrity of its members. Albert knew that if the people saw the Judiciary Committee in action on this important issue they would come to realize that the members of

The Judiciary Committee, chaired by Peter Rodino, investigated the Watergate burglary and the White House cover-up.

Congress were not mediocrities or incompetents. "No decision I could ever make would be more significant for my country," he said. "In an impeachment inquiry, two institutions would be judged, not one. We would examine the president, and the American people would examine us."[55]

As a matter of fact, a poll taken early in 1974 revealed that eight out of ten individuals interviewed felt that Congress was failing to do a satisfactory job as the nation's governing body.[56]

On February 6, 1974, the House authorized the Judiciary Committee to investigate whether grounds existed for the impeachment of Richard Nixon. Several weeks later, on March 1, the Watergate grand jury indicted seven former Nixon advisers and aides, and Judge Sirica subsequently directed that the evidence be turned over to the Judiciary Committee. On April 11, the committee voted 33 to 3 to subpoena the tapes of conversations held in February, March and April 1973. Five days later Special Prosecutor Jaworski issued a subpoena for sixty-four tapes. Nixon refused, but he released over a thousand pages of edited conversations to the Judiciary Committee on April 30. They hardly satisfied the members, who demanded the actual tapes. In late May 1974, after the failure of two more subpoenas, they sent a stern letter to the President, reminding him that he was not the judge of what constituted a proper inquiry into his own impeachment or what evidence should be allowed in such an inquiry. Nixon responded on June 10 in a letter to Rodino, declaring that he was "determined to do nothing which . . . would render the executive branch henceforth and forever more subservient to the legislative branch, and would thereby destroy the constitutional balance."[57]

On July 24, 1974, the Supreme Court, on an appeal from the Special Prosecutor's order to turn over the tapes, bypassing the Court of Appeals, rendered a unanimous decision (8 to 0, with William Rehnquist abstaining), stating that the President must surrender evidence in a criminal proceeding.

When the House Judiciary Committee ended its closed investigatory phase, it scheduled public viewing for July 24, 25, 26, 27, 29 and 30, during which days it would debate whether impeachment recommendations should be sent to the House floor. The decision to televise the committee's meetings engendered strong objections by members, and it took many impassioned pleas from the floor to convince a majority that such a momentous event should be open to the public.

Convince them, they did. On July 22 the House amended the rules by a roll call vote of 346 to 40 to permit televising the debates. The committee

Hugh D. Scott, Jr., of Pennsylvania, the Senate minority leader; Senator Barry M. Goldwater of Arizona; and John J. Rhodes, the House leader of the Republican Party, issue a public statement regarding Watergate and Nixon's possible impeachment.

itself agreed to open their proceedings by a vote of 31 to 7, on condition that the networks not allow commercial messages to interrupt the deliberations. On the evening of July 24, the televised debate began.

The American public avidly watched the likes of Barbara Jordan, Paul Sarbanes, Jack Brooks, Elizabeth Holtzman and others "wrestle publicly with their own consciences and their nation's future." They came to recognize, said Speaker Albert, that rather remarkable and talented individuals served in the House of Representatives, and that the system worked, just as the Founders had intended.[58] One of the most impressive members of the committee was Barbara Jordan, an African-American member from Texas, who gave a compelling speech on the constitutional basis for the impeachment of a President. "The Constitution charges the President with the task of taking care that the laws be faithfully executed," she intoned in her mellifluous voice, "and yet the President has counseled his aides to commit perjury, willfully disregarded the secrecy of grand jury proceedings, concealed surreptitious entry, and attempted to compromise a Federal judge while publicly displaying his cooperation with the processes of criminal justice."[59]

Not until July 27, 1974, did the House Judiciary Committee vote the first of three articles of impeachment, 27 to 11, with 7 Republicans siding with the majority. This article recommended impeachment on the grounds that Nixon "engaged personally and through his subordinates and agents in a course of conduct designed to delay, impede, and obstruct the investigation" of the Watergate burglary, to "cover up, conceal, and protect those responsible," and to "conceal the existence and scope of other unlawful covert activities." On July 29 a second article of impeachment was adopted by a vote of 28 to 10, accusing the President of "violating the constitutional rights of citizens, impairing the due and proper administration of justice in the conduct of lawful inquiries, and of contravening the law governing agencies of the executive branch and the purposes of these agencies." Finally, on July 30, by a vote of 21 to 17, Nixon was charged with defiance of committee subpoenas, thus impeding the impeachment process. But the committee voted down, 26 to 12, an article accusing him of usurping congressional war powers by bombing Cambodia.[60]

On August 5, Nixon released the transcripts of three conversations with H. R. Haldeman, White House chief of staff, recorded on June 23, 1972. These conversations took place six days after the break-in and proved to be what was called the "smoking gun," because they revealed that Nixon had been aware of the cover-up and had personally ordered a halt to an FBI investigation into the Watergate break-in. The eleven Republicans who voted against impeachment now said they would change their votes.

The vulgarity of the language used by the President in these tapes shocked many Americans. They revealed a foul-mouthed, bigoted man who had disgraced his office. The general public now realized that Nixon had betrayed his oath to preserve, protect and defend the Constitution of the United States.

On August 7, 1974, the House voted 385 to 25 to permit radio and television live coverage of the impeachment debate on the floor. At the same time Nixon met with three leading Republicans in Congress: John J. Rhodes, the House leader of the Republican party, Hugh D. Scott, Jr., of Pennsylvania, the Senate minority leader, and Senator Barry M. Goldwater of Arizona, who told him that he could not expect more than ten votes against his impeachment in the House, and not more than fifteen in the Senate against his removal. Rhodes later said that the trip up Pennsylvania Avenue to meet with Nixon at the White House "was the most trying ordeal of his 30 years in Congress."[61]

Around the country there were repeated calls for Nixon to step down. The next day, August 8, in a television address, the President announced his resignation, declaring that he "no longer had a strong enough political base" to persevere. The resignation took effect on the following day, and the House of Representatives accepted the report of the impeachment inquiry on August 20.

Gerald Ford immediately took the oath of office and nominated Nelson Rockefeller as the new Vice President. The nomination was approved by both houses of Congress, according to the procedure described in the 25th Amendment to the Constitution. "Our long national nightmare is over," Ford declared. "Our great republic is a government of laws and not of men."[62] Ford's and Rockefeller's advance in the executive branch of government represented the first time in American history that neither the President or Vice President had been elected by the people.

A month later, on September 8, 1974, Ford gave Nixon an unconditional pardon. He denied that a "deal" had been struck in testimony given on October 17 before the House Judiciary Subcommittee on Criminal Justice. Rather, he insisted that it was his wish to end the controversy and restore peace in the country. At the same time, many of Nixon's aides were convicted of conspiracy, obstruction of justice, perjury and violating federal campaign laws, and received varying prison sentences.[63]

THE NATION WAS shocked again when, at 2:00 a.m. in the morning of October 7, 1974, the Washington police stopped a Lincoln Continental (the same type automobile that congressmen had been receiving from the Ford Motor Company at reduced leasing rates) near the Jefferson Memorial. One of the five passengers in the car was an intoxicated Wilbur Mills, the Chairman of the Ways and Means Committee, his face bruised and his nose bloody. Another passenger, Annabel Battistella, jumped out of the car and plunged into the Tidal Basin. It soon developed that Battistella was a thirty-eight-year-old stripper who performed as "Fanne Fox, the Argentine Fire-cracker" at the local Silver Slipper. After secluding himself for a few days, Mills reemerged and apologized to his family and constituents. But on November 30, he appeared drunk onstage with Fanne Fox at a Boston strip club. When asked if his behavior in a burlesque theater would hurt him, Mills replied, "This won't ruin me . . . nothing can ruin me."[64] Three days later he entered the Bethesda Naval Hospital suffering from "exhaustion." He later resigned his chairmanship of Ways and Means Committee and publicly admitted that he was being treated for alcoholism. He was replaced as chairman by Al Ullman of Oregon.

Wilbur Mills had been a superb legislator. Diligent and imaginative, he worked hard and helped to finance many of the social reforms put forward by the Johnson administration. He was a "hero" to the members of the Ways and Means Committee, even to those of the opposition. According to Republican Barber Conable of New York, who served on the committee, Mills "practiced the kind of bipartisan, consensus politics" that made a Republican member "feel like he was an important member of the committee from the start." Mills worked closely with John Byrnes of Wisconsin, the ranking Republican on the committee, and their "cooperative relationship" generated the bipartisanship that was so characteristic of Ways and Means under his direction. Mills "wanted to stretch the tent so that everybody could get in it." And the bills he reported to the full House invariably passed "because he worried about winning." He would roam the floor, "making sure that influential members were able to accept this or that provision of the bill." If they had objections, Mills would return to his committee and say, "Fellows, we have to change the bill. We are going to have trouble." And he would suggest "this or that potential change." Put simply, said Conable, "he went through an informal democratic process to be sure he was not going to be defeated on the floor with respect to any detail."[65]

It took enormous skill to chair a committee successfully, even a sub-committee, and years of experience. Women members had a particularly

Wilbur Mills, a distinguished chairman of the Ways and Means Committee whose career ended tragically in scandal.

difficult time gaining the political clout that would advance them to a chairmanship. At first, having a woman lording it over a group of male colleagues seemed most improper. It invited all manner of vulgar comment. Even so, in this era of change, they could not be denied the opportunity indefinitely, and by the mid-1970s, a few of them had achieved the prize. And that required additional changes of some procedures. What to call them? "We had a very powerful member of the House," remembered a future Speaker, Tom Foley. Her name was Leonor Sullivan of Missouri, and she chaired the Merchant Marine and Fisheries Committee during the 93rd and 94th Congresses (1973–1977). Witnesses who came before the committee would often say, "Good morning, Madam Chair."

"Bang, bang, bang, bang" sounded across the room, as the gavel, wielded by the chair, repeatedly hit the wooden desk. "Please address the chair correctly," ordered Sullivan.

"I'm sorry, I'm sorry," stammered the witness. "Good morning, Madam Chairperson."

The gavel struck again. "Bang, bang, bang, bang."

Finally, "a pitying staff member would whisper something in the witness's ear."

The witness brightened. "I'm very sorry, Madam Chairman."

"She wanted to be called Chairman," laughed Foley, "and her theory, I think, was, when women become general officers or admirals in service, there's not a special title for them. . . . She felt that the title, Chairman, was a rank, and not a gender designation. She wanted to have the same rank as males."[66]

Unfortunately, women in the House had "to wage virtually every battle alone" to obtain their rights, remarked a new member from Colorado, Pat Schroeder. "The assumption was that we should be so appreciative of being allowed into the hallowed halls of Congress, we'd fall on our knees in gratitude for every crumb." The first time that Schroeder wandered onto the outside porch of the House chamber for some fresh air during a debate, "I could hear a lot of *harrumphing* behind me. . . . They felt 'letting' women on the House floor was bad enough" without having to endure further invasions of privileged areas.[67]

There were some women in the House who really drove men to distraction, and seemed to take delight in validating every prejudice the men felt about having them in Congress. Bella Abzug of New York was perhaps the most notorious. She was a feisty, passionate, loud-mouthed combatant, and any male who gave her cause for complaint soon felt the lash of her tongue.

Southern House members were particularly uncomfortable with the female presence in their midst, and when Pat Schroeder was placed on the Armed Services Committee, its chairman, F. Edward Hébert of Louisiana,

Pat Schroeder and Ron Dellums were forced to share a single chair because the chairman of the Armed Services Committee, F. Edward Hébert, objected to their presence on his committee.

said to her, "I hope you aren't going to be a skinny Bella Abzug." Hébert tried to block Schroeder's appointment and the appointment of Ron Dellums of California, an African-American, to his committee. When he failed, he took his revenge by announcing that "while he might not be able to control the makeup of the committee, he could damn well control the number of chairs in his hearing room. . . . He said that women and blacks were worth only half of one 'regular' member, so he added only one seat to the committee room and made Ron and me share it. Nobody else objected, and nobody offered to scrounge up another chair."[68] The fact that in the 1970s not another member of the committee offered an objection deeply offended Schroeder. Either they agreed with Hébert about having a woman and a black as colleagues or they were afraid to challenge his authority.

Such were the problems women faced in the early years of their arrival in Congress. Nevertheless, their number has steadily increased. By 1975 they had formed the first Congressional Women's Caucus, to sponsor legislation directly affecting children, women and health care.

An issue of particular interest to women suddenly arose that would bedevil the country for years to come. In 1973, the Supreme Court, in *Roe v. Wade,* struck down state abortion laws as a violation of the rights of privacy guaranteed under the 14th Amendment to the Constitution. Later, in June 1977, Henry J. Hyde, Republican of Illinois, introduced a rider to an appropriations bill in the House which outlawed the use of Medicaid funds to pay for abortions except where the life of the mother was endangered. It passed 207 to 164. Around the country the number of legal abortions had increased dramatically, setting off a national debate between those who were "pro-life" and those favoring a choice. Every future appointment to the Supreme Court brought concern as to a candidate's position on the Roe decision.

In Congress, women simply wanted to be treated equally, both in the House and in the Democratic Caucus and Republican Conference. And their persistence helped bring about further reforms of House procedures and rules. At the next meeting of the Democratic Caucus from December 2 to 5, 1974, following the Wilbur Mills scandal, a number of important changes were adopted, including that of requiring secret ballot elections of all chairmen. In effect this drove the final nail into the coffin of the seniority system, which for decades had determined access to positions of power. One immediate result of this reform was the removal of Hébert as chairman of the Armed Services Committee. He was replaced by Mel Price of Illinois, and both Schroeder and Dellums got their own seats in the meeting room. Moreover, in 1992, Dellums became chairman of this committee.[69]

House Republicans voted on April 29, 1975, to open their Conference meetings to the public, and the Democrats followed suit on September 9. In deciding leadership, the Republicans unanimously re-elected John J. Rhodes of Arizona as minority leader and Robert H. Michel of Illinois as minority whip, replacing Leslie C. Arends who retired.

ONE IMPORTANT RESULT of the Watergate scandal was passage of the Campaign Finance Law in 1974. Among many things, it established spending limits and required full disclosure of campaign contributions and expenses. Another result was the massive defeat of Republicans in the midterm elections of 1974. In the House, the Republicans lost 40 seats; 92 new representatives were elected, of whom 71 were Democrats. These "Watergate babies," as Tip O' Neill called them, were "highly sophisticated and talented . . . and independent, and they didn't hesitate to remind you that they were elected on their own, often without any help from the Democratic party." In not a few cases they defeated incumbents in the primaries. "They were not steeped in the old traditions of, you know, by your grace and favor, Mr. Chairman," commented Foley. Veterans of the House called them "outsiders" who had not come up through regular channels, like state legislatures or city councils or county offices. They had never "rung doorbells, or driven people to the polls, or stayed late stuffing envelopes at campaign headquarters," remarked Tip O'Neill, who was struck by how many of them told him they decided to run for office because of Vietnam, Watergate or environmental issues. They said they had had no interest in politics until Robert Kennedy ran for office in 1968.[70]

These Watergate babies met together over four days at the start of the 94th Congress in January 1975, and invited every chairman to address them. They came to the House "with unbelievable, for the time, unbelievable assertiveness." They were "unbelievably uppity." Some of the chairmen declared that they were "too busy" to accept the invitation, whereupon they were informed that if they failed to appear the group would vote en masse against them in the Caucus. "It was mind boggling."[71] These chairmen immediately found time to oblige them.

At the Democratic Caucus meeting, chaired by Phillip Burton, a motion by Don Edwards was offered to abolish the old House Un-American Activities Committee. Burton called for a voice vote, then, without many knowing what had happened, pounded his gavel and declared the motion adopted. Between them, Burton and Edwards had "abolished the most infamous and anti-democratic committee of the postwar era."[72]

To some it looked as though the Democrats had a veto-proof Congress after the 1974 midterm election, until they remembered that between thirty and forty conservatives of their party regularly voted with the Republicans who had remained loyal to the Ford administration.

President Ford and the Republican Party were scarred not only by the Nixon pardon but also by the high inflation rate and rising consumer prices, a trade deficit, a falling stock market, a slowdown in manufactures and increased unemployment. In addition, Congress and Ford wrangled for over a year on the appropriate manner by which to deal with the nation's dependence on energy before the President reluctantly signed the Energy Policy and Conservation Act of 1975, which, among other things, required improved energy efficiency in automobiles and other consumer products.

AND MORE SCANDALS erupted. One that drew bemused attention occurred in May 1976, when the *Washington Post* ran a front-page article in which it was claimed that one Elizabeth Ray had been kept on the House payroll as a House Administration Committee secretary, but that her only duties involved servicing Chairman Wayne Hays's sexual needs. "I can't type. I can't file. I can't even answer the phone," she was reported to have said. And she was paid $14,000 a year.[73] At first Hays, an arrogant, abrasive fellow whom the Steering Committee had considered dumping, denied the charge, but then he asked the House Ethics Committee to investigate the matter, admitting he had a "personal relationship" with Ms. Ray. On September 1, he submitted a letter of resignation from Congress to Speaker Albert.

Such scandals triggered additional reforms. The House Administration Committee, on June 28, 1976, adopted a series of orders to implement

Caucus proposals that did not require House action. It demanded a strict accounting of salaries and duties of staff employees and monthly submission of reports about how House funds were spent. It also eliminated postage stamp allowances, currently at $1,140 a year, and ended the practice of allowing members to convert unused stationery and travel allowances into cash for their personal use.[74]

As for the Ethics Committee, many members complained that it "too often sidestepped or ignored" action on standards because of "the operation of the buddy system or because of the reluctance of individual members to criticize colleagues." John J. Flynt, chairman of the Committee, admitted that it was "never pleasant or enjoyable to sit in judgement of one's peers." Besides, to expel a member required a two-thirds vote. And the Ethics Committee usually wanted a formal, sworn statement of complaint from a member of Congress before investigating any misconduct, something most members were reluctant to do. As a consequence, many Americans doubted that Congress had the will to properly police itself.[75]

ON A HAPPIER note, the nation celebrated its bicentennial on July 4, 1976, with many festive events and parades, including a massive display of sailing ships in the New York harbor.

ON OCTOBER 24, 1976, the *Washington Post* claimed that South Korean agents dispersed between $500,000 and $1 million in cash and gifts to members of Congress for the purpose of providing "a favorable legislative climate" toward South Korea. Over the next several months, an investigation by the Commission on Administrative Review, which had been created following the Wayne Hays scandal and was chaired by David R. Obey of Wisconsin, resulted in the adoption by the House on March 2, 1977, of a new Ethics Code by a vote of 402 to 22.[76] One of the provisions of the code limited to 15 percent the amount of a member's official salary he or she might earn from employment outside Congress; another provision limited honoraria from public speeches to $750. But the country at large continued to lose faith in the ability of Congress to enforce its Ethics Code. Although a number of congressmen were subsequently indicted on charges of conspiracy, bribery, mail fraud and acceptance of illegal gratuities, the Ethics Committee recommended nothing more than censure, which the House reduced to reprimand when the accused denied any intentional wrongdoing.

However, the series of scandals that surfaced in 1976 seemed to have little impact on the presidential election of that year. Democrats nominated former governor of Georgia Jimmy Carter, after Hubert Humphrey decided against running, and Carter chose Senator Walter Mondale of Minnesota as his running mate. The Republicans nominated Ford, despite a strong bid to replace him by Ronald Reagan, the governor of California. In place of Rockefeller, who withdrew, they named Senator Robert Dole of Kansas. Despite the many economic advantages the Democrats seemed to enjoy, despite Watergate and the Nixon pardon, and despite the frequent quarrels between Ford and Congress, especially the one over energy, Carter barely won the election. He received 297 electoral votes to Ford's 240. Happily for the Democrats, they retained control of both houses of Congress. In the House there were now 292 Democrats and 143 Republicans, and in the Senate the Democrats held a 62 to 38 advantage.

In June 1976, at the start of the election campaign, Speaker Carl Albert announced that he would not seek another term as a member of the House of Representatives. As Speaker, he presided over a rapidly changing House in which authority was more widely distributed among the members, and the Democratic Caucus and Republican Conference had been revitalized. His most unique contribution as Speaker was that he "reached out beyond the city of Washington, and became a figure in national and international parliamentary affairs." His predecessor, John McCormack, "wasn't a feature on the social scene of Washington. He was a devoted husband, and all that he wanted to do was go home at the end of the day and enjoy dinner with his wife." Albert, declared Tom Foley, "started making trips abroad, to Asia, to Korea, to the Philippines, to Japan, to the UK, to the Soviet Union, to Romania, to Yugoslavia. This was a new kind of outreach for House Speakers. And, I think it started an era in which Speakers of the House were not sort of internally limited by the House. . . . And he did it very well. He had an interest in foreign affairs and different cultures."[77]

Over the past several years, Albert had informed Tip O'Neill at least half a dozen times that he, O'Neill, would succeed him as Speaker when he stepped down, but it still came as a shock to O'Neill when Albert announced his retirement. At the time of the formal announcement, the majority leader was in California helping to raise funds for the party. He was sitting around the pool of the hotel when one of the congressional candidates came running in with the news. "Tip," he said, "I just heard on the radio that Carl Albert is retiring. Let me be the first one to support you for Speaker."

Without question, O'Neill had been ambitious for the Speakership since he arrived in the House. So he immediately started rounding up commitments, only to find, to his delight, that he had no opposition.[78] He was a man his colleagues respected and loved. They knew he had no personal agenda other than serving in the House and helping his party. He was a politician to his fingertips. He was easily elected when Congress reconvened in January 1977.

As Speaker, Tip O'Neill made himself accessible at all times. He appeared on the House floor at the start of each session. He enjoyed conversing with other House members, including those of the opposition.[79] "He

Three Democratic Speakers, Tip O'Neill, Carl Albert, and John McCormack, who presided over a House in which the members of both parties usually maintained cordial and friendly relations.

had little ego and no animosity toward anyone. He ruled by humor and anecdote."[80] And he had been carefully groomed for the position. After all, he was the only member to serve in all four positions of the party leadership: Campaign Committee chair, whip, majority leader and now Speaker—to say nothing of the many years he served on the Rules Committee.

But according to Republican Henry Hyde of Illinois, Tip had only two close Republican friends in Congress: Bob Michel of Illinois and Silvio Conte of Massachusetts. "We [Republicans] were barely tolerated by Tip O'Neill, who was bitterly partisan."[81]

If the selection of Speaker went easily, the contest for majority leader turned into a bitter brawl. At first there were only three candidates: Burton, Bolling and Majority Whip John McFall. Burton and Bolling loathed each other and worked to block each other's election. In an effort to improve his standing among Democrats and refute his reputation for aloofness, Bolling began holding dinner parties at his home. Many thought him arrogant. Indeed, he was. "If I told him they just discovered an atom bomb under the Capitol," recounted one member, "he'd say, 'Yes, I knew it was there all the time.' "[82]

Tip liked none of the three for majority leader. He distrusted Burton, thought him "crazy" and "revolutionary," and maybe even feared him. He knew Bolling from his days on the Rules Committee and could not stomach his arrogance. And McFall, whom he liked, did not have the votes to be chosen.

Tip needed another candidate. At the moment it looked as though Burton would win, hands down. For the Speaker to openly oppose him could have and probably would have catastrophic consequences. Besides, he did not relish the thought of breakfasting every morning with a man who, according to one aide, "would reach over and rip your lungs out," if he disagreed with your policy or strategy.[83]

So, working through an aide, Tip asked Rostenkowski and a few others to find a better candidate. After hurried conversations with the membership, they decided that Jim Wright of Texas, an outstanding floor orator and manager, was the only man to beat Burton. Rostenkowski invited Wright to Chicago to meet Mayor Daley, who had previously thrown his support to Bolling. Convinced that he should switch his support, Daley encouraged other big-city mayors to follow his lead and lean on their congressional delegates to vote for Wright.[84]

Realizing his opportunity for advancement in the party had arrived, Wright announced his candidacy on July 27, 1976. He figured that McFall was "beatable," Burton had lusted for the job for the last two years but had not yet locked it up, and Bolling . . . well Bolling was the "child prodigy of Sam Rayburn . . . and you can't be that forever."[85]

With the stakes so high, and the bitterness among the contestants so intense, the election rivaled that of the presidency in 1976. When the Democratic Caucus convened in January 1977 and the balloting began for the position of majority leader, it still looked as though Burton would win. Indeed, the first vote seemed convincing. Burton garnered 106 votes to 81 for Bolling, 77 for Wright, and 31 for McFall. That knocked out McFall. On the second ballot, Burton gained one vote, reaching 107, but Wright moved up to second place by winning 95, and Bolling came in last with 93.

Bolling was thus eliminated. And his friends were deeply shocked. Some of them blamed Burton for manipulating Wright's rise and swore to get even. Burton knew he was in danger as Bolling and other enemies fanned out among the members, urging them to switch to Wright. It slowly dawned on the crowd that this was not a simple matter of a routine party contest. With such a sharp contrast in personalities between the flamboyant Burton and the cool managerial skill of Wright, they recognized that "they were deciding the future direction of the Democratic party in Congress and possibly beyond for years to come."[86]

The balloting began again. The tension in the room was almost unbearable. As the ballots were counted it appeared to be a dead heat. Then, when there was only one ballot yet to count, Charlie Wilson reached into the box and pulled it out. It was for Jim Wright.

People screamed, then started chanting: Wright, WRIGHT, *WRIGHT*. He had defeated the supposed champion, 148 to 147. About 50 of Bolling's 93 supporters switched to Wright.

Wright recalled that "two fellows came in the door holding up one finger with smiles on their faces. It dawned on others before it did me, I think, because I was suddenly surrounded by people reaching over, shaking hands, congratulating me. I was overwhelmed by a tide of emotion and then when the announcement was made, I was still in a state of euphoria."

The voting was so close that the chair, Tom Foley, did not want to announce it, but rather call for a recapitulation. "This is too close. We've got to be absolutely sure." But Burton would not allow it. "Either announce it, Mr. Chairman, or I'm going down and taking the microphone right now and conceding. . . . I think he was convinced he'd lost it, and he didn't want to go through the emotional agony of another," said Foley.

Bolling went home and had two stiff drinks: one in condolence, and one in celebration.[87]

The towering liberal, the titan for reform had been narrowly defeated. Those who voted against him saw him as too manipulative, too driven, too ambitious and too contentious. "Phil had people who would walk on water with him," claimed Foley. "But he also unnecessarily antagonized members . . . by losing his temper and then he'd go back and apologize." Said Rostenkowski, ". . . he was too liberal for me."[88]

The leadership then went on to beat back another attempt to make the whip elective. Instead O'Neill and Wright appointed John Brademas to succeed McFall as whip, and Rostenkowski as deputy whip. Having backed the winner, Rostenkowski was rewarded by being restored to a leadership position.

When, as the new Speaker, O'Neill walked into his office he found it completely unfurnished. At that time, the Speaker was permitted to take everything in his office and ship it to a site of his choosing where it could be reassembled to replicate what he had in the Capitol. The setup resembled a presidential library, so to speak. As Speaker, O'Neill, along with the Vice President and chief justice, had the right to borrow historic artifacts from the government. One of the things O'Neill borrowed was a huge oak desk from the Smithsonian Institution. It had belonged to Grover Cleveland. "During my years as Speaker," O'Neill recalled, "that desk dominated my office and was a terrific conversation piece." When President Ronald Reagan later saw it, he told the Speaker that he had once played Grover Cleveland in the movies. "No, Mr. President," O'Neill replied, "you're thinking of Grover Cleveland Alexander, the ball player." It happened that O'Neill had just seen the movie on late-night television.[89]

O'Neill met Jimmy Carter in Georgia. He and a number of other party leaders visited the newly elected President to discuss policy. Carter explained his program and his desire to see it enacted by Congress, whereupon Tip O'Neill advised him to consult with House committee chairmen. But the President-elect dismissed the suggestion, claiming there was no need. If necessary, he said, he would appeal over their heads to the people. "At that precise moment Tip knew they were in trouble."[90]

As Carter's inauguration approached, the Speaker learned that his family had been given seats in the back row at the event, whereupon he called to speak to Hamilton Jordan, a Carter aide, who was managing the inaugural.

"Is this Hannibal Jerkin [sic]," O'Neill asked. "This is Tip O'Neill. I'm Speaker of the House. You may not be aware of this, but I am your host for the inaugural. Now it has come to my attention . . . you've given my family these seats in the very back. You certainly have the right to do that, since you are running the inaugural, but I do want you to know that, if that happens, for the first ninety days, nothing this administration wants will go through the House. Because the power to recognize is solely the Speaker's, and I will recognize no one who wants to help an operation this stupid. So, you can either decide to change where my family is sitting, or you can decide to go to Georgia until sometime shortly after April."[91]

Undoubtedly, the seats were changed.

Once Carter was inaugurated, he came to the Speaker's office to learn about Congress and how it operated. Unfortunately, said O'Neill, the new President did not have a strong staff and never seemed able to build popular support—or even build support among Democrats in Congress. Therefore, despite the large majorities in both houses, little of note was accomplished during his administration. According to O'Neill, Carter's people came from the south and "just didn't understand Irish or Jewish politicians, or the nuances of city politics." A southerner is a "sweet talker who can skin you alive with his charm." A northerner, on the other hand, "is far more blunt and rambunctious. Whereas the northerner enjoys conflicts and will actually seek them out, the southerner does his best to avoid political quarrels and skirmishes."[92]

Carter had a poor relationship with Congress, agreed Barber Conable. He would inform the members what he wanted "and that was the end of it." No follow-through. He did not "participate in the process." He was good at detail, "but he didn't have a clear vision for the country, and he wound up judging the Congress and not leading it."[93] John Murtha of Pennsylvania claimed that Jimmy Carter knew "more about more things than any President in the history of the United States. . . . And yet . . . he . . . didn't pat you on the back; hell, he just didn't get along with people."[94]

In midterm, Carter reshuffled his cabinet and forced the resignations of several members. He also tried to micromanage his administration and found it an impossible task. The result triggered a lack of confidence in his leadership by the public and, insisted O'Neill, a loss of twelve House seats and three Senate seats in the 1978 midterm election.

Carter also held a particularly unfortunate domestic economic summit at Camp David, a presidential retreat, with over a hundred participants of varying backgrounds. Out of that summit came a speech by the President in which he described a national malaise or a "crisis of confidence," of stagnation and paralysis. It set a tone that profoundly discouraged many Americans.[95]

To make things worse, a sting operation conducted by the FBI between July 1979 and January 1980 targeted several members of Congress. The bureau decided to check reports that legislators took bribes in exchange for official favors. A front organization named Abdul Enterprises Ltd. (called Abscam) solicited business by claiming that its agents represented Arab business men who were prepared to exchange money for legislative favors. FBI agents dressed as Arab sheiks videotaped their meetings with the Congressmen, but many later criticized the procedure as an entrapment. Six House members were subsequently indicted and found guilty in 1980 and 1981. The first to be indicted was Michael "Ozzie" Myers, Democrat of Pennsylvania, who was found guilty on August 30, 1980, of bribery, conspiracy and interstate travel to aid racketeering. The others included Richard Kelly, Republican of Florida; John W. Jenrette, Democrat of South Carolina; Raymond F. Lederer, Democrat of Pennsylvania; John M. Murphy, Democrat of New York; and Frank Thompson, Jr., Democrat of New Jersey. Murphy was chairman of the House Merchant Marine and Fisheries Committee, and Thompson was chair of the House Administration Committee. This sting was one of the largest investigations involving members of Congress and included more than $400,000 in cash.

A month later, on October 2, 1980, the House, by a vote of 376 to 30, voted to expel Myers. He had the distinction of being the first member to be expelled since 1861. As for the other members caught in the sting, all but Lederer and Williams lost their bid for reelection before they could be brought to trial or investigated by the Ethics Committee. Lederer was subsequently convicted in January 1981 and resigned from the House to prevent expulsion.[96]

For the Carter administration, things went steadily downhill. In foreign affairs it suffered a particularly devastating blow in Iran, despite its success in September 1978 in helping to end the hostilities between Israel and Egypt. The trouble began when the Shah of Iran fled the country after a revolt by Islamic fundamentalists. When he was admitted to the United

States on October 22, 1979, to obtain medical treatment, Ayatollah Khomeini urged his followers to demonstrate. Hundreds of militant students stormed the U.S. Embassy in Tehran and demanded the return of the shah for trial, but Carter refused to extradite him and froze all Iranian assets in the United States. The militants took fifty-two American hostages. With the exception of thirteen female and black Americans, these hostages were held in captivity for 444 days. A halfhearted attempt at rescue in April 1980 ended in failure, and eight U.S. servicemen died in the effort. For the next year the crisis dominated the news and American foreign policy.

In the presidential contest of 1980, these many disasters provided the Republican ticket of Ronald Reagan and George H. W. Bush with an unexpected landslide over Carter and Mondale. Reagan won 43 states for 489 electoral votes to Carter's six states for 49 electoral votes. So complete was the victory from the outset of the counting that Carter conceded the election even before the final results from the West Coast were tabulated. The Republicans also captured the Senate, 53 to 46 (with 1 independent), gaining 12 seats; but the Democrats retained control of the House, 243 to 192. Still, the Republicans had won 33 additional seats, and because of the Dixie-Republican alliance, as it was frequently called, the tone and style of the lower chamber became increasingly conservative. "Many of the initiating, leading, influential liberals were defeated in the House," Conable remarked. Of particular pleasure for Republicans was the electoral defeat of the majority whip, John Brademas of Indiana, and Al Ullman of Oregon, chairman of the Ways and Means Committee, who were seen by their constituents as too close to "the mess in Washington."[97]

Did this election constitute a mandate? O'Neill did not think so. "Ronald Reagan didn't win the 1980 election as much as Jimmy Carter lost it," he said. "Despite my affection and respect for Carter, the fact is that by election day a great many Americans couldn't wait to get rid of him." Against a really strong candidate in a robust economy, O'Neill averred, "Ronald Reagan would have had no more chance of being elected president of the United States than the man in the moon."[98]

In the House Democratic Caucus, O'Neill was unopposed for reelection as Speaker, as was majority leader Jim Wright of Texas. Wright then announced that Thomas S. Foley of Washington would succeed Brademas as whip. Dan Rostenkowski was O'Neill's and Wright's first choice for whip because there was no one better "at counting the house," but Rostenkowski announced that he preferred to serve as chairman of the Ways and Means Committee, replacing Al Ullman. "Everything that's going to happen is going to be in the economic area," Rostenkowski told Tip O'Neill. "And I want to be where the action is. Tip, for the next four years they'll be talking about the chairman of the Ways and Means Committee. They won't be talking about some goddamned whip."

"Don't do this to me," pleaded O'Neill.

"Okay, I won't do this to you. I'll take the whip's job. But you've got Sam Gibbons [next in line] as chairman of the Ways and Means Committee."

"Oh Jesus," cried O'Neill. "He's a loose cannon!"

"There you go," responded Rostenkowski.

"Take the chairman of the Ways and Means Committee," commanded O'Neill.[99]

The Republican Conference chose Bob Michel as minority leader, succeeding John J. Rhodes, who resigned, and Trent Lott of Mississippi as whip. Jack Kemp of New York was named chairman of the Republican Conference and Richard Cheney of Wyoming defeated Marjorie S. Holt of Maryland for chairman of the Republican Policy Committee.

The House Democrats were demoralized following this election and prepared to deal with Reagan's announced intention of cutting domestic spending in order to increase the military budget. But according to those in California who knew him best, Reagan was "all bark and no bite." As governor of California, despite his supposed conservatism, he had actually increased spending and raised taxes. The Speaker met with the House Republican leadership and agreed to a schedule for consideration of Reagan's so-called supply-side economics, a system his Vice President, George Bush, had termed "voodoo economics" during the primaries. According to Reagan, lower taxes would bolster the economy and lead to prosperity.

Both James Jones, the new chairman of the House Budget Committee, and Rostenkowski, the new chairman of Ways and Means, were exceedingly anxious to avoid defeat in their first outings on the floor as chairmen of these important committees, and therefore were willing to compromise with the administration. But Reagan had no intention of compromising. He wanted his economic program enacted just as he had put it forward.[100]

Reagan never had much interest in the details of legislation, but he was superb at fighting for them. He pleaded with members of Congress over the phone; he worked through his staff and a "savvy team of congressional liaison men;" and he frequently addressed the American people on television to support his program. "All in all," commented Tip O'Neill, "the Reagan team in 1981 was probably the best run political operating unit I've ever seen."[101]

And that spelled trouble for House Democrats.

18

The Conservative Revolution, 1981–2001

OR THE FIRST time in American history the inauguration of a President took place on the West Lawn of the Capitol building. Thousands crowded the area to watch the proceedings, while many more followed it on television. Speaking to the nation, Ronald Reagan, the oldest person to be elected chief executive—he was less than a month away from turning 70—declared that "government is not the solution to our problem; government is the problem." He further remarked that it was time "to get government back within its means, and to lighten our punitive tax burden."[1] As one of his first directives he ordered a freeze on government hiring of civilian employees, and two months later announced that thirty-seven thousand government jobs would be eliminated. Minutes after Reagan finished his inaugural address, the fifty-two American hostages were released by the Iranian government in what appeared to be a final rebuke to Jimmy Carter.

Because of his popularity, the House Democratic leadership were more than anxious to work with the new President, but they were overwhelmed by his deft political maneuvering that minimized their numerical strength and achieved incredible successes during his first year in office. Reagan inherited an economy crippled by high inflation and high interest rates. At the time the prime lending rate fluctuated between 20 and 20.5 percent.

The President was determined to lower taxes, which he insisted would stimulate economic growth and productivity, and to increase the size and strength of the armed forces so that they could face down the Soviet Union, or what he called the "evil empire." To achieve these goals, he first directed his staff to impose strict party discipline. In the past, at least two or even three dozen Republicans, mainly from the Northeast, frequently voted for Democratic measures. We "could always count on" them, said O'Neill. No longer. "After 1980 we lost them—along with the southern Democrats. As a result, the huge majority we had enjoyed during the Carter years disappeared. . . . The new president jumped in with both feet." A master politician, Reagan provided extraordinary leadership of Congress. Some House members claimed that they saw Reagan more during his first few months in office than they could recall seeing Jimmy Carter during his entire administration.[2]

O'Neill remembered receiving a tremendous number of letters—more than he had in his whole career—begging him to give the President's program a fair hearing. And the press repeated this message. "As Speaker, I could have refused to play ball with the Reagan administration by holding up the president's legislation in the Rules Committee. But in my view, this wasn't a politically wise thing to do." So O'Neill decided to give Reagan breathing space, despite his "strong opposition" to the chief executive's program. "I was afraid that the voters would repudiate the Democrats if we didn't give the president a chance to pass his program. After all, the nation was still in an economic crisis and people wanted immediate action."[3]

In one of their first meetings, the Speaker told the President that he looked forward to working with him, reminding him that he had always been on good terms with Republicans. As a matter of fact, O'Neill and Bob Michel, the Republican minority leader, regularly played golf and gin rummy together. "On trips, boy, he'd always want to play gin rummy during the whole trip. He was a good gin player," reported Michel, "very good." "I tried to tell the younger members, gosh, you just don't see that today, but at that time, why, you did, you know, you socialized with one another. It made a lot of difference in how you got things done."[4]

As for the President, Tip recorded, this socializing worked perfectly. "Despite our various disagreements in the House, we were always friends after six o'clock and on weekends." Reagan rather liked what O'Neill had suggested during their initial meeting and thereafter he would frequently begin a telephone conversation by saying, "Hello, Tip, is it after six o'clock?"

"Absolutely, Mr. President," the Speaker would respond.

Over the course of eight years, Tip and Reagan "had a lot of disagreements. Some of our arguments," O'Neill recollected, "got pretty heated. One time we were going at it pretty good at a White House leadership breakfast and Al Simpson, the Republican whip, stopped us.

"'You two Irishmen are confusing us,' he said. 'You give out with all that Irish charm, telling stories and swapping jokes, then you get in here and start all this fighting. I can't keep up.' Of course, the argument stopped. He was right. You have to learn to disagree without being disagreeable."

On the whole, O'Neill reported, "we managed to maintain a pretty good friendship."[5]

This mutual respect and willingness to avoid "being disagreeable" seeped down to House members. "Speaker Tip O'Neill and President Reagan would be competitive and partisan in their business dealings and cordial after hours," declared Donald Sundquist, a Republican from Tennessee, "and the same was true for most of the rest of us. After the House adjourned, everybody was decent to each other and could share a laugh."[6]

The Democratic leadership was taken by surprise when the administration put all its proposals into one huge package, the Economic Recovery Act of 1981, rather than separate bills. The bill was so complicated that it passed before the members knew what they were voting for. Reagan "could have put us into war and we might not have discovered it for weeks." On July 29, Dan Rostenkowski warned the members that if they accepted the President's bill "we accept his dominance of our House for the months ahead. We surrender to the political and economic whim of his White House." After the House approved the tax cut package, 282 to 95, Rostenkowski lectured his colleagues. "Make no mistake about it, this is the President's bill. It outlines a

These two "Irishmen," President Reagan and Speaker O'Neill, fought many a political battle but always had a drink together when they met after 6:00 p.m.

bold—and risky—economic strategy. Only time will tell whether the risks involved . . . were worth taking."[7]

The leadership managed to salvage some items, but the damage done was "enormous." A staggering total of forty-eight Democrats, most of them southern conservatives who called themselves "Boll Weevils," broke ranks and voted for the measure, while only one Republican defected. These Boll Weevils included Phil Gramm of Texas, Robert Stump of Arizona, Charles Stenholm of Texas and Charles Whitley of North Carolina, among others, who regularly met once a week in the office of G. V. Montgomery of Mississippi to plot strategy. "We saved Ronald Reagan's programs his first four years," boasted Montgomery.[8] Because "there were enough Boll Weevil Democrats, we controlled the agenda on economic issues," explained Dick Cheney, "and I think that's significant."[9]

"In 1981," sighed O'Neill, "everything I had fought for, everything I had believed in, was being cast aside." Medicare and student loans were lowered, child nutrition programs were cut, and unemployment compensation was reduced. The Speaker was particularly offended by the fact that many "weak-kneed members of my party" willingly deserted "our basic principles" and voted with the administration. A number of them explained that their constituents wanted them to support the President and they were "scared stiff" of being out of step with the country.[10]

By the summer the nation slipped into a recession due to a tight monetary policy pursued by the Federal Reserve Board and the astronomically high interest rates. By December 1981, some 9 million Americans were unemployed. The prime lending rate stood at 15 percent.

Passage of the tax bill and the Budget Reconciliation measure, which projected reduced spending by the government over the next three years, prompted Reagan to declare that his proposals represented "an end to the excessive growth in government bureaucracy and government spending and government taxing."[11] But the huge loss of revenue that resulted forced the administration to ask the Congress to raise the debt ceiling above the trillion-dollar mark. The legislature complied, lifting the ceiling to $1,079,800,000,000 through September 30, 1982. By the time this 97th Congress closed its first session on December 16, 1981, the federal deficit was headed beyond $100 billion and the economy was in decline.[12]

The nation almost lost its chief executive when John W. Hinckley, Jr., son of a Colorado oil executive, attempted to assassinate Reagan. The President was shot in the chest at 2:30 p.m. on March 30, 1981, while emerging from the Washington Hilton Hotel, but fortunately he recovered and was released from the hospital on April 11. Hinckley was later found not guilty of any crime by reason of insanity and he was duly incarcerated.

This near brush with death hardly slowed the energetic chief executive. He drove through Congress the greatest increase in defense spending in

American history, along with the greatest cutback in domestic programs and the largest tax cuts this country had ever experienced.

O'Neill had no intention of adopting what Reagan called "supply-side economics"—namely, lowering taxes to encourage investments and increasing the deficit—as a means of achieving prosperity. To him it was the same policy pursued by Herbert Hoover. Since "politics is the art of repackaging," said the Speaker, Reagan had done nothing more than wrap an old philosophy a little differently and sell it to the American people. "Ronald Reagan was Herbert Hoover with a smile," he claimed. However, Jim Jones, the new chairman of the Budget Committee, and Dan Rostenkowski, who headed the Ways and Means Committee, "were eager to compromise with the administration," according to O'Neill, and wanted to avoid at all costs any defeat in their first tests on the floor as committee chairmen.[13]

But they both took a beating.

And a significant segment of the public was literally watching the course of House events on television. Tip O'Neill said that his decision in 1979 to permit live, televised coverage of the House of Representatives was "one of the best decisions I ever made." Sam Rayburn used to say that microphones and cameras would detract from the dignity of the chamber. Quite the opposite, argued O'Neill. It has led "to a tremendous improvement in the image of the House."[14] The electorate came to realize that many of their Representatives were hardworking, intelligent men and women. And several of the members recognized how they could enhance their reputations throughout the country. By a vote of 342 to 44, the House adopted a resolution on October 27, 1977, directing the Speaker to proceed with the "expansion of an experimental closed-circuit test of TV coverage."[15]

Television first came into the House on March 19, 1979, and Representative Albert Gore, Jr., of Tennessee was the first Congressman to speak before the cameras. He assured his viewers and his colleagues seated around him that this new medium would "change this institution" and "revitalize representative democracy."[16]

But there was a downside. "Once television was in place," explained Charles Johnson, the House parliamentarian from 1994 to 2004, "members were less willing to take on their opponents and to potentially be embarrassed, preferring, instead, to have prescripted speeches and then sit down. And that's virtually all you see now."[17] Today, rarely, if ever, does a speech on the House floor change a single vote. Members are more likely to direct their remarks at an unseen television audience, not their colleagues.

The beginning of public television proved to be particularly innovative; cameras recorded entire sessions, morning and night. The Cable Satellite Public Affairs Network (C-SPAN) introduced continuous coverage of Congress, both House and Senate. One disadvantage was the fact that members who in the past spent part of the afternoon on the floor listening to the debates now watched them intermittently on TV in their offices.

Young, conservative Republicans were the first to appreciate the opportunity provided by C-SPAN of speaking directly to their constituents and the public at large. They discussed important issues, frequently bypassing committees and the party leadership. The most aggressive and creative of these new Republicans was Newt Gingrich of Georgia, a former history professor, who won election in 1978 and had a natural affinity for television. Born in Pennsylvania, raised on army bases in Europe and America, he earned a doctorate in Modern European History from Tulane University. "I am an example," he said, "one of many, that you can be born without money, learning, and [by] brute persistence, you can rise in America, and you can have an impact out of all proportion of probability. And that's what makes America such a uniquely creative society."[18] After several failures, he arrived in the House where he founded the Conservative Opportunity Society (COS), a group of young Republicans committed to a conservative agenda of less government and lower taxes and generally called "Gingrich's Guerillas" by the leadership.[19]

The COS members began their attack on the Democrats on January 23, 1984, the day the second session of the 98th Congress convened. Starting in 1983 they sometimes met in one another's office, but never in Gingrich's. "You can't be as strong a personality as I am and be at the center simultaneously," he later declared. "So I always wanted someone else to be chairman. I always wanted somebody else to organize meetings. I always wanted somebody else to take the lead." Such men as Robert S. Walker of Pennsylvania, Dan Coates of Indiana, Vin Weber of Minnesota, Daniel Lungren of California, Judd Gregg of New Hampshire, Connie Mack of Florida and Duncan Hunter of California breakfasted together every Wednesday in the Cannon Building, Room 124.[20] They were regularly joined by Dave Gribbin, the administrative assistant to Dick Cheney, the highly conservative member from Wyoming. "He [Gribbin] was viewed as sort of the pipeline to me," claimed Cheney, "because of my ties to the Wednesday Group, the liberal Republican organization in the House." Cheney had been approached by Barber Conable of New York to join the Wednesday Group, otherwise known as the SOS Club, a group of eighteen more moderate Republicans who also met for breakfast on Wednesday morning to exchange information and discuss policy and party affairs.[21] "I said no, I said I don't want to do that," remembered Cheney. "I'm a conservative, I'm from Wyoming, it's not really my bag."

"Dumb move, bad mistake," Conable responded. "You need to be in the Wednesday Group. You'll automatically have ties with all the conservatives, that's your crowd, but you need to be plugged into and wired with us. And we'll be better if you become a part of our organization than we would be without you." Convinced, Cheney joined and consequently became a bridge between the COS and the liberal and more moderate Republicans, all the while maintaining his status with regular conservatives. "I was the grease between the grinding gears to some extent." Gingrich would "see me when he wanted access lots of times to the leadership, and Bob [Michel] would use me as a buffer to try to make sure that those eager young beavers didn't tip and exceed their responsibilities." Cheney's rise in party leadership, first as Republican Party policy chairman, then chairman of the Republican Conference, then minority whip, was due "I think in part because I did have these kinds of relationships, with COS, with the senior membership, with the Wednesday Group, and also, obviously, with the conservatives."[22] But there were other reasons. According to Henry Hyde of Illinois, Cheney was "very smart, very shrewd, very serious . . . he wasn't a back slapper. . . . He had command of whatever he was dealing with. A very able guy."[23]

At the breakfast meetings of the COS, the members made plans to harass Democrats. Gingrich was particularly vitriolic in denouncing Democrats as "ruthlessly partisan in changing the rules of the House, stacking committees, apportioning staff and questioning the [Reagan] administration."[24] He charged that the House itself had been corrupted under Democratic rule. To Cheney, Gingrich was "a pain in the ass," but "he had this enormous drive and this fundamental belief that we would be the majority, and that was a gift."[25]

Most remarkable was Gingrich's determination to restore the legislature to the central position it enjoyed when the nation was founded under the Constitution. Over two centuries the executive branch had absorbed much of the leadership that Congress once exercised. Gingrich thought he could and should restore a proper balance between the two branches. "The Congress in the long run can change the country more dramatically than the President," he told the *Congressional Quarterly* in 1979. "I think that's healthy. One of my goals is to make the House the coequal of the White House."[26]

C-SPAN was especially useful for Gingrich. "I figured out," he declared, "if I could start making speeches on C-Span, then I would reach a dramatically bigger audience than people who flew five hundred miles to speak to a Kiwanis club."[27] He and the other "Guerillas" would give short one-minute jabs at the Democrats in the morning and longer "Special Order"*

[*A Special Order entitled a member to take the floor after the House has finished its business and speak for an hour on any subject of his or her choosing. The House is usually empty by then, and these speeches are intended strictly for home consumption.]

jabs in the evening. "And, so, I would go over in the afternoon and I'd give an hour-long speech on some topic. I like philosophizing and theorizing, and there's a market in America, I wouldn't say it's a giant market, but there's a market for the politician as teacher, for people who want to know what did that mean, as opposed to just what is your polemic."[28]

The number of one-minute speeches increased from 110 in March 1977 to 344 by March 1981.[29] The strategy of the COS involved repeated confrontations with the Democratic leadership, especially before the TV cameras. But this type of activity only produced an incivility within the chamber and drove members further apart. It "will poison the national dialogue and cripple democratic debate," warned David Obey, Democrat of Wisconsin.[30]

And so it did. Slowly, the poison of confrontation and personal attack worked through the institution, and within a few years destroyed all vestiges of courtesy and civility among the members.

Most often the cameras showed only the person speaking and viewers therefore presumed that he or she was addressing a full house when actually the chamber was empty. Viewers also assumed that the Democrats had no response to the charges leveled against them, when in fact they were absent. Infuriated by the tactics of the COS, Speaker O'Neill, on May 10, 1984, ordered the cameras to pan across the empty room the next time one of the "Guerillas" launched into a tirade to show he was speaking to an empty room.

At one point, remembered Gingrich, "we decided to go after Eddie. He was O'Neill's roommate, Eddie Boland" of Massachusetts. Why Boland? "Because he had offered the Boland amendment" that barred federal funds from supporting anticommunist rebels in South America. Gingrich singled him out in a dramatic speech that also questioned his patriotism. "But our purpose in talking was to see if we could actually get him [Boland] to come down to debate us. Because we understood that the dumbest thing he could do was come down and debate us. I mean we were backbench nobodies. . . . Now we had no idea that the person who would do it would be Tip. And Tip just went berserk."[31]

Outraged, the Speaker tongue-lashed Gingrich, citing the attack against his friend as "the lowest thing" he had witnessed in Congress.[32] His verbal barrage grew so hot and violent that O'Neill was officially chastised on May 15 for using derogatory language, and it was stricken from the record. It was the first time since 1797 that a Speaker was reproached because of his language.[33]

Foolishly, Tip had taken the bait, and now Gingrich responded calmly. The Georgia representative consulted at length with his advisers about "how to be very careful" and how not to let his emotions show. He rose and on a point of personal privilege asked to speak. Because O'Neill was the object of the response he had to surrender the chair. And while Gingrich was explaining "why I have been attacked and how badly I feel about being attacked," Tip stood on the floor listening. "His friends couldn't get him off the floor. I mean, the correct thing for O'Neill to do is get off the floor. Give the kid his moment. . . . And O'Neill stands there and gets madder and madder. And we finally have this interchange where he's pointing at me and yelling. . . . But I'm not shouting. I stayed very calm. . . . It was the first time a lot of Republican activists had ever seen a Republican on the House floor fighting. In all these years, they felt like they'd been taking the punches. . . . Anyway, it was a great moment. Well, and, because of C-SPAN, it's fabulous television."[34]

"Congress has always been an exceedingly polite society," O'Neill later acknowledged, "where even my justified rebuke of Newt Gingrich constituted unacceptably bad conduct. Because the House of Representatives includes 435 members from all regions of the country who hold a wide range of political philosophies, it's critical that members treat each other with respect. Attacking another member when he's not there to respond, while pretending that the House was in session, is a gross violation of our code of behavior."[35]

A new era had begun, an era of incivility and personal attack and partisanship that would dominate House proceedings for the remainder of the century and beyond.

WHEN REAGAN PROPOSED slicing Social Security benefits in his 1981 budget proposal, the Speaker lashed back on television and accused Republicans of attempting to balance the budget on the backs of the elderly. Reagan retreated and on March 25, 1983, Congress passed legislation that prevented the Social Security system from going bankrupt. O'Neill was thereafter seen by the public as the kindly defender of the weak, not the hard-hearted, big-city, machine politician, as portrayed by Gingrich and his cohorts. But the real hero of Social Security was Claude Pepper of Florida, chairman of of the House Select Committee on Aging. He played a pivotal role in shaping the final bill.

One thing Democrats learned about Reagan after several skirmishes was the fact that he "would compromise at the right time." He was not "hard-nosed" all the time as some thought, said John Murtha, Democrat of Pennsylvania. On a $15 billion proposed slash of defense funds, for example, "we knew that he was willing to compromise, but he didn't compromise until the end. I mean he fought it right through to the end and then he would compromise."[36]

But Reagan did advance such extraordinary budget and tax cuts as to significantly alter government policy. Personal income taxes were trimmed 25 percent across the board over 33 months. Starting in 1985, tax rates,

Speaker Tip O'Neill, Majority Leader Jim Wright and chairman of the Ways and Means Committee, Dan Rostenkowski, voicing their opposition to President Reagan's proposed tax cut.

personal exemptions and regular deductions were to be indexed to reflect cost of living increases; the capital gains tax was reduced from 28 to 20 percent; and the amounts which could be excluded from estate and gift taxes were increased. As for the budget, such areas as education, health, housing, environment, food stamps, school meals, the National Endowment for the Arts and Humanities, and urban aid programs were slashed. To many, it seemed like a conservative revolution to match the liberal revolution of the New Deal–Fair Deal era.

The Reagan administration also sought a massive buildup of the military. Despite Democratic efforts to move at a slower pace, the President increased the defense budget from $180.5 billion to $279 billion. Funding was provided to rebuild the navy, purchase bombers and missiles and construct a space-based strategic defense system, popularly known as "Star Wars." As a result, the deficit soared from $79 billion in 1981 to $185 billion in 1986, forcing Reagan to go to Congress and ask for a tax increase. Even with this increase, the deficit continued to climb, reaching a high of $290 billion at its peak. The national debt tripled.[37] Later, Dick Cheney would boast that "Reagan proved deficits don't matter."[38]

Democrats recovered somewhat from the "debacle of 1980" in the congressional election of 1982 by gaining 26 House seats. There were now 269 Democrats to 166 Republicans in the House. The Senate held 46 Democrats and 54 Republicans. During the election, Democrats pounded Republicans on their voting record, especially on Social Security.

ON APRIL 18, 1983, terrorists bombed the U.S. embassy in Beirut, Lebanon, killing 63 people. Six months later, on October 23, terrorists bombed the Marine Corp compound in that country, killing 241 marines and sailors. Reagan took action on February 7, 1984, when he ordered the withdrawal of marines from Lebanon.

Still the President remained popular and won easy reelection in 1984, along with his running mate, George H. W. Bush,[39] over the Democrat, Walter Mondale of Minnesota, capturing all but Mondale's home state and the District of Columbia. For the first time, at Mondale's suggestion, a major party chose a woman, Representative Geraldine A. Ferraro of New York, to run as Vice President, but she was unable to provide significant electoral support.

In the 1984 election, the Republicans gained fourteen House seats, but the Democrats managed to retain control. In his State of the Union Address, President Reagan again asked for further cuts in domestic spending and increased appropriations for the military.

WHEN ACTIVIST PRESIDENTS such as Reagan assume office and exercise masterly political skills, Congress must constantly stand guard for increased encroachment by the President on the basic powers of the House and Senate because of the danger that these powers can be absorbed or redistributed to the advantage of the chief executive. The classic example was the way the President had come to dominate the preparation of the budget. The enactment of the Budget and Accounting Act of 1921 mandated that an annual budget be submitted to Congress. To assist the process, it established a Bureau of the Budget within the Treasury Department. During the New Deal and World War II, President Roosevelt acted so aggressively that he assumed the principal role in deciding budgetary matters. He moved the bureau out of the Treasury and brought it closer to the White House. With the conclusion of World War II, Congress repeatedly passed legislation restricting presidential control of the nation's finances, such as the Budget and Impoundment Control Act in 1974, which limited the executive's ability to impound funds passed by Congress.

Another example was the control and distribution of funds in foreign affairs. In his efforts to support anticommunist forces in South America, President Reagan tried to overthrow the Marxist Sandinista regime in Nicaragua by providing military assistance and funds to the counterrevolutionary anti-Sandinista (or Contra) forces. Twice, in 1982 and 1983, Congress barred assistance to the Contras; the "Boland amendment" (which triggered the Gingrich-O'Neill fracas) to the spending bill passed on October 12, 1984, forbade the Pentagon, CIA, or other intelligence agencies from furnishing "military equipment, military training or advice, or other support for military activities, to any group or individual, not part of a country's armed forces, for the purpose of overthrowing the Government of Nicaragua."[40] This amendment was reenacted in 1985 and extended through the 1986 fiscal year.

To circumvent this restriction, the administration used funds from secret arms sales to Iran, along with other assistance provided by foreign governments and private individuals, to support the Contra effort to overthrow the Sandinistas. It began in the spring of 1985 when Israeli intelligence informed the American government that Shiite Muslims were willing to assist the release of western hostages held in Lebanon in exchange for arms to be sold to Iran. On January 17, 1986, Reagan approved covert arms sales to Iran through the CIA, ordering the CIA Director, William J. Casey, not to tell the Congress about it, thus inaugurating a systematic conspiracy to deceive Congress and cover up the activities of members of the National Security Council (first established in 1947) who were funneling the funds to the Contras.

Reagan also asked Congress for $100 million in Contra aid, and he and his aides worked tirelessly to win its passage. Reagan himself spent hours on the telephone with "swing voters," urging their support. The debates on the floor were particularly heated, acrimonious, and extremely partisan. When Democrats rose to speak against giving the President what he requested, Republicans would demand the floor to respond and when it was refused they jeered and stamped their feet. Henry Hyde of Illinois looked straight at the majority section of the House and predicted that "History . . . is going to assign to you Democrats the role of pallbearers at the funeral of Democracy in Central America." But O'Neill replied that today's vote was "a matter of conscience, not of politics."[41] The House rejected the President's request, 222 to 210, on March 20, 1986.

A new phase in the developing scandal began with the diversion of funds from the Iranian arms sale to the Contras and the administration's encouragement of foreign and private sources of support. This action in the minds of some congressional leaders violated the spirit and possibly the letter of the law, an impeachable offense. A three-man commission, appointed by the President on November 26 and headed by former Texas Senator John Tower, a Republican, identified Robert McFarlane, former director of the National Security Council, his successor, Rear Admiral John M. Poindexter, and his aide, Lieutenant Colonel Oliver North, along with Casey, as the men responsible for arranging the sale to Iran and diverting the profits from the sale to the rebels fighting the Sandinista government of Nicaragua. The commission also criticized Reagan for remaining out of contact with what was happening in his administration. A joint House–

Senate report accused Reagan of permitting "a cabal of zealots" to engage in activities that showed contempt for the law. "There is something wrong if the president doesn't know what is going on in the basement of the White House," growled Senator Robert Byrd, Democrat from West Virginia.[42]

At least four laws were "blatantly" violated: the National Security Act, the Arms Export Control Act, the Department of Defense Appropriations Act, and the Anti-Terrorism Act. "So flagrant was the flouting of law" that any number of Democratic congressmen demanded that impeachment proceedings be undertaken against the President. "Whenever you went into a group of Democratic members," remembered Jim Wright, the majority leader, "you were hearing, 'impeachable offense. Impeach.' There were movements to have hearings on it. Every committee could have a little piece of jurisdiction over one of the laws that were violated. . . . I thought, they're going to have a circus here. They're going to wind up with nothing but a three-ring or ten-ring circus. . . . I have lived through the impeachment of Nixon, and I didn't want to see that revived in our country again."[43]

Once the scandal became public, Oliver North systematically shredded all written evidence before Congress could subpoena the documents.

The investigations by Congress were angry, partisan affairs, but they did document that the Reagan administration had "lied to and deceived Congress and the public; scorned the constitutional rights and responsibilities of Congress in the conduct of foreign policy; [and] abdicated the conduct of that policy to private, profit-seeking persons."[44] But, said Tip O'Neill, "we're not going to go through another impeachment. It's too hard on the country. We're not going to do it." According to John Murtha, "that's exactly what he said. That's how simple it was, and we didn't go through with it. I think he [Reagan] might have been impeached. That was just as serious, if not more serious, than the Watergate."[45] Jim Wright agreed. The "last thing our country needed was an impeachment outcry or a frontal challenge to the president's personal integrity." Besides, "he had only two years left to be President. We were getting everything we wanted here in the House. We were overriding his vetoes on the water bill, the highway bill, and the trade bill."[46]

But the situation became explosive. The possibility of impeachment drove Republicans to near violence. "I mean people like Cheney would have been furious," remembered Gingrich. "I mean the House Republicans would have gone berserk. It wasn't like Nixon. . . . In Nixon's case you have tapes of the President himself. And members realized he had lied to them personally."[47]

Reagan accepted full responsibility for the affair, declaring that he had sent aid to Iran in the hope of improving relations, not to free hostages in Lebanon. Aides swore he had not been informed of the secret arrangement of funneling funds to the Contras, but McFarlane implied in his testimony before the House Foreign Affairs Committee on December 8, 1986, that Reagan did. "I find it hard to imagine that it was undertaken without higher authority," McFarlane declared.[48]

Meanwhile, the U.S. Court of Appeals for the District of Columbia appointed Lawrence E. Walsh as independent counsel, and his investigation led to the indictment of fourteen individuals, all of whom were convicted. McFarlane pleaded guilty to four counts of illegally withholding information from Congress and was sentenced to two years probation and was fined $20,000. Poindexter resigned, North was fired, and both men were indicted. On May 4, 1989, North was convicted of three felonies, including destroying and falsifying official documents, and acquitted of nine other charges. He was fined and put on probation for two years, but a federal judge overturned the findings and dismissed the charges. A federal appeals court also threw out the felony convictions of Poindexter. President George Herbert Walker Bush pardoned two others in 1992. Caspar Weinberger, the secretary of defense, was charged with four counts of perjury and making false statements, but President Bush pardoned him after first making sure that Democrats would not protest.[49]

Walsh issued a three-volume *Final Report on the Iran/Contra Matter,* which said that there was no credible evidence that Reagan had violated any criminal statute. "Nevertheless, he set the stage for the illegal activities of others by encouraging and, in general terms, ordering support of the contras . . . when funds for the contras were cut off by the Boland amendment." Reagan instructed McFarlane to keep the Contras alive, "body and soul," which when passed on to North was interpreted by him as a clear "invitation to break the law." The *Report* concluded that Reagan, the secretaries of state and defense, the director of the CIA and their assistants "skirted the law, some of them broke the law, and almost all of them tried to cover up the President's willful activities."[50]

Was Reagan guilty of an impeachable offense? "I believe the truth is that he was not really focused on what he was saying" to his aides or agreeing to, "and had no memory of it," concluded Jim Wright. "That's what I believe."[51]

After a long and bitter struggle, Congress, on June 25, 1986, authorized $300 million in economic assistance to Central American countries, $70 million of which went to the Contras in military aid. Throughout the debate, the rancor in Congress reached unprecedented heights. Bob Michel, the minority leader, felt extreme discomfort with the confrontational style of the COS. "Be gentlemanly," he pleaded, "and once you've made your point, get on with the business of governing."[52]

But by this time some Republicans were not paying much attention to Bob Michel; they looked to Gingrich to provide the agenda and drive to overturn Democratic control of the House. Not all Republicans, of course.

Dick Cheney, for example, felt that Michel provided the kind of leadership necessary for the time and under the circumstances in which the Republicans were forced to operate. These were years in which "46 Republicans in the House was all we had. And Bob did what he had to do under those circumstances, and it was a different era."[53]

Indeed. But it was an era Gingrich and the COS had sworn to end.

LEADERSHIP OF A different kind came from the White House. Reagan wanted to reform the tax code in 1985, but Rostenkowski's committee reported out a bill that, according to Cheney, "didn't look anything like what Reagan wanted." Still the President asked Republican House members to pass it anyway and send it to the Republican Senate "where they'd clean it up. But a lot of us in the House did not want to vote for that bad Democratic bill. We were opposed to it, but we didn't want to be directly against the President. So . . . some of us, Trent Lott and I and some others, organized an effort and we killed the rule, sent the whole thing back to committee."

At that point Reagan sent a message that he wanted to speak to the House Republicans. In the meantime, a terrible airplane accident occurred at Gander, Newfoundland, and over two hundred troopers from the 101st Airborne Division, "coming back from Europe or the Middle East," were killed.

Reagan went to the memorial service at Fort Campbell, Kentucky "and then came straight to the Hill to speak to the House Republicans. We had all the Republicans jammed in a big committee room in the Rayburn building."

The President walked in "and started talking about what it means to be an American, about patriotism and sacrifice and talked about that [memorial] service event. There wasn't a dry eye in the place." Then Reagan paused. "Now, gentlemen, about that tax bill."

"That's all he said. Members started jumping up and saying, 'I'm with you, Mr. President.' 'You can count on me, Mr. President.' "

Henry Hyde "led the charge. Seventy House Republicans switched from being against the rule to [being] for the rule and they brought the bill back up that afternoon or the next day and passed it, and sent it over to the Senate." All Reagan had to do was say, "Now, gentlemen, about that tax bill" and "that was enough."[54]

Small wonder Reagan was known as the "Great Communicator."

The Senate, of course, made radical changes to the bill, but in a joint conference the House and Senate versions were reconciled in a series of compromises. Rostenkowski chaired the conference and controlled the agenda by stating that he would accept the lower Senate tax rates if the reforms initiated by the House would prevail. "If [we] have one mission," he said, "it's to guarantee fairness for middle-income families." The House passed this most sweeping tax-reform measure since the 1940s by a vote of 292 to 136 on September 25, 1986, and the Senate agreed two days later.[55]

As the quarreling within Congress mounted, Tip O'Neill announced that he was stepping down as Speaker and leaving his beloved House. The party and the nation, he said, needed new leadership. "I could have stayed on indefinitely, but I had no great desire to end up as a tottering old congressman. In my younger days, I used to feel that both Rayburn and McCormack had remained on the job too long, and this was one mistake I was determined to avoid." Besides, there was Jim Wright to think about. He had been a loyal majority leader since 1977. He deserved "his day in the sun, too."[56]

And the record Tip left was impressive. The years O'Neill presided over the House were years in which an efficient legislative operation slowly evolved. But it required strong leadership. Take, for example, the 99th Congress (1985–1987). It revised the tax code more completely than at any time since World War II; it enacted stiffer environmental regulations; it raised student aid; and it revised the immigration law. To a large extent the success resulted from the fact that bills were brought to the floor with limitations on the amendments that could be proposed. In the past bills were amended to death and took months to debate. Together with the Rules Committee, the Speaker made sure both debate and amendments were kept under tight control. Debate was reduced to a few days, leaving members with a sense of pride that the House, unlike the Senate, functioned intelligently and swiftly.

All of this changed when Jim Wright became Speaker. He was initially seen as agreeable, obliging, and easy to meet and converse with. He was a superb orator, and he loved the House. He honestly believed that "the House is the raw essence of the nation."[57]

But as Speaker he worsened the relationship between the two parties. He excluded Republicans from any involvement in House business, intensifying the angry exchanges on the floor over appropriations, taxes, housing, health and sundry other issues. It was even known that Democrats on a particular committee "went into a back room and approved a bill that hadn't even been written—they approved it 'in concept.' I'd never heard of such a thing," complained Sundquist of Tennessee, a member of that committee. "Not only did they not consult with us, we had no paperwork. They approved a bill that they described to us but hadn't even written!"[58]

Then Wright did something that really infuriated the Republicans. On October 29, 1987, he delayed a vote on a reconciliation bill that raised taxes in order to reduce the budget deficit by $40 billion over two years. Under normal circumstances, announcement of the results of the balloting was delayed fifteen minutes to give stragglers an opportunity to cast their votes. When the fifteen minutes expired on the reconciliation bill, the measure

The bushy-browed Speaker, Jim Wright, was hounded out of office on charges that he violated the standards of the Ethics Committee.

had lost 205 to 206. Republicans reveled. They shouted at Wright to declare the bill defeated. But he stood silently on the dais. Minutes passed. Finally, a voice rang out, "Hold the vote!" Democrat Jim Chapman of Texas rushed down the aisle and switched his vote by asking for a green card. At that moment, Wright shouted at Bonior, "Take back that damn red card." Then, in what seemed to some as a triumphant voice, he cried, "if there are no other members in the chamber who desire to vote . . ." Republicans booed. Trent Lott slammed his fist against a lectern and nearly shattered it. But Wright continued, "Or if there are no other members who desire to change their vote, on this vote the yeas are 206 to 205."[59]

The bill passed. Republicans exploded, but it did them little good. Chapman was subsequently rewarded with a seat on the Appropriations Committee.[60]

Anger and resentment in the House rose to a new level. "The degree of partisanship, the strength of feeling, is more than it has been," claimed Dick Cheney. "We had our problems with Tip O'Neill, too, but with Wright it is somehow more bitter."[61] "Deep down," argued Vin Weber, Wright was seen as a "mean-spirited person, ruthless in the truest sense of the word." Partisan dislike of O'Neill was ideological, he continued, but with Wright it was personal. Without intending to do so, Wright "really became a catalyst for bringing the whole Republican Party over to our [Gingrich's] side," claimed Robert Walker. "It galvanized the GOP around activist tactics."[62]

Even Democrats had problems with the new Speaker. John Murtha compared Wright's style of operation with that of Tip O'Neill. Tip "told you what he wanted done the first of the year and never interfered with how you got it done. Jim Wright, on the other hand, not only told you what he wanted you to do, he told you how he wanted you to do it." As a result, "Jim didn't get along as well."[63]

Cheney declared to a *National Journal* reporter that Wright was "a heavy-handed son of a bitch . . . and he will do anything he can to win at any price, including ignoring the rules, bending rules, writing rules, denying the

House the opportunity to work its will. It brings disrespect to the House it-self. There's no sense of comity left. Why should you, if you are a Republican, and given the way Republicans are treated, think of a Democrat as a col-league? They aren't colleagues."[64]

They aren't colleagues! That comment marked a sad moment in the his-tory of the House of Representatives.

EMOTIONS WERE RUBBED raw when Wright got involved in attempting to work out a peace agreement to settle the raging battle in Nicaragua. He met with the leftist president of Nicaragua, Daniel Ortega, in Washington three times from November 11 to November 13, 1987, triggering criticism that he was interfering in foreign policy matters that should be left to the executive. For several years, Reagan had refused to meet officially with the Nicaraguan leftists. Wright insisted he was not attempting to negoti-ate with Ortega, and that he had met with him and Cardinal Miguel Obando, the Catholic Church's intermediary between the Nicaraugan president and the Contras, at their request. "I hope the administration will understand that I am not trying to usurp its role and that I am not under any illusion that I am a diplomat."[65] But "from negative comments emanating from the White House," he later wrote, "it slowly became clear to me that highly placed people in the administration did not want a peaceful settlement in Nicaragua. They actually wanted the talks to break down so they could use the 'failure' of the peace efforts as an excuse for renewing the war."[66]

House Republicans stormed over this "meddling" in diplomatic affairs, and attacks on the Speaker intensified, especially when Republicans named Gingrich as the minority whip in March 1989. Cheney or Lott should have been elected because they were senior, but Cheney chose to accept the invi-tation to become secretary of defense, and Lott moved to the Senate. "I couldn't allow another member of the Michel wing . . . to get into the chain of succession," Gingrich figured. "Michel is a very fine man," he admitted. "A man I can respect a great deal." But "he had adopted a model of politics in which it was virtually inevitable we'd be a minority. I thought my mis-sion was to make us a majority."

Gingrich immediately got on the phone and instructed his staff to "track down the maximum number of Republican phone numbers . . . and by 8 on Monday, I had fifty-five pledges," and that was "before anybody else had thought about running." He even considered "taking Michel on . . . be-cause Michel and George H. W. Bush had clearly polarized against me, and had used every element of the leader's power and every element of the Pres-ident's power to try to beat me. . . . I was clearly now the dominant figure in the House party."[67] In fact, Gingrich was elected by a bare majority, 87 to 85, over Edward Madigan of Illinois.

Gingrich toured the country, calling Wright a "crook," and even went so far as to file charges against the Speaker with the House Ethics Committee, demanding an investigation into Wright's personal finances.[68] The committee had an equal number of Republicans and Democrats, so it was not so easy to manipulate its investigation.

On April 17, 1989, the Ethics Committee released a statement in which Wright was charged with sixty-nine instances in five broad categories of violating House gift and income rules. One involved a claim that the Speaker's wife had business dealings with a wealthy friend in which no work was involved and for which she had received $145,000 over ten years, presumably to influence legislation, which constituted an illegal gift. Another, and possibly a more important charge, was Wright's "sweetheart" arrangement with the publishers of his book, *Reflections of a Public Man,* a collection of his public speeches, which paid him 50 percent royalties and which was sold to lobbyists in lots of a thousand copies.

As the Wright scandal heated up, the majority whip, Tony Coelho of California, announced on May 26, 1989, that he would resign rather than face an investigation into his financial affairs, first reported by an article in *Newsweek* magazine. It was now becoming obvious that support for Wright as Speaker was melting away, and, to make matters worse, he was blamed for the public outrage over the attempt of the House to raise members' salaries from $89,500 to $135,000, which failed to pass.[69] To top things off, Cheney and Michel had filed charges before the Ethics Committee in September 1988, accusing Wright of "disclosing classified information inappropriately in connection with Central America."[70]

Democrats found faults as well. Wright acted arbitrarily, expanding the whip system and appointing a deputy whip without consulting the whip who had been elected in the Caucus. He named a nonfreshman to the Steering and Policy Committee to represent the freshmen, a position traditionally assigned to a newcomer. Worse, he delayed reappointments to the Rules Committee, remarking, "I just wanted them to remember they were the Speaker's appointees."[71]

The Democrats "were so concerned about public opinion," declared John Murtha, "the fact that it looked like Jim had done something wrong" that they distanced themselves from him. "I mean compared to some of the things that other people have been charged with, it was nothing and it was unfortunate."[72] The false accusations, said Wright, were "so aggravating that I was up in the middle of the night, shaking with anger, just trembling and angry. My blood pressure was going up." In addition, the cost of a lengthy legal proceeding that could run as high as $500,000 troubled him. He did not have that kind of money, and "I wasn't going to beg for money." He realized, of course, that "this thing is dividing people in the House. I'm not going to be able to get anything done of a constructive nature. And there's too much divisiveness." Faced with the fact that he could no longer expect support from Democrats, Wright made his decision.[73]

He strode into the House on May 31, 1989. He was one of the best orators in Congress, and everyone appreciated that fact, so the chamber was packed and anticipation ran high. No one except his closest advisers knew what he would do. In an emotional speech in which his voice frequently broke and tears welled up in his eyes, he resigned his position as Speaker. In an hour-long address, he begged the members of his party not to seek revenge on his behalf. "All of us in both political parties must resolve to bring this period of mindless cannibalism to an end."[74]

His action marked the first abdication of a Speaker during his tenure in office. When he also resigned his seat as a member of Congress, the Ethics Committee dropped its investigation.

Wright was replaced as Speaker by Tom Foley of Washington on June 6, 1989. Foley first arrived in the House in 1965 from a conservative-leaning district in the state of Washington. A soft-spoken, likable, moderate Democrat, he was elected chairman of the Democratic Caucus in 1977 and three years later was picked by Speaker O'Neill to succeed John Brademas as whip. An effective operator in negotiating a two-year budget agreement with the Reagan administration, he was chosen majority leader in 1986 without opposition, although some Republicans attempted to smear him.[75]

Richard Gephardt of Missouri was advanced as majority leader. He first came to the House in 1976 and won a seat on the Ways and Means Committee. As a member of that committee and several other leadership-appointed task forces, he displayed an uncanny knack for building consensus within the Democratic Party, and sometimes with Republicans as well. He was known as a pragmatic progressive. At the beginning of his fifth term in the House he was elected chairman of the Democratic Caucus in 1984 and unsuccessfully sought the Democratic nomination for President

The genial Tom Foley, one of only two Speakers in the history of the House to lose reelection while serving as Speaker.

in 1988. His popularity among his Democratic colleagues in the House was demonstrated by the fact that many of them endorsed his candidacy and worked for him in their districts.

William Gray of Pennsylvania, an African-American, was named as whip, the first black member of the House to win that leadership position.[76] Steny H. Hoyer of Maryland succeeded Gray as Chairman of the Democratic Caucus.

Partisanship in Congress had now reached such an intense level that it was next to impossible for the two parties to agree on any important issue. The art of compromise was fast disappearing. And what happened tended to validate the "scorched earth" methods employed by the COS and Gingrich. Motives were questioned, integrity challenged, and stinging, pejorative remarks were regularly heard on the floor. After Wright's resignation, the "mindless cannibalism" in the House grew noticeably worse. "There's an evil wind blowing in the hall of Congress today," worried Jack Brooks of Texas. "We've replaced comity and compassion with hatred and malice."[77]

In an attempt to reverse the deteriorating relations between the two parties and reactivate the need for compromise, Speaker Foley held weekly meetings with Bob Michel, the minority leader. "And the thing about Tom that really surprised me," declared Michel, "was that he suggested that when we have our weekly meetings, we'll alternate offices. He said, 'I'll come over to your office one week and you come over to mine the next week,' and that's the way we operated and that was never heard of before."[78]

THE EVENTS THAT boiled over and dramatically altered relationships in Congress occurred during the closing days of the Reagan administration and into the following years. But a number of important pieces of legislation were enacted prior to Reagan's departure from office. First, an Income Tax Reform Act was passed on October 22, 1986. This act removed millions of low-income Americans from the tax rolls, eliminated a number of allowed deductions and tax shelters, designated capital gains as income, reduced the corporate tax rate from 46 percent to 34 percent, and combined a number of personal income brackets.

The second was passage of the Japanese-American Reparations Act on August 10, 1988, which provided $20,000 to each surviving Japanese-American who had been interned in a relocation camp during World War II.

Welfare reform provided another significant achievement for the 100th Congress. Among other things, states were required to establish education, work and training programs for adult welfare recipients. This Congress closed its last session with the approval of a $2.7 billion omnibus antidrug bill.[79]

THE PERIOD FROM JANUARY 6, 1987, to January 3, 1989, marked the years of the 100th Congress, a fact that reminded members and the country at large that the House of Representatives and the Senate had been operating and guiding this nation for two centuries. As part of that commemoration, the massive *Biographical Directory of the United States Congress, 1774–1989* was published by a Joint Bicentennial Commission, a work that provided information on all the executive officers, names of delegates of the Continental Congresses, census apportionment of representatives, the basic facts about all one hundred Congresses, and biographical sketches of every man and woman who served in Congress. It was a notable achievement.

Of particular moment during the final year of Reagan's tenure as President was the signing in early December 1987, with Mikhail Gorbachev, the Soviet Union's democratically minded premier, of the Intermediate Nuclear Forces (INF) Treaty, the first nuclear disarmament agreement between the two countries, which banned intermediate range weapons from the nuclear arsenals of both countries. The arms buildup by the United States under Reagan placed a heavy strain on the ability of the Russians to maintain an equal balance of military power and helped convinced them to sign the INF Treaty.

By the time George Herbert Walker Bush defeated his Democratic opponent, Michael Dukakis, in the presidential election of 1988—the first sitting Vice President to capture the White House since Martin Van Buren in 1836—the internal weaknesses of the Soviet Union began to manifest themselves in the political upheavals that erupted in eastern Europe. In Poland a non-Communist government was formed in 1990; in Lithuania, Latvia and Estonia, the people demanded autonomy from Russia; Hungary declared itself a free republic, as did Czechoslovakia, Romania, Uzbekistan, Ukraine, Georgia, Azerbaijan and Armenia; in East Germany, thousands of people fled to West Germany through the open borders of Czechoslovakia, Hungary and Poland. On December 22, 1989, the Brandenburg Gate was reopened, and the infamous wall separating East and West Berlin was torn down, thus symbolically ending the Cold War.

As the Soviet Union crumbled, a new threat to world peace occurred on August 2, 1990, when the dictator of Iraq, Saddam Hussein, seized the border country of Kuwait. The U.N. ordered Saddam to withdraw his troops and set a deadline for compliance, while at the same time the United States rushed troops to Saudi Arabia. Bush busied himself in creating a coalition of many nations, and Congress passed a joint resolution on January 12, 1991, by a vote in the House of 250 to 183, authorizing the President to employ force to carry out the sanctions imposed by the U.N. By the end of 1990, an army of 500,000 had been deployed in the area.

This Gulf War, as it came to be called, provided one occasion when Democrats and Republicans engaged in a "thoughtful and impressive" three-day debate over the resolution. Despite their differences, they held a "full discussion," which was described as "dignified, often moving," with some members offering prayers for the country, the President and the troops. Foley remembered Bob Michel coming up to the Speaker's chair "with tears in his eyes. He said, 'This is the hardest vote I think I've ever had to cast because I'm putting young men and women at risk and I know it. But I think it's the right thing to do.' He and I voted differently on the bill, but it was a sense of, I think, the mutual respect the Republicans and Democrats throughout the House had with the differing opinions of their colleagues on an issue of enormous importance to the country."[80] Those who did object to the resolution argued that only Congress may declare war and that the President risked impeachment if he violated the Constitution by ignoring the rights of the legislative branch.

On January 16, 1991, a military attack, known as Operation Desert Storm, was initiated against Iraq. The coalition forces achieved almost immediate success, and on February 25, Saddam agreed to withdraw his troops from Kuwait and accept the terms of a cease-fire. He also accepted the U.N. resolution calling for the destruction or removal of all Iraq's chemical and biological weapons.

Because of Congress's failure to protect its constitutional jurisdiction in foreign affairs, three Presidents—Reagan, Bush and Clinton—took advantage of it by sending troops into Lebanon, Grenada, Libya, Kuwait, Bosnia, Kosovo, Serbia and Yugoslavia without any legislative authorization. In taking action they cited resolutions from the U.N. or NATO. The War Powers Resolution was simply ignored.

BACK IN THE House of Representatives the members resumed their partisan attack on each other in early 1991 when the Republicans publicized a report by the General Accounting Office (GAO) in which it was revealed that 325 sitting and former members of the House overdrew their accounts in the House Bank and paid no penalty. The House Bank was a kind of checking service in which members deposited their salaries and drew against them. When overdrafts occurred they were covered from the general pool and the individuals involved were not charged for issuing bad checks.

Sensing they had a politically explosive issue, the Republicans demanded an investigation by the Ethics Committee. They insisted that the names of the guilty be made public. Democrats snorted their derision since no federal funds were involved, and no crime had been committed. But Republicans persisted in their attack. With the C-SPAN cameras following his every move, James Nussle of Iowa appeared on the floor with a paper bag over his head and demanded to know who had issued these overdrafts.

Speaker Foley was reluctant to allow the finances of the members to be turned over to a special prosecutor and suffered mounting criticism for inept leadership. Some demanded his resignation. Bob Michel tried to halt Republican attacks but could not. In the violence of the partisan warfare that ensued, the House was no longer a place for a moderate like Michel. "I always felt," he later reported, "that I didn't have to step on people's toes or run over people. . . . My normal inclination was always to talk to the other side."

No more. A new era of personal assault was gathering momentum. "I thought, oh shucks, I've been around here for 38 years. I'm done." So, without regret, he chose to end his career at the close of the 103rd Congress.[81]

A great many other representatives also left—and not of their own volition. In the presidential election of 1992, George Bush, who was seeking reelection, was narrowly defeated by the Democratic candidate, Bill Clinton. In addition, the largest turnover in the House in forty years occurred. Forty-four members of the lower chamber were defeated in the primaries or general election, and over a hundred new members of the House were elected. The number of women in the House increased from 28 to 47. Of those individuals named in the bank "scandal," 77 were defeated or retired. Republicans gained 9 seats in the House, but the Democrats retained control, 258 to 176 Republicans and 1 Independent. One positive result was the creation in 1992 of a house administrator to oversee financial (payrolls) and nonlegislative (internal mail) matters.

Bush's defeat came in part from the economic downturn that had only begun to correct itself as the election ended; from his reversal of a promise not to raise taxes ("Read my lips, no new taxes") when he agreed to a budget deal with Democrats to raise $134 billion in new taxes over five years, an action that horrified conservatives in his party; and from the almost frightening display at the Republican nominating convention of extreme religious views that seemed to have emerged within the party.

IT IS A sad fact that from 1975 to 1990 the number of scandals involving federal officers who were indicted for corruption skyrocketed over 1,000 percent. Many were guilty of accepting personal gifts, campaign contributions, and other gratuities such as luxury hotel accommodations, golf outings and the like—all paid for by lobbyists or private individuals. Some members were unwittingly guilty of continuing practices that had been outlawed by the Ethics Committee. And whenever it suited their needs, both political parties exploited these activities in their attacks on one another, and generated an atmosphere of intense partisanship that weakened the authority and power of the House of Representatives.

Following the House Bank affair came the Post Office scandal. A grand jury found evidence that funds had been embezzled, that cocaine had been sold and that stamps provided to members had been exchanged for cash. Dan Rostenkowski was indicted on embezzlement, fraud and cover-up charges, which he denied. But the Democratic Caucus forced him to resign as chairman of the Ways and Means Committee just at a moment when his forceful leadership was most needed by the new Clinton administration.

PRESIDENT CLINTON HAD appointed his wife, Hillary Rodham Clinton, to head a task force to provide a comprehensive health-care system. That plan was unveiled by the President in a nationally televised speech before a joint session of Congress. To say the least, it was incredibly complicated, and the bill as offered in the House ran to over thirteen hundred pages. Several committees itched to get their hands on it, and the party leadership unwisely referred it to three separate committees with jurisdictional claims: Ways and Means, Education and Labor, and Energy and Commerce. Secondary referrals went to seven subcommittees that were charged with examining specific sections of the bill. John Dingell chaired the Energy and Commerce Committee; the new chairman of Ways and Means was Sam Gibbons, the very man Tip O'Neill referred to as a "loose cannon." It was a botched arrangement and a recipe for defeat.

Neither one of these three committees came up with a bill that could pass muster. Despite the good intentions of many committee members, time finally ran out. Congress began its delayed August recess in 1994 without completing work on a health-care bill and the issue was declared dead for the remainder of the year. Actually, the issue was beyond resuscitation.[82]

The health-care fiasco only added fuel to the Republican contention that the institution had been corrupted by continuous Democratic rule for the past forty years. The scandals of the last few years increased public anger over the behavior of federal officials, and Gingrich kept reminding the electorate that it was time for a change. Through his political action committee (GOPAC) he recruited young, energetic Republicans to run for office, raised money to help them in their campaigns and sent them training tapes.[83] On September 27, 1994, some three hundred Republican congressional incumbents and challengers to Democratic incumbents gathered on the steps of the Capitol and unveiled Newt Gingrich's "Contract with America," by which they promised to cleanse the House of Representatives of its corruption in the first hundred days of the next Congress if they won forty new seats.

During the presidential election of 1992 there had been repeated allegations of Clinton's extramarital affairs that had conservatives, particularly in the South and Midwest, outraged. Furthermore, President Clinton's policy of dealing with homosexuals in the military ("Don't ask, don't tell") and the failed attempt at a universal health-insurance plan swelled the growing army of angry, conservative, reform-minded Republicans who demanded change.

And change did come—with a wallop. Democrats hardly knew what hit them. In the midterm election of 1994 they lost some 52 seats and not a single incumbent Republican failed to win reelection. Even Speaker Foley was defeated; Rostenkowski lost in a very close election; and Jack Brooks of Texas, the chairman of the Judiciary Committee, failed in his bid for reelection. The Republicans captured control of the House, 230 to 204, and the conservative revolution began in earnest.

Speaker Foley was the first sitting Speaker to lose reelection since Galusha A. Grow of Pennsylvania in 1862. Foley's district had always been marginal, of course, but the National Rifle Association targeted him for his support of a crime bill that carried an assault weapon ban, and its efforts went a long way in defeating him. Others claimed that he paid little attention to the needs and interests of his constituents but, recalled Gingrich, he was also "a man who had never acquired the reins of power." He "never built his machine."[84]

Gingrich, of course, was hailed as the wizard who had engineered this extraordinary victory.[85] "Newt should be given great credit. He was the visionary that knew it was possible and made it possible," said Bob Livingston, a future Speaker-designate of the Republican party.[86] In March 1989, Gingrich had been elected whip by a bare margin, 87 to 85, over Edward Madigan of Illinois when Dick Cheney surrendered that position to become secretary of defense. Then, when Bob Michel left the House in 1994, Gingrich became minority leader. Actually, he skipped that position. "I'm the only person in modern times who went from being minority whip to being Speaker."[87]

With Michel's support and acquiescence, Gingrich took over leadership of the party in the summer. "Michel was a very, very good manager of his own transition," admitted Gingrich.[88] The Republican Conference also elected Richard Armey of Texas as majority leader and Tom DeLay, whom Dick Cheney described as "maybe the best vote counter I've ever encountered in the House," as whip.[89] The Democrats named Gephardt as minority leader, David Bonior of Pennsylvania as whip, and Vic Fazio as Caucus chairman.

In the House election on January 4, 1995, Gingrich was chosen Speaker, 228 to 202 for Gephardt, in a roll call vote. His parents, wife and children watched from the gallery, which was filled with cheering Republicans. Indeed, it was such a momentous occasion that the Capitol Building was packed with visitors and reporters. Republicans now ruled the House after forty years in the desert, and recaptured the Senate 53 to 47, which they had not done since 1986.

When the Speaker-elect was presented to the House, Republicans erupted with shouts and foot-stamping. Gephardt passed the gavel to Gingrich, remarking on the nation's ability to peacefully transfer power without conflict. "With resignation but with resolve," he said, "I hereby end 40 years of Democratic rule of the House. You are now my Speaker. Let the great debate begin."[90]

Republicans in the House were ecstatic. Now, at long last, they sat in the seat of power, and they had many scores to settle with their Democratic foes. They opened the new Congress with a marathon fourteen-and-a-half-hour session, the kind of performance that would dominate the year.[91] Gingrich immediately set to work changing many House rules. He reduced committee staffs by a third and chose committee chairmen according to their ability to realize goals, not their seniority. Chairmen could hold their positions for no more than three consecutive terms, and the Speaker could serve no more than four consecutive terms, a proposal adopted by the House, 355 to 73, without a single dissenting Republican vote. Legislation was initiated on Social Security, welfare reform, budget, a tax cut, crime, defense and illegal drugs. Three committees—District of Columbia, Merchant Marine and Fisheries, and Post Office and Civil Service—were eliminated, and many more subcommittees. Proxy voting by which committee chairman controlled the votes of absent members was abolished; more committees were open to the public, and the first independent audit of House books got under way. The office of door-keeper was abolished and its functions transferred to the sergeant at arms. The Speaker's staff literally went around and knocked on every door in the Capitol "to find out" what was going on in each room. "I mean, we Republicans didn't know how many rooms there were."[92] "For a freshman Congressman," declared Paul N. McCloskey of California, "particularly a Republican in the minority during the 40 years between 1954 and 1994, there was a golden rule of expected silence."[93] No more.

The Speaker convinced most Republicans to pledge support for his clearly defined agenda in the "Contract." "We had three hundred and fifty candidates sign the Contract, voluntarily. . . . The Contract was not a platform. Platform says what we believe in. Contract said what we will vote on. This was conscious on my part because I wanted to do two things as soon as we took control. I wanted to radicalize the House. . . . The second was, I needed something that [Richard] Armey could run." Gingrich was busy trying to balance the budget and work on reforming Medicare, so Armey took over and "actually ran the House for the first hundred days," with the Contract as a guide.[94] It was a stupendous start for Gingrich in what would become his turbulent tenure as Speaker.

"I think it was Dick's idea to come up with a Contract with America," declared Bob Livingston. "The rest of us pitched in and created it. . . . Newt fleshed it out. I mean clearly, he was a major player in making it happen." Livingston himself wrote the defense plank.[95]

The House enacted most of the items of the Contract, except the one

Newt Gingrich, the architect of the conservative revolution in the House that began with the overthrow of Democratic rule in the mid-term election of 1994.

that called for adopting a constitutional amendment to limit members' terms to twelve years, and a missile defense in outer space, but very few got through the Senate. However, the Congressional Accountability Act passed, which held Congress subject to federal law regarding workers' rights, and the Senate ultimately agreed to the prohibition of unfunded mandates and it became law.[96]

One important innovation originated with the David Obey Commission in 1976 in an effort to reform the business processes of the House. Little significant change came of the commission's report until the Republicans took control in 1995. According to Jay Eagen, the chief administrative officer since the 105th Congress, James Nussle of Iowa led a Transition Task Force that created a chief administrative officer and took "a number of functions that were either independent entities or under the clerk or under the sergeant at arms or affiliated with the Committee on House Administration and centralized them under one officer." Today there are approximately seven hundred individuals involved in the operation, working in four business divisions. "We do everything from information technology to finances," said Eagen, "to human resources, to contracting and procurement of services and equipment and then administering those contracts."[97] The chief administrative officer is elected by the entire House at the beginning of each Congress, just like the clerk, sergeant at arms, and chaplain.

SINCE THE TENURE of chairmen of committees and subcommittees was now limited to six years, competition for these chairs became a regular occurrence. The GOP Steering Committee, headed by J. Dennis Hastert of Illinois, who became Speaker in 1999, later hit upon a new technique to fill these slots. Each candidate would be interviewed. "The candidates will be given an opportunity to discuss their legislative agenda, oversight agenda, how they intend to organize the committee, and their communication strategy," Hastert explained. The Steering Committee would then make the selections and forward them to the full Republican Conference for final approval.[98]

Gingrich, meanwhile, pressed for a balanced budget. Failing to get a constitutional amendment that would mandate this goal, he insisted that a balance between income and expenditure could be accomplished by 2002. The chairman of the House Budget Committee, John Kasich of Ohio, reported out a bill that trimmed $1 trillion in spending cuts over the next seven years. Among other things, it eliminated such executive departments as Education, Commerce and Energy, along with nearly three hundred federal programs. In a party-line vote the House passed the measure, 238 to 219, but the Senate failed to agree on many of these eliminations.

Now it was the Democrats' turn to lambast the majority party. In the House, declared Harry A. Johnston, Democrat from Florida, "the minority party does not legislate—it is that simple." It may slow down legislation and maybe "fine-tune" a bill, "but it never plays an activist role in shaping the laws of the country."[99] Men like John Dingell and John Murtha, both strong chairmen, had no idea what it was like to be in the minority. "And so the pain level was extraordinary. None of them had ever been in the minority in Congress, not in forty years."[100]

Leon Panetta of California accused Gingrich of trying to pressure the President into following the lead of the House, knowing that a presidential veto could not be overridden since it took a two-thirds vote. He charged Gingrich with attempting to hold a gun to the President's head and threatening "to shut down the government" if the Republicans "did not get their tax cuts to help the rich and cut spending that would help the young, the old, the poor and the needy."[101] Clinton encouraged House Democrats to hammer away at Republican attempts to slash the budget. And where the GOP appeared rigid and unreasonable about fiscal matters, the President seemed more open to compromise as he slowly nudged his party away from its extreme liberalism to a more centrist position. Later he would say that "the era of big government is over."[102]

• • •

WHEN CLINTON VETOED a stopgap spending bill, funding for most government offices ran out on November 13, 1995. As a result, almost eight hundred thousand federal workers were ordered home. Vital services like law enforcement continued, but a wide range of government operations—from tourist attractions such as the National Gallery of Art, Yosemite, Yellowstone, Smoky Mountains and Grand Canyon National Parks to the processing of Social Security applications—were shut down. If the only way we could demonstrate "that we were really going to balance the budget" was by closing the government, said Gingrich, then so be it. Otherwise, "you never would have gotten Clinton and his staff to realize how deadly serious we were." And "it was really hard to exaggerate how systematically routinely dishonest Clinton was, and how really good he was at it." The President would agree on one day to balance the budget and "the next morning" he would say that "he didn't actually quite mean that. And this went on all the time."

That tactic left Gingrich far behind. "I'm not fast enough. I mean, Clinton's tactically much faster than I." So "I had to plant stakes in the ground and say, okay, when you're done dancing, here's reality."[103]

The public reacted to the shutdown with horror and anger. It was probably more the *idea* of a government shutdown than the closing of tourist sites that offended them. For the most part they blamed the Republicans for the outrage, but Gingrich declared that "all the president has to do . . . is commit to a seven year balanced budget" and the government would begin to function again.[104]

Then the Speaker made a colossal mistake. At a breakfast meeting with reporters he revealed that he had triggered the shutdown in part because Clinton had snubbed him on an overseas diplomatic trip to attend the funeral of the assassinated prime minister of Israel, Yitzak Rabin, by making him and Senate majority leader Bob Dole exit the plane from the rear door.

Reporters guffawed. Newspapers around the country highlighted the story. The *New York Daily News* on November 16, 1995, carried the headline, "CRY BABY," and below the headline was a cartoon showing Gingrich as a screaming baby in diapers with a caption that read, "Newt's tantrum. He closed down the government because Clinton made him sit at back of the plane." On the House floor, Democrats paraded a blow-up of the cartoon, much to the amusement and delight of sympathetic visitors in the gallery. The angry opposition voted 231 to 173 to stop Democrats from bringing the blow-up into the chamber. It was disrespectful, undignified, and a violation of House rules, they bellowed. Gingrich had now become the villain of the shutdown drama.[105]

Gingrich later admitted that holding the breakfast meeting with reporters was "stupid. If you were listing the dumbest things I did . . . that would be on the short list."[106]

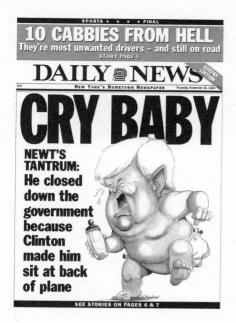

Newt Gingrich admitted that the press conference he held that triggered this cartoon was one of the dumbest things he did in his entire career.

After a weekend of talks between the opposing sides, a truce was announced on Sunday evening, November 19, sending federal employees back to work on Monday. A continuing resolution was passed to cover expenses through December 15, as the House labored for the next four weeks to reach a budget deal with the White House. But recriminations and accusations brought all attempts at a reconciliation to a halt and, at midnight on December 15, the government shut down once again—just in time for Christmas! This time it lasted for twenty-one days.

With a quarter of a million federal employees locked out, Congress recessed and went home to spend the holidays. They soon heard from their constituents. By the time they returned in January they knew that the so-called Republican revolution was in trouble. "Enough is enough," cried Senator Bob Dole of Kansas.[107] Even Gingrich capitulated. He told the Republican Conference on January 5, 1996, that it was time to end the shutdown. Later that day the House and Senate passed a series of funding bills that reopened the government and ended the battle between Congress and the White House, a battle Clinton clearly won.[108]

And with a booming economy and falling deficits, Clinton was reelected to a second term in 1996 over Senator Dole. The Republicans lost three House seats. In the midterm election of 1998 they would lose five more.

The public obviously found Republicans guilty of a spiteful action and saw Newt Gingrich as the principal player in manipulating this outrage. The party's majority was slowly shriveling, and to many Republicans the fault lay strictly with the Speaker. Gingrich's style, which tended to be confrontational, loud and aggressive, did not help him. "The problem for the party," complained one Republican, "is that Newt is the face of the party."[109]

Complicating the Speaker's problems were the continuing attacks by the Democrats about his alleged violation of ethics rules. A special counsel for the Ethics Committee looked into Gingrich's TV appearances and the college course he taught to determine if tax-deductible money had been diverted from his political action committee, GOPAC. There was the question of whether he had violated any tax law. And the hefty advance he had received from a publisher to write a book also came under sharp criticism. The upshot of the investigation was a recommendation that he be reprimanded and fined. On January 21, 1997, by a vote of 395 to 28, the House both fined him $300,000 and reprimanded him, the first sitting Speaker to be so chastised.

In the following months an unsuccessful coup to unseat Gingrich was attempted by some of the most extreme conservative Republicans and senior leaders. But then came the disappointing results of the 1998 midterm election. "Instead of gaining seats," said Bob Livingston, chairman of the Appropriations Committee, "we lost five. I was furious. That's because I'd worked my butt off all year to campaign and raised a ton of money. And they were all turned into anti-Clinton ads and that's not what I'd raised them for. I said that I'd raised the money to spend it on pro-Republican ads. We didn't talk about what we had done right. We talked about what he [Clinton] had done wrong! And we blew it!"

"A lot of people started talking to me," remembered Livingston. A number of Republicans said to him, "Run, run, run." Matt Salmon of Arizona claimed "he would not vote for Gingrich under any circumstance. And that kind of started the ball rolling"[110]

The ball quickly gained momentum. Livingston reached a decision and informed Gingrich that "I'm going to run against you. I said that at about ten o'clock in the morning," on November 6, 1998. "By two o'clock, he [Gingrich] announced that he was not going to run again."[111] He withdrew as a candidate for Speaker in the 106th Congress and resigned his seat. Forthwith, the Republican Conference on November 18 chose Livingston to succeed him. There was no opposition.

Aside from Gingrich, one reason for the disappointing results of the election for Republicans was the continued economic health of the nation, which allowed Clinton to present not only a balanced budget for 1998 but a surplus as well.

ON FRIDAY AFTERNOON, July 24, 1998, a dreadful tragedy occurred in which for the first time two U.S. Capitol police officers were killed in the line of duty. A forty-two-year-old lone gunman, Russell Eugene Weston, a diagnosed paranoid schizophrenic from Rimini, Montana, entered the Capitol through the Document Room Door on the ground floor at 3:40 p.m., walked around the metal detector and shot the guard, Officer Jacob J. Chestnut, in the head with a .38 caliber pistol. He then dashed up a short flight of stairs, rounded a corner and followed a woman down a hallway leading to the office complex of Tom DeLay, the majority whip. Inside the office, another Capitol police offficer, Detective John M. Gibson, assigned to provide security for DeLay, confronted him. The two fired at one another at almost point-blank range. During the exchange, a tourist, Angela Dickerson, was wounded in the face and arm, Gibson was killed and Weston himself was critically shot. The shooting "sent panicked bystanders diving for cover," turning "the midsummer peace of the Capitol grounds into pandemonium." The gunman was subdued by several other officers who rushed to the scene. He was later charged with the murder of Chestnut and Gibson, but he was subsequently found to be incompetent to stand trial and confined to a psychiatric hospital.

The following Tuesday, the bodies of Chestnut and Gibson lay in honor* in the Capitol Rotunda, with Chestnut the first African-American to receive this recognition. All day, from 8:00 a.m. to 7:00 p.m., the public paid its respects.

A brief memorial service was held at 3:00 p.m. atttended by the President, Vice President, members of the House and Senate and other dignitaries. Tributes to the slain officers were given by President Clinton, Speaker Gingrich, Senate Majority Leader Trent Lott, and the Capitol police chief Gary Abrecht. In his remarks, Clinton said that the officers had "consecrated this house of freedom." Gingrich commented: "I want to emphasize that this building is the keystone of freedom, that it is open to the people because it is the people's building. No terrorist, no deranged person, no act of violence will block us from preserving our freedom and keeping this building open to people from all over the world."

Members of the victims' families sat close by, many of them weeping, while hundreds of standing police officers and congressmen stood at attention. "It was a death in the family," said Senator Trent Lott.[112]

SINCE THE BEGINNING of the Clinton administration, Republicans had conducted no fewer than thirty-seven investigations into the operations of the White House—such as its travel office and the involvement by the Clintons in the Whitewater land scheme in Arkansas—in an effort to find cause to introduce impeachment proceedings. Then the President did something incredibly stupid as well as immoral, and he was soon overwhelmed by personal scandal, long rumored, involving his sex life. He was sued by Paula Jones, a former employee when he served as governor of Arkansas, for sexual harassment. Worse, he was accused of inappropriate behavior with a

---

*This is protocol. Lying in state is reserved for those entitled to a state funeral.

White House intern, Monica Lewinsky—in the Oval Office, no less. Kenneth Starr was appointed by Attorney General Janet Reno to investigate and, in testimony before a grand jury in January 1998, Clinton swore he had had no improper relations with Lewinsky, a denial he repeated many times to his cabinet and members of Congress, among others.

The State of the Union address gave him the opportunity to go on television and remind the American people that he had produced the first balanced budget in thirty years and that they were the recipients of an unbroken period of economic prosperity. Opinion polls recorded his steadily mounting approval rating. "I think the American people," declared Republican senator Robert E. Bennett of Utah, "have come to the conclusion that they do not want to drive the president out of office just because he's not faithful to his wife, and they turned off all the rest of it."[113]

But the truth soon emerged. Continued revelation of incriminating evidence finally forced the President to admit in a televised appearance on August 17, 1998, that he had indeed carried on an "inappropriate" affair with Lewinsky. Still, he insisted that he had done nothing illegal. Several weeks later, on September 9, the day the House returned from its recess, Starr's office delivered thirty-six boxes of documents to the House, including two copies of the investigator's report and supporting evidence, and argued that Clinton's actions "may constitute grounds for impeachment."[114]

During the summer of 1998, prior to the midterm election, "our polls were fine," claimed Bob Livingston. "And then, about the end of August, Newt made a decision. . . . He made the decision along with Dick Gephardt, who participated in it, to take all of the grand jury transcripts and put them on the Internet, *all* of the information. And I'm convinced, with the wisdom of the American people," Livingston continued, "that they sensed a degree of unfairness there. Public attitude switched from being totally against Clinton to against the Republicans, right about the first of September."[115] That was another reason for the midterm loss of five seats, leaving the Republicans with a slim six-member majority in the 106th Congress.

On October 8, 1998, the House passed a resolution 258 to 176, instructing the Judiciary Committee, chaired by Henry Hyde of Illinois, to examine the evidence and decide whether the President had committed impeachable offenses "or whether it was just something personal and not a matter of national concern."

Hearings by the thirty-seven-member committee were "quite contentious, and things were heating up," declared Hyde. The committee included old-line liberals like John Conyers of Michigan and Barney Frank of Massachusetts, and hard-line conservatives like Bob Barr of Georgia and Charles Canady of Florida. But in Henry Hyde the committee had a chairman who was respected by members of both parties, and he succeeded in maintaining a degree of civility during the most heated debates in the committee.

As far as Republicans were concerned, according to Hyde, the charges "had nothing to do with sex and everything to do with perjury and swearing under oath," but the Democrats "were successful in defining the issue as a very personal one that lying about is not that uncommon," that sexual misbehavior is not a high crime or misdemeanor.[116]

Several Democrats warned the Republicans of a backlash. "As you judge the president of the United States," cautioned Charles Rangel of New York, "the voters will be judging you on November the 3rd." Then a rapid-fire series of events unfolded. Gingrich resigned, Clinton reached a monetary settlement with Paula Jones and the Republicans chose Robert Livingston as Speaker-designate.[117]

After studying the evidence presented, Hyde and his committee decided on December 11–12 that Clinton had indeed "committed perjury and obstructed justice." Furthermore, they agreed that "it would be a dereliction of duty if we didn't proceed . . . with impeachment with a view towards removing him from office." They voted 21 to 16 for impeachment, but recognized that ousting Clinton from office "was a long shot at best," since it required a two-thirds vote in the Senate.[118]

Livingston and the new Republican leadership also favored pushing ahead with impeachment. The Speaker-designate remembered speaking to a number of doubtful members and convincing them to stand with the committee. The basic charge, he told them, "had nothing to do with the sexual peccadilloes. It had to do with the fact that he [Clinton] lied before the grand jury, and because people in the military and other agencies had done exactly what he did and were in prison."[119]

The irony of pushing ahead with this action when Reagan escaped impeachment over Iran-Contra probably did not cross the minds of committee members. The Republican members were determined to get rid of Clinton at all cost.

The committee presented its report on impeachment to the full House, and for thirteen and a half hours over two days, December 18 and 19, the chamber reverberated with cries of protest and indignation from Democrats and vigorous arguments supporting the charges from Republicans. Democrats contended that censure was the appropriate course of action to take, but that suggestion was shot down on a procedural vote, 230 to 204, whereupon the Democrats walked out of the chamber in protest.

When it was revealed that Livingston had also committed adultery, it electrified the entire nation. Here were two of the leaders of the government, Clinton and Livingston, disgraced by their actions. Livingston decided to do something about it. He entered the House chamber on December 19 and made a speech that stunned his audience. He began by saying how "I very much regret the enmity and the hostility that has been bred in the halls of Congress for the last months and year. I want so very much to pacify and

cool our raging tempers and return to an era when differences were confined to the debate, not to a personal attack or assassination of character." He
said, "I am proud to serve in this institution, and I respect every member of
this body."

Then he turned to the Clinton impeachment proceedings and expressed
his belief that the President had perjured himself. "To the President I would
say, sir, you have done great damage to this nation" but "you have the power
to terminate that damage and heal the wounds that you have created. You,
sir, may resign your post."

Democrats shouted, "No, no, no." Then they chanted, "You resign. You
resign."

Livingston held up his right hand as a signal that he had more to say. "I
can only challenge you in such fashion," he went on, "if I am willing to heed
my own words. So I must set the example that I hope President Clinton will
follow. I will not stand for Speaker of the House," he said. "I shall vacate my
seat in approximately six months into the 106th Congress."[120]

There was stunned silence. Then he turned and left the chamber as his
colleagues rose to give him a standing ovation.

Several Democrats thought his action as misguided as Clinton's impeachment. "It is a surrender to a developing sexual McCarthyism," fumed
Jerrold Nadler, a Democrat from New York. Minority leader Richard Gephardt "rushed to the cloak room and got on the phone with the President."[121]
Then he returned to the chamber and spoke with passion and conviction as
he connected the Livingston decision with Clinton's impeachment. "We are
now rapidly descending into a politics where life imitates farce. Fratricide
dominates our public debate and America is held hostage with tactics of
smear and fear. Let all of us here today say no to resignation, no to impeachment, no to hatred, no to intolerance of each other, and no to virtuous
self-righteousness."[122] But his speech, in Livingston's opinion, "was ridden
with crocodile tears."[123]

Meanwhile Tom DeLay and Bill Paxon of New York began working the
floor to round up support for J. Dennis Hastert of Illinois, the deputy whip,
to replace Livingston. They urged their colleagues to speak to Hastert, who
was sitting in the back row of the chamber, and convince him to run for the
Speakership. One by one Paxon ushered Republican lawmakers to the remote area to urge Hastert to stand for the office. There was no question that
this hulking, lumbering, six-foot-tall man with an engaging smile was a popular choice and unsullied by ethical blemishes, something desperately
needed at this juncture. "I see myself," Hastert explained in an interview, "as
a person who throughout my career has listened to people and tried to understand the issues they want to talk about. I try to bring people together; I
see that as my role."[124] He was nominated unanimously by the Republican
Conference on January 5, 1999, and elected by the House the following day.

The debate over the impeachment of President Clinton having concluded, it was time to take a formal vote. Democrats returned to the chamber, but the outcome was predictable. By a vote of 228 to 206 the House of Representatives impeached the President on the charge of perjury before a grand jury about his affair with Lewinsky, and a vote of 221 to 212 on the obstruction of justice charge in the Paula Jones suit in that he allegedly helped to conceal evidence and tamper with witnesses. Then the House, by a vote of 228 to 190, created a thirteen-member committee, chaired by Hyde, to serve as managers for the impeachment trial in the Senate. Members of the Judiciary Committee constituted the entire thirteen-member team.

Looking back, Hyde admitted to "an error in judgment on my part: my inability to say no to people who wanted to be managers" at the trial. Any number of them "pleaded with me to be a manager and I found it difficult to turn them down, so we ended up with a surplus of managers." It was "unwieldy." Worse, "we found ourselves the proverbial skunk at the garden party: nobody wanted us. The senators wanted to get it over with in a hurry, and following the polls and finding that this impeachment was not the most popular move in the world," they sought to end it quickly. "They limited the

Henry Hyde (center) and the Judiciary Committee that served as managers for the President Clinton impeachment trial in the Senate.

number of witnesses we could produce; we couldn't put anybody on the stand unless they okayed it; and there was nobody really enthusiastic for what we were doing, including our own [Senate Republican] leadership."[125]

The managers felt hamstrung. But what could they do? They had little choice. Under these trying circumstances, they realized getting a conviction would be next to impossible.

The trial in the Senate began on January 7, 1999. Chief Justice William Rehnquist, complete with gold-stripe-sleeved black robe right out of Gilbert and Sullivan, presided. According to Hyde, Democratic senator Robert Byrd of West Virginia would not let the prosecutors call Monica Lewinsky as a witness to testify. He refused his permission, and so "we couldn't bring her in to answer questions. To do it right, we should have had her in, we should have had some of these other people. The President himself might well have been a witness. But there was a quiet hostility towards us over trying the case."

"When they said we couldn't have Lewinsky," Hyde declared, "I should have held a press conference and said, 'They're tying our hands and feet. This is not a trial as the Constitution provides; they won't let us call witnesses.' And I would have called the President as a witness. Fight that out, let the chief justice rule on that."[126]

To open the proceedings, Hyde reminded the Senators of their duty as impartial jurors. "You are seated in this historic chamber . . . to listen to the evidence as those who must sit in judgment. To guide you in this grave duty, you've taken an oath of impartiality." Representative James Rogan of California managed the perjury case, and Representative Asa Hutchinson of Arkansas the obstruction of justice. Edward Bryant of Tennessee presented a chronological history of the events that led to the investigation by Kenneth Starr. All three insisted that Clinton had lied under oath to a federal judge, disgraced his office and deserved punishment just like any other ordinary citizen. Rogan replayed some of the President's testimony before the grand jury; Hutchinson used charts to argue obstruction of justice; and Bryant showed a video of Clinton taking the oath of office on the Capitol steps.

James Sensenbrenner of Wisconsin provided an overview of the managers' case, promising "all kinds of little nuggets—lots of stuff you haven't heard before." Actually, nothing new was revealed, and as the hours passed the senators could be seen fidgeting or taking notes or gesturing for a glass of water, but not a single one of them "so much as whispered" during the opening arguments.

The defense was a high-powered group of eight individuals, headed by Charles Ruff, the White House counsel. In his summation, Ruff contended that the managers' vision was too dark. "I believe it to be a vision more focused on retribution, more designed to achieve partisan ends." Our vision, he continued, is different, and "we know the pain the president has caused our society and his family and his friends, but we know, too, how much the president has done for this country."

In any comparison of the presentations by the prosecution and defense, there could be little doubt that the prosecution had failed to convince two-thirds of the senators to vote to remove Clinton from office. To many observers, it did appear to be a matter of partisan hatred for a morally flawed President and a desire to exact retribution.

After nearly five weeks of testimony and deliberation, the Senate voted against removal of the President on February 9, 1999, and acquitted him. Ten Republicans and all forty-five Democrats voted not guilty to the charge of perjury; on the charge of obstruction of justice, the Senate split, 50 to 50. Later Clinton declared that he was "profoundly sorry" for what he had imposed on the Congress and the American people.

The failure of the prosecution prompted both Bob Livingston and Newt Gingrich to point an accusing finger at Kenneth Starr. "Starr was an academic," said Livingston, "and not a criminal prosecutor. . . . I think had he been a criminal prosecutor, he would *not* have allowed the information [about Clinton's sexual affairs] to get on the Internet." The case should have been about perjury, nothing more. "Starr," Gingrich declared, ". . . actually diminished the importance of the issue and made it human, rather than legal."[127]

The intense partisanship generated by the scandal and trial carried forward to the presidential election of 2000 when Al Gore, the sitting Vice President, was defeated by the Republican George W. Bush, son of the former President, as a result of the Supreme Court involving itself in the election by awarding Florida's disputed vote to Bush, even though he had lost the popular vote nationwide by more than a half million. The House remained Republican, but the Senate was split down the middle, 50 to 50. It was only the deciding vote of Vice President Richard Cheney that kept nominal control of the upper house in Republican hands.

THE HORROR THAT occurred on September 11, 2001, when terrorists commandeered several planes and rammed two of them into the World Trade Center in New York City, killing three thousand people, and another plane dove into the Pentagon, killing and wounding scores of individuals, had the effect of uniting the country in its determination to end terrorism in the world. President Bush sent troops into Afghanistan that toppled the Taliban regime but failed to capture the leading terrorist, Osama bin Laden.

This new century began with the nation at war, a war in which U.S. troops in Afghanistan have continued to combat insurgents, a war that soon escalated with the invasion of Iraq on March 20, 2003. And by 2005 the end of U.S. military involvement in those two countries was nowhere in sight.

Epilogue

A S THE NATION moved from the latter decades of the twentieth century to the twenty-first century, the profile of Congress, and especially the House of Representatives, had changed substantially. In 1967, just after passage of the Voting Rights Act of 1965, there were only five African-Americans in the House; but by 1993, at the start of the 103rd Congress, there were thirty-eight, sixteen of whom came from southern states and another four from border states. In 1969, the Congressional Black Caucus was formed with nine members, and by 1985 that number rose to twenty. To illustrate how dramatic the change in the House had become, there were five standing committees and two select committees chaired by African-Americans in the 99th Congress (1985–1987). Of other minorities, there were nineteen Hispanics by 1995, one Native American, and seven Asian-Americans in the House and two Asian-Americans in the Senate. By 2004 there were 42 African-Americans and 27 Hispanics in the House. As for women, their numbers in the House increased from eleven in 1965 to forty-eight in 1993 and 70 in 2004.

Throughout the nation's history, change has been a constant. The Founders created a republic, but, with the steady expansion of the suffrage over two centuries, the country evolved into a democracy. This fact was most particularly reflected in the House of Representatives, which developed from an institution in 1789 of 65 white, mostly Anglo-Saxon and Protestant men from the middle and upper classes of society to today's 435 men and women of every class, nationality, race and religion.

Quite a feat in two hundred years! And further changes will undoubtedly follow.

Percentage-wise, the 435 representatives today are not proportionate to the percentages of women, blacks, Hispanics and Asians in the total population of the United States. In 2005, women were not represented in the House in the number commensurate with their actual number in American society. The 2000 census shows that women comprise 50.9 percent of a total U.S. population of 281,421,906. But their representation in the House is only 16.09 percent. Compared to other democracies around the world, where women are generally represented in much larger numbers, the United States lags behind. According to the November 28, 2005, issue of *Newsweek* magazine, the United States ranks 67th in female representation among world governments. The same disproportion is true for minorities. African-Americans are 12.3 percent of the U.S. population, while their representation in the House is 9.66 percent. Hispanics represent 12.5 percent of the population, but only 6.20 percent in the House.

In another respect, the extraordinary evolution of the country is illustrated by the amount of money spent to run the country. The 1st Congress appropriated a little over two million dollars. Through August 2005, the 109th Congress had appropriated 2.255 trillion dollars—and that figure did not include the cost of repairing the damage inflicted by Hurricanes Katrina, Rita and Wilma. In 1789, the national debt ran to slightly more than 50 million dollars. In 2005, it is 7.918 trillion—and mounting. From millions to trillions is quite a leap.[1]

THE PROCEEDINGS OF the House are much more open today, much more public. The debates on the floor and the committee hearings are regularly attended by visitors. As much as prudence will allow, secrecy has been reduced substantially.

The religious complexion of Congress also changed. Roman Catholics rose from 87 Representatives in 1965 to 118 in the 103rd Congress, and most of them were Democrats. In 2005, there were 155 Catholics in the 109th Congress, of whom 132 were House members. For the first time, a Roman Catholic priest was chosen in 2000 as House chaplain. As for Jews, in 1963, there were only 9 members in the House. By 1993 there were 23, and in 2005, there were 37 in Congress, of whom 26 were members of the House. Protestant denominations suffered a corresponding loss, the greatest among Methodists and Presbyterians.[2]

A sampling of the membership of the present-day Congress reveals that the 435 representatives and 100 senators clearly represent a cross section of American life. In the 109th Congress (2005–2007), the members had engaged in every conceivable profession. Not surprisingly, the largest number of them were lawyers, followed by public servants, such as mayors, state governors, state legislators, cabinet secretaries, an ambassador and state and federal judges. Next in number were those in business, agriculture and education. Medicine was particularly well represented. There were medical doctors, nurses, psychologists, a psychiatrist, dentists, an optometrist, a pharmacist and two veterinarians. Also present were sheriffs, state troopers, police officers, firemen, probation officers, and FBI and CIA agents. Accountants, six ministers, musicians, radio and television broadcasters, airline pilots, an astronaut, and football and baseball players were among the members of this Congress. From the blue-collar and white-collar classes came a carpenter, meat cutter, taxicab driver, a steelworker, ironworker, paper-mill worker, cement-plant worker, an exterminator, an orchard worker, auctioneers, vintners, bank tellers, a hotel clerk, a hotel bellhop, a racetrack blacksmith, a cowboy and a magician.[3] Quite a list, one truly representative of a broad spectrum of occupations in every part of the country.

Interestingly, a study completed in 2005 found that 43 percent of the members who leave government to return to private life register as lobbyists. That had not happened before. As late as the 1980s, few lawmakers became lobbyists because they considered it beneath their dignity. But a sea-change had occurred in the past few years. Unquestionably, the enormous salaries and the growing demand for lobbying services by industry account for the change. But control of the executive and legislative branches of government by the Republican Party after 2000 may also have had something to do with it. Following George W. Bush's election, the largest number of lawmakers ever recorded flooded into the lobbying field. Half of the members to leave government after that election registered to lobby, and they frequently found employment with lobbies that had foreign governments as clients! "Access equals power in Washington," said Frank Clemente, director of Congress Watch, "and few people have greater access than a former member of Congress."[4]

ANOTHER IMPORTANT CHANGE in the House during the modern period was the alteration of the workweek. "We used to work from noon Mondays until three o'clock on Fridays," remembered John Murtha.[5] Members moved to Washington, brought their families, learned to live with the discomforts and benefits of life in the District of Columbia and, most important of all, got to know their colleagues, frequently crossing party lines to make friends. Indeed, Donald Rumsfeld said he had "as many friends who were Democrats as I did who were Republicans."[6] He played paddleball with the opposition, and Rostenkowski usually drove home to Chicago on weekends with two Republican colleagues: the minority leader, Bob Michel, and Harold Collier.

No more. For one thing, they see less of each other. Representatives frequently flee the city at the first opportunity. With the arrival of jet air flights, members found they could fly home for an extended weekend, including those from such distant districts as Hawaii and Alaska. Families chose to remain home in their districts rather than disrupt the schooling of children and separate themselves from relatives and friends for long periods of time. Taking advantage of this situation to save money while in Washington, several House members now sleep in their offices and shower in the physical-fitness complex (the facility has a locker room, a gym and a swimming pool) behind an unmarked locked door in the basement of the Rayburn Office Building. Only members have access to this complex. In addition, the sharp increase in partisanship in the 1980s and 1990s, and the personal abuse members flung at one another in debate, made the House an unpleasant place to spend one's time. Socializing across party lines has become a rarity. Members hardly know one another. Friendships are frequently limited to colleagues one serves with on committees.[7]

Geographically, the members became divided without anyone directing it. They did not share the same "watering holes," explained Henry Hyde of Illinois. At the state level, he said, "after the session, you go to the same bars and restaurants and you intermingle. Whereas in Washington, they're dispersed physically. The Republican club is on one side and the Democrat club is on another and never the twain shall meet."[8]

As a result of these many changes, the workweek in the House of Representatives was reduced to two days and one night. Members left town late Thursday or early Friday and did not return until Monday or early Tuesday. They were said to belong to the "Tuesday Through Thursday Club."[9] By the beginning of the twenty-first century, reported the *Washington Post*, members had "Monday, Friday and most of Tuesday free of Washington-based duties, roughly their average workweek this year." Mondays are called "Proforma Mondays," meaning it counts as a legislative day but nothing gets done, nobody is present in the House. Frequently what happens is that the Speaker pro tem calls the House in session, approves the minutes of the previous day, and then adjourns. Said one representative, "Given all the issues and problems the country faces, it's scandalous that we're only coming in to work three days a week, and even then most of the time we're renaming post offices."[10]

It is not uncommon, if a federal holiday falls on a Monday, such as Columbus Day, for Congress to take the entire week off. It is called "District Work Period," the official euphemism for "recess." The 4th of July week is known as "Independence Day District Work Period," and the entire month of August is called the "Summer District Work Period."

And speaking of euphemisms, the junkets around the world that members regularly take are called Codels, meaning congressional delegations.

WHEN DID THE workweek reduction occur? Bob Livingston credits Newt Gingrich with the change. "Newt said, 'Stay home and campaign,' and they did." That was the way to end Democratic rule and make the Republicans the majority party.

"The nation is a full-time nation," lectured Livingston. "And Congress should be a full-time Congress. My feeling is very strong that if you want to be a local politician, run for local office. If you want to run this country," he continued, "you've got to be here. You've got to be here five days a week. You've got to make sure your committee system is observant, that you're participating in those committees and subcommittees, and that they're providing oversight, maintenance, and structure of the country. And I don't see that happening." But the members "don't want to come here, except when absolutely necessary."

"One of the biggest failings in the House right now," Livingston continued, "is lack of oversight because their schedule doesn't permit adequate attention for oversight. And I think that there's a real problem that empowers the staff. They get arrogant, and change becomes more difficult."

Since much of the workload necessarily shifted to members of the staff, their number increased tremendously during the last quarter of the twentieth century. A congressman in 1960 had a budget of $20,000 for staff salaries. By the middle of the 1990s it was $515,760.[11] Today there are 17,800 paid staffers and an additional 7,000 unpaid interns and fellows. The staff often writes the legislation that goes before the full House for approval. It is not uncommon for members to vote on bills they have not read or studied or know much about. "Unfortunately, it's far too frequent," Livingston sighed. They simply follow the direction of the leadership.[12]

ANOTHER IMPORTANT DEVELOPMENT that took place in Congress was the steady drift of southerners from the Democratic Party to the Republican Party. For years southerners had frequently voted with their conservative friends in the Republican Party, but after the civil rights reforms during the Johnson administration the South slowly built up a solid Republican base. J. Strom Thurmond, the senator from South Carolina, was one of the more prominent legislators to switch parties. During the election of 1964 he abandoned his previous allegiance to the Democratic party and aided Barry Goldwater in his unsuccessful bid for the presidency against Lyndon Johnson. He was soon followed by others until the South, by the end of the century, was represented overwhelmingly in Congress by Republicans. If the truth be told, John Murtha explained, "we did part of that ourselves. We drove them out. When I say we drove them out, these liberals were very, very hard on the Southern Democrats. . . . They wanted them to toe the line" and vote for issues that would defeat them in their districts. "Many of them gave up because they . . . realized . . . if they voted with us, they lost their election."[13]

Although Washington had physically changed for the better during the second half of the twentieth century—what with the introduction of air-conditioning in virtually every building; the completion of the Kennedy Center for the Performing Arts that brought theater, opera, a symphony orchestra, concerts and touring artists to town; the arrival of upscale shops, businesses and restaurants; the construction of new hotels, homes and apartments, and many other amenities—still members of Congress chose to return to their hometowns for long weekends where they could enjoy their families, see to the needs of their constituents and, perhaps most important, campaign for reelection. Representatives do need to win election every two years—that is, if they want a long tenure—so getting home to campaign as often as possible becomes a necessity.

Unfortunately, the rivalries, the incivility, and partisan discord in Congress that had dominated the final decade of the twentieth century extended into the twenty-first. Part of the reason for the continuation of partisanship, as both Foley and Michel attest, is the fact that because of gerrymandering* in the states during the past few decades there exist "only 35 competitive seats out of the 435, and it's too bad." The same people are elected over and over, reducing the number of individuals who might bring fresh ideas, insights and enthusiasm to Congress. There should be more contests between opposing political views, said Foley, so that the people can decide which party they wish to have represent them in Congress. More competitive seats would allow the democratic system to function as it should.[14]

Another reason for the reduction of competitive seats is the fact that incumbents have the advantage of what Bill Thomas of California called "the campaign finance incumbent protection system." Incumbents usually have more money with which to campaign, he points out. For one thing, taxpayer dollars are spent by incumbents on franked mail to their constituents. In 1973–74, he reported, the amount of money for franked mail came to about $40 million, and rose to $130 million in the 1989–90 election. Incumbents in 1989–90 spent $163 million to win reelection compared to $36 million by challengers who tried to unseat them. Obviously, as far as money goes toward deciding elections, it is much more difficult for a challenger to wage a successful campaign than it is for an incumbent.[15] And that fact was amply demonstrated in the 2004 election when only seven House incumbents were defeated.

---

*Gerrymandering is a procedure by which a political district is drawn so that it contains the largest number of partisans for either the Republican or Democratic Party. Probably the first was the "salamander-shaped" district of Essex, north of Boston, Massachusetts, that Federalists dubbed a "gerrymander" after Governor Elbridge Gerry. This particular gerrymander first appeared in the *Boston Gazette* of March 26, 1812. *Encyclopedia of the United States Congress* (New York, 1995) 2: 908–912.

But franking reform in 1989 reduced expenditures by 70 percent from $113 million to $34 million in 2004. Of that $34 million, the House spent 89 percent of it and the Senate 11 percent.[16] Still, it is interesting that in an election year the frank is double the normal expenditure. Today, the House Ethics Committee has strict rules about members using the frank for campaign purposes. Members are forbidden to frank any mass mailing less than 90 days before the date of a primary or general election in which the member is a candidate for public office.

IN THE COURSE of its history, over the last century and a half, the two branches of government—executive and legislative—have usually been divided between the Democratic and Republican Parties. Either the House was Democratic and the Senate Republican, or vice versa; or the executive was Republican and one or the other or both houses were Democratic, or vice versa. The American people appear to favor a "divided government" as a way of preventing one-party rule. With one-party rule, the legislative and executive branches usually operate in lockstep. Such a setup invariably results in the dominance of the executive. Congress surrenders a great deal of its power and authority, and submits to the direction of the President.

Obviously, there are advantages and disadvantages to both divided government and one-party rule. Divided government usually means limited government, frequently leaving many problems unresolved. One-party rule, on the other hand, can provide a great deal of legislation that can be beneficial to the country as a whole, and do it quickly. But it also can lead to an "arrogance of power" and diminish the possibility of compromise between the two competing parties. Put another way, divided government can provide real checks and balances on absolute power.

Which to choose? Which is preferable? The people must decide. It depends on what they want and need at any given time.

THE HOUSE HAS faced many challenges in the past and successfully met them. It will take especially strong leadership and determination on the part of many individuals to end the partisan rancor that now exists and restore what has been lost. But it can be done. Intense partisanship is not new to the Congress. It existed in the past and was vanquished. It will again.

The institution of the House as the world's greatest arena for open and democratic legislation is mocked when, as Speaker McCormack said, members forget that they "have been highly honored by being selected by five hundred thousand or six hundred thousand of [their] constituents to come to Washington and represent them in the House. If the day comes when, rain or shine, cold or hot, windy or calm, you come to the capital and you see that great structure set out against the sky, and you are not deeply honored and proud to have this rare opportunity of service, then quit, just quit. Because if you lose your awe of this great privilege, you don't belong."[17]

Members need to have a deep, emotional attachment to the House, McCormack insisted. They need to know its history and respect its traditions. As John Murtha of Pennsylvania exclaimed when asked about his feelings, "I love it. I mean every day when I come to work, I just can't help myself. I love this job."[18]

From the beginning of the Republic, noted Speaker Nicholas Longworth, "it has been the duty of every freeborn voter to look down upon us and the duty of every freeborn humorist to make jokes about us." Mark Twain did it best when he said in jest that the United States had no criminal class "except, of course, for Congress."[19] But the electorate needs to remember that for the most part they are served by intelligent men and women who are hardworking and dedicated.

For all its faults, as David McCullough rightly remarked in his speech before a joint session of the House and Senate on March 2, 1989, Congress "has not been the unbroken parade of clowns and thieves and posturing windbags so often portrayed."[20] Over the past two centuries the members have accomplished remarkable feats. They established a democratic government representing free people of every race and creed; they built roads, canals, highways and railroads; they ended slavery and child labor; they created Social Security, the G.I. Bill, Medicare and voting rights protection. They guided the country's expansion westward across a three-thousand-mile continent and passed the Homestead and Morrill Land Grant Acts. They aided the nation's evolution from an agricultural to an industrial society. They made possible the transformation of a fragile collection of individual states into a colossus that presently dominates the globe. They have served the American people extremely well.

NEWT GINGRICH RELATED the true story about two reporters from *Pravda* who visited Washington. As Speaker, he showed them around the Capitol and brought them into the House chamber. One of the reporters asked to mount the rostrum, and Gingrich gave his permission. The reporter not only climbed up the rostrum, he also sat down in the Speaker's chair. He looked around the empty chamber and after several minutes descended. "I have sat at the center of freedom," he declared.[21]

That is what the House of Representatives has created over the past two centuries: a center of freedom.

Much of the good that has occurred resulted from the fact that individuals of opposing positions agreed to accommodate one another in order to achieve important goals for the benefit of the American people. The history of the House demonstrates repeatedly that when members fail or refuse to compromise they invite disaster.

In *The Federalist Papers,* Number 57, James Madison wrote: "The aim of every political Constitution is, or ought to be, first, to obtain for rulers, men who possess most wisdom to discern, and most virtue to pursue the common good of the society, and in the next place, to take the most effectual precautions for keeping them virtuous, whilst they continue to hold their public trust."

There are exceptions, of course, but for the most part Madison's prescription for service in the House of Representatives has been fairly met throughout its long history. What is more, most members recognize that they have been given a gift by their constituents to serve them, and that they have an obligation in the relatively brief time allotted them to make a difference in advancing the public welfare and adding to the glory of this center of freedom.

What a fabulous challenge! What a golden opportunity!

List of Speakers (1789–2005)

CONGRESS	SPEAKER	STATE	DATE ELECTED
1st	Frederick A.C. Muhlenberg	Pennsylvania	Apr. 1, 1789
2nd	Jonathan Trumbull	Connecticut	Oct. 24, 1791
3rd	Frederick A.C. Muhlenberg	Pennsylvania	Dec. 2, 1793
4th–5th	Jonathan Dayton	New Jersey	Dec. 7, 1795
6th	Theodore Sedgwick	Massachusetts	Dec. 2, 1799
7th–9th	Nathaniel Macon	North Carolina	Dec. 7, 1801
10th–11th	Joseph B. Varnum	Massachusetts	Oct. 26, 1807
12th–13th	Henry Clay[1]	Kentucky	Nov. 4, 1811
13th	Langdon Cheves	South Carolina	Jan. 19, 1814
14th–16th	Henry Clay[2]	Kentucky	Dec. 4, 1815
16th	John W. Taylor	New York	Nov. 15, 1820
17th	Philip P. Barbour	Virginia	Dec. 4, 1821
18th	Henry Clay[3]	Kentucky	Dec. 1, 1823
19th	John W. Taylor	New York	Dec. 5, 1825
20th–22nd	Andrew Stevenson	Virginia	Dec. 3, 1827
23rd	John Bell	Tennessee	June 2, 1834

(continued)

CONGRESS	SPEAKER	STATE	DATE ELECTED
24th–25th	James K. Polk	Tennessee	Dec. 7, 1835
26th	Robert M.T. Hunter	Virginia	Dec. 16, 1839
27th	John White	Kentucky	May 31, 1841
28th	John W. Jones	Virginia	Dec. 4, 1843
29th	John W. Davis	Indiana	Dec. 1, 1845
30th	Robert C. Winthrop	Massachusetts	Dec. 6, 1847
31st	Howell Cobb	Georgia	Dec. 22, 1849
32nd–33rd	Linn Boyd	Kentucky	Dec. 1, 1851
34th	Nathaniel P. Banks	Massachusetts	Feb. 2, 1856
35th	James L. Orr	South Carolina	Dec. 7, 1857
36th	William Pennington	New Jersey	Feb. 1, 1860
37th	Galusha A. Grow	Pennsylvania	July 4, 1861
38th–40th	Schuyler Colfax	Indiana	Dec. 7, 1863
40th	Theodore M. Pomeroy[4]	New York	Mar. 3, 1869
41st–43rd	James G. Blaine	Maine	Mar. 4, 1869
44th	Michael C. Kerr[5]	Indiana	Dec. 6, 1875
44th–46th	Samuel J. Randall	Pennsylvania	Dec. 4, 1876
47th	J. Warren Keifer	Ohio	Dec. 5, 1881
48th–50th	John G. Carlisle	Kentucky	Dec. 3, 1883
51st	Thomas B. Reed	Maine	Dec. 2, 1889
52nd–53rd	Charles F. Crisp	Georgia	Dec. 8, 1891
54th–55th	Thomas B. Reed	Maine	Dec. 2, 1895
56th–57th	David B. Henderson	Iowa	Dec. 4, 1899
58th–61st	Joseph G. Cannon	Illinois	Nov. 9, 1903
62nd–65th	James Beauchamp Clark	Missouri	Apr. 4, 1911
66th–68th	Frederick H. Gillett	Massachusetts	May 19, 1919

(*continued*)

CONGRESS	SPEAKER	STATE	DATE ELECTED
69th–71st	Nicholas Longworth	Ohio	Dec. 7, 1925
72nd	John N. Garner	Texas	Dec. 7, 1931
73rd	Henry T. Rainey[6]	Illinois	Mar. 9, 1933
74th	Joseph W. Byrns[7]	Tennessee	Jan. 3, 1935
74th–76th	William B. Bankhead[8]	Alabama	June 4, 1936
76th–79th	Sam Rayburn	Texas	Sept. 16, 1940
80th	Joseph W. Martin, Jr.	Massachusetts	Jan. 3, 1947
81st–82nd	Sam Rayburn	Texas	Jan. 3, 1949
83rd	Joseph W. Martin, Jr.	Massachusetts	Jan. 3, 1953
84th–87th	Sam Rayburn[9]	Texas	Jan. 5, 1955
87th–91st	John W. McCormack	Massachusetts	Jan. 10, 1962
92nd–94th	Carl B. Albert	Oklahoma	Jan. 21, 1971
95th–99th	Thomas P. O'Neill, Jr.	Massachusetts	Jan. 4, 1977
100th–101st	James C. Wright, Jr.[10]	Texas	Jan. 6, 1987
101st–103rd	Thomas S. Foley	Washington	June 6, 1989
104th–105th	Newt Gingrich	Georgia	Jan. 4, 1995
106th–109th	J. Dennis Hastert	Illinois	Jan. 6, 1999

SOURCE: *Biographical Directory of the U.S. Congress*, Congressional Research Service.

1. Resigned from the House of Representatives, January 19, 1814.
2. Resigned on October 28, 1820.
3. Resigned from the House of Representatives, March 6, 1825.
4. Elected Speaker, March 3, 1869, and served one day.
5. Died in office, August 19, 1876.
6. Died in office, August 19, 1934.
7. Died in office June 4, 1936.
8. Died in office, September 15, 1940.
9. Died November 16, 1961.
10. Resigned from the House of Representatives, June 6, 1989.

Clerks of the House (1789–2005)

CONGRESS	CLERK	STATE	DATES
1st–4th	John Beckley	Virginia	1789–1797
5th	Jonathan W. Condy	Pennsylvania	1797–1799
6th	John H. Oswald	Pennsylvania	1799–1801
7th–9th	John Beckley	Virginia	1801–1807
10th–13th	Patrick Magruder	Maryland	1807–1815
13th–17th	Thomas Dougherty	Kentucky	1815–1822
17th–22nd	Matthew St. Clair Clarke	Pennsylvania	1822–1833
23rd–25th	Walter S. Franklin	Pennsylvania	1833–1838
25th–26th	Hugh A. Garland	Virginia	1837–1841
27th	Matthew St. Clair Clarke	Pennsylvania	1841–1843
28th	Caleb J. McNully	Ohio	1843–1845
28th–29th	Benjamin B. French	New Hampshire	1845–1847
30th–31st	Thomas J. Campbell	Tennessee	1847–1850
31st	Richard M. Young	Illinois	1850–1851
32nd–34th	John W. Forney	Pennsylvania	1851–1856

CONGRESS	CLERK	STATE	DATES
34th	William Cullom	Tennessee	1856–1857
35th–36th	James C. Allen	Illinois	1857–1860
36th	John W. Forney	Pennsylvania	1860–1861
37th	Emerson Etheridge	Tennessee	1861–1863
38th–43rd	Edward McPherson	Pennsylvania	1863–1875
44th–46th	George M. Adams	Kentucky	1875–1881
47th	Edward McPherson	Pennsylvania	1881–1883
48th–50th	John B. Clark, Jr.	Missouri	1883–1889
51st	Edward McPherson	Pennsylvania	1889–1891
52nd–53rd	James Kerr	Pennsylvania	1891–1895
54th–61st	Alexander McDowell	Pennsylvania	1895–1911
62nd–65th	South Trimble	Kentucky	1911–1919
66th–71st	William Tyler Page	Maryland	1919–1931
72nd–79th	South Trimble	Kentucky	1931–1947
80th	John Andrews	Massachusetts	1947–1949
81st–82nd	Ralph R. Roberts	Indiana	1949–1953
83rd	Lyle O. Snader	Illinois	1953–1955
84th–89th	Ralph R. Roberts	Indiana	1955–1967
90th–94th	W. Pat Jennings	Virginia	1967–1977
94th–97th	Edmund L. Henshaw, Jr.	Virginia	1977–1983
98th–99th	Benjamin J. Guthrie	Maryland	1983–1987
100th–103rd	Donnald K. Anderson	California	1987–1995
104th–106th	Robin H. Carle	Idaho	1995–1998
105th–109th	Jeff Trandahl	South Dakota	1998–2005
109th	Karen Haas	Maryland	2005–present

SOURCE: Office of the Clerk, U.S. House of Representatives.

Sergeants at Arms of the House (1789–2005)

CONGRESS (YEARS)	SERGEANT AT ARMS, STATE	DATE ELECTED
1st (1789–91)–9th (1805–07)	Joseph Wheaton, RI	May 12, 1789
10th (1807–09)	Thomas Dunn, MD	Oct. 27, 1807
11th (1809–11)–18th (1823–25)	Thomas Dunn, MD John O. Dunn, DC	— Dec. 6, 1824
19th (1825–27)–22nd (1831–33)	John O. Dunn, DC	—
23rd (1833–35)	Thomas B. Randolph, VA	Dec. 3, 1833
24th (1835–37)–26th (1839–41)	Roderick Dorsey, MD	Dec. 15, 1835
27th (1841–43)	Eleazor M. Townsend, CT	June 8, 1841
28th (1843–45)	Newton Lane, KY	Dec. 7, 1843
29th (1845–47)	Newton Lane, KY	—
30th (1847–49)	Nathan Sargent, VT	Dec. 8, 1847
31st (1849–51)–32nd (1851–53)	Nathan Sargent, VT Adam J. Glossbrenner, PA	— Jan. 15, 1850
36th (1859–61)	Adam J. Glossbrenner, PA Henry W. Hoffman, MD	— Feb. 3, 1860

CONGRESS (YEARS)	SERGEANT AT ARMS, STATE	DATE ELECTED
37th (1861–63)	Edward Ball, OH	Jul. 5, 1861
38th (1863–65)–43rd (1873–75)	Nathaniel G. Ordway, NH	Dec. 8, 1863
44th (1875–77)–46th (1879–81)	John G. Thompson, OH	Dec. 6, 1875
47th (1881–83)	George W. Hooker, VT	Dec. 5, 1881
48th (1883–85)–50th (1887–89)	John P. Leedom, OH	Dec. 4, 1883
51st (1889–91)	Adoniram J. Holmes, LA	Dec. 2, 1889
52nd (1891–93)	Samuel S. Yoder, OH	Dec. 8, 1891
53rd (1893–95)	Herman W. Snow, IL	Aug. 7, 1893
54th (1895–97)	Benjamin F. Russell, MO	Dec. 2, 1895
55th (1897–99)	Benjamin F. Russell, MO	—
56th (1899–1901)–61st (1909–11)	Henry Casson, WI	Dec. 4, 1899
62nd (1911–93)	Ulysses S. Jackson, IN Charles F. Riddell, IN	Apr. 4, 1911 Jul. 18, 1921
63rd (1913–95)—65th (1917–19)	Robert B. Gordon, OH	Apr. 7, 1913 Dec. 6, 1915
66th (1919–21)–71st (1929–31)	Joseph G. Rogers, PA	May 19, 1919
72nd (1931–33)–79th (1945–47)	Kenneth Romney, MT	Dec. 7, 1931 —
80th (1947–49)	William F. Russell, PA	—
81st (1949–51)–82nd (1951–53)	Joseph H. Callahan, KY	Jan. 3, 1949 Jan. 3, 1951

(continued)

CONGRESS (YEARS)	SERGEANT AT ARMS, STATE	DATE ELECTED
83rd (1953–55)–92nd (1971–73)	William F. Russell, PA[1] William R. Bonnell, PA[2] Zeake W. Johnson, Jr., TN[3]	Jan. 3, 1953 Jan. 5, 1955 Jan. 3, 1957 Jan. 7, 1959 Jan. 3, 1961 Jan. 9, 1963 Jan. 4, 1965 Jan. 10, 1967 Jan. 3, 1969 Jan. 21, 1971
	Kenneth R. Harding, VA	Oct. 1, 1972
93rd (1973–75)	Kenneth R. Harding, VA[4]	Jan. 3, 1973 Jan. 14, 1975 Jan. 4, 1977
96th (1979–81)	Benjamin J. Guthrie, MD (acting)	Jan. 15, 1979
97th (1981–83)	Benjamin J. Guthrie, MD	Jan. 5, 1981
98th (1983–85)–102nd (1991–93)	Jack Russ, MD[5]	Jan. 3, 1983 Jan. 3, 1985 Jan. 6, 1987 Jan. 3, 1989 Jan. 3, 1991
	Werner W. Brandt, VA[6]	
103rd (1993–95)	Werner W. Brandt, VA	Jan. 5, 1993
104th (1995–97)–108th (2003–05)	Wilson "Bill" Livingood, PA	Jan. 4, 1995 Jan. 7, 1997 Jan. 6, 1999 Jan. 3, 2001 Jan. 7, 2003

SOURCE: *Biographical Directory of the United States Congress, Congressional Directory*, various editions.

1. Died, July 7, 1953.
2. Appointed, September 15, 1953.
3. Resigned, September 30, 1972.
4. Resigned, February 29, 1980.
5. Resigned, 1992.
6. Appointed, March 12, 1992.

Chaplains of the House
(1789–2005)

DATE	NAME	DENOMINATION
May 1, 1789	The Reverend William Lynn	Presbyterian
Jan. 4, 1790	The Reverend Samuel Blair	Presbyterian
Nov. 5, 1792	The Reverend Ashbel Green	Presbyterian
Nov. 17, 1800	The Reverend Thomas Lyell	Methodist
Dec. 7, 1801	The Reverend William Parkinson	Baptist
Nov. 5, 1804	The Reverend James Laurie	Presbyterian
Dec. 1, 1806	The Reverend Robert Elliot	Presbyterian
Oct. 26, 1807	The Reverend Obadiah Bruen Brown	Baptist
May 22, 1809	The Reverend Jesse Lee	Methodist
Nov. 4, 1811	The Reverend Nicholas Sneathen	Methodist
Nov. 2, 1812	The Reverend Jesse Lee	Methodist
Sept. 19, 1814	The Reverend Obadiah Bruen Brown	Baptist

(continued)

DATE	NAME	DENOMINATION
Dec. 4, 1815	The Reverend Spencer Houghton Cone	Baptist
Dec. 2, 1816	The Reverend Burgess Allison	Baptist
Nov. 18, 1820	The Reverend John Nicholson Campbell	Presbyterian
Dec. 3, 1821	The Reverend Jared Sparks	Unitarian
Dec. 2, 1822	The Reverend John Brackenridge	Presbyterian
Dec. 1, 1823	The Reverend Henry Biddleman Bascom	Methodist
Dec. 6, 1824	The Reverend Reuben Post	Presbyterian
Dec. 6, 1830	The Reverend Ralph Randolph Gurley	Presbyterian
Dec. 5, 1831	The Reverend Reuben Post	Presbyterian
Dec. 3, 1832	The Reverend William Hammett	Methodist
Dec. 2, 1833	The Reverend Thomas H. Stockton	Methodist
Dec. 1, 1834	The Reverend Edward Dunlap Smith	Presbyterian
Dec. 7, 1835	The Reverend Thomas H. Stockton	Methodist
Dec. 5, 1836	The Reverend Oliver C. Comstock	Baptist
Sept. 4, 1837	The Reverend Septimus Tustin	Presbyterian
Dec. 4, 1837	The Reverend Levi R. Reese	Methodist
Dec. 2, 1839	The Reverend Joshua Bates	Congregationalist
Dec. 7, 1840	The Reverend Thomas W. Braxton	Baptist
May 31, 1841	The Reverend John W. French	Episcopalian

DATE	NAME	DENOMINATION
Dec. 6, 1841	The Reverend John Newland Maffit	Methodist
Dec. 5, 1842	The Reverend Frederick T. Tiffany	Episcopalian
Dec. 4, 1843	The Reverend Isaac S. Tinsley	Baptist
Dec. 4, 1844	The Reverend William M. Daily	Methodist
Dec. 1, 1845	The Reverend William Henry Milburn	Methodist
Dec. 7, 1846	The Reverend William T.S. Sprole	Presbyterian
Dec. 6, 1847	The Reverend Ralph Gurley	Presbyterian
Dec. 1, 1851	The Reverend Littleton F. Morgan	Methodist
Dec. 6, 1852	The Reverend James Gallagher	Presbyterian
Dec. 5, 1853	The Reverend William Henry Milburn	Methodist
Jul. 4, 1861	The Reverend Thomas H. Stockton	Methodist*
Dec. 7, 1863	The Reverend William Henry Channing	Unitarian
Dec. 4, 1865	The Reverend Charles B. Boynton	Congregationalist
Mar. 4, 1869	The Reverend John George Butler	Presbyterian
Dec. 6, 1875	The Reverend S.L. Townsend	Episcopalian
Oct. 15, 1877	The Reverend John Poise	Methodist
Dec. 3, 1877	The Reverend W.P. Harrison	Methodist
Dec. 5, 1881	The Reverend Frederick Dunglison Power	Disciples of Christ

(continued)

DATE	NAME	DENOMINATION
Dec. 3, 1883	The Reverend John Summerfield Lindsay	Episcopalian
Dec. 7, 1885	The Reverend William Henry Milburn	Methodist
Aug. 7, 1893	The Reverend Samuel W. Haddaway	Methodist
Dec. 4, 1893	The Reverend Edward B. Bagby	Christian
Dec. 2, 1895	The Reverend Henry N. Couden	Universalist
Apr. 11, 1921	The Reverend James Shera Montgomery	Methodist
Jan. 3, 1950	The Reverend Bernard Braskamp	Presbyterian
Jan. 10, 1967	The Reverend Edward G. Latch	Methodist
Jan. 15, 1979	The Reverend James D. Ford	Lutheran
Mar. 23, 2000	The Reverend Daniel P. Coughlin	Roman Catholic

SOURCE: *Biographical Directory of the U.S. Congress; Congressional Directory,* various editions.

*From 1855 to 1861 the local clergy in the District of Columbia conducted the opening prayer. Thereafter, the House has elected a chaplain at the beginning of each Congress.

Doorkeepers of the House (1789–1995)

CONGRESS (YEARS)	DOORKEEPERS, STATE	DATE ELECTED
1st (1789–91)–3rd (1793–95)	Gifford Dalley	—
4th (1793–97)–16th (1819–21)	Thomas Claxton	—
17th (1821–23)–21st (1829–31)	Benjamin Birch, MD	—
22nd (1831–33)–25th (1837–39)	Overton Carr, MD	—
26th (1839–41)—27th (1841–43)	Joseph Follansbee, MA	—
28th (1843–45)	Jesse E. Dow, CT	—
29th (1845–47)	Cornelius S. Whitney, DC	—
30th (1847–49)	Robert E. Horner, NJ	—
31st (1849–51)	Robert E. Horner, NJ	—
32nd (1851–53)–33rd (1853–55)	Z.W. McKnew, MD	—
34th (1855–57)	Nathan Darling, NY	—
35th (1857–59)	Robert B. Hackney, VA	—
36th (1859–61)	George Marston, NH	—

(continued)

CONGRESS (YEARS)	DOORKEEPERS, STATE	DATE ELECTED
37th (1861–63)	Ira Goodnow, VT	—
38th (1863–65)	Ira Goodnow, VT	—
39th (1865–67)	Ira Goodnow, VT	—
40th (1867–69)	Charles E. Lippincott, IL	—
41st (1869–71)–43rd (1873–75)	Otis S. Buxton, NY	—
44th (1875–77)	John H. Patterson, NJ	—
45th (1877–79)	Charles W. Field, GA	—
46th (1879–81)	Charles W. Field, GA	—
47th (1881–83)	Walter P. Brownlow, TN	—
48th (1883–85)	James W. Wintersmith, TX	—
49th (1885–87)	Samuel Donaldson, TN	—
50th (1887–89)	A.B. Hurd, MS	—
51st (1889–91)	Charles E. Adams, MD	—
52nd (1891–93)	Charles H. Turner, NY	—
53rd (1893–95)	A.B. Hurd, MS	—
54th (1895–97)–56th (1899–1901)	William J. Glenn, NY	—
57th (1901–03)–61st (1909–11)	Frank B. Lyon, NY	—
62nd (1911–93)–65th (1917–19)	Joseph J. Sinnott, VA	—
66th (1919–21)–71st (1929–31)	Bert W. Kennedy, MI	—
72nd (1931–33)–78th (1943–45)	Joseph J. Sinnott, VA	—
79th (1945–47)	Ralph R. Roberts, IN	—
80th (1947–49)	M.L. Meletio, MO	—
81st (1949–51)–82nd (1951–53)	William M. Miller, MS	Jan. 3, 1949 Jan. 3, 1951
83rd (1953–55)	Tom Kennamer, MO	Jan. 3, 1953

CONGRESS (YEARS)	DOORKEEPERS, STATE	DATE ELECTED
84th (1955–57)–93rd (1973–75)	William M. Miller, MS*	Jan. 5, 1955
		Jan. 3, 1957
		Jan. 7, 1959
		Jan. 3, 1961
		Jan. 9, 1963
		Jan. 4. 1965
		Jan. 10, 1967
		Jan. 3, 1969
		Jan. 21, 1971
	James T. Malloy, NY (acting)	Jan. 3, 1973
94th (1975–77)–103rd (1993–95)	James T. Malloy, NY	Jan. 14, 1975
		Jan. 4, 1977
		Jan. 15, 1979
		Jan. 5, 1981
		Jan. 3, 1983
		Jan. 3, 1985
		Jan. 6, 1987
		Jan. 3, 1989
		Jan. 3, 1991
		Jan. 5, 1993

SOURCE: *Biographical Directory of the United States Congress, Congressional Directory,* various editions.

*Resigned, December 31, 1974.

Chief Administrative Officers of the House (1995–2005)

CONGRESS (YEARS)	DIRECTOR OF NONLEGISLATIVE AND FINANCIAL SERVICES, STATE	DATE APPOINTED
102nd (1991–93)– 103rd (1993–95)	Leonard P. Wishart, III, NJ	Dec. 28, 1992
104th (1995–97)	Scott M. Faulkner, WV*	Jan. 4, 1995
	Jeff Trandahl, SD (acting)	Nov. 23, 1996
105th (1997–99)	Jeff Trandahl, SD (acting)	
	James M. Eagen, III, PA	Aug. 1, 1997
106th (1999–2001)– 108th (2003–05)	James M. Eagen, III, PA	Jan. 6, 1999 Jan. 3, 2001 Jan. 7, 2003

SOURCE: *Congressional Directory*, various editions; H. Rept. No. 97-HOC-12 (September 24, 1997).

*Resigned, November 22, 1996.

APPENDIX

7

Parliamentarians of the House

PARLIAMENTARIANS		
70th (1928)	Lewis Deschler	1928
71st (1929–31)–92nd (1971–73)	Lewis Deschler	
93rd (1973–75)	Lewis Deschler William Holmes Brown	1974
94th (1975–77)–102nd (1991–93)	William Holmes Brown	
103rd (1993–95)	William Holmes Brown Charles W. Johnson	1994
104th (1995–97)–107th (2001–03)	Charles W. Johnson	
108th (2003–05)	Charles W. Johnson John V. Sullivan	May 31, 2004*

SOURCE: Raymond W. Smock, "House Parliamentarian," in Donald C. Bacon, Roger H. Davidson, and Morton Keller eds., *The Encyclopedia of the United States Congress* (New York, 1995), 1522–1523; *Congressional Record*, various editions.

Congressional Record (May 20, 2004), H3394.

8

Majority and Minority Leaders (1899–2006)

CONGRESS	MAJORITY LEADER	MINORITY LEADER	YEARS
56th	Sereno E. Payne (R-NY)	James D. Richardson (D-TN)	(1899–1901)
57th	Sereno E. Payne (R-NY)	James D. Richardson (D-TN)	(1901–1903)
58th	Sereno E. Payne (R-NY)	John Sharp Williams (D-MS)	(1903–1905)
59th	Sereno E. Payne (R-NY)	John Sharp Williams (D-MS)	(1905–1907)
60th	Sereno E. Payne (R-NY)	John Sharp Williams (D-MS)	(1907–1908)
60th	Sereno E. Payne (R-NY)	James Beauchamp Clark (D-MO)	(1907–1909)
61st	Sereno E. Payne (R-NY)	James Beauchamp Clark (D-MO)	(1909–1911)
62nd	Oscar W. Underwood (D-AL)	James R. Mann (R-IL)	(1911–1913)
63rd	Oscar W. Underwood (D-AL)	James R. Mann (R-IL)	(1913–1915)

CONGRESS	MAJORITY LEADER	MINORITY LEADER	YEARS
64th	Claude Kitchin (D-NC)	James R. Mann (R-IL)	(1915–1917)
65th	Claude Kitchin (D-NC)	James R. Mann (R-IL)	(1917–1919)
66th	Frank W. Mondell (R-WY)	James Beauchamp Clark (D-MO)	(1919–1921)
67th	Frank W. Mondell (R-WY)	Claude Kitchin (D-NC)	(1921–1923)
68th	Nicholas Longworth (R-OH)	Finis J. Garrett (D-TN)	(1923–1925)
69th	John Q. Tilson (R-CT)	Finis J. Garrett (D-TN)	(1925–1927)
70th	John Q. Tilson (R-CT)	Finis J. Garrett (D-TN)	(1927–1929)
71st	John Q. Tilson (R-CT)	John N. Garner (D-TX)	(1929–1931)
72nd	Henry T. Rainey (D-IL)	Bertrand H. Snell (R-NY)	(1931–1933)
73rd	Joseph W. Byrns (D-TN)	Bertrand H. Snell (R-NY)	(1933–1935)
74th	William B. Bankhead (D-AL)	Bertrand H. Snell (R-NY)	(1935–1937)
75th	Sam Rayburn (D-TX)	Bertrand H. Snell (R-NY)	(1937–1939)
76th	Sam Rayburn (D-TX)	Joseph W. Martin, Jr. (R-MA)	(1939–1940)
76th	John W. McCormack (D-MA)	Joseph W. Martin, Jr. (R-MA)	(1940–1941)
77th	John W. McCormack (D-MA)	Joseph W. Martin, Jr. (R-MA)	(1941–1942)
78th	John W. McCormack (D-MA)	Joseph W. Martin, Jr. (R-MA)	(1943–1945)

(continued)

CONGRESS	MAJORITY LEADER	MINORITY LEADER	YEARS
79th	John W. McCormack (D-MA)	Joseph W. Martin, Jr. (R-MA)	(1945–1947)
80th	Charles A. Halleck (R-IN)	Sam Rayburn (D-TX)	(1947–1949)
81st	John W. McCormack (D-MA)	Joseph W. Martin, Jr. (R-MA)	(1949–1951)
82nd	John W. McCormack (D-MA)	Joseph W. Martin, Jr. (R-MA)	(1951–1953)
83rd	Charles A. Halleck (R-IN)	Sam Rayburn (D-TX)	(1953–1955)
84th	John W. McCormack (D-MA)	Joseph W. Martin, Jr. (R-MA)	(1955–1957)
85th	John W. McCormack (D-MA)	Joseph W. Martin, Jr. (R-MA)	(1957–1959)
86th	John W. McCormack (D-MA)	Charles A. Halleck (R-IN)	(1959–1961)
87th	John W. McCormack (D-MA)	Charles A. Halleck (R-IN)	(1961–1962)
87th	Carl B. Albert (D-OK)	Charles A. Halleck (R-IN)	(1962–1963)
88th	Carl B. Albert (D-OK)	Charles A. Halleck (R-IN)	(1963–1965)
89th	Carl B. Albert (D-OK)	Gerald R. Ford (R-MI)	(1965–1967)
90th	Carl B. Albert (D-OK)	Gerald R. Ford (R-MI)	(1967–1969)
91st	Carl B. Albert (D-OK)	Gerald R. Ford (R-MI)	(1969–1971)
92nd	Hale Boggs (D-LA)	Gerald R. Ford (R-MI)	(1971–1973)
93rd	Thomas P. O'Neill, Jr. (D-MA)	Gerald R. Ford (R-MI)	(1973)

CONGRESS	MAJORITY LEADER	MINORITY LEADER	YEARS
93rd	Thomas P. O'Neill, Jr. (D-MA)	John J. Rhodes (R-AZ)	(1974–1975)
94th	Thomas P. O'Neill, Jr. (D-MA)	John J. Rhodes (R-AZ)	(1975–1977)
95th	James C. Wright, Jr. (D-TX)	John J. Rhodes (R-AZ)	(1977–1979)
96th	James C. Wright, Jr. (D-TX)	John J. Rhodes (R-AZ)	(1979–1981)
97th	James C. Wright, Jr. (D-TX)	Robert H. Michel (R-IL)	(1981–1983)
98th	James C. Wright, Jr. (D-TX)	Robert H. Michel (R-IL)	(1983–1984)
99th	James C. Wright, Jr. (D-TX)	Robert H. Michel (R-IL)	(1985–1986)
100th	Thomas S. Foley (D-WA)	Robert H. Michel (R-IL)	(1987–1988)
101st	Richard A. Gephardt (D-MO)	Robert H. Michel (R-IL)	(1989–1990)
102nd	Richard A. Gephardt (D-MO)	Robert H. Michel (R-IL)	(1991–1992)
103rd	Richard A. Gephardt (D-MO)	Robert H. Michel (R-IL)	(1993–1994)
104th	Richard K. Armey (R-TX)	Richard A. Gephardt (D-MO)	(1995–1996)
105th	Richard K. Armey (R-TX)	Richard A. Gephardt (D-MO)	(1997–1998)
106th	Richard K. Armey (R-TX)	Richard A. Gephardt (D-MO)	(1999–2000)
107th	Richard K. Armey (R-TX)	Richard A. Gephardt (D-MO)	(2001–2002)
108th	Tom DeLay (R-TX)	Nancy Pelosi (D-CA)	(2003–2005)
109th	Tom DeLay (R-TX) Roy Blunt (R-MO), temporary John Boehner (R-OH)	Nancy Pelosi (D-CA)	(2005–Present)

Democratic Whips (1899–2005)

CONGRESS	NAME	STATE	DATE
56th	Oscar W. Underwood	Alabama	1899–1901
57th	James T. Lloyd	Missouri	1901–1903
58th	James T. Lloyd	Missouri	1903–1905
59th	James T. Lloyd	Missouri	1905–1907
60th	James T. Lloyd	Missouri	1907–1909
61st	N/A		1909–1911
62nd	N/A		1911–1913
63rd	Thomas M. Bell	Georgia	1913–1915
64th	N/A		1915–1917
65th	N/A		1917–1919
66th	N/A		1919–1921
67th	William A. Oldfield	Arkansas	1921–1923
68th	William A. Oldfield	Arkansas	1923–1925
69th	William A. Oldfield	Arkansas	1925–1927
70th	William A. Oldfield	Arkansas	1927–1929*
70th	John McDuffie	Alabama	1927–1929
71st	John McDuffie	Alabama	1929–2931
72nd	John McDuffie	Alabama	1931–1933

CONGRESS	NAME	STATE	DATE
73th	Arthur H. Greenwood	Indiana	1933–1935
74th	Patrick J. Boland	Pennsylvania	1935–1937
75th	Patrick J. Boland	Pennsylvania	1937–1939
76th	Patrick J. Boland	Pennsylvania	1939–1941
77th	Patrick J. Boland	Pennsylvania	1941–1943
77th	Robert Ramspeck	Georgia	1941–1943
78th	Robert Ramspeck	Georgia	1943–1945
79th	Robert Ramspeck	Georgia	1945–1947
79th	John J. Sparkman	Alabama	1945–1947
80th	John W. McCormack	Massachusetts	1947–1949
81st	J. Percy Priest	Tennessee	1949–1951
82nd	J. Percy Priest	Tennessee	1951–1953
83rd	John W. McCormack	Massachusetts	1953–1955
84th	Carl Albert	Oklahoma	1955–1957
85th	Carl Albert	Oklahoma	1957–1959
86th	Carl Albert	Oklahoma	1959–1961
87th	Carl Albert	Oklahoma	1961–1963[†]
87th	Thomas Hale Boggs	Louisiana	1961–1963
88th	Thomas Hale Boggs	Louisiana	1963–1965
89th	Thomas Hale Boggs	Louisiana	1965–1967
90th	Thomas Hale Boggs	Louisiana	1967–1969
91st	Thomas Hale Boggs	Louisiana	1969–1971
92nd	Thomas P. O'Neill, Jr.	Massachusetts	1971–1973
93rd	John J. McFall	California	1973–1975

(continued)

CONGRESS	NAME	STATE	DATE
94th	John J. McFall	California	1975–1977
95th	John W. Brademas	Indiana	1977–1979
96th	John W. Brademas	Indiana	1979–1981
97th	Thomas S. Foley	Washington	1981–1983
98th	Thomas S. Foley	Washington	1983–1985
99th	Thomas S. Foley	Washington	1985–1987
100th	Tony Coelho	California	1987–1989
101st	Tony Coelho	California	1989
101st	William (Bill) H. Gray, III	Pennsylvania	1989–1991
102nd	William (Bill) H. Gray, III	Pennsylvania	1991–1993
102nd	David E. Bonior	Michigan	1991–1993
103rd	David E. Bonior	Michigan	1993–1995
104th	David E. Bonior	Michigan	1995–1997
105th	David E. Bonior	Michigan	1997–1999
106th	David E. Bonior	Michigan	1999–2001
107th	David E. Bonior	Michigan	2001–2003
107th	Nancy Pelosi	California	2001–2003
108th–present	Steny Hoyer	Maryland	2003–present

SOURCE: *Biographical Directory of the U.S. Congress*, Congressional Research
Service.

*Resigned.
†Elected as Speaker in 1971.

Republican Whips (1897–2005)

CONGRESS	NAME	STATE	DATE
55th–58th	James A. Tawney	Minnesota	1897–1905
59th–60th	James E. Watson	Indiana	1905–1909
61st–62nd	John W. Dwight	New York	1909–1913
63rd	Charles H. Burke	South Dakota	1913–1915
64th–65th	Charles M. Hamilton	New York	1915–1919
66th–67th	Harold Knutson	Minnesota	1919–1923
68th–71st	Albert H. Vestal	Indiana	1923–1931
72nd	Carl G. Bachmann	West Virginia	1931–1933
73rd–78th	Harry L. Englebright	California	1933–1943*
78th–93rd	Leslie C. Arends	Illinois	1943–1975
94th–96th	Robert H. Michel	Illinois	1975–1981
97th–100th	Trent Lott	Mississippi	1981–1989
101st	Dick Cheney	Wyoming	1989†
101st–103rd	Newt Gingrich	Georgia	1989–1995
104th–107th	Tom DeLay	Texas	1995–2003
108th–present	Roy Blunt	Missouri	2003–present

SOURCE: *Biographical Directory of the U.S. Congress,* Congressional Research Service.

*Died in office, May 13, 1943.
†Resigned, March 17, 1989, to become secretary of defense.

Organizing the House

TODAY WHEN A new Congress convenes, the members organize themselves according to the following procedure.

After it is established that a quorum is present via an electronic count, the clerk of the previous Congress calls for nominations for the office of Speaker. Both majority and minority parties put forward their candidates, usually by the chair of their respective Republican Conference and Democratic Caucus. The clerk then selects tellers and a roll call ensues with each member rising from his or her chair and casting his or her vote by calling out the name of their choice. The nominees themselves usually vote "present." A vote for themselves is regarded as a departure from tradition.

When the balloting concludes, the clerk announces the results of the vote and names the person elected. Then the clerk appoints a committee to escort the Speaker-elect to the chair. This committee usually consists of party leaders from both parties and members of the Speaker's state delegation. The committee and the Speaker-elect leave the chamber, line up outside and then march back into the chamber, walking down the center aisle to the rostrum as the other members rise and applaud their new Speaker.

The defeated candidate introduces the Speaker-elect to the House. The Speaker-elect then addresses the House from the chair. This is ordinarily the only time the Speaker addresses the House from the chair. If he wishes to participate in a debate on any issue during the session he normally surrenders the chair to someone else, steps down and speaks from the well of the House, just like any other member.

Next, the Speaker-elect announces that he is ready to take the oath of office and invariably designates the dean of the House to administer the oath. The dean is the person who has served the longest as a representative. This designation is considered an honor, but the Speaker-elect may choose someone else, if he so wishes.

After taking the oath himself, the Speaker asks all the other members to rise to take the oath of office, which he administers en banc (altogether).

Now the House is officially ready to conduct business, and the first order of the day is the introduction of Resolution Number 1 to choose the clerk, sergeant at arms, chaplain and chief administrative officer (CAO).* Resolution Number 1 is offered by the majority leader

The names of the individual designees for these four positions are read. They line up in the well and the Speaker administers the oath of office. With that task concluded, the House has completed its organization.

---

*The CAO position was established in 1994. The business of the clerk had become so enormous that such duties as finance, maintenance, supplies, and so on were switched to the newly created office of the CAO.

12

Counting the Electoral Votes for President and Vice President

T HE PROCESS BEGINS with the Speaker calling the House to order. The Vice President and members of the Senate arrive at the lobby of the House. A staff member from the back of the House calls out, "Mr. Speaker, the Vice President and senators of the United States." Members of the House rise as the Vice President and senators walk down the center aisle. The senators sit with the representatives and the Vice President joins the Speaker on the rostrum.

The Vice President is the president pro tempore of the Senate and is referred to as "Mr. President." He then calls the tellers from the House and Senate to come to the rostrum and read the results of the election contained in the certificates submitted by each state. The tellers are not staff. They are members of the chamber they represent. In the 2004 presidential election there were two members from each house reading the certificates in rotation.

The parliamentarian hands each certificate in alphabetical order to the President, who hands it to a teller. The teller takes the certificate and, before a microphone, reads, "Mr. President, the certificate of the electoral votes from the state of Alabama seems to be regular, in form and authentic and it appears therefrom that ___ of the state of ___ received X number of votes for President, and ___ of the state of ___ received X number of votes for Vice President." This procedure is followed for each of the states read alphabetically.

In the 2004 election, when the tellers got to the state of Ohio, about a dozen members of the House—all of them Democrats—rose and objected to the counting of Ohio's vote. "For what purpose do you rise?" the president pro tem asked. "For the purpose of objecting to the counting of the vote of Ohio as read." The president pro tem asked if the objection was reduced to writing and if any senator also objected, since at least one member from each house must challenge the vote. The objection had been written and one senator did rise, whereupon the president pro tem ended the joint session and ordered the senators to return to their own chamber to determine the position of the Senate on the objection. Each house had to decide for itself whether to count Ohio's votes.

In the House the Speaker called the members to order and directed that the debate would last two hours, with each member speaking no longer than five minutes. The time was divided equally between the two parties. At the conclusion of the debate there was a call for the ayes and nays on the question of accepting the objection to counting Ohio's vote as presented in its certificate. A roll call vote was then demanded by electronic voting, and the result was 267 no votes and 31 yes votes.

The Vice President and Senators returned; the Senate also rejected the objection, and the counting of the electoral votes continued.

At the end of the procedure the Vice President announces the results of the counting of electoral votes.

Organization and Operation of the Whip

TODAY THE REPUBLICAN whip[1] has 16 deputy whips and 60 regional whips. There is a whip for every three or four members. The whip selects the deputy and regional whips. Among Democrats, the organization of the office was reformed in 2003, and the whip now has a senior chief deputy whip, 6 chief deputy whips, 30 senior whips, 40 assistant whips and 24 regional whips.

"On bills that we think are competitive," explained Roy Blunt, the Republican majority whip for the 108th and 109th Congresses, within ten or fifteen minutes on the floor "you can get your initial whip count." For example, one of the whips will approach a member of his party and ask, "On the energy bill tomorrow [which the leadership supports], are you a yes, a no, a lean yes, a lean no, undecided?" If the member says "anything but yes," then the whip will respond, "Well, what do you need to know? What is wrong with the bill? Do you need more information?" Or the whip may say, "Why are you undecided?" or "Why are you leaning against it?" At that point "I get together with the chief deputy whip and our deputy whips and say, "Okay, how do we clean this list up? How do we go back to everybody who's not a yes and be sure that they're moving to the yes category?" There are some members "I can get that the Speaker can't get; the Speaker can get members I can't get. We usually don't involve the Speaker unless it" becomes a necessity.

The value and importance of the whip was commented on by Robert Novak of the *Chicago Sun-Times* on November 27, 2003. The bill providing prescription drug benefits under Medicare, he wrote, would have been easily defeated by Republicans, save for the "most efficient party whip operation in congressional history."

Speaker Hastert has said, "I've never made it a practice to try to buy somebody with a project," such as "roads and bridges and schools." Members "ought to vote for something because of the policy. And to buy people off just doesn't work." The Speaker talks to individual members usually in his office. On the Medicare bill, for example, Speaker Hastert talked with one conservative "four different times that afternoon, and three times on the floor that evening. I still didn't get his vote, but you know, I felt it was my job to go after him as many times as I could to make sure I got my point across." Because of his persistence with various other members, "I picked up probably 25 to 30 votes three days before [the final vote], and also I picked up probably a half a dozen votes on the floor. People said, 'I won't vote until the end to see how things go.' And then, at the end, we had to unlock a couple of votes" by reminding them that "for the future of this country this is the right thing to do."

14

Routing Legislation Through Congress

IN SENDING LEGISLATION passed by the House to the Senate, the bill is first engrossed—that is, typed in the office of the enrolling clerk and printed in the Government Printing Office. After that the printed copy is signed by the clerk of the House and walked by one of the "reading clerks" to the Senate chamber. When that clerk arrives at the other end of the Capitol he waits at the rear of the chamber until one of the Senate clerks on the dais notices him. The Senate clerk then walks up the center aisle and stands alongside him. Not until the presiding officer of the Senate nods approval does the clerk announce, "Mr. President, a message from the House." The House clerk then steps forward, bows to the presiding officer and says, "Mr. President, I am directed by the House to deliver to the Senate [at this point he would cite the bill number and its basic contents] in which the concurrence of the Senate is requested." Then, handing the bill to the Senate clerk, he bows again and exits the chamber. The Senate clerk then brings the document to the dais, and the presiding officer asks unanimous Senate consent to have the bill both read and referred to the appropriate committee for action.

Once the bill has been passed by the Senate a message to that effect is sent to the House. The bill is then enrolled and put on parchment. The clerk and Speaker sign it, and it is delivered back to the Senate for the signature of the president pro tem. Once signed, it is sent to the President in the White House.

Electronic Voting

THE VOTING IN the House of Representatives by electronic means was established by the Legislative Reorganization Act of 1970 and implemented in 1973. Members now vote electronically by going to one of the 44 voting stations attached to various chairs scattered about the chamber, inserting his or her encrypted vote-ID card into the slot of the machine and choosing one of three options: "yea," "nay," or "present." The machine records the vote and displays it and the votes of all the other members on a large viewing board on the wall behind the press gallery and above the Speaker's rostrum. Each member's name is illuminated with one of three colors: red if the vote is nay, green if it is yea, and yellow if it is present/absent.

If a member wishes to change his or her vote during the last five minutes of the vote, he or she hands a paper ballot to the tally clerk, who then changes the vote electronically. The paper ballot is green for yea, red for nay and amber for present.

On the two side walls of the chamber are score screens showing the resolution or bill number, how much time is left for the voting, and the number of yeas, nays and present that have been cast as the voting progresses.

SOURCE: *Washington Post,* Janurary 24, 1973.

Committees of the House and Joint Committees of the 109th Congress

COMMITTEES OF THE HOUSE

Agriculture, Appropriations, Armed Services, Budget, Energy and Commerce, Financial Services, Government Reform, Homeland Security, House Administration, International Relations, Judiciary, Resources, Rules, Science, Small Business, Standards of Official Conduct, Transportation and Intrastructure, Veterans Affairs, Ways and Means and Permanent Select Committee on Intelligence

JOINT COMMITTEES WITH THE SENATE

Joint Economic Committee, Joint Committee on the Library of Congress, Joint Committee on Printing and Joint Committee on Taxation

Pages

P AGES SERVE AS support staff for the members of the House of Representatives, principally as messengers. They are students in their junior year of high school who are at least sixteen years of age. To qualify for an appointment, they must have a grade point average of no less than 3.0 from an accredited school and must be sponsored by a member of Congress. In 1982, a Page Board was created to ensure that the Page Program is "conducted in a manner that is consistent with the efficient functioning of the House and welfare of the Pages." The Page Program includes the House Page Residence Hall and the House Page School. It is administered by the Office of the Clerk. Pages attend a separate school in the Library of Congress, which offers a typical junior-year course of study. The pages are required to purchase uniform clothing, gray slacks or skirts, navy jacket, white shirt. A uniform tie is provided by the Office of the Clerk. Senate pages wear navy slacks or skirts.

Today pages are appointed by the offices of the Speaker and minority leader. At first they were selected exclusively by the majority leadership, including those who worked in the minority cloakroom. The Speaker set up a Personnel Committee to decide which representatives might name pages. Democrats tended to ask senior members to perform the task, while Republicans rotated the appointments among all their members so that eventually everyone had a chance to choose a page if he or she so desired.

Speakers Sam Rayburn and Joseph Martin altered the system somewhat by permitting the minority leadership to pick 4 pages to answer

The page school in the early twentieth century.

phones in the minority cloakroom. That number was increased to 5 in 1967 and has slowly climbed until today it stands at 24. In 2005 some 72 pages have been authorized during the winter and spring congressional sessions, and 78 during the summer. At present there are 31 girls and 36 boys for a total of 67, a number less than the full complement. The first African-American page, Frank Mitchell, was appointed by Representative Paul Findley of Illinois on April 14, 1965. Speaker Carl Albert appointed Felda Looper, the first female House page, on May 14, 1973, although Gene Cox, daughter of Representative Eugene Cox, served as a page for three hours on the opening day of the 79th Congress on January 3, 1939, and was paid $4 for her work.

Pages today receive a yearly salary of $17,540, with a monthly gross salary of $1,462, and pay the government $400 a month for room and meals.

SOURCE: Jim Oliver, assistant manager, Republican cloak room, to author, December 6, 2004, January 24, February 28, 2005; Jeff Trandahl, Clerk of the House, to author, December 7, 2004; Wren Ivester, assistant manager, Democratic cloak room, to author, March 9, 2005.

Credits: Photographs and Illustrations

The illustrations appearing in this book are courtesy of:

p. 11—Library of Congress (LOC), Prints and Photographs Division (PPD): LC-USZ62-1686; p. 13—LOC PPD: LC-USZ6-832; p. 14—LOC PPD: LC-USZ62-83085; p. 15—LOC PPD: LC-USZ62-4795; p. 21—LOC PPD: LC-USZ62-9580; p. 31—LOC PPD: LC-USZ62-13004, LC-USZ62-3462; p. 42—U.S. Senate Historical Office; p. 49—LOC Reproduction Number: HABS, PA51-Phila, 6A-5; p. 51—LOC PPD: LC-USZ62-4793; p. 61—LOC PPD: LC-USZ62-4416; p. 63—LOC PPD: LC-USZ62-1551, LC-USZ62-9242; p. 67—LOC, Geography and Maps Division (GMD): G3850 1792.E41 Vault, Digital ID g3850 ct000299; p. 74—Architect of the Capitol (AOC) Photographic Records Image (PRI): 60636; p. 82—LOC PPD: LC-USZ62-33234; p. 87—LOC PPD: LC-DIG-ppmsca-0078, LC-USZC4-247; p. 91—LOC PPD: LC-USZ62-5083; p. 95—LOC PPD: LC-USZ62-28108; p. 97—LOC PPD: LC-USZ62-5314; p. 99—AOC PRI: 70000; p. 108—AOC PRI: 113330E; p. 125—LOC PPD: LC-USZ62-2342; p. 130—LOC PPD: LC-DIG-cwpbh-06504; p. 134—LOC PPD: LC-DIG-cwpbh-02619; p. 145—LOC PPD: LC-DIG-cwpbh-00511; p. 153—LOC PPD: LC-USZ62-38851; p. 157—AOC PRI: 5066; p. 160—LOC PPD: LC-USZ62-54709; p. 163—LOC PPD: LC-USZ62-20023; p. 169—LOC PPD: LC-USZ62-33710; p. 171—LOC PPD: LC-DIG-cwpbh-01194; p. 172—LOC PPD: LC-USZC4-7987; p. 179—AOC PRI: 70619; p. 182—LOC PPD: LC-DIG-cwpbh-01935; p. 185—LOC PPD: LC-DIG-cwpbh-01037; p. 187—LOC PPD: LC-USZ62-38215; p. 202—U.S. National Archives (USNA): III-B-4279; p. 205—USNA Center for Legislative Archives: SEN 40C-A2, RG 46, Records of the United States Senate; p. 208—LOC PPD: LC-DIG-cwpbh-00664; p. 209—LOC PPD: LC-USZ62-2814; p. 211—LOC PPD: LC-DIG-cwpbh-03911; p. 230—LOC PPD: LC-DIG-cwpbh-04482; p. 235—LOC PPD: LC-DIG-cwpbh-04036; p. 237—LOC PPD: LC-USZ62-66358; p. 239—Poore, Benjamin Perley. *Perley's Reminis-*

cences. Volume II. Philadelphia, Hubbard Brothers Publishers Inc., 1886. pg. 514; p. 247—LOC PPD: LC-USZ62-89505; p. 249—LOC PPD: LC-USZC4-2708, LC-USZ62-108128; p. 260—LOC PPD: LC-USZ62-1819; p. 261—LOC PPD: LC-H814-T01-L03-009; p. 268—LOC PPD: LC-USZ62-132233; p. 273—LOC PPD: LC-DIG-ggbain-02778; p. 274—LOC PPD: LC-DIG-ggbain-05519; p. 277—LOC PPD: LC-USZ62-94179; p. 286—LOC PPD: LC-USZ62-67319; p. 291—LOC PPD: LC-USZ62-68318; p. 292—LOC PPD: LC-USZ62-52250; p. 302—LOC PPD: LC-USZ62-110525; p. 305—LOC PPD: LC-USZ62-26186; p. 308—U.S. Senate Historical Office: "Bonus Marchers in Front of the Capitol, 1932"; p. 310—LOC PPD: LC-USZ62-85214; p. 314—LOC PPD: LC-USZ62-87966; p. 323—LOC PPD: LC-USZ62-109680; p. 331—Corbis: U630113ACME; p. 342—LOC PPD: LC-USZ62-126515; p. 347—LOC PPD: LC-USZ62-127913; p. 349—LOC PPD: LC-USZ62-17268; p. 364—LOC PPD: LC-USZ62-114945; p. 367—Office of Photography, U.S. House of Representatives, Rules Committee; p. 370—LOC PPD: LC-USZ62-107877;p.372—LOC PPD:LC-USZ62-92317;p.376—LOC PPD:LC-USZ62-90127; p. 377—LOC PPD: LC-USZ62-122149; p. 399—LOC PPD: LC-U9-10364-37; p. 404—LOC PPD: LC-USZ62-107876; p. 409—Office of Representative John Conyers: "Congressional Black Caucus, May 1971"; p. 413—Corbis: U1651309-13; p. 418—LOC PPD: LC-U9-25383-33; p. 422—USNA: "LBJ Library Photo" Serial number 9346-23A; p. 427—LOC PPD: LC-USZ62-100089; p. 431—LOC PPD: LC-U9-23069-20; p. 439—Office of Photography, U.S. House of Representatives; p. 440—USNA: E 3356-07A (Nixon: Last Day Collection); p. 443—LOC PPD: LC-USZ62-99537; p. 445—R. Michael Jenkins, Congressional Quarterly, Inc.; p. 450—Carl Albert Center Congressional Archives, University of Oklahoma: AlMcOn; p. 459—Ronald Reagan Presidential Library: C12755-22A; p. 466—Corbis: U2048059; p. 473—LOC PPD: LC-USZ62-122171; p. 476—Office of Photography, U.S. House of Representatives: Thomas F. Foley; p. 484—Associated Press; p. 487—*New York Daily News* front page 11/16/1995: 5G900K9W; p. 492—Office of the House Committee on the Judiciary; p. 542—LOC PPD: LC-USZ61-1898; Insert p. 1—LOC PPD: LC-USZ62-2566; Insert p. 2—LOC PPD: LC-USZ62-2770; Insert p. 3—LOC PPD: LC-USZC4-530, LC-USZ62-4702; Insert p. 4—Samuel F. B. Morse, *The House of Representatives,* 1822, Oil on canvas, 86-7/8 × 130-5/8 in (220.7 x 331.8 cm), Corcoran Gallery of Art, Washington, D.C., Museum Purchase, Gallery Fund, 11.14; Insert p. 5—LOC PPD: LC-USZ62-110213; Insert p. 6—U.S. Senate Collection Number: 33.0006; Insert p. 7—U.S. Capitol Historical Society: *100th Congress*; Insert p. 8—AOC

Notes

PROLOGUE

1. Henry Steele Commager, ed., *Documents of American History* (New York, 1963), 1, 15–16.
2. Quoted in Francis J. Bremer, *John Winthrop: America's Forgotten Founding Father* (New York, 2003), 179.
3. Commager, *Documents of American History*, 1, 100.
4. Ibid., 111.
5. Ibid., 133.
6. Most colonial legislatures also met in secret.
7. Adrianne Koch, ed., *Notes of Debates in the First Federal Convention of 1787* (Athens, Ohio, 1966), 39.
8. Commager, *Documents of American History*, 1, 139.
9. Only George Mason and Edmund Randolph of Virginia and Elbridge Gerry of Massachusetts did not add their signatures.
10. North Carolina delayed its approval and Rhode Island did not attend the convention.
11. March 4 remained the date for the start of each new administration until the passage of the 20th Amendment on February 6, 1933, when it was changed to January 20.

CHAPTER I. INAUGURATING A NEW GOVERNMENT, MARCH–APRIL 1789

1. Quoted in Winfred Bernhard, *Fisher Ames, Federalist and Statesman* (Chapel Hill, N.C., 1965), 76.
2. Quoted in Raymond Smock, "The House of Representatives: First Branch of the New Government," in Joel Silbey, ed., *The Congress of the United States: Its Origins and Early Development* (New York, 1991), 156.

3. Charlene Bangs Bickford and Kenneth R. Bowling, *Birth of the Nation: The First Federal Congress, 1789–1791* (Madison, Wisc., 1989), 4. Needless to add, there were accusations of electoral fraud right at the very beginning of this new government, which remained a factor throughout the entire history of Congress.

4. The first census was held in 1790 and 1791 and was used to reapportion the 3rd Congress. Bickford and Bowling, *Birth of the Nation*, 5.

5. Ibid., 9.

6. The location of the building is variously given as Wall and Nassau and Wall and Broad. Both are correct. Kenneth R. Bowling and Helen E. Veit, eds., *Documentary History of the First Federal Congress: The Diary of William Maclay and Other Notes on Senate Debates* (Baltimore, 1988), 9:3, n. 1, say Wall and Nassau; but Ray Smock's article "The House of Representatives," 155, says it was on Wall and Broad.

7. Federal Hall fell into decay and was torn down in 1812; but later the government purchased the property and built a Greek Revival building that now serves as the Federal Reserve Bank of New York. Today it includes a museum run by the National Park Service.

8. Peter Muhlenberg to Benjamin Rush, April 20, 1789, quoted in Charlene Bangs Bickford et al., eds., *Documentary History of the First Federal Congress, 1789–1791, Correspondence, First Session, March–May 1789* (Baltimore, 2004), 15: 300. Peter Muhlenberg was the brother of Frederick Muhlenberg, the first Speaker of the House.

9. Frederick Muhlenberg said that "the Building is really elegant & well designed—for a Trap—but I still hope, however well contrived we shall find Room to get out of it." Frederick Muhlenberg to Benjamin Rush, March 5, 1789 in ibid., 37.

10. Quoted in Bickford and Bowling, *Birth of the Nation*, 10.

11. "A Communication from New York," quoted in Margaret C. S. Christman, *The First Federal Congress, 1789–1791* (Washington, D.C., 1989), 105.

12. Henry Adams, *History of the United States,* quoted in James R. Sharp, *American Politics in the Early Republic: The New Nation in Crisis* (New Haven, 1993), 20.

13. Fisher Ames to George Richards Minot, March 25, 1789, in Seth Ames, ed., *Works of Fisher Ames* (Boston, 1854), 1:31–32.

14. Elias Boudinot to Hannah Boudinot, May 15, 1789, in Bickford et al., *Documentary History of the First Federal Congress, 1789–1791, Correspondence*, 15:557.

15. Smock, "House of Representatives," 155.

16. Fisher Ames to George Richards Minot, April 4, 1789, in Ames, *Works*, 1:33.

17. Smock, "House of Representatives," 156–157.

18. Bickford and Bowling, *Birth of the Nation*, 12.

19. Fisher Ames to William Tudor, April 25, 1789, in Bickford et al., *Documentary History of the First Federal Congress, 1789–1791, Correspondence*, 15:351.

20. Fisher Ames to George Richards Minot, May 3, 1789, in Ames, *Works*, 1:35.

21. Catherine Greene to Jeremiah Wadsworth, April 18, 1789, *Documentary History of the First Federal Congress, 1789–1791, Correspondence*, 15: 280.

22. David P. Currie, *The Constitution in Congress: The Federalist Period, 1789–1801* (Chicago, 1997), 118.

23. Elias Boudinot to his wife, April 14, 1789, in *Documentary History of the First Federal Congress, 1789–1791, Correspondence,* 15:260.

24. Smock, "House of Representatives," 157.

25. In 2003 the clerk's staff numbered 285. Earlier, before reforms were instituted, the figure had climbed to 1,000. A complete list of clerks of the House from the 1st to the 109th Congress can be found in Appendix 2.

26. Bickford and Bowling, *Birth of the Nation,* 18. The *Annals of Congress,* which William W. Seaton and Joseph Gales, Jr., began publishing in 1834, were taken primarily from Lloyd's *Congressional Register,* as long as it was published, and then from Fenno's *Gazette.* The *Annals* include debates from the first session of the 1st Congress to the first session of the 18th Congress. The *Register of Debates in Congress* succeeded the *Annals* and it, in turn, was replaced in 1833 by the *Congressional Globe,* published by Francis P. Blair. In 1873 Congress decided that the *Congressional Record* would be produced by the Government Printing Office. Bickford et al., *Documentary History of the First Federal Congress, Debates in the House of Representatives,* 10: xxiii; Donald C. Bacon, Roger H. Davidson, and Morton Keller, eds. *The Encyclopedia of the United States Congress,* 2:993.

27. Smock, "House of Representatives," 2: 157–158.

28. James Kent to Elizabeth Hamilton, December 2, 1832, Hamilton-McLane Papers, LC, quoted in Bickford and Bowling, *Birth of the Nation,* 18.

29. Alexander White to James Madison, August 25, 1789, in *Documentary History of the First Federal Congress, 1789–1791, Correspondence,* 16:1399.

30. *Journal of the House of Representatives,* 1st Congress, 1st session, 6.

31. John Page to St. George Tucker, April 5, 1789, Bickford et al., *Documentary History of the First Federal Congress, 1789–1791, Correspondence,* 15:201.

32. *Journal of the House of Representatives,* 1st Congress, 1st session, 8–10.

33. In 2003 the sergeant at arms had a staff of eighty. See Appendix 3 for a complete list of the sergeants at arms from the 1st Congress (1789–1791) to the 109th Congress (2005–2007).

34. For a complete list of doorkeepers from the 1st to the 103rd Congresses, when the position was terminated, see Appendix 5.

35. A complete list of the chaplains, with their denominations, from the 1st to the 109th Congresses can be found in Appendix 4.

36. Linda De Pauw, ed., *Documentary History of the First Federal Congress, House of Representatives Journal* (Baltimore, 1977), 3:7–9.

37. This Oath Act was the first piece of legislation enacted by Congress and signed by the President. It passed the Senate on May 7, the House on May 18, and was signed by President Washington on June 1.

38. See Appendix 11 for House procedures as practiced today.

39. David McCullough, *John Adams* (New York, 2001), 392.

40. James M. Banner, Jr., "John Adams," in James M. McPherson, ed., *To the Best of My Ability* (New York, 2000), 22.

41. De Pauw, ed., *Documentary History of the First Federal Congress, House of Representatives Journal* (Baltimore, 1977), 3:14–15.

42. Bickford and Bowling, *Birth of the Nation*, 21.

43. De Pauw, ed., *Documentary History of the First Federal House Journal*, 3:17.

44. McCullough, *Adams*, 401.

45. Fisher Ames to William Tudor, April 26, 1789, in Bickford et al., *Documentary History of the First Federal Congress, 1789–1791, Correspondence*, 15:365.

46. James Flexner, *George Washington and the New Nation, 1783–1793* (Boston, 1969), 3:182.

47. Fisher Ames to George Richards Minot, May 14, 1789, in Ames, *Works*, 1:36.

48. Flexner, *Washington*, 3:187.

49. James Madison to Thomas Jefferson, June 30, 1789, in Bickford et al., *Documentary History of the First Federal Congress, 1789–1791, Correspondence*, 16:890.

50. Flexner, *Washington*, 3:187.

51. Robert Morris to Mary Morris, March 4, 1789, in Bickford et al., *Documentary History of the First Federal Congress, 1789–1791, Correspondence*, 15:15.

52. Fisher Ames to George Richards Minot, May 3, 1789, in Ames, *Works*, 1:34.

53. Bowling and Veit, *Documentary History of the First Federal Congress: The Diary of William Maclay*, 9:13.

54. Quoted in Gordon S. Wood, "George Washington," in McPherson, *To the Best of My Ability*, 310.

55. Flexner, *Washington*, 3:183–184.

56. Henry Wynkoop to Reading Beatty, May 1789, in Bickford et al. *Documentary History of the First Federal Congress, 1789–1791, Correspondence*, 15: 425.

CHAPTER II. THE FIRST SESSION OF THE 1ST CONGRESS, MARCH–SEPTEMBER 1789.

1. Irving Brant, *James Madison: Father of the Constitution, 1787–1800* (Indianapolis, 1941–1961), 3:246; Fisher Ames to George Richards Minot, May 3, 1789, in Seth Ames, ed., *Works of Fisher Ames* (Boston, 1854), 36.

2. *Annals of Congress*, 1st Congress, 1st session, 109.

3. Fisher Ames to George Richards Minot, May 27, 29, 1789, in Ames, *Works*, 1:44–45, 50.

4. Alexander White to Horatio Gates, June 1, 1789, in Charlene Bangs Bickford et al., eds., *Documentary History of the First Federal Congress, 1789–1791, Correspondence, First Session, March–May 1789* (Baltimore, 2004), 16:682.

5. Ames to Minot, May 27, 29, 1789, in Ames, *Works*, 1: 44–45, 50.

6. Fisher Ames to George Richards Minot, May 29, 1789, in Ames, *Works*, 1:48.

7. *Congressional Register*, 1: 136–137.

8. Ames to Minot, May 27, 1789, in Ames, *Works*, 1: 45.

9. James Madison to Edmund Pendleton, April 19, James Madison to Thomas Jefferson, May 23, 1789, in Bickford et al., *Documentary History of the First Federal Congress, 1789–1791, Correspondence*, 15: 285, 619.

10. William Smith to Gabriel Manigault, June 7, 1789, and Tristam Lowther to James Iredell, May 9, 1789, in ibid., 16: 718, 15: 493.

11. Charlene Bangs Bickford and Kenneth R. Bowling, *Birth of the Nation: The First Federal Congress, 1789–1791* (Madison, Wisc., 1989), 33. The House bureaucracy

today is truly staggering. Each representative, for example, can hire 18 permanent staff members and four part-time assistants. Multiply that by 435 House members and 5 additional nonvoting members and the number runs into the thousands. And this does not include staffers on standing committees.

12. Ibid., p. 35.

13. John Page to St. George Tucker, July 23, 1789, in Bickford et al., *Documentary History of the First Federal Congress, 1789–1791, Correspondence,* 16: 110.

14. Thomas Fitzimmons to Benjamin Rush, June 2, 1789, in ibid., 15: 686.

15. Joel H. Silbey, " 'Our Successors Will Have an Easier Task': The First Congress Under the Constitution, 1789–1791," *The Congress of the United States: Its Origins and Early Development* (New York, 199), 127.

16. Brant, *Madison,* 3: 258–259; *Annals of Congress,* 1st Congress, 1st session, 387. It should be pointed out that President Ronald Reagan neglected to superintend the conduct of his staff during the Iran-Contra scandal.

17. Ames to Minot, May 31, 1789, in Ames, *Works,* 1:52.

18. Andrew Jackson was the first President to dismiss a cabinet officer after he refused to resign. Several Senators complained but Jackson established the precedent that he had the right to dismiss members of the executive department for whatever reason he deemed necessary.

19. Margaret C. S. Christman, *The First Federal Congress, 1789–1791* (Washington, D.C., 1989) 137.

20. In the interim John Jay, the secretary of foreign affairs under the Articles, unofficially conducted the department's business.

21. The ordinance was first passed by the Congress under the Articles of Confederation on July 13, 1787.

22. Theodore Sedgwick to Pamela Sedgwick, August 20, 1789, in Bickford et al., *Documentary History of the First Federal Congress, 1789–1791, Correspondence,* 16:1361.

23. *Annals of Congress,* 1st Congress, 1st session, 449–450.

24. William Smith to Edward Rutledge, August 5, 1789, in Bickford et al., *Documentary History of the First Federal Congress, 1789–1791, Correspondence,* 16: 1327.

25. Richard Bland Lee to Leven Powell, March 29, 1789, in ibid., 15:146.

26. Fisher Ames to Timothy Dwight, June 11, 1789, in ibid., 1:52–53.

27. Bruce Ragsdale, "History of the House of Representatives," manuscript, Library of Congress, chap. 2:8; Charles B. Bickford and Helen Veit, eds., *Documentary History of the First Federal Congress, Legislative Histories* (Baltimore, 1986), 4:1–48; Kenneth R. Bowling, "A Tub to the Whale," *Journal of the Early Republic* 8 (Fall 1988): 223–251.

28. Fisher Ames to George Richards Minot, July 8, 1789, in Bickford et al., *Documentary History of the First Federal Congress, 1789–1791, Correspondence,* 16:978.

29. *Congressional Register,* 2:215–216.

30. Frederick A. Muhlenberg to Benjamin Rush, August 18, 1789, in Bickford et al., *Documentary History of the First Federal Congress, 1789–1791, Correspondence,* 16:1348.

31. Fisher Ames to Thomas Dwight, June 11, 1789, in Ames, *Works,* 1:53.

32. The seat of the American government changed many times. During the Revolution there was Philadelphia, Baltimore, and Lancaster and York, Pennsylvania. After the war the government resided in Philadelphia but moved to Princeton, New Jersey, where it remained from June 30, 1783, to November 4, 1783. Then in November it moved to Annapolis, Maryland, where it remained from November 26, 1783, to June 3, 1784. Congress agreed to alternate meeting places between Annapolis and Trenton, New Jersey, until it could agree on a permanent capital. The government remained in Trenton from November 1, 1784, to December 24, 1784. Then Congress gave up the idea of shuttling back and forth between cities and in January 1785 it moved to New York City.

33. Comte de Moustier to Comte de Montmorin, April 7, 1789, in Bickford et al., *Documentary History of the First Federal Congress, 1789–1791, Correspondence,* 15:219.

34. *New York Daily Advertiser,* July 27, 1789; Leonard to Silvanus Bourn, August 16, and William Smith to Gabriel Manigault, June 7, 1789, in Bickford et al., *Documentary History of the First Federal Congress, 1789–1791, Correspondence,* 16: 1060, 1332, 718.

35. As Madison told Jefferson earlier in the session, "the proceedings of the new Congress are so far marked with great moderation and liberality, and will disappoint the wishes and predictions of many who have opposed the Government. The spirit which characterizes the House of Reps. in particular is already extinguishing the honest fears which considered the system as dangerous to republicanism." James Madison to Thomas Jefferson, May 27, 1789, in Bickford et al., *Documentary History of the First Federal Congress, 1789–1791, Correspondence,* 15:639.

36. Fisher Ames to Minot, June 23, 1789, in Ames, *Works,* 1:66.

37. Ibid., 1:61.

CHAPTER III. NEW YORK, PHILADELPHIA AND IDEOLOGICAL CONFLICT, 1790–1797

1. John Page to Robert Page, March 16, 1789, in Charlene Bangs Bickford et al., eds., *Documentary History of the First Federal Congress, 1789–1791, Correspondence First Session, March–May 1789* (Baltimore, 2004), 15:71.

2. Abigail Adams to Mary Cranch, August 9, 1789, in Stewart Mitchell, ed., *New Letters of Abigail Adams, 1788–1801* (Boston, 1947), 19.

3. Abigail Adams to Mary Cranch, July 27, 1790, in ibid., 55.

4. Perhaps the first known lobbyist was the Reverend Manasseh Cutler, who served as an agent and member of the Ohio Company of Associates, a collection of Massachusetts investors. He labored successfully with Congress to buy public land in the Northwest Territory at rock-bottom prices.

5. Fisher Ames to George Richards Minot, October 30, 1789, in Seth Ames, ed., *Works of Fisher Ames* (Boston, 1854), 1:74.

6. Fisher Ames to the Rev. J. Freeman, January 9, 1790, quoted in Winfred Bernhard, *Fisher Ames, Federalist and Statesman* (Chapel Hill, N.C.), 121.

7. Several months later on May 29, 1790, Rhode Island overcame its hesitation, ratified the Constitution and entered the Union as the thirteenth state.

8. Bickford et al. *Documentary History of the First Federal Congress House of Representatives Journal*, 3:252–254.

9. *Annals of Congress,* 1st Congress, 1st session, I:929.

10. Ron Chernow, *Alexander Hamilton* (New York, 2004), 301–302.

11. Ibid., 295–308.

12. *Annals of Congress,* 1st Congress, 2nd session, 1131–1132.

13. William Neilson to John Chaloner, February 17, 1790, Chaloner Papers, Clement Library, University of Michigan, quoted in Charlene Bangs Bickford and Kenneth R. Bowling, eds., *Birth of the Nation: The First Federal Congress, 1789–1791* (Madison, Wisc., 1989), 64.

14. *Annals of Congress,* 1st Congress, 2nd session, 1234.

15. Quoted in Irving Brant, *James Madison: Father of the Constitution, 1787–1800* (Indianapolis, 1941–1961), 3:299.

16. Theodore Sedgwick to Pamela Sedgwick, March 4, 1790, quoted in Bickford and Bowling, *Birth of the Nation*, 95.

17. Ames to William Tudor, March 3, 1790, quoted in Bernhard, *Fisher Ames*, 139.

18. Brant, *Madison,* 3:305.

19. John Quincy Adams to John Adams, April 5, 1790, in Washington C. Ford, ed., *Writings of John Quincy Adams* (New York, 1913–1917), 1:50.

20. *Annals of Congress,* 1st Congress, 2nd session, 1453–1464.

21. Kenneth R. Bowling and Helen E. Veit, eds., *Documentary History of the First Federal Congress: The Diary of William Maclay and Other Notes on Senate Debates* (Baltimore 1988), 9:226.

22. Ibid., 9:215.

23. *Annals of Congress,* 1st Congress, 2nd session, 1577.

24. Bowling and Veit, *Documentary History Maclay Diary* 9:241.

25. *Gazette of the United States,* April 14, 1790, quoted in ibid., 8:1007.

26. Abraham Baldwin to Joel Barlow, May 8, 1790, quoted in Margaret C. S. Christman, *The First Federal Congress, 1789–1791* (Washington, D.C., 1989), 178.

27. Thomas Cushing to Benjamin Goodhue, April 17, 1790, quoted in Bickford and Bowling, *Birth of the Nation*, 68.

28. This congressional joint rule continued for the next half century.

29. George Washington to the Marquis de la Luzerne, August 10, 1790, Washington Papers, Library of Congress.

30. James Madison to James Monroe, June 1, 1790, quoted in Brant, *Madison,* 3: 312.

31. Quoted in H. A. Washington, ed., *The Writings of Thomas Jefferson* (Philadelphia, 1869–71), 1: 274–276, 7: 226.

32. Brant, *Madison,* 3: 315.

33. See Jacob E. Cooke, "The Compromise of 1790," *William and Mary Quarterly* (October 1970) and Kenneth R. Bowling, "Dinner at Jefferson's: A Note on Jacob E. Cooke's 'The Compromise of 1790,' " and the rebuttal by Cooke in *William and Mary Quarterly* (October 1971): 523–545, 629–648. Hamilton's most recent biographer, Ron Chernow, accepts the Jefferson interpretation. Chernow, *Hamilton,* 328–331. See also Brant, *Madison,* 3: 314–318.

34. Elbridge Gerry to James Monroe, June 25, 1790, in W. C. Ford, ed., "Letters of Elbridge Gerry," *New England Historical and Genealogical Register,* 2: 436.

35. Quoted in Christman, *First Federal Congress,* 186, 188.

36. Quoted in Brant, *Madison,* 3: 314–315.

37. Washington to Luzerne. August 10, 1790, Washington Papers, Library of Congress.

38. David Currie, *The Constitution in Congress: The Federalist Period* (Chicago, 1997), 134.

39. William Few to Edward Telfair, January 15, 1791, quoted in Bickford and Bowling, *Birth of the Nation,* 96.

40. Thomas Jefferson to Robert R. Livingston, February 4, 1791, in Julian P. Boyd, ed., *The Papers of Thomas Jefferson* (Princeton, 1950), 19: 241.

41. Bowling and Veit, *Documentary History, First Federal Congress, Maclay Diary,* 9: 331.

42. Theodore Sedgwick to Pamela Sedgwick, January 28, 1791, quoted in Christman, *First Federal Congress,* 196–198; Kenneth R. Bowling, "The Federal Government and Republican Court Move to Philadelphia," in Bowling and Donald R. Kennon, eds., *Neither Separate Nor Equal* (Athens, Ohio, 2000) 17; Abigail Adams to Abigail Adams Smith, December 26, 1790, in C. F. Adams, ed., *Letters of Mrs. Adams* (Boston, 1841), 210–212.

43. Theodore Sedgwick and Pamela Sedgwick, January 28, 1791, quoted in Christman, *First Federal Congress,* 197.

44. Abigail Adams to Mary Cranch, January 9, 1791, in Mitchell, ed., *New Letters of Abigail Adams,* 67.

45. Theodore Sedgwick to Pamela Sedgwick, January 9, 1791, quoted in Kenneth R. Bowling, "Federal Government and Republican Court Move to Philadelphia," in Bowling and Donald R. Kennon, *Neither Reporter Nor Equal* (Athens, Ohio, 2000), 12.

46. Abigail Adams to Mary Cranch, February 5, 1792, in Mitchell, ed., *New Letters of Abigail Adams,* 77.

47. Richard N. Rosenfeld, *American Aurora: A Democratic-Republican Returns* (New York, 1997), 9.

48. Theodore Sedgwick to his wife, January 9, 1791, quoted in Christman, *First Federal Congress,* 199.

49. Fisher Ames to Timothy Dwight, December 12, 1790, in Ames, *Works,* 1: 89.

50. James R. Sharp, *American Politics in the Early Republic: The New Nation in Crisis* (New Haven, Conn., 1993), 38.

51. Quoted in Christman, *First Federal Congress,* 200.

52. Ibid., 205.

53. For a full account of this incident, see Thomas P. Slaughter, *The Whiskey Rebellion: Frontier Epilogue to the American Revolution* (New York, 1986).

54. Bickford and Bowling, *Birth of the Nation,* 64.

55. Bowling and Veit, *Documentary History, First Federal Congress, Maclay Diary,* 9: 347.

56. William Few to Edward Telfair, January 15, 1791, quoted in Christman, *First Federal Congress,* 209.

57. Dumas Malone, *Jefferson and the Rights of Man* (Boston, 1951), 325.

58. Ibid., 339–341

59. Hamilton communicated his "Report on the National Bank" to the House on December 14, 1790. See *Annals of Congress*, 1st Congress, 3rd session, 2082–2112.

60. De Pauw, ed., *Documentary History, House Journal,* 1st Congress, 3: 775.

61. Raymond W. Smock, *Report of the Commission on the Bicentenary of the U.S. House of Representatives* (Washington, 1986), 1.

62. Charles Francis Adams, ed., *The Works of John Adams, Second President of the United States* (Boston, 1851), 9: 485, 511.

63. Noble E. Cunningham, Jr., "John Beckley: An Early American Party Manager," in Joel Silbey, ed., *The Congress of the United States: Its Origins and Early Development* (New York, 1991), 404–405.

64. Chernow, *Hamilton,* 374–379.

65. George C. Chalou, "St. Clair's Defeat, 1792," in Arthur M. Schlesinger, Jr., and Roger Bruns, eds., *Congress Investigates: A Documentary History, 1792–1974* (New York, 1975), 1: 3.

66. The ratio was changed in President Andrew Jackson's administration to 16 to 1, which brought gold back into circulation.

67. The position was raised to cabinet rank in the Jackson administration.

68. *Annals of Congress*, 2nd Congress, 2nd session, 834–840; Dumas Malone, *Jefferson and the Ordeal of Liberty* (Boston, 1962), 22.

69. Fisher Ames to Timothy Dwight, January, 1793, and Fisher Ames to George Richards Minot, February 20, 1793, in Ames, *Works,* 1: 127, 128.

70. *Annals of Congress*, 1st Congress, 1st session, 331–334; Bernhard, *Fisher Ames,* 222–223.

71. Fisher Ames to Christopher Gore, February 25, 1794, in Ames, *Works,* 1: 135.

72. Stanley Elkins and Eric McKitrick, *The Age of Federalism* (New York, 1993), 420; Sharp, *American Politics in the Early Republic,* 119.

73. *Annals of Congress*, 4th Congress, 1st session, 450.

74. Ibid., 400–401.

75. Ibid., 426, 760–761.

76. Jack Rakove, *James Madison and the Creation of the American Republic* (New York, 2002), 140.

77. *Annals of Congress*, 4th Congress, 1st session, 1239–1263.

78. Sharp, *American Politics in the Early Republic,* 132.

79. Fisher Ames to Christopher Gore, January 10, 1795, in Ames, *Works,* 1: 161.

80. Fisher Ames to Timothy Dwight, January 5, 1797, and Fisher Ames to Gore, October 5, 1796, in Ames, *Works,* 1: 201, 213.

81. Previous Speakers had begun the practice of placing loyalists on the important committees, but Sedgwick institutionalized the practice. See Norman K. Risjord, "Partisanship and Power: House Committees and the Powers of the Speaker, 1789–1801," *William and Mary Quarterly* (October 1992): 49, 628–651.

82. Thomas Jefferson wrote a parliamentary manual in 1800 that was later adopted by the House.

CHAPTER IV. A NEW BEGINNING IN WASHINGTON, 1798–1807.

1. Ron Chernow, *Alexander Hamilton* (New York, 2004), 553–566.
2. Raymond Walters, Jr., *Albert Gallatin: Jeffersonian Financier and Diplomat* (New York, 1957), 97, 100.
3. *Annals of Congress*, 5th Congress, 2nd session, 1034.
4. Henry Adams, *Life of Albert Gallatin* (New York, 1943), 191–193.
5. *Annals of Congress*, 5th Congress, 1st session, 947.
6. This law was repealed in 1802 and the naturalization law of 1795 was reenacted.
7. This law expired in 1800.
8. Quoted in David McCullough, *John Adams* (New York, 2001), 505. Limited to two years, the Sedition Act expired in 1801.
9. Richard N. Rosenfeld, *American Aurora: A Democratic-Republican Returns* (New York, 1997), 160.
10. *Annals of Congress,* 5th Congress, 2nd session, 2008–2014.
11. Ibid., 2110; E. James Ferguson, ed., *Selected Writings of Albert Gallatin* (Indianapolis, 1967), 173, 182; Walters, *Gallatin,* 182.
12. Walters, *Gallatin,* 112.
13. *Annals of Congress*, 5th Congress, 2nd session, 2093, 2107–2111.
14. Henry Steele Commager, *Documents of American History* (New York, 1963), 1:178–184.
15. Adams, *Gallatin,* 221.
16. *Annals of Congress,* 5th Congress, 2nd session, 1631–1642.
17. Ibid., 6th Congress, 1st session, 712.
18. William C. Allen, *History of the United States Capitol* (Washington, 2001), 41.
19. Ibid., 6–7.
20. Ibid., 9, 10.
21. James Sterling Young, *The Washington Community, 1800–1828* (New York, 1966), 22.
22. James H. Hutson, *To Make All Laws: The Congress of the United States, 1789–1989* (Washington, 1989), 11.
23. Benjamin Rush to John Adams, March 19, 1789, in Charlene Bangs Bickford et al., eds., *Documentary History of the First Federal Congress, 1789–1791, Correspondence, First Session*, March–May 1789 (Baltimore, 2004), 15:80.
24. Gouverneur Morris to the Princess de la Tour et Taxis, December 14, 1800, cited and translated in Anne Carey Morris, ed., *The Diary and Letters of Gouverneur Morris* (New York, 1888), 2:394–395.
25. Quoted in Constance M. Green, *Washington* (Princeton, 1962), 23.
26. Pierre-Charles L'Enfant to George Washington, June 22, 1791, quoted in Allen, *History of the United States Capitol, 9.*
27. *Congressional Quarterly Guide to Congress* (Washington, 2001), II, 728.
28. Allen, *History of the United States Capitol*, 19–20.
29. Walters, *Gallatin*, 126, 127.
30. Edmund Quincy, *Life of Josiah Quincy* (Boston, 1874), 186–188.
31. Cynthia D. Earman, "Remembering the Ladies: Women, Etiquette and Diversions in Washington City, 1800–1814," in *Washington History* 12:105–106.

32. McCullough, *Adams,* 550.

33. *Journal of the House of Representatives,* 6th Congress, 2nd session, 791–792.

34. Alexander Hamilton to Oliver Wolcott, Jr., December 16, 1800, quoted in Noble Cunningham, *In Pursuit of Reason: The Life of Thomas Jefferson* (Baton Rouge, 1987), 233.

35. Alexander Hamilton to James Bayard, January 16, 1801, quoted in ibid., 234.

36. Albert Gallatin to his wife, February 5, 1801 quoted in Adams, *Gallatin,* 260.

37. Thomas Jefferson to James Monroe, February 15, 1801, in Paul Leicester Ford, ed., *The Works of Thomas Jefferson* (New York, 1904–1905), 7:491.

38. Albert Gallatin to his wife, February 16, 1801, quoted in Adams, *Gallatin,* 262.

39. M. L. Davis, *Memoirs of Burr* (Freeport, NY, 1970), 2:129–133.

40. James Bayard to Allen McLane, February 17, 1801, *AHA Report for 1913,* 2:128–129.

41. James D. Richardson, ed., *A Compilation of the Messages and Papers of the Presidents* (Washington, 1897), 1:310.

42. Margaret Bayard Smith, *First Forty Years of Washington Society,* ed. Gaillard Hunt (New York, 1906), 25.

43. Allen, *History of the United States Capitol,* 45–47.

44. Smith, *First Forty Years of Washington Society,* 13–14.

45. James Hutson, *Religion and the Founding of the American Republic* (Washington, 1998), 84–87

46. William Henry Sparks, *The Memories of Fifty Years* (Philadelphia, 1889), 227.

47. *Annals of Congress,* 9th Congress, 1st session, 561.

48. Thomas Jefferson to Barnabas Bidwell, July 5, 1806, Jefferson Papers, Library of Congress. See also Cunningham, *In Pursuit of Reason,* 250.

49. Quoted in Robert A. McCaughey, *Josiah Quincy, 1772–1864: The Last Federalist* (Cambridge, Mass., 1974), 49.

50. Roger Griswold to his wife, January 25, 1802, Roger Griswold Papers, Yale University Library.

51. Thomas Jefferson to Robert Livingston, April 18, 1802, in Ford, *Works of Thomas Jefferson,* 9:364–365.

52. *Annals of Congress,* 7th Congress, 2nd session, 339.

53. Dumas Malone, *Jefferson the President: First Term, 1801–1805* (Boston, 1970), 302. On the Louisiana Purchase, see also Alexander DeConde, *This Affair of Louisiana* (New York, 1976).

54. Thomas Jefferson to John Breckinridge, August 12, 1803, in Ford, *Works of Thomas Jefferson,* 10:5, 7.

55. William Plumer, *Memorandum of Proceedings in the U.S. Senate,* ed. Everett S. Brown (New York, 1969), 13.

56. *Annals of Congress,* 8th Congress, 1st session, 385–420, 432–433.

57. Ibid., 409, 436–437.

58. Adams, *Gallatin,* 318.

59. Prior to the vote five senators withdrew from the chamber.

60. *Annals of Congress,* 8th Congress, 1st Session, p. 674; Thomas Jefferson to Joseph Nicholson, May 13, 1804, in Washington, *Writings of Thomas Jefferson,* 4: 486; Cunningham, *In Pursuit of Reason,* 272.

61. Quoted in Richard H. Dabney, *John Randolph* (Chicago, 1898), 46.

62. John Quincy Adams, *Memoirs,* ed. Charles Francis Adams (Philadelphia, 1874–1877), 1:359.

63. See William Rehnquist, *The Historic Impeachments of Samuel Chase and President Andrew Johnson* (New York, 1992).

64. Adams, *Memoirs,* 1:370.

65. Cunningham, *In Pursuit of Reason,* 281.

CHAPTER V. HENRY CLAY AND THE ASCENDANCY OF THE HOUSE
OF REPRESENTATIVES, 1806–1821

1. William C. Allen, *History of the United States Capitol* (Washington, 2001), 72.

2. Total appropriations for the south wing from March 3, 1803, through April 1808 came to $330.000. Ibid., 71, 74.

3. Josiah Quincy to his wife, February 26, March 3, 1808, in Edmund Quincy, *Life of Josiah Quincy* (Boston, 1874), 134, 136.

4. Dumas Malone, *Jefferson the President: Second Term, 1805–1809* (Boston, 1974), 5:545.

5. *Annals of Congress,* 11th Congress, 1st Session, 579–582.

6. Henry Clay to James Monroe, November 13, 1810, in James F. Hopkins et al., eds., *The Papers of Henry Clay* (Lexington, Ky., 1959–1993), 1:498.

7. Nathan Sargent, *Public Men and Events* (Philadelphia, 1875), 1:130.

8. John W. Forney, *Anecdotes of Public Men* (New York, 1970), 1:194.

9. Quincy, *Life of Josiah Quincy,* 255.

10. Robert V. Remini, *Henry Clay: Statesman for the Union* (New York, 1991), 83.

11. Langdon Cheves to Henry Clay, July 30, 1812, in Hopkins et al., eds., *Papers of Henry Clay,* 1:700.

12. *Annals of Congress,* 12th Congress, 1st session, 596–602.

13. Ibid., 1451–1461.

14. James D. Richardson, *A Compilation of the Messages and Papers of the Presidents* (Washington, D.C., 1897), 1:490.

15. Henry A. Wise, *Seven Decades of the Union* (Freeport, N.Y., 1871), 53.

16. *Annals of Congress,* 12th Congress, 1st session, 1617, 1625–1637.

17. For the latest study of the war, see Walter R. Borneman, *1812: The War That Forged a Nation* (New York, 2005).

18. Margaret Bayard Smith to Mrs. Kirkpatrick, August [1814], in Gaillard Hunt, ed., *First Forty Years of Washington Society* (New York, 1906), 103–104.

19. Ibid., 109.

20. Ibid., 104.

21. Ibid., 109.

22. Allen, *History of the United States Capitol,* 107–108.

23. February 18, March 4, 1815.

24. *Annals of Congress,* 13th Congress, 3rd session, 1155.

25. Henry A. Wise, *Seven Decades of the Union* (Philadelphia, 1881), 63.

26. *Annals of Congress,* 14th Congress, 1st Session, 832.

27. Bruce Ragsdale, "History of the House," manuscript, in the Library of Congress, chap. 4, 15.

28. Gerald Gamm and Kenneth Shepsle, "Emergence of Legislative Institutions: Standing Committees in the House and Senate, 1810–1825," *Legislative Studies Quarterly* 14 (February, 1989): 39–66.

29. Ralph C. H. Catterall, *The Second Bank of the United States* (Chicago, 1903), 10–21.

30. *Annals of Congress,* 14th Congress, 1st session, 866–868; Remini, *Clay,* 143.

31. *Annals of Congress,* 14th Congress, 1st session, 866.

32. On the Compensation Act, see C. Edward Skeen, *"Vox Populi, Vox Dei"*: The Compensation Act of 1816," *Journal of the Early Republic* 6 (Fall 1986): 253–274.

33. Joseph Story to Ezekiel Bacon, March 12, 1818, in William Story, ed., *Life and Letters of Joseph Story* (Boston, 1851), 1:311.

34. *Annals of Congress,* 15th Congress, 2nd session, 631–655; Remini, *Clay,* 164–165.

35. *Annals of Congress,* 15th Congress, 2nd session, 1204.

36. Allen, *History of the United States Capitol,* 51–52, 127–137.

37. Henry Clay to Leslie Combs, February 5, 1820, and Henry Clay to Adam Beatty, January 22, 1820, in Hopkins, ed., *Papers of Henry Clay,* 2: 774, 766.

38. *Annals of Congress,* 16th Congress, 1st session, 424, 427–430, 831–833.

39. William Plumer, Jr., to William Plumer, Sr., February 12, 1820, in Everett Somerville Brown, ed., *The Missouri Compromise and Presidential Politics, 1820–1825* (St. Louis, 1926), 8–9; *Annals of Congress,* 16th Congress, 1st session, 1210; Glover Moore, *Missouri Controversy, 1819–1821* (Lexington, Ky., 1953), 93.

40. William Plumer to his father, March 1820, in Brown, *Missouri Compromise,* 14; Moore, *Missouri Controversy,* 104.

41. Carl J. Vipperman, *William Lowndes and the Transition of Southern Politics* (Chapel Hill, N.C., 1989), 249.

42. William Henry Sparks, *The Memories of Fifty Years* (Philadelphia, 1889), 230.

43. Langdon Cheves to Henry Clay, March 3, 1821, in Hopkins, ed., *Clay Papers,* 3: 58.

CHAPTER VI. A DEMOCRATIZED HOUSE, 1822–1846

1. Washington C. Ford, ed., *Writings of John Quincy Adams* (New York, 1913–1917), 4: 375–378, 526–531.

2. Margaret Bayard Smith to Mrs. Kirkpatrick, January 1819, in Margaret Bayard Smith, *First Forty Years of Washington Society,* ed. Gaillard Hunt (New York, 1906), 146–147.

3. John Fairfield to his wife, June 11, 1836, and December 28, 1835, in Arthur G. Staples, ed., *The Letters of John Fairfield* (Lewiston, Me., 1922), 42, 141.

4. Ibid., 20–21.

5. Nathan Sargent, *Public Men and Events* (New York, 1875), 1:118, 2:47–48.

6. John W. Forney, *Anecdotes of Public Men* (New York, 1970), 1:115.

7. Sargent, *Public Men and Events,* 2:22.

8. Henry Clay to Peter B. Porter, February 15, 1824, in James F. Hopkins, ed.,

The Papers of Henry Clay (Lexington, Ky.), 3:640; Robert V. Remini, *Henry Clay: Statesman for the Union* (New York, 1991), 236.

9. Henry Clay to Peter B. Porter, December 7, 1824, in Hopkins, ed., *Papers of Henry Clay*, 3: 892.

10. John Quincy Adams, *Memoirs,* ed. Charles Francis Adams (Philadelphia, 1874–1877), 6:464–465; Remini, *Clay,* 258.

11. Bruce Ragsdale, "House of Representatives," manuscript, Library of Congress, chap. 4, 22; Merrill D. Peterson, *The Great Triumvirate* (New York, 1987), 341–342.

12. Andrew Jackson to William B. Lewis, February 14, 1825, Miscellaneous Jackson Papers, New York Historical Society.

13. James D. Richardson, *A Compilation of the Messages and Papers of the Presidents* (Washington, D.C., 1897), 2:866–882.

14. *Journal of the House of Representatives,* 19th Congress, 2nd session, 389–404.

15. Silas Wright, Jr., to Azariah C. Flagg, April 7, 1828, Flagg Papers, New York Public Library.

16. A. H. Shepperd to Bartlett Yancey, April 17, 1828, Yancey Papers, University of North Carolina Library.

17. Daniel Webster to Joseph E. Sprague, April 13, 1828, in Claude H. Van Tyne, ed., *The Letters of Daniel Webster* (New York, 1902), 135–136.

18. *Register of Debates,* 20th Congress, 1st session, 2700, 2708.

19. Robert V. Remini, *The Election of Andrew Jackson* (New York, 1963), 178.

20. Ibid., 187–188.

21. Smith, *First Forty Years of Washington Society,* 295.

22. Richardson, *Messages and Papers,* 2:1010–1011.

23. Ibid., 1025.

24. *Journal of the House of Representatives,* 21st Congress, 1st session, 726–730.

25. Ibid., 1145–1156; U.S. *Statutes,* 4:411–412.

26. Dumas Malone, *Jefferson and the Ordeal of Liberty* (Boston, 1962), 318, 456.

27. Robert S. Walker, "A Look at the Rules of the House," in Lou Frey, Jr., and Michael T. Hayes, eds., *Inside the House: Former Members Reveal How Congress Really Works* (Lanham, N.Y., 2001), 249.

28. Donald R. Kennon and Rebecca M. Rogers, *The Committee on Ways and Means: A Bicentennial History, 1789–1989* (Washington, D.C., 1989), 99.

29. Ibid., 111.

30. Robert V. Remini, *Andrew Jackson and the Course of American Freedom* (New York, 1981), 366.

31. *Journal of the House of Representatives,* 22nd Congress, 1st session, 3851.

32. Richardson, *Messages and Papers,* 2:1140–1153.

33. *Journal of the House of Representatives,* 23rd Congress, 1st session, 3474–3477; William Rives to Levi Woodbury, May 26, 1834, Woodbury Papers, Library of Congress.

34. Quoted in Joel H. Silbey, "Congress in a Partisan Political Era," in Julian E. Zelizer, ed., *The American Congress* (Boston and New York, 2004), 142.

35. Quoted in Kennon and Rogers, *Committee on Ways and Means,* 97–98.

36. Alexis de Tocqueville, *Democracy in America* (New York, 1945), 1:204.

37. John Fairfield to his wife, April 27, 1836, in Staples, *Letters of John Fairfield,* 122.

38. Benjamin F. Perry, *Reminiscences of Public Men* (Philadelphia, 1883), 305.

39. John Fairfield to his wife, December 8, 1835, December 5, 15, 1836, in Staples, *Letters of John Fairfield*, 26, 31, 147.

40. *Washington Globe,* February 3, 4, April 13, 1835; *New York Evening Post,* February 4, 1835.

41. Accounts of the duel can be found in Don Seitz, *Famous American Duels* (New York, 1929), 251–283; and Myra L. Spaulding, "Dueling in the District of Columbia," *Records of the Columbia Historical Society* 29–30 (1928): 186–210.

42. *National Intelligencer,* February 16, 1838.

43. John Fairfield to his wife, February 23, 26, 1838, in Staples, *Letters of John Fairfield*, 202–229.

44. *Congressional Globe,* 25th Congress, 2nd session, House Report No. 750, 1–2. See Appendix 15 for further information about House pages.

45. Richardson, *Messages and Papers,* 2:1304, 1305, 1309.

46. Ibid., 2:1203–1206.

47. *Congressional Globe,* 24th Congress, 1st session, 498–499; Leonard L. Richards, *The Life and Times of Congressman John Quincy Adams* (New York, 1986), 121.

48. *Congressional Globe,* 24th Congress, 1st session, 409.

49. Ibid., 27th Congress, 2nd session, 506; *National Intelligencer,* February 11, 15, 1842; Robert V. Remini, *John Quincy Adams* (New York, 2002), 140.

50. *Congressional Globe,* 27th Congress, 2nd session, 168–215.

51. Sargent, *Public Men and Events,* 2:143–145.

52. Ibid., 2:145–146.

53. *Congressional Globe,* 27th Congress, 2nd session, 214–15. See also Lynn H. Parsons, "Censuring Old Man Eloquent: Foreign Policy and Disunion, 1842," *Capitol Studies* 3 (Fall 1975): 89–106. For Adams's account, see Adams, *Memoirs,* 11:70–88.

54. Sargent, *Public Men and Events,* 2:168.

55. Adams, *Memoirs,* 12:116.

56. *Rochester (New York) Daily Democrat,* February 10, 1842; *Philadelphia U.S. Gazette,* quoted in the *New York Tribune,* February 1, 1842; *New York Evening Post,* January 28, 1842; *Washington Globe,* February 4, 1842.

57. Donald A. Ritchie, *Press Gallery: Congress and the Washington Correspondents* (Cambridge, Mass., 1991), 30–31.

58. Sargent, *Public Men and Events,* 2:287–290.

59. *Congressional Globe,* 29th Congress, 1st session, 791.

60. Benjamin Brown French, *Witness to the Young Republic: A Yankee's Journal,* eds. John McDonough and Donald Cole (Hanover, N.H., 1989), 192; Sargent, *Public Men and Events,* 2:310–311.

61. Abraham Lincoln, *Speeches and Writings, 1832–1858,* ed. Don E. Fehrenbacher, (New York, 1989), 176.

62. Sargent, *Public Men and Events,* 2:332. Today this room is reserved for female members of Congress.

CHAPTER VII. THE STRUGGLE TO SAVE THE UNION, 1846–1860

1. James D. Richardson, ed., *A Compilation of the Messages and Papers of the Presidents* (New York, 1907), 4:456.
2. David M. Potter, *The Impending Crisis, 1848–1861* (New York, 1976), 18–20.
3. *Congressional Globe,* 29th Congress, 1st Session, 1211–1213; Potter, *Impending Crisis,* 20.
4. *Congressional Globe,* 29th Congress, 1st session, 1217.
5. Ibid., 1217–1218; Potter, *Impending Crisis,* 21, 22; Charles Buxton Going, *David Wilmot, Free-Soiler* (Gloucester, Mass., 1966), 100.
6. *Boston Whig,* August 15, 1846, quoted in Frank Otto Gatell, *John Gorham Palfrey and the New England Conscience* (Cambridge, Mass., 1963), 130–131.
7. Michael F. Holt, "The Slavery Issue," in Julian E. Zelizer, *The American Congress,* 194.
8. *Congressional Globe,* 29th Congress, 2nd session, appendix, 139; Milo Milton Quaife, ed., *The Diary of James K. Polk* (Chicago, 1910), 2:75, 288–290, 299.
9. *Congressional Globe,* 29th Congress, 2nd session, 178–180, 187–188, and appendix, 116–119; Potter, *Impending Crisis,* 66.
10. *Congressional Globe,* 29th Congress, 2nd session, 573.
11. Ibid., appendix, 278–282.
12. Potter, *Impending Crisis,* 68; *Congressional Globe,* 29th Congress, 2nd session, Appendix, 119–120, 76–80, 86, 134–136, 246, 281.
13. Robert V. Remini, *Henry Clay: Statesman for the Union* (New York, 1991), 698.
14. Eric Foner, *Free Soil, Free Labor, Free Men* (New York, 1970), 124–125; Remini, *Clay,* 706.
15. John Niven, *John C. Calhoun and the Price of Union* (Baton Rouge, 1988), 323–325.
16. Potter, *Impending Crisis,* 87.
17. John W. Forney, *Anecdotes of Public Men* (New York, 1970), 1:57, 165
18. Michael F. Holt, *The Rise and Fall of the American Whig Party* (New York, 1999), 467–468.
19. Holman Hamilton, *Prologue to Conflict: The Crisis and Compromise of 1850* (New York, 1966), 40.
20. *Congressional Globe,* 31st Congress, 2nd session, 38.
21. Quoted in Holt, *American Whig Party,* 467–468.
22. Ibid., 470–471.
23. Nathan Sargent, *Public Men and Events* (New York: 1875), 2:351.
24. *Congressional Globe,* 31st Congress, 1st session, 26.
25. Ibid., 256, 351.
26. Holt, *American Whig Party,* 471–472.
27. Holman Hamilton, " 'The Cave of the Winds' and the Compromise of 1850," in Joel Silbey, ed., *The United States Congress in a Partisan Political Nation, 1841–1896* (New York, 1991), 1:339.
28. *Congressional Globe,* 31st Congress, 1st session, appendix, 115–127.
29. *New York Herald,* November 21, 1850.
30. *Congressional Globe,* 31st Congress, 1st session, 200–205.

31. Hamilton, *Prologue to Conflict,* p. 67.

32. Richard Crallé, ed., *The Works of John C. Calhoun* (New York, 1857), 4:573.

33. *Congressional Globe,* 31st Congress, 1st session, 476ff; Robert V. Remini, *Daniel Webster: The Man and His Time* (New York, 1997), 669–671.

34. Robert W. Johannsen, *Stephen A. Douglas* (New York, 1973), 294–303.

35. Fletcher Webster, ed., *The Private Correspondence of Daniel Webster* (Boston, 1857), 2:369–370.

36. *Congressional Globe,* 31st Congress, 1st session, 1562.

37. Ibid., 1682–1687, 1695–1704.

38. *Washington Globe,* September 6, 1850.

39. Benjamin Perley Poore, *Perley's Reminiscences of Sixty Years in the National Metropolis* (Tecumseh, Mich., 1886), 1:384–385; *National Intelligencer,* August 10, September 9, 1850.

40. *Congressional Globe,* 31st Congress, 1st session appendix, 940.

41. Sargent, *Public Men and Events,* 2:376–377.

42. *Congressional Globe,* 33rd Congress, 1st session, 239–240.

43. Potter, *Impending Crisis,* 151; *Congressional Globe,* 32nd Congress, 2nd session, 7, 474–475, 542–544, 556–565.

44. *Congressional Globe,* 33rd Congress, 1st session, 1254–1255, and app., 193–197; Alexander H. Stephens to Thomas W. Thomas, May 23, 1854, quoted in Holt, *American Whig Party,* 820–821.

45. Quoted in Johannsen, *Stephen A. Douglas,* 434.

46. For a detailed analysis of the rise of the Republican Party, see William E. Gienapp, *The Origins of the Republican Party, 1852–1856* (New York, 1987).

47. Roy F. Nichols, *Blueprint for Leviathan: American Style* (New York, 1963), 85.

48. Michael F. Holt, "The Antimasonic and Know Nothing Parties," in Arthur M. Schlesinger, Jr., ed., *The History of U.S. Political Parties* (New York, 1973), 1:575–620.

49. A reference to the temperance movement that began during the Jacksonian era.

50. Quoted in Johannsen, *Stephen A. Douglas,* 460–461.

51. Holt, *American Whig Party,* 951–954.

52. Abraham Lincoln to Joshua Speed, August 29, 1855, in Ray P. Baker, ed., *The Collected Works of Abraham Lincoln* (Springfield, Ill., 1953), 2:320–323.

53. *New York Times,* June 15, 1855.

54. Tyler Anbinder, *Nativism and Slavery: The Northern Know Nothings and the Politics of the 1850s* (New York, 1992), 220–245; Arthur M. Schlesinger, Jr., and Fred Israel, eds., *History of American Political Parties* (New York, 1971), 2:1094.

55. Roger A. Bruns, "The Assault on Charles Sumner," in Schlesinger and Bruns, eds., *Congress Investigates: A Documentary History, 1792–1974* (New York, 1975), 2:817.

56. *National Intelligencer,* June 3, 1857; Schlesinger and Bruns, *Congress Investigates,* 2:816.

57. *Congressional Globe,* 34th Congress, 1st session, House Report No. 182, app., 137.

58. Preston S. Brooks to J. H. Brooks, May 23, 1856, Brooks Papers, University of South Carolina Library.

59. *Congressional Globe,* 34th Congress, 1st session, House Report No. 182, p. 23.

60. P. S. Brooks to J. H. Brooks. May 23, 1856, Brooks Papers, University of South Carolina Library.

61. Schlesinger and Bruns, *Congress Investigates,* 2:815–818.

62. *Congressional Globe,* 34th Congress, 1st session, 831–833.

63. Schlesinger and Bruns, *Congress Investigates,* 2:827–828. See also David Herbert Donald, *Charles Sumner and the Coming of the Civil War* (New York, 1960), 294–297.

64. *Frank Leslie's Illustrated Newspaper,* quoted in "An Account of a Brawl on the Floor of the House of Representatives," in Raymond W. Smock, ed., *Landmark Documents on the U.S. Congress* (Washington, 1999), 193–194.

65. Potter received this nickname when he was challenged to a duel and chose bowie knives as the weapons of choice.

66. Poore, *Perley's Reminiscences,* 1:532–536.

67. "An Account of a Brawl on the Floor of the House of Representatives," in Raymond W. Smock, ed., *Landmark Documents in the U.S. Congress* (Washington, D.C., 1999), 193.

68. William C. Allen, *History of the United States Capitol* (Washington, D.C., 2001), 185, 187, 196, 199.

69. Ibid., 206, 207, 209, 211.

70. Benjamin Brown French, *Witness to the Young Republic: A Yankee's Journal,* eds. John McDonough and Donald Cole (Hanover, N.H., 1989), 223; Mary Jane McLane, *Life in Washington and Life Here and There* (Philadelphia, 1985), 238–239.

71. Allen, *History of the United States Capitol,* 229, 230.

72. Ibid., 178–179.

73. A four-inch main was installed in the upper story.

74. Allen, *History of the United States Capitol,* 215–218, 242.

75. Ibid., 366–367.

76. Ibid., 242.

77. O. O. Stealey, *Twenty Years in the Press Gallery: A Concise History of Important Legislation from the 48th to the 58th Congress* (New York, 1906), 331.

78. These portraits still hang in the House chamber. Lafayette is honored because he was the first foreign visitor to speak before the House members.

79. Donald A. Ritchie, *Press Gallery: Congress and the Washington Correspondents* (Cambridge, Mass., 1991), 60.

80. McLane, *Life in Washington,* 2; Sara Pryor, *Reminiscences of Peace and War* (Freeport, N.Y., 1908), 4, 42.

81. Poore, *Perley's Reminiscences,* 2:25–27.

82. Robert W. Johannsen, ed., *The Lincoln-Douglas Debates of 1858* (New York, 1965), 88.

83. Ollinger Crenshaw, "The Speakership Contest of 1859–1860: John Sherman's Election: A Cause of Disruption?" in Joel H. Silbey, ed., *The Congress of the United States, 1789–1989, The United States Congress in a Partisan Political Nation, 1841–1896,* 2:326.

84. Potter, *Impending Crisis,* 389–390; James F. Rhodes, *History of the United States from the Compromise of 1850* (London, 1910), 2:420.

85. McLane, *Life in Washington*, 352.
86. Rhodes, *History of the United States*, 2:420.
87. Pryor, *Reminiscences of Peace and War*, 94.
88. Ibid., 98.
89. Rhodes, *History of the United States*, 2:426.
90. For an analysis of roll call votes in Congress from 1836 to 1860, see Thomas B. Alexander, *Sectional Stress and Party Strength: A Computer Analysis of Roll-Call Voting in the United States House of Representatives, 1836–1860* (Nashville, 1967).

CHAPTER VIII. THE CIVIL WAR, 1860–1865

1. James G. Blaine, *Twenty Years of Congress from Lincoln to Garfield* (Norwich, Conn., 1884), 1:215.
2. Quoted in Frank L. Klement, *The Limits of Dissent: Clement L. Vallandigham and the Civil War* (New York, 1998), 48.
3. Joel H. Silbey, *A Respectable Minority: The Democratic Party in the Civil War Era, 1860–1868* (New York, 1977), 34.
4. *Congressional Globe*, 36th Congress, 2nd session, 1461.
5. A "card" was a signed announcement of the members' intention to resign and was addressed and delivered to the Speaker.
6. Blaine, *Twenty Years of Congress*, 1:242–243.
7. Ibid., 243.
8. S. S. Cox, *Eight Years in Congress, 1857–1865* (New York, 1865), 24.
9. Seven were from Alabama, one from Florida, eight from Georgia, four from Louisiana, five from Mississippi, six from South Carolina, and two from Texas.
10. Robert D. Ilisevich, *Galusha A. Grow: The People's Candidate* (Pittsburgh, 1988), 198.
11. *Congressional Globe*, 36th Congress, 2nd session, 1432–1433.
12. James D. Richardson, *A Compilation of the Messages and Papers of the Presidents* (New York, 1907), 4: 3206–3213.
13. Abraham Lincoln, *Speeches and Writings, 1832–1858*, ed. Don E. Fehrenbacher (New York, 1989), 167.
14. Benjamin Perley Poore, *Perley's Reminiscences of Sixty Year in the National Metropolis* (Tecumseh, Mich., 1886), 75. The companies were the National Light Infantry from Pottsville, Pennsylvania; the Washington Artillerists, also from Pottsville; the Ringgold Light Artillery of Reading, Pennsylvania; the Logan Guards of Lewistown, Pennsylvania; and the Allen Infantry of Allentown, Pennsylvania. Heber S. Thompson, *The First Defenders* (n.p., 1910), 7.
15. Curtis Clay Pollock to Emily Clay Pollock, April 19, 1861, quoted in Leo L. Ward, "First Defenders Answered Lincoln's Call 137 Years Ago," in *Pottsville Republican*, April 18, 19, 1998. Pollock was wounded in the shoulder in the assault on Petersburg, Virginia, and died from lockjaw on June 23, 1864, at the age of twenty-two.
16. Thompson, *First Defenders*, 14.
17. Arthur M. Schlesinger, Jr., and Roger Bruns, eds., *Congress Investigates: A Documentary History, 1792–1974* (New York, 1975), 2: 226.

18. Thompson, *First Defenders,* 15.

19. Ibid., 16–17.

20. Quoted in William C. Allen, *History of the United States Capitol* (Washington, D.C., 2001), 314.

21. Mark E. Neely, *The Fate of Liberty: Abraham Lincoln and Civil Liberties* (New York, 1991), 11; *Congressional Globe,* 37th Congress, 1st session, 3.

22. Klement, *Limits of Dissent,* 76; *Congressional Globe,* 37th Congress, 1st session, 130.

23. Blaine, *Twenty Years of Congress,* 1:324; Ilisevich, *Galusha A. Grow,* 202–203

24. *Congressional Globe,* 37th Congress, 1st session, 5.

25. Ilisevich, *Galusha A. Grow,* 204.

26. Noah Brooks, *Washington, D.C., in Lincoln's Time* (Chicago, 1971), 27.

27. Ibid.; Poore, *Perley's Reminiscences,* 2: 101; George S. Boutwell, *Reminiscences of Sixty Years in Public Affairs* (New York, 1968), 10.

28. Hans L. Trefousse, *Thaddeus Stevens: Nineteenth-Century Egalitarian* (Chapel Hill, N.C., 1997), 113.

29. James M. McPherson, *Battle Cry of Freedom: The Civil War Era* (New York, 1988), 339–345.

30. When Johnson resigned four months later to become the governor of Tennessee, no other loyal southerner remained in Congress to replace him.

31. McPherson, *Battle Cry of Freedom,* 363–364.

32. Poore, *Perley's Reminiscences,* 2:103.

33. Mark E. Neely, Jr., "The Civil War," in Julian E. Zelizer, ed., *The American Congress* (Boston, 2004), 212.

34. Schlesinger and Bruns, eds., *Congress Investigates,* 2:1207–1208.

35. *Congressional Globe,* 37th Congress, 2nd session, 1589–1590, 1613–1623, 1629–1649, and app., 88–94, 101–103.

36. Quoted in Leonard P. Curry, *Blueprint for Modern America: Nonmilitary Legislation of the First Civil War Congress* (Nashville, 1968), 42–43.

37. Quoted in McPherson, *Battle Cry of Freedom,* 505.

38. Ibid., 506.

39. Quoted in ibid., 517.

40. Quoted in ibid., 561.

41. Quoted in Joanna D. Cowden, *"Heaven will Frown on Such a Cause As This": Six Democrats Who Opposed Lincoln's War* (Lanham, Md., 2001), 1, 6.

42. Quoted in Trefousse, *Thaddeus Stevens,* 130–131.

43. McPherson, *Battle Cry of Freedom,* 610–611.

44. Ibid., 627–645.

45. Noah Brooks, *Washington, D.C. in Lincoln's Time* (Chicago, 1971), 74. Brooks was a contemporary news reporter.

46. Ibid., 322–323. Brumidi continued painting murals and frescoes throughout the Capitol building, including hallways, until his death in 1880 at the age of seventy-five.

47. Crawford initially intended to include a liberty cap, but Secretary of War Jefferson Davis objected because the cap was a symbol of freed slaves. Crawford died in 1857, but he had completed the plaster model for the statue in his Rome studio.

48. Allen, *History of the United States Capitol*, 325–326. The dome includes 8,909,200 pounds of ironwork and 5,214,000 pounds of supporting masonry. It cost $1,047,291. The statue alone cost $23,796.82 and weighs approximately 15,000 pounds.

49. Thomas V. Walter to Amanda Walter, December 2, 1863, quoted in ibid., 327.

50. Henry L. Dawes to Electra Dawes, December 8, 1863, Dawes Papers, Library of Congress; Herman Belz, "The Etheridge Conspiracy of 1863: A Projected Conservative Coup," in Joel Silbey, ed., *The Congress of the United States: Its Origins and Early Development* (New York, 1991), 587, 589.

51. Belz, "Etheridge Conspiracy," 591.

52. Ibid., 598; Asher C. Hinds, *Precedents of the House of Representatives of the United States* (Washington, D.C., 1907), 1:68–74; Henry L. Dawes to his wife, December 7, 1863, Dawes Papers, Library of Congress.

53. Belz, "Etheridge Conspiracy," 599.

54. These territories included Arizona, Colorado, Dakota, Idaho, Montana, Nebraska, Nevada, New Mexico, Utah and Washington.

55. *Congressional Globe*, 38th Congress, 1st session, 4–5; Belz, "Etheridge Conspiracy," 599–600.

56. Belz, "Etheridge Conspiracy," 600.

57. Brooks, *Washington, D.C.*, 30.

58. Schlesinger and Bruns, eds., *Congress Investigates*, 2:231.

59. Ibid., 236.

60. Brooks, *Washington*, 98–99.

61. Schlesinger and Bruns, eds., *Congress Investigates*, 2:236.

62. Trefousse, *Stevens*, 137.

63. Brooks, *Washington, D.C.* 184–187.

64. Secretary of State William Seward announced on December 18, 1865, that the 13th Amendment had been adopted, following the action by Oregon, the twenty-seventh state to ratify it.

65. Quoted in Ernest B. Furgurson, *Freedom Rising: Washington in the Civil War* (New York, 2004), 350–351.

66. Richardson, *Messages and Papers*, 5:3478.

67. Champ Clark, *My Quarter Century of American Politics* (New York, 1920), 206; Donald R. Kennon and Rebecca M. Rogers, *The Committee on Ways and Means: A Bicentennial History, 1789–1989* (Washington, D.C., 1989), 167.

68. Poore, *Perley's Reminiscences*, 2:169.

69. Blaine, *Twenty Years of Congress*, 2:7–8, 15.

70. Thaddeus Stevens to Andrew Johnson, May 16, 1865, quoted in Trefousse, *Thaddeus Stevens*, 163–164.

71. Benjamin B. Kendrick, *The Journal of the Joint Committee of Fifteen on Reconstruction* (New York, 1969), 138.

CHAPTER IX. RECONSTRUCTION, 1865–1867

1. Benjamin B. Kendrick, *The Journal of the Joint Committee of Fifteen on Reconstruction* (New York, 1969), 17–18.

2. Ibid., 139.

3. Ibid., 140–141.

4. *Harper's New Monthly Magazine* (December 1865): 128.

5. LaWanda Cox and John H. Cox, *Politics, Principle, and Prejudice, 1865–1866* (New York, 1963), 141–142.

6. Hans L. Trefousse, *Andrew Johnson: A Biography* (New York, 1989), 237–238.

7. Emily Edson Briggs, *The Olivia Letters: Being Some History of Washington City for Forty Years* (New York, 1906), 11.

8. Cox and Cox, *Politics, Principle, and Prejudice*, 141–142.

9. *Congressional Globe*, 39th Congress, 1st session, 3. See also Edward McPherson, *The Political History of the United States of America During the Period of Reconstruction* (New York, 1972), x.

10. *Congressional Globe*, 39th Congress, 1st session, 3, 4, 5; George S. Boutwell, *Reminiscences of Sixty Years in Public Affairs* (New York, 1968), 7; Hans L. Trefousse, *Thaddeus Stevens: Nineteenth-Century Egalitarian* (Chapel Hill, N.C., 1997) 175–176; Benjamin Perley Poore, *Perley's Reminiscences of Sixty Years in the National Metropolis* (Tecumseh, Mich., 1886), 2:211.

11. *Congressional Globe,* 39th Congress, 1st session, 72–75.

12. Eric McKitrick, *Andrew Johnson and Reconstruction* (New York, 1960), 258.

13. *Congressional Globe,* 39th Congress, 1st session, 72–75, House Report No. 30, pt. 2, 30–31, 55–56; Trefousse, *Thaddeus Stevens,* 176.

14. The nine House members consisted of Radicals Thaddeus Stevens, George S. Boutwell of Massachusetts, and Elihu B. Washburne of Illinois; Moderates Justin S. Morrill, John A. Bingham of Ohio, Roscoe Conkling of New York and Henry T. Blow of Missouri; and Democrats Andrew J. Rogers of New Jersey and Henry Grider of Kentucky. Trefousse, *Thaddeus Stevens,* 176.

15. Quoted in Eric Foner, *Reconstruction: America's Unfinished Revolution, 1863–1877* (New York, 1988), 247.

16. *Congressional Globe*, 39th Congress, 1st session, 72–75; Trefousse, *Thaddeus Stevens,* 177. Over in the Senate Charles Sumner, who had recovered from the beating "Bully Brooks" had administered, declared that the South had committed "state suicide." Sumner was considered "too ultra" in his views and was therefore left off the joint committee. Foner, *Reconstruction, 239.*

17. Ibid., 243; *Congressional Globe,* 39th Congress, 1st session, 299, 655, 688.

18. Trefousse, *Thaddeus Stevens,* 181; Shelby M. Cullom, *Fifty Years of Public Service* (Chicago, 1911), 150.

19. Foner, *Reconstruction,* 243–244.

20. Ibid., 245.

21. Ibid., 250–251

22. *Congressional Globe,* 39th Congress, 1st session, 1861.

23. Ibid., 2nd session, 1761.

24. Foner, *Reconstruction,* 231–232

25. Ibid., 251; *Congressional Globe,* 39th Congress, 1st session, 1755–1760.

26. Ibid., 3148; Foner, *Reconstruction,* 254–255.

27. Ibid.

28. *Congressional Globe,* 39th Congress, 1st session, 2765; Foner, *Reconstruction,* 257, 258.

29. Ibid., 261.

30. Ibid., 261–262.

31. Carl Schurz, *The Reminiscences of Carl Schurz* (New York, 1907–1908), 3: 243; Trefousse, *Andrew Johnson,* 262–266.

32. Quoted in Foner, *Reconstruction,* 271.

33. Alvin M. Josephy, *On the Hill: A History of the American Congress* (New York, 1979), 227.

34. Foner, *Reconstruction,* 273.

35. *Congressional Globe,* 39th Congress, 2nd session, 250–253.

36. Ibid., 1213–1215.

37. Foner, *Reconstruction,* 274.

38. Quoted in Josephy, *On the Hill,* 228.

39. McKitrick, *Johnson and Reconstruction,* 493–494.

40. Ibid., 500.

41. David Miller De Witt, *The Impeachment and Trial of Andrew Johnson* (Madison, Wisc., 1967), 344–345, 347; *Congressional Globe,* 40th Congress, 2nd session, 1610.

42. De Witt, *Impeachment and Trial,* 359.

43. Ibid., 358.

44. *Congressional Globe,* 40th Congress, 2nd session, 1337.

45. Raymond W. Smock, ed., *Landmark Documents on the U.S. Congress* (Washington, D.C., 1999), 217–221. De Witt, *Impeachment and Trial,* 379.

46. Poore, *Perley's Reminiscences,* 2:229.

47. In Louisiana he was known as "Beast" Butler because of his decrees when serving as military commander of the state.

48. Boutwell, *Reminiscences,* 119–120.

49. De Witt, *Impeachment and Trial,* 382, 385, 386, 388.

50. Briggs, *Olivia Letters,* 48, 49.

51. De Witt, *Impeachment and Trial,* 395–396.

52. Briggs, *Olivia Letters,* 34.

53. *Congressional Globe,* 40th Congress, 2nd session, 1612–1613; De Witt, *Impeachment and Trial,* 416, 466, 483.

54. De Witt, *Impeachment and Trial,* 513.

55. Trefousse, *Andrew Johnson,* 319.

56. Ibid., 326

57. Ibid., 327.

58. Editorial, "Dissenting Senators," in *Harper's Weekly,* June 6, 1868, 354.

59. Robert W. Cherny, *American Politics in the Gilded Age, 1868–1900* (Wheeling, Ill., 1997), 49.

60. David W. Blight, *Race and Reunion: The Civil War in American Memory* (Cambridge, Mass., 2001), 100–102.

61. Quoted in ibid., 105.

62. Bruce A. Ragsdale and Joel D. Treese, *Black Americans in Congress, 1870–1989* (Washington, D.C., 1990), 31–32, 45, 81, 117–118, 145, 149; Briggs, *Olivia Letters*, 274.

63. John W. Forney, *Anecdotes of Public Men* (New York, 1970), 1:216, 321–322.

64. Blight, *Race and Reunion*, 114.

65. Foner, *Reconstruction*, 455.

66. U.S. *Statutes at Large*, 1871, 16: 566.

67. Harry James Brown and F. D. Williams, eds., *The Diary of James A. Garfield* (East Lansing, Mich., 1967–1981), 2:258.

68. Foner, *Reconstruction*, 533; *Congressional Record*, 43rd Congress, 1st session, 344, 382.

69. Ibid., 334, 379, 381.

70. Ibid., 407–410.

71. Foner, *Reconstruction*, 555–556. In 1883 the Supreme Court struck down the Civil Rights Act of 1875 as unconstitutional, insisting that the federal government could not regulate individual behavior in matters of race relations.

72. In the case *United States v. Reese* in 1876, the Supreme Court ruled that the 15th Amendment did not give anyone the right to vote. It merely guaranteed that racial discrimination would not be employed to prevent anyone from exercising the right to vote.

73. The Supreme Court ruled that states had withheld voting rights from certain classes of males (the propertyless blacks, criminals) and were within their rights to withhold suffrage from all women.

74. Mary Gabriel, *Notorious Victoria: The Life of Victoria Woodhull, Uncensored* (Chapel Hill, N.C., 1998), 69–70, 73, 82–83; Nancy E. McGlen and Karen O'Connor, *Women's Rights: The Struggle for Equality in the Nineteenth and Twentieth Centuries* (New York, 1983), 49.

75. Quoted in Cherny, *American Politics in the Gilded Age*, 58.

76. Both candidates received more popular votes than any previous presidential candidate. Keith Ian Polakoff, *The Politics of Inertia: The Election of 1876 and the End of Reconstruction* (Baton Rouge, 1973), 199–200.

77. Blight, *Race and Reunion*, 136.

78. Quoted in Theodore Clarke Smith, *The Life and Letters of James Abram Garfield* (Hamden, Conn., 1968), 1:613.

79. *New York Sun*, November 9, 1876; entry for November 12, 1876, in T. Harry Williams, ed., *The Diary of a President, 1875–1881: Covering the Disputed Election, the End of Reconstruction and the Beginning of Civil Service* (New York, 1964), 50–51.

80. Polakoff, *Politics of Inertia*, 221–222.

81. Ibid., 269–270.

82. Ibid., 280, 283–284; Poore, *Perley's Reminiscences*, 2: 325, 330–331.

83. Polakoff, *Politics of Inertia*, 286, 289.

84. The hotel was owned by the city's wealthiest black resident, James Wormley.

85. Polakoff, *Politics of Inertia*, 309, 310.

CHAPTER X. THE GILDED AGE, 1869–1895

1. More recent historians are uncomfortable with the term because it tends to emphasize the scandals and "obscure" some aspects of the era that had "great and long-term significance." See, for example, Robert W. Cherny, *American Politics in the Gilded Age, 1868–1900* (Wheeling, Ill., 1997), 2.

2. Quoted in Donald R. Kennon and Rebecca M. Rogers, *The Committee on Ways and Means: A Bicentennial History, 1789–1989* (Washington, 1989), 174.

3. *House Journal,* 42nd Congress, 3rd session, 429.

4. *Congressional Globe,* 42nd Congress, 3rd session, 11–12.

5. "Affairs of the Union Pacific Railroad Company," U.S. House of Representatives, House Report No. 77, in ibid., 15–23.

6. Ibid., i–xix.

7. Ibid., 497.

8. J. B. Crawford, *The Crédit Mobilier of America: Its Origins and History* (Boston, 1880), 215–216.

9. *Congressional Globe,* 42nd Congress, 3rd session, 2100.

10. Harry James Brown and F. D. Williams, eds., *The Diary of James A. Garfield* (East Lansing, Mich., 1967–1981), 2:254.

11. Although one visitor argued that only about twenty-five members were worth their salaries, "most could not make more than half as much by the sale of their talents in any other capacity." Frank G. Carpenter, *Carp's Washington* (New York, 1960), 27.

12. O. O. Stealey, *Twenty Years in the Press Gallery: A Concise History of Important Legislation from the 48th to the 58th Congress* (New York, 1906), 17–18.

13. Stephen Stathis, *Landmark Legislation, 1774–2002* (Washington, D.C., 2003), 111.

14. Eric Foner, *Reconstruction: America's Unfinished Revolution* (New York, 1988), 523.

15. Ronald M. Peters, Jr., *The American Speakership: The Office in Historical Perspective* (Baltimore, 1990), 56; Edward Stanwood, *James Gillespie Blaine* (Boston, 1905), 119.

16. William S. McFeely, *Grant: A Biography* (Norwalk, Conn., 1987), 410–416.

17. Ibid., 432–436, 440.

18. Davis Saville Muzzey, *James G. Blaine: A Political Idol of Other Days* (Port Washington, N.Y., 1934), 83–84, 89–90.

19. Ibid., 91.

20. Ibid., 92.

21. Ibid., 83–84.

22. Ibid., 94.

23. *Congressional Record*, 44th Congress, 1st session, 3602–3617.

24. Muzzey, *Blaine*, 94–95.

25. Alvin M. Josephy, *On the Hill: A History of the American Congress* (New York, 1979), 263.

26. Champ Clark, *My Quarter Century of American Politics* (New York, 1920), 1:275–276.

27. Quoted in Kathryn Jacob, *Capital Elites: High Society in Washington, D.C., after the Civil War* (Washington, D.C., 1995), 54.

28. Benjamin Perley Poore, *Perley's Reminiscences of Sixty Years in the National Metropolis* (Tecumseh, Mich., 1886), 2:261–263; Carpenter, *Carp's Washington*, 5–7.

29. Mary Clemmer Ames, *Ten Years in Washington* (Hartford, Conn., 1873), 72–73.

30. Ibid.

31. Poore, *Perley's Reminiscences*, 2:261–263; Jacob, *Capital Elites*, 61–62.

32. Poore, *Perley's Reminiscences*, 2:263.

33. Ibid., 2:522.

34. Jacob, *Capital Elites*, 69–70.

35. Stealey, *Twenty Years in the Press Gallery*, 42.

36. Quoted in Cherny, *American Politics*, 56.

37. Poore, *Perley's Reminiscences*, 2:315–316.

38. Although by the 1850s the Rules Committee had begun to assume greater authority when it briefly became a standing committee during the 31st and 32nd Congresses.

39. Woodrow Wilson, *Congressional Government* (New Brunswick, N.J., 2000), 79.

40. James A. Garfield, "A Century of Progress," *Atlantic Monthly* 40 (1877): 61.

41. Theodore Clarke Smith, ed., *Life and Letters of James A. Garfield* (New Haven, 1925), 675; *Congressional Record,* 45th Congress, 3rd session, 2381.

42. James D. Richardson, *A Compilation of the Messages and Papers of the Presidents* (Washington, D.C., 1897), 7:523. 531.

43. Leonard D. White, *The Republican Era, 1869–1901: Study in Administrative History* (New York, 1958), 35–38.

44. Garfield, *Life and Letters,* 684.

45. Noah Brooks, *Statesmen: Men of Achievement* (New York, 1893), 330; David S. Barry, *Forty Years in Washington* (Boston, 1924), 80.

46. H. Wayne Morgan, *From Hayes to McKinley: National Politics, 1877–1896* (Syracuse, N.Y., 1969), 120.

47. A. Hoogenboom, *Outlawing the Spoils: A History of the Civil Service Reform Movement, 1865–1883* (Urbana, Ill., 1961), 249–251.

48. Morgan, *From Hayes to McKinley,* 162–164.

49. When this exclusion act expired in 1892, the Geary Act extended it for another ten years, and this extension, made permanent in 1902, required each Chinese resident, such as a teacher or merchant, who was exempt from the Exclusion Act to register and obtain a certificate of residence. In 1943 Congress repealed all the exclusion acts.

50. James A. Barnes, *John G. Carlisle: Financial Statesman* (New York, 1931), 68–72.

51. Ibid., 48–49.

52. Stealey, *Twenty Years in the Press Gallery*, 44.

53. Ibid., 51.

54. Barnes, *John G. Carlisle,* 77.

55. Cherny, *American Politics*, 32, 75.

56. Quoted in Donald A. Ritchie, *Press Gallery: Congress and the Washington Correspondents* (Cambridge, Mass., 1991), 137.

57. Clark, *My Quarter Century of American Politics,* 206.

58. Stealey, *Twenty Years in the Press Gallery*, 11.

59. Edward Winslow Martin, *Behind the Scenes in Washington* (New York, 1873), 221.

60. Poore, *Perley's Reminiscences,* 2:513–515.

61. Carpenter, *Carp's Washington,* 13.

62. Ibid., 15.

63. Ibid., 24.

64. Cherny, *American Politics,* 81–82, 83, 84.

65. Ibid., 601–602.

66. Quoted in Margaret Susan Thompson, *The "Spider Web": Congress and Lobbying in the Age of Grant* (Ithaca, N.Y., 1985), 48, 49, 51.

67. Sargent, *Public Men and Events* (Philadelphia, 1875), 2: 48.

68. Carlton Jackson, *Presidential Vetoes, 1792–1945* (Athens, Ga., 1967), 149.

CHAPTER XI. "CZAR" REED AND "UNCLE JOE" CANNON, 1888–1910

1. Champ Clark, *My Quarter Century of American Politics* (New York, 1920), 1: 277; William A. Robinson, *Thomas B. Reed, Parliamentarian* (New York, 1930), 132, 133; Josephy, *On the Hill,* 260, 279.

2. *Congressional Record,* 47th Congress, 1st session, 4306; Robinson, *Reed,* 87.

3. Robinson, *Reed,* 197–198; *Washington Post,* December 3, 1889.

4. Thomas B. Reed, "Rules of the House of Representatives," *Century Magazine* 37:792–795. See also his article "Obstruction in the National House," *North American Review* 149:421–428.

5. L. White Busby and Katherine Graves Busby, *Uncle Joe Cannon: The Story of a Pioneer American* (New York, 1927), passim. See also Sarah A. Binder, *Minority Rights, Majority Rule: Partisanship and the Development of Congress* (Cambridge, U.K., 1997).

6. During the first eighty years of the history of the House, the clerk called out the full name of the members. Then in 1879 the clerk shortened it by using the honorific "Mister" followed by the surname. To shorten it even further, the clerk in 1911 simply called the members by their surnames only. Today few roll calls are necessary, except for the election of the Speaker, but when they are held only the surname is used. Neil MacNeil, *Forge of Democracy The House of Representatives* (New York, 1963), 57; Donnald K. Anderson, clerk of the House from 1987 to 1995, to the author, September 29, 2004.

7. O. O. Stealey, *Twenty Years in in the Press Gallery: A Concise History of Important Legislation from the 48th to the 58th Congress* (New York, 1906), 81.

8. Joseph G. Cannon, "Dramatic Scenes in My Career in Congress: When Reed Counted a Quorum," *Harper's Magazine* 140 (March 1920): 436.

9. *Congressional Record,* 51st Congress, 1st session, 948–951.

10. Ibid., 951.

11. United States Congress, House Committee on Rules, *A History of the Committee on Rules: 1st to 97th Congress, 1789–1981* (Washington, D.C., 1983), 71.

12. Robinson, *Reed,* 220–224; Josephy, *On the Hill,* 261.

13. Robinson, *Reed.* Quoted in Samuel W. McCall: *The Life of Thomas Brackett Reed* (Boston, 1914) 82–83.

14. Clark, *My Quarter Century of American Politics*, 290.
15. Robinson, *Reed*, 132–133.
16. *Washington Post*, March 1, 12, 1890; *New York Times*, March 12, 1890.
17. H. Wayne Morgan, *William McKinley and His America* (Syracuse, N.Y., 1963), 130.
18. Samuel W. McCall, *The Life of Thomas Brackett Reed* (Boston, 1914), 115.
19. H. Wayne Morgan, *From Hayes to McKinley: National Politics, 1877–1896* (Syracuse, N.Y., 1969) 335–345, 349–356.
20. Tom E. Terrill, *The Tariff, Politics, and American Foreign Policy, 1874–1901* (Westport, Conn., 1973), 161–164.
21. Henry Steele Commager, *Documents of American History* (New York, 1963), 2: 136.
22. Reed's biographer, William A. Robinson, says that in an article in the *North American Review* in March 1892, Reed made no claim to authorship of the quotation. Robinson, *Reed*, 251.
23. Morgan, *From Hayes to McKinley*, 355.
24. Joseph Gurney Cannon, *The Memoirs of Joseph Gurney "Uncle Joe" Cannon* (Danville, Ill, 1996), 102.
25. S. Walter Martin, "Charles F. Crisp, Speaker of the House," *The Georgia Review* 8 (Summer 1954), 167; Stealey, *Twenty Years in the Press Gallery*, 106.
26. Barnes, *Carlisle*, 101.
27. Robinson, *Reed*, 284.
28. Stephen Stathis, *Landmark Legislation, 1774–2002* (Washington, D.C., 2003), 138.
29. Morgan, *From Hayes to McKinley*, 454.
30. Ibid., 458–459.
31. Festus P. Summers, *William M. Wilson and Tariff Reform* (New Brunswick, N.J., 1953), 184–185.
32. Robinson, *Reed*, 307–310.
33. Summers, *William M. Wilson and Tariff Reform*, 184–185.
34. Robinson, *Reed*, 321.
35. Morgan, *From Hayes to McKinley*, 477.
36. Commager, *Documents of American History*, 2: 178.
37. Morgan, *From Hayes to McKinley*, 521–523.
38. A complete listing of Republican and Democratic whips from the 56th to the 109th Congress can be found in Appendix IX and Appendix X.
39. *Congressional Record*, 55th Congress, 2nd session, 1628. Quoted in Robinson, *Reed*, 364–365.
40. Ibid., 365.
41. James Conaway, *America's Library: The Story of the Library of Congress, 1800–2000* (Washington, D.C., 2000), 75. According to a report issued in 2000, the library now holds 110 million volumes.
42. The building was given the name Thomas Jefferson Building on June 13, 1980, by the then Librarian of Congress, Daniel Boorstin. Behind the building an "Annex" was built in 1939 and is now called the John Adams Building. Across the street, facing Independence Avenue, the James Madison Building, opened to the public

in 1980, houses huge collections of manuscripts, maps, newspapers, prints, photo-graphs and audio materials.

43. William C. Allen, *History of the United States Capitol* (Washington, D.C., 2001), 298, 308.

44. The building was officially named the Cannon House Office Building in 1962 to honor Speaker Joseph Cannon. Two additional office buildings were later erected: the Longworth Building (named in honor of Speaker Nicholas Longworth), com-pleted in 1933, and the Rayburn Building (named in honor of Speaker Sam Ray-burn), completed in 1965.

45. H. Wayne Morgan, *McKinley and His America* (Kent, Ohio, 2003), 222–225; Com-mager, *Documents of American History,* 2: 186–187.

46. Morgan, *McKinley and His America,* 272–278; Robinson, *Reed,* 359, 360.

47. Robinson, *Reed,* 159.

48. McCall, *Reed,* 234.

49. *Congressional Record,* 55th Congress, 2nd session, 6019.

50. Commager, *Documents of American History,* 2:187.

51. Bacon et al., eds., *Encyclopedia of the United States Congress,* 964.

52. McCall, *Reed,* 371; *Washington Post,* February 26, 1899.

53. Robinson, *Reed,* 370.

54. Stealey, *Twenty Years in the Press Gallery,* 146.

55. Bruce A. Ragsdale and Joel D. Treese, *Black Americans in Congress, 1870–1989* (Washington, D.C., 1990), 160.

56. Quoted in Alvin M. Josephy, *On the Hill: A History of the American Congress* (New York, 1979), 277; McCall, *Reed,* 302.

57. Stathis, *Landmark Legislation,* 150.

58. Interview in *Review of Reviews* from 1903, quoted in Blair Belles, *Tyrant from Il-linois* (New York, 1951), 8.

59. C. W. Thompson, *Party Leaders of the Time* (New York, 1906), 177; Scott William Rager, "Uncle Joe Cannon: The Brakeman of the House of Representatives," in Roger H. Davidson et al., eds., *Masters of the House: Congressional Leadership over Two Centuries* (Boulder, Colo., 1998), 66.

60. William R. Gwinn, *Uncle Joe Cannon: Archfoe of Insurgency* (New York, 1957), 177.

61. Scott William Rager, "Uncle Joe Cannon," in Davidson et al., eds., *Masters of the House,* 66, 67.

62. George Norris, *Fighting Liberal: The Autobiography of George W. Norris* (Lincoln, Neb., 1945), 11.

63. Rager, "Uncle Joe Cannon," 67.

64. *Congressional Record,* 61st Congress, 2nd session, 3436.

65. Norris, *Fighting Liberal,* 110. See also Richard Lowitt, *George W. Norris: The Persis-tence of a Progressive* (Urbana, Ill., 1971).

66. *Congressional Record,* 61st Congress, 2nd session, 3304; MacNeil, *Forge of Democ-racy,* 79.

67. A complete listing of the majority and minority leaders of the Republican and Demo-cratic Parties from the 56th to the 109th Congress can be found in Appendix 8.

68. MacNeil, *Forge of Democracy,* 81.

69. Charles W. Thompson, *Party Leaders of the Time* (New York, 1906), 149–150.

70. Rager, "Uncle Joe Cannon," 65.

71. Alice R. Longworth, *Crowded Hours* (New York, 1933), 170. As late as the 1960s, spittoons were distributed to the members.

72. MacNeil, *Forge of Democracy*, 98.

73. Rager, "Uncle Joe Cannon," 67–68.

74. Quoted in Richard and Lynne Cheney, *Kings of the Hill: Power and Personality in the House of Representatives* (New York, 1983), 125.

75. He was furious when muckraker David Graham Phillip described the Senate as "a den of plutocrats" in a series of articles in the *Cosmopolitan* magazine. Ellen Fitzpatrick, "Muckraking and Its Aftermath," in *Muckraking: Three Landmark Articles* (New York, 1994), 113.

76. *Congressional Record*, 56th Congress, 1st session, 7.

77. Carl E. Hatch, *The Big Stick and the Congressional Gavel: A Study of Theodore Roosevelt's Relations with His Last Congress, 1907–1909* (New York, 1967), 37, 70–71.

78. U.S. Congress, House Committee on Rules, *History of the Committee on Rules* 10.

79. Rager, "Uncle Joe Cannon," 75–76.

80. Cited in ibid., 77.

81. And his resolution did not qualify under the rules of Calendar Wednesday.

82. Norris, *Fighting Liberal*, 113.

83. Ibid., 117–118.

84. Alice Roosevelt Longworth, *Crowded Hours* (New York, 1933), 174.

85. *Congressional Record*, 61st Congress, 2nd session, 3292, 3425–3433. For a complete discussion of the Cannon revolt, see United States Congress, House Committee on Rules, *A History of the Committee on Rules* (Washington, D.C., 1983).

CHAPTER XII. THE SPEAKER ECLIPSED AND REVIVED, 1910–1928

1. L. White Busby and Katherine Graves Busby, *Uncle Joe Cannon: The Story of a Pioneer American* (New York, 1927), 269.

2. William Rager, "Uncle Joe Cannon: The Brakeman of the House of Representatives," in Roger H. Davidson et al., eds., *Masters of the House* (Boulder, Colo., 1998), 80.

3. William C. Allen, *History of the United States Capitol* (Washington, D.C., 2001), 396.

4. Cordell Hull, *The Memoirs of Cordell Hull* (New York, 1948), 46.

5. Ibid., 59, 62.

6. Ibid.

7. Evans C. Johnson, *Oscar W. Underwood: A Political Biography* (Baton Rouge, La., 1980), 140.

8. Hull, *Memoirs*, 64.

9. Oscar King Davis, "Where Underwood Stands: An Interview with the Democratic Leader of the House," *Outlook* 99 (September, 23, 1911): 199.

10. Robert W. Woolley, "Underwood of Alabama: Democracy's New Chieftain," *American Review of Reviews* 44 (September 1911): 298.

11. Hull, *Memoirs*, 62. Cannon also allowed the minority party to decide committee assignments, but subject to his veto.

12. Ibid.

13. Almost from the beginning of the Republic, few ex-senators became members of the House, "but there has been a constant procession of House members to the Senate." Thomas Reed once said that House members went to the Senate to retire. But Champ Clark offered five reasons for the "procession": "First, the longer term; second, Senators being fewer, their votes are more important; third, patronage; fourth, participation in treaty-making power; fifth, greater social recognition." Champ Clark, *My Quarter Century of American Politics* (New York, 1920), 219.

14. Alvin M. Josephy, *On the Hill: A History of the American Congress* (New York, 1990), 294.

15. John Milton Cooper., Jr., *The Warrior and the Priest: Woodrow Wilson and Theodore Roosevelt* (Cambridge, Mass., 1983), 235.

16. Arthur Link, *Wilson and the Progressive Era* (New York, 1954), 35.

17. So called because he supposedly preferred the cactus over the Texas wildflower.

18. Donald R. Kennon and Rebecca M. Rogers, *Committee on Ways and Means: A Bicentennial History, 1789–1989* (Washington, D.C., 1989), 251.

19. Link, *Wilson and the Progressive Era*, 41.

20. Stephen W. Stathis, *Landmark Legislation, 1774–2002* (Washington, D.C., 2003), 169.

21. Link, *Wilson and the Progressive Era*, 70, 74–75.

22. Neil MacNeil, *Forge of Democracy: The House of Representatives* (New York, 1963), 252.

23. Link, *Wilson and the Progressive Era*, 214.

24. Alex Matthews Arnett, *Claude Kitchin and the Wilson War Policies* (Boston, 1937), 90, 160.

25. Ibid., 92.

26. Link, *Wilson and the Progressive Era*, 225–251.

27. Quoted in Hannah Josephson, *Jeannette Rankin, First Lady in Congress: A Biography* (Indianapolis, 1974), 57.

28. Ellen Maury Slayden, *Washington Wife: Journal of Ellen Maury Slayden from 1897–1919* (New York: 1962), 298–299.

29. Ibid., 299.

30. Quoted in J. P. Tumulty, *Woodrow Wilson As I Knew Him* (New York, 1921), 259.

31. Quoted in Arnett, *Kitchin*, 227.

32. Quoted in ibid., 235, 245–246.

33. Josephson, *Rankin*, 75–76.

34. Ibid.

35. Arnett, *Kitchin*, 236.

36. The House passed the prohibition on September 23, 1918, by a vote of 171 to 34.

37. Center for Legislative Archives, National Archives and Records Administration, *Our Mothers Before Us: Women and Democracy* (Washington, 1998), 5–6.

38. "Women Pioneers on Capitol Hill, 1917–1934: Women in Congress," manuscript, Office of History and Preservation, U.S. House of Representatives, 1, forthcoming.

39. Ibid., 2, 5. Edith Nourse Rogers of Massachusetts took her deceased husband's

seat in a special election in 1925. No one expected her to last. But she fooled them. She served in the House from 1925 to 1960. Jill S. Pollack, *Women on the Hill: A History of Women in Congress* (New York, 1996), 44. Other widows who succeeded to their deceased husband's seats in Congress include Florence Prag Kahn, Margaret Chase Smith, Frances Bolton, Maurine Neuberger and Lindy Boggs.

40. Donald C. Bacon, "Nicholas Longworth: The Genial Czar," in Davidson et al., eds., *Masters of the House,* 127; Richard Cheney and Lynne Cheney, *Kings of the Hill* (New York, 1983), 144–146.

41. Alice R. Longworth, *Crowded Hours* (New York, 1933), 281.

42. Ibid., 322.

43. John D. Hicks, *Republican Ascendancy, 1921–1933* (New York, 1960), 21.

44. David M. Kennedy, *Freedom from Fear: The American People in Depression and War, 1929–1945* (New York, 1999), 18.

45. Longworth, *Crowded Hours,* 313, 315.

46. From "Cassiday, Capitol Bootlegger," *Washington Post,* October 24, 1930. The representative in question could have been "Cactus Jack" Garner or Nicholas Longworth, both heavy drinkers if not alcoholics.

47. *Washington Post,* November 1, 1929; July 23, October 24, 25, 26, 1930.

48. Ibid., March 5, 1925.

49. "Women Pioneers on Capitol Hill," 5.

50. Jill S. Pollack, *Women on the Hill: A History of Women in Congress* (New York, 1996), 49–50.

51. Carol Felsenthal, *Alice Roosevelt Longworth* (New York, 1988), 135.

52. President Warren G. Harding, inaugural address, March 4, 1921, quoted in Robert J. Banis, ed., *Inaugural Addresses: Presidents of the United States* (Chesterfield, Mo., 2001), 226–233.

53. *New York Times,* November 11, 1923; Woodrow Wilson, radio address, November 10, 1923, quoted in Arthur S. Link, ed., *The Papers of Woodrow Wilson* (Princeton, N.J., 1992) 68: 466–467.

54. Floyd Millard Riddick, *The United States Congress: Organization and Procedures* (Manassas, Va., 1949), 123.

55. John Higham, *Strangers in the Land: Patterns of American Nativism, 1860–1925* (New Brunswick, N.J., 1955), 311.

56. Cheney and Cheney, *Kings of the Hill,* 150–151.

57. *Congressional Quarterly's Guide to Congress* (Washington, D.C., 2000), 56.

58. *Congressional Record,* 68th Congress, 1st session, 1137.

59. Ibid., 949.

60. Ibid., 1896–1902, 5657.

61. 68th Congress, 1st session, 5918–5920.

62. Stathis, *Landmark Legislation,* 186.

63. "The LaFollette Platform of 1924," in Commager, *Documents of American History,* 2: 375–377.

64. Arthur M. Schlesinger, Jr., *The Crisis of the Old Order, 1919–1933* (Cambridge, Mass., 1957), 98.

65. Bacon, "Longworth," 131.

66. Schlesinger, *Crisis of the Old Order,* 102.

67. Cheney and Cheney, *Kings of the Hill,* 152.

68. Bacon, "Longworth," 129.

69. Robert Tailey, "So This Is Congress," *Baltimore Post,* May 30, 1924.

70. Bacon, "Longworth," 134.

71. Although Longworth had been married to Alice Roosevelt for eighteen years, they never had a child. Not until 1925. He was cheered when he entered the House chamber after his daughter's birth, even though many members gossiped that the biological father was Senator William Borah. The rumor was so widespread that Alice herself jokingly acknowledged that the infant, Paulina, bore a striking resemblance to Uncle Joe Cannon. Alice betrayed her husband more than once, the last time when she destroyed his papers after he died, along with his invaluable Stradivarius violin.

72. William Tyler Page, "Mr. Speaker Longworth," in *Scribner's Monthly Magazine* (March 1928): 272–280.

73. Bacon, "Longworth," 131.

74. Ibid., 134.

75. *Congressional Record,* 69th Congress, 1st session, 382; Cheney and Cheney, *Kings of the Hill,* 154.

76. *Congressional Record,* 69th Congress, 1st session, 387, 388.

77. Bacon, "Longworth," 134.

78. Clinton W. Gilbert in "The Daily Mirror of Washington," *Philadelphia Public Ledger,* March 2, 1926, quoted in Bacon, "Longworth," 135.

79. *New York Herald Tribune,* April 10, 1931.

80. The name "derived from Longworth's first public office on the Cincinnati school board." Carol Felsenthal, *Alice Roosevelt Longworth* (New York, 1988), 159. This hideaway (Room H-128) was one of the Speaker's perks. It is one flight down from the House chamber. It was the room where Harry Truman was found on April 12, 1945, and asked to hurry to the White House where he learned that FDR was dead and that he was now the President of the United States.

81. Frances Spatz Leighton, *Fishbait: The Memoirs of the Congressional Doorkeeper* (Englewood Cliffs, N.J., 1977), 55. According to Fishbait Miller, Speaker Longworth was "one of the greatest womanizers in history on Capitol Hill." Miller came to the House two years after Longworth died but heard many stories about the former Speaker during his forty-two years of service.

CHAPTER XIII. THE GREAT DEPRESSION, THE NEW DEAL AND THE OUTBREAK OF WAR, 1928–1941

1. Arthur M. Schlesinger, Jr., *The Crisis of the Old Order, 1919–1933* (Cambridge, Mass., 1957), 129.

2. Bruce A. Ragsdale and Joel D. Treese, *Black Americans in Congress, 1870–1989* (Washington, D.C., 1990), 36; Eliot M. Rudwick, "Oscar De Priest and the Jim Crow Restaurant in the U.S. House of Representatives," *Journal of Negro Education* 35 (Winter 1966): 77–82.

3. David M. Kennedy, *Freedom From Fear: The American People in Depression and War, 1929–1945* (New York, 1999), 44.

4. *Baltimore Sun,* April 10, 1931, quoted in Donald C. Bacon, "Nicholas Longworth: The Genial Czar," in Roger H. Davidson et al., eds., *Masters of the House* (Boulder, Colo., 1998), 140.

5. Quoted in Alvin M. Josephy, *On the Hill: A History of the American Congress* (New York, 1979), 316.

6. William Starr Myers and Walter H. Newton, *The Hoover Administration: A Documentary Narrative* (New York, 1936), 149–150.

7. Howard Zinn, *La Guardia in Congress* (New York, 1958), 209ff.

8. Kennedy, *Freedom from Fear,* 83–85.

9. Stephen W. Stathis, *Landmark Legislation, 1774–2002* (Washington, D.C., 2003), 196.

10. William E. Leuchtenburg, *Franklin D. Roosevelt and the New Deal* (New York, 1963), 13–14.

11. Kennedy, *Freedom from Fear,* 63.

12. Schlesinger, *Crisis of the Old Order,* 314.

13. Quoted in Leuchtenburg, *Roosevelt and the New Deal,* 9.

14. Quoted in ibid., 30.

15. Ibid., 41.

16. Quoted in James T. Patterson, *Congressional Conservatism and the New Deal* (Lexington, Ky., 1967), 5, 7.

17. Later, Harry L. Hopkins, Felix Frankfurter and Samuel I. Rosenman became important advisers to FDR.

18. Arthur M. Schlesinger, Jr., *The Coming of the New Deal* (New York, 1959), 2–25.

19. *Congressional Record,* 73rd Congress, 1st session, 206, 209, 211, 214.

20. Quoted in D. B. Hardeman and Donald C. Bacon, *Rayburn: A Biography* (Austin, Tex., 1987), 154.

21. Thomas P. O'Neill, Jr., *Man of the House: The Life and Political Memoirs of Speaker Tip O'Neill* (New York, 1987), 129.

22. *Congressional Record,* 73rd Congress, 1st session, 4190.

23. Leuchtenburg, *Roosevelt and the New Deal,* 61.

24. Lawrence Elliott, *Little Flower: The Life and Times of Fiorello La Guardia* (New York, 1983), 72.

25. Booth Mooney, *Roosevelt and Rayburn* (Philadelphia, 1971), 54.

26. Donald R. Kennon and Rebecca M. Rogers, *The Committee on Ways and Means: A Bicentennial History, 1789–1989* (Washington, D.C., 1989), 280.

27. Leuchtenburg, *Roosevelt and the New Deal,* 116.

28. MacNeil, *Forge of Democracy: The House of Representatives* (New York, 1963), 291.

29. Kennedy, *Freedom from Fear,* 270.

30. Quoted in Hardeman and Bacon, *Rayburn,* 179.

31. Kennedy, *Freedom from Fear,* 328–329.

32. Ibid., 331–334.

33. Quoted in Leuchtenburg, *Roosevelt and the New Deal,* 233.

34. Ibid., 234.

35. Kennedy, *Freedom from Fear,* 340.

36. Patterson, *Congressional Conservatism,* 277–279.

37. Ibid., 181.
38. Arthur M. Schlesinger, Jr., and Roger Bruns, eds., *Congress Investigates: A Documentary History* (New York, 1975), 4:2925, 2929, 2935.
39. Leuchtenburg, *Roosevelt and the New Deal,* 280.
40. Joseph W. Martin, *My First Fifty Years in Politics* (New York, 1960), 82–83.
41. Ibid., 272–273.
42. Kennedy, *Freedom from Fear,* 426–432.
43. Hardeman and Bacon, *Rayburn,* 227, 245.
44. Martin, *My First Fifty Years in Politics,* 91, 92.
45. Kennedy, *Freedom from Fear,* 455–456.
46. Ibid., 469.
47. *Christian Science Monitor,* January 7, 1941.
48. Quoted in Hardeman and Bacon, *Rayburn,* 261–262.
49. Ibid.
50. Ibid., 264.
51. Ibid., 267–270.
52. Kennedy, *Freedom from Fear,* 516–523.
53. *Congressional Record,* 77th Congress, 1st session, 9504–9505.
54. Hardeman and Bacon, *Rayburn,* 275–277.

CHAPTER XIV. THE HOT AND COLD WARS, 1941–1952

1. Roland Young, *Congressional Politics in the Second World War* (New York, 1956), 29; Stephen W. Stathis, *Landmark Legislation, 1774–2002* (Washington, D.C., 2003), 220.
2. "Women in Congress, 1917–2005," Office of History and Preservation, U.S. House of Representatives, forthcoming.
3. Years later Congress tried to redress this wrong in 1988 by granting each survivor a flat sum of $20,000.
4. David M. Kennedy, *Freedom from Fear: The American People in Depression and War, 1929–1945* (New York, 1999), 492–564.
5. Joseph W. Martin, *My First Fifty Years in Politics* (New York, 1960), 100–101.
6. Randolph E. Paul, *Taxation in the United States* (Boston, 1954), 297.
7. Donald R. Kennon and Rebecca M. Rogers, *The Committee on Ways and Means: A Bicentennial History, 1789–1989* (Washington, D.C., 1989), 302.
8. Roland Young, *Congressional Politics in the Second World War* (New York, 1956), 22–23.
9. Ibid., 24, 47.
10. *Congressional Record,* 78th Congress, 1st session, 10.
11. Bruce J. Dierenfield, *Keeper of the Rules: Congressman Howard W. Smith of Virginia* (Charlotte, Va., 1987), 103.
12. Young, *Congressional Politics,* 19–21.
13. Kennedy, *Freedom from Fear,* 484–488.
14. Ibid., 682–685.
15. Young, *Congressional Politics,* 140.
16. Kennon and Rogers, *Committee on Ways and Means,* 305.

17. Kennedy, *Freedom from Fear*, 786–787.

18. David McCullough, *Truman* (New York, 1996), 341–342.

19. Carl Albert, *Little Giant* (Norman, Okla., 1990), 172.

20. James C. Wright to the author, July 27, 2005.

21. *Adam by Adam: The Autobiography of Adam Clayton Powell, Jr.* (New York, 1991), 71.

22. Thomas P. O'Neill, Jr., *Man of the House: The Life and Political Memoirs of Speaker Tip O'Neill* (New York, 1987), 127. Today this room contains nothing relating to Rayburn, except perhaps a small round mural on the wall with a star and the words "State of Texas."

23. Josephy, *On the Hill*, 340.

24. *Congressional Record*, 79th Congress, 1st Session, 3389.

25. Kennedy, *Freedom from Fear*, 638–642, 647.

26. *Committee on Un-American Activities, Hearings Regarding the Communist Infiltration of the Motion Picture Industry*, 80th Congress, 1st session (Washington, D.C., 1947), 217.

27. Robert K. Carr, *The House Committee on Un-American Activities* (Ithaca, N.Y., 1998), 56, 101.

28. Martin Gilbert, *Churchill: A Life* (London, 1991), 866.

29. Stathis, *Landmark Legislation*, 230.

30. Today there are twenty-one House standing committees.

31. D. B. Hardeman and Donald C. Bacon, *Rayburn: A Biography* (Austin, Tex., 1987), 319. In 2004 there were 18,098 lobbyists representing 17,728 clients. I am grateful to Jeff Trandahl, former clerk of the House of Representatives, for this information.

32. Clarence Brown related this story to Neil MacNeil; it can be found in MacNeil's *Forge of Democracy: The House of Representatives* (New York, 1963), 103.

33. Congressional Research Service et al., *A History of the Committee on Rules* (Washington, D.C., 1983), 154.

34. *Washington Post*, June 23, 1949; *New York Times*, January 21, 1951.

35. Kennedy, *Freedom from Fear*, 642–643.

36. MacNeil, *Forge of Democracy*, 295–296.

37. McCullough, *Truman*, 565–566.

38. Quoted in ibid., 548.

39. Ibid., 562–565.

40. For the election of 1948, see ibid., 624ff.

41. *Congressional Record*, 81st Congress, 1st session, A6.

42. Ibid., 706; 2nd session.

43. U.S. Senate, Select Committee to Study Censure Charges, Hearings on S. Res. 301, 1–16, quoted in Arthur Schlesinger, Jr., and Roger Bruns, eds., *Congress Investigates*, 5: 3903; Thomas C. Reeves, *The Life and Times of Joe McCarthy* (New York, 1982), 660–662.

44. McCullough, *Truman*, 834–856.

45. Extended accounts of the renovation can be found in the *Washington Post*, February 15, June 19, 1949; January 1, 1951. Pursuant to House Resolution 740, passed

on September 27, 1962, the motto "In God We Trust" was attached to the wall directly behind and above the Speaker's rostrum. The thirteen stars were replaced with twelve stars for purely decorative purposes, six stars on each side of the motto.

46. *Congressional Quarterly's Guide to Congress* (Washington, D.C., 2000), 67.

CHAPTER XV. THE GATEKEEPER AND THE FIGHT FOR CIVIL RIGHTS, 1953–1961

1. Stephen E. Ambrose, *Eisenhower: The President* (New York, 1984), 115.
2. Donald R. Kennon and Rebecca M. Rogers, *The Committee on Ways and Means: A Bicenntenial History, 1789–1989* (Washington, D.C., 1989), 312.
3. Gary W. Reichard, *The Reaffirmation of Republicanism: Eisenhower and the Eighty-Third Congress* (Knoxville, 1975), 98.
4. Ibid.; Reichard, *Reaffirmation of Republicanism,* 101–103; "The Congress: Maneuvers on the Hill," *Time,* June 1, 1953, 14; Alfred Steinberg, *Sam Rayburn: A Biography* (New York, 1975) 281.
5. Reichard, *Reaffirmation of Republicanism,* 129–132.
6. *Washington Post,* March 2, 1954; February 22, 2004.
7. Stephen W. Stathis, *Landmark Legislation, 1774–2002* (Washington, D.C., 2003), 240–241.
8. Ronald M. Peters, Jr., *The American Speakership: The Office in Historical Perspective* (Baltimore, 1997), 130.
9. Carl Albert, "The Speakership in My Time," in Ronald M. Peters, Jr., ed., *The Speaker: Leadership in the U.S. House of Representatives* (Washington, D.C., 1994), 183.
10. Democrats reformed the organization of the office in 2003, which provided the whip with a senior chief deputy whip, 7 chief deputies, 30 senior whips, 40 assistant whips and 24 regional whips.
11. Carl Albert, *Little Giant* (Norman, Okla., 1990), 199, 203, 205, 207.
12. O'Neill, *Man of the House: The Life and Political Memoirs of Speaker Tip O'Neill* (New York, 1987), 204.
13. Albert, *Little Giant,* 209, 211.
14. Clem Miller, *Member of the House: Letters of a Congressman* (New York, 1962), 93.
15. O'Neill, *Man of the House,* 157.
16. In June 2005 the Senate formally apologized for failing to enact antilynching legislation.
17. O'Neill, *Man of the House,* 138.
18. Albert, *Little Giant,* 227; Carl Albert, interview, reported in the *Washington Post,* August 19, 1958.
19. Dierenfield, *Keeper of the Rules,* 138.
20. James A. Robinson, *The House Rules Committee* (Indianapolis, 1963), passim.
21. Albert, *Little Giant,* 223–225; Bruce J. Dierenfield, *Keeper of the Rules: Congressman Howard W. Smith of Virginia* (Charlottesville, 1987), 136–137.
22. Richard Bolling, *House Out of Order* (New York, 1965), 176.

23. Ibid., 177.

24. D. B. Hardeman and Donald C. Bacon, *Rayburn: A Biography* (Austin, Tex., 1987), 419.

25. Ibid.

26. Robert Dallek, *Lone Star Rising: Lyndon Johnson and His Times, 1908–1960* (New York, 1991), 496; Robert A. Caro, *The Years of Lyndon Johnson: Master of the House* (New York, 2000), 3:785–786. South Carolina's Strom Thurmond was the principal author of the manifesto.

27. *Congressional Record*, 84th Congress, 2nd session, 4459–4464.

28. *Congressional Quarterly Almanac*, 1956, 458–460.

29. Ibid., 460.

30. Ibid., 461.

31. These included George W. Andrews of Alabama, Oren Harris of Arkansas, A. Sydney Herlong, Jr., of Florida, James C. Davis of Georgia, Noble Gregory of Kentucky, F. Edward Hebert of Louisiana, William Colmer and John Bell Williams of Mississippi, Graham Barden of North Carolina, James P. Richards of South Carolina, Tom Murray of Tennessee, O. Clark Fisher of Texas, and Smith, Watkins M. Abbitt and Burr P. Harrison of Virginia.

32. Telephone interview between Bruce J. Dierenfield and A. Sydney Herlong, September 11, 1983, in Dierenfield, *Keeper of the Rules*, 152.

33. Interview between Carl Elliot and Bruce J. Dierenfield, January 23, 1984, in ibid., 152.

34. Ibid.

35. Hardeman and Bacon, *Rayburn*, 420.

36. Bolling, *House Out of Order*, 181.

37. Hardeman and Bacon, *Rayburn*, 420–421.

38. Ibid., 421.

39. James C. Wright to the author, July 27, 2005.

40. Peters, *American Speakership*, 132–133.

41. Albert, *Little Giant*, 233.

42. Ibid., 234.

43. Ibid., 233–234.

44. Dallek, *Lone Star Rising*, 496.

45. *Congressional Quarterly Almanac*, 1957, 554.

46. Albert, *Little Giant*, 213.

47. Ibid., 215–217.

48. Ibid., 222.

49. Carl Vinson Institute of Government, *Carl Vinson: A Legacy of Public Service Institute of Government*, (Athens, Ga., 2002), 90; Albert, *Little Giant*, 222.

50. Ibid., 223–225.

51. Ibid., 225.

52. *Congressional Quarterly Almanac*, 1957, 556.

53. Bolling, *House Out of Order*, 185.

54. They promised to help him kill a school construction bill that he found unacceptable.

55. *Congressional Quarterly Almanac,* 1957, 559.

56. *Washington Post,* June 20, 1957; *Congressional Quarterly Almanac,* 1957, 558–559; *Congressional Record,* 85th Congress, 2nd session, 9518.

57. Caro, *Johnson,* 3:914–916; Dallek, *Lone Star Rising,* 524–528.

58. Quoted in *A History of the Committee on Rules,* 173; the remark has also been attributed to Rayburn.

59. Dierenfield, *Keeper of the Rules,* 158.

60. Ambrose, *Eisenhower,* 407–413.

61. Caro, *Johnson,* 3: 893.

62. *Congressional Quarterly Almanac,* 1958, 290–291.

63. Dallek, *Lone Star Rising,* 562.

64. Allen, *History of the Capitol,* 420–433; William Allen to author, November 15, 2005.

65. Albert, *Little Giant,* 237.

66. *Time* magazine quoted in Neil MacNeil, *Forge of Democracy: The House of Representatives* (New York, 1963), 79.

67. Albert, *Little Giant,* 238.

68. Ibid., 239.

69. Ibid., 240.

70. Hardeman and Bacon, *Rayburn,* 455; Albert, *Little Giant,* 240.

71. Hardeman and Bacon, *Rayburn,* 459.

72. Albert, *Little Giant,* 242.

73. Ibid., 243; Hardeman and Bacon, *Rayburn,* 462.

74. Ibid., 402–403; Albert, *Little Giant,* 242–243.

75. Jerome Doolittle, "The Gentleman from Georgia Goes Home," *Saturday Evening Post* 237 (December 5, 1964): 26.

76. Hardeman and Bacon, *Rayburn,* 464–465; Dierenfield, *Keeper of the Rules,* 182–183; Albert, *Little Giant,* 244.

CHAPTER XVI. THE GREAT SOCIETY, VOTING RIGHTS AND VIETNAM, 1961–1969

1. D. B. Hardeman and Donald C. Bacon, *Rayburn: A Biography* (Austin, Tex., 1987), 348.

2. "The Leadership of Sam Rayburn," *House Document* 247, 87th Congress, 1st session, xv, 2, 3, 117–118.

3. Ibid., 19.

4. James C. Wright to the author, July 27, 2005.

5. *Congressional Quarterly Almanac,* 1961, 69.

6. Ibid.

7. Ibid., 224.

8. Ibid.

9. Ibid., 74; ibid., 1962, 234. Impacted aid, whereby the government paid part of the cost of constructing and operating schools on behalf of children of parents who either worked or lived on federal property, was also part of this bill.

10. Ibid., 1961, 161.

11. Bruce J. Dierenfield, *Keeper of the Rules: Congressman Howard W. Smith of Virginia* (Charlottesville, 1987), 186.

12. Carl Albert, *Little Giant* (Norman, Okla., 1990), 269.

13. Neil MacNeil, *Forge of Democracy: The House of Representatives* (New York, 1963), 122.

14. *Congressional Quarterly Almanac,* 1962, 145.

15. Robert Michel to the author, January 19, 2005.

16. *Congressional Quarterly Almanac,* 1962, 145.

17. Ibid., 146.

18. Ibid., 146, 64–65.

19. MacNeil, *Forge of Democracy,* 397.

20. Dierenfield, *Keeper of the Rules,* 187; *Congressional Quarterly Almanac,* 1962, 64–65.

21. Robert Dallek, *An Unfinished Life: John F. Kennedy, 1917–1963* (New York, 2003), 514–518.

22. *Congressional Quarterly Almanac,* 1963, 336.

23. Quoted in James L. Sundquist, *Politics and Policy* (Washington, 1968), 261.

24. Ibid., 262.

25. Dallek, *Unfinished Life,* 604.

26. Donald Rumsfeld to the author, June 21, 2005.

27. Jerald ter Horst, *Gerald Ford and the Future of the Presidency* (New York, 1974), 81; Rumsfeld to the author, June 21, 2005; Henry Z. Scheele, "Prelude to the Presidency; An Examination of the Gerald R. Ford–Charles A. Halleck House Minority Leadership Contest," *Presidential Studies Quarterly* 25 (Fall 1995): 770.

28. James M. Cannon, "Gerald R. Ford," in Roger H. Davidson et al., eds., *Masters of the House* (Boulder, Colo., 1998), 260.

29. Rumsfeld to the author, June 21, 2005.

30. *Congressional Quarterly Almanac,* 1963, 61.

31. Quoted in Hugh Davis Graham, *The Civil Rights Era: Origins and Development of National Policy, 1960–1972* (New York, 1990), 134; *Congressional Quarterly Almanac,* 1964, 343.

32. Robert Dallek, *Flawed Giant: Lyndon Johnson and His Times, 1961–1973* (New York, 1998), 60–62.

33. Ibid., 345.

34. Ibid., 377.

35. Dierenfield, *Keeper of the Rules,* 194.

36. Carl M. Brauer, "Women, Activists, Southern Conservatives, and the Prohibition of Sex Discrimination in Title VII of the 1964 Civil Rights Act," *Journal of Southern History* 49 (February, 1983): 46, 49–51.

37. Dierenfield, *Keeper of the Rules,* 198.

38. Dallek, *Flawed Giant,* 120.

39. *Congressional Quarterly Almanac,* 1964, 377, 378.

40. Dallek, *Flawed Giant,* 11–121.

41. *Congressional Quarterly Almanac,* 1964, 66.

42. Rumsfeld to the author, June 21, 2005.

43. Ibid.

44. Gerald Ford, *A Time to Heal* (New York, 1979), 77.

45. Rumsfeld to the author, June 21, 2005.

46. Ibid.

47. Scheele, "Prelude to the Presidency," 767–785.

48. Ford, *Time to Heal,* 67.

49. Rumsfeld to the author, June 21, 2005.

50. *Congressional Quarterly Almanac,* 1965, 25.

51. Stathis, *Landmark Legislation,* 264–69.

52. Thomas P. O'Neill, Jr., *Man of the House: The Life and Political Memoirs of Speaker Tip O'Neill* (New York, 1987), 186.

53. Donald R. Kennon and Rebecca M. Rogers, *The Committee on Ways and Means: A Bicentennial History, 1789–1989* (Washington, D.C., 1989), 322.

54. Graham, *Civil Rights Era,* 165.

55. *Congressional Quarterly Almanac,* 1965, 538.

56. Ibid., 540.

57. Ibid., 556.

58. Ibid., 540, 557; Dierenfield, *Keeper of the Rules,* 202–203.

59. *Congressional Quarterly Almanac,* 1965, 559–561.

60. Ibid., 573.

61. Dierenfield, *Keeper of the Rules,* 204.

62. Tom Foley, "The Foley Speakership," in Walter Oleszek, ed., *The Cannon Centenary Conference: The Changing Nature of the Speakership* (Washington, D.C., 2005), 69–70.

63. These precepts were formulated from a study by Professor Richard F. Fenno, Jr., and can be found in James S. Fleming, *Window on Congress: A Congressional Biography of Barber B. Conable, Jr.* (Rochester, N.Y., 2004), 76–84.

64. Thomas Foley to the author, January 18, 2005.

65. Charles Neu, *America's Lost War: Vietnam: 1945–1975* (Wheeling, Ill., 2005), 78–80.

66. *Congressional Quarterly Almanac,* 1965, 74.

67. Ibid., 7.

68. Neu, *America's Lost War,* 119.

69. Albert, *Little Giant,* 301.

70. Dallek, *Flawed Giant,* 398–399; Julian E. Zelizer, *Taxing America: Wilbur D. Mills, Congress, and the State, 1945–1975* (Cambridge, U.K., 1998), 1.

71. Congressional Research Service et al., *A History of the Committee on Rules* (Washington, D.C., 1983), 201–203.

72. *Congressional Quarterly Almanac,* 1966, 75.

73. Charles V. Hamilton, *Adam Clayton Powell, Jr.* (New York, 1991), 447–449.

74. Ibid., 460–468.

75. *Congressional Quarterly Almanac,* 1968, 202.

76. Ibid., 1969, 1022.

77. Ibid., 1968, 658.

78. Ibid.

79. Ronald M. Peters, Jr., *The American Speakership: The Office in Historical Perspective* (Baltimore, 1997), 147, 149; Richard Bolling, *House Out of Order* (New York, 1965), 74–76.

80. Dallek, *Flawed Giant*, 514–515; Neu, *America's Lost War*, 130–139.

81. Dallek, *Flawed Giant*, 519–530.

82. Ibid., 522–525, 533; *Congressional Quarterly Almanac*, 1968, 782.

83. Ibid., 592; Neu, *America's Lost War*, 149, 152.

84. *Congressional Quarterly Almanac*, 1969, 24.

85. Quoted in Nelson W. Polsby, *How Congress Evolves: Social Bases of Institutional Change* (New York, 2004), 38.

86. Peters, *American Speakership*, 149.

87. Bolling, *House Out of Order*, 74–76; Peters, *American Speakership*, 149.

88. Ibid., 150.

CHAPTER XVII. SCANDAL, WATERGATE AND REFORM, 1969–1980

1. *Congressional Quarterly Almanac*, 1969, 1017.

2. Ibid., 1019.

3. Ibid., 1017.

4. Ibid., 164–165.

5. Robert Sherrill, "We Can't Depend on Congress to Keep Congress Honest," *New York Times*, July 19, 1970.

6. *Congressional Quarterly Almanac*, 1969, 1024.

7. *New York Times*, June 10, 17, 18, 27, July 3, 10, 1970; *Congressional Quarterly Almanac*, 1970, 66.

8. Gerald Ford, *A Time to Heal* (New York, 1979), 81.

9. *New York Times*, editorial, December 27, 1968; Marjorie Hunter, "7 House Democrats Begin Jockeying for Election as Floor Leader," in *New York Times*, May 30, 1970.

10. Ronald M. Peters, Jr., *The American Speakership: The Office in Historical Perspective* (Baltimore, 1997), 151.

11. *Congressional Quarterly Almanac*, 1970, 68–69.

12. Sherrill, "We Can't Depend on Congress."

13. Ibid.

14. *Congressional Quarterly Almanac*, 1973, 33.

15. Five of the eight convictions of conspiracy, bribery and perjury against Dowdy were later reversed by an appellate court. Three counts of perjury remained.

16. Sherrill, "We Can't Depend on Congress."

17. Ibid.

18. Stathis, *Landmark Legislation*, 280.

19. Peters, *American Speakership*, 153.

20. Steven S. Smith and Christopher J. Deering, *Committees in Congress* (Washington, D.C., 1990), 47.

21. John Jacobs, *A Rage for Justice: The Passion and Politics of Phillip Burton* (Berkeley, Calif., 1995), xxi.

22. Unrecorded teller votes between 1970 and 1971 dropped from 51 to 2. Julian Zel-

izer, *On Capitol Hill: The Struggle to Reform Congress and Its Consequences* (New York, 2004), 128.

23. Dan Rostenkowski to the author, July 1, 2004.

24. Peters, *American Speakership*, 153, 156, 158.

25. Thomas P. O'Neill, *Man of the House: The Life and Political Memoirs of Speaker Tip O'Neill* (New York, 1987), 215–216.

26. Rostenkowski to the author, July 1, 2004.

27. *New York Times*, January 20, 1971.

28. *Congressional Quarterly Almanac*, 1971, 10.

29. *New York Times*, January 4, 20, 1971. The Republicans naturally picked Ford as minority leader and Leslie C. Arends as whip.

30. *Congressional Quarterly Almanac*, 1971, 130.

31. Ibid., 17.

32. Ibid., 890–891.

33. Ibid., 1970, 706; ibid., 1971, 656–657.

34. Ibid., 1971, 722; ibid., 1973, 258.

35. Jacobs, *Rage for Justice*, 239.

36. Ibid., 240

37. *Congressional Quarterly Almanac*, 1973, 27.

38. Ibid., 45.

39. Carl Albert, "The Speakership in My Time," in Ronald M. Peters, Jr., ed., *The Speaker: Leadership in the U.S. House of Representatives,* (Washington, 1994), 191.

40. *Congressional Quarterly Almanac*, 1973, 27, 45.

41. Ibid., 31. But the Steering and Policy Committee, it should be remembered, was "firmly under the control of the leadership"—that is, the Speaker, the majority leader, the caucus chairman, the whip and the deputy whip. Carl Albert, *Little Giant* (Norman, Okla., 1990), 347; Zelizer, *On Capitol Hill*, 166.

42. Peters, *American Speakership*, 177.

43. *Congressional Quarterly Almanac*, 1973, 755–756, 760–769; ibid., 1974, 634.

44. Ibid., 1974, 634–637.

45. Peters, *American Speakership*, 184.

46. *Congressional Quarterly Almanac*, 1974, 638.

47. Charles Johnson to the author, March 9, 2005. And these reforms demonstrated "the determination of the Congress to defend its own prerogatives against the claims of an over-reaching executive branch." Peters, *American Speakership,* 179.

48. Ibid., 188–189.

49. Ford, *Time to Heal,* 105.

50. Ibid., 67.

51. *Congressional Quarterly Almanac*, 1973, 33.

52. Ibid., 1974, 871.

53. O'Neill, *Man of the House,* 245, 249.

54. *Congressional Quarterly Almanac*, 1974, 869.

55. Albert, *Little Giant,* 362, 364.

56. *Congressional Quarterly Almanac*, 1974, 867.

57. Ibid., 871–872.

58. Albert, *Little Giant*, 365–366.

59. Debate on Articles of Impeachment, July 24, 25, 26, 27, 29, 30, 1974, 93rd Congress, 2nd session, quoted in Raymond W. Smock, *Landmark Documents on the U.S. Congress* Washington, D.C., 1991) 493.

60. "Impeachment of Richard M. Nixon" in *House Report* 93–105, in Smock, *Landmark Documents*, 488–495.

61. *Washington Post*, August 26, 2003.

62. Quoted in Stephen W. Stathis, *Landmark Legislation, 1774–2000* (Washington, D.C., 2003), 287.

63. These aides had frequently alienated members of the House by attempting to "discipline" those who criticized the White House by blocking invitations to state dinners or Sunday prayer breakfasts. Ford said he had learned from Rayburn to "disagree without being disagreeable. . . . Nixon's aides never understood that, and it developed into one of the worst failings of his Administration." Ford, *Time to Heal*, 89.

64. Zelizer, *On Capitol Hill*, 159, 165.

65. James S. Fleming, *Window on Congress: A Congressional Biography of Barber B. Conable, Jr.* (Rochester, N.Y., 2004), 114–116.

66. Thomas Foley to the author, January 18, 2005.

67. Pat Schroeder, *24 Years of House Work . . . and the Place Is Still a Mess: My Life in Politics* (Kansas City, 1998), 31–32.

68. Ibid., 40–41.

69. Ibid., 57.

70. Foley to the author, January 18, 2005; O'Neill, *Man of the House*, 282.

71. Foley to the author, January 18, 2005.

72. Jacobs, *A Rage for Justice*, 265.

73. *Congressional Quarterly Almanac*, 1976, 25.

74. Ibid., 26.

75. Ibid., 23–25.

76. On July 23, 1976, freshman representative Allen T. Howe, a Democrat from Utah, was found guilty of soliciting sex for hire from two undercover officers pretending to be prostitutes. He was sentenced to thirty days in prison and a $150 fine and was defeated in the 1976 election. Ibid., 26.

77. Foley to the author, January 18, 2005.

78. O'Neill, *Man of the House*, 272.

79. Richard Cheney to the author, December 22, 2004.

80. Gary Hymel, one of Tip O'Neill's administrative assistants, to the author, June 2, 2004.

81. Henry Hyde to the author, December 15, 2004.

82. Jacobs, *Rage for Justice*, 300.

83. Ibid., 302.

84. Dan Rostenkowski to the author, June 3, 2005.

85. Jacobs, *Rage for Justice*, 301–302, 304, 309, 311.

86. Ibid., 318–320.

87. Ibid., 321–322, 324; James C. Wright to the author, July 27, 2005; Foley to the author, January 18, 2005.

88. Ibid; Rostenkowski to the author, June 3, 2005.

89. O'Neill, *Man of the House*, 333.

90. Interview with Gary Hymel, June 2, 2004.

91. Newt Gingrich to the author, July 13, 2004. Speaker Gingrich had this story on good authority. He said it is a "true story."

92. O'Neill, *Man of the House*, 305.

93. Fleming, *Window on Congress*, 261, 272.

94. John Murtha to the author, March 14, 2005.

95. *Congressional Quarterly Almanac*, 1980, 20.

96. Zelizer, *On Capitol Hill*, 201–204.

97. Fleming, *Window on Congress*, 268; *Congressional Quarterly Almanac*, 1980, 13-B.

98. O'Neill, *Man of the House*, 336.

99. Rostenkowski to the author, July 1, 2004.

100. Ibid.

101. O'Neill, *Man of the House*, 344–345.

CHAPTER XVIII. THE CONSERVATIVE REVOLUTION, 1981–2001

1. Paul D. Erickson, *Reagan Speaks: The Making of an American Myth* (New York, 1985), 139–145.

2. Thomas P. O'Neill, Jr., *Man of the House: The Life and Political Memoirs of Speaker Tip O'Neill* (New York, 1987), 341.

3. Ibid., 344.

4. Robert Michel to the author, January 19, 2005. John Murtha, Democrat from Pennsylvania, a thirty-year veteran of the House, agreed with Michel. "Today is the most partisan I've ever seen," he declared. In the old days "you got along, there was comity." Now, "it's business dealings, rather than any kind of personal dealings at all, and it's too bad." John Murtha to the author, March 14, 2005.

5. O'Neill, *Man of the House*, 333, 335; Tip O'Neill and Gary Hymel, *All Politics Is Local* (New York, 1994), 184.

6. Don Sundquist, "A Governor's Reflections on Life in the U.S. House," in Lou Frey, Jr., and Michael T. Hayes, eds., *Inside the House: Former Members Reveal How Congress Really Works* (Lanham, N.Y., 2001), 312.

7. *Congressional Quarterly Almanac*, 1981, 21, 91, 103.

8. G. V. Montgomery, "Wielding Influence as a Conservative Democrat," in Frey and Hayes, *Inside the House*, 154. The Boll Weevils were later succeeded by the Blue Dogs. Where the Boll Weevils sprang mainly from the South, the Blue Dogs came "from all over the country," said Montgomery. Ibid., 155.

9. Richard Cheney to the author, December 22, 2004.

10. O'Neill, *Man of the House*, 345, 349.

11. Stephen W. Stathis, *Landmark Legislation, 1774–2002* (Washington, D.C., 2003), 310.

12. *Congressional Quarterly Almanac*, 1981, 14, 21; Stathis, *Landmark Legislation*, 313.

13. O'Neill, *Man of the House*, 344.

14. Ibid., 288.

15. *Congressional Quarterly Almanac,* 1977, 826. Prior to the arrival of television, House members got breaking news from a ticker tape in the Speaker's lobby, just outside the House chamber.

16. Quoted in Julian Zelizer, *On Capitol Hill: The Struggle to Reform Congress and Its Consequences* (New York, 2004), 208.

17. Charles Johnson to the author, March 9, 2005.

18. Newt Gingrich to the author, July 13, 2004.

19. Zelizer, *On Capitol Hill,* 206, 212.

20. Gingrich to the author, July 13, 2004.

21. James S. Fleming, *Window on Congress: A Congressional Biography of Barber B. Conable, Jr.* (Rochester, N.Y., 2004), 83.

22. Cheney to the author, December 22, 2004.

23. Henry Hyde to the author, December 15, 2004.

24. Quoted in Zelizer, *On Capitol Hill,* 212.

25. Gingrich to the author, July 13; Cheney to the author, December 22, 2004.

26. Quoted in Judith Warner and Max Berley, *Newt Gingrich: Speaker to America* (New York, 1995), 178.

27. Ibid.

28. Gingrich to the author, July 13, 2004.

29. Zelizer, *On Capitol Hill,* 214.

30. Quoted in ibid.

31. Gingrich to the author, July 13, 2004.

32. Zelizer, *On Capitol Hill,* 214; O'Neill, *Man of the House,* 354.

33. *Congressional Quarterly Almanac,* 1984, 208.

34. Gingrich to the author, July 13, 2004.

35. O'Neill, *Man of the House,* 354–355.

36. Murtha to the author, March 14, 2005.

37. Fleming, *Window on Congress,* 305–306.

38. James Goldsborough, "Passing the Bill to Our Children," *San Diego Union-Tribune,* January 19, 2004.

39. As a freshman representative from Texas in 1967, George Bush won a seat on the Ways and Means Committee, a very rare occurrence for a first-term congressman. With his later election as President, Bush became the eighth Ways and Means member in history to attain the White House.

40. Stathis, *Landmark Legislation,* 314.

41. *Congressional Quarterly Almanac,* 1986, 400.

42. Ibid., 1986, 415.

43. Jim Wright, "Challenges That Speakers Face," in Ronald M. Peters, Jr., ed., *The Speaker: Leadership in the U.S. House of Representatives* (Washington, D.C., 1994), 233–234; James C. Wright to the author, July 27, 2005; *Congressional Quarterly Almanac,* 1986, 400.

44. Bacon, ed., *Encyclopedia of the United States Congress,* 3: 1159; Stathis, *Landmark Legislation,* 327; Wright, "Challenges That Speakers Face," 234.

45. Murtha to the author, March 14, 2005.

46. Bacon, *Encyclopedia of the United States Congress,* 3: 1159; Stathis, *Landmark Leg-*

islation, 327; Wright, "Challenges That Speakers Face," 234; Wright to the author, July 27, 2005.

47. Gingrich to the author, July 13, 2004.

48. *Congressional Quarterly Almanac,* 1986, 431.

49. Murtha to the author, March 14, 2005.

50. Raymond W. Smock, ed., *Landmark Documents on the U.S. Congress* (Washington, D.C., 1999), 588, 589, 591, 593.

51. Wright to the author, July 27, 2005. Bob Livingston also suggests that Reagan's mental faculties had begun to fade due to the Alzheimer's disease that afflicted him. Bob Livingston to the author, September 27, 2005.

52. Warner and Berley, *Newt Gingrich,* 102.

53. Cheney to the author, December 22, 2004.

54. Ibid.

55. *Congressional Quarterly Almanac,* 1986, 491, 518.

56. O'Neill, *Man of the House,* 371.

57. Quoted in John M. Barry, *The Ambition and the Power: The Fall of Speaker Wright* (New York, 1989), 58.

58. Sundquist, "Governor's Reflections," 311.

59. David Hawkins, "After Criticizing Jim Wright in '87, GOP Used His Tactic," *Congressional Quarterly, Today,* November 22, 2003, 4; Barry, *Ambition and the Power,* 471–472.

60. Later, on November 25, 2003, the Republicans, now in the majority, repeated this tactic. During a vote on the Medicare drug bill, Speaker Hastert held up the balloting for three hours until sufficient votes had been secured to win passage of the measure, 220 to 215. One Republican representative claimed he was offered a bribe to vote for the bill. Jonathan E. Kaplan, "Hastert Hits Back on Medicare Vote and Ethics, *The Hill,* March 17, 2004.

61. Nelson W. Polsby, *How Congress Evolves: Social Bases of Institutional Change* (New York, 2004), 134.

62. Quoted in Mel Steely, *The Gentleman from Georgia: The Biography of Newt Gingrich* (Macon, Ga., 2000), 88.

63. Murtha to the author, March 14, 2005.

64. Quoted in Barry, *Ambition and the Power,* 482.

65. *Congressional Quarterly Almanac,* 1987, 130; Jim Wright, *Balance of Power: Presidents and Congress from the Era of McCarthy to the Age of Gingrich* (Atlanta, 1996), 467–469.

66. Wright, "Challenges That Speakers Face," 132.

67. Gingrich to the author, July 13, 2004.

68. Wright, *Balance of Power,* 474.

69. James L. Merriner, *Mr. Chairman: Power in Dan Rostenkowski's America* (Carbondale, Ill., 1999), 236.

70. Cheney to the author, December 22, 2005. The charges "never came to a head because he [Wright] stepped down before it got to that point."

71. Polsby, *How Congress Evolves,* 133.

72. Murtha to the author, March 14, 2005.

73. Wright to the author, July 27, 2005.

74. *Congressional Record,* 101st Congress, 1st session, 10440.

75. Ronald M. Peters, Jr., *The American Speakership: The Office in Historical Perspective* (Baltimore, 1997), 281–282; *Congressional Quarterly Almanac,* 1989, 41.

76. *Washington Post,* May 28, 1989; *Congressional Quarterly Almanac,* 1989, 1376–1383.

77. Quoted in Julian E. Zelizer, ed., *The American Congress: The Building of Democracy* (Boston, 2004), 718.

78. Michel to the author, January 19, 2005.

79. *Congressional Quarterly Almanac,* 1988, 23, 25.

80. Tom Foley, "The Foley Speakership," in Walter Oleszek, ed., *The Cannon Centenary Conference: The Changing Nature of the Speakership* (Washington, D.C., 2005), 73–74.

81. Michel to the author, January 19, 2005.

82. *Congressional Quarterly Almanac,* 1994, 13, 43–48.

83. Gingrich to the author, July 13, 2004.

84. Gephardt "didn't have that much power against the chairmen, either," according to Gingrich. "And so you had this vacuum. . . . [Nancy] Pelosi [minority leader of the 108th and 109th Congresses] is beginning to fill it. But, it was never fully filled until Pelosi came on." Gingrich to the author, July 13, 2004.

85. Barbara Sinclair, "Tip O'Neill and Contemporary House Leadership," in Roger H. Davidson, et al., eds., *Masters of the House* (Boulder, Colo., 1989), 313.

86. Livingston to the author, September 27, 2005. It could be argued, surmised Dick Cheney, that the 1994 cataclysm "was sort of the culmination of the Reagan revolution, that Reagan had set in motion forces in the '80s presidential contests that inspired a lot of people to get into politics. You'll find a lot of those members got started back in that period of time. And it's had a lasting significance in the country and it finally came to fruition in the House in the mid-'90s." Cheney to the author, December 22, 2004.

87. Gingrich to the author, July 13, 2004.

88. Ibid.

89. Cheney to the author, December 22, 2004.

90. *Congressional Quarterly Almanac,* 1995, 1–3.

91. Ibid.

92. Ibid.

93. Quoted in Frey and Hayes, *Inside the House,* 53.

94. Gingrich to the author, July 13, 2004.

95. Livingston to the author, September 27, 2005.

96. Gingrich was particularly proud of helping to set up the Thomas System with William Thomas of California, chairman of the Joint Committee on the Library, by which "you can go online and pull up every document in the U.S. House, every committee report, every record of hearings, every vote on the House floor, every bill that's been introduced for each Congress starting in 1995. All of it for free.

"One of the proudest moments in my career was when Bill Archer got up and announced that he was introducing the tax bill, and read the Web site at which you could pick up the bill. So, here he is talking, on C-SPAN, and I think over a hundred thousand copies were downloaded the first afternoon by people all over the country. That, to me, was, in a sense, computer age populism." Gingrich to the author, July 13, 2004.

97. Jay Eagen to the author, January 6, 2005.

98. David H. Davidson and Walter J. Oleszek, *Congress and Its Members* (Washington, D.C., [1994], 208–209; Theodore Van Der Meid, legal counsel to Speaker J. Dennis Hastert, to the author, March 8, 2005.

99. Harry A. Johnston, "Power in the U.S. House and the Florida State Senate," in Frey and Hayes, ed., *Inside the House,* 189.

100. Gingrich to the author, July 13, 2004.

101. Quoted in Steely, *Gentleman from Georgia,* 307.

102. *Congressional Quarterly Almanac,* 1996, D-5.

103. Gingrich to the author, July 13, 2004.

104. Quoted in *Congressional Quarterly Almanac,* 1995, 11-4.

105. Ibid., 1–23.

106. Gingrich to the author, July 13, 2004.

107. *Congressional Quarterly Almanac,* 1995, 11-6.

108. There are some in Congress who believe that Gingrich could have won the struggle with Clinton had he held out longer. When he caved in, many conservative Republicans were offended and deserted him. Billy Pitts, Rules Committee chief of staff, to the author, October 19, 2004.

109. Quoted in Zelizer, *On Capitol Hill,* 261.

110. Livingston to the author, September 27, 2005.

111. Ibid.

112. *Washington Post,* July 25, 26, 27, 28, 29, 1998; *The Standard-Times,* New Bedford, MA, July 26, 1998. Actually, Christopher Shermon Eney was the first Capitol Police officer to be killed on duty. He was shot accidentally by another officer in a training exercise on August 24, 1984.

113. *Congressional Quarterly Almanac,* 1998, 12–13.

114. Ibid., 12–15.

115. Livingston to the author, September 27, 2005.

116. Hyde to the author, December 15, 2004.

117. *Congressional Quarterly Almanac,* 1998, 12–15.

118. Hyde to the author, December 15, 2004; *Congressional Record,* 105th Congress, 2nd session, 1998.

119. Livingston to the author, September 27, 2005.

120. *Congressional Quarterly Almanac,* 1998, 12–34.

121. Livingston to the author, September 27, 2005.

122. *Congressional Quarterly Almanac,* 1998, 12–47.

123. Livingston to the author, September 27, 2005.

124. *Washington Post,* January 5, 1999.

125. Hyde to the author, December 15, 2004.

126. Ibid.

127. Livingston to the author, September 27, 2005; Gingrich to the author, July 13, 2004.

EPILOGUE

1. Congressional Research Service to author, November 9, 2005.
2. These statistics are taken from Stanley I. Kutler, ed., *Encyclopedia of the United States in the Twentieth Century* (New York, 1996), 1:365, and Mildred L. Amer, *Membership of the 109th Congress: A Profile,* Congressional Research Services Report (Washington, D.C., 2005).
3. Amer, ibid.
4. *Washington Post,* July 27, 2005.
5. John Murtha to the author, March 14, 2005.
6. Donald Rumsfeld to the author, June 22, 2005.
7. Ibid.; Dan Rostenkowski to the author, July 1, 2004; Martha Cooper, wife of Representative Andrew Cooper, to the author, May 18, 2005.
8. Henry Hyde to the author, December 15, 2005.
9. James L. Merriner, *Mr. Chairman: Power in Dan Rostenkowski's America* (Carbondale, Ill., 1999), 94.
10. *Washington Post*, May 11, 2004.
11. Merriner, *Mr. Chairman,* 82.
12. Bob Livingston to the author, September 27, 2005.
13. Murtha to the author, March 14, 2005.
14. Tom Foley to the author, January 18; Robert Michel to the author, January 19, 2005.
15. Bill Thomas, "Making Elections More Competitive: Election Reform Under a Republican Congress," pp. 41–49 in "The Republican Congress: A Manifesto in the House of Representatives," January, 1992, in the Robert H. Michel Papers, Leadership Series, Box 15, Folder, 102nd Congress, Everett Dirksen Congressional Center, Pekin, Illinois.
16. Congressional Research Service Report to Congress, Updated to March 1, 2005.
17. Foley to author, January 18, 2005.
18. Murtha to the author, March 14, 2005.
19. Jim Wright, "Challenges That Speakers Face," in Ronald M. Peters, ed., *The Speaker: Leadership in the U.S. House of Representatives* (Washingtoin, D.C., 1994), 242.
20. The occasion was the commemoration of the bicentenary of Congress. His speech is quoted in *Final Report of the Commission on the Bicentenary of the U.S. House of Representatives,* 101st Congress, 2nd session, House Report, 101–815, 27.
21. Newt Gingrich to the author, July 13, 2004.

APPENDIX 6. CHIEF ADMINISTRATIVE OFFICERS OF THE HOUSE

1. Mildred L. Amer, *Membership of the 109th Congress: A Profile,* Congressional Research Services Report (Washington, D.C., 2005).

APPENDIX 13. ORGANIZATION AND OPERATION OF THE WHIP

1. Roy Blunt to the author, December 8, 2003; J. Dennis Hastert to the author, December 8, 2003.

APPENDIX 17. PAGES

1. Office of the Clerk, "Information on the House Page Program," 1.

Index